# DYNAMIC STRATEGIC RESOURCES

# THE STRATEGIC MANAGEMENT SERIES

STRATEGIC THINKING
Leadership and the Management of Change
Edited by
JOHN HENDRY AND GERRY JOHNSON
WITH JULIA NEWTON

COMPETENCE-BASED COMPETITION
Edited by
GARY HAMEL AND AIMÉ HEENE

BUILDING THE STRATEGICALLY-RESPONSIVE ORGANIZATION
Edited by
HOWARD THOMAS, DON O'NEAL, ROD WHITE AND DAVID HURST

STRATEGIC RENAISSANCE AND BUSINESS TRANSFORMATION
Edited by
HOWARD THOMAS, DON O'NEAL AND JAMES KELLY

COMPETENCE-BASED STRATEGIC MANAGEMENT
Edited by
AIMÉ HEENE AND RON SANCHEZ

STRATEGIC LEARNING AND KNOWLEDGE MANAGEMENT
Edited by
RON SANCHEZ AND AIMÉ HEENE

STRATEGY STRUCTURE AND STYLE
Edited by
HOWARD THOMAS, DON O'NEAL AND MICHEL GHERTMAN

STRATEGIC INTEGRATION
Edited by
HOWARD THOMAS AND DON O'NEAL

STRATEGIC DISCOVERY
Edited by
HOWARD THOMAS, DON O'NEAL AND RAUL ALVARADO

MANAGING STRATEGICALLY IN AN INTERCONNECTED WORLD
Edited by
MICHAEL A. HITT, JOAN E. RICART I COSTA AND ROBERT D. NIXON

Further titles in preparation

STRATEGIC FLEXIBILITY: MANAGING IN A TURBULENT ECONOMY
Edited by
GARY HAMEL, C.K. PRALAHAD, HOWARD THOMAS AND DON O'NEAL

NEW MANAGERIAL MINDSETS: ORGANIZATIONAL TRANSFORMATION AND STRATEGY IMPLEMENTATION
Edited by
MICHAEL A. HITT, JOAN E. RICART I COSTA AND ROBERT D. NIXON

DYNAMIC STRATEGIC RESOURCES: DEVELOPMENT, DIFFUSION AND INTEGRATION
Edited by
MICHAEL A. HITT, PATRICIA GORMAN CLIFFORD, ROBERT D. NIXON AND KEVIN P. COYNE

THE STRATEGIC MANAGEMENT SERIES

# DYNAMIC STRATEGIC RESOURCES

## Development, Diffusion and Integration

Edited by

Michael A. Hitt,
Patricia Gorman Clifford,
Robert D. Nixon and Kevin P. Coyne

JOHN WILEY & SONS, LTD
Chichester · New York · Weinheim · Brisbane · Singapore · Toronto

*National* 01243 779777
*International* (+44) 1243 779777
e-mail (for orders and customer service enquiries): cs-books@wiley.co.uk
Visit our Home Page on http://www.wiley.co.uk
or http://www.wiley.com



*Other Wiley Editorial Offices*

John Wiley & Sons, Inc., 605 Third Avenue,
New York, NY 10158-0012, USA

WILEY-VCH Verlag GmbH, Pappelallee 3,
D-69469 Weinheim, Germany

Jacaranda Wiley Ltd, 33 Park Road, Milton,
Queensland 4064, Australia

John Wiley & Sons (Asia) Pte Ltd, 2 Clementi Loop #02-01,
Jin Xing Distripark, Singapore 129809

John Wiley & Sons (Canada) Ltd, 22 Worcester Road,
Rexdale, Ontario M9W 1L1, Canada

***Library of Congress Cataloging-in-Publication Data***
Dynamic Strategic Resources / edited by Michael A. Hitt ... [et al.].
p. cm. -- (The Strategic management series)
"The contributions in this volume are based on papers from the 1998 Strategic Management Society Conference held in Orlando, Florida"--P.
Includes bibliographical references and index.
ISBN 0-471-62533-7 (hardback : alk. paper)
1. Strategic Planning Congresses. 2. Industrial Management Congresses. I. Hitt, Michael A. II. Strategic Management Society. Conference (1998 : Orlando, Fla.) III. Series.
HD30.28.T343 1999
656.4'012--dc21 99-32599
CIP

***British Library Cataloguing in Publication Data***

A catalogue record for this book is available from the British Library

ISBN 0-471-625337

Typeset in 10/12 Palatino from the author's disks by MCS Ltd, Salisbury, Wiltshire.
Printed and bound in Great Britain by Biddles Ltd, Guildford and King's Lynn.
This book is printed on acid-free paper responsibly manufactured from sustainable forestry, in which at least two trees are planted for each one used for paper production.

# Contents

# Contributors

PAUL BIERLY
*James Madison University, College of Business, MSC 0205, Harrisonburg, VA 22807, USA*

MARGARET BRUCE
*Department of Textiles, UMIST, PO Box 88, Manchester M60 I QD, UK*

SUZANNE M. CARTER
*365 College of Business Administration, University of Notre Dame, PO Box 399, Notre Dame, IN 46556-0399, USA*

PATRICIA GORMAN CLIFFORD
*School of Business Administration, University of Connecticut at Stamford, Room 390, One University Place, Stamford, CT 06901-2315, USA*
(Dr. Clifford was employed at McKinsey and Company during the development of this book.)

KEVIN P. COYNE
*McKinsey and Company, Suite 4600, Georgia-Pacific Center, 133 Peachtree Street, N.E., Atlanta, GA 30303, USA*

ANTONIO DAVILA
*IESE, University of Navarra, Avenida Pearson 21, Barcelona 08034, Spain*

PAOLA DUBINI
*SDA, Bocconi, Via Bocconi 8, 20136 Milano, Italy*

RODOLPHE DURAND
*Goizueta Business School, Emory University, 1300 Clifton Road, Atlanta, GA 30322, USA*

MICHAEL A. HITT
*Lowry Mays College and Graduate School of Business, Department of Management, Texas A&M University, College Station, TX 77843-4221, USA*

BIRGIT H. JEVNAKER
*Norwegian School of Management BI, Department of Innovation and Economic Organization, PO Box 580, N-1302 Sandvika, Norway*

THOMAS KEIL
*Institute of Strategy and International Business, Helsinki University of Technology, PO Box 9500, 02015 HUT, Finland*

ERIC H. KESSLER
*Pace University, Lubin School of Business, New York, NY 10038-1598, USA*

KENTARO KOGA
*School of Commerce, Waseda University, Nishi-waseda 1-6-1, Shinjuku-ku, Tokyo 169-5021, Japan*

RICHARD LEIFER
*Rensselaer Polytechnic Institute, School of Management, 110 8th St, Troy, NY 12180-3590, USA*

IAN C. MACMILLAN
*University of Pennsylvania, Snider Entrepreneurial Research Center, 409 Vance Hall, 3733 Spruce St., Philadelphia, PA 19104-6374, USA*

SARAH J. MARSH
*Northern Illinois University, Department of Management, Wirtz Hall, DeKalb, IL 60115, USA*

RITA GUNTHER MCGRATH
*703 Uris Hall, Columbia University Graduate School of Business, 3022 Broadway, New York, NY 10027, USA*

JOE NANDHAKUMAR
*Department of Management, University of Southampton, Southampton S017 1BJ, UK*

ROBERT D. NIXON
*A.B. Freeman School of Business, Tulane University, New Orleans, LA 70118-5669, USA*

Moacir de Miranda Oliveira Junior
*Pontificia Universidade Católica de São Paulo, ESPM FEA—Departamento de Administracão, Rua Monte Alegre, 984 São Paulo, SP 05014-901, Brazil*

Annette L. Ranft
*Wake Forest University, The Wayne Calloway School of Business and Accountancy, Box 7285, Winston-Salem, NC 27109-7285, USA*

Mark Rice
*Rensselaer Polytechnic Institute, School of Management, 110 8th St., Troy, NY 12180-3590, USA*

Frank T. Rothaermel
*Department of Management and Organization, UW Business School, Box 353200, University of Washington, Seattle, WA 98195-3200, USA*

Wm. Gerard Sanders
*Marriott School of Business, 769 TNRB, Brigham Young University, Provo, UT 84602, USA*

Mirela Schwarz
*Department of Management, University of Southampton, Southampton SO17 1BJ, UK*

Mohan Subramaniam
*University of Connecticut, School of Business, 368 Fairfield Road, U-41MG, Storrs, CT 06269-2041, USA*

Frans A.J. van den Bosch
*Department of Strategy and Business Environment, Rotterdam School of Management, Erasmus University Rotterdam, PO Box 1738, 3000 DR Rotterdam, Netherlands*

Raymond A. van Wijk
*Department of Strategy and Business Environment, Rotterdam School of Management, Erasmus University Rotterdam, PO Box 1738, 3000 DR Rotterdam, Netherlands*

N. Venkatraman
*Information Systems Department, School of Management, Boston University, 595 Commonwealth Avenue, Boston, MA 02215, USA*

Jonathan Wilson
*Surrey European Management School, University of Surrey, Guildford, Surrey GU2 5XH, UK*

# Series Preface

The Strategic Management Society was created to bring together, on a worldwide basis, academics, business practitioners, and consultants interested in strategic management. The aim of the Society is the development and dissemination of information, achieved through its sponsorship of the annual international conference, special interest workshops, the *Strategic Management Journal*, and other publications.

The Society's annual conference is a truly international meeting, held in recent years in Stockholm, Barcelona, Toronto, London, Paris, Mexico City, Chicago and Phoenix. Each conference deals with a broad, current theme, within which specific sub-themes are addressed through keynote speeches and discussion panels featuring leading experts from around the world.

The Strategic Management Book Series is a cooperative effort between the Strategic Management Society and John Wiley & Sons. The series focuses on cutting edge concepts/topics in strategic management theory and practice. The books emphasize building and maintaining bridges between theory and practice in strategic management. The work published in these books generates and tests theories of strategic management; and additionally, it demonstrates how to learn, understand and apply these theories in practice. The books in the series represent the products of Strategic Management Society sponsored Mini-Conferences and best volumes from the annual International Strategic Management Society Conferences.

The contributions in this volume are based on papers from the 1998 Strategic Management Society Conference held in Orlando, Florida, USA. The contributors represent an excellent set of authors from many regions of the world, specifically Asia, Europe, North America and South America. The following paragraphs provide an overview of the contents of this important book.

Prior research suggests that core competencies are critical to firm performance. Core competencies are based on a firm's capabilities that, in turn, are derived from the firm's resources. Because of the importance of firm resources to competitive advantage, this book examines the management of strategic resources. The book addresses two major themes: (1) resource strategy and firm performance; and (2) the development, commitment and governance of firm resources.

Successful firms build competitive advantages from their core competencies. Not only do they develop unique and valuable competencies but they also configure (integrate) their competencies in new and flexible ways and thereby renew themselves by facilitating the development and implementation of new strategies. Intangible resources such as corporate culture and firm reputation may be especially useful in this regard. Heterogeneous firm resources can be useful not only in developing a firm's competitive strategy but also aid the movement into new international markets (international strategy).

To develop and sustain a set of heterogeneous and valuable resources, a firm must manage them effectively. Managing strategic resources involves developing, allocating and governing the firm's resources. The internal development of resources requires that firms build (learn) knowledge and then exploit that knowledge. One means of accessing knowledge is through external networks (social capital). In fact, these external networks (for example, strategic alliances) can be used to expand the creative capability of the firm and thereby help the firm to maintain a superior competitive position. Allocating resources to new projects is a critical decision for the future performance of firms. Effective allocation of resources allows them to be leveraged to create competitive advantages. Goals for the use of resources not only serve as a benchmark to evaluate performance but also help coordinate among different functions and serve as a catalyst for organizational learning.

Thus, this book provides multiple perspectives on the creation and outcomes of strategic resources and how they can be managed to produce sustainable competitive advantages. The chapters herein provide an in-depth examination of how strategic resources are developed and managed to create value in business organizations.

# 1

# The Development and Use of Strategic Resources

MICHAEL A. HITT, ROBERT D. NIXON, PATRICIA GORMAN CLIFFORD, KEVIN P. COYNE

## INTRODUCTION

When Edith Penrose suggested in 1959 that returns achieved by firms could be attributed to the resources held by those firms, her contemporaries, largely industrial organization economists, were not persuaded. Such ideas were antithetical to the thinking in the field of economics at the time. Economists largely assumed that firm resources were relatively homogeneous within industries and that firms deviating from industry norms would experience performance declines—not enhancements.

Fortunately, several strategic management scholars began to adopt and extend her ideas in the early 1980s, thus the concept of heterogeneous firm attributes was more readily embraced. Since that time, a significant body of research has developed suggesting that firm resources, capabilities and competencies help firms gain competitive advantages that, in turn, produce higher performance (Wernerfelt, 1984; Barney, 1986, 1991; Rumelt, 1991; Amit & Schoemaker, 1993). This work argues that firms hold heterogeneous and idiosyncratic resources on which their individual strategies are based. When these strategies are successful in leveraging firm resources to gain a competitive advantage that is then sustained over

*Dynamic Strategic Resources: Development, Diffusion and Integration.*
Edited by Michael A. Hitt, Patricia Gorman Clifford, Robert D. Nixon and Kevin P. Coyne.

time, the firms achieve higher economic returns than others (Arora & Gambardella, 1997).

Prior to the development of the resource-based view of the firm, the industrial organization economic approach dominated the thinking in the strategic management field. The IO approach emphasizes inter-industry firm homogeneity, and attributes competitive advantage to barriers to entry, order of entry (i.e., first mover advantage), and interfirm transaction costs. However, this approach has been unable to explain many phenomena that have occurred over time. The resource-based view of the firm has been an important development in the field of strategic management, because it provides potential answers to what some refer to as the defining question of this field, "Why do some organizations perform better than others?" (Barnett, Greve & Park, 1994).

To take a fairly recent example, during a severe recession in the early 1990s, all US domestic airlines lost substantial amounts of money, except for one. Southwest Airlines continued to make a profit when all of its competitors' financial performance suffered. Special resources that its competitors did not have enabled Southwest Airlines to achieve abnormal positive returns during poor economic times and relative to all its competitors (Hitt, Ireland & Hoskisson, 1999). Those resources were effectively leveraged to implement its integrated low cost and differentiation strategy, which, by virtue of the idiosyncratic resources, has not been successfully imitated.

Because of the theoretical and more recent empirical work, the field understands that leveraging resources is important to gain a sustainable competitive advantage. While there are multiple typologies of resource characteristics necessary to develop sustainable competitive advantages, most authors have integrated them into four critical ones: (1) the resources must be valuable, (2) the resources must be rare, (3) the resources must be difficult or impossible (i.e., prohibitively costly) to imitate by competitors, and (4) the resources must be nonsubstitutable by other types of resources (Barney, 1991).

Resources can be distinguished as tangible or intangible. Tangible resources include financial resources and physical resources, whereas intangible resources include assets such as skills, knowledge, managerial capabilities, and firm reputation. Most authors argue that intangible resources are more likely to produce sustainable competitive advantages than physical resources because they are often very difficult to understand and imitate. The nature of intangible resources is often socially complex. Thus, it is difficult to understand how these resources are created and why they are valuable. Furthermore, the relationship between intangible resources and firm performance is often causally ambiguous (Coff, 1997). Southwest Airlines' primary and most valuable resources are its human capital and its corporate culture. It is difficult to imitate a corporate culture because of the inability to identify and/or replicate its primary bases. It is socially complex because it involves multiple parts such as many human interactions, both formal and informal rules, policies and norms, and a large set of behavioral actions. Because Southwest Airlines is perceived as an excellent place to work, often it has hundreds of applications for a single position opening. As a result, managers within Southwest Airlines are able to select high-quality employees and those who will best fit with and help sustain its corporate culture.

Over the past 15 years, the resource-based view has provided an intriguing lens for the study of firms, their processes and their performance —with particular emphasis on how firm resources interplay with firm strategy to produce different outcomes. The chapters which follow emphasize several important topics. They examine how resources lead to competitive advantage and other outcomes. They also focus on how resources serve as a base for strategies which, in turn, produce specific firm outcomes. Several chapters explore how firms develop critical resources while others examine the governance of resources and resource commitment. Next, we examine resources, strategy and outcomes.

## Organizational Resources: Outcomes and Strategy

### Firm Resources and Outcomes

Capabilities represent a set of integrated resources used to perform important activities. These capabilities are embedded in the skills and knowledge of a firm's employees (Hitt, Ireland & Hoskisson, 1999). A firm's competencies are based on its capabilities, organizational routines and ability to learn (Praest, 1998). Core competencies then are the activities that firms perform especially well and provide a potential source of competitive advantage. As a result, core competencies are critical to firm performance. However, they cannot remain static because of the dynamic and complex new competitive landscape (Hitt, Keats & DeMarie, 1998). Firms must develop dynamic core competencies (Lei, Hitt & Bettis, 1996). They must continuously develop their competencies and/or be prepared to change and develop new ones, to maintain a competitive edge. Sometimes, as the competitive landscape changes, existing competencies must be de-emphasized or abandoned and new and valuable competencies developed in order to remain competitive.

The dynamism of core competencies and its implications are acknowledged in Oliveira's chapter. Oliveira explains the characteristics of core competencies in detail but specifically focuses on the importance of knowledge development and learning to sustain the dynamic character of core competencies. In particular, Oliveira explains the firm as an agent of knowledge creation and transfer and then explores different types of knowledge created by firms. To be most valuable, knowledge must be diffused throughout the organization. Tacit and collective knowledge, the basis of most core competencies, is accumulated in employee skills and embedded in technical systems (e.g., software, databases and formal procedures) and values and norms. Therefore, Oliveira argues that knowledge management is critical to developing and sustaining a dynamic and resource-based competitive advantage.

Building on Oliveira's chapter, Marsh and Ranft explain how knowledge-based resources can be used to enter new markets. As product life cycles become shorter and competitive advantages and market shares diminish through aggressive actions by competitors, new market entry opportunities may be critical. Firms must have the appropriate resources to enter and succeed in new product markets. Marsh and Ranft empirically examined several research hypotheses regarding the relationship between different knowledge-based resources and mode of entry into product markets. They found acquisitions were used to enter new markets that were high in uncertainty and required substantial tacit knowledge for success. Those firms using internal development to enter new markets that required substantial tacit knowledge performed poorly. Their results suggest that while transferring tacit knowledge may be difficult using alliances and acquisitions, it may be even more difficult to create such knowledge through internal development. This suggests that tacit knowledge may be acquired in a less costly and more timely manner through alliances or acquisition than by developing such knowledge alone.

The chapter by Durand explores the contributions of inimitable, nontransferable and nonsubstitutable resources to firm performance. Using a sample of 2875 firms in 50 different industries representing 13 separate industrial sectors, he found that the inimitability and nontransferability of productive resources both positively affect a firm's market performance. Furthermore, he found nonsubstitutable supplier relationships also to increase the firm's market performance, but because of the costs involved in building the relationship, the same variable had a negative effect on return on sales. Conversely, nonsubstitutable customer relationships had a positive effect on return on sales but a negative effect on market performance because they prevent the firms from targeting a wider consumer market. In other words, the consumer in this case has significant power over the firm. Durand's results provide strong support for the resource-based view of the firm by showing a direct linkage between a firm's resources and its performance.

## THE INTERPLAY BETWEEN RESOURCES AND STRATEGY

The resource-based view of the firm suggests that firms use resources to build competencies upon which their strategies are based. In this way, firms' strategies are derived from their resources. For example, prior research has shown that firm diversification strategies may be shaped by idiosyncratic firm competencies (Hitt & Ireland, 1985; Montgomery & Wernerfelt, 1988; Henderson & Cockburn, 1994). Leonard-Barton (1992) argues that managerial systems and organizational values and norms allow firms to develop and implement strategies that help them respond to their environment. Henderson and Cockburn (1994) argue that some firms have an architectural competence that allows them to integrate existing competencies in new and flexible ways in order to develop new competencies. Thus, some firms have the capability to renew themselves by constantly developing existing competencies or building new ones that subsequently allow them to develop and implement new strategies.

Schwarz and Nandhakumar describe how strategy is developed based on corporate culture in a newly transformed organization. Drawing on Barney's (1986) work, they argue that a firm's cultural context provides a source of competitive advantage in developing strategic ideas through its effects on strategic thinking in the organization. That is, it shapes the quality of strategic decisions. They examined these ideas in a field study that involved observing and interviewing organizational members in their daily work, decision-making processes and strategically important meetings. Their research provides an in-depth examination of how culture and strategy interactively developed after a major restructuring and reengineering of a firm. Strategic ideas evolved from strategic debate characterized by brainstorming sessions, mind maps, critics group evaluation, workshops and formal and informal meetings. After a specific strategic decision was made, a coherent strategic plan was developed in order to transform the strategic ideas into action. The process of developing the plan was largely shaped by cultural factors. Of course, cultural factors also shape the strategic debate from which the strategic ideas evolved. For example, the language used to communicate ideas in strategic debates was conditioned by the cultural environment. Their conclusions suggest that the culture affected the content quality, pace of development and maturity of strategic ideas.

Garrone and Rossini (1998) found that entry into new markets was based on firm-specific capabilities. In particular, diversification into new markets was centered on product competencies and complementary assets such as financial resources. Resources may actually drive some strategies. For example, excess resources and capabilities within firms may drive managers to search for new products and services and new market opportunities (Miles *et al.*, 1997). The chapter by Wilson examines how different industries and different customer values require different resources. Wilson contrasts the contingency and resource-based views of the firm to account for differences in performance between firms within the same industry. Results of Wilson's research suggest that firm performance can best be understood by integrating contingency and resource-based approaches. Specifically, his research showed that heterogeneous resources develop and interact with market-related forces, particularly consumer preferences, to produce a competitive advantage. Thus, firms integrate information from the market (their consumers) and use their resources to develop a strategy to satisfy market needs/demands.

Rao (1994) argues the importance of reputation, a firm-specific resource, to competitive advantage. For example, he suggests that reputations can significantly contribute to performance differences among firms because they are rare, socially complex and difficult to imitate. Firms, then, can use positive reputations as a resource upon which to build their strategies. For example, they may use the strength of their reputation to enter a new market and the reputation may help firms build brand identity with customers. Reputations provide legitimacy to firms, particularly in new markets. However, based on the work described in Carter and Sanders' chapter, firms must be careful to follow an appropriate strategy to maintain or improve their corporate reputation. While reputation affects strategy as suggested by Rao (1994), Carter and Sanders argue that strategy affects a firm's reputation. They suggest that strategic actions provide signals to external constituents about managerial decisions and thus influence the constituents' perception of the firm's reputation. In particular, they studied the effects of acquisitions and divestitures on firms' reputations. They found firms divesting businesses in order to refocus on more closely related businesses and that those engaged in limited acquisitions tended to have less positive reputations. Because they control for prior performance, these results have potentially significant implications. However, they also found the level of firm diversification to moderate the relationships between the strategic actions and firm reputation. In fact, firms that were more diversified had a positive relationship between the strategic actions of acquisition and divestiture and firm reputation. Carter and Sanders concluded that constituents likely viewed the diversified firms as possessing the necessary skills to create value from both types of strategic actions. They suggest that some firms do have particular skills in conducting acquisitions and likely divestitures as well. Thus, reputation may be an important corporate resource but can be affected by strategic actions, suggesting that strategies and resources are reciprocally interdependent.

Other strategies, such as moving into new international markets (international diversification), may also be based on resources. Prior research has suggested that firms having an excess of resources, such as new innovative products, may enter international markets to help capture economies of scale and scope (Hitt, Hoskisson & Kim, 1997). However, other resources such as managerial capabilities may be critical in implementing international diversification effectively. For example, Murtha, Lenway and Bagozzi (1998) argue that global mindsets and managerial capabilities to consider complex interactions and differences in international markets may be critical to the successful implementation of international strategies. The Dubini and MacMillan chapter examines how firms globalize. In fact, these authors argue that the road to globalization is, indeed, rugged and that the globalization process is far from orderly. Firms that diversify into international markets must deal with the dual problem of achieving fit in each local landscape while also simultaneously developing fit with a global environment. They suggest that many of these landscapes in which the firms must compete are quite rugged. Dubini and MacMillan argue that patterns of globalization are influenced by a firm's specific competence base along with the competitive landscapes in which they operate. They use the global appliance industry as an example of the concepts noted, and explain several ways in which firms align competencies with opportunities in these new markets. First, they transfer competencies between operations in different local competitive landscapes. Sometimes they acquire the necessary competencies to compete in a particular landscape. At other times, they make investments in alliances that provide access to specific competencies needed to compete in particular local landscapes. Dubini and MacMillan argue that the ruggedness in local markets (competitive landscapes) thus tends to constrain globalization of firms. Thus, firms do not necessarily move smoothly into new markets. They tend to enter new international markets and then adapt and develop the resources necessary to compete effectively before they move into other new international markets. Perhaps this is the problem to which Murtha, Lenway and Bagozzi (1998) referred in the need for managerial capabilities to understand and manage complex interactions and differences in international markets. Dubini and MacMillan conclude that the development of a global strategy was an evolutionary process orchestrated by the firm's attempts to fit both local and global landscapes simultaneously while reacting to competitors' countermoves and other environmental dynamics.

## Organizational Resources: Development, Commitment and Governance

In order to have a set of heterogeneous and valuable resources, a firm must either acquire them or develop them. To develop intangible resources, the ones that are the most difficult to imitate, largely requires learning and the building of knowledge (Teece, Pisano & Shuen, 1997). This means that firms must have the capability to learn. Some refer to this capability to learn as absorptive capacity (Cohen & Levinthal, 1990). Learning is cumulative and often self-reinforcing. That is, firms build on their existing knowledge base (Schilling, 1998).

## Development of Resources

Some of the critical knowledge in organizations is tacit. This means that people hold it but cannot articulate this knowledge to others. As a result, it can only be learned by performing the actions. Thus, much knowledge may be acquired through "learning by doing" (Pisano, 1994). However, perhaps most important is to have the organization configured to support such learning. In other words, a firm's organizational structure and strategy can facilitate its learning (Henderson & Cockburn, 1994). This may be seen in the chapter by van den Bosch and van Wijk. They argue that firms must both exploit their existing knowledge and explore for new knowledge simultaneously. They recommend the network structure (N-form) as a means to facilitate knowledge sharing and creation processes in an organization. They suggest that the N-form facilitates horizontal knowledge flows between interdependent organizational units as opposed to the vertical flow in more traditional organization structures. Thus, the N-form enables high levels of coordination and integration of knowledge. In turn, these characteristics often lead to higher levels of knowledge exploration through the internal networks within the firm. Van den Bosch and van Wijk's case study research supported their expectations. As quoted by these authors, "The process by which knowledge is created and utilized in organizations may be the key inimitable resource managers need to appreciate if not understand ..." (Schendel, 1996: 3).

The networks may be internal as noted by van den Bosch and van Wijk or they may be external. Regardless, the relationships built through these networks lead to the development of social capital (Nahapiet & Ghoshal, 1998). The term social capital applied to these relationships implies that the relationships create value for the firm. That is, the networks of relationships constitute a valuable resource for the firm. Nahapiet and Ghoshal (1998) argued that social capital facilitates the creation of new intellectual capital. In particular, it helps firms in creating and sharing the intellectual capital or knowledge, similar to the arguments of van den Bosch and van Wijk. These relational resources can be especially valuable when they are rare, durable, difficult to imitate and nontradable (Dierickx & Cool, 1989). This is because they tend to be tacit and ambiguous and lead to a form of social complexity

(Barney, 1991; Reed & DeFillippi, 1990). The chapter by Rothaermel describes a form of social capital in what he calls creative cooperation. In effect, Rothaermel's research tests two different models regarding the nature of competition that follows a technological discontinuity, creative destruction and creative cooperation. Rothaermel describes creative cooperation as extensive cooperation among firms to adapt to a radical technological change. He argues that the process of creative cooperation allows industry performance to improve following the discontinuity. However, while the process of creative destruction can provide a competitive advantage to individual firms, it often leads to a decline in industry performance. Therefore, creative cooperation actually produces a form of industry-specific social capital.

Other forms of cooperation that can create social capital include strategic alliances. These provide firms with the opportunity to acquire assets, and capabilities/competencies that may not be easily accessible in factor markets. Among the assets that can be acquired are intangible resources such as reputation. The relationships in strategic alliances reduce barriers by facilitating resource information exchange (Oliver, 1997). Thus, tacit knowledge can be acquired through human capital transfers between partners in a strategic alliance. As a result, alliances allow partners the potential to learn knowledge from other partners in the alliance, assuming that these partners are accommodating in allowing the transfer of this knowledge (Gulati, 1998). The chapter by Jevnaker and Bruce describes the use of strategic alliances to expand the creative capability of the firm. These authors focus on a firm's collaboration with industrial design consultants. They argue that this alliance is a strategic relational activity and represents a fragile corporate asset. They suggest that a good relationship between the partners in this alliance can strengthen the product name and quality image (its reputation) in the market. Of course, this is in addition to the value created by management of risk and sharing of costs, both of which may be especially important with radically new designs. They also suggest that these alliances help firms to reduce uncertainty.

The chapter by Bierly and Kessler also suggests that alliances and network structures can help firms to maintain a superior competitive position, particularly in dynamic environments in which most firms exist today. In particular, Bierly and Kessler test a number of hypotheses related to the timing of entry into strategic alliances and the effect of such timing on acquiring resources such as knowledge and the outcome of innovation from strategic alliances. They analyzed over 650 strategic alliances in the pharmaceutical industry from 1988 to 1995, concluding that there are different types of alliances based on timing of entry. For example, there are early stage alliances and later stage alliances, as well as some in between. Often, they found that the timing of the alliance was context driven and played an important role in the technological learning of the firm. Bierly and Kessler also argue that the governance of these alliances can be quite important.

## Resource Governance and Commitment: Producing Innovation

Firms collaborating in strategic alliances are seeking mutual benefits by pooling their complementary resources and capabilities. They seek to obtain advantages and share the value created by building and maintaining reciprocal interdependencies between the partners. To do so, they must build collective interest as opposed to self-interest, build trust and create reciprocal exchanges among the partners (Lado, Boyd & Hanlon, 1997). However, transferring firm-specific resources and skills is difficult and complex (Anand & Singh, 1997). Furthermore, when partners acquire knowledge in these alliances, the bargaining power may shift, thereby eliminating this partner's dependence on the other partner. In these cases, without trust, the independent partner may take advantage of the other and control or leave the alliance to become a competitor (Inkpen & Beamish, 1997). When firms are in an alliance to create innovation, skills sharing is particularly important because of the likely heterogeneity of the capabilities in R&D of the separate partners (Sakakibara, 1997). However, the resource sharing in R&D alliances designed to produce innovation leaves partners particularly vulnerable. As a result, the governance of these relationships may be critical to the success of such an undertaking.

The governance of R&D and the importance of social capital is discussed in the chapter by Keil. Keil notes that prior analysis of the governance for R&D has been dominated by a focus on transaction costs. If firms conduct R&D solely internal to the firm, the type of oversight required is hierarchical governance. However, in intermediate arrangements, R&D may be conducted collaboratively with an external partner as suggested above. While we may analyze this situation through a transaction cost framework, Keil argues that there are several deficiencies with this approach. Most importantly, it tends to ignore the value that can be created through collaborative activities. That is, transactions may have costs but they also have potential benefits. Therefore, Keil argues for the use of a social capital approach. As communicated earlier, a social capital approach examines the value created by the social relationships, thereby allowing the effective integration and collaborative use of complementary resources and capabilities.

Teece, Pisano and Shuen (1997) argue that firms successful in the global marketplace have demonstrated and implemented timely, rapid and flexible product innovation. Furthermore, they suggest that the capability to effectively coordinate and redeploy internal and external competencies to accomplish such innovation is critically important. Thus, competence is important as a source of competitive advantage in research and development productivity. Henderson and Cockburn's (1994) research found that firm capabilities and competencies explained a substantial amount of variance in research productivity across firms they examined. The last set of chapters in this book describes the allocation of resources in investment to produce innovation and the capabilities and competencies necessary to create appropriate innovation for gaining and maintaining competitive advantage.

McGrath and Dubini's chapter describes the allocation of resources to new research projects. Thus, the commitment of resources to these projects becomes critical to their survival and ultimate success. McGrath and Dubini contrast a rational decision process for allocating resources to new projects with a real options approach. Real options logic suggests that small investments in a project can be made in order to create the right but not the obligation to participate in future opportunities. If the project becomes successful, the option can be exercised and the company would then commit to a full-scale new project. However, if the project failed, losses are limited. They argue that investing in real options can not only create a preemptive strategy, but also reduce the uncertainty related to this strategy. McGrath and Dubini believe that real options logic provides a more realistic view of investing in new development projects and can be more effectively applied by managers than an assumed rational decision process.

In an earlier chapter, we noted the use of resources to expand into international markets and that operating in international markets also produced some resources. The Subramaniam and Venkatraman chapter describes the influence of tacit international knowledge on global new product development capabilities. These authors argue the importance of global new product development. One of the key elements in successful new product development is the ability to transfer knowledge and deploy it across national borders. In doing so, it can provide advantages over competitors in these markets. Their research provided strong support for the leveraging of tacit international market knowledge to build a global new product development capability. They integrated tacit overseas information in the global new product design through information processing mechanisms. They also note that a firm's ability to integrate this new knowledge in order to build capabilities is limited by the firm's *relative* absorptive capacity, a concept proposed by Lane and Lubatkin (1998).

Koga and Davila's chapter focuses on the role of performance goals in new product development. Koga and Davila argue that performance goals have several purposes. First, they serve as a benchmark for rewards to product designers, thereby overcoming potential agency problems. Second, performance goals guide actual performance and facilitate the planning and coordination among business functions involved in new product development. Third, performance goals can serve as a catalyst for organizational learning among workers involved in new product development, in order to achieve the goal. The authors' research did not provide support for the use of performance goals to alleviate the agency problem or to facilitate coordination. However, it showed strong support for the argument that performance goals guide and facilitate organizational learning to achieve the targets. Therefore, the use of goals facilitate the building of organizational knowledge and capabilities in order to produce innovation.

The final chapter, by Leifer and Rice, emphasizes a very interesting and potentially important premise. These authors explain how mature firms can build the capability to produce what they refer to as breakthrough innovation. Leifer and Rice note the importance of innovation in the current competitive environment, making it important for firms, even those in mature industries, to become more innovative. That is, innovation is required to be strategically competitive in most global markets. Leifer and Rice's chapter reports on a multicase, three-year longitudinal study of 12 ongoing breakthrough innovation projects in 10 large, mature firms. They identified five tactics that fostered breakthrough innovation. These included stimulating attractive ideas, promoting opportunity recognition, evaluating and screening breakthrough innovations, creating incubating organizational structures and catalyzing individual initiatives. These are described in detail and have substantial managerial implications. They conclude that conventional management techniques are unsuitable in most of these cases until uncertainty can be reduced substantially. This means that conventional management techniques are largely inappropriate until the innovation can be introduced to the market. Innovative capabilities, thus, may warrant special attention to be maximally leveraged as firm resources.

In summary, this book focuses on the development, use and oversight of strategic resources. The resource-based view of the firm has become a popular, if not dominant, focus in strategic management. However, there have been few in-depth examinations of this approach to strategic management within firms. This book provides multiple perspectives on the creation and outcomes of strategic resources as well as how they can be developed, allocated and used to produce sustainable competitive advantages in firms. As a result, the chapters presented in this book provide a valuable in-depth view of how strategic resources can be developed and leveraged to create value in business organizations.

## REFERENCES

Amit, R. & Schoemaker, P.J.H. (1993). Strategic assets and organizational rent. *Strategic Management Journal*, **14**, 33–46.

Anand, J. & Singh, H. (1997). Asset redeployment, acquisitions and corporate strategy in declining industries. *Strategic Management Journal*, **18** (Special Issue), 99–118.

Arora, A. & Gambardella, A. (1997). Domestic markets and international competitiveness: generic and product-specific competencies in the engineering sector. *Strategic Management Journal*, **18** (Special Issue), 53–74.

Barnett, W.P., Greve, H.R. & Park, D.Y. (1994). An evolutionary model of organizational performance. *Strategic Management Journal*, **15** (Special Issue), 11–28.

Barney, J.B. (1986). Strategic factor markets: Expectations, luck and business strategy. *Management Science*, **31**, 1231–1241.

Barney, J.B. (1991). Firm resources and sustained competitive advantage. *Journal of Management*, **17**, 99–120.

Coff, R.W. (1997). Human assets and management dilemmas: Coping with hazards on the road to resource-based theory. *Academy of Management Review*, 22, 374–402.

Cohen, W.N. & Levinthal, D.A. (1990). Absorptive capacity: A new perspective on learning and innovation. *Administrative Science Quarterly*, **35**, 128–152.

Dierickx, I. & Cool, K. (1989). Asset stock accumulation and sustainability of competitive advantage. *Management Science*, **35**, 1504–1511.

Garrone, P. & Rossini, A. (1998). The role of technological and product capabilities in a new high-tech business: The case of cellular services. *Journal of High Technology Management Research*, **9**, 285–307.

Gulati, R. (1998). Alliances and networks. *Strategic Management Journal*, **19** (Special Issue), 293–317.

Henderson, R. & Cockburn, I. (1994). Measuring competence? Exploring firm effects in pharmaceutical research. *Strategic Management Journal*, **15** (Special Issue), 63–84.

Hitt, M.A., Hoskisson, R.E. & Kim, H. (1997). International diversification: Effects on innovation and firm performance in product-diversified firms. *Academy of Management Journal*, **40**, 767–798.

Hitt, M.A. & Ireland, R.D. (1985). Corporate distinctive competence, strategy, industry and performance. *Strategic Management Journal*, **6**, 273–293.

Hitt, M.A., Ireland, R.D. & Hoskisson, R.E. (1999). *Strategic Management: Competitiveness and Globalization*. Cincinnati, OH: SouthWestern Publishing.

Hitt, M.A., Keats, B.W. & DeMarie, S.M. (1998). Navigating in the new competitive landscape: Building strategic flexibility and competitive advantage in the 21st century. *Academy of Management Executive*, **12**(4), 22–42.

Inkpen, A.C. & Beamish, P.W. (1997). Knowledge, bargaining power, and the instability of international joint ventures. *Academy of Management Review*, 22, 177–202.

Lado, A.A., Boyd, N.G. & Hanlon, F.C. (1997). Competition, cooperation, and the search for economic rents: A syncretic model. *Academy of Management Review*, 22, 110–141.

Lane, P.J. & Lubatkin, N. (1998). Relative absorptive capacity and interorganizational learning. *Strategic Management Journal*, **19**, 461–477.

Lei, D., Hitt, M.A. & Bettis, R. (1996). Dynamic core competences through meta-learning and strategic context. *Journal of Management*, 22, 549–569.

Leonard-Barton, D. (1992). Core capabilities and core rigidities: A paradox in managing new product development. *Strategic Management Journal*, **13**, 111–125.
Miles, R.E., Snow, C.C., Mathews, J.A., Miles, G. & Coleman, H.J., Jr. (1997). Organizing in the Knowledge Age: Anticipating the cellular form. *Academy of Management Executive*, **11**(4), 7–20.
Montgomery, C.A. & Wernerfelt, B. (1988). Diversification, Ricardian rents, and Tobin's Q. *Rand Journal of Economics*, **19**, 623–632.
Murtha, T.P., Lenway, S.A. & Bagozzi, R.P. (1998). Global mindsets and cognitive shifts in a complex multinational corporation. *Strategic Management Journal*, **19**, 97–114.
Nahapiet, J. & Ghoshal, S. (1998). Social capital, intellectual capital, and the organizational advantage. *Academy of Management Review*, **23**, 242–266.
Oliver, C. (1997). Sustainable competitive advantage: Combining institutional and resource-based views. *Strategic Management Journal*, **18**, 697–714.
Penrose, E.T. (1959). *The Theory of the Growth of the Firm*. New York: Wiley.
Pisano, G.P. (1994). Knowledge, integration, and the locus of learning: An empirical analysis of process development. *Strategic Management Journal*, **15** (Special Issue), 85–100.
Praest, N. (1998). Changing technological capabilities in high-tech firms: A study of the telecommunications industry. *Journal of High Technology Management Research*, **9**, 175–193.
Rao, H. (1994). The social construction of reputation: Certification contests, legitimation and the survival of organizations in the American automobile industry, 1895–1912. *Strategic Management Journal*, **15** (Special Issue), 29–44.
Reed, R. & DeFillippi, R.J. (1990). Causal ambiguity, barriers to imitation and sustainable competitive advantage. *Academy of Management Review*, **15**, 88–102.
Rumelt, R. (1991). How much does industry matter? *Strategic Management Journal*, **12**, 167–185.
Sakakibara, M. (1997). Heterogeneity of firm capabilities and cooperative research and development: An empirical examination of motives. *Strategic Management Journal*, **18** (Special Issue), 143–164.
Schendel, D.E. (1996). Editor's introduction to the 1996 Winter Special Issue: Knowledge and the firm. *Strategic Management Journal*, **17** (Special Issue), 1–4.
Schilling, M.A. (1998). Technological lockout: An integrative model of the economic and strategic factors driving technology success and failure. *Academy of Management Review*, **23**, 267–284.
Teece, D.J., Pisano, G. & Shuen, A. (1997). Dynamic capabilities and strategic management. *Strategic Management Journal*, **18**, 509–534.
Wernerfelt, B. (1984). A resource-based view of the firm. *Strategic Management Journal*, **5**, 171–180.

# Organizational Resources: Outcomes and Strategy

# 2

# Core Competencies and the Knowledge of the Firm

MOACIR DE MIRANDA OLIVEIRA JUNIOR

## INTRODUCTION

This paper helps the reader to understand how knowledge management can contribute to a firm's development of sustainable competitive advantage. Two basic assumptions underlie this work. The first is that knowledge is a resource that can and must be managed to improve the firm's performance. The second assumption is that an organization's wellspring of new knowledge is always an organizational learning process, which the company can and must try to influence. The challenge presented is to discover how the organizational learning process can be stimulated and the firm's knowledge managed to develop the firm's core competencies in a superior way.

The paper is structured in three main sections. The first section deepens the link between the knowledge of the firm and its core competencies, showing knowledge as a resource that contributes to the development of competencies. In the second section the notion that the firm's main role is the efficient management of its knowledge is presented, as well as knowledge taxonomy and its strategic implications for the firm's management. The third section argues that theories of knowledge creation, integration and combination can be applied to the development of

*Dynamic Strategic Resources: Development, Diffusion and Integration.*
Edited by Michael A. Hitt, Patricia Gorman Clifford, Robert D. Nixon and Kevin P. Coyne.

strategically relevant collective knowledge and core competencies. Finally, concluding remarks are presented.

## Resources and Competitive Advantage

In the first part of this section the main implications of the resource-based view of the firm for the definition of the firm's core competencies are presented. The second part discusses what are the firm's strategic competencies and presents the ways through which the firm's core competencies and its knowledge are linked.

### Resource-Based View of the Firm

The challenge in discovering how firms develop and maintain competitive advantage is one of the central research streams in strategic management theory. In the last 15 years a framework for strategy that combines both internal and external analysis of the organization has emerged, and its basic premise is that its resources drive a company's performance. This framework is the so-called "resource-based view of the firm". This approach proposes that resources are the main determinant of the competitiveness of the firm, in opposition to the approach of industry analysis (Porter, 1980), in which the main determinant of the firm's competitiveness is its industry position.

Resource endowment has a long tradition in economics, an important early work in this field being that of Penrose (1959), which saw firms as broader sets of resources. The actual discussion is rooted in Wernerfelt's (1984) work, which presents resources as anything that could be thought of as a strength or weakness of the firm, or as those (tangible and intangible) assets which are tied semi-permanently to the firm. Wernerfelt's (1984) approach presents a way of using resources as the main source of competitive advantage, through the development of what the author called "resource position". By resource position the author meant the possibility of using resources to develop a competitive position more difficult for others to catch up with. The author gives some examples of resources: brand names, in-house knowledge of technology, employment of skilled personnel, trade contacts, machinery, efficient procedures, capital, etc.

Another important contribution is the perspective that "a major contribution of the resource-based model is that it explains long lived differences in firm profitability that cannot be attributed to differences in industry conditions. (...) So long as the assets are imperfectly mobile, inimitable, and nonsubstitutable, other firms will not be able to mimic its strategy.'' (Peteraf, 1993: 186). Indeed, the conditions outlined above are reinforced by Barney's (1991) assertion that ''firms cannot expect to 'purchase' sustained competitive advantages on open markets (...). Rather, such advantages must be found in the rare, imperfectly imitable, and non-substitutable resources already controlled by a firm''. This follows conditions presented by Dierickx and Cool (1989: 1510) that state that strategic assets are nontradeable, nonimitable and nonsubstitutable.

The need for a resource difficult to imitate, transfer, buy, sell or substitute (Wernerfelt, 1984; Barney, 1991; Dierickx & Cool, 1989; Peteraf, 1993) that must have a systemic integration with other resources is therefore the main contribution of the resource-based view of the firm to the development of sustainable competitive strategy. In a more comprehensive way, Schoemaker and Amit (1997) present the distinctive characteristics of strategic assets, including:

- Difficult to trade or imitate
- Scarce, durable, and not easily substituted
- Complementary to one another (that is, one asset's value increases as another asset's value increases)
- Specialized to the firm (hard to transfer)
- In line with the future strategic industry factors
- Creating value for the firm's shareholders (appropriable).

From a resource-based perspective core competencies can form the basis of firm-specific advantages, especially across borders (Lei, Hitt & Bettis, 1996), and this is the subject of the next part of this section.

## Core Competencies

Resources may be tangible or intangible, and sometimes it is difficult even to identify the resource we are referring to, but in this discussion ''the notion that some resources commanded by a firm, particularly those which are intangible, can be a result of processes by which a firm creates or acquires knowledge about its operations, that is to say, processes of organizational learning'' is of particular interest (Drummond, 1997: 12–13). Some examples of intangible resources are ''organizational knowledge'' or ''trust between management and labor'', that ''cannot be traded or easily replicated by competitors since they are deeply rooted in the organization's history and culture. Such assets accumulate slowly over time. (...) The more firm-specific, the more durable the assets are and the harder they are for competitors to imitate.'' (Schoemaker & Amit, 1997: 374).

The resource-based view of the firm and, more specifically, the development of intangible resources establish important connections with the work of Prahalad and Hamel (1990). Wernerfelt (1994: 171) regards Prahalad and Hamel's (1990) work as being "single-handedly responsible for diffusion of the resource-based view into practice". These authors say that, more important than the development of well-defined strategic business units with their artificial boundaries that obstruct the spreading of knowledge in the company, is the "ability to build, at lower cost and more speedily than the competitors, the core competencies that spawn unanticipated products" (Prahalad & Hamel, 1990: 81). These authors understand core competencies as "the collective learning in the organization, especially how to co-ordinate diverse production skills and integrate multiple streams of technologies" (Prahalad & Hamel, 1990: 82). In other words, core competence is "a bundle of skills and technologies that enables a company to provide a particular benefit to customers" (Hamel & Prahalad, 1994: 199), and represents a "sum of learning across individual skills sets and individual organizational units" (Hamel & Prahalad, 1994: 203), rather than a single discrete skill or technology.

The core competence concept is not new. Leonard-Barton (1992: 111–112) explains that "various authors have called them distinctive competencies (Snow and Hrebiniak, 1980; Hitt and Ireland, 1985), core or organizational competencies (Prahalad and Hamel, 1990; Hayes, Wheelright and Clark, 1988), firm-specific competence (Pavitt, 1991), resource deployments (Hofer and Schendel, 1978), and invisible assets (Itami, with Roehl, 1987)". Despite the terminology, what is clear is that the concept is a useful tool to help us understand how resources are associated with firms' performance.

To recognize the core competence of the firm, it is necessary to understand why a firm has superior returns, and what are the distinctive capabilities that sustain it. In order to better understand Prahalad and Hamel's proposition, Rumelt (1994: xvi) cites the following main features of the firm's core competencies:

1. *Corporate span*. Core competencies span business and products within a corporation. Put differently, powerful core competencies support several products or businesses.
2. *Temporal dominance*. Products are but the momentary expression of a corporation's core competencies. Competencies are more stable and evolve more slowly than products do.
3. *Learning by doing*. Competencies are gained and enhanced by work.
4. *Competitive locus*. Product-market competition is merely the superficial expression of a deeper competition over competencies.

The flip side of core competencies, or core capabilities, is core rigidities. Core rigidities inhibit innovation and "are activated when companies fall prey to insularity or overshoot an optimal level of best practices." (Leonard-Barton, 1995: 55). The management task is to search and develop a new core resource when the actual core is still doing well. IBM's problems in recent years are an example. The failure in renewing its core competencies on the manufacturing, marketing and servicing of large mainframe computers before the market deterioration, made these competencies become core rigidities, and the firm has now to develop new core competencies to become competitive again (Hitt, Keats & DeMarie, 1998).

Core competencies must have a dynamic nature in order to prevent them from becoming core rigidities, mainly in turbulent and chaotic environments: "Dynamic refers to the capacity to renew competencies so as to achieve congruence with the changing business environment; certain innovative responses are required when time-to-market and timing are critical, the rate of technological change is rapid, and the nature of future competition and markets difficult to determine" (Teece, Pisano & Shuen, 1997: 515). Dynamic core competencies require organizational learning for their development and continuous updating (Hitt, Keats & DeMarie, 1998). Learning occurs in the firm and in the firm's network (at a corporate level), and multinational firms have an advantage over local firms as their subsidiaries operate in different environments, facing different threats and opportunities, and giving a greater possibility of learning and thus increasing their competitive advantage (Bartlett & Ghoshal, 1986).

The same is also true in relation to interorganizational learning, through collaborations and alliances (Hamel, 1991; Inkpen, 1996; Child & Faulkner, 1998), where partners can exchange knowledge and learn with each other; such learning can therefore be a vehicle for new organizational learning and for renewal of the firm's core competencies.

In this work it is proposed that collective tacit knowledge is the root of the firm's core competencies and the outcome of processes of knowledge sharing, mainly know-how socialization, that occurs through observation, imitation and practice (Nonaka & Takeuchi, 1995) within and between firms. As these knowledge-sharing processes should occur in ways that can be controlled by the firm, and as they are connected to work practices, they are idiosyncratic to the firm(s) and easier to protect. The sustainability of the advantage given by the core competency is also a function of the collective knowledge, mainly tacit know-how, integrated within it. This idea expands Grant's (1996) proposition that "the broader the scope of the knowledge integrated within a capability, then the more difficult imitation becomes" (Grant, 1996: 117).

The resource-based view of the firm presents an important contribution to the understanding of how intangible assets can constitute the basis of a competitive strategy and how to identify what are the strategic assets or core competencies that will secure superior returns to the company in the future. However, as firm-specific resources receive more emphasis, "questions of how they can be acquired and developed become increasingly relevant, which is the domain of learning" (Moingeon & Edmondson, 1996: 9). It is also the domain of skill acquisition and the management of knowledge, believed to lay the greatest potential for contributions to strategy (Teece, Pisano & Shuen, 1997). The next section of the paper addresses the question of how the organizational learning theory and the knowledge of the firm theory can be helpful to the development of firm-specific resources and mainly of the firm's core competencies.

## The Firm as an Agent of Knowledge Creation and Transfer

Theories of the firm are conceptualizations about the real world that try to explain and predict the firm's behavior. Every theory is designed to address a particular set of its characteristics and behaviors (Grant, 1996). Relevant contributions to the challenge of providing a better comprehension of the firm's behaviors are found in the history of companies (Chandler, 1962) and in organizational theory (Morgan, 1986), among others. Attempts at integrating economics and organizational approaches are found in the behavioral theory of the firm (Cyert & March, 1963) and the evolutionary theory of the firm (Nelson & Winter, 1982). New theories of the firm have appeared that try to explain what are the determining factors of the firm's success. The resource-based view of the firm, discussed in the first section, is among these theoretical attempts.

Recently, some researchers have begun working on the deepening of the resource-based approach, to constitute a knowledge-based perspective. This proposition appeared in the 1990s as a result of the confluence of some research streams, and is still in its first stages of development: "The emerging 'knowledge-based view' is not, as yet, a theory of the firm (...) To the extent that it focuses upon knowledge as the most strategically important of the firm's resources it is an outgrowth of the resource-based view. At the same time, knowledge is central to several quite distinct research traditions, notably *organizational learning*, the *management of technology*, and *managerial cognition*." (Grant, 1996: 110—emphasis as in the original). These research fields heavily influence the knowledge-based theory. The learning theory gives considerable attention to how organizations learn, but much less to the implication that organizations already "know" something (Kogut & Zander, 1992). Despite this, the comprehension of learning as the process that changes the state of knowledge of an individual or organization (Sanchez & Heene, 1997) makes both fields "not detachable". Research on technological innovation and diffusion (e.g., Rogers, 1983; von Hippel, 1988; Cohen & Levinthal, 1990) is seminal for the emergent knowledge perspective. The distinction of individual tacit knowledge (Polanyi, 1966) from collective tacit knowledge, presented in today's literature by Weick and Roberts (1993) and Spender (1996), gives substance to the formulation of strategic implications on these types of knowledge for the firm's performance. Finally, the knowledge-based approach deepens the more relevant role that knowledge must play in organizations and society (Bell, 1973; Toffler, 1990; Quinn, 1992; Drucker, 1993, among others), from the point of view of strategic management.

The firm's definition adopted in this work is aligned with recent theoretical developments, which understand knowledge as the main strategic asset in the firm. The main role of the firm is to manage this asset in order to improve organizational performance. This work follows Kogut and Zander's (1993: 627) definition that sustains that "firms are social communities that serve as efficient mechanisms for the creation and transformation of knowledge into economically rewarded products and services". The company is understood as a knowledge stock that consists basically of codified and applicable knowledge as well as knowledge related to coordination of actions in the organization. What will determine the firm's success is its efficiency in the transformation of knowledge as ideas into knowledge that can be applied, in comparison with the efficiency of other companies in this process (Kogut & Zander, 1993).

The view of the company as an agent of knowledge creation and transfer points to the need for a definition of organizational knowledge. In the next part of this section the knowledge concept and its constitutive aspects are discussed.

## The Knowledge Concept

The knowledge concept is not consensual. The history of philosophy, since the classical Greek period, is associated with an endless search for the meaning of the concept of knowledge. Nonaka (1994: 15) affirms the traditional epistemology to adopt a definition of knowledge as "justified true belief". Related to the same question of "what is knowledge?", Grant (1996: 110) states that "since this question has intrigued some of the world's greatest thinkers from Plato to Popper without the emergence of a clear consensus, this is not an arena in which I choose to compete", and proposes that the recognition that there are many types of knowledge relevant to the firm is enough for managerial discussion on the theme. The definition adopted in this paper understands knowledge as the "set of beliefs held by an individual about causal relationships among phenomena" (Sanchez,

Heene & Thomas, 1996: 9), understanding causal relationships as cause-and-effect relationships between imaginable events or actions and likely consequences of those events or actions. Organizational knowledge is defined as "the shared set of beliefs about causal relationships held by individuals within a group" (Sanchez & Heene, 1997: 5).

Sanchez and Heene (1997) explain that the intentions of these definitions are threefold: first, to explain that the strategic relevance of knowledge is never given, absolute or deterministic, but exists only as beliefs, based on evaluations of possible causal relationships between phenomena; second, to recognize that knowledge originates and exists in individuals' minds, but organizations can have knowledge in several ways that is understood by more than one individual in the company; and finally, to "refocus the concept of knowledge on conscious mental processes (beliefs) rather than lower-level neural processes at the level of sensory-motor co-ordination" (Sanchez & Heene, 1997: 5). At this stage it is important to clarify the concepts of tacit and explicit knowledge, and of its constitutive elements. In the next part these concepts are presented.

## Components of the Firm's Knowledge

The distinction between kinds of knowledge presented by Polanyi (1966) and put under an economic and business approach by Nelson and Winter (1982) is basic for actual research on knowledge in management theory. Nonaka (1994), referring to Polanyi's work, states that the primary distinction is between two kinds of knowledge: "tacit knowledge" and "explicit knowledge". Explicit—or codified—knowledge refers to knowledge that is transmittable in formal, systematic language, while tacit knowledge has a personal quality, which makes it more difficult to formalize and communicate. "Tacit knowledge is deeply rooted in action, commitment, and involvement in a specific context" (Nonaka, 1994: 16). Polanyi (1966) tends to define knowledge in terms of its difficulty to communicate, but this is not a consensual perspective. "Tacit does not mean knowledge that *cannot* be codified (see Nonaka's treatment); it is best defined as 'not yet explained'" (Spender, 1996: 58—emphasis as in the original), meaning that there are some dimensions of tacit knowledge that must be better explored.

Spender (1996) suggests that tacit knowledge in the workplace activity usually has three components: the *conscious*, the *automatic*, and the *collective*. The conscious component is that more easily codified, as the individual can understand what he or she is doing. In the automatic component the individual does not have consciousness about what he is applying, and the activity is performed in an unconscious way ("taken-for-granted knowledge"). The collective component relates to the knowledge developed by the individual and shared with others in the workplace, but also to that knowledge that is part and parcel of the social system. Spender (1996) adds to these three components of tacit knowledge another category, understood as "scientific" or "objective" (and more easily understood), and presents a matrix of types of knowledge (Exhibit 2.1).

Spender (1996) argues that each type of organizational knowledge can provide the basis for competitive advantage, and this work is discussed below.

It has been stated that the knowledge of the firm can be explicit or tacit, and the latter can be conscious, automatic or collective. But this is not the only approach to understanding the dimensions of organizational knowledge. Another approach suggests a twofold typology that distinguishes the knowledge of the firm in two parts: information and know-how. "By information we mean knowledge that can be transmitted without loss of integrity once the syntactical rules required for deciphering it are known. Information includes facts, axiomatic propositions, and symbols" (Kogut & Zander, 1992: 386). Kogut and Zander quote von Hippel (1988) to define know-how as the "accumulated practical skill or expertise that allows one to do something smoothly and efficiently" and explain that the key word in the definition is "accumulated", as it implies that know-how must be learned and acquired.

It seems clear that a relationship can be established between the concepts of information and explicit knowledge on the one hand, and between know-how and tacit knowledge on the other. If information is based on syntactical rules, it is codified and explicit in a comprehensible and socially accessible way in the company. As know-how is an "accumulated" ability, it means that this expertise in "how to do" is not always easily explained, which establishes a nexus with the notions of tacit knowledge in its automatic and collective dimensions. This assertion is reinforced by Grant (1996: 111—emphasis as in the original) that identifies "*knowing how* with *tacit knowledge*, and *knowing about* facts and theories with *explicit knowledge*" and explains that explicit knowledge is revealed by its communication, and tacit knowledge is revealed through its application, meaning that the critical

| | *Individual* | *Social* |
|---|---|---|
| *Explicit* | Conscious | Objectified |
| *Implicit* | Automatic | Collective |

Exhibit 2.1 Types of organizational knowledge. (Source: Spender, 1996: 64)

distinction between the two types of knowledge is related to their transferability and to the mechanisms for this.

The existing knowledge in different companies differs in its dimensions, and these differences must reflect the value and strategic utility of this knowledge. In the next part, relevant aspects of knowledge transfer are presented, taxonomy for knowledge is introduced, and the implications of the nature of knowledge for its management are discussed.

## Knowledge Transfer

Companies have knowledge distributed and shared for all, but there are also several stocks of knowledge that belong to individuals, small groups or functional areas. Organizations look for codification and simplification of this knowledge in order to make it more widely accessible. On a more basic level, the establishment of a common language by individuals and groups in companies is fundamental in order to express and articulate common beliefs, connecting individual beliefs and creating a structure for organizational knowledge. Companies codify this knowledge through different means (e.g. manuals, engineering drawings) in an attempt to provide a structure to knowledge. Through codification, organizations can improve the apprehensibility of knowledge and thus its transfer between groups within the organization and even across its borders (Sanchez & Heene, 1997).

Apprehensibility in knowledge transfer processes is also enhanced by the receptor's "absorptive capacity", that is largely a function of the level of prior related knowledge, not in any single individual but in links across a mosaic of individual capabilities (Cohen & Levinthal, 1990). For firms' alliances the concept of "partner-specific absorptive capacity" refers to the firm's "ability to recognize and assimilate valuable knowledge from a particular alliance partner", and this capacity is a "function of (1) the extent to which partners have developed overlapping knowledge basis and (2) the extent to which partners have developed interaction routines that maximize the frequency and intensity of sociotechnical interactions" (Dyer & Singh, 1998: 665).

Knowledge can be distinguished between personal, group, organizational and network knowledge. The teaching of know-how and information among individuals requires interaction within small groups, often through the development of a unique language and code. Among groups, when the transfer of knowledge is within the same function, the problems of different professional languages are attenuated. But when the transfer among groups involves different functions (e.g. from development to production), and the shared codes of professional groups differ, the codification process plays a central role. "To facilitate this transfer, a set of higher-order organizing principles act as mechanisms by which to codify technologies into a language accessible to a wider circle of individuals" (Kogut & Zander, 1992: 389). These principles are called higher-order as they facilitate the integration of the whole company. Therefore, firms can be understood as "communities" where knowledge can be communicated and combined by a common language and organizing principles.

The problem of moving the knowledge in the company may also be distinguished as mobility both within the "communities of practice"—a group in which know-how is shared and needs to work together to put it in practice—and between the communities (Brown & Duguid, forthcoming). Within communities, knowledge is continuously embedded in practice; thus producing and propagating knowledge are almost indivisible, as the members have the same beliefs, language and organizing principles. Between communities of practice, since usually each community has different beliefs about the work and the world and a distinct shared conduct code, these differences often imply difficulties for knowledge transfer. A study of Hewlett-Packard's approach to quality is a good example. The firm was quite successful in identifying its "best" practices, but not so successful in moving them (Cole, forthcoming, quoted in Brown & Duguid) because of problems related to different language and organizing principles (Kogut & Zander, 1992) and distinct shared conduct codes (Brown & Duguid, forthcoming) among groups.

Communities of practice are generated from social interactions, which go beyond the internal and external boundaries imposed by organizations (Brown & Duguid, 1991). Within the network of interacting companies, the know-how transfer implies long-term relationships, which demand the development of a common code learnt and shared by the companies involved (Kogut & Zander, 1992). This assertion is reinforced by the comprehension that "a firm may choose to seek advantages by creating assets that are specialized in conjunction with the assets of an alliance partner". One of the three types of asset specificity identified is the "human asset specificity", that refers to "transaction-specific know-how accumulated by transactors through long-standing relationships (e.g., dedicated supplier engineers who learn the systems, procedures, and the individuals idiosyncratic to the buyer). Human cospecialization increases as alliance partners develop experience working together and accumulate specialized information, language, and know-how. This allows them to communicate efficiently and effectively, which reduces communication and errors, thereby enhancing quality and increasing speed to market" (Dyer & Singh, 1998: 662). The development of a common code shared by firms, which facilitates knowledge transfer, can therefore itself constitute an advantage for the partners in a cooperative relationship.

Knowledge transfer can act as a tool for improving the firm's performance, but it is a "double-edged sword". In efforts to replicate actual and new knowledge, a central paradox appears: codification and simplification of knowledge also induce the likelihood of imitation (Kogut & Zander, 1992). Knowledge transfer is a desired and necessary strategy to the firm's development, but the facility of imitation by competitors will corrode the company's advantage.

Deliberate transfer of knowledge must be distinguished from the diffusion of strategically relevant knowledge that escapes the firm's control. Companies need to keep control over this diffusion that can reduce the strategic relevance of the company's competencies (Sanchez, 1997). This is the same premise of the distinction between voluntary and involuntary transfer. Features that restrict involuntary transfer tend also to inhibit voluntary transfer, while actions to facilitate voluntary transfer can also facilitate involuntary transfer (Winter, 1987), and managers have to perceive the risks associated with this paradox.

A taxonomy of organizational knowledge can contribute to clarifying the question of how to restrict involuntary transfer without inhibiting voluntary transfer, presenting dimensions for analysis of the nature of knowledge that could facilitate this task.

## Organizational Knowledge Taxonomy

All firms own several sets of knowledge but, for each company, and perhaps for each industry, there is a kind or just a few kinds of knowledge that are strategically relevant. A taxonomy of organizational knowledge, and its subsequent strategic implications, could be useful for managers in understanding what are the characteristics of the sets of knowledge that can provide an advantage to the firm. Winter (1987) presents a taxonomy of organizational knowledge (see Exhibit 2.2) where a position near the left of a continuum is an indicator that the knowledge may be difficult to transfer, whereas a position near the right is indicative of ease of transfer.

The first of these continua ranges from highly tacit knowledge to fully articulable knowledge. On the one hand, individual skills are highly tacit and even the person who owns the knowledge cannot give a useful explanation of its rules. On the other hand, fully articulable knowledge can be communicated from its possessor to another person, who becomes as much "in the know" as the originator (Winter, 1987).

The first subdimension of the Tacit/Articulable continuum is Teachable/Not teachable. Tacit skills may be teachable even though not articulable. Winter (1987: 171) explains that "successful learning presupposes the willingness of the pupil to engage in a series of trial performances and to

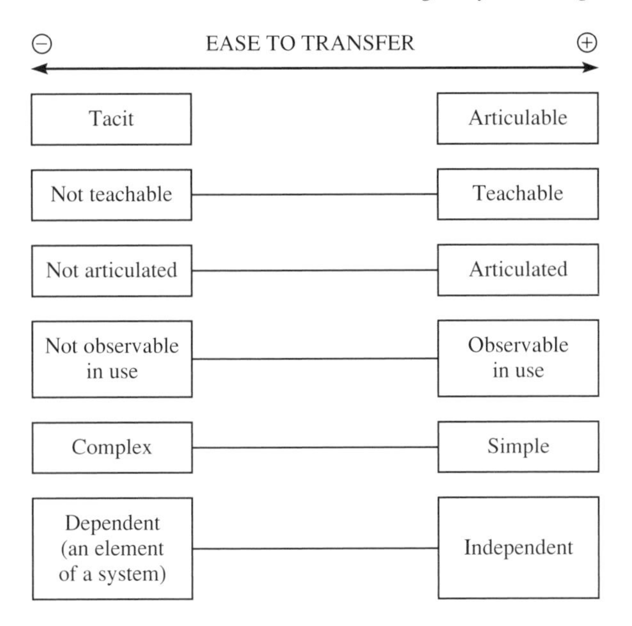


EXHIBIT 2.2 Taxonomic dimensions of knowledge assets. (Source: Adapted from Winter, 1987: 170)

attend to the teacher's critique of the errors made in these trials. Teachers may also provide a model performance of the skill, which provides the pupil with an opportunity for imitative learning." (One example is *on-the-job* training in multinational consulting companies, where junior consultants follow senior consultants in their work, in order to learn the appropriate procedures and attitude in dealing with clients.) The second subdimension is Not articulated/Articulated, which distinguishes between articulable knowledge that *is* articulated and *is not* articulated. Articulable knowledge that is not articulated can simply "change to another company" in an employee's head, or "be forgotten" as time goes on.

The second of the major continua concerns observability in use. It relates to the extent of knowledge exposition necessary for the knowledge to become useful to anybody outside the company. The design of a product launched in the market is a secret difficult to keep if the product is made available for purchase (and also can be freely observed).

The dimension Complex/Simple means the amount of information required to characterize the item of knowledge in question. This dimension is related to the amount of interacting elements in a specific activity or product, where a smaller amount of elements implies a greater simplicity and transfer facility. The Dependent/Independent dimension has the same assumption. When a knowledge set is already available to be useful alone, it is also more easily transferred. Winter (1987) gives the example of a pocket calculator and a microcomputer module to exemplify the extremes that go from a totally independent element to an element that is just one part of a more complex system.

In another piece of research, designed to define the attributes of knowledge to be considered in decisions on technology transfer internally or externally to the company, Kogut and Zander (1993) defined the attributes "codifiability", "teachability" and "complexity" as the main ones to be considered. For codifiability the author understands the extent to which the knowledge has been articulated in documents. For teachability, it is the ease by which know-how can be taught to new workers. Complexity relates to the number of critical and interacting elements embraced by an entity or activity.

Another proposition, focused on the utilization of the knowledge to value creation within the company, is presented by Grant (1996). These are the characteristics of the knowledge presented:

1. *Transferability*. Relates to the possibility of knowledge transfer within and between companies.
2. *Capacity for aggregation*. Also related to knowledge transfer. Relates to the possibility of the transferred knowledge being aggregated to knowledge previously existing in the company. The "absorptive capacity" (Cohen & Levinthal, 1990) of the recipient is central.
3. *Appropriability*. Refers to the ability of the owner of a resource to receive a return equal to the value created by that resource.
4. *Specialization in knowledge acquisition*. As the human brain has limited capacity to acquire, store and process knowledge, individual specialists in particular areas of knowledge are necessary to allow knowledge to be acquired.
5. *The knowledge requirements of production*. Makes the assumption that the critical input in production and primary source of value is knowledge.

Each of the above knowledge taxonomies and characteristics presented (Winter, 1987; Kogut & Zander, 1993; Grant, 1996) must be analyzed for the definition of the pertinent strategy for the firm. Key complementary dimensions to determine the strategic importance of the knowledge in the firms are: (1) value creation, meaning the possibility of the specific knowledge to bring rents to the company; (2) transferability, understood as the likelihood of the firm's use of the knowledge in the company's network, internally or in cooperation with partners; and (3) inimitability, related to the risk of competitors reproducing that kind of knowledge and therefore eroding the company's advantage. A more detailed analysis of the strategic implications of the knowledge taxonomy presented is the subject of the next part.

## Strategic Implications of Knowledge Taxonomy

There are three main points about the intrinsic nature of the knowledge that are relevant to the strategic action: (1) the definition of what knowledge is really worthy to be developed by the company; (2) how the firm can share the knowledge—when it is possible—that will sustain its advantage; and (3) how the knowledge that constitutes the firm's advantage will be protected. The nature of the knowledge is fundamental for these definitions. This topic analyses some possibilities for strategic action related to the nature of the knowledge, defined for its dimensions and characteristics that were discussed in the previous part.

Knowledge that is more easily transferred may constitute the basis for business expansion, but also for involuntary diffusion of knowledge. When the company's advantage is sustained by explicit knowledge, the strategy of the firm must recognize that it is prone to be accessible and mobile, and in order to retain control over this knowledge the firm must establish patents, contracts, accords of commitment, etc. (Spender, 1996). In this sense, the best action may be the quick expansion of knowledge application within the company, and even in the market, using accords of licensing or partnerships related to the technological or organizational competencies involved (Winter, 1987). By doing this the company can achieve the consequent returns related to its unique competitive advantage, before the competitors are able to put a similar product on the market. Firms must extract returns because competitors could develop a better product that makes their product obsolete; this also explains why some firms cannibalize their own product with frequent innovations, so as not to lose their own customers (the author thanks the reviewers for these insights). The same strategy of quick expansion of knowledge application to explore the research and development period may be applied to processes if, for example, it seems unlikely that the secrecy of a process may be maintained for a long time.

Risks related to observability in use in productive processes may be diminished not only by restricting the possibilities of observability, but also by compartmentalizing knowledge within the company. The possibilities of controlling observability and resisting reverse engineering in products "are illustrated by the practice of 'potting' integrated circuit devices—encasing them in a resin that cannot be removed without destroying the device" (Winter, 1987: 174).

When an individual or small group owns the knowledge, the strategic action of the company must be driven to avoid the "appropriation" of this knowledge by the individuals. One possible action is to ensure that the company owns the necessary complementary assets for the superior performance of this knowledge. Kogut and Zander (1992) give the example of artists in the recording market whom, besides talent, also need a distribution network. This also applies in the case of advantage based on automatic knowledge, as in a high-performance professional, where the strategy must focus on how to integrate this special individual knowledge with the complementary assets in the company (Spender, 1996). The same applies to the independence of knowledge. To acquire the control of co-specialized complementary assets of a system is one way of self-protecting independence and involuntary knowledge transfer (Winter, 1987).

Related to Grant's (1996) taxonomy, relevance to production can justify more controls and not codification of knowledge, in order to make involuntary knowledge more difficult to transfer. Due to specialization, knowledge production—meaning creation of new knowledge, acquisition of existing knowledge, and storage of knowledge (Grant, 1996)—requires individual specialists in particular areas of knowledge, and the company must contract these individuals to facilitate the knowledge production process. Appropriability could help the firm to define whether the company must or must not invest in the development of a given knowledge. Tacit knowledge is not directly appropriated because it may only be imperfectly transferred—it is more commonly acquired through practice, which makes its transfer slow, costly and uncertain—and because of this it can be appropriated only through its application to productive activity. Explicit knowledge suffers from the problem that one who acquires it can resell it without losing it, and also from the problem that the act of marketing it makes it available for potential buyers. The firm must focus on the development of explicit knowledge that can be retained, such as patents or copyrights (Grant, 1996), and also on the development of collective tacit knowledge, which it is harder to transfer but easier to protect, as will be explained below.

An important distinction is perceived when the firm's advantage is based on collective knowledge. In this case, the strategic problems related to identifying, sharing and protecting relevant knowledge are of less intensity, as nobody alone can "take the knowledge home", nor is it easy for competitors to imitate this knowledge, by putting together a high-performing team, for example (Spender, 1996). This assertion has a common ground with the understanding that, despite the fact that know-what and know-how (defined as the ability to put know-what into practice) work together, they circulate separately. Know-what is the explicit knowledge that may be shared by several, and as it circulates easily it is often hard to protect. "Know-how, by contrast, embedded in work practice (usually *collective* work practice) is *sui generis* and thus relatively easy to protect" (Brown & Duguid, forthcoming: 2—emphasis as in the original). They circulate separately because it is relatively easy for a member of a high-performing group, for example, to explain "what" they do, but it can be very difficult to explain "how" they do it.

Collective know-how is more difficult to circulate and transfer, and the more it is embedded in the work practice, the less relevant is the departure of one or some of the members of this collective (to another company, for example). Members of such a collective are like parts of a buzzword: most of the buzzword together makes much more sense than one piece isolated; in a dynamic social context, the incorporation of a new piece to a position that is lacking is easier than the development of the whole. Collective knowledge can confer a sustainable competitive advantage to the firm when it is rooted not only in know-what, but mainly in collective know-how, grounded in practice and experience in a specific context, and developed dynamically from a firm-specific accumulation of learning and skills, depending on the firm's history and direction (Lei, Hitt & Bettis, 1996). Know-how is an "accumulated" ability (von Hippel, 1988), an expertise in "how to do" that is not always easily explained, that establishes a nexus with the notion of tacit knowledge—revealed only through its application (Grant, 1996)—in its automatic and collective dimensions (Spender, 1996).

The core competence of the firm is rooted mainly in sets of collective know-how (or collective knowledge that is tacit) developed through learning across individual skill sets, individual organizational units and partnerships with other firms, gained and enhanced by work practice, that must be dynamic in nature to attend to the continuously changing market demands. The next part of this section discusses the origins of collective knowledge in the company, with a focus on collective know-how as the basis of the firm's core competencies.

## Development and Integration of the Knowledge of the Firm

Actions related to knowledge creation and transfer must be directed to the development of the firm's strategic capabilities (or competencies). The nature of the knowledge aggregated to the competencies will be decisive for the sustainability of the competitive advantage conferred by that competence. Collective knowledge is more easily protected, giving a greater possibility of maintenance of the firm's advantage for longer. Processes of collective knowledge creation and integration, sustained by common language and symbols, may be vital sources of development of the firm's advantage. The final part of this main section discusses the nature of the collective knowledge of the company and the mechanisms of development of this knowledge.

## Collective Knowledge

A central question is whether knowledge is an individual or a collective possession. Nonaka (1994: 17) states that "At a fundamental level, knowledge is created by individuals. An organization cannot create knowledge without individuals", and that the company's role is to organizationally amplify the knowledge created by individuals, crystallizing it as part of the knowledge network of the company. However, this is not a consensual point of view. The proposition that tacit knowledge has a collective component diverges from this statement in a fundamental aspect. Spender (1996) identifies essentially epistemological questions about whether knowledge is collective, personal or social, and contrasts Nonaka's and Polanyi's approach to knowledge with Vygotsky's (1962): "While Polanyi presumed activity yielded tacit knowledge that remained private, Vygotsky argued that activity shaped consciousness in ways that were social and were eventually reflected in language and social structure. Thus, practical knowledge is not only integrated with practice, as Polanyi suggests, it is also integrated with the consciousness of the community of practitioners" (Spender, 1996: 59). This is a central argument to the vision of knowledge as a social construction, based on language and practices that are understood and communicated to other members in society.

Brown and Duguid (1991) highlight the relevance of relationships between individuals, which goes beyond the internal and external boundaries imposed by organizations. The authors present the "community of practice" concept to highlight the way in which people actually work as opposed to the formal job prescriptions or task-related procedures that are specified by the organization. The proposition that understands the firm as a community of practice rejects the vision of knowledge transfer traditionally implicit in the managerial literature that isolates the knowledge from the practice. On the contrary, this approach develops a vision of knowledge as a social construction, where what is learnt is deeply embedded within the conditions in which it is learnt (Brown & Duguid, 1991).

Knowledge is embedded in work practice, but communities do not dismiss the idea of individual knowledge. "Individual and collective knowledge in this context bear on one another much like the parts of individual performers to a complete musical score, the lines of each actor to a movie script, or the roles of team to overall performance of a team and a game" (Brown & Duguid, forthcoming). The whole task will be carried out only if each one knows its part, and it makes sense only when all parts are put together. Kogut and Zander (1992: 385) reinforce this presumption, stating that "the knowledge of the firm must be understood as socially constructed, or, more simply stated, as resting in the organizing of human resources'' and, because of this, difficult to imitate and redeploy. This article is aligned with the propositions by Brown and Duguid (1991), Kogut and Zander (1992) and Spender (1996) that understand the knowledge of the firm as the result of specific interactions occurring between individuals in an organization, and therefore a socially constructed asset.

Collective knowledge is developed in interactions between individuals that belong to groups within and even between companies, and is therefore created and revealed in practice, and shared in work groups. Each firm or partnership develops idiosyncratic collective knowledge, sustained by common language and symbols, through unique interactions in a specific context. Collective knowledge that is tacit and embedded in work practice, and therefore know-how, can be highly inimitable. When it also helps the firm to create value, it will be the basis of the firm's core competencies.

The idea that competencies are embedded in the organizational routines and practices, and because of this cannot be traded or imitated, reinforces the above assertion. Competencies are obscured from view because much of their knowledge component is tacit and dispersed along four dimensions (Day, 1997):

1. Accumulated employee knowledge and skills.
2. Knowledge embedded in technical systems, including software, linked databases and formal procedures.
3. Management systems that exist to create and control knowledge.
4. The values and norms that dictate what information is to be collected, what types are most important, and how it is to be used.

A good example is Wal-Mart's competence to manage a cross-docking logistics system, which gives the company a significant edge over Kmart. ''The system is part of a broader customer pull system that starts with individual stores placing their orders based on store-movement data. These orders are gathered and filled by suppliers in full truckloads. These loads are delivered to Wal-Mart's warehouses, where they are sorted, repacked, and dispatched to stores. The transfer from one loading dock to another takes less than 48 hours, sharply cutting the usual inventory and handling costs (...) Kmart knows full well what Wal-Mart has accomplished with its logistics system and can readily buy the hardware and software, but has been unable to match the underlying capability'' (Day, 1997: 59). Wal-Mart's processes are not readily visible because they cut across different organizational units, reducing the observability in use (Winter, 1987). And since much of the collective knowledge is tacit and dispersed among many individuals, a competitor cannot acquire the requisite knowledge simply by staffing with the best people available (Day, 1997), which means that it is useful only as an element of a system (Winter, 1987).

The most important implication of this discussion about collective knowledge is that it can, and must, be valued as a source of sustainable competitive advantage. Collective knowledge has the necessary attributes to make it difficult for competitors to imitate, to trade or to substitute. The forms of creation and integration of strategically relevant collective knowledge must be the object of close attention on behalf of companies. The final section considers these themes.

## Knowledge Creation and Integration

It is possible to distinguish several levels of social interaction through which knowledge is created in the organization, and it is important that the company be able to identify the levels of social interaction that could generate relevant knowledge. Nonaka and Takeuchi (1995) present a Model of Knowledge Conversion (Exhibit 2.3), as an explanation of how knowledge is created and how knowledge creation can be managed.

By "socialization", Nonaka and Takeuchi (1995) mean the conversion of tacit knowledge interaction between individuals, mainly through observation, imitation and practice. The key to acquiring knowledge in this way is shared experience. "Combination" is a mode of knowledge conversion that involves different bodies of explicit knowledge held by individuals (the exchange mechanisms may be meetings, telephone conversations and computer systems) that make possible the reconfiguration of the existing information, leading to new knowledge. "Internalization" is the conversion of explicit knowledge into tacit knowledge, in which the authors identify some similarities with the notion of "learning", and "externalization" is the conversion of tacit knowledge into explicit knowledge, a relatively undeveloped concept, as the authors understand.

| | *To* Tacit Knowledge | *To* Explicit Knowledge |
|---|---|---|
| *From* Tacit Knowledge | Socialization | Externalization |
| *From* Explicit Knowledge | Internalization | Combination |

Exhibit 2.3 Four modes of knowledge conversion. (Source: Nonaka & Takeuchi, 1995: 62)

The approach of knowledge creation by Nonaka (1994) and Nonaka and Takeuchi (1995) establishes an important nexus with the work of Brown and Duguid (1991). "Attempts to solve practical problems often generate links between individuals who can provide useful information. The exchange and development of information within these evolving communities facilitates knowledge creation by linking the routine dimensions of day-to-day work with active learning and innovation" (Nonaka, 1994: 23–24). The communities play a key role in the socialization process presented by Nonaka and Takeuchi (1995), where the tacit knowledge among individuals is integrated, which constitutes an important step in the development of collective knowledge in the firm.

Nonaka (1994) and Nonaka and Takeuchi (1995) state that the four modes of knowledge conversion must be managed in an articulated and cyclic way, and call the set of four processes the Spiral of Knowledge Creation. In the spiral, knowledge starts at the individual level, moves up to the group level, and then to the firm level. As the knowledge spirals upward in the organization, it may be enriched and extended as individuals interact with each other and with their organizations. The creation of organizational knowledge requires the sharing and dissemination of individual experiences. In alliances, each process provides an avenue for managers to gain exposure to knowledge and ideas outside their traditional organizational boundaries (Inkpen, 1996).

Nonaka (1994) explains that there are several "triggers" that induce the modes of knowledge conversion. Socialization is normally started with the building of a "team" or "field" of interaction, which facilitates the sharing of members" perspectives and experiences. Successive rounds of meaningful "dialogue" can trigger externalization, where the utilization of "metaphors" can be applied to help members articulate their own perspectives and thereby reveal hidden tacit knowledge. Combination is facilitated by "coordination" between members of the team and other sections of the organization and the "documentation" of existing knowledge. Internalization can be stimulated by processes of "learning by doing" where individuals experience sharing explicit knowledge that is gradually translated, through interaction and a process of trial-and-error, into different aspects of tacit knowledge.

Knowledge creation, as proposed in the Model of Knowledge Conversion, makes the assumption that knowledge is created from tacit and explicit knowledge previously existing in the organization. This assumption is also the basis of the "combinative capabilities" concept. "Creating new knowledge does not occur in abstraction from current capabilities. Rather, new learning, such as innovations, are products of a firm's *combinative capabilities* to generate new applications from existing knowledge" (Kogut & Zander, 1992: 391—emphasis as in the original). In this sense, companies normally learn in areas related to those of their actual practice, and the knowledge advances through recombination of previously existing knowledge.

Grant (1996) reinforces this idea, stating that the primary role of the organization is knowledge integration. The coordination mechanisms of specialists' knowledge are the path to this integration. The author presents four mechanisms capable of integrating specialist knowledge: (1) rules and directives, (2) sequencing, (3) routines, and (4) group problem solving and decision-making. The relation between the "knowledge integration" approach and the competitive advantage generated is that the development of capabilities in the company is the outcome of knowledge integration. It depends, therefore, on the organization's ability in aligning and integrating the knowledge of many specialist individuals. Understanding the firm's strategically relevant capabilities as the outcome of knowledge integration puts a special emphasis on collective knowledge, whether in the form of language, shared meaning, or mutual recognition of knowledge domains.

## Concluding Remarks

The central thesis of this chapter is that the core competencies of the firm are rooted mainly in collective know-how, that is tacit because it is embedded in work practice, and that is developed through learning-by-doing in firm-specific contexts or in specific inter-firm collaborative contexts. Since know-how is tacit, "sticky", and difficult to codify, it is also hard for competitors to imitate. This proposition extends the existing literature on core competencies and knowledge management in two principal ways. First, a relationship between collective knowledge—mainly know-how—and the firm's core competencies is presented, as a means by which knowledge management can contribute to the firm's development of sustainable competitive advantage. Second, related to the strategic problems of knowledge transfer, share and protection, it is explained that the idiosyncratic ways by which know-how is created, transferred and developed (mainly through stimulated firm-specific social interactions and also through inter-firm specific relationships) make these strategic problems less relevant. Both statements present openings for future research developments and strategic action.

## Acknowledgements

This theoretical paper is part of a PhD research project currently being carried out at the University of São Paulo, Brazil. Part of the research was carried out in an exchange programme at the University of Cambridge, UK. The author thanks Professor Maria Tereza Leme Fleury and Professor John Child for their supervision, thanks the CAPES for sponsoring the research in England and the Sasakawa Fellowship Fund for sponsoring the research in Brazil, and thanks the FIA-FEA/USP for sponsoring the trip to the 1998 SMS Conference. The author is especially grateful to the reviewers for their insightful comments. Eventual errors are solely due to the author.

## REFERENCES

Barney, J.B. (1991). Firm resources and sustained competitive advantage. *Journal of Management*, **17**, 99–120.

Bartlett, C.A. & Ghoshal, S. (1986). Tap your subsidiaries for global reach. *Harvard Business Review*, **64**(4), 87–94.

Bell, D. (1973). *The Coming of Post-Industrial Society*. New York: Basic Books.

Brown, J.S. & Duguid, P. (1991). Organizational learning and communities-of-practice: Towards a unified view of working, learning, and innovation. *Organization Science*, **2**, 40–57.

Brown, J.S. & Duguid, P. (forthcoming). Organizing knowledge. *California Management Review*, 1–27.

Chandler, A.D. (1962). *Strategy and Structure: Chapters in the History of the American Industrial Enterprise*. Cambridge, MA: MIT Press.

Child, J. & Faulkner, D. (1998). *Strategies of Co-operation: Managing Alliances, Networks, and Joint Ventures*. New York: Oxford University Press.

Cohen, W. & Levinthal, D. (1990). Absorptive capacity: A new perspective on learning and innovation. *Administrative Science Quarterly*, **35**, 128–152.

Cole, R. (forthcoming). *The Quest for Quality Improvement: How American Business Met the Challenge*. New York: Oxford University Press.

Cyert, R.M. & March, J.G. (1963). *A Behavioral Theory of the Firm*. Englewood Cliffs, NJ: Prentice-Hall.

Day, G.S. (1997). Maintaining the competitive edge: Creating and sustaining advantages in dynamic competitive environments. In G.S. Day & D.J. Reibstein (eds), *Wharton on Dynamic Competitive Strategy*, New York: Wiley.

Dierickx, I. & Cool, K. (1989). Asset stock accumulation and sustainability of competitive advantage. *Management Science*, **35**(12), 1504–1513.

Drucker, P. (1993). *Post-Capitalist Society*. Oxford: Butterworth Heinemann.

Drummond, A. (1997). *Enabling conditions for organizational learning: A study in international business ventures*. Unpublished PhD thesis, The Judge Institute of Management Studies, University of Cambridge.

Dyer, J.H. & Singh, H. (1998). The relational view: Cooperative strategy and sources of interorganizational competitive advantage. *Academy of Management Review*, **23**(4), 660–679.

Grant, R.M. (1996). Toward a knowledge-based theory of the firm. *Strategic Management Journal*, **17**, 109–122.

Hamel, G. (1991). Competition for competence and inter-partner learning within international strategic alliances. *Strategic Management Journal*, **12**, 83–103.

Hamel, G. & Prahalad, C.K. (1994). *Competing for the Future*. Boston, MA: Harvard Business School Press.

Hayes, R.H., Wheelwright, S.C. & Clark, K.B. (1988). *Dynamic Manufacturing: Creating the Learning Organization*. New York: Free Press.
Hitt, M. & Ireland, R.D. (1985). Corporate distinctive competence, strategy, industry and performance. *Strategic Management Journal*, **6**(2), 171–180.
Hitt, M.A., Keats, B.W. & DeMarie, S.M. (1998). Navigating in the new competitive landscape: Building strategic flexibility and competitive advantage in the 21st century. *Academy of Management Executive*, **12**(4), 22–42.
Hofer, C.W. & Schendel, D. (1978). *Strategy Formulation: Analytical Concepts*. St Paul, MN: West Publishing.
Inkpen, A.C. (1996). Creating knowledge through collaboration. *California Management Review*, **39**(1), 123–140.
Itami, H. & Roehl, T. (1987). *Mobilizing Invisible Assets*. Cambridge, MA: Harvard University Press.
Kogut, B. & Zander, U. (1992). Knowledge of the firm, combinative capabilities, and the replication of technology. *Organization Science*, **3**(3), 383–397.
Kogut, B. & Zander, U. (1993). Knowledge of the firm and the evolutionary theory of the multinational corporation. *Journal of International Business Studies*, Fourth Quarter, 625–645.
Lei, D., Hitt, M.A. & Bettis, R. (1996). Dynamic core competences through meta-learning and strategic context. *Journal of Management*, **22**(4), 549–569.
Leonard-Barton, D. (1992). Core capabilities and core rigidities: A paradox in managing new product development. *Strategic Management Journal*, **13**, 111–125.
Leonard-Barton, D. (1995). *Wellsprings of Knowledge: Building and Sustaining the Sources of Innovation*. Boston, MA: Harvard Business School Press.
Moingeon, B. & Edmondson, A. (1996). Organizational learning as a source of competitive advantage. In B. Moingeon, & A. Edmondson (eds), *Organizational Learning and Competitive Advantage*, London: Sage.
Morgan, G. (1986). *Images of Organization*. Beverly Hills, CA: Sage.
Nelson, R. & Winter, S. (1982). *An Evolutionary Theory of Economic Change*. Cambridge, MA: Harvard University Press.
Nonaka, I. (1994). A dynamic theory of organizational knowledge creation. *Organization Science*, **5**(1), 14–37.
Nonaka, I. & Takeuchi, H. (1995). *The Knowledge Creating Company*. New York: Oxford University Press.
Pavitt, K. (1991). Key characteristics of the large innovating firm. *British Journal of Management*, **2**, 41–50.
Penrose, E.T. (1959). *The Theory of Growth of the Firm*. London: Basil Blackwell.
Peteraf, M.A. (1993). The cornerstones of competitive advantage: A resource-based view. *Strategic Management Journal*, **14**, 179–191.
Polanyi, M. (1966). *The Tacit Dimension*. London: Routledge & Kegan Paul.
Porter, M. (1980). *Competitive Strategy*. New York: Free Press.
Prahalad, C.K. & Hamel, G. (1990). The core competence of the corporation. *Harvard Business Review*, May–June, 79–91.
Quinn, J.B. (1992). *Intelligent Enterprise: A Knowledge and Service Based Paradigm for Industry*. New York: Free Press.
Rogers, E. (1983). *The Diffusion of Innovations*. New York: Free Press.
Rumelt, R. (1994). Foreword. In G. Hamel & A. Heene (eds), *Competence-Based Competition*. New York: Wiley, xv–xix.
Sanchez, R. (1997). Managing articulated knowledge in competence-based competition. In R. Sanchez & A. Heene (eds), *Strategic Learning and Knowledge Management*, Chichester: Wiley.

Sanchez, R. & Heene, A. (1997). A competence perspective on strategic learning and knowledge management. In R. Sanchez & A. Heene (eds), *Strategic Learning and Knowledge Management*, Chichester: Wiley.
Sanchez, R., Heene, A. & Thomas, H. (1996). Towards the theory and practice of competence-based competition. In R. Sanchez, A. Heene & H. Thomas (eds), *Dynamics of Competence-Based Competition*, Oxford: Elsevier.
Schoemaker, P.J.H. & Amit, R. (1997). The competitive dynamics of capabilities: Developing strategic assets for multiple futures. In G.S. Day & D.J. Reibstein (eds), *Wharton on Dynamic Competitive Strategy*, New York: Wiley.
Snow, C.C. & Hrebiniak, L.G. (1980). Strategy, distinctive competence, and organizational performance. *Administrative Science Quarterly*, **25**, 317–335.
Spender, J.-C. (1996). Competitive advantage from tacit knowledge? Unpacking the concept and its strategic implications. In B. Moingeon & A. Edmondson (eds), *Organizational Learning and Competitive Advantage*, London: Sage.
Teece, D.J., Pisano, G. & Shuen, A. (1997). Dynamic capabilities and strategic management. *Strategic Management Journal*, **18**, 509–533.
Toffler, A. (1990). *Powershift: Knowledge, Wealth and Violence at the Edge of the 21st Century*. New York: Bantam Books.
von Hippel, E. (1988). *The Sources of Innovation*. Cambridge, MA: MIT Press.
Vygotsky, L.S. (1962). *Thought and Language*. Cambridge, MA: MIT Press.
Weick, K.E. & Roberts, K.H. (1993). Collective minds in organizations: Heedful interrelating on flight decks. *Administrative Science Quarterly*, **38**, 357–381.
Wernerfelt, B. (1984). A resource based view of the firm. *Strategic Management Journal*, **5**, 171–180.
Wernerfelt, B. (1994). The resource-based view of the firm: Ten years after. *Strategic Management Journal*, **16**, 171–174.
Winter, S. (1987). Knowledge and competence as strategic assets. In D. Teece (ed.), *The Competitive Challenge—Strategies for Industrial Innovation and Renewal*, Cambridge, MA: Ballinger.

# 3

# Why Resources Matter: An Empirical Study of the Influence of Knowledge-Based Resources on New Market Entry

SARAH J. MARSH, ANNETTE L. RANFT

## INTRODUCTION

In recent years, the growing consensus by managers and strategy researchers is that some of the most important resources and capabilities in a firm are based on knowledge. Knowledge may take the form of information, data, or dynamic capabilities (Nonaka, 1994). For example, knowledge about how to interpret changes in customer desires or how to integrate the skills necessary for new product development, can be critical to the firm's ability to succeed. The successful management of knowledge-based resources is considered central to competitive advantage, especially in many of today's high-technology industries (Stewart, 1997). High-profile companies, such as Cisco Systems and Microsoft, for example, pursue

*Dynamic Strategic Resources: Development, Diffusion and Integration.*
Edited by Michael A. Hitt, Patricia Gorman Clifford, Robert D. Nixon and Kevin P. Coyne.

numerous alliances and acquisitions each year to access knowledge-based resources for new product development (Wysocki, 1997).

The importance of knowledge-based resources and capabilities to competitive advantage is not restricted to high-profile, high technology corporations such as Microsoft and Cisco Systems, however. For example, in a recent corporate move in the auto industry, Trans Mart, Inc., of Florence, Alabama was acquired by Aftermarket Technology Corp., of Aurora, Illinois. Trans Mart's 70 telemarketers represented the "crown jewels" that Aftermarket Technology sought to access through the acquisition (Wysocki, 1997). This group of telemarketers not only had unique telemarketing capabilities, but they also had "almost encyclopedic knowledge of transmissions in used cars ... [and they knew how to sell it] through cold-calling to mom-and-pop repair shops." (Wysocki, 1997: 1). This example illustrates two knowledge-based resources. First, the *information* about transmissions illustrates one type of knowledge-based resource. Second, the *capability* of the telemarketers to market that information to a specific group illustrates a more dynamic knowledge-based resource (Lei, Hitt & Bettis, 1996).

Competitive advantage that is based on knowledge-based resources and capabilities may be more sustainable than competitive advantage established through financial and physical resources. The firm's knowledge-based resources are often tacit, or implicit and non-codified, thereby creating knowledge barriers and making them difficult for competitors to imitate (Miller & Shamsie, 1996). In addition, the underlying knowledge giving rise to valuable capabilities may not be separable from the individuals or teams that develop and apply the resources to the firm's competitive situation (Winter, 1987). These less mobile resources are more likely to form the basis for competitive advantage, unlike more mobile physical and financial resources (such as land, equipment, or capital), because their value cannot be bid away (Peteraf, 1993).

When firms enter new markets, the firm's knowledge-based resources and capabilities can play a significant role. As product life cycles shrink and competitive advantages are diminished through aggressive imitation by competitors, decisions about entry become critical. These forces require firms to enter markets more frequently to sustain growth in revenues and profits, and this increased rate of entry creates additional pressure on the resources of the firm. A firm that accesses and exploits its knowledge-based resources effectively may be more successful when entering new markets.

Previous research has begun the process of exploring how knowledge-based resources and capabilities contribute to a firm's competitive advantage, but little existing research has examined how a firm accesses the knowledge-based resources and capabilities required in new markets. This study extends the developing body of research about how the nature of the firm's resources and capabilities influences managers' decisions and firm

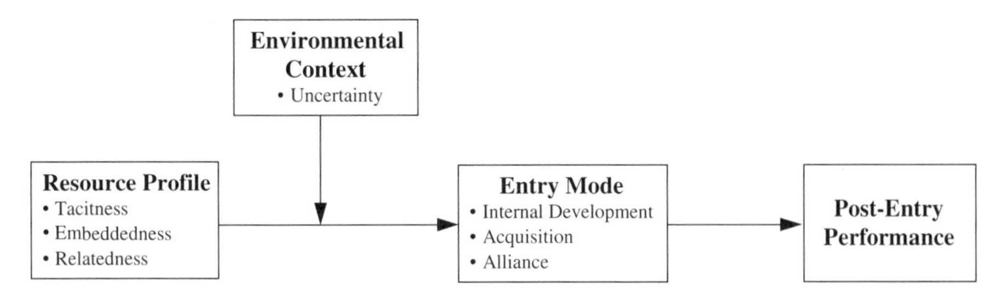


FIGURE 3.1 Research model

performance by focusing on how firms obtain different types of knowledge-based resources needed for new market entry. Specifically, this research addresses two primary research questions:

1. Does the type and location of the resources and capabilities required in a new market influence how a firm enters the market?
2. Does post-entry performance vary based on how firms access the resources and capabilities needed to enter new markets?

We develop our theoretical framework using the resource-based and knowledge-based perspectives of the firm. An underlying premise of this framework is that in addition to physical and financial resources, firms frequently need less tangible, knowledge-based resources which vary in their level of tacitness and embeddedness. We propose that the type of resources needed and the degree to which they are tacit and embedded influence how firms decide to access the resources they need to succeed in a new market. We also argue that the uncertainty in the new market influences the long-term valuation of required resources, and therefore influences managers' decisions about entry mode choice. The model is shown in FIGURE 3.1.

## ENTERING NEW MARKETS

Entry into a new market is the culmination of a process in which new resources and capabilities are accessed and integrated into the firm. The decision about how to access these resources can take three general forms: internal development, acquisition, or alliance.

The decision to enter through each entry mode carries with it a set of tradeoffs regarding the level of commitment or investment required, the speed of entry into the new market, the potential reward, and the range of resources accessed. First, the level of commitment or investment required by the entrant firm varies across each mode (Kogut, 1991; Auster, 1992; Haspeslagh & Jemison, 1991). In the internal development and acquisition modes, the level of investment may be large, because the entrant firm bears the full cost of entry. On the other hand, while investments in internal development activities can take the form of iterative and incremental investments (Yip, 1982) that conform to the resource constraints in the firm, acquisitions often involve "take it or leave it" decisions (Haspeslagh & Jemison, 1991) that involve the lump-sum investment of large amounts of capital. In addition, acquisitions often involve paying a premium to successfully acquire the target (Jemison & Sitkin, 1986), leading to increased uncertainty about the returns generated by the acquisition. The decision to enter through alliance may be "reversible" through termination of the agreement (Kogut, 1991), minimizing the level of commitment and risk associated with the entry.

Second, the speed of the entry is often enhanced through acquisition or alliance because the target or the alliance partner may be already established in the new market. When entering through acquisition or alliance, the target or partner may already have developed key resources and capabilities, minimizing the time and additional investment required to enter the new market (Kogut, 1991; Hitt *et al.*, 1996; Lei, Hitt & Bettis, 1996).

The reward associated with each entry mode reflects the level of potential benefits that accrue to the entrant firm as a result of entry. The rewards of entry can vary with entry mode. Most directly, the alliance mode allows the firm to share development costs and potential losses, as well as future profits, with a partner (Kogut, 1991). Sharing the profits from any entry venture with an alliance partner lowers the potential rewards for each partner relative to the rewards for entry through internal development or acquisition. The internal development and acquisition modes may provide other benefits by offering the opportunity for the firm to share or leverage its resources and capabilities in a way that is difficult for competitors to replicate (Teece, Pisano & Shuen, 1997; Teece, 1982). Thus, the firm's current resources and capabilities may influence the overall level of benefits associated with each entry mode.

Finally, each mode of entry may offer a different range of resources and capabilities for entering a new market (Harrigan, 1985; Hill & Hellriegel, 1994). Internal development activities can be limited by the range of resources and capabilities available within the firm, while acquisition and alliance partners can offer a wide range of resources and capabilities to the entrant firm (Harrison *et al.*, 1991; Hill & Hellriegel, 1994). A firm with highly specialized resources and capabilities, for example, may be limited in its ability to enter a new market, and, therefore, it may enter through acquisition or alliance modes that can provide a wider range of resources and capabilities necessary to enter the new market.

## Linking Resources with New Market Entry

The firm's resources and capabilities have gained increased attention as researchers investigate the key factors associated with firm behavior and performance. The resource-based approach argues that the firm's resources and capabilities[1] are the basis for competitive advantage. These resources may consist of physical and financial resources, but they may also include less tangible resources that are based on human and organizational capital.

A firm's resource base is composed of tangible physical resources (such as plant and equipment, access to raw materials, or geographic location), financial resources, and less tangible resources (Penrose, 1959). A firm's competitive advantage is the result of the productive combination and use of all its resources, whether physical, financial, human, or organizational. The underlying knowledge that managers use when combining and integrating the firm's resources is arguably the most important resource for the firm (Conner & Prahalad, 1996).

From the resource-based perspective, competitive advantage can be sustained to the extent that the resources used to create the competitive advantage are rare, valuable, nonsubstitutable and difficult to imitate (Barney, 1991). Resources and capabilities that are rare, valuable, nonsubstitutable, and difficult to imitate frequently result from a firm's superior ability to access, develop, and integrate knowledge (Grant, 1996). Resources and capabilities based on knowledge and the organizational capital necessary to integrate knowledge are often tacit, or implicit and non-codifiable (Reed & DeFillippi, 1990). Tacit resources and capabilities are often "invisible assets" (Itami, 1987) that are difficult to identify, observe, and articulate (Winter, 1987), making them "sticky" or difficult to transfer or replicate (Collis, 1991; Teece, Pisano & Shuen, 1997). Tacit resources are often important to competitive advantage because they are causally ambiguous, that is, they conform to a set of rules not known to the person following them (Polanyi, 1962). This ambiguity makes it difficult for competitors to replicate these types of resources. Tacit resources are most often developed through individual or shared experience (Nelson & Winter, 1982; Nonaka, 1994; Polanyi, 1962), and they are, therefore, difficult to replicate without recreating the experiences that led to their development.

When entering new markets, a firm must identify and access the resources and capabilities necessary to compete in the new market. Each of the three primary modes of entry provides different means of accessing resources required in the new market. For example, internal development may provide a firm the opportunity to *create* or *develop* the resources and capabilities needed in a new market by investing in the development of knowledge and capabilities of its current employees, technical systems, and management systems.

Alternatively, the firm may choose to acquire another firm to *access* the resources and capabilities necessary to compete in the new market. While not all acquisitions represent entry, the acquiring firm may identify the acquired business as one that already has necessary resources and capabilities to compete in a new market. These existing resources may provide a base for expansion in a new market and create synergy between an acquirer's current businesses and the acquired business (Yip, 1982).

Finally, the firm may choose to form an alliance with another firm in order to *share* the resources and capabilities necessary to enter the new market. Strategic alliances have been defined in many ways in the literature and researchers often characterize alliances as a continuum of cooperative agreements. These agreements may include a variety of legal forms, such as independent joint ventures, limited cross-equity ownership, minority equity stakes, technical licensing and development agreements, know-how and patent licensing agreements, and distribution or marketing agreements (Astley & Brahm, 1989; Borys & Jemison, 1989; Contractor & Lorange, 1988; Nohria & Garcia-Pont, 1991). In each of these legal forms, the primary objective is to provide access to the partner's resources and share knowledge to achieve some joint outcome (Badaracco, 1991).

When entering new markets, firms may recognize the need to develop or obtain tacit resources and capabilities to succeed in a new market. These firms face the challenge of trying to internally develop assets which cannot be codified or easily transferred, and are, therefore, most often developed through experience (Lei, Hitt & Bettis, 1996; Reed & DeFillippi, 1990). This development takes time and may delay a firm's entry into a new market in a timely fashion. Accessing these resources through acquisition or alliance may be preferred because the target or partner has already developed the resources through its previous experience, thereby minimizing the time and risk associated with trying to replicate the successful experience. Therefore, we predict the following hypothesis:

> H1: The higher the tacitness of required resources, the higher the probability of acquisition or alliance relative to internal development.

The location of valuable resources and capabilities can also contribute to competitive advantage by making them difficult to imitate. Embedded resources are dependent upon a social system of a team of individuals, their relationships, and their networks (Leonard-Barton, 1992; Badaracco, 1991). These resources and capabilities reside in the human and organizational capital of the firm, and they are dependent upon the coordination of a large number of interdependent skills and assets (Reed & DeFillippi, 1990). Inseparable from the social and/or physical systems of the organization

(Winter, 1987), embedded resources are based on know-how about which no single individual has full knowledge. Embedded resources frequently give rise to communities of practice where each individual contributes a specialized subset of knowledge and knows who to turn to for expertise outside his or her subset (Brown & Duguid, 1992; Pentland, 1992). Because embedded resources are socially complex, any change to the organizational context in which they reside may alter the social relationships and networks that give rise to their value. Embedded resources are difficult to imitate because they are often developed over time, and the process through which they are developed creates a "path dependence" that inhibits rapid imitation (Lei, Hitt & Bettis, 1996).

When entering a new market, a firm that does not have the required embedded resources and capabilities is at a disadvantage because creating them requires development of an entire social system. Acquisition of a firm that has valuable embedded resources or entering into an alliance with one alleviates the necessity to build these socially complex resources from the ground up. Therefore, we predict that:

> H2: The higher the embeddedness of the required resources, the higher the probability of acquisition or alliance relative to internal development.

When firms enter new markets that require resources and capabilities that are related to their current resource base, they have an advantage with respect to the internal development of new resources. Internal development may capture economies of scope and scale (Farjoun, 1998; Teece, 1982), but the firm may also benefit because it can develop the new, related capabilities more rapidly and/or more efficiently than its competitors (Markides & Williamson, 1994).

The firm's ability to internally develop new resources is enhanced by the relatedness of its current resource profile, because the firm can build on its current resource base. The ability to build on the firm's current resource and knowledge base creates relatively high levels of absorptive capacity that enable the firm to recognize, assimilate, and apply external information (Cohen & Levinthal, 1990). The systems, structures, and processes that the firm already has in place serve as platforms to extending its knowledge and developing new knowledge necessary for succeeding in the marketplace. On the other hand, acquisitive entry into a new market that requires unrelated resources and capabilities may provide more certainty for managers entering a new market they do not understand well (Hitt, *et al.*, 1996). Therefore, we predict that:

> H3: The more related the resources required to compete in the new market are to the current resources in the firm, the higher

the probability of internal development relative to acquisition and alliance.

The competitive environment faced by the entrant firm can also influence the value of any given resource (Collis & Montgomery, 1985; Peteraf, 1993). Uncertainty in the new market environment raises the risks associated with accessing the resources to enter the new market. In new market environments where there is high uncertainty, the long-term value of a resource may be difficult to predict. Entry into an uncertain environment through internal development may involve redirecting resources and capabilities already employed to an initiative with rewards that are uncertain and difficult to quantify. Because acquisitions are lump-sum investments that are difficult to reverse (Haspeslagh & Jemison, 1991), entry through acquisition may be considered risky in new markets characterized by a high degree of uncertainty. The commitment of resources to enter through alliance, on the other hand, is typically lower than outright acquisition of the partner (Auster, 1992), minimizing the risk associated with entering an uncertain environment.

In new market environments where the long-term value of a resource is uncertain, relatively rapid, short-term access to valuable resources may be preferable to the potential liability of long-term ownership. Entry into unpredictable environments is especially risky when the investments required are large, discrete, and/or irreversible. High investment costs of acquisition and internal development are irreversible and become less attractive in an uncertain environment. Because we had previously predicted that the tacitness of the resource would influence a firm's preference for acquisition and alliance over internal development, we are predicting an interaction between tacitness and new market uncertainty. Or, more formally:

H4: The higher the uncertainty in the new market environment and the higher the tacitness of the required resources, the higher the probability of alliance relative to internal development and acquisition.

The research model assumes that managers make rational decisions that lead to improved firm performance in the new market. We argue that while no particular entry mode will lead to higher performance, entry mode decisions that address the differences in the type and location of the required resources, as discussed above, will positively influence post-entry performance. Therefore, we predict that:

H5: Firms that conform to the predictions made in this model will have higher post-entry performance in the new market.

## Research Methodology

Survey data collected directly from top managers of the entrant firms were employed to measure variables relating to the resources required in the new market, their relatedness to the firm's current resources, the environmental context, entry mode choice, and post-entry performance. A separate survey of experts was used to measure the tacitness and embeddedness of the resources. Archival data about the firm's financial resources and survey data about the intended speed of entry were included as control variables. Data were collected on 90 domestic new market entry events in multiple industries. Thirty-one of the entries were through internal development, 38 through acquisition, and 21 through alliance. Consistent with the recent increased attention on alliances, 20 of the alliances occurred after 1991. Linear regression and multinomial logistic regression analysis were used to test the hypotheses.

### Sample Selection

The sample was derived from the universe of domestic new market entries by publicly held US firms between 1985 and 1997. Analysis of archival data in over 1200 company press releases, 250 annual reports, and 590 industry reports resulted in the identification of 613 entry events by publicly held US firms. The items selected for content analysis were identified electronically through the Lexis database using a keyword search strategy (e.g., entry, new market, diversification, internal development, *de novo*, acquisition, alliance, and joint venture). A new market entry was selected if it involved selling a new product and/or targeting a new customer base.

### Survey Administration

Data collection occurred through surveys administered to top managers of entrant firms and an expert panel. The names and addresses of the CEO of each entrant firm, and, when appropriate, the chief divisional or subsidiary officer of the entering unit, were identified using *Corporate Affiliations Plus*, *Ward's Directory*, and *Compact Disclosure*. Officers in charge of corporate strategy were also identified, when possible. The expert panel was composed of three researchers with experience in investigating knowledge-based resources.

Pre-tests of the survey by practicing managers were conducted. The administration of the survey was then performed consistent with techniques that maximize the response rate (Dillman, 1978). Pre-notification letters

identifying the new market about which we would be seeking information were sent. The first mailing of the survey occurred one week later. Reminder cards were sent to all potential respondents. A second mailing of the survey was sent to non-respondents. Follow-up phone calls were made to encourage non-respondents to complete and return the survey.

Several steps were taken to increase the respondents' ability to recall accurate information. For example, respondents were asked about a specific new market entry. Questions about facts or concrete events are subject to less error than questions about past opinions or beliefs (Glick *et al.*, 1990; Golden, 1992; Miller, Cardinal & Glick, 1997). Respondents were also motivated to provide accurate information by ensuring the confidentiality of their responses and promising a summary of the project results for all respondents.

A total of 693 surveys were delivered to potential respondents, and 175 responses (26%) were received in response to the administration of the survey instrument. These responses included 101 completed surveys (15%) and 74 responses (11%) indicating that company policy prevented survey completion or that personnel knowledgeable about the entry event were no longer employed by the firm. Missing data on key variables and financial data reduced the number of usable surveys to 90. The survey response rate is consistent with the average response rate of 10–12% when surveys are sent to top executives (Hambrick, Geletkanycz & Frederickson, 1993).

T-tests showed no significant differences between respondents and non-respondents with respect to long-term debt/equity, return on assets, or current ratio in the year prior to entry. The median sales of the entrant firms in the year of entry was $578 million.

## Measures

The tacitness, embeddedness, and relatedness of the firm's resources and capabilities and those necessary to compete in the new market were measured using a comprehensive list of resources and capabilities which was developed based on existing items used in the strategy, marketing, and operations literatures (Dess & Davis, 1984; Hitt & Ireland, 1985; Conant, Mokwa & Varadarajan, 1990; Kohli, Jaworski & Kumar, 1993; Kohli & Jaworski, 1990; Hall, 1992; King, 1996; Nayyar, 1992). Resources and capabilities articulated in prominent conceptual articles about the resource-based perspective and how the firm's resources influence firm behavior and performance were also included (Markides & Williamson, 1994, 1996; Verdin & Williamson, 1994; Miller & Shamsie, 1996). The items reflect functional capabilities used in previous research, such as "ability to forecast market growth" and "effectiveness of service network or delivery systems"

(Hill & Hellriegel, 1994; Biggadike, 1976; Yip, 1982; Snow & Hrebiniak, 1980; Hitt & Ireland, 1985), as well as the "higher-level" (Brumagim, 1994) or integrative capabilities highlighted in the resource-based literature, such as "ability to share knowledge across functional areas" and "ability to serve a wide geographical range of markets" (Brumagim, 1994; Grant, 1996; Nelson & Winter, 1982; Kogut & Zander, 1992). In addition, items included physical and financial resources such as "plant and equipment", "favorable locations", and access to "financial capital". Duplicate items identified in the literature were removed and a comprehensive set of 68 items representing physical and knowledge-based resources comprised the final list.

## Relatedness

In the survey administered to top managers in the new entrant firms, respondents were asked: "In your judgment, how much of each resource or capability was required to succeed in the new market when it was entered?" and "In your judgment, how much of each resource or capability was present in the firm prior to the firm's entry into the new market?" on a 7-point Likert-type scale (1 = extremely low level and 7 = extremely high level). The survey questions were placed in a side-by-side format to help assure that respondents evaluated the same resource/capability for each question.

The following formula demonstrates how the relatedness measure was operationalized:

$$\frac{1}{g}\sum_{j=1}^{g}(R_{fj}-R_{nj})(R_{nj}) \qquad (3.1)$$

where:

$g$ = number of items
$R_f$ = score for resource/capability present in firm prior to entry
$R_n$ = score for resource/capability required in the new market
$j$ = index for resource/capability items.

The measure weighted the difference between the amount of each resource/capability present and the amount of each resource/capability required by the amount required, so that differences in the relative importance of the resources/capabilities across entries could be reflected in the data. Only negative differences were included in the calculation, based on the premise that having more of a given resource/capability than required would not mitigate the absence of other required resources/capabilities. In other words, if a firm had an extremely high level of "product or market-specific functional experience" (or a score of 7) prior to entry, when only a moderate level (score of 4) was required for the new market, this excess resource/capability would not compensate for a moderate level of "R&D Capability" (score of 4), when an extremely high level was required in the new market (score of 7).

## Tacitness and Embeddedness

Three researchers in different geographic locations served as expert panelists, based on their previous research experience relating to knowledge-based resources. The expert panelists evaluated separately the tacitness and embeddedness of each of the 68 resources and capabilities. The tacitness score reflects how important "learning from experience" is likely to be in the development of the resource or capability (1 = not at all important and 7 = extremely important). Similarly, the embeddedness score reflects how important "social networks" were likely to be in developing or accessing the resource or capability (1 = not at all important and 7 = extremely important). Average correlations between the expert panelists' scores on tacitness and embeddedness of the 68 resources and capabilities were highly significant (tacitness: $r = .44$, $p < .001$; embeddedness: $r = .55$, $p < .001$). The tacitness and embeddedness scores from the panelists were then averaged to create tacitness and embeddedness scores for each of the 68 resources and capabilities.

The measures for tacitness and embeddedness for each entry event were then calculated by averaging the tacit or embedded scores for only those resources and capabilities in which the respondents indicated that there was a difference between the firm's current capabilities and those needed for entry into the new market. By averaging the scores, a higher tacitness or embeddedness score indicates that the firm needed a higher level of tacit or embedded resources, without regard to the size of the gap (or degree of relatedness) between the firm's current resources and those needed in the new market.

## Uncertainty

The measure for environmental uncertainty was created by averaging multiple items developed from the extant literature (Miller & Friesen, 1984; Duncan, 1972). Survey respondents were asked to rate the predictability of changes in the new market for seven items (changes in customer tastes, production or service technologies, product technology, competitors' strategies, distribution methods, supplier demands, and government regulation). The Cronbach's alpha coefficient was .76, exceeding the minimum acceptable level of .70 recommended by Nunnally (1978).

### Dependent Variable

Data about the mode of entry employed to enter the new market were taken directly from the survey instrument. A definition of each entry mode was provided and respondents indicated which mode of entry best described the initial entry into the new market; 83% of the cases conformed with the data collected during review of press releases during the sample selection.

### Control Variables

The level of internal funds available and the speed of entry were included as control variables. The level of internal funds was included as a control variable based on previous evidence suggesting that financial resources influence entry mode choice (Chatterjee, 1990). The measure reflects the liquidity and debt capacity of the firm. The level of internal funds was measured by subtracting the firm's current liabilities and long-term debt from current assets, and dividing this number by the firm's market value in the year prior to the entry.

In addition, because acquisitions are well established as a rapid way to access new resources and capabilities (Hill & Jones, 1998; Hitt, Ireland & Hoskisson, 1996), the intended speed of entry, as measured on the survey by a 7-point Likert-type scale item, was also included as a control variable.

### Performance

Performance in the new market was measured using survey data in order to capture performance information about the specific entry event, information that is not available in archival measures of overall firm or divisional performance. Performance in the new market was measured using three items. Respondents were asked to indicate the performance in the new market relative to their expectations and relative to competitors, as well as the length of time required to achieve performance goals in the new market relative to their expectations when entering the new market. The performance measure was calculated by averaging the scores on the three items. The alpha coefficient for the three measures is .82.

## Results

Table 3.1 shows descriptive statistics and Pearson correlations. Three key relationships should be noted. First, there is a nearly perfect correlation

TABLE 3.1 Descriptive statistics and Pearson correlations ($n = 90$)[a]

| Variable | Mean | SD | 1 | 2 | 3 | 4 | 5 | 6 | 7 |
|---|---|---|---|---|---|---|---|---|---|
| 1 Tacitness | 3.39 | 1.38 | 1.00 | | | | | | |
| 2 Embeddedness | 2.94 | 1.19 | 0.99** | 1.00 | | | | | |
| 3 Uncertainty | 3.82 | 1.01 | 0.16 | 0.16 | 1.00 | | | | |
| 4 Relatedness | −.67 | .32 | −0.90** | −0.90** | −0.13 | 1.00 | | | |
| 5 Internal funds | −.37 | .12 | −0.03 | −0.05 | 0.00 | 0.05 | 1.00 | | |
| 6 Speed of entry | 5.70 | 1.16 | 0.01 | −0.01 | 0.10 | 0.04 | −0.10 | 1.00 | |
| 7 Post-entry performance | 4.12 | 1.47 | −0.28** | −0.28** | −0.03 | 0.20† | 0.08 | −0.07 | 1.00 |

[a] Significance levels:
† $p < .10$
** $p < .01$.

between the tacitness and the embeddedness of resources ($r = .99$, $p < .001$); those resources that are developed through experience are also likely to be located in social networks and relationships among individuals and groups within and outside the organization. Conceptually, tacitness and embeddedness are separate constructs (Winter, 1987). Tacit knowledge, or knowledge that is difficult to codify and articulate, may be located in a single individual, that is, it is not necessarily embedded in a network of individuals. On the other hand, embedded resources and capabilities are necessarily tacit; codifying the capabilities that are based on a group of individuals and their relationships is nearly impossible. The empirical distinction, however, between the two constructs could not be achieved. For this reason, the results that follow will discuss only the results relating to tacitness.

Second, a strong correlation exists between relatedness and tacitness.[2] This correlation indicates that firms entering new markets that are highly related to their current businesses may be less likely to need tacit resources ($r = -.90$, $p < .001$). Or, conversely, firms that enter markets that are less related to their current businesses are more likely to need tacit resources.

Finally, the level of post-entry performance shows a strongly negative correlation with tacitness ($r = -.28$, $p < .008$). The relatedness of the new market to the firm's current businesses shows a moderately positive correlation with post-entry performance ($r = .20$, $p < .06$), unlike previous studies which found very little evidence of a linkage between relatedness and performance (Biggadike, 1976; Yip, 1982; Sharma & Kesner, 1996).

Multinomial logistic regression was conducted to test the first four hypotheses. The results shown in TABLE 3.2 show that the control variables, internal funds and the speed of entry, had the predicted and significant effects. Firms with high levels of internal funds were more likely to enter through internal development (ID) and acquisition (AQ) than alliance (AL) (ID/AL: $b = 5.01$, $p < .05$; AQ/AL: $b = 9.98$, $p < .003$). As anticipated, firms entering rapidly were more likely to enter through acquisition than internal development ($b = .70$, $p < .006$).

As shown in TABLE 3.2, no relationship was found between the tacitness of resources needed in the new market and entry mode choice ($\chi^2 = .07$, 2 df, $p < .96$). Thus, no support was found for H1 and H2. Because relatedness and tacitness had a highly negative correlation, the tests for relatedness (H3) were conducted separately, as shown in TABLE 3.3. The results show no significant influence on entry mode choice based on relatedness ($\chi^2 = .05$, 2 df, $p < .98$), offering no support for H3.

The results suggest that the interaction of tacitness and uncertainty has a significant effect on entry mode choice ($\chi^2 = 11.99$, 2 df, $p < .003$). To calculate the influence of the interaction, different values for the tacitness and uncertainty variables were used to calculate the change in the

TABLE 3.2 Summary of multinomial logistic regression results[a] (Model 1)

| Variable[c] | Internal Development (ID) vs Alliance (AL) | | | | Acquisition (AQ) vs Alliance (AL) | | | | Internal Development (ID) vs Acquisition (AQ)[b] | | | |
|---|---|---|---|---|---|---|---|---|---|---|---|---|
| | B | SE | B | SE | B | SE | B | SE | B | SE | B | SE |
| Tacitness (H1) | −.13 | .22 | −.06 | .22 | −.15 | .22 | −.02 | .24 | .02 | .19 | −.04 | .21 |
| Uncertainty† | .21 | .31 | .30 | .36 | .41 | .31 | .81 | .39* | −.21 | .26 | −.51 | .31 |
| Tacitness × Uncertainty (H4)** | | | .23 | .24 | | | .76 | .27** | | | −.53 | .22** |
| Internal funds** | 4.82 | 2.55† | 5.01 | 2.57* | 8.98 | 3.13** | 9.98 | 3.40** | −4.16 | 2.88 | −4.98 | 3.09 |
| Speed of entry** | −.32 | .26 | −.28 | .28 | .30 | .28 | .41 | .31 | −.62 | .24 | −.70 | .25** |
| Constant | 3.74 | 2.13† | 3.05 | 2.03 | 1.15 | 2.24 | −1.23 | 2.59 | 2.59 | 1.81 | 4.28 | 2.14* |
| **Model** $\chi^2$ (8 df, N = 90) | 20.71** | | | | | | | | | | | |
| **Model** $\chi^2$ (10 df, N = 90) | | | 32.70*** | | | | | | | | | |

[a] Summarized results show regression coefficient estimates (B), standard errors (SE), and significance level using Wald statistic.
[b] The analysis was rerun with acquisition specified as the reference group to generate these regression coefficients.
[c] Significance level of the variable was calculated by comparing the change in log-likelihood when the variable is removed from model with interaction. Significance levels:
† $p < .10$
* $p < .05$
** $p < .01$
*** $p < .001$

TABLE 3.3 Summary of multinomial logistic regression results[a] (Model 2)

| Variable[c] | Internal Development (ID) vs Alliance (AL) | | Acquisition (AQ) vs Alliance (AL) | | Internal Development (ID) vs Acquisition (AQ)[b] | |
|---|---|---|---|---|---|---|
| | B | SE | B | SE | B | SE |
| Relatedness (H3) | .08 | .93 | .20 | .95 | −.12 | .82 |
| Uncertainty | .18 | .31 | .39 | .30 | −.21 | .26 |
| Internal funds** | 4.88 | 2.54* | 9.00 | 3.11** | −4.12 | 2.86 |
| Speed of entry* | −.32 | .26 | 2.96 | .28 | −.62 | .24** |
| Constant | 3.51 | 2.10† | .92 | 2.22 | 2.59 | 1.80 |
| **Model** $\chi^2$ (8 df, N = 90) | 20.26** | | | | | |

[a] Summarized results show regression coefficient estimates (B), standard errors (SE), and significance level using Wald statistic.
[b] The analysis was rerun with acquisition specified as the reference group to generate these regression coefficients.
[c] Significance level of the variable was calculated by comparing the change in log-likelihood when the variable is removed. Significance levels:
† $p < .10$
* $p < .05$
** $p < .01$

probabilities of each entry mode choice. When the tacitness and uncertainty values are increased to the 75th percentile, the probability of alliance decreases 4%, the probability of internal development decreases 14%, and the probability of acquisition increases 16%, relative to the main effect of tacitness. In other words, when tacitness and uncertainty are high, the use of acquisitions to enter new markets increases relative to internal development and alliance. These results are contrary to the predictions made in H4, which predicted that alliances would be the entry mode of choice.

To test whether firms that conform to the predictions made in this model have higher performance, several tests were conducted with the full sample and with subgroup samples of internal development, acquisition, and alliances. Using the full sample, linear regression of tacitness on post-entry performance suggests that high levels of tacitness have a significant and negative effect on post-entry performance ($b = -.30$, $F = 7.42$, $p < .008$), as shown in TABLE 3.4. Tacitness explained nearly 8% of the variance in post-entry performance.

Separate subgroup analyses were conducted using the same linear regression model for each mode. As shown in TABLE 3.4, these analyses reveal that tacitness has a significantly negative effect on post-entry

TABLE 3.4 Summary of regression analysis (dependent variable = Post-Entry Performance)

| Independent variable | Sample size[a] | b | $R^2$ | F | Significance |
|---|---|---|---|---|---|
| (Constant), tacitness | 90 (all entries) | −.30 | .078 | 7.41 | p < .008 |
| (Constant), tacitness | 31 (ID entries) | −.42 | .140 | 4.74 | p < .038 |
| (Constant), tacitness | 38 (AQ entries) | −.22 | .049 | 1.85 | p < .182 |
| (Constant), tacitness | 21 (AL entries) | −.15 | .032 | .62 | p < .440 |
| (Constant), relatedness | 90 (all entries) | .93 | .040 | 3.70 | p < .057 |
| (Constant), relatedness | 31 (ID entries) | 1.36 | .075 | 2.36 | p < .136 |
| (Constant), relatedness | 38 (AQ entries) | .71 | .027 | .99 | p < .325 |
| (Constant), relatedness | 21 (AL entries) | .59 | .028 | .55 | p < .468 |

[a] ID = Internal Development, AQ = Acquisition, AL = Alliance.

performance for those firms entering through internal development (b = −.42, F = 4.73, p < .04). This effect is quite strong, especially given the small sample size (n = 31). The effect of tacitness on performance for entries through acquisition and alliance shows no significant effect (AQ: b = −.22, F = 1.85, p < .18; AL: b = −.15, F = .62, p < .44).

In addition, using the full sample, linear regression of relatedness on post-entry performance shows that relatedness has a marginally significant and positive effect on performance (b = .93, F = 3.69, p < .06). As shown in TABLE 3.4, relatedness showed no significant effect on post-entry performance based on the three subgroups of internal development, acquisition, and alliance.

In an alternative test of the performance effects, the tacitness score was used to predict entry mode, and the post-entry performance of those firms that had entered using the predicted mode was compared to those firms that had entered through a different mode. To conduct this test, the overall sample was split using those firms with the highest and lowest tacitness scores (top and bottom third). Firms were then placed into two groups: (1) those that entered into the predicted mode, and (2) those that did not enter using the predicted mode. Analysis showed no significant difference in post-entry performance between those firms that conformed to the model's predictions of entry mode based on tacitness and those that entered through other modes (F = .05, n = 60, p < .82). The results were similar when the mean level was used to split cases into high and low tacitness groups. A similar procedure was used to examine the impact of relatedness. This analysis also showed no significant difference in post-entry performance between those firms that conformed to the model's predictions of entry mode based on relatedness (F = .68, n = 59, p < .41).

## Discussion

This research set out to increase our understanding of how the type, the tacitness, and the embeddedness, of the firm's resources and capabilities influence firm behavior and performance when entering new markets. The empirical results of this study suggest that tacit resources are "invisible assets" (Itami, 1987) that are "sticky" and difficult to develop due to the causal ambiguity about how they are created and the need for direct experience in creating them (Badaracco, 1991). Those firms that needed higher levels of tacit resources and capabilities were more likely to suffer lower levels of post-entry performance. The need for resources and capabilities that are located in social networks or relationships among people also inhibits post-entry performance, due to the difficulty of transferring or replicating these resources.

When exploring the influence of tacitness for each of the three modes, performance in new markets entered through internal development was more negatively influenced than entries through acquisition or alliance. The evidence suggests that tacit resources needed to enter new markets successfully represent significant barriers to high performance. Conversely, for those firms that already have the necessary resources, tacit resources can provide significant sources of competitive advantage.

These findings suggest that while transferring tacit resources through acquisition or alliance may be difficult (Ranft & Zeithaml, 1999), tacit resources may be easier to transfer than to create through internal development activities. Firms that need tacit resources must go through the time-consuming efforts required to develop the new resources and capabilities through experience (Polanyi, 1962), thereby inhibiting successful performance in the new market. This study suggests that a firm will benefit if decisions about entry mode reflect the type of resources and capabilities it requires in the new market. More specifically, if the firm needs to access tacit resources, it will be better served to enter through acquisition or alliance than internal development.

This research also found a highly negative correlation between relatedness and tacitness. That is, when firms needed resources and capabilities to enter the new market, the resources and capabilities they needed were highly tacit. One potential explanation is that tacit resources and capabilities are, in fact, "invisible assets" (Itami, 1987), therefore, when respondents report how much of a tacit resource is in the firm, they have difficulty identifying it. Previous research has found that managers' perceptions vary systematically by level (King & Zeithaml, 1998; Ireland, *et al.*, 1987). Because top managers are more focused on preparing the firm for the future, they may perceive the firm's resources and capabilities differently than middle managers, who are more focused on the application of current resources and capabilities (King & Zeithaml, 1998). Tacit resources and capabilities may be especially difficult for top managers to see, based on their distance from the actual application of these resources and capabilities.

The evidence suggests that financial resources do play a role in entry mode choice when the alliance mode is considered. This study found, as did Chatterjee (1990), that financial resources did not influence the choice between internal development and acquisition. However, the choice of alliance over the alternative modes was significantly influenced by the availability of internal funds. Thus, alliances are attractive when the firm's access to financial resources is limited.

In spite of this evidence about the influence of different types of resources on performance, why don't managers make decisions about entry mode choice that conform with the arguments made in this paper? The evidence in this research suggests that the type of resources needed has little influence on entry mode choice. The interaction of tacitness and the uncertainty in the new market led managers to use acquisitions, not alliances to enter the new market, contrary to our predictions. The explanations for our findings may be both substantive and/or related to the operationalization of this research.

One explanation may be that entry mode choice decisions reflect a large range of factors that extend well beyond the limited number of variables in the model used in this study. Although the resource-based and knowledge-based views provide support for the careful consideration of the nature of the resources and capabilities needed to enter the new market, other factors may dominate in strategic decisions about entry mode choice. Key factors in the external environment, such as the amount of competitive rivalry or stage in the product life cycle, may have significant influences on entry mode choice which were not included in this research. Other factors, such as managerial cognition of the environment, recent managerial experiences, managerial preferences, dominant industry practices, or governmental constraints, may also influence entry strategies (Koza & Lewin, 1998).

In addition, the tacitness and embeddedness measures were developed using expert panelists, not the decision makers themselves. The actual level of tacitness or embeddedness of the firm's resources and capabilities may vary, depending on the industry or the firm. The methods used in this study could not accommodate this type of variation.

Finally, using the firm's resources and capabilities to explain firm behavior focuses on economic and strategic factors as drivers of strategic decisions. It requires an assumption that managers' decisions reflect an intimate and objective understanding of the firm's resources and capabilities as well as how to exploit and combine those resources and capabilities to maximize profits. If this assumption about the decision-makers is relaxed, the power of the resource-based perspective as a predictor of firm behavior is greatly reduced. In addition, previous literature suggests that other cognitive biases (e.g., escalation of commitment or framing) may influence strategic decision-making in ways that are inconsistent with the economic and strategic factors (Bateman & Zeithaml, 1989; Schwenk, 1984). The empirical evidence regarding the effect of tacitness on post-entry performance supports the possibility that economic and strategic criteria may not be the dominant drivers of the decision-making process.

This research begins to explore the opportunities and challenges of managing knowledge-based resources in the context of new market entry. The evidence suggests that knowledge-based resources are difficult to develop internally, and, therefore, firms may be better served if they access such resources through acquisition and alliance when entering new markets. Firms will be best served if the strategic decisions that managers make reflect the very real challenges associated with developing and applying knowledge-based resources. We hope that this research serves as a basis for future examination of the role that knowledge-based resources play in important strategic decisions.

## Notes

1. In this study, resources and capabilities are used interchangeably to mean the assets, abilities, organizational processes, information, and knowledge controlled by the firm (Barney, 1991).
2. An alternative measure of tacitness using a threshold measure was calculated for every resource where the amount of resource needed exceeded 4 on the 7-point scale. The alternative measure was also negatively correlated with relatedness ($p < .001$).

## References

Astley, W.G. & Brahm, R.A. (1989). Organizational designs for post-industrial strategies: The role of interorganizational collaboration. In C. Snow (ed.), *Strategy, Organization Design, and Human Resources Management*, Greenwich, CT: JAI Press, 233–270.

Auster, E.R. (1992). The relationship of industry evolution to patterns of technological linkages, joint ventures, and direct investment between U.S. and Japan, *Management Science*, **38**(6), 778–792.

Badaracco, J.L., Jr. (1991). *The Knowledge Link: How Firms Compete through Strategic Alliances*. Boston, MA: Harvard Business School Press.

Barney, J.B. (1991). Firm resources and sustained competitive advantage. *Journal of Management*, **17**, 99–120.

Bateman, T.S. & Zeithaml, C.P. (1989). The psychological context of strategic decisions: A model and convergent experimental findings. *Strategic Management Journal*, **10**, 59–74.

Biggadike, R.E. (1976). *Corporate diversification: Entry, strategy, and performance.* Doctoral Dissertation, Harvard Business School, Boston, MA.
Borys, B. & Jemison, D.B. (1989). Hybrid arrangements as strategic alliances: Theoretical issues in organizational combinations. *Academy of Management Review,* **14**(2), 234–249.
Brown, J.S. & Duguid, P. (1992). Organizational learning and communities of practice: Toward a unified view of working, learning, and innovation. *Organization Science,* 2, 40–57.
Brumagim, A.L. (1994). A hierarchy of corporate resources. *Advances in Strategic Management,* **10A**, 81–112.
Chatterjee, S. (1990). Excess resources, utilization costs, and mode of entry. *Academy of Management Journal,* **33**(4), 780–800.
Cohen, W.M. & Levinthal, D.A. (1990). Absorptive capacity: A new perspective on learning and innovation. *Administrative Science Quarterly,* **35**, 128–152.
Collis, D.J. (1991). A resource-based analysis of global competition: The case of the bearings industry. *Strategic Management Journal,* **12**, 49–68.
Collis, D.J. & Montgomery, C.A. (1995). Competing on resources: Strategy in the 1990s. *Harvard Business Review,* July–August, 118–128.
Conant, J.S., Mokwa, M.P. & Varadarajan, P.R. (1990). Strategic types, distinctive marketing competencies and organizational performance: A multiple measures-based study. *Strategic Management Journal,* **11**, 365–383.
Conner, K. & Prahalad, C.K. (1996). A resource-based theory of the firm: Knowledge versus opportunism. *Organization Science,* **7**, 77–501.
Contractor, F.J. & Lorange, P. (1988). Why should firms cooperate? The strategy and economics basis for cooperative ventures. In F. Contractor & P. Lorange (eds), *Cooperative Strategies in International Business,* Lexington, MA: Heath, 3–30.
Dess, G.G. & Davis, P.S. (1984). Porter's (1980) generic strategies as determinants of strategic group membership and organizational performance. *Academy of Management Journal,* **27**(3), 467–488.
Dillman, D.A. (1978). *Mail and Telephone Surveys: The Total Design Method.* New York: Wiley.
Duncan, R.B. (1972). Characteristics of organizational environments and perceived environmental uncertainty. *Administrative Science Quarterly,* **17**, 313–327.
Farjoun, M. (1998). The independent and joint effects of the skill and physical bases of relatedness in diversification. *Strategic Management Journal,* **19**, 611–630.
Glick, W.H., Huber, G.P., Miller, C.C., Doty, D.H. & Sutcliffe, K.M. (1990). Studying changes in organizational design and effectiveness: Retrospective event histories and periodic assessments. *Organization Science,* **1**, 293–312.
Golden, B.R. (1992). The past is the past—or is it? The use of retrospective accounts as indicators of past strategy. *Academy of Management Journal,* **35**, 848–860.
Grant, R.M. (1996). Prospering in dynamically-competitive environments: Organizational capability as knowledge integration. *Organization Science,* **7**(4), 375–387.
Hall, R. (1992). The strategic analysis of intangible resources. *Strategic Management Journal,* **13**(2), 135–144.
Hambrick, D.C., Geletkanycz, M.A. & Frederickson, J.W. (1993). Top executive commitment to the status quo: Some test of its determinants. *Strategic Management Journal,* **14**(6), 401–418.
Harrigan, K.R. (1985). Coalition strategies: A framework for joint ventures. *Academy of Management Proceedings,* 16–20.
Harrison, J., Hitt, M.A., Hoskisson, R.E. & Ireland, R.D. (1991). Synergies and post-

acquisition performance: Differences versus similarities in resource allocations. *Journal of Management*, **17**, 173–190.

Haspeslagh, P.C. & Jemison, D.B. (1991). *Managing Acquisitions: Creating Value through Corporate Renewal*. New York: Free Press.

Hill, C.W.L. & Jones, G.R. (1998). *Strategic Management: An Integrated Approach*, (4th edn.), Boston, MA: Houghton Mifflin.

Hill, R.C. & Hellriegel, D. (1994). Critical contingencies in joint venture management: Some lessons from managers. *Organization Science*, **5**(4), 594–607.

Hitt, M.A. & Ireland, R.D. (1985). Corporate distinctive competence, strategy, industry and performance. *Strategic Management Journal*, **6**, 273–293.

Hitt, M.A., Ireland, R.D. & Hoskisson, R.E. (1996). *Strategic Management: Competitiveness and Globalization*. Minneapolis/St Paul: West Publishing.

Hitt, M.A., Hoskisson, R.E., Johnson, R.A. & Moesel, D.D. (1996). The market for corporate control and firm innovation. *Academy of Management Journal*, **39**(5), 1084–1119.

Ireland, R. D., Hitt, M.A., Bettis, R.A. & DePorras, D.A. (1987). Strategy formulation processes: Differences in perceptions of strength and weakness indicators and environmental uncertainty by managerial level. *Strategic Management Journal*, **8**, 469–485.

Itami, K. (1987). *Mobilizing Invisible Assets*. Cambridge, MA: Harvard University Press.

Jemison, D.B. & Sitkin, S.B. (1986). Corporate acquisitions: A process perspective. *Academy of Management Review*, **11**, 145–163.

King, A.W. (1996). *Managers' perceptions of organizational competencies and firm performance*. Unpublished Doctoral Dissertation, University of North Carolina at Chapel Hill, NC.

King, A.W. & Zeithaml, C.P. (1998). *Competencies, ambiguity, and firm performance: A model and empirical evidence*, Working Paper.

Kogut, B. (1991). Joint ventures and the option to expand and acquire. *Management Science*, **37**(1), 19–32.

Kogut, B. & Zander, U. (1992). Knowledge of the firm, combinative capabilities, and the replication of technology. *Organization Science*, **3**(3), 383–397.

Kohli, A.K. & Jaworski, B.J. (1990). Market orientation: The construct, research propositions, and managerial implications. *Journal of Marketing*, **54**(2), 1–18.

Kohli, A.K., Jaworski, B.J. & Kumar, J. (1993). MARKOR: A measure of market orientation. *Journal of Marketing Research*, **30** (November), 467–477.

Koza, M.P. & Lewin, A.Y. (1998). The co-evolution of strategic alliances. *Organization Science*, **9**(3), 255–264.

Lei, D., Hitt, M.A. & Bettis, R. (1996). Dynamic core competences through meta-learning and strategic context. *Journal of Management*, **22**(4), 549–570.

Leonard-Barton, D. (1992). Core capabilities and core rigidities: A paradox in managing new product development. *Strategic Management Journal*, **3**, 111–125.

Markides, E.C. & Williamson, P.J. (1994). Related diversification, core competences and corporate performance. *Strategic Management Journal*, **15** (special issue, Summer), 149–165.

Markides, E.C. & Williamson, P.J. (1996). Corporate diversification and organizational structure: A resource-based view. *Academy of Management Journal*, **39**(2), 340–367.

Miller, C.C., Cardinal, L.B. & Glick, W.H. (1997). Retrospective reports in organizational research: A reexamination of recent evidence. *Academy of Management Journal*, **40**, 189–204.

Miller, D. & Friesen, P. (1984). *Organizations: A Quantum View*. Englewood Cliffs, NJ: Prentice Hall.
Miller, D. & Shamsie, J. (1996). The resource-based view of the firm in two environments: The Hollywood film studios from 1936 to 1965. *Academy of Management Journal*, **39**(3), 519–543.
Nayyar, P.R. (1992). On the measurement of corporate diversification strategy: Evidence from large U.S. service firms. *Strategic Management Journal*, **13**(3), 219–235.
Nelson, R. & Winter, S. (1982). *An Evolutionary Theory of Economic Change*. Cambridge, MA: Belknap Press.
Nohria, N. & Garcia-Pont, C. (1991). Global strategic linkages and industry structure. *Strategic Management Journal*, **12**, 105–124.
Nonaka, I. (1994). A dynamic theory of organizational knowledge creation. *Organization Science*, **5**, 14–37.
Nunnally, J.C. (1978). *Psychometric Theory*, (2nd edn.) New York: McGraw-Hill.
Penrose, E. (1959). *The Theory of Growth of the Firm*. Oxford: Blackwell.
Pentland, B.T. (1992). Organizing moves in software support. *Administrative Science Quarterly*, **37**, 527–548.
Peteraf, M.A. (1993). The cornerstones of competitive advantage. *Strategic Management Journal*, **14**(3), 179–192.
Polanyi, M. (1962). *Personal Knowledge: Towards a Post-Critical Philosophy*. Chicago, IL: Chicago University Press.
Ranft, A. & Zeithaml, C.P. (1999). *Preserving and transferring knowledge-based resources during post-acquisition implementation*, Working Paper.
Reed, R. & DeFillippi, R.J. (1990). Causal ambiguity, barriers to imitation, and sustainable competitive advantage. *Academy of Management Review*, **15**(1), 88–102.
Schwenk, C.R. (1984). Cognitive simplification processes in strategic decision-making. *Strategic Management Journal*, **5**, 111–128.
Sharma, A. & Kesner, I. (1996). Diversifying entry: Some ex ante explanations for postentry survival and growth. *Academy of Management Journal*, **39**(3), 635–677.
Snow, C.C. & Hrebiniak, L.G. (1980). Strategy, distinctive competence, and organizational performance. *Administrative Science Quarterly*, **25**(2), 317–336.
Stewart, T.A. (1997). Brain power: Who owns it ... how they profit from it. *Fortune*, 17 March, 105–110.
Teece, D.J. (1982). Towards an economic theory of the multiproduct firm. *Journal of Economic Behavior and Organization*, **3**, 39–63.
Teece, D.J., Pisano, G. & Shuen, A. (1997). Dynamic capabilities and strategic management. *Strategic Management Journal*, **18**(7), 509–533.
Verdin, P.J. & Williamson, P.J. (1994). Core competences, competitive advantage and market analysis: Forging the links. In G. Hamel & A. Heene (eds), *Competence-Based Competition*, New York: Wiley.
Winter, S. (1987). Knowledge and competence as strategic assets. In D. Teece (ed.), *The Competitive Challenge: Strategies for Industrial Innovation and Renewal*, New York: Harper and Row, 159–184.
Wysocki, Jr., B. (1997). Why an acquisition? Often, it's the people. *Wall Street Journal*, 6 October.
Yip, G.S. (1982). Diversification entry: Internal development versus acquisition. *Strategic Management Journal*, **3**, 331–345.

# 4

# The Relative Contributions of Inimitable, Non-Transferable and Non-Substitutable Resources to Profitability and Market Performance

RODOLPHE DURAND

## INTRODUCTION

In the explanation of firm performance, proponents of the resource-based view have developed an analysis defending the dominance of firm effects over industry effects. The resource-based view (RBV) seeks to better understand the drivers behind differences in profitability by understanding differences between firms (Wernerfelt, 1984; Barney, 1991; Amit & Schoemaker, 1993).

*Dynamic Strategic Resources: Development, Diffusion and Integration.*
Edited by Michael A. Hitt, Patricia Gorman Clifford, Robert D. Nixon and Kevin P. Coyne.

RBV interprets these differences in profitability as stemming from variety in the sources of rents accruing to firms, which are themselves affected by differences in the control and management of strategic resources (Winter, 1987, 1995). A firm is considered a unique bundle of resources, and its cost position may in fact be more a function of its resource portfolio than of its market position (Wernerfelt, 1984; Rumelt, 1984).

Empirical studies often address the impact of resource endowment on firm performance (Wernerfelt & Montgomery, 1988; Balakrishnan & Fox, 1993). Researchers try to understand the complex interplay between different types of resources, which leads to increases in performance. A firm's strategic moves are often reinterpreted from the resource-based viewpoint: for instance, integration means controlling new bundles of resources in addition to controlling cost (Chatterjee, 1990); diversification implies not only hedging risk but also preserving the relatedness of the resource portfolio (Markides & Williamson, 1994). However, rather few empirical studies have tried to differentiate the various sources of competitive advantage. Although qualitative differences between resources underlying production theoretically explain firm heterogeneity (Penrose, 1959), these relationships have not been empirically studied extensively enough.

This lack of empirical studies is the motivation for this paper. Had we a clear taxonomy of the resources, their properties and their impact on performance, we could analyze specifically the firms' peculiarities and explain in detail the determinants of performance. This paper distinguishes three kinds of resources, three properties and three performance variables. In order to understand the connection between a firm's resources and its competitive position, we primarily need to understand the influence of each resource on performance variables.

This study shows that knowing the properties of a firm's resources—including the properties of the firm's exchange relationships with suppliers and customers—is critical to understanding the firm's performance. We test the hypotheses of the RBV on a large sample of French firms (2875 firms within 50 industries). In particular, we show that inimitability and non-transferability of productive resources consistently contribute to increase both the firm's profitability and its market performance. However, maintaining exchange relationships that are non-substitutable entails a trade-off for the rent-seeking firm, between profitability on the one hand and market position on the other.

The paper is organized as follows. We begin by presenting the model and setting up the hypotheses to be tested. In the next section, we describe the data and methodology. We then detail the results. Finally, we offer some concluding remarks on the strategic implications of the results for sustaining a competitive advantage.

# Research Model

## Dependent Variables of Performance

Most empirical studies focus on only one indicator of performance in spite of the well-known theoretical and empirical drawbacks of this choice (Venkatraman & Ramunajam, 1986; Schmalensee, 1989; Capon, Farley & Hoenig, 1990). The shortcoming of single-variable models can be overcome by introducing at least two or three performance variables in the empirical models. Many variables are available. First, an evaluation of the profitability of a firm is frequently used. Price Cost Margin or Return on Sales are the most common indicators, useful in assessing the way the firm is able to monitor its costs. A second indicator of profitability is an evaluation of the use of the assets (operation and financial structure). Stock valuation, return on equity (ROE) and return on assets (ROA) are valuable indicators of how efficiently management has utilized the firm's resources. Finally, another traditional assessment of a firm's performance consists of market performance, i.e. either growth of sales or market power (using the relative market share).

We use three performance variables in our model: margin, profitability and market performance. We will distinguish the multiple effects of a firm's resource portfolio on its performance by considering these three variables in our model. Indeed, the effects of each resource can be detailed for each performance variable. Moreover, these variables have causal relationships among themselves that we must acknowledge. The literature has shown that high market performance is a precondition for high margin and high profitability to occur in many industries (Mancke, 1974; Schmalensee, 1989). In addition, a firm with high margins should experience higher profitability, all other conditions being equal. Thus, we expect two positive causal relationships. First, the higher a firm's market performance, the higher the margins and profitability of that firm. Second, high margins are likely to cause a high profitability.

Hypotheses on performance

H1: The higher a firm's market performance, the better the firm's margin and profitability.

H2: The higher a firm's margin, the higher a firm's profitability.

## Resources, Properties and Performance

Many authors describe a firm's resources either by their nature or by their properties (Wernerfelt, 1984; Barney, 1986; Dierickx & Cool, 1989; Grant,

1991; Amit & Schoemaker, 1993; Teece, Pisano & Shuen, 1997). For instance, some authors distinguish the nature of resources as financial, productive, organizational and human resources (Penrose, 1959; Barney, 1991).

When dealing with manufacturing firms, at least three kinds of resources are essential to exhibit the features of these firms. First, the *productive resources*, which correspond to the nature of the technological assets and aptitudes of the firm, are likely to be the main source of differences in the actualization of rent potential. Many authors have studied a firm's technological basis as a fundamental criterion for explaining competitive advantage and performance (Nelson & Winter, 1982; Levin, Cohen & Mowery, 1985; Teece, 1986; von Hippel, 1988; Sanchez, 1995; Christensen, 1994; Teece, Pisano & Shuen, 1997). These productive resources include tangible assets as well as intangible capabilities. Second, the *exchange relationships*, which deal with the links between the focal firm and its suppliers and customers, are a natural source of explanation of the level of performance (Verdin & Williamson, 1994; Levinthal & Myatt, 1994; Powell & Dent-Micallef, 1997; Poppo & Zenger, 1998). Numerous costs (research, information, negotiation, and so on) as well as several benefits (learning, time and quality management, for instance) are associated with the management of exchange relationships. The nature of the exchange relationships is likely to impact the level of the costs incurred and the amount of the benefits derived; hence the firm's performance (Larson, 1992). Third, the *level of internal coordination* within a firm can provide it with an advantage by allowing it to better actualize the rent potential of its resources (Chandler, 1962; Galbraith, 1972). The circulation of strategic information, the diffusion of reports, and the implementation of adequate organizational structures principally characterize internal coordination (Moingeon & Edmondson, 1996).

We acknowledge that this breakdown may be restrictive. But these elements (productive resources, exchange relationships, and internal coordination) seem to constitute the basic components absolutely necessary to define a firm (Demsetz, 1995). Without one of them, the definition would be incomplete to study the rationales of a firm's performance. Nevertheless, complementary information should be included when dealing with specific strategic decisions. For instance, the degree of coherence between resources must be included in the study of diversification (Teece *et al.*, 1994) or past experience in the study of FDI (Shaver, Mitchell & Yeung, 1997). However, for a descriptive and comparative analysis of firm performance, we estimate that the examination of these three elements consists of a necessary first test to empirically support or deny the RBV of firm performance.

Therefore, in this study, a firm's resource portfolio corresponds to the set of a firm's productive resources, a firm's exchange relationships, and a firm's internal coordination. More specifically, we detail below the influence a firm's resource portfolio has on each of the three performance variables. We formulate the corresponding hypotheses.

## Productive Resources and Performance

The RBV emphasizes the role productive resources play in the appropriation of rents by manufacturing firms. Productive resources, i.e. the technology as well as the knowledge and aptitudes used by the firm in the operation process, are the manufacturing firm's main assets. Theory suggests that the less imitable a firm's productive resources, the more likely the firm will create differential rents, i.e. will be able to outperform its rivals (Barney, 1991; Grant, 1991). The effect of inimitability is similar, namely positive, for each of the three performance variables. Inimitability brings about higher margins and best profitability. In addition, a firm which has inimitable productive resources, will be able to achieve better market performance. This is accomplished by tapping into the firm's specific productive resources in order to create a competitive advantage in production scale, scope, or flexibility.

But the productive resources also need to be not easily transferable to other companies (Penrose, 1959; Amit & Schoemaker, 1993; Peteraf, 1993). The absence of an accurate market valuation for strategic factors is a reason for a firm both to develop a competitive advantage and to appropriate differential rents. Causal ambiguity exists in evaluating the strategic value of a firm's productive resources (Lippman & Rumelt, 1982). As with inimitability, the non-transferability is a condition that favors the three performance variables, according to the RBV (Barney, 1991; Grant, 1991).

Hypotheses 3

H3a: The more inimitable a firm's productive resources, the better the firm's performance (margin, profitability, and market performance).

H3b: The less transferable a firm's productive resources, the better the firm's performance (margin, profitability, and market performance).

## Exchange Relationships and Performance

Not having extended the aforementioned reasoning from the productive resources to the exchange relationships is one of the main shortcomings of the RBV (Dyer & Singh, 1998). Some studies have dealt specifically with the vertical relationships in different industries and question strategic decisions using the RBV (Cool & Henderson, 1996; Mudambi & Helper, 1998). To the best of our knowledge, however, no article has concurrently studied the effects of supplier and customer relationships on multiple performance variables.

First, we must mention that we consider the exchange relationships to be resources. Many authors have studied the relationships between suppliers, customers, and the focal firm. We define the focal firm as the firm involved in supplier and customer relationships, as described in Porter's competitive analysis model. Porter (1980) considered these relationships as adversarial and countervailing forces. The one who has the most bargaining power achieves higher performance to the detriment of the other. Williamson (1975, 1985) developed transaction cost theory on the idea that the costs associated with the management of exchange relationships explain organizational and industrial structures. However, Williamson's unit of analysis does not directly concern a firm's performance. Moreover, Williamson's agents are opportunistic by nature.

## Supplier Relationship

The RBV may renew these traditional views of exchange relationships. Instead of considering the power or the costs associated with the supplier/customer relationship, the RBV suggests that the quality of this resource can lead to differential rents (Verdin & Williamson, 1994; Walsh *et al.*, 1996). More precisely, having been able to build a non-substitutable relationship with its supplier provides a source of rents to a firm that helps the firm to compete (Conner, 1991). Information sharing, trust, and co-development are factors that create a non-substitutable supplier relationship (Dyer & Singh, 1998). This relationship supports a firm's competitive advantage and contributes to the firm's market performance. However, the creation of a non-substitutable relationship demands time, coordination, trust, patience, and money (Larson, 1992). The effects on a focal firm's margins and profitability should not be as positive as they were on market performance (Walker & Poppo, 1991). Therefore, building a non-substitutable supplier relationship will diminish a firm's profitability but improve the firm's market performance.[1]

In a nutshell, neither the transaction cost theory nor Porter analysis adequately explains the effect of supplier relationships on a firm's performance. On one hand, the transaction costs are not necessary borne by only one of the two firms involved in the exchange relationship. Also the effects of transaction costs on each performance variable may differ. On the other hand, Porter's bargaining power theory is too restrictive when analyzing the different performance indicators, because supplier/client relationships are much more complex than pure antagonistic relationships. The RBV of the exchange relationships better characterizes the rent potential the focal firm owns. This view enables one to differentiate between the cost incurred in order to develop this specific relationship—which reduces margin and profitability—and the benefits the focal firm will derive from it in terms of market performance.

Hypotheses 4

H4a: The less substitutable the supplier relationships, the better the firm's market performance.

H4b: The less substitutable the supplier relationships, the lower the firm's margin and profitability.

## Customer Relationship

It appears that the RBV argument developed for the exchange relationship between a firm and its suppliers can be adapted for the relationship between the focal firm and its customers. Creating a non-substitutable relationship with its customers means making the firm's products appealing and essential for customers, creating a specific link between customer and firm which induces confidence, satisfaction, reputation, and trustfulness between both economic actors. This will benefit the focal firm, because the firm can charge the customer a premium for having access to this non-substitutable relationship. The customer willingly pays this premium to reduce its risks (in quality, delays, and stable procurement) and to contract with a supplier that caters to its specific needs. However, in terms of market performance, the fact that the focal firm targets some customers deprives the firm of being able to target a wider market. Consequently, the positive effect on margins and profitability is likely to be counterbalanced by reduced market performance, resulting from the need for the firm to narrow its target market in order to develop these intense and non-substitutable customer relationships.

Hypotheses 5

H5a: The less substitutable the customer relationships, the lower the firm's market performance.

H5b: The less substitutable the customer relationships, the better the firm's margin and profitability.

## Internal Coordination

It is difficult to assume a direct link between the level of internal coordination and the three firm performance variables. We expect the relationship between the level of internal coordination and performance to be indirect. In fact, assessing the level of internal coordination in our generic model cannot give a clear indication of its direct effect on performance. Internal coordination should enable a firm to improve its efficiency, but it concurrently creates associated management costs (Chandler, 1962; Galbraith, 1972; Walker & Poppo, 1991; Larson, 1992). Consequently, we assume that a high level of internal coordination creates a climate in which the use of resources is efficient and effective, thus leading to inimitability, non-transferability and non-substitutability of the other resources

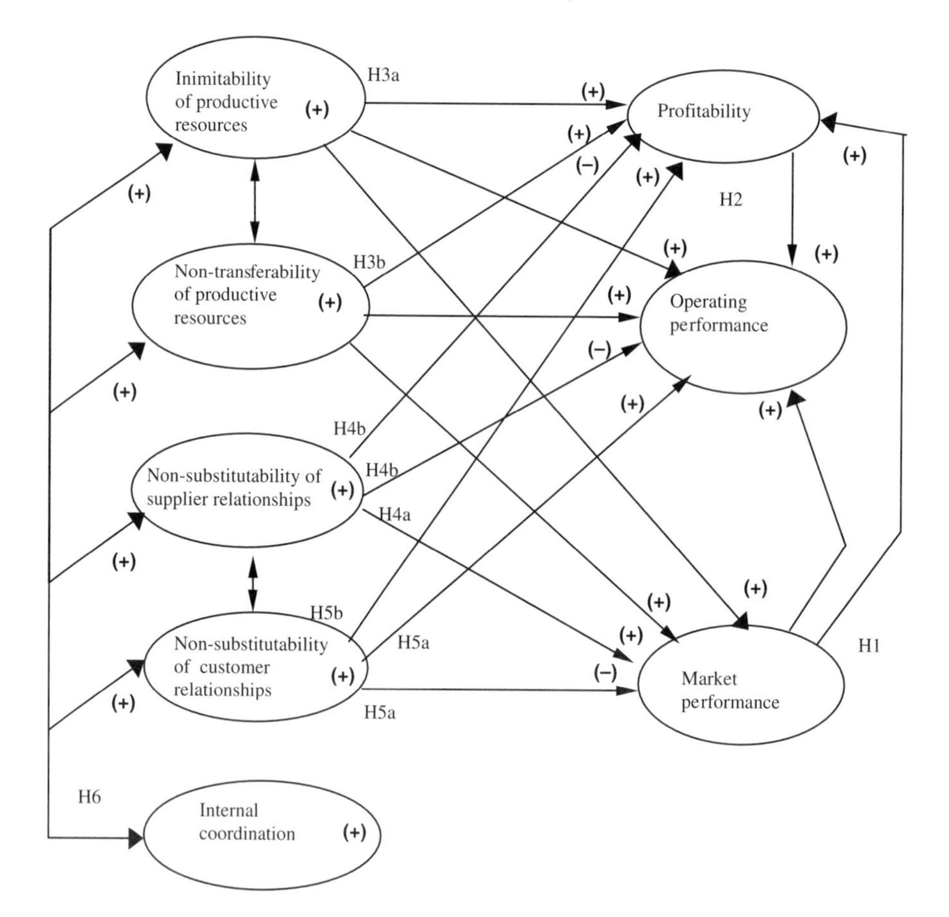


Figure 4.1 Theoretical model

(McGrath, McMillan & Venkatraman, 1995). Thus, a high level of internal coordination within a firm facilitates the actualization of the rent potential of its other idiosyncratic resources (inimitable and non-transferable productive resources, and non-substitutable exchange relationships), which in turn positively impact the performance of the firm.

Hypothesis 6

H6: The level of internal coordination within a firm is positively correlated with its other resources (productive resources and exchange relationships) but does not have a direct impact on the firm's performance variables.

FIGURE 4.1 provides a template for the theoretical model of the causal scheme of the relative contributions of inimitable, non-transferable, and non-substitutable resources to profitability and market performance. It integrates the three resources (productive resources, exchange relationships, and internal coordination) with the dependent variables (margin, profitability, and market performance).

## DATA AND ESTIMATION

### DATA AND SAMPLE

The data used in this research were gathered by the French central bank, the Bank of France, in 1995 and 1996. The Bank of France launched this survey in order to complement its traditional financial analysis of risk for small to medium-sized firms with an in-depth evaluation of these firms' strategy, for which public data are often rare. Qualitative data were collected in face-to-face interviews with CEOs, using a computer-aided questionnaire. For this kind of survey, the top manager is considered the person with the most comprehensive knowledge about strategy and performance (Hambrick, 1981). These interviews were conducted by specially trained Bank of France employees. The questionnaire dealt chiefly with the following topics: the business environment, the firm's strategy in each business, and internal organization and management features.

Fifty industries within 13 industrial sectors are represented in this survey (TABLE 4.1). The majority of companies are small and medium-sized industrials (from 30 to 2000 employees) that tend to be focused on one or two four-digit "SIC code equivalent" industries. The survey represents a random sample of small to medium-sized manufacturing firms and of

TABLE 4.1 Descriptive statistics: breakdown of the sample by industrial sector

| Industrial sector (European nomenclature) | N | % |
|---|---|---|
| Food and kindred products | 483 | 16.8 |
| Broadwoven fabrics and textile mill products | 342 | 11.9 |
| Leather goods and footwear | 66 | 2.3 |
| Wood products | 37 | 1.3 |
| Paper and allied products | 257 | 8.9 |
| Chemical and allied products | 134 | 4.7 |
| Rubber and plastic products | 170 | 5.9 |
| Stone, clay, and glass products and nonferrous metals | 90 | 3.1 |
| Fabricated metal products | 459 | 16.0 |
| Industrial machinery and equipment | 293 | 10.2 |
| Electronic and other electric equipment | 229 | 8.0 |
| Transportation equipment | 116 | 4.0 |
| Miscellaneous | 199 | 6.9 |
| Total | 2875 | 100 |

industries that have primarily small to medium-sized firms (TABLE 4.2). Nonetheless, we can expect that our results will be similar for larger public companies.

In order to minimize the possible effects of outliers in the sample for this study, we included only the industries (four-digit SIC code equivalent) for which at least 15 firms were competing. In order to prevent the study from being biased by diversification effects, we removed firms for which the main business represented less than 70% of their sales. Finally, we eliminated firms with missing data. The size of our final sample was 2875 firms, operating in 50 industries.

TABLE 4.2 Descriptive statistics: breakdown of the sample by firm size

| Decile | No. of employees | Annual revenue (FF million) |
|---|---|---|
| 1 | 42 | 21.8 |
| 2 | 48 | 30.3 |
| 3 | 60 | 40.4 |
| 4 | 76 | 53.2 |
| median | 94 | 71.6 |
| 6 | 121 | 94.1 |
| 7 | 165 | 134.2 |
| 8 | 240 | 207.7 |
| 9 | 404 | 430.8 |

# VARIABLES

## Dependent Variables

We selected three variables for performance. First, margin was measured by the firm's return on sales (ROS). Variable ROS is an average for the years 1995 to 1997. Second, the proxy for profitability was the 1995–1997 average value of the firm's return on assets (ROA).

Finally, market performance was evaluated using two variables, KEYPOS and BCG. KEYPOS is an indicator calculated by the Bank of France, which estimates a firm's relative position among rivals. At the beginning of the questionnaire, each CEO defines within a provided list the key success factors (KSF) of their industries. At the end of the questionnaire, on the same list, CEOs evaluate their company on a five-point Likert scale. The Bank of France methodological services then calculate KEYPOS as a weighted average of the distance between the competitive advantage acknowledged by the CEOs and the KSF of the industry. BCG is the ratio between a firm's market share and the main competitor's market share. Together, KEYPOS and BCG estimate a firm's market performance.

## Inimitability of Productive Resources

We used two variables for the operationalization of the inimitability of productive resources. First, the degree of flexibility characterizes the endowment a technological base provides a firm (Sanchez, 1995). Following several studies, we assumed that the more flexible a firm's technology, the less imitable were its productive resources (Kogut & Zander, 1992; Christensen, 1994). If a technology enables a firm to greatly differentiate its production, then the firm has the capability to manage flexibility, complexity, and operations in such a way that competitors are unlikely to easily imitate (Sanchez & Mahoney, 1996). The proxy DIFF estimates the degree of product differentiation provided by a firm's technology basis.

Second, we created an indicator, DESTIME, as a proxy for the "Time Compression Diseconomies" a new competitor will incur in trying to imitate a firm's productive resources (Dierickx & Cool, 1989). A firm trying to accumulate strategic resources in a minimized period of time will stumble upon inevitable friction costs. These costs are time compression diseconomies (TCD), which reduce the imitability of a firm's productive resources (Dierickx & Cool, 1989). Creation of DESTIME consists of three steps (see the Appendix for complete questions). (1) The CEOs determined the strategic dimensions that primarily affected their firm's cost of production. CEOs' choices included the size of units of production, the volume of activity, the specificity of the technology, privileged access to a source of procurement, and labor productivity. (2) The CEOs then evaluated TCD as the difficulty a new entrant faces in imitating their firm on every dimension of production chosen in step 1 using a five-point Likert scale. (3) Finally, we calculated DESTIME as a compounded average of the value of the advantage corresponding to the selected strategic dimensions (see Appendix).

### Non-Transferability of Productive Resources

We used three variables as proxies for the non-transferability of productive resources. Non-transferability must be built within the firm and R&D is the main factor enabling the productive resources to be non-transferable. In order to assess the non-transferability of productive resources within a firm, CEOs are asked which functions they focus on in order to compete against rivals. If they quote R&D as a high priority, this indicates that their firm is developing specialized assets, specific resources, and idiosyncratic aptitudes. Each of these factors increases the non-transferability of a firm's productive resources. Therefore, the FUNR&D variable represents the priority CEOs gave the R&D function in comparison with other functions (marketing, procurement, etc.).

However, this measure alone is not sufficient to highlight how R&D and non-transferable productive resources are related. Hence, a more quantitative measure of R&D has to be included. Accordingly, we used an evaluation of the level of a firm's R&D expenditures and compared it to the industrial average. The resulting variable, R&DREL, shows how a firm is building specific productive resources, which are neither easily valued by the market nor transferable (Barney, 1986). The formulation of a strategic objective regarding R&D, combined with effective above-average R&D expenditures, characterizes a commitment to obtaining non-transferable resources.

Finally, we created a third indicator concerning the nature of a firm's productive resources. We assumed that there were two kinds of resources, those directly connected to production (cost, quality, and technical performance) and those dealing with sales (brand image, delays, and complementary services). Resources linked to production require more resource stocks than sales resources require (Dierickx & Cool, 1989). In addition, productive resources precede sales resources, and they have stocks that are not as easily eroded as the stocks of sales resources. "In general, only variables that have the nature of a stock, as opposed to a flow, can carry a credible threat, and the more so, the slower the stock is decaying over time" (Dierickx & Cool, 1989: 1508). Therefore, by evaluating the difference between the stocks of the resources linked to sales (supposedly more transferable) and the stocks of resources linked to production (assumed to be less transferable), we created another proxy, DEGTRANS, for the non-transferability of productive resources. For more detail on the calculation of DEGTRANS, see the Appendix.

## Non-Substitutability of Supplier Relationships

Three observable variables serve to evaluate the non-substitutability of supplier relationships. First, CEOs appraised the two switching costs describing their exchange relationship. The switching cost incurred by the firm is SCSup, and the switching cost the supplier incurs if it wants to change its customer (i.e. the focal firm) is SCSupCus. Applying RBV to these exchange relationships leads to the conclusion that when both switching costs are high, a special relationship unites both players. This relationship is non-substitutable.

Second, to solidify this interpretation, we add a third variable, COMPSup. COMPSup measures the level of competitive pressure the focal firm exerts over its supplier. Competitive pressure occurs for companies that systematically require competitive bids in procurement rather than giving priority to past suppliers. If the firm prefers a less competitive mode of selecting its suppliers, the firm and the supplier are involved in a non-substitutable relationship, especially if both switching costs are high.

## Non-Substitutability of Customer Relationships

Symmetrically to the operationalization of non-substitutable supplier relationships, we used the switching costs incurred between the focal firm and its customers for the operationalization of non-substitutable customer relationships. SCCus represents the cost incurred by the firm if it changes one of its main customers. SCCusSup is an evaluation of the cost for a customer if it chooses to change its supplier (i.e. the focal firm). As before, when both switching costs are high, a non-substitutable exchange relationship is likely to exist between both players.

Secondly, to support this measure, we added a variable that evaluates the focal firm's level of commitment to its customers (ADAPT). If the focal firm has consented to some specific investment for maintaining good relationships with its customer, the focal firm is involved in a non-substitutable relationship since its investments are likely to have lower value for another customer. Consequently, the three observable variables together indicate the degree of non-substitutability of the customer relationship.

## Internal Coordination

The level of diffusion of a firm's strategic objectives within the organization (DIFOBJ) is an indicator of the level of internal coordination. The better informed the members of the organization are, the higher the level of a firm's internal coordination. Accordingly, the presence and efficiency of managerial accounting and reporting increase the quality of internal coordination; this is especially true for small and medium-sized firms. Specifically, the deeper this information is distributed within a company, the better the level of the company's internal coordination. DIFINFO is the variable that evaluates the diffusion of managerial accounting information within a firm. DIFOBJ and DIFINFO focus on the communication component of the coordination mechanisms. In order to add information to our construct regarding the structure of the organization, the third variable estimates how often the firm uses transversal modes of coordination. Transversal modes of coordination include different liaison roles, similar to the role of a project manager (Galbraith, 1972). Consequently, the frequency with which a firm makes use of these coordinating mechanisms (COORD) gives an indication of the level of sophistication of the firm's internal coordination. Altogether, these three variables enabled us to assess the level of internal coordination.

## Control Variables

We control our model from three major effects. First, we included variables regarding the level of concentration inside the industry. Industry concentration was measured as the four-firm concentration ratio at the four-digit SIC equivalent level. We also controlled for the effects of industry growth. Industry growth measurement was the industry's annual change in sales, expressed as a percentage, for the three years preceding the survey.

Second, we analyzed the significance of the average differences of independent variables according to firm size. It appeared that the fourth quartile (firms with more than 200 employees) presented some significant differences in comparison with the other quartiles. Consequently, we created two subsamples. We studied the effects of a firm's size on our model by testing the theoretical model on each subsample.

Finally, we analyzed the impact of the sector. We used the French statistical classification developed by INSEE that distinguishes four general categories of manufacturing industries: food and agro-industries, consumer goods industries, intermediary industries, and equipment industries. We tested our theoretical model on each industrial sector.

## Model

Integration of the different elements (observable variables, resources, and performance variables) requires a model that incorporates the causal links between explanatory variables and dependent variables, the relationships among the set of explanatory variables, and the relationships within the dependent variables. We used Lisrel for estimating the different parameters and fit indexes. Lisrel explicitly differentiates between observed and latent variables, and estimates the quality of the constructs (Bollen, 1989). It requires both explicitly stating the correspondence between observed and latent variables and specifying the relationships among theoretical constructs precisely. Lisrel gives fit indexes for the overall model (GFI, AGFI, RMR, total coefficient of determination) and for each causal relationship (coefficients, T-values, and squared multiple correlations for structural equations). Specifically, due to the nature of our variables, we used the polychoric matrix and the WLS procedure of estimation, as recommended by Joreskog and Sorbom (1989).

# Results

The correlation matrix is presented in Table 4.3. No result appears to question the use of our variables. On the contrary, correlations among the observable variables supposed to operationalize an explanatory variable are high. Variables are ordinal, and most of them are not normal. We conducted a Principal Component Analysis on our observable variables in order to pre-test the quality of the representation of the resource portfolio. Results are provided in Table 4.4. Signs and loadings are well oriented. The axes obtained by this procedure correspond to the expected explanatory variables. Therefore, the observable variables are the expression of the latent variables.

The loadings $\lambda_x$ and $\lambda_y$ represent the estimation by Lisrel of the relationships between latent variables and observable variables. Our assumptions are well supported by these loadings (Table 4.5). The coefficients are relatively high (seven out of ten are equal to or greater than 0.6), and all the signs conform to our hypotheses, as the Principal Component Analysis had previously indicated. T-values are very significant. Furthermore, the total coefficient for X-variables, which measures the overall quality of these relationships, is very good (0.96).

Regarding the squared multiple correlations for structural equations, ROS presents a significant but relatively low coefficient (7%), whereas ROA and market performance both have remarkably high coefficients (57% and 39%). Overall, the total coefficient of determination is highly satisfactory (42%). Fit

TABLE 4.3 Correlation matrix

| | ROS | ROA | KEYPOS | BCG | FUNRD | DEGTRANS | R&DREL | DESTIME | DIFF | COMPSup | SCSupCus | CTFR | ADAPT | SCusSup | Scus | CCORD | DIFINFO |
|---|---|---|---|---|---|---|---|---|---|---|---|---|---|---|---|---|---|
| ROA | **0.5978**<br>Sig ,000 | | | | | | | | | | | | | | | | |
| **KEYPOS** | **0.0651**<br>Sig ,000 | **0.0828**<br>Sig ,000 | | | | | | | | | | | | | | | |
| **BCG** | **0.0695**<br>Sig ,000 | **0.0874**<br>Sig ,000 | **0.1435**<br>Sig ,000 | | | | | | | | | | | | | | |
| **FUNRD** | 0.0507<br>Sig, 002 | 0.0057<br>Sig, 721 | 0.0657<br>Sig ,000 | 0.0828<br>Sig ,000 | | | | | | | | | | | | | |
| **DEGTRANS** | −0.0032<br>Sig, 832 | −0.0279<br>Sig, 068 | −0.1221<br>Sig ,000 | −0.0636<br>Sig ,000 | **−0.1239**<br>Sig ,000 | | | | | | | | | | | | |
| **R&DREL** | 0.0387<br>Sig, 014 | 0.006<br>Sig, 705 | 0.0078<br>Sig, 613 | 0.0435<br>Sig, 014 | **0.1036**<br>Sig ,000 | **−0.0655**<br>Sig ,000 | | | | | | | | | | | |
| **DESTIME** | 0.054<br>Sig ,000 | 0.0186<br>Sig, 224 | 0.0152<br>Sig, 311 | 0.0287<br>Sig, 096 | 0.0676<br>Sig ,000 | −0.0112<br>Sig, 463 | −0.003<br>Sig, 849 | | | | | | | | | | |
| **DIFF** | 0.0962<br>Sig ,000 | 0.0681<br>Sig ,000 | 0.1615<br>Sig ,000 | 0.0868<br>Sig ,000 | 0.2052<br>Sig ,000 | −0.1276<br>Sig ,000 | 0.0652<br>Sig ,000 | **0.1564**<br>Sig ,000 | | | | | | | | | |
| **COMPSup** | 0.0093<br>Sig, 544 | −0.0165<br>Sig, 283 | −0.0633<br>Sig ,000 | 0.0114<br>Sig, 508 | 0.0384<br>Sig, 017 | 0.0339<br>Sig, 027 | −0.001<br>Sig, 949 | 0.0653<br>Sig ,000 | 0.0108<br>Sig, 480 | | | | | | | | |
| **SCSupCus** | 0.0199<br>Sig, 192 | 0.0598<br>Sig ,000 | 0.0646<br>Sig ,000 | 0.0844<br>Sig ,000 | 0.0382<br>Sig, 017 | −0.0288<br>Sig, 059 | 0.0085<br>Sig, 588 | 0.0657<br>Sig ,000 | 0.0684<br>Sig ,000 | **−0.0682**<br>Sig ,000 | | | | | | | |
| **SCSup** | 0.0117<br>Sig, 445 | −0.0128<br>Sig, 404 | 0.0145<br>Sig, 334 | 0.0401<br>Sig, 020 | 0.0735<br>Sig ,000 | −0.0043<br>Sig, 781 | 0.036<br>Sig, 022 | 0.03<br>Sig, 051 | 0.0846<br>Sig ,000 | **−0.122**<br>Sig ,000 | **0.1686**<br>Sig ,000 | | | | | | |
| **ADAPT** | 0.0579<br>Sig ,000 | 0.0275<br>Sig, 071 | −0.0251<br>Sig, 091 | −0.0038<br>Sig, 822 | 0.1113<br>Sig ,000 | −0.0069<br>Sig, 652 | 0.0499<br>Sig, 001 | 0.059<br>Sig ,000 | 0.0869<br>Sig ,000 | 0.0519<br>Sig, 001 | 0.0223<br>Sig, 142 | 0.0969<br>Sig ,000 | | | | | |
| **SCCusSup** | 0.0498<br>Sig, 001 | 0.0219<br>Sig, 155 | 0.0559<br>Sig ,000 | 0.031<br>Sig, 074 | 0.1068<br>Sig ,000 | −0.0365<br>Sig, 018 | 0.0619<br>Sig ,000 | 0.0848<br>Sig ,000 | 0.1713<br>Sig ,000 | 0.0318<br>Sig, 040 | 0.0637<br>Sig ,000 | 0.1745<br>Sig ,000 | **0.2063**<br>Sig ,000 | | | | |
| **SCCus** | −0.0117<br>Sig, 441 | −0.0263<br>Sig, 083 | −0.0209<br>Sig, 159 | 0.0022<br>Sig, 900 | 0.0408<br>Sig, 011 | −0.016<br>Sig, 291 | 0.0331<br>Sig, 034 | 0.0135<br>Sig, 375 | −0.0043<br>Sig, 778 | −0.0074<br>Sig, 629 | 0.04<br>Sig, 008 | 0.1113<br>Sig ,000 | **0.2176**<br>Sig ,000 | **0.1753**<br>Sig ,000 | | | |
| **COORD** | 0.0496<br>Sig, 001 | 0.0099<br>Sig, 519 | 0.0084<br>Sig, 577 | 0.0466<br>Sig, 007 | 0.0618<br>Sig ,000 | 0.0163<br>Sig, 290 | 0.0592<br>Sig ,000 | 0.0717<br>Sig ,000 | 0.0516<br>Sig, 001 | 0.051<br>Sig, 001 | 0.043<br>Sig, 005 | 0.0261<br>Sig, 091 | 0.0786<br>Sig ,000 | 0.074<br>Sig ,000 | 0.0483<br>Sig, 002 | | |
| **DIFINFO** | 0.0031<br>Sig, 842 | −0.0043<br>Sig, 784 | 0.0007<br>Sig, 963 | 0.0632<br>Sig ,000 | 0.0522<br>Sig, 001 | −0.0277<br>Sig, 076 | 0.0281<br>Sig, 079 | 0.0709<br>Sig ,000 | 0.0414<br>Sig, 008 | 0.0495<br>Sig, 002 | 0.0969<br>Sig ,000 | 0.0512<br>Sig, 001 | 0.0428<br>Sig, 006 | 0.0395<br>Sig, 012 | 0.0281<br>Sig, 069 | **0.2149**<br>Sig ,000 | |
| **DIFOBJ** | −0.0126<br>Sig, 419 | −0.0214<br>Sig, 168 | 0.0245<br>Sig, 106 | 0.0081<br>Sig, 642 | 0.0509<br>Sig, 002 | 0.0064<br>Sig, 678 | 0.0568<br>Sig ,000 | 0.0502<br>Sig, 001 | 0.0154<br>Sig, 321 | 0.0859<br>Sig ,000 | 0.0422<br>Sig, 006 | 0.0122<br>Sig, 435 | 0.0308<br>Sig, 046 | 0.0534<br>Sig, 001 | 0.0063<br>Sig, 681 | **0.2384**<br>Sig ,000 | **0.2655**<br>Sig ,000 |

TABLE 4.4 Principal Component Analysis[a]

| | Factor 1 | Factor 2 | Factor 3 | Factor 4 | Factor 5 |
|---|---|---|---|---|---|
| ADAPT | **.72723** | .11642 | .05624 | −.12668 | .08372 |
| SCCusSup | **.70472** | .02288 | −.10200 | .00582 | −.12084 |
| SCCus | **.61175** | .05960 | −.16607 | −.10755 | .33282 |
| DIFOBJ | .01607 | **.71904** | .04391 | −.02269 | .06738 |
| DIFINFO | .01521 | **.69830** | −.14023 | −.05694 | .08001 |
| COORD | .17128 | **.69067** | .03820 | −.08564 | .05987 |
| SCSup | .28320 | .04579 | **−.67693** | −.05294 | .07234 |
| SCSupCus | .00491 | .14968 | **−.65605** | .04465 | .23506 |
| COMPSup | .10959 | .17171 | **.62266** | .15418 | .31387 |
| DEGTRANS | .04687 | .05371 | .06950 | **.66485** | −.02576 |
| R&DREL | .12639 | .19544 | −.03820 | **−.56612** | −.15833 |
| FUNRD | .16936 | .09460 | .03119 | **−.55430** | .29057 |
| DESTIME | .05471 | .13375 | −.02049 | .03291 | **.74011** |
| DIFF | .12909 | .01585 | −.13128 | −.46549 | **.60363** |

[a] Percentage of inertia represented by the axes: 50.2%.

TABLE 4.5 Parameters from Lisrel: operationalization of the latent variables

| Latent variable | X variable | Loading $\lambda_x$ |
|---|---|---|
| Inimitability of productive resources | DESTIME | .391[a] |
| | DIFF | 1 |
| Non-transferability of productive resources | R&DREL | .451[a] |
| | FUNRD | 1 |
| | DEGTRANS | −.658[a] |
| Non-substitutability of customer relationship | SCSup | .593[a] |
| | SCSupCus | 1 |
| | COMPSup | −.597[a] |
| Non-substitutability of supplier relationship | SCCus | 1 |
| | SCCusSup | .424[a] |
| | ADAPT | .564[a] |
| Internal coordination | DIFINFO | 1 |
| | DIFOBJ | 1[a] |
| | COORD | .938[a] |
| | **Y variable** | **Loading $\lambda_y$** |
| Margin | ROS | 1 |
| Profitability | ROA | 1 |
| Market | KEYPOS | .659[a] |
| Performance | BCG | 1 |

[a] Significant at 1%.

indexes (GFI, AGFI and RMR) confirm an excellent global fit of the model, given the size of the sample and the nature of the variables (Baumgartner & Homburg, 1996; Hulland, Chow & Lam, 1996).

## CAUSAL RELATIONSHIPS

### Productive Resources

Causal relationships are shown in FIGURE 4.2. H3a and H3b receive strong support. Inimitability of productive resources impacts positively ROS (+0.181) and market performance (+0.243). Non-transferability of productive resources greatly impacts market performance (+0.46) but seems to have little significant effect on margin and ROA.

### Exchange Relationships

Regarding supplier relationships, H4a and H4b are confirmed. Non substitutable supplier relationships give leverage to a firm increasing its market performance (+0.166). However, the cost of developing such a relationship obliterates margins, since the focal firm must incur costs (information, communication, and coordination) to build the relationship. As expected, then, the impact on ROS is negative and significant (−0.095).

We expected converse effects on performance variables regarding customer relationships (H5a and H5b). The results confirmed these hypotheses. A non-substitutable customer relationship increases ROS (+0.121) but decreases a firm's market performance (−0.275) by preventing the firm from targeting a wider market.

### Internal Coordination

In the Lisrel model, we left "free" the relationships between internal coordination and the dependent variables. None of the coefficients were significant. Therefore, as expected, there is no significant direct effect between the level of coordination and either profitability or market performance. However, the relationships between the level of internal coordination and the other resources are positive (from 0.15 to 0.23). These correlations indicate that the higher the level of internal coordination, the more likely the resources are to be inimitable, non-transferable and non-substitutable. Accordingly, in order to develop inimitable, non-transferable, and non-substitutable resources, a firm requires high levels of internal coordination. These results provide strong support for H6.

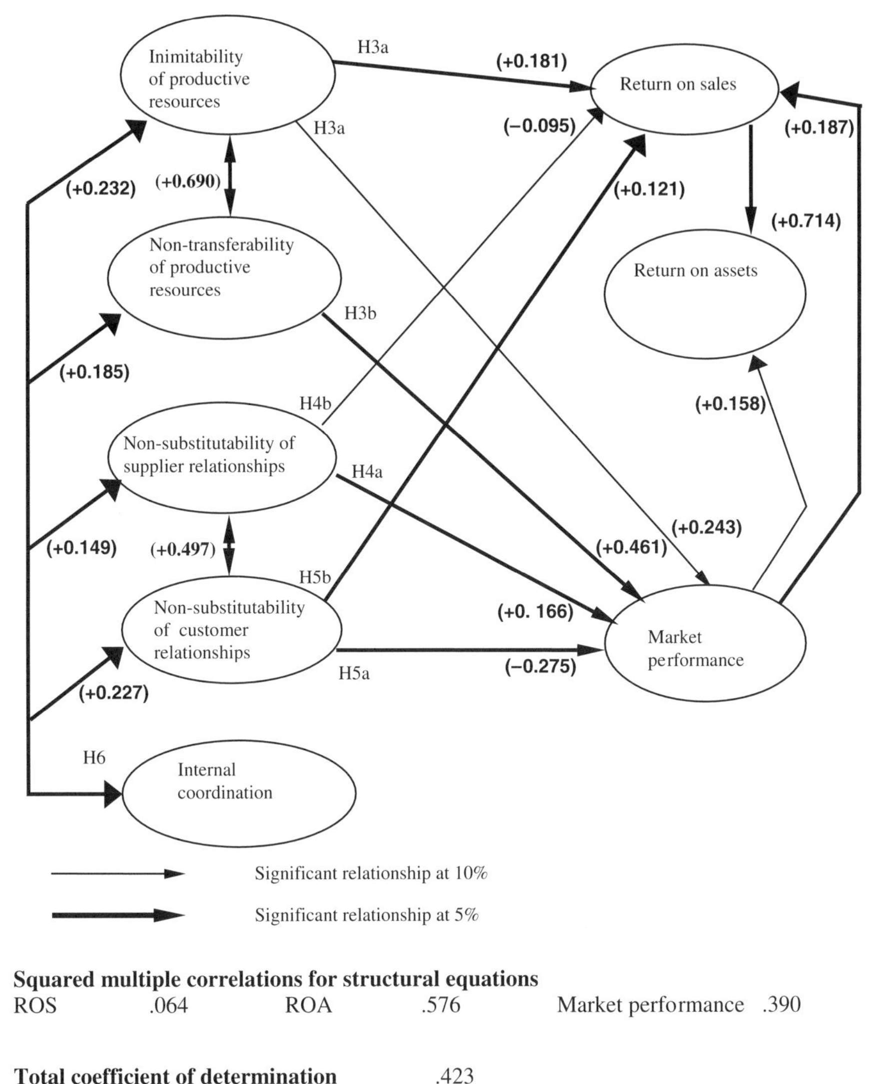


**Squared multiple correlations for structural equations**

ROS .064 ROA .576 Market performance .390

**Total coefficient of determination** .423

**Global fit indexes**

GFI .990 AGFI .984 RMR .030

$\chi^2$ 324 df 93

FIGURE 4.2 Lisrel results

### Performance Variables

The relationships linking market performance to both ROS and ROA are positive and significant (+0.19 and +0.16). It appears, therefore, that market performance positively affects profitability, as assumed by H1. The relationship between ROS and ROA is positive and significant (+0.71), conforming to H2.

The squared multiple correlation, which expresses the quality of explanation of a dependent variable, is high for ROA (57%), although no exogenous explanatory variables have a significant direct impact on ROA. According to our results, only ROS and market performance directly "cause" ROA. Consequently, we tested another model, creating a new dependent latent variable, using both ROS and ROA as proxies. All the preceding results were confirmed, suggesting the robustness of the model. The squared multiple correlation for the new performance variable is 9% and the total coefficient of determination for the two-dependent-variable model is 40.2% (compared to 42% with the three-dependent-variable model).

## Additional Comments

### System Effect

Correlation between inimitability and non-transferability of the productive resources (0.7) and correlation between the two exchange relationships (0.5) are both high. We interpret these results as a reinforcement effect between related resources, i.e. productive resources and exchange relationships (see Figure 4.2). The more inimitable a firm's productive resources are, the higher the degree of non-transferability of these resources. The more non-substitutable the relationships a firm has with its suppliers, the more likely the firm is to have non-substitutable customer relationships. These two aforementioned reinforcement effects, when combined with the positive effect of internal coordination on the four other resources, create an overall system effect.

### Direct and Indirect Effects

No masked effect appeared from the analysis of the direct, indirect and total effects provided by Lisrel. On the contrary, two additional results emerged that complement the overall coherence of the model. First, there is an indirect and significant effect that links non-transferable productive resources with ROS (+0.265). Second, inimitable productive resources have a significant indirect effect on ROA (+0.134).

### Control Variables

Industry growth has a positive impact on profitability, but a non-significant effect on market performance. On the contrary, market concentration impacts significantly (and negatively) market performance but has no significant effect on profitability. This last result indicates that the more concentrated the industry, the more intense the competition, and then the more difficult it is for a firm to achieve high market performance.

We tested our theoretical model on two subsamples, according to firm size. No discrepancies appeared in the results between small and larger firms. This result confirms the validity of the RBV analysis of performance, since no size bias is found between smaller and larger firms.

Finally, four additional models were tested based upon the sector in which a firm competes: food and agro-industries, consumer goods industries, intermediary industries, and equipment industries. Again, the structure of the results was found to be stable. No differences appeared in signs or coefficients. Yet, it is worth noting some nuances in the significance of the relationships, according to the sector. These nuances provide a more fine-tuned analysis of the results, in accordance with the specificity of the sectors. For instance, the significance of the exchange relationships was preponderant for the "intermediary industries" that principally produce by-products to be used by other industries.

## Discussion

In this discussion section, we review our results and take a step back in order to place them in the perspective of a firm's competitive position. At this point, nevertheless, we feel it is necessary to comment on two limitations of the study.

## Limitations

The first limitation of our study concerns the use of secondary data. We did not collect the data for this study, but instead used data already available, which had been gathered by the Bank of France's services. As a consequence, many additional questions that could have greatly contributed to the operationalization of latent variables in the model could not be asked.

The second limitation relates to the use of CEOs' answers. Researchers suggest cross-evaluating the answers using other methods when possible. Unfortunately, we could not cross-validate the CEOs' answers. However, previous studies have shown that subjective data is worthwhile when evaluating general strategic issues and performance (Hambrick, 1981; Venkatraman & Ramanujam, 1986). According to Tull and Hawkins (1980) personal interviews are advantageous for handling complex questions, collecting large amounts of data, and obtaining in-depth information. In addition, the Bank of France uses trained interviewers in order to attenuate over-confident and careless answers. Face-to-face interviews led by trained interviewers tend to reduce the inconsistency of individual answers (deLeeuw, Hox & Snijkers, 1995).

## CONTRIBUTIONS

This paper is one of the first cross-sectional studies to test the RBV on a large representative sample of non-US industries. The overall fit of the model is notably high (over 40%), and the causal links validate the RBV of performance. Our study confirms that each firm's resources each contributes differently to its performance. Some are more important to market performance, while others are vital to profitability. In particular, the non-transferability and the inimitability of a firm's productive resources (technology, levels of R&D expenditures, accumulated experience, and time diseconomies) are positively linked to the observed performance variables, but especially to market performance.

Second, the non-substitutability of the exchange relationships is linked in a complex way with a firm's performance. The relationship between the focal firm and its supplier is considered non-substitutable when both switching costs between the firm and the supplier are high, and when the firm prefers the continuity of long-term relationships with its suppliers rather than short-term competition among potential suppliers (Dyer & Singh, 1998). These high switching costs indicate that a specific relationship exists between both companies. In this case, we found that building this relationship has a cost and lowers profitability, but enables the focal firm to obtain better market performance (Mudambi & Helper, 1998). Conversely, the non-substitutability of the relationships with the customers implies the firm targets specific customers—consequently the firm can charge a premium to these customers over and above the costs of the specific investments incurred to offer adapted products. Therefore, in the case of customer non-substitutability, the margins and profitability are positively influenced while market performance will be reduced. Thus, in either case, managing the non-substitutability in exchange relationships entails a tradeoff for the rent-seeking firm between market performance and profitability.

Third, we found that internal coordination does not have a direct impact on the performance variables. However, as expected, strong positive coefficients with the explanatory variables confirms that internal coordination is a catalyst for the enhancement of the non-transferability, the inimitability and the non-substitutability of the other resources.

Finally, we would like to emphasize the importance of considering multiple variables of performance in empirical studies. Too often, general results proceed from significant relationships linking explanatory variables to either market performance or profitability variables. This study clearly illustrates the real complexity underlying the analysis of firm performance. More specifically, some explanatory variables may have opposite effects on each of these performance variables. Only appropriate methods such as, for instance, Lisrel makes it possible to distinguish between these multiple effects.

## Conclusion

This study provides managers with a clarification of the relationships linking their firm's resources and performance. Three principal lessons can be drawn from our study. First, managers must enable the firm to develop idiosyncratic productive resources, using continuous flows of R&D investment in order to build economies of time, to incite innovations, and to increase the flexibility of its technological base. Inimitable and non-transferable resources ensure that the company develops a source of differential rents, which competitors are unlikely to easily imitate. Second, as an interface, the focal firm should increase the switching cost of its different exchange relationships. Investing in suppliers' non-substitutability is costly in terms of immediate profitability, but the investment pays back in terms of market performance. With customers, investment in non-substitutability has a positive impact on profitability. Third, managers willing to pursue a resource-based strategy should improve the level of internal coordination within the firm. By diffusing clear objectives, using managerial accounting and transversal coordination, managers can induce a system effect, improving the properties of all the other resources, and creating an *efficient* bundle of resources.

## Note

1. The non-substitutability is a matter of degree. Exchange relationships are more or less substitutable. We mean here "the less substitutable they are, the better for a firm's market performance".

## References

Amit, R. & Schoemaker, P. (1993). Strategic assets and organizational rent. *Strategic Management Journal*, **14**(1), 33–46.

Balakrishnan, S. & Fox, I. (1993). Asset specificity, firm heterogeneity and capital structure. *Strategic Management Journal*, **14**(1), 3–16.

Barney, J. (1986). Strategic factor markets: Expectations, luck, and business strategy. *Management Science*, **42**, 1231–1241.

Barney, J. (1991). Firm resources and sustained competitive advantage. *Journal of Management*, **17**, 99–120.

Baumgartner, H. & Homburg, C. (1996). Applications of structural equation modeling in marketing and consumer research: A review. *International Journal of Research in Marketing*, **13**, 139–161.

Bollen, K.A. (1989). *Structural Equations with Latent Variables*. New York: Wiley.

Capon, N., Farley, J.U. & Hoenig, S. (1990). Determinants of financial performance: A meta-analysis. *Management Science*, **36**(10), 1143–1159.

Chandler, A.D. (1962). *Strategy and Structure*. Cambridge, MA: MIT Press.

Chatterjee, S. (1990). Excess resources, utilization costs, and mode of entry. *Academy of Management Journal*, **33**, 780–800.

Christensen, J.F. (1994). Analyzing the technological base of the firm. Paper presented at Conférence Eunetics, September, Strasbourg, France, published in R. Sanchez, A. Heene & H. Thomas (eds), *Dynamics of Competence-Based Competition*, Pergamon (1996).

Conner, K.R. (1991). A historical comparison of resource-based theory and five schools of thought within industrial organization economics: Do we have a new theory of the firm? *Journal of Management*, **17**, 121–154.

Cool, K. & Henderson, J. (1996). Factor regression analysis, power and profits in supply chains. Mimeo, reprinted in M. Ghertman, J. Obadia & J.L. Arregle (eds), *Statistical Models for Strategic Management*, Kluwer Publications.

DeLeeuw, E., Hox, J. & Snijkers, G. (1995). The effect of computer-assisted interviewing on data quality. *Journal of the Market Research Society*, **37**, 325–345.

Demsetz, H. (1995). *The Economics of the Business Firm*. Cambridge: Cambridge University Press.

Dierickx, I. & Cool, K. (1989). Asset stock accumulation and sustainability of competitive advantage. *Management Science*, **35**, 1504–1511.

Dyer, J. & Singh, H. (1998). The relational view: Cooperative strategy and source of inter-organizational competitive advantage. *Academy of Management Review*, **23**, 660–680.

Galbraith, J. (1972). Organization design: An information processing view. In J.W. Lorsch & P.R. Lawrence (eds), *Organization Planning, Cases and Concepts*, Homewood, IL: Irwin, 49–74.

Grant, R.M. (1991). The resource-based theory of competitive advantage: Implications for strategy reformulation, *California Management Review*, Spring, 114–135.

Hambrick, D.C. (1981). Strategic awareness within top management teams. *Strategic Management Journal*, **2**, 153–173.

Hulland, J., Chow, Y. & Lam, S. (1996). Use of causal models in marketing research: A review. *International Journal of Research in Marketing*, **13**, 181–197.

Joreskog, K. & Sorbom, D. (1989). *Lisrel 7, a Guide to the Program and Applications*. SPSS, Inc.

Kogut, B. & Zander, U. (1992). Knowledge of the firm, combinative capabilities and the replication of technology. *Organization Science*, **3**, 383–397.

Larson, A. (1992). Network dyads in entrepreneurial settings: A study of governance exchange relationships, *Administrative Science Quarterly*, **37**, 76–102.

Levin, R., Cohen, W. & Mowery, D. (1985). R&D appropriability, opportunity and market structure: new evidence on some Schumpeterian hypotheses. *American Economic Review*, **75**, 20–25.

Levinthal, D.A. & Myatt, J. (1994). Co-evolution of capabilities and industry: The evolution of mutual fund processing. *Strategic Management Journal*, **15**, 45–62.
Lippman, S. & Rumelt, R. (1982). Uncertain imitability: An analysis of interfirm differences in efficiency under competition. *Bell Journal of Economics*, **13**, 418–443.
Mancke, R.B. (1974). Causes of the interfirm profitability differences: A new interpretation of the evidence. *Quarterly Journal of Economics*, **88**, 181–193.
Markides, C. & Williamson, P. (1994). Related diversification, core competences and corporate performance. *Strategic Management Journal*, **15**, 149–165.
McGrath, R.G., McMillan, I. & Venkatraman, S. (1995). Defining and developing competence: A strategic process paradigm. *Strategic Management Journal*, **16**, 251–275.
Moingeon, B. & Edmondson, A. (1996). *Organizational Learning and Competitive Advantage*, London: Sage.
Mudambi, R. & Helper, S. (1998). The close but adversarial model of supplier relations in the U.S. auto industry. *Strategic Management Journal*, **19**, 775–792.
Nelson, R. & Winter, S. (1982). *An Evolutionary Theory of Economic Change*, Boston, MA: Harvard University Press.
Penrose, E. (1959). *The Theory of the Growth of the Firm*. Oxford: Basil Blackwell.
Peteraf, M. (1993). The cornerstones of competitive advantage: a resource-based view. *Strategic Management Journal*, **14**, 179–191.
Poppo, L. & Zenger, T. (1998). Testing alternative theories of the firm: Transaction cost, knowledge based and measurement explanations for make-or-buy decisions in information services. *Strategic Management Journal*, **19**, 853–877.
Porter, M.E. (1980). *Competitive Strategy*. New York: Free Press.
Powell, T.C. & Dent-Micallef, A. (1997). Information technology as competitive advantage: The rôle of human, business and technology resources. *Strategic Management Journal*, **18**, 375–405.
Rumelt, R. (1984). Toward a strategic theory of the firm. In X. Lamb (ed.), *Competitive Strategic Management*, Englewood Cliffs, NJ: Prentice-Hall, 556–570.
Sanchez, R. (1995). Strategic flexibility in product competition. *Strategic Management Journal*, **16**, 135–159.
Sanchez, R. & Mahoney, J. (1996). Modularity, flexibility, and knowledge management in product and organization design. *Strategic Management Journal*, **17**, (Winter Special Issue), 63–76.
Schmalensee, R. (1989). Inter-industry studies of structure and performance. In R. Schmalensee & R. Willig (eds), *Handbook of Industrial Organization*, vol. 2, Amsterdam: North Holland, 951–1009.
Shaver, J.M., Mitchell, W. & Yeung, B. (1997). The effect of own-firm and other-firm experience on foreign direct investment survival in the US, 1987–92. *Strategic Management Journal*, **18**, 811–824.
Teece, D. (1986). Profiting from technological innovation: Implications for integration, collaboration, licensing and public policy. *Research Policy*, **15**, 285–305.
Teece, D., Pisano, G. & Schuen, A. (1997). Dynamic capabilities and strategic management. *Strategic Management Journal*, **18**, 509–535.
Teece, D.J., Rumelt, R. Dosi, G. & Winter, S. (1994). Understanding corporate coherence: Theory and evidence. *Journal of Economic Behavior and Organization*, **23**, 537–556.
Tull, D.S. & Hawkins, D. (1980). *Marketing Research: Measurement and Method*, New York: MacMillan.
Venkatraman, N. & Ramanujam, V. (1986). Measurement of business performance in strategic research: A comparison of approaches. *Academy of Management Review*, **11**, 801–814.
Verdin, P. & Williamson, P. (1994). Core competences, competitive advantage and

market analysis: Forging the links. In G. Hamel A. Heene (eds), *Competence-based Competition*, Chichester: Wiley, 77–111.
Von Hippel, E. (1988). *The Sources of Innovation*. Oxford: Oxford University Press.
Walker, G. & Poppo, L. (1991). Profit centers, single-source suppliers, and transaction costs. *Administrative Science Quarterly*, **36**, 66–88.
Walsh, S., Boylan, R., Morone, J. & Paulson, A. (1996). Core capabilities and strategy, empirical evidence for the semiconductor silicon industry. In H. Thomas & D. O'Neal (eds), *Strategic Integration*, Chichester: Wiley, 149–166.
Wernerfelt, B. (1984). A resource-based view of the firm. *Strategic Management Journal*, **5**, 171–180.
Wernerfelt, B. & Montgomery, C.A. (1988). Tobin's q and the importance of focus in firm performance, *American Economic Review*, **78**, 246–251.
Williamson, O.E. (1975). *Markets and Hierarchies: Analysis and Antitrust Implications*, New York: Free Press.
Williamson, O.E (1985). *The Economic Institutions of Capitalism*, New York: Free Press.
Winter, S. (1987). Knowledge and competence as strategic assets. In D. Teece (ed.), *The Competitive Challenge*, Cambridge, MA: Ballinger, 159–184.
Winter, S. (1995). Four Rs of profitability: Rents, resources, routines and replication. In C. Montgomery (ed.), *Resource-based and Evolutionary Theories of the Firm*, Boston, MA: Kluwer Academic, 147–178.

## Appendix. Operationalization of Variables

### Non-Imitability of Productive Resources

**Variable DIFF**

Relative to your main competitors, your technological base enables you to differentiate your production

| less | | | | more |
|---|---|---|---|---|
| 1 | 2 | 3 | 4 | 5 |

**Variable DESTIME**

$$\text{DESTIME} = \frac{\sum_{i,j} \text{FACT}_i \times \text{EVAL}_j}{\sum_i \text{FACT}_i}$$

where FACT corresponds to the binary answer (0 or 1) to the following question:
Among these factors, indicate which have most influenced your production costs during the past two years:

1. Size of production unit
2. Volume of production
3. Use of specific technology

4. Privileged access to a supply source
5. Labor productivity.

EVAL is the answer to an additional question evaluating the time diseconomies for new competitors for each of the selected items:

1. The difficulties for new competitors to reach a sufficient plant size are:

| low | | | | high |
|---|---|---|---|---|
| 1 | 2 | 3 | 4 | 5 |

2. The difficulties for new competitors to reach a sufficient cumulated volume of production are (same scale)
3. The difficulties for new competitors to have access to your production technologies are (same scale)
4. The difficulties for new competitors to find equivalent conditions of raw material or component access are (same scale)
5. The difficulties for new competitors to reach a similar labor productivity level are (same scale).

## Non-Transferability of Productive Resources

**Variable R&DREL**

$$R\&DREL_i = R\&D_i - R\&D_{NAF}$$

where $R\&D_i$ is firm i's R&D expenditure as a percentage of sales, and $R\&D_{NAF}$ is the average of all the firms' R&D expenditure as a percentage of sales in the industry, at the four-digit SIC level (French equivalent is NAF).

**Variable FUNRD**
Please indicate which functions primarily enabled your firm to sustain a competitive position in your market?

Technological development    graded from 1 to 3
Marketing
Finance
Procurement

**Variable DEGTRANS**
DEGTRANS results from the following formula:

$$DEGTRANS = \frac{\sum_{d,e,f} RjS \times S_{d,e,f}}{\sum_{d,e,f} RjS} - \frac{\sum_{a,b,c} RjS \times S_{a,b,c}}{\sum_{a,b,c} RjS}$$

The higher the DEGTRANS value, the more a firm focused on developing likely transferable productive resources. Two questions were asked:

1. First, in order to determine the Strategic Resources (RjS):
   What are the factors on which you have focused your efforts during the past two years? Binary answers. Several possible answers among
   (a) price/cost
   (b) quality
   (c) technical performance, innovation
   (d) brand image, reputation
   (e) delays
   (f) additional services.
   Thus, $RjS_{a,b,c}$ are cost, quality and technical performance; and $RjS_{d,e,f}$ are brand image, delays, and additional services.
2. Second, in order to estimate the value of the stocks (S) of strategic assets:
   For each of the selected resources, evaluate your position relative to your main competitors (five-point Likert scale, with 5 a very high competitive advantage).

## NON-SUBSTITUTABILITY OF SUPPLIER RELATIONSHIP

**Variable SCSup**
For your firm, changing your main suppliers will entail switching costs that are

low high
1 2 3 4 5

**Variable SCSupCus**
For your main suppliers, the loss of you as a customer will have consequences that are

low high
1 2 3 4 5

**Variable COMPSup**
You systematically prefer to put your suppliers in competition rather than giving priority to the continuity of your relationships:

complete disagreement complete agreement
1 2 3 4 5

## Non-Substitutability of Customer Relationships

**Variable SCCus**
For your firm, the costs incurred for replacing one of your main customers are

low high
1 2 3 4 5

**Variable SCCusSup**
For your main customers, the loss of you as a supplier will entail switching costs that are

low high
1 2 3 4 5

**Variable ADAPT**
To satisfy your main customers, you adapted by making specific investments for them that are

low high
1 2 3 4 5

## Internal Coordination

**Variable DIFOBJ**
The objectives followed by top management are communicated to all employees:

complete disagreement complete agreement
1 2 3 4 5

**Variable DIFINFO**
Managerial accounting service develops and diffuses to the middle managers reporting tables, analytical accounting results, and business plans:

complete disagreement complete agreement
1 2 3 4 5

**Variable COORD**
The firm has implemented specific means of transversal coordination (inter-service coordinator, team workshop, and committee):

seldom permanently
1 2 3 4 5

# 5

# The Evolution of Strategy in a Newly Transformed Organization: The Interplay Between Strategy Development and Corporate Culture

MIRELA SCHWARZ, JOE NANDHAKUMAR

It has been widely recognized that the strategy development process involves generating strategic ideas which present a potential source of sustained competitive advantage (e.g. Barney, 1986, 1991; Hart & Banbury, 1994). The strategy development process involves a complex dynamic process with various influences (e.g. Pettigrew, 1985b, 1990, 1992). Papadakis and Barwise (1997: 291) claim that the literature on strategy decision process has not yet been able to resolve the question of what "the key influences on the process of making strategic decisions" are.

Many authors, such as Sworder (1995), Rhodes (1995), Van den Ven (1992) and Fiol (1991), suggest that corporate culture is an important issue

*Dynamic Strategic Resources: Development, Diffusion and Integration.*
Edited by Michael A. Hitt, Patricia Gorman Clifford, Robert D. Nixon and Kevin P. Coyne.

for generating successful strategic ideas. Barney (1986), for example, argues that a particular cultural context presents a source of competitive advantage in developing strategic ideas. However, limited academic work has explored the relationship between the strategy formulation and the corporate culture (e.g. Chen, Sawyers & Williams, 1997; Nwachukwu & Vitell Jr., 1997; Sworder, 1995; Rhodes, 1995; Kono, 1994; Schwartz & Davis, 1981). This lack of academic research in strategy decision process is somewhat surprising given the increasing interest in corporate culture.

The main aim of this chapter is to explore the core research question of how strategic ideas evolve in a newly transformed organization and how they are shaped by the corporate culture. The primary contribution of this research lies in the development of a new theoretical conceptualization of the interplay between the evolution of strategic ideas and cultural context. The rich insights gained from this study are finally used to outline some implications for theories into strategy development and practice of managing the process of strategy development.

## Literature Review

### Strategic Ideas

Much of the literature on strategic decision processes agrees that the early, formative steps in decision making are crucial because they guide the search for solutions (e.g., Cyert & March, 1963; Bower, 1972; Witte, 1972; Mintzberg, Raisinghani & Theoret, 1976; Quinn, 1981; Lyles, 1981; Nutt, 1984, 1986; Pettigrew, 1985a; Hickson *et al.*, 1986). One of these important formative steps in decision making is generating strategic ideas, which evolve out of strategic thinking. In the strategy literature a common language for describing strategic ideas and strategic thinking is just beginning to emerge (e.g. Garratt, 1995).

Strategic ideas are seen as the outcome of the strategic thinking process. Strategic ideas are described as "dominant images we hold in our minds" (Sworder, 1995: 72), "the gem of an idea" (Mintzberg, 1995: 68) or "breakthrough insights" (Rhodes, 1995: 92). Evolution of strategic ideas requires creative, lateral and inductive thinking among its strategic thinkers (Mintzberg, 1995). In addition, "nonlinear thinking" and "strategic flexibility" are important issues in the development of strategic ideas (Hitt, Keats & DeMarie, 1998: 26–28). Mintzberg characterizes strategic thinkers as "innovative entrepreneurs", who are able to think creatively and inductively and challenge "conventional wisdom". Strategic thinkers are described by some researchers as "direction-givers" (e.g., Sworder, 1995; Garrat, 1995). Strategic thinking is applied not only at the "board level"

(Sworder, 1995; Mintzberg, 1995) but also in other organizational and managerial levels.

## Strategic Ideas and Corporate Culture

Many authors (e.g. Rhodes, 1995; Sworder, 1995) claim that studies on organizational decision making seldom address the interplay between strategic ideas and corporate culture. The strategy development process involves a range of strategic ideas, which shape the future of an organization. As has been emphasized by many authors (e.g. Barney, 1991; Hart & Banbury, 1994) the strategy decision-making process itself presents a potential source of sustained competitive advantage. Many practitioners claim that successful strategies are seen as evolving out of corporate culture which acknowledges and rewards individuals by identifying their aspirations with value systems embedded in the organizational context (e.g. Deal & Kennedy, 1982).

Although some of the literature suggests that the fit between strategy and culture is essential to the success of an organization (Fiol, 1991; van den Ven, 1992; Barney, 1986; Lorsch, 1986; Schwartz & Davis, 1981; Shrivastava, 1985), only limited research has been done to investigate the relationship between strategy development and corporate culture (e.g. Chen, Sawyers & Williams, 1997; Nwachukwu & Vitell Jr., 1997; Kono, 1994, Schwartz & Davis, 1981; Shrivastava, 1985).

When organizational members work on strategy development, they usually bring in their values, ideas, beliefs, experience and knowledge as part of units of data which they feed into the debate to shape the process of generating strategic ideas (e.g. Rhodes, 1995; Sworder, 1995). Furthermore Sworder (1995) recognized the impact of attitudes, habits, beliefs and self-esteem on the quality of strategic thinking. He identified habits as "ingrained thinking patterns developed over time" (1995: 72) which shape the quality of strategic thinking. In addition, he claims that beliefs and opinions can operate as "sensors" (1995: 73) in the strategic thinking process which help us to identify strategic ideas.

## Corporate Culture

Since the 1980s, there has been an increasing interest in corporate culture as demonstrated in the popularity of books such as *Corporate Cultures* (Deal & Kennedy, 1982) and *Theory Z* (Ouchi, 1981) and in the academic management literature (e.g. Pettigrew, 1979; Schein, 1985). In the literature, however, there is no consensus on the meaning of corporate culture and its application in organizational studies. One main reason lies in the conflicting metaphors of culture, which are based on different underlying assumptions.

The view of culture adopted in this work is that of a root metaphor (Smircich, 1983; Morgan, 1986). This approach views organizations as culture-producing phenomena as opposed to having a culture. This conception supports a sense-making perspective of corporate culture. Researchers following this cultural perspective acknowledge the definition of culture as ''shared meanings, shared understandings and shared sense making'' (Morgan, 1986: 128). This view is derived from the symbolic conception of culture, which focuses on the interpretation of symbols and symbolic action. This view that corporate culture is a system of ''publicly and collectively accepted meanings'' (Pettigrew, 1979: 574) is visible (Schein, 1985) and represents the social bond that holds the organization together (Smircich, 1983).

Leadership plays an important role in shaping the corporate culture (e.g. Clark, 1972; Pettigrew, 1979; Sathe, 1985; Schein, 1985) and provides key insights into why organizations work in the way they do. Although organizational members may leave the organization and new ones are taking over their position, the management preserves knowledge, behaviors, norms and values over time (Daft & Weick, 1984). One main management task is to construct and maintain systems of shared beliefs and meanings (Pfeffer, 1981; Morgan, 1986). Culture provides a sense of identity to its organizational members (Deal & Kennedy, 1982) and supports gaining commitment and generating motivation (Smircich, 1983).

## Research Site and Methodology

This study was carried out during 1997–98 in an electronic manufacturing company (SRS—a pseudonym) based in Germany, which is part of a leading international electronic manufacturing company. SRS recently went through major strategic and organizational changes that led to a strategic reorientation of their business activities. The organization changed their main strategy that affected the services they delivered to their customers. Our study followed the strategy evolution process for 12 months, from the origin of the strategic idea to strategy development.

### Research Methodology

The research approach adopted in this chapter is based on grounded theory methodology (Glaser & Strauss, 1967; Martin & Turner, 1986; Turner, 1983; Strauss & Cobin, 1990) which has been widely used in organizational research (e.g. Pettigrew, 1990; Ancona, 1990; Kahn, 1990; Elsbach & Sutton, 1992; Orlikowski, 1993). Using grounded theory methodology, this study seeks to offer a theoretical interpretation of the process of strategy creation from the cultural perspective. This methodology is also seen as inductive, contextual and processual (Martin & Turner, 1986), which fits with the interpretative research approach adopted in this research.

## Data Collection

The field study employed a variety of "engaged" data-gathering methods (Orlikowski, 1993; Nandhakumar & Jones, 1997) involving unstructured and semi-structured interviews, non-participant observations and documentation review, in which researchers have extensive contact with the research phenomena. From June 1997 to July 1998, an average of 2 weeks every 2 months was spent on the field site, observing and interviewing organizational members during their daily work, decision-making process, and strategically important meetings; 77 interviews were conducted with 11 members of the company each lasting an average of one and a half hours. Each interviewee was interviewed several times during the research period. Table 5.1 provides details regarding the number of interviews and the positions of the interviewees.

The people interviewed at SRS were the main actors involved in the strategy creation and implementation process—in this case the managing directors, CEO, members of the middle management and other individual

Table 5.1 Number of interviews conducted at SRS and the positions of the interviewees

| Positions of interviewees | Number of interviews |
|---|---|
| CEO | 5 |
| Senior Manager Sales | 3 |
| Senior Manager Finance | 2 |
| Senior Manager Product A | 3 |
| Senior Manager Product B | 4 |
| Senior Manager Planning | 2 |
| Senior Manager SRS | 25 |
| Sales personnel | 8 |
| Service technician | 10 |
| Product manager | 8 |
| External consultant | 7 |
| **Total** | 77 |

organizational members (cf. Chakravarthy & Doz, 1992; Pettigrew, 1992). The interviews focused on understanding organizational members' meaningful experiences with the strategy creation and implementation process and their perceptions of the transformation and change before the study period. Some of the interviews were tape-recorded and were subsequently transcribed. Detailed notes were also taken during the interviews.

The use of in-depth interviews as the main type of data collection was supplemented with observation, informal discussion and document reviews. Observation was carried out in particular by attending workshops, formal and informal meetings, conversations and discussions relating to strategic issues. These sessions lasted in general between two and five hours, occasionally the entire day. Informal conversations with the interviewees and other staff members were held while the researcher spent some additional time in the company, for example attending social events and observing the daily activities in the CEO's office and taking notes of the events and conversations relating to strategic decisions. After every session, extensive notes were taken, which were then written up into a case study describing the strategy development process of SRS as well as important aspects of the organizational and cultural context.

## Data Analysis

The data were analyzed using the techniques of grounded theory (Glaser & Strauss, 1967), which provided guidelines for the classification of and commentary on qualitative data. The analytical technique of reading and rereading field notes and identifying possible concepts evolving out of the empirical findings is called the open coding process (Strauss & Cobin, 1990). All identified themes were put together and organized in possible categories or main headlines with meaningful labels (Strauss & Cobin, 1990).

Maintaining the categories with the concepts was an iterative process. Since the beginning of the research process, new themes were always added and sometimes categories were reconstituted under different labels. This approach helped to organize and analyze the field notes. It also helped to classify the different meanings of the phenomena generating strategic ideas and therefore helped to identify the importance of strategic debate within the process of generating strategic ideas in a particular cultural atmosphere.

The iteration between data and concepts in the field study ended when enough categories and associated concepts had been identified. This stage was achieved when no additional data were collected at SRS, and no additional concepts and categories evolved out of the existing empirical data. The developed categories and concepts explain how the strategy evolution process occurred (cf. Glaser & Strauss, 1967).

While this in-depth study in one organization enables us to gain insights into the complex dynamic process of strategy development, it also means that we must be cautious about generalizing from this single study. As Nandhakumar and Jones (1997) argue, the generalization from the research reported should be seen as explanations of particular phenomena derived from interpretive research in specific organizational settings, which may be valuable in the future in other organizations and contexts. The understanding gained in this study therefore provides a basis for understanding similar phenomena in other settings, rather than enabling the prediction of behavior in other contexts.

The case study presented in the next section of this chapter focuses on the strategy development process in the participating company (SRS). The company name and some details about organizational members have been disguised in order to follow the ethical limits and confidentiality agreements with the company involved.

## Case Study: SRS

### Company Background

SRS, a company based in Germany, is part of a leading manufacturer of high- and medium-voltage substations, which belongs to one of the big international electronic manufacturing companies in the world. SRS provided after-sales service to high- and medium-voltage substations, electrical networks and high-current systems of utility companies or energy providers. The services were first provided for the local market and were then expanded to cover most other parts of the world, such as Eastern and Western Europe, North and South America, the Far East and the Southeast Asian markets.

### Transformation

Between 1990 and 1992 the international manufacturer of substations (RS) went through major reengineering changes, which particularly involved a review of the existing products and services as well as of markets and customers. During this restructuring period it was identified that the after-sales service was a major weakness and threat to maintain competitive advantage on the market and to retain the existing customers. For example, if the service of a power plant was interrupted due to technical defects it was vital for the customer that the repair was done as quickly and reliably as possible. Often a power plant distributes electricity to a whole city and any interruption causes a strong negative economic effect on the city as well as for the energy provider.

As a result of the reengineering activities a new service organization (SRS) was established within the international manufacturer of substations at the end of 1992. The new organization was responsible for all after-sales service activities in Europe and had around 100 employees. The new service organization became a separate department within the international manufacturer of substations with Schneider as the managing director. The after-sales service activities involved simple repair, spare part deliveries and maintenance services for high- and medium-voltage substations and electrical networks.

In 1994 SRS became a profit center within RS, with a 40% increase in the number the of staff. The whole organization was occupied with activities such as recruitment of new employees, development of new marketing material and establishing an infrastructure for further growth. The SRS profit center started to develop and establish its own infrastructure in terms of EDP facilities and accounting, reporting and budgeting systems in order to be able to run the service business independently of the other departments within RS.

In 1996 the SRS profit center became an independent organization with about 350 staff providing services for the parent company and other organizations. The annual sales revenue showed a remarkable increase from $115 million in 1994 to $329 million in 1996. The organization was now responsible for all service activities around the world. In addition it was announced that it would be the training center for all service units of RS substations in 50 countries all over the world. In order to coordinate and control all activities, the infrastructure was enhanced by introducing new information systems and laptops for the service staff, with connection to headquarters.

## Cultural Context

The organizational culture evolving in SRS was seen as "competitive and performance-oriented". It was a "young" culture, which began to evolve with the foundation of SRS at the end of 1992. The SRS manager, Schneider, in his mid-fifties, became the head of the new SRS service department in 1992, and later manager of the profit center in 1994 and then head of the new worldwide Business Service Unit in 1996. Schneider had profound knowledge of the product substation, and was aware of the latest market developments. His management style was open and participatory and encouraged a climate of creativity and innovation without major restrictions. He gave his employees as much freedom as possible with regard to their daily activities, their time and their budget. As long as the daily work resulted in planned sales and profit, he hardly interfered in their daily working life. Schneider showed a cooperative, democratic leadership style in which he favored norms that called for collaborative and competitive spirit.

The relationship between organizational members and Schneider was very open and based on trust. The organizational members of SRS accepted Schneider's authority. Among themselves they had a strong solidarity. Schneider was open for *ad hoc* meetings and informal interaction. The nature of interaction could be described as competitive, friendly, a little provocative but also supportive. The organizational members had no hesitation in approaching Schneider or other employees for advice and help.

Observing the daily working life of the staff and managers showed that people approached other staff and managers without fear, to talk about problems or new ideas. Everywhere doors were open, and when people passed through the corridor they exchanged words with each other, such as: "how is that job in Kuwait going?" or "did Karl help you out with your problem?".

The working culture was highly cooperative and informative and focused on problem solving and teamworking. The values of the organization called for cooperation among the employees, trust, pioneering work, enthusiasm for work, customer orientation and "fighting spirit" to compete in the market, and modest competition among the employees. In the day-to-day business there was an ethos of sharing problems and ideas in an atmosphere of free and open exchange. This was often due to lack of sufficient experience and knowledge among individual employees to carry out the required tasks on their own. This ethos was fostered by ritualistic informal "lunches", coffee breaks in the office, and after-office-hours visits to public houses. The function of all these meetings and social events was to affirm the mutual interest of employees and Schneider, and to increase solidarity between the employees, which meant that a closer working and social relationship among the organizational members was achieved along with sharing of their value system.

## International Service Strategy Development

SRS developed an international service strategy for all substation businesses around the world. The aim was to provide more customized after-sales services, which could start from financial management, engineering planning or simple repair work to a retrofit job. The following events and processes describe the development of the international service strategy of SRS.

## Market Implications

The managing director, Schneider, used to meet regularly with his customers and such meetings were often accompanied by social events. During these meetings, most of which took place outside Germany, he often received information regarding the customers' satisfaction with SRS's service and their needs and requirements. SRS's customers demanded more than just repair and maintenance work; for example, they wanted to outsource most of their in-house service activities and all-round service, which covered technical, security-oriented and ecologically friendly maintenance activities and financial advice. This trend was subsequently confirmed in a customer survey.

SRS carried out a market analysis of international organizations that are known for having a professional, efficient and successful after-sales service, such as in the airline or office equipment industry. The intention behind this analysis, according to Schneider, was to get an idea of how a successful professional service works in a highly competitive industry sector.

## Initial Ideas

Schneider's initial ideas for an international after-sales service strategy were mainly initiated by talking to customers and further developed by the organizational members. Schneider was convinced that the key success factor for any strategy to be accepted within the organization was to communicate and present the strategy effectively and adequately to the key decision-makers within the RS organization. As he pointed out, "it is so essential to communicate right the first time when you articulate the idea, otherwise it will be killed immediately". He therefore looked for professional support in formulating and presenting his initial strategic idea. He approached an external consultant, who was specialized in public relations and marketing activities. Schneider had several meetings with the consultant, explaining his business, giving him all the market information and laying out some of his ideas for the new service strategy.

The external consultant reformulated Schneider's initial strategic idea into simpler words to make them accessible to an audience which did not have the same professional background, and presented the ideas in professional-looking presentation charts. The written report (including the contents of the strategic idea and the main benefits for the customers and organization) was presented to the organizational members of SRS.

## Evolution of the Initial Strategic Ideas

Schneider then organized a meeting with his managers and presented his idea using colored overhead charts. During the whole presentation he emphasized that he was not sure if the idea was applicable and realistic. He was asking for advice and more detailed information rather than informing them that this was his new idea. As one of the organizational members recalled: "... he said in this meeting ... it is a nice idea, but he didn't really know how he could use it. As we were faced with the day-to-day business, it was very important for him to get our input. We felt very flattered, challenged and ... and we loved that."

After the meeting Schneider asked the management team to think about the ideas he had presented and to develop a strategy concept including a business plan for the implementation. His intention was that they should go through the same procedure as he did with the external consultant by talking through the ideas, formulating them, and identifying weaknesses and potentials of the ideas. Further, he wanted to make sure that he got the commitment of the organizational members for his initial idea which should subsequently be the organization's vision.

The organizational members involved in the strategic meetings and discussions felt encouraged to be asked to develop a strategy and business plan for an international service organization. The organizational members worked hard, and intensively, in teamwork and were very engaged. When they started to work out the details of the concept each organizational member started to involve other employees into a face-to-face discussion. In the whole process they worked only with a few senior employees whom they trusted to ensure that the idea was not spreading throughout the organization. The organizational members elaborated and abandoned some of Schneider's ideas, but also developed some new strategic ideas.

The final concept of the internationally oriented service strategy was described in terms of contents of the services, organizational structure, management, resources, customer benefits, sales and profit forecasts. A report was then produced for presentation purposes.

After a month, the middle management team met Schneider to present their concepts. Karl, who was Schneider's most favored manager, presented the idea, claiming: "well, I presented the concept because I am the one who speaks [Schneider's] language and knows how to deal with his difficult personality, in particular when he asks some nasty questions." He is very demanding and likes to provoke people in meetings in order to find out if they can present solid argument. Schneider was satisfied with the way the organizational members elaborated his ideas and came up with new ones. Some of the senior employees were consulted and the final version was written up in the form of a report.

### Conflicts and Adjustments of Ideas

Later, a meeting between Schneider and the CEO of the parent company was arranged. Schneider presented the new service strategy for the new SRS organization to the CEO, whereby his presentation focused on the potentially strong increase of sales and profits with the new service strategy. Schneider argued that the organization had problems in achieving the sales and profit goals that were agreed with the headquarters. Therefore he thought this issue might be one of the key factors to convince the CEO to accept the new service concept.

The CEO showed an interest in the strategy concept and in particular in the profit and sales forecasts. He hesitated to make it public and suggested to Schneider that he should discuss this concept with other senior managers to get their agreement and commitment. The CEO expressed his concerns that he would like to have enough supporters within the senior management before he agreed to proceed with further actions.

Schneider organized several meetings with managing directors within the organization. He chose to meet the senior managers after office hours to have a more relaxed atmosphere. He took his presentation paper slides with him and discussed them with the manager. During these communications he was always keen to point out the benefits for the other managers and that there will be no conflict of interest. These meetings were described by Schneider as "rather unfriendly, I had the feeling I was on a battlefield". Every time Schneider discussed the new service strategy with one of the senior managers he went back to his organizational members and asked them to elaborate some more details.

Schneider's objective was to convince a critical mass of general managers, to gain their support for his new service strategy. During these formal and informal meetings Schneider was faced with different interests and fears concerning a more powerful service organization that might lead to any loss of power for the other managing directors. Schneider recalled that during the meeting: "I had to convince the general management by selling them the idea that it might be also useful for their business or at least that it will not harm them. But also I had to make sure that they don't get the impression that it might be very successful and that my position might increase in the organization". The general managers feared that Schneider could gain a more powerful position than he had. Their perception was that he did not agree with their business policy and procedure and would, therefore, be a threat for their business. Schneider hence described all these meetings as "*Seiltanz*" [rope walking].

During the same period Schneider started to arrange and hold these discussion meetings with the senior managers in the sales department, and received a service contract for a full service, maintenance and retrofit job. This was the first service contract as such. Schneider did not inform any senior managers, nor the CEO about this work. He thought "they might have forced me to reject this contract ... and if we would have failed to deliver the requested service my whole strategy would be gone". The reason for his fear was that part of this job was usually handled by the sales department. As he decided to carry it out within the SRS organization, he was aware that the sales revenue would not be accounted for in the sales department. He feared that the sales revenue issue would in the end destroy SRS's future strategy. In order to keep the contract confidential he used the necessary infrastructure, such as staff and spare parts from the companies of RS abroad in Northern Europe and South East Asia. In each of the contacted organizations he had his "friends". In this way it was not known to the organization that the actual strategy was already partly implemented, with foreign resources.

## Strategic Decisions

After half of the general managers had agreed to the concept, Schneider had another meeting with the CEO and informed him about the current agreement of the majority of senior managers. As a result the CEO agreed to present this concept during the next meeting at headquarters in July 1997 where all business units of the world would be present. In November 1997, Schneider presented the new service strategy at the second annual general meeting of all business units of the international electronic engineering company by showing a specially designed PR film. Schneider engaged a PR agency to develop a marketing film of the strategy concept. The presentation was a success and the response was very positive.

The result was that the international headquarters announced that all service activities were converged into a new "Service & Retrofit" Business Unit worldwide, with the central service headquarters in Germany. Schneider headed the new Business Unit as well as keeping the position of managing director of the service organization in Germany. With this announcement all service activities were displayed on the worldwide accounting and budgeting system to follow its sales and profit development.

After the announcement from the international headquarters that the service organization operated as an international Business Unit responsible for all service activities, Schneider organized a big celebration for his employees. He involved the same management team that elaborated his initial strategy vision to carry out the necessary work.

## Analysis and Discussion

In this section we discuss our grounded theory analysis of the evolution of strategic ideas from a cultural perspective at the SRS organization. The key themes identified are presented along with their underlying concepts and relationships. "Strategic Debate", which emerged as the main theme of the empirical analysis, provided a conceptualization for the evolution of strategic ideas. At SRS, Strategic Debate was characterized by brainstorming sessions, mind maps, critiques, group evaluation work, workshops, and formal and informal meetings. This included any form of discussion and communication where strategic ideas were discussed, questioned and further developed and explored.

### Strategic Debate

The process of Strategic Debate involves generating, elaborating or abandoning strategic ideas. Figure 5.1 illustrates our conceptualization of

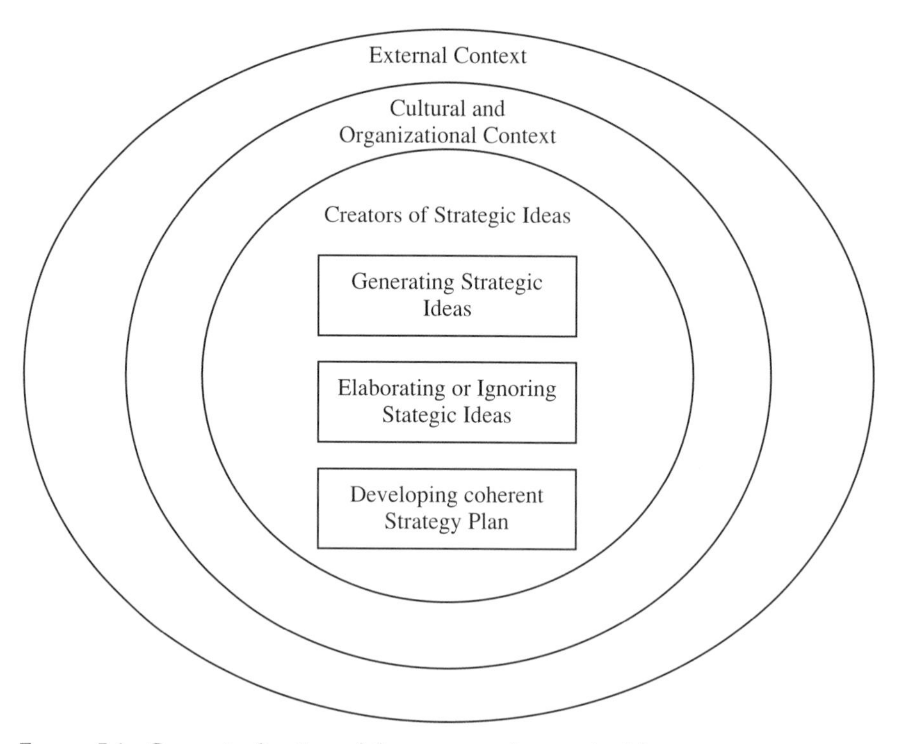


Figure 5.1 Conceptualization of the process of strategic debate

the process of Strategic Debate where strategic ideas are generated. The evolution of strategic ideas shows three dimensions: generating strategic ideas, elaborating or abandoning them, and developing a coherent strategy plan.

## Generating Strategic Ideas

The origin of the initial strategic ideas was shaped by many external factors such as market developments and customer demands; by organizational and cultural context such as the evolving competitive culture within SRS; and by individual-level factors such as key players' personality, experience and knowledge of the business and products. For example, at SRS, the strategic ideas generated by Schneider were mainly shaped by discussion with customers and organizational members, by competitors and by his own experience of the product and the business. In addition, the interaction with the external consultant influenced the formulation and articulation of strategic ideas, as Schneider noted that it enabled him to translate his "picture into simple words". The evolving competitive culture within SRS shaped Schneider's initial idea. For example, Schneider recalled that: "I was interested in expanding the service activities because I wanted to have a more powerful position ... the same as sales and finance director, work with advanced technology and qualified people ... I had to create an interesting job for myself".

Schneider described the process of developing his ideas as "a puzzle" where all the little parts came together over a period of time. Schneider carried out his thinking process in a "mentally" solitary manner, and occasionally "parts of the puzzle" were discussed with customers or organizational members to explore its practicality. It had become impossible to trace back the exact time when the initial ideas evolved, according to the manager. The initial idea was further developed by the organizational members, whereby new strategic ideas evolved. This process of evolving new strategic ideas occurred at different stages during the whole strategy development process. It was not a one-time activity; rather it was unintentionally repeated during the strategic debates.

## Elaborating or Abandoning Strategic Ideas

This dimension in the evolution of strategic ideas involves major activities such as creative questioning, criticizing, creative answering, information gathering and synthesizing. During discussion with the external consultants some of the strategic ideas of the SRS manager were further elaborated or neglected, or new ideas evolved.

The Strategic Debate among the organizational members and the SRS manager was characterized by posing questions, suggesting new ideas, adjusting existing ideas, elaborating or abandoning existing ideas, and gathering more information with regard to a particular idea. For example, one organizational member described the process as: "... a lot of discussion about all the details, split up in sub-groups to work out some details, met again and discussed the details, raised open, sometimes resolved questions and discussed where we could get some information. We often used our existing network around the world to get some advice or we got back to our 'oldies' whom we often found very useful because of their long-term experience and knowledge". The arguments, information and ideas were mainly based on existing knowledge and experience of individual organizational members, on the organizational and cultural context as well as the external context.

This process was shaped by cultural factors such as the trusting relationships between Schneider and the organizational members. For example, one organizational member stated: "I trusted Schneider, that his initial idea would be good for us. During our discussions he relied on our judgement and welcomed our suggestions. There was a mutual trust between us that helped to focus and concentrate on exploring the idea of an independent service department".

## Developing a Coherent Strategy Plan

This dimension involves developing a coherent strategy plan based on the strategic ideas. For example, at SRS the strategic ideas were transformed into a strategy and business plan that included the business scope and goals, range of services, resource policy and investment plan.

This process was shaped by cultural factors such as the different value systems and conflicting relationships between other senior managers and the CEO within the parent company. As stated by Schneider, "we had to develop a written plan where all managers agree to it. We carried out several meetings and every time we changed some wording, or the language ... and at the end we had a diplomatic paper which attempted to consider the interest of all parties". This often led to a readjustment or reformulation of some strategic ideas in order to avoid conflicts within the parent company.

The strategic ideas were generated, explored and modified by different organizational members with different knowledge and experience as well as personality. At SRS, Schneider and other organizational members participating in the Strategic Debate contributed with their knowledge and experience, as well as with their personality, values, beliefs, emotional commitments and attitudes to the process of Strategic Debate. The Strategic

Debate thus served as a platform for communication and selling the ideas to individual organizational members, in particular to those who made the final strategic decisions and to those who were responsible for implementing the new strategy.

In all three dimensions of evolution of strategic ideas the leadership played an important part. For example, through Schneider's managerial and communication style he motivated and encouraged organizational members to express their concern, criticism and questions with regard to strategic ideas and to contribute and participate actively in the discussion. He also created an open and respectful atmosphere during the discussion in which all employees had the right to express their opinions and views without being interrupted, embarrassed or not heard. He tried to manage the different personalities and communication styles by introducing common respect among the organizational members, despite their different views and opinions. Schneider therefore took over the role of facilitator during this process.

## The Constituents of Strategic Debates

Our analysis into the nature of factors influencing the evolution of strategic ideas led to the development of four sub-themes which explained the dynamics and complexity of Strategic Debate. The first sub-theme comprises "Strategic Warriors" which includes all participants participating in generating strategic ideas. "Patterns of Interaction" emerged as a second sub-theme and focused on the way and form in which the Strategic Warriors interacted and communicated with each other during the Strategic Debate. The third theme is "Strategic Language" which is used by the Strategic Warriors to articulate and communicate strategic issues and ideas. The final sub-theme is "Strategic Synthesis" which supports the elaboration of existing ideas.

### Strategic Warriors

The first sub-theme, Strategic Warriors, comprised organizational members who are involved and participated in the strategic debate. We use the term "warriors" from Schneider's portrayal of the organizational members involved in the strategic debate. He argued that: "... they had to operate, discuss, argue and fight like warriors in all the debates until the implementation was finished." At SRS, there were four main groups of Strategic Warriors: the manager (Schneider), the external consultant, organizational members who participated in the strategic debate, and the senior managers and CEO of the parent company. The Strategic Warriors had different knowledge and expertise of the business, and different personalities, which were expressed in their beliefs, values and interests. The Strategic Warriors participating in and contributing to the strategic debate represented the essential source out of which strategic ideas were generated.

The SRS manager, Schneider, had a profound knowledge of the company's products and the business that was based on his 25 years of experience. He strongly believed that there was an urgent need for a change in the after-sales service worldwide. He was very open-minded, expressing his ideas without any hesitation (even if he ignored them at the next moment). He had a strong capacity to borrow and adapt ideas from elsewhere, in particular from discussion with others such as customers. His communication style was open, respectful and encouraging. Schneider formulated and developed the initial strategic ideas which initiated the whole process of Strategic Debate.

Another Strategic Warrior, the external consultant, was specialized in public relation and marketing activities. He had no particular experience in the SRS business. His main interest (being involved in the evolution of the new strategy), according to his own statement, was "to build up a new long term client relationship with Schneider .... It might open up some new business opportunities." The manager Schneider characterized the consultant as "being very trustful, reliable, working hard ... and has sometimes crazy ideas". The consultant helped Schneider to articulate his ideas into words and coherent stories. The business relationship between the external consultant and the manager developed into a trustful friendship.

All organizational members participating in the evolution of strategic ideas represented the third group of Strategic Warriors. They were selected by the manager mainly by asking them directly to contribute to the strategic debate, or by encouraging them to express their opinions or by motivating them to express their views. They determined which strategic ideas would be elaborated or ignored. They were also in charge of generating new strategic ideas. The majority of the organizational members were young, in their thirties, highly qualified with various functional backgrounds. Their main interest was "to gain a lot of experience and to pursue all possible existing career opportunities". They were open to change, looking out for new opportunities and challenges. These organizational members were later responsible for the implementation of the strategy.

The fourth group of Strategic Warriors included the senior managers and CEO of the parent company who made the final decisions on the realization of SRS international strategies. Each senior manager represented one business area within the parent company, such as planning and engineering, finance and sales. Their main interests, as stated by one of the managers, were "to do business as usual ... strengthen my own position and make sure that I keep my job till my pension ...". Schneider's plan to establish a new business area was perceived as a possible threat by the senior managers. As stated by one of them: "we had the impression that Schneider wants to take over some of our businesses and reduce our power within the whole organization". In addition there were personal resentments against the manager which were due to Schneider's quick career development, different management and communications style and background in comparison to the other senior managers.

Since the beginning of the 1990s the parent company had experienced a decrease in sales and profit. The CEO's main interest was "to open up new business opportunities to increase sales and profit, and to avoid closure of this location". He was interested in SRS's strategy as it opened up new markets with new sales and profit opportunities.

### Patterns of Interaction

The second sub-theme within Strategic Debate was "Patterns of Interaction". This illustrated how the four different groups of Strategic Warriors interacted and communicated with each other during the Strategic Debates.

The interaction between the SRS manager and the external consultant was important in creating the opportunity for Schneider to formulate his mental representations into words and to present them in communicable and sellable form to third parties. The focus was to translate his strategic ideas into sellable concepts, which could be understood by all organizational members within the parent company. For that purpose the external consultant transformed Schneider's words into simpler words and used simple presentation forms for communicating the ideas. The prior aim here was to gain the commitment and agreement for the strategic ideas.

The external consultant took over the role of a translator at the early stages of the evolution of strategic ideas. During the workshops with the manager he was mainly listening, giving the manager the possibility to talk confidentially about his ideas. In addition he reformulated the ideas of Schneider using much simpler words for an audience who did not have the same professional background. During this phase he sometimes contributed to generating new ideas even though he had no particular industrial expertise of SRS business. On some occasions he stimulated Schneider to generate new ideas.

The interaction between Schneider and the organizational members participating in the evolution of strategic ideas led to a strategy plan. During the Strategic Debate Schneider took over the role of a facilitator and referee. With the support of other organizational members, he developed an open, friendly and encouraging working and communication atmosphere. For example, he encouraged other employees to express their views, pose questions, exchange information and learn from other people. By pushing his employees to express their own views in the daily business he coached them to think critically. In this way he gave them the opportunity to revise, to develop or to change their perspectives. Schneider took every opportunity to influence the atmosphere of a particular debate and interaction among the organizational members. He stimulated the debate in ways that often had a positive influence on the flow of generating strategic ideas. For example, he used to write unpopular ideas on a special board and leave them until the beginning of the implementation of the strategy. The aim was to ensure that these ideas were not lost and reviewed at a later stage.

The Strategic Warriors also took over the main role of a communicator or messenger of the new SRS strategy. The interaction between Schneider and other Strategic Warriors was also influenced by different thinking styles, in particular when generating new strategic ideas, or elaborating or abandoning the existing ones. Each member took a different approach to developing and formulating strategic ideas. The interaction among the organizational members was very much influenced by Schneider's style of communication and behavior.

The role of the fourth group of Strategic Warriors, the senior managers and the CEO of the parent company, was to decide if the SRS strategy could be realized or not. The interaction between Schneider and the senior managers and CEO was shaped by different interests and powers. For example, Schneider had several face-to-face meetings with senior managers where the politics and interests of each senior manager and their organizational unit played an essential role during the discussion. After each meeting with the senior managers Schneider went back to his organizational members in order to make some changes in their written strategy concept. He asked them to elaborate some more details or adjust or change some issues which came up during these meetings with senior managers. The strategy paper was also changed several times, mainly by reformulating phrases that might appear as a potential conflict of interest. The CEO was the main driving force behind the adjustment and reformulation process of the existing strategic ideas. He informed Schneider at an early stage that in order to get a commitment from the CEO the manager would have to get consent of at least half of the senior managers for SRS's strategy.

The interaction patterns were heavily influenced by the existing corporate culture. For example, the Strategic Debate process drew on many routinized practices regarding preparation, communication and control of meetings that were established over time. In addition the knowledge about each organizational member's personality, working style and problem-solving approach, as well as thinking style, shaped the interaction patterns. As one organizational member stated: "... because I know my colleagues quite well ... for example, I know how they think and what their reaction means, even when they appear to be negative about something in the first instant—I know how to communicate with them ... that they take my idea seriously and listen to it." The interaction between the organizational members in their daily life was shaped by trust and the shared belief that the establishment of an independent service department is a successful idea supported by the leadership.

## Strategic Language

The third sub-theme of Strategic Debate was Strategic Language. Strategic Language comprised words, phrases and expressions which were used by participants during a strategic debate to express and communicate strategic issues and ideas. The Strategic Language was used as a medium by the Strategic Warriors to articulate and communicate strategic ideas. Strategic Debate happened through Strategic Language. Strategic Language could be in written or spoken form. For example, at SRS, Strategic Language was used in the form of presentations, reports, minutes, discussion, views and opinions.

Strategic Language facilitates the exchange of knowledge and the transformation of tacit knowledge into articulated knowledge. Tacit knowledge is understood as non-verbalized, intuitive and unarticulated knowledge, whereas articulated knowledge represents knowledge which has been expressed in some written or spoken form. Others had access to the existing tacit knowledge within the organization through Strategic Language and the willingness of organizational members to articulate their knowledge. The use of Strategic Language therefore led to articulated knowledge. This process was important for generating strategic ideas and presents a major step towards shared knowledge. At SRS, for example, every organizational member had a particular tacit knowledge about the business due to their experience and background. By expressing their views and opinions about strategic ideas they were encouraged to articulate their tacit knowledge in the form of opinions, criticism, perspectives, suggestions or new strategic ideas.

Strategic language enabled organizational members to reach a common understanding of the shared meanings of the strategic ideas. The language used also reflected the contextual understanding of the strategic ideas discussed. Strategic Language presented a prerequisite to understanding the context and meanings of the strategic ideas. On the other hand, it is important to have an effective debate about the contents and quality of the strategic ideas. At SRS discussion about the meaning of the different strategic ideas was essential for the organizational members. As pointed out by one organizational member, "... everybody wanted to understand what the different strategic ideas really meant. It was like looking for a common definition or description of the ideas ...". Organizational members' understanding and interpretation, however, was influenced by their knowledge and experience of the business and their disciplines as well as their intellectual thinking capability.

The use of Strategic Language was conditioned by the local cultural atmosphere. The communication culture within the organization shaped the Strategic Language used during the Strategic Debates. The communication within SRS was open, friendly, argumentative, tactful and respectful. Even if one of the organizational members disagreed with the views expressed by another member, the discussion proceeded in a friendly and respectful manner and language. Strategic Warriors used various terms, wording and definitions, as well as assumptions with regard to each individual service activity in SRS, to reformulate the strategic ideas and to out maneuver and avoid conflicts within the organization. In addition, the shared belief among Strategic Warriors that Schneider's initial idea would be successful led to the use of confident language throughout the organization. One organizational member from the sales department recalled that "the people [in SRS] talked about the new ideas like they already carried them out ... like they are already real."

### Strategic Synthesis

The final sub-theme of Strategic Debate was Strategic Synthesis. Strategic Synthesis represented an organizational, intellectual and social mechanism which mainly elaborates the "raw" strategic ideas into "mature" strategic ideas. The Strategic Synthesis process comprised elements such as questioning, reviewing, exchanging information and knowledge, listening, thinking, criticizing, disagreeing and processing the shared knowledge. Strategic Synthesis requires the fusion of all these activities with the individual thinking and communication styles in order to process the complexities, discontinuities and contradictions of the strategic ideas.

At SRS organizational members were encouraged to discuss critical issues and views. One organizational member described the process of one typical strategic debate as: "... first somebody presented a theme, issue or idea. Then everybody was encouraged to give his view on it. People started to provide criticism, but in a tactful way, by for example adding some additional points to it and suggesting some changes. In important strategic meetings one would always find that all functions of the organization were presented to ensure that we heard and listened to all opinions and different perspectives. That's very helpful!".

The Strategic Warriors who carried out Strategic Synthesis came from different disciplines and departments. They had different knowledge, experience, perspectives and beliefs that were reflected in a discussion. By sharing their knowledge during the debates they contributed to further elaboration of the ideas. Organizational members' input, as pointed out by Schneider: "... was essential during the development process ... not only in resolving issues, but in identifying unanticipated deficiencies as well as further potential applications of the ideas".

The Strategic Synthesis process demanded intellectual flexibility and conceptual thinking abilities of the organizational members to contribute effectively to the process. At SRS the Strategic Warriors were motivated, encouraged and sometimes urged by the manager to participate in the debate with new thoughts and perspectives. A passive participation was perceived by all organizational members as "irresponsible".

Different perspectives, knowledge and beliefs led to partly controversial, conflicting and provocative arguments and ideas. This polarity and multitude of perspectives encouraged the organizational members at SRS to assess their business and to develop ideas beyond their existing views. Different views also supported the process of elaborating or abandoning existing ideas or even generating new ideas. The manager of SRS often introduced polarized views by provoking sometimes "obscure ideas" or by supporting the critical views of organizational members.

The Strategic Synthesis process demanded of its organizational members the ability to mentally distance themselves by stepping back from the strategic ideas discussed. This was seen as necessary to allow for "mental time and space" to review and process the contents and meanings of strategic ideas. As recalled by Schneider: "After several intensive strategic debates it was very important to come all together in a relaxed atmosphere where we had a drink together and just talked about totally different things". A disruption physically as well as mentally from intense involvement in the strategic debate was often experienced as "refreshing our minds", as stated by one organizational member.

The leadership played an important role in contributing to the effectiveness of Strategic Synthesis. For example, at SRS the manager encouraged intuition, expressing ideas, learning from failures, handling the stress of change and keeping everyone fresh and stimulated and involved. Schneider facilitated the different thinking and communication styles of the organizational members to ensure "not to let die any ideas". With this style of leadership the manager created an open cultural atmosphere which led to the active participation of the organizational members during the Strategic Synthesis process and to fostering an idea-making climate. The shared belief among organizational members of SRS and Schneider led to the strong commitment and involvement of everyone. This influenced the willingness and degree of participation throughout the Strategic Synthesis process.

## Theoretical Conceptualization of the Evolution of Strategic Ideas

Figure 5.2 summarizes our theoretical conceptualization of the evolution of Strategic Ideas through Strategic Debate. Strategic Warriors, Patterns of Interaction, Strategic Language, and Strategic Synthesis represent sub-themes of Strategic Debate emerging from the data analysis.

The strategic literature recognizes that strategy development can occur in a form of discussion and conversation (e.g. Liedtka & Rosenblum, 1996; Schwenk, 1997). This study supports the claim that strategy development occurs in the form of a "Debate". We suggest in addition a new theoretical framework for developing strategic ideas through Strategic Debate, involving four major themes: "Strategic Warriors", "Patterns of Interaction", "Strategic Language" and "Strategic Synthesis".

Strategic Warriors were the main contributors to the strategic ideas. As illustrated by many authors in the strategic management field, there are different organizational members with different knowledge, expertise and position involved in the strategy development process (e.g. Mintzberg & McHugh, 1985; Eisenhardt & Bourgeois, 1988; Wooldridge & Floyd, 1990; Hitt, Keats & DeMarie, 1998). There is also evidence that the personality of organizational members and their beliefs and attitudes shape the strategy development process (e.g. Sworder, 1995; Rhodes, 1995). In this study

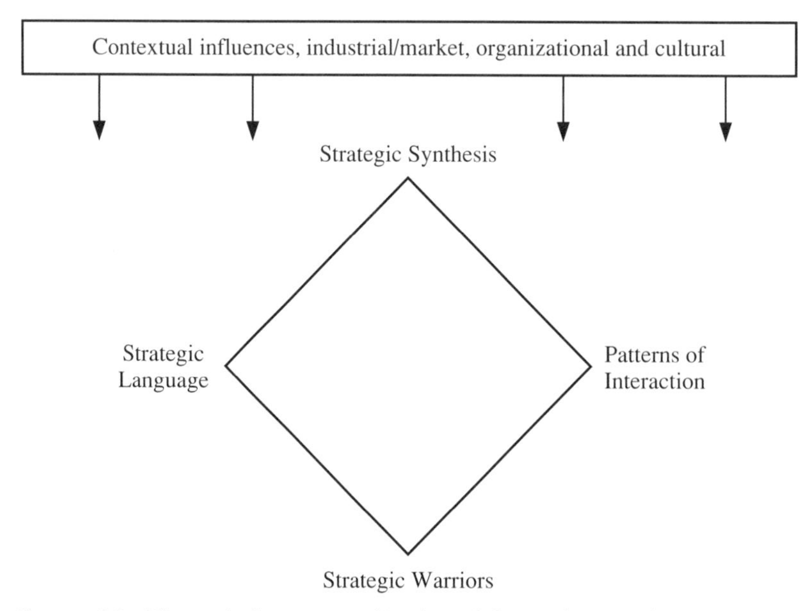


Figure 5.2 Theoretical conceptualization of the evolution of strategic ideas

Strategic Warriors each posed particular knowledge, experience and knowhow of the business as well as a particular personality with specific beliefs and attitudes with regard to the business. By using Strategic Language they shared their knowledge and shaped the development of strategic ideas. The patterns of interaction and the process of Strategic Synthesis offered the possibilities for organizational members to influence existing strategic ideas by elaborating or abandoning the ideas or even generating new ones.

The strategic literature recognizes that politics and different interests of parties involved in strategy development (e.g. Pettigrew, 1985a; Eisenhardt & Bourgeois, 1988; Sharfman & Dean, 1994; Pettigrew & NcNulty, 1995; Dean & Sharfman, 1996) influence the outcome of strategy development. In this study we support this view and suggest that the "Patterns of Interaction" which consider the politics and different interests of organizational members is a key element in influencing the strategy development process. In addition Patterns of Interaction represented the communication culture within an organization. The Strategic Language was used as a medium for members to interact with each other. The Patterns of Interaction influenced the effectiveness of the Strategic Synthesis process.

Strategic Language facilitated the exchange of knowledge and the transformation of tacit into articulated knowledge among the creators of the strategic ideas (cf. Nonaka & Takeuchi, 1995). We suggest that this transformation process occurs through Strategic Language. Strategic Language was used by the Strategic Warriors to support the process of understanding the context and meaning of the different strategic ideas among the organizational members. Strategic Language was used as a medium to facilitate the Strategic Synthesis process and the interaction among Strategic Warriors.

Many studies also claim that the strategy development process is a "learning process" (e.g. Jones, 1994). This study supports such claims and suggests further that Strategic Synthesis, as part of the strategic development process, is represented as an organizational, intellectual and social process. In this process all the necessary disciplines are presented, and elaborate the strategic ideas into competitive, realizable, effective strategies. Strategic Language was the medium to facilitate the synthesis process, Strategic Warriors were the main actors, and the pattern of interaction characterized the way in which Strategic Warriors communicated and interacted with each other in this process.

## CONCLUSIONS

In this chapter, we have presented the findings of a grounded theory study on the evolution of strategy in a newly transformed organization. The theoretical framework presented provided a conceptualization of the complex dynamic processes of the evolution of strategic ideas. This framework provided one way of explaining the influence of the cultural context on evolution of strategic ideas. The dynamic relationship between strategic ideas and cultural context was represented through Strategic Debate, the key theme that emerged from the study, and its four constituent themes: Strategic Warriors, Patterns of Interaction, Strategic Language and Strategic Synthesis. In conclusion, we outline some implications for practice, by drawing on the rich insights gained from this study.

## Flow of Generating Strategic Ideas

The findings indicated that the flow of generating strategic ideas was influenced by strategic discussion carried out in a particular cultural context. An open, highly participative strategic debate could enhance the development of strategic ideas. This study illustrated that strategic debates were a means of facilitating strategic thinking. The process of Strategic Debate indicated that the working and communication culture and the leadership style could influence the strategy development process. The individual organizational members who shaped the working and communication culture present a valuable resource in the strategy development process. In order to initiate the strategic debate and to have creative questions, an appropriate culture, which motivates employees to contribute and participate, should be in place. The existing culture could therefore shape the degree and form of the participation of the organizational members involved in generating strategic issues and lead to a competitive advantage.

The strategic literature recognizes that strategic decision making is a group process based on discussion (e.g. Papadakis & Barwise, 1997). In order to improve the strategic debate process Schwenk (1997) suggests encouraging group members to express their views, avoiding being overcritical towards the views of others, and appointing a member who is responsible for protecting the views of organizational members who disagree with the majority. Schwenk also recommends a team-building session during the strategic debate whereby the common objectives of the group are agreed and negative emotions are cleared (cf. Eisenhardt, Kahwajy & Bourgeois, 1997).

In practice, this would suggest not only that the technique for carrying out strategic debate should be improved but that there must be an increased awareness within organizations for the importance of Strategic Debate or any other form of strategic conversations.

As discussed earlier, the existing cultural context within an organization was influential in generating strategic ideas. This has several implications for managers. First, it is important to create an open atmosphere for discussing controversial views, which would recognize each organizational member's views. Second, it is essential to establish a climate in which all participants feel comfortable. Third, it is necessary to develop a particular communication and working culture which allows exchange of different and controversial views without constraining the process of generating strategic ideas. Finally, it is important to have adequate leadership and skills in carrying out a strategic debate successfully. Training of organizational members in how to carry out such conversations should occur at an early stage.

## Matching the Intellectual, Social and Cultural Resources

This study showed that the organizational members who were involved in the Strategic Debate ("Strategic Warriors") represented an influential group in the process of generating strategic ideas. As widely claimed by other authors, generating strategic ideas is not an exclusive task for executive managers in the current business context. There is also evidence that the importance of wider participation, in particular of middle management, is essential in order to successfully develop strategy (e.g. Burgelman, 1983; Schilit, 1987; Nonaka, 1988; Eisenhardt & Bourgeois, 1988). It is claimed that greater involvement of organizational members in strategic processes seems to alleviate coordination problems and more effectively focuses members' activities and resources on the implementation of the strategy (Guth & MacMillan, 1986; Wooldridge & Floyd, 1990).

This study supports the call for a good mixture of participants with different functional knowledge and experiences related to the business of an organization. We suggest in addition that a situational match of existing intellectual, social and cultural resources represented in the Strategic Warriors is significant in achieving competitive advantage for a company in developing successful strategies. The intellectual resources are presented in knowledge, experience, thinking and communication style, which have an important impact on the quality of the ideas in the Strategic Debate process. The social resources are presented in the relationship, trust, interaction and knowledge about each individual organizational member, which have an impact on the process of sharing tacit knowledge. The cultural resources are represented through the Strategic Warriors' personalities and characters which affect the quality and pace of the strategy development process.

This would suggest a need to consider the different intellectual, social and cultural backgrounds of the organizational members involved in the Strategic Debate. This understanding may also help the management to form the best match among the organizational members who are participating in generating strategic ideas. In addition this understanding may help the management to manage and lead the participants' contribution, communication and discussion efficiently.

## Quality of the Strategic Ideas

We have already discussed how an open-minded and participative interaction positively influenced the quality of the evolved strategic ideas. Dean and Sharfman (1996) found that politics might influence the outcome of strategic decisions or the decision effectiveness. In their earlier study, Sharfman and Dean (1994) found that political behavior was less likely to occur when managers or organizational members contributing to the strategic decisions had developed interpersonal trust which seems to limit the need for political behaviors. Although trust among the Strategic Warriors at SRS was strongly developed and supported by a strong team spirit, the diverse politics within the parent company were influential during the evolution of the strategic ideas. The different interests and politics were considered by reformulating or readjusting the ideas.

Further, our study also supports the claim that cultural aspects such as attitudes, habits, beliefs and emotional commitments influence the quality of strategic thinking (Sworder, 1995). Rhodes (1995) recognizes that among organizational members there are different thinking faculties of individuals, groups and organizations. In our study the Strategic Warriors had different characteristic thinking styles which determined and guided their approach in generating strategic ideas. Different thinking styles in a group of individuals during the Strategic Debates present a valuable resource in the strategy development process. This, combined with a leadership style that acknowledges, recognizes and manages these different thinking styles, has a positive impact on the quality of the strategic ideas and can lead to a competitive advantage.

## Pace of Generating Strategic Ideas

We found that a common Strategic Language influences the pace of generating strategic ideas. Strategic Language enabled the meanings and understanding of the strategic ideas to be communicated effectively among the organizational members. Rhodes (1995) acknowledges that a common language in strategic thinking enables organizational members to work more effectively.

The sharing of tacit knowledge, the process of transforming tacit knowledge into articulated knowledge, and finally the management skills required to manage this transformation process are key success factors in generating new strategic ideas.

This claim for a common strategic language may have implications for the business world. Managers may need to ensure a common understanding of the strategic vocabularies used in the Strategic Debate. It is important to pay attention to different ways of understanding among participants and to the meanings of strategic ideas and the terms used.

## Maturity of Strategic Ideas

The Strategic Synthesis process within the Strategic Debate influenced the further elaboration of the strategic issues. The process of Strategic Synthesis enabled organizational members to identify strategic ideas that are negligible or important for further elaboration. As recognized in the strategy literature (e.g. Rhodes, 1995; Sworder, 1995; Mintzberg, 1995) Strategic Synthesis requires intellectual flexibility and conceptual thinking abilities among its organizational members who were involved in the strategic debate. The intellectual flexibility and capability of the organizational members played an important factor in generating strategic ideas. The intellectual flexibility and capability of organizational members participating in the Strategic Synthesis process presents another key resource for achieving competitive advantage for a firm.

## Acknowledgements

The authors would like to thank the organizational members involved in this study for their time and cooperation during this project. The authors also wish to acknowledge the valuable comments and suggestions made by editors on an earlier version of this chapter.

## References

Ancona, D. (1990). Outward bound: Strategies for team survival in an organization. *Academy of Management Journal*, **33**(2), 334–365.

Barney, J.B. (1986). Organizational culture: Can it be a source of sustained competitive advantage? *Academy of Management Review*, **11**, 656–665.

Barney, J.B. (1991). Firm resources and sustained competitive advantage. *Journal of Management*, **17**(1), 99–120.

Bower, J.L. (1972). *Managing the Resource Allocation Process: A Study of Corporate Planning and Investment*. Boston, MA: Harvard Business School Press.

Burgelman, R.A. (1983). A model of the interaction of strategic behavior, corporate context and the concept of strategy. *Academy of Management Review*, **8**(1), 61–70.

Chakravarthy, B.S. & Doz, Y. (1992). Strategy process research: Focusing on corporate self-renewal, *Strategic Management Journal*, **13** (Special Issue), 5–14.

Chen, A.Y.S., Sawyers, R.B. & Williams, P.F. (1997). Reinforcing ethical decision making through corporate culture. *Journal of Business Ethics*, **16**, 855–865.

Clark, B.R. (1972). The organizational saga in higher education. *Administrative Science Quarterly*, **17**, 178–184.

Cyert, R.M. & March, J.G. (1963). *A Behavioral Theory of the Firm*, Englewood Cliffs, NJ: Prentice-Hall.

Daft, R.L. & Weick, K.E. (1984). Toward a model of organizations as interpretation systems. *Academy of Management Review*, **9**, 284–295.

Deal, T.E. & Kennedy, A.A. (1982). *Corporate Cultures*. Reading, MA: Addison-Wesley.

Dean, J.W. & Sharfman, M.P. (1996). Does decision making matter? A study of strategic decision making effectiveness. *Academy of Management Journal*, **39**(2), 368–396.

Eisenhardt, K.M. & Bourgeois, L.J. (1988). Politics of strategic decision making in high-velocity environments: Toward a midrange theory. *Academy of Management Journal*, **31**, 737–770.

Eisenhardt, K.M., Kahwajy, J.L. & Bourgeois, L.J. (1997). Taming interpersonal conflict in strategic choice: How top management teams argue but still get along. In V. Papadakis & P. Barwise (eds), *Strategic Decisions*, Boston, MA: Kluwer Academic Publishers.

Elsbach, K.D. & Sutton, R.I. (1992). Acquiring organizational legitimacy through illegitimate actions: A marriage of institutional and impression management theories. *Academy of Management Journal*, **35**(4), December, 699–738.

Fiol, C.M. (1991). Managing culture as a competitive resource: An identity-based view of sustainable competitive advantage. *Journal of Management*, **17**(1), 191–211.

Garratt, B. (1995). *Developing Strategic Thought—Rediscovering the Art of Direction-Giving*. San Francisco, CA: McGraw-Hill.

Glaser, B.G. & Strauss, A.L. (1967). *The Discovery of Grounded Theory: Strategies for Qualitative Research*. New York: Aldine Publishing.

Guth, W.D. & MacMillan, I.C. (1986). Strategy implementation versus middle management self interest. *Strategic Management Journal*, **7**, 313–327.

Hart, S. & Banbury, C. (1994). How strategy-making processes can make a difference. *Strategic Management Journal*, **15**, 251–269.

Hickson, D., Butler, R., Gray, D., Mallory, G. & Wilson, D. (1986). *Top Decisions: Strategic Decision Making in Organizations*. San Francisco, CA: Jossey Bass.

Hitt, M.A., Keats, B.W. & DeMarie, S.M. (1998). Navigation in the new competitive landscape: Building strategic flexibility and competitive advantage in the 21st century. *Academy of Management Executive*, **12**(4), 22–42.

Jones, M.R. (1994). Learning the language of the market: Information systems strategy formation in a UK district health authority. *Accounting, Management and Information Technologies*, **4**(3), 119–147.

Kahn, W.A. (1990). Psychological conditions of personal engagement and disengagement at work. *Academy of Management Journal*, **33**(4), 692–724.

Kono, T. (1994). Changing a company's strategy and culture. *Long Range Planning*, **27**(5), 85–97.
Liedtka, J.M. & Rosenblum, J.W. (1996). Shaping conversations: Making strategy, managing change. *California Management Review*, **39**(1), 141–157.
Lorsch, J.W. (1986). Managing culture: The invisible barrier to strategic change. *California Management Review*, **28**(2), 95–109.
Lyles, M.A. (1981). Formulating strategic problems: empirical analysis and model development. *Strategic Management Journal*, **2**, 61–75.
Martin, P.Y. & Turner, B.A. (1986). Grounded theory and organizational research. *Journal of Applied Behavioural Research*, **22**(2), 141–157.
Mintzberg, H. (1995). Strategic thinking as "seeing". In B. Garratt (ed.), *Developing Strategic Thought*, San Francisco, CA: McGraw-Hill.
Mintzberg, H. & McHugh, A. (1985). Strategy formation in an adhocracy. *Administrative Science Quarterly*, **30**, 160–197.
Mintzberg, H., Raisinghani, D. & Theoret, A. (1976). The structure of unstructured decision processes. *Administrative Science Quarterly*, **21**(2), 246–275.
Morgan, G. (1986). *Images of Organization*. Beverly Hills, CA: Sage.
Nandhakumar, J. & Jones, M. (1997). Too close for comfort? Distance and engagement in interpretive information systems research. *Information Systems Journal*, **7**, 109–131.
Nonaka, I. (1988). Toward middle-up-down management. *Sloan Management Review*, **29**(3), 9–18.
Nonaka, I. & Takeuchi, H. (1995). *The Knowledge-Creating Company: How Japanese Companies Create the Dynamics of Innovation*, New York: Oxford University Press.
Nutt, P.C. (1984). Types of organizational decision processes. *Administrative Science Quarterly*, **29**(3), 414–450.
Nutt, P.C. (1986). The tactics of implementation. *Academy of Management Journal*, **29**(2), 230–261.
Nwachukwu, S.L.S. & Vitell, S.J. Jr. (1997). The influence of corporate culture on managerial ethical judgements. *Journal of Business Ethics*, **16**, 757–776.
Orlikowski, W.J. (1993). Case tools as organizational change: Investigating incremental and radical changes in system development. *MIS Quarterly*, **17**, 309–340.
Ouchi, W.G. (1981). *Theory Z: How American Business Can Meet the Japanese Challenge*. Reading, MA: Addison-Wesley.
Papadakis, V. & Barwise, P. (1997). Research on strategic decisions: Where do we go from here? In V. Papadakis & P. Barwise (eds), *Strategic Decisions*, Boston, MA: Kluwer Academic Publishers.
Pettigrew, A.M. (1979). On studying organization culture. *Administrative Science Quarterly*, **24**, 570–581.
Pettigrew, A.M. (1985a). Culture and politics in strategic decision making and change. In J.M. Pennings (ed.), *Strategic Decision Making in Complex Organizations*, San Francisco, CA: Jossey Bass.
Pettigrew, A.M. (1985b). *The Awakening Giant: Continuity and Change at ICI*. Oxford: Blackwell.
Pettigrew, A.M. (1990). Longitudinal field research on change: Theory and practice. *Organization Science*, **1**(3), 267–292.
Pettigrew, A.M. (1992). The character and significance of strategy process research. *Strategic Management Journal*, **13**, 5–16.
Pettigrew, A.M. & McNulty, T. (1995). Power and influence in and around the boardroom. *Human Relations*, **48**(8), 845–873.

Pfeffer, J. (1981). Management as symbolic action; the creation and maintenance of organizational paradigms. In L.L. Cummings & B.M. Staw (eds), *Research in Organizational Behavior*, Greenwich, CT: JAI Press.
Quinn, J.B. (1981). Managing strategic change. *Sloan Management Review*, Spring, 19–34.
Rhodes, J. (1995). The processes of thinking strategically. In B. Garratt (ed.), *Developing Strategic Thought*, San Francisco, CA: McGraw-Hill.
Sathe, V. (1985). *Culture and Related Corporate Realities*. Homewood, IL: Irwin.
Schein, E.H. (1985). *Organizational Culture and Leadership*. San Francisco, CA Jossey-Bass.
Schilit, W.K. (1987). An examination of the influence of middle-level managers in formulating and implementing strategic decisions. *Journal of Management Studies*, **24**(3), 307–320.
Schwartz, H. & Davis, S.M. (1981). Matching corporate culture and business strategy. *Organisational Dynamics*, Summer, 30–48.
Schwenk, C. (1997). Diversity, eccentricity and devil's advocacy. In V. Papadakis & P. Barwise (eds), *Strategic Decisions*, Boston, MA: Kluwer Academic Publishers.
Sharfman, M.P. & Dean, J.W. (1994). Political behavior in strategic decision making. *Proceedings of the Decision Sciences Institute Annual Meetings*, Honolulu, Hawaii.
Shrivastava, P. (1985). Integrating strategy formulation with organizational culture. *Journal of Business Strategy*, **5**(3), 103–111.
Smircich, L. (1983). Concepts of culture and organisational analysis. *Administrative Science Quarterly*, **28**, 339–358.
Strauss, A. & Cobin, J. (1990). *Basics of Qualitative Research: Grounded Theory, Procedures and Techniques*. Newbury Park, CA: Sage.
Sworder, C. (1995). Hearing the baby's cry: It's all in the thinking. In B. Garratt (ed.), *Developing Strategic Thought*, San Francisco, CA: McGraw-Hill.
Turner, B.A. (1983). The use of grounded theory for the qualitative analysis of organizational behaviour. *Journal of Management Studies*, **20**(3), 333–348.
Van de Ven, A.H. (1992). Suggestions for studying strategy process: A research note. *Strategic Management Journal*, **13** (Special Issue), 169–188.
Witte, E. (1972). Field research on complex decision making process—the phase theory. *International Studies of Management and Organization*, 156–182.
Wooldridge, B. & Floyd, S.W. (1990). The strategy process, middle management involvement, and organizational performance. *Strategic Management Journal*, **11**, 231–241.

# 6

# Different Industries and Different Customer Values Require Different Resources: Towards the Marriage of Strategic Positioning Theory and the Resource-Based View of the Firm

JONATHAN WILSON

## INTRODUCTION

One of the main goals in the development of theory in the field of corporate strategy is to create models which account for differences in performance between firms in the same industry. The implication is that the better the model the greater the levels of explanation of this variance. A number of distinct themes have been developed in this quest. These themes fall into two major categories, namely the contingency and resource-based views of

*Dynamic Strategic Resources: Development, Diffusion and Integration.*
Edited by Michael A. Hitt, Patricia Gorman Clifford, Robert D. Nixon and Kevin P. Coyne.

the firm. They are not necessarily treated as mutually exclusive by authors, so there is considerable overlap in the way in which they are used. Some authors also do not explicitly claim to be developing theory in one domain or the other, but it is clear from their approach that their presuppositions arise from one or the other.

The model presented in this paper synthesizes these two schools of thought. In essence the new approach hypothesises that the more successful firms in an industry will perform better on a selected number of customer values, and in turn those values will depend on a prioritised set of resources. In other words a causal chain exists between the performance on a set of prioritised firm outputs, and this performance depends upon a certain set of prioritised resources.

The implication is that successful firms will have not only identified their output priorities but also emphasised certain resources in support of those outputs. The story line goes further to suggest that what comprises a successful marriage of the resource and positioning-based theories will vary between different industries. The new model is thus a step towards the marriage of both the previous theoretical approaches, contributes to our understanding of why some companies perform better than others, and confirms that indeed when it comes to tailoring strategy one size certainly does not fit all.

The new model is operationalised and tested empirically through a questionnaire-based survey of four different UK industries. Two of these are service industries and two are manufacturing industries. The service industries include UK-based financial services and logistic services. The manufacturing industries include UK-based automotive component and electronic components manufacturing. In all, 104 companies of mixed size participated in the survey. The analytical part of the paper is an investigation of the relationships between firm performance on outputs visible to the customer in the marketplace. The analysis of these relationships deals with the importance of the firms' positioning strategy to business performance. The analytical section goes on to examine the relationships between types of firm resources and performance on the output values of the firm.

The major statistical tool used is structural equation modelling. Comparisons of the positioning-based relationships and the resource-based relationships are made between industries to see whether the priorities within the model vary by industry type, in other words to confirm that in tailoring strategy for successful firms one size does not fit all. The survey questionnaire was developed from data gathered from in-depth interviews with senior executives. The responses in the questionnaire were triangulated with data gathered from secondary sources, with cross-validation built into the questionnaire itself, and directly from customers of the participating firms.

The story concludes by demonstrating that what are important output values of the firm (positioning) in relation to business performance do indeed vary considerably between industries. Furthermore the resource types that are required to support these outputs vary between industries within those sectors.

The evidence shows clearly that strategies need careful tailoring along the positioning and resource dimensions to fit different industries if superior performance is to be achieved.

## THEMES FROM THE LITERATURE

The two major themes in the literature are the contingency approach (Venkatraman & Prescott, 1990; Lenz, 1980; Hambrick & Lei, 1985) and the resource approach (Barney, 1991; Wernerfelt, 1984). Hambrick and Lei (1985: 765) have defined contingency as an approach which is different from the universalistic and situation specific in that it recognises certain classes of settings for which generalisations can be made. The Hambrick and Lei (1985) study has argued for the need to prioritise contingency variables relative to business performance as a basis for justifying their significance. To build contingency theory under this definition requires that the researcher develop variables which demarcate the "high performance" classes from which strategic generalisations can be made. It is the variety of variables used in developing the theoretical classes which has given rise to the large number of sub-themes of contingency theory. Sub-themes that have been shown to have good explanatory power within the contingency approach are the congruency (Venkatraman, 1990; Fiegenbaum, Hart & Schendel, 1996) and competency approaches (Hitt & Ireland, 1986; McGrath, MacMillan & Venkatraman, 1995), as well as the environmental approach (Ansoff, 1987; Dess, Ireland & Hitt, 1990; Miller, 1987a; Kotha & Nair, 1995; Rumelt, 1991; Kim & Campbell, 1995). In addition a strong sub-theme of the contingency approach is the positioning theory (Porter, 1980, 1985, 1996).

This study develops another contingency view from this literature, namely consumer (or customer) preferences, which is labelled the "output-based view of the firm". In this way it develops a market-orientated approach to understanding firm performance. The output-based view is concerned with consumer preferences in so far as they determine the relative value of the outputs of the firm. They are used as the primary prioritising mechanism between the firm's competitive position in the industry and the importance of the underlying resources that create the firm's output. Consumer preferences require interpretation by managers (the firm). How effectively managers understand actual consumer preferences and translate them into resource priorities is possibly a key explanation of differences in firm performance. Of all the contingency approaches the positioning sub-theme is probably most important to the market advantage of the firm, with the resources theme fundamental to both firm cost and revenue competitiveness. Therefore this study is focused on the development and testing of a parsimonious model that integrates both the resource-based view of the firm and positioning theory as a powerful means of explaining differences in firm performance.

The nomenological tree shown in FIGURE 6.1 provides an overview of the development of the contingency and resource-based theories, which underpin the development of this study's approach to explaining differences in firm performance. The detail of each component is discussed in the text following.

The study of corporate strategy draws on theories from a wide range of disciplines, but probably none is more important than that of industrial economics. The seminal works of Mason (1939), Bain (1959) and Scherer (1970) provide the basis of much of the work of later strategists. The

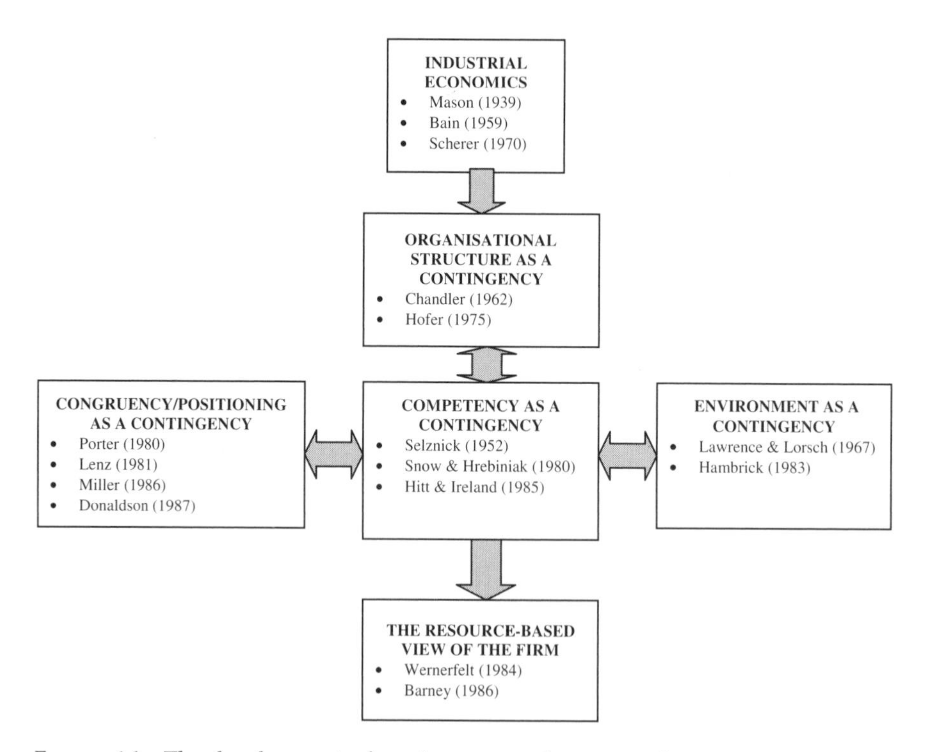


FIGURE 6.1 The development of contingency and resource theory

underpinnings of both the contingency and resource views of the sources of economic rent were already contained within these earlier works. More than that, these earlier works recognised the importance of the relationships between contingencies and resources (Scherer, 1970).

Organisational structure as a contingency variable explaining differences in firm performance was derived from industrial economics and brought to the fore in the 1960s and 1970s. This research emphasis spawned the more recent focus on congruency, competence, positioning and the environment as contingencies that explain differences in business performance.

In some ways the field of corporate strategy has returned to its economic roots in the development of the resource-based view of the firm as introduced and elaborated on by Wernerfelt (1984), Barney (1986) and Peteraf (1993). This study builds on both these streams. In the first instance it is related to the contingency approach by using underlying consumer preferences as a powerful contingency in determining which tangible and intangible product and service features produced by the firm have value. This approach has obvious microeconomic roots. This has been called the "market system" in the literature (Scherer, 1970). This market-facing approach is the basis by which the underlying resources are prioritised. This study therefore embraces both contingency and resource theory into an exploratory model that attempts to explain patterns of relationships and differences in firm performance.

## Some Limitations of the Positioning Theory

The positioning theory came to prominence in the 1980s (Porter, 1980, 1985). It suggests that through the use of a variety of analytical tools the market/industry environment can be understood to the point where strategic choices can be made as to the nature of the strategic business unit's competitive advantage—known as generic strategies. Porter (1996) refined this approach by drawing a distinction between "strategic positioning" (and the need for strategic choice) and "operational effectiveness". In Porter's view the strategic choice (position) drives the operational decisions and should guide the necessary trade-offs in the underlying operational capabilities. This approach has been criticised as being too narrow and prescriptive and the analytical content useful only as an input into the strategic process rather than its objective (Mintzberg, Ahlstrand & Lampel, 1998). Strategy, from this point of view, is essentially an inductive process, not a deductive process.

This paper argues that the major weakness of the positioning theory lies elsewhere. The positioning theory suggests that strategic choice (positioning) be made on a broad basis in the context of the industry. The problem is that individual customers/consumers probably buy products and services on criteria which are much more refined than those suggested by broad generic strategies. It is possible that a lack of refinement in the positioning approach results in a large "gap" between the intended strategy and the realised strategy because developing the required supporting tangible and intangible resources cannot be done on such a generalised basis. Additionally, customers will probably have a number of heterogeneous criteria on which they make their selections. Market segmentation is an attempt to find patterns or "bundles" of similar preferences. These preferences will change over time. Some of these preferences will change from being "order winning" to "order qualifying" (Hill, 1993). The relative importance of these criteria will also change within each bundle of preferences. Indeed, the relative size of consumer preference bundles will change over time. Strategic choice, it is argued here, should be made primarily on the basis of an ongoing knowledge of these consumer preferences.

As a result, current positioning theory has possibly caused as many problems for the strategic process as it has helped solve problems because it has not given sufficient weight to the detailed understanding of current and future customer preferences. For example, attempting to describe strategy in terms of broad differentiation or cost leadership or even describing strategic choice in terms of customer service, efficiency, innovation and quality is not a refined enough statement of consumer preferences on which to base strategic choice. Strategic choice made at the level of an industry analysis will be woefully inadequate in linking into functional strategies that have to make congruent trade-offs and produce the very specific customer "order winning" performance. Positioning theory and the strategic choice that this implies need to be built up from knowledge of current and future "customer specific" preferences. A successful firm's position in an industry may be interpretable in terms of generic strategies, but the firm probably got there by a fine-grained, sometimes emergent and sometimes deliberate, understanding of consumer preferences, on which strategic choices were built.

In summary the main weakness of the positioning theory is that it is built on aggregate understanding of the industry, typically in terms of cost leadership or broad differentiation, rather than on fine-grained understanding of consumer preferences. One of the major consequences of this is that the strategic choices made at strategic business unit level, using an aggregate industry analytical approach, can carry no effective meaning at a functional strategy level. The most appropriate linkage in deciding the nature of a firm's outputs and the consequent nature of its resources is therefore probably current and future consumer preferences.

## SOME LIMITATIONS OF THE RESOURCE-BASED APPROACH

The development of the resource-based view is possibly something of a reaction to the positioning theory. It takes a decidedly inward-looking approach to finding explanations as to why certain firms outperform others. This is illustrated in the definition provided by Barney (1991), where the focus is on assets, capabilities, etc., that improve efficiency and effectiveness. The role of the market as the prioritisation mechanism is at best implied.

The key characteristic of these resources, and the reason for their economic value, is their heterogeneous distribution among competing firms. The resource-based view therefore differs from the industrial or structured view of the firm, in that it does not make the assumption that there is homogeneity of resources between firms in an industry or that any differences are short lived (Barney, 1991: 100).

The resource-based view of the firm strengthens the theoretical justification for searching for richer explanations of the divergence in firm performance in examination of heterogeneous resources, strategies and the relationships between them. The central issue in the resource-based view is heterogeneity (Peteraf, 1993).

Applying this view, heterogeneity is therefore a necessary but not sufficient condition for differences in firm performance. The underlying question is "what is the relative importance of these attributes and is there a logical sequencing of their ordinal positions?". It may be that the attribute that "it exploits opportunities and/or neutralises threats in a firm's environment" (Barney, 1991: 105), i.e. it is valuable, is a precondition to the usefulness of the other attributes. This attribute of value also has characteristics of its own. For example, it could be argued that it is inherently market (customer) orientated—it either generates unique value for the customer (opportunity) or limits competitors' access to those customers (threat). In other words, the value which the resource generates is based on market outcomes of those resources. On the other hand, the other three resource attributes mentioned by Barney (1991) are inherently supply orientated. For example, the characteristics of rareness, inimitability, and non-substitutability are characteristics of supply. The importance of these "supply" attributes is consequently not based on the strength of these attributes but is derived from their relationship (impact) on the *a priori* value attribute. For example, if a resource has little impact on the external opportunity or threats facing the firm, then regardless how rare, inimitable, and non-substitutable the resource is, it will have little economic value. The growing literature on the resource-based view of the firm does not yet appear to have fully discussed the relationship between these resource attributes. Peteraf (1993) describes four similar theoretical conditions that underlie competitive advantage. In this analysis the sources of competitive advantage relate to internal and supply-related resources. Peteraf does not extend this analysis outward in terms of the "value" requirement as defined by Barney (1991), but only implies this requirement. It is assumed that these resources produce the "right" outputs. As Peteraf (1993: 188) clearly states: "The resource-based model is fundamentally concerned with the internal accumulation of assets, and with asset specificity".

While the resource-based view correctly stresses heterogeneity, it is limited in its explanatory power, by not relating those internal resources to heterogeneous market-related outputs. If these two aspects can be combined (the external examination of heterogeneous firm outputs and their relationship to internal heterogeneous resources) then a richer causal model of differences in firm economic performance could be constructed.

The literature does show some evidence of development along these lines. For example, Mehra (1996) recognised the importance of combining both a market-orientated approach and a resource-based approach in a study to determine whether strategic group analysis is better using one rather than the other in explaining differences in performance. The question which Mehra does not answer is which comes first, market-led strategies or resource-led strategies? With reference to global competition he implies that resources come first (Mehra, 1996: 308).

The products or services on which a company competes may be constrained by the firm's history (Barney, 1991), but consideration needs to be given to the notion that what defines a sustainable resource is *a priori* market led. Strategic change and the consequent re-engineering of business processes, competencies and resources is often justified on the basis of shifts in market preferences (Mathur, 1988; Ramaswami, Flynn & Nilakanta, 1993).

The effectiveness of unique resource endowments is logically prescribed by the evolving patterns of marketplace preferences. As Levitt's (1960) classic article pointed out, what is required is a focus on customers' needs rather than products—a state of "marketing myopia". A strong focus on resources may lead to the same consequences as marketing myopia, a form of "resource myopia"; or as Miller (1990) suggested in his book *The Icarus Paradox*, companies can become so focused in accumulating resources in a specialised area that they lose sight of fundamental change in the marketplace. The internal orientation of the resource-based view may also lead to strategic inertia (Ghemawat, 1991).

Creating unique and valuable visible outputs in the marketplace is external evidence that the firm possesses the appropriate unique internal resources. Customers and competitors alike will see these marketplace outputs—this is unavoidable in an open economy. The ability of the firm to sustain its market uniqueness will be a function of the uniqueness of the appropriate resources. The development of a theory that adequately relates the market positioning view and the resource-based view has yet to emerge. In particular a research approach that leads from heterogeneous market outputs (based on customer preferences) to heterogeneous resources is yet to be specified.

In sum, the resource-based view is lacking in definition of what defines value—heterogeneity in itself being necessary but insufficient. It is argued here that resources have value in the first instance on a derived basis. They derive their value from the nature of consumer preferences—a measure external to the firm itself.

## Towards a Marriage of the Positioning Theory and the Resource-Based View of the Firm—the Output-Based View of the Firm

The argument developed from the literature is that differences in firm performance can be explained through a combination of firm resources and output values, where firm resources derive their importance from the relative value of the firm's outputs. These outputs in turn derive their prioritisation from "bundles" of customer preferences. Congruency between these factors will have an important role in determining performance. In addition, resource advantages are not directly related to competitive advantage but are indirectly manifest through cost and market advantages. It needs to be noted that the explanatory power of such a model (see Figure 6.2) depends on the economic/industry context in which it is being applied, because the model assumes that consumer preferences matter in the way resources are developed and allocated within the economy/industry. In economies/industries where open market processes are weak (i.e. consumer preferences are limited in some way), the model would possibly have less explanatory power.

This model gives emphasis to the importance of consumer preferences in determining the priorities of both firm efficiency (cost advantage) and market advantage (output values). Market advantage, as reflected in the firm's relative performance on "visible to the customer" output values, will determine the quality of the revenues the firm earns (price premium and volume). Firm efficiency determines the cost base of the firm. These two factors in combination give rise to the quality of the firm's business performance (competitive advantage). There is also an interaction effect between the cost and market advantages; for example, volume can sometimes facilitate efficiency.

The importance given to a firm's resources is derived from the relative importance of the firm's cost and market advantages. The resource

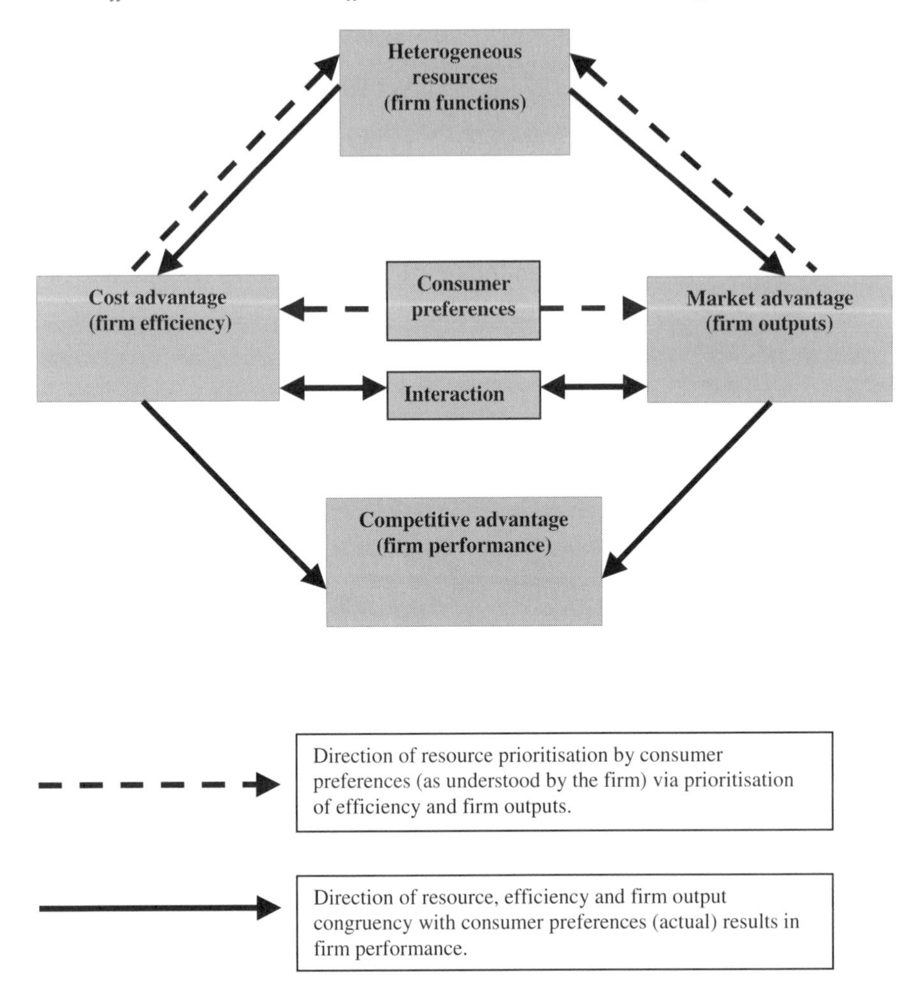


FIGURE 6.2 The relationships between resources, outputs, efficiency and performance—the output-based view of the firm

advantage of a firm, in this model, is linked only indirectly to the firm's competitive advantage through its cost and market advantages.

## PROPOSITIONS

The development of propositions follows a deliberate pattern in this study. They begin with the highest possible level of aggregation and progressively examine the relationships identified in the theoretical model in greater and greater detail.

> Controlling proposition. Competitive advantage is the product of a heterogeneous set of market, cost and resource advantage variables and such a model has better fit properties as the level of industry aggregation is reduced.

The main objective of this study is to create a model which explains a significant proportion of the variability in business performance. The above proposition claims that resource advantage is the most fundamental level of competitive advantage as it is the basis for creating either a cost or a market advantage or both. Cost and market advantages are intermediate-level advantages which combine to determine the overall competitive advantage of the firm. In simultaneous combination, these exogenous unobserved variables should explain a high proportion of business performance. This approach of identifying a number of potential contingency variables and testing them simultaneously is not new.

As Grinyer, McKiernan and Yasai-Ardekani (1988) showed in their study of contingent variables in the UK electrical engineering industry, a conjoint analysis of "contingent strategic, market, planning, and organisational contingencies" (p. 298) accounted for a high proportion of business performance.

This study provides a similar methodology, but rather than using such a broad eclectic selection of contingent variables, it confines itself to and justifies resource, cost and market advantage variables. This study implies that a systematic understanding of output values, efficiency and resource variables is the appropriate route to a prioritised understanding of the other variables used by Grinyer, McKiernan and Yasai-Ardekani which are largely aspects of firm tangible and intangible resources. This study also implies that the theoretical model will fit the data to a significantly greater degree at an industry level, as Grinyer, McKiernan and Yasai-Ardekani (1988) found in their study.

To test this proposition, structural equation modeling is deployed.

> Proposition 1: output values and business performance. There is a positive relationship between output values, efficiency, price and business performance. These relationships are heterogeneous and have greater explanatory power as the level of industry aggregation is reduced.

This proposition is derived from the revenue-related concepts in the theoretical model, namely output values and price, and the cost-related concept, namely efficiency. The basic notion is that these concepts do not have equal importance to business performance. It is the heterogeneous nature of these relationships which is of primary interest in the understanding of the sources of competitive advantage (Venkatraman, 1990).

This proposition also extends the analysis of the heterogeneous nature of the relationships by examining variations between industries. The strategic reference points (Fiegenbaum, Hart & Schendel, 1996) could possibly vary between industries and consequently explain differences in importance of underlying competencies between industries.

The final point that this proposition makes is that the explanatory power of the model should increase as the level of industry aggregation is reduced.

> Proposition 2: output values, efficiency and functional impact. There is a positive relationship between output values, efficiency, price and functional impact. These relationships are heterogeneous and have greater explanatory power as the level of industry aggregation is reduced.

This proposition suggests that the relative importance of functions is not static between and within industries. The purpose of this proposition is to enable a degree of generalisation of the output-based view of the firm. On the one hand, not only does the relationship of functions to output values vary, but on the other it also varies across and within industries. Consequently important functions and competencies in one industry will not be as important in another. This has strong implications for strategic management at the corporate, strategic business unit (SBU) and functional levels (Hitt, Ireland & Stadter, 1982).

The central notion to this proposition is that the relative importance of functions varies by its impact on the output values. The importance of this proposition derives from the possible insights that may be obtained into the functional resources that form the basis of core competencies and competitive advantage (McGrath, MacMillan & Venkatraman, 1995; Snow & Hrebiniak, 1980).

Finally, these propositions combine to test the theoretical model developed in this study. They relate resources (as embodied in functions) to both cost and market advantages and these in combination relate to the firm's business performance or competitive advantage.

## Methodology

Data were collected by means of a postal survey of four UK industries. These were electronic components manufacturing, automotive components manufacturing, financial services and logistics services industries. Pre-pilot survey interviews were held with 12 executives from these industries to determine the most appropriate items to measure business performance, efficiency, output values and functions. These items were also examined in relation to prior studies. From this examination a pilot survey instrument was developed which was tested on 30 companies. The survey instrument was adjusted and used in the main survey. The survey instrument was built mainly on seven-point Likert scales

The use of Likert scales is generally accepted in strategy research without reducing accuracy with respect to objective measures (Dess & Robinson, 1984; Miller & Friesen, 1983; Bourgeois, 1985). The central point in the scale (4) was anchored to the industry average (Dean & Snell, 1996) to provide an external benchmark against which firms could rate themselves. This increased the objective nature of the scale and allowed for later triangulation of the responses with financial data collected from independent sources.

Market share, return on investment and return on sales were the financial performance measures used for identifying the relative importance of the output values as described in the theoretical model.

## Measuring Functional Effectiveness

Functional effectiveness is defined as the relative effectiveness of key functions in the creation of the output values and efficiency in relation to the industry average. These broadly relate to Porter's (1980, 1985) primary value chain activities. This study examines purchasing, R&D, operations, distribution, marketing and sales, and after-sales support functions for their effectiveness across the value outputs and efficiency.

## Measuring Output Values

Output values are those values that are identifiable in the marketplace that have value to the customer. They are the tangible and intangible features of the products and services that are offered to the customer for which the customer is prepared to pay. Not all outputs from the firm will necessarily have value to the customer in this definition. Likewise, all relevant customer needs may not be met by the output of the firm. The output values measured in this study are to be found in the structural equation models. The customer responsiveness output value is parsimoniously constructed from variables, confirmed in the pre-survey interviews and cited frequently in prior studies. These criteria apply to all the output values in this study. Three of these customer responsiveness variables are visible in the marketplace and two are strong proxies for visible customer responsiveness output values, although they are not directly observable.

Price is also included as it represents the exchange value between the firm and the customer (Olshavsky, Aylesworth & Kempf, 1995). Total revenue is a function of total units sold multiplied by unit price. Consequently the ability to successfully charge a price that is higher than the industry average represents a premium which directly impacts on firm performance. However, price is not an output value of the firm as defined in this study.

A further questionnaire was created from the output variables as described in the structural equation model and sent to a customer of the supplier for triangulation purposes.

The theoretical model shows two other factors which are not output values but nevertheless have a strong influence on business performance. These are price and cost, i.e.

$$\text{Profit} = \text{revenues} - \text{costs} \tag{6.1}$$

and

$$\text{Revenues} = \text{unit price} \times \text{volume} \tag{6.2}$$

The price variable was measured using a seven-point Likert scale with industry average as the mid-point. The cost factors were measured by a number of efficiency variables. Thus the ability of the firm to generate revenues in this model is a function of its performance on output values.

The range of size of company captured in this study was from very large to very small (as measured by number of employees on the returned questionnaires). By capturing this range, size effects on the results could be measured. The size distribution in the selected SIC codes was expected to be positively skewed with a high proportion of small firms in each sector. As a result of this population distribution, by selecting the top 500 by sales size in each industry, a high proportion of the total turnover in each sector should have been captured.

## Results

Table 6.1 shows the number of usable responses (and descriptive statistics) that were achieved after reminder mailings and follow-up telephone calls.

The major explicit reason for non-return of questionnaires was company policy, which dictated non-participation in research. This was confirmed by a follow-up telephone call to non-respondents. The low response rate from the financial services industry could arise from the inherently

TABLE 6.1 Usable response rate and descriptive statistics

| | Electronic components manufacturing | Automotive components manufacturing | Financial services | Logistics services | Total |
|---|---|---|---|---|---|
| Supplier questionnaires | 596 | 577 | 540 | 539 | 2252 |
| Usable returns | 39 | 24 | 13 | 28 | 104 |
| Percentage | 6.5% | 4.2% | 2.4% | 5.2% | 4.6% |
| Number of employees | 5–2000 | 9–2000 | 24–24 000 | 5–8500 | — |
| Mean no. of employees | 226.7 | 531.7 | 2426.2 | 1046.0 | — |
| Skewness | 3.2 | 1.1 | 3.6 | 2.6 | — |
| <100 employees (%) | 51.3 | 37.5 | 7.7 | 57.1 | — |
| <300 employees (%) | 84.6 | 54.2 | 53.8 | 75.0 | — |

manufacturing bias in the value chain approach in the questionnaire construction. The wording of the questionnaire attempted to adjust for this bias. Nevertheless, using a single questionnaire across service and manufacturing industries has been noted as problematic in prior studies (Bart & Habib, 1991). There was no strong indication in the pilot study that this would be a problem in this study.

The distribution figures shown in TABLE 6.1 clearly show the predominance of small to medium-sized firms by count in the returned questionnaires. The distribution is positively skewed in all cases. For example, in the electronic component manufacturing industry 84.6% of the number of respondents had 300 or fewer employees, and firms of fewer than 100 employees accounted for 51.3% of the distribution. This positive skewness possibly reflects the firm size distribution in the industry as a whole and is similar to results found in other studies of this type (Miller & Friesen, 1982). Whether the larger firms have different relationships within the theoretical model was tested and found to be not significant.

The number of respondents is adequate for inferential statistics (Mazen, Hemmasi & Lewis, 1987), although higher numbers of financial services firms could be sought in future research through a tailored survey instrument. The findings are the first indicative results for these UK industries in this type of study.

The use of small data sets is not uncommon in this type of study. Grinyer, McKiernan and Yasai-Ardekani (1988), in a study of the UK electrical engineering industry, collected data from 45 companies. From this data set they construct regression models with average return on investment (and other business performance measures) as the dependent variable and up to nine independent variables. Interestingly they found company- and market-specific factors to be good predictor variables of business performance.

### Scale Reliability

The scales developed for this study included scales for financial performance and scales for output values and efficiency. To test the degree to which they are unidimensional, Cronbach's alpha tests were carried out (Dean & Snell, 1996). A summary is given in TABLE 6.2. These reliability tests give good evidence that the variables included in the scales were unidimensional on the grounds suggested by Van de Ven and Ferry (1979).

To additionally understand the reliability of the scales, the relationships in this study were examined both using the scales and at the individual scale item level. This gave a more detailed picture of the strength of individual items that made up the scale. This was also important in building parsimonious confirmatory structural equation models. It enabled a more discriminatory approach in the use of the underlying factors.

### Triangulation

A major criticism of the use of Likert scales is their subjective characteristic. Likert scales were used in this study to capture a number of variables including business performance. The business performance ratings were triangulated post-survey with financial data collected from available sources and for those companies which were recorded in these sources. The subjective financial performance measures were verified.

The suppliers were the main respondents in this research. They had evaluated their performance on output values using seven-point Likert scales. They were asked to supply the name of a customer so that the suppliers' ratings could be checked. A questionnaire was sent to these customers using the same output value, efficiency and price scales as the suppliers used. These supplier performance ratings were verified by this

TABLE 6.2 Scale reliability analysis

| Scale Description | Cronbach's alpha | Number of items in scale | Construct type |
|---|---|---|---|
| Financial | .6802 | 3 | Narrow |
| Customer responsiveness | .6526 | 5 | Moderate |
| Innovation | .8049 | 4 | Moderate |
| Quality | .7285 | 3 | Moderate |
| Efficiency | .7407 | 4 | Moderate |

procedure. It is interesting to note that the suppliers consistently rated themselves higher than their customers. While this reflects potential bias in the responses, this bias is nevertheless consistent.

## A Consolidated Structural Equation Model—the Base Case

The following is a description of the major components of the structural equation model, which is based on the theoretical model of this study.

### The Composition of the Unobserved Exogenous ''Resource Advantage'' Variable

The theoretical model in this study suggests that there is a relationship between functional effectiveness and the resources that underpin functions. For example, an extreme case would be where the resources of a function were difficult to duplicate, the skills within a function were difficult to imitate, and the level of investment planned for the function sustained both difficulty to imitate and duplicate resource characteristics. Additionally these resources are leveraged by the function's high impact on the value delivered to the customer and high levels of functional effectiveness. Such a combination of functional resources and impact translates into a ''resource advantage'' and is observed as functional effectiveness. The structural equation model is further built up, as ''resource advantage'' is also related to exogenous variables called ''market advantage'', ''cost advantage'' and finally ''competitive advantage''.

This study does not attempt to examine in any depth the underlying tangible and intangible variables that give rise to a resource advantage. The degree of functional effectiveness is the outcome of resource advantage. This study only looks at how functional effectiveness co-varies with resource advantage. Understanding how functional effectiveness co-varies with resource advantage is one way of prioritising functions and thereby providing an ordinal approach to the later examination of the underlying tangible and intangible resources.

If, for example, the operations function's effectiveness is found to co-vary strongly with resource advantage, then future research could examine the nature of the tangible and intangible resources within the operations function to determine how it generates a resource advantage. The variables that could be used in such a study could include technology types, skill levels and planning processes. There is substantial literature justifying these items (Skinner, 1974; Corsten & Will, 1993; Wheelwright, 1984; Berry, Hill & Klompmaker, 1993; Kim & Arnold, 1992).

Factor analysis is carried out on the functional effectiveness scores to confirm the existence of an underlying construct, which is labelled "resource advantage". The use of factor analysis will help to reduce the number of functional effectiveness scores to be included in the industry-specific models. This data reduction process is an aid to developing a parsimonious model which reflects the unique cross-functional combination of underlying resources, which gives rise to the "resource advantage".

TABLE 6.3 shows the results of a factor analysis of the functional effectiveness scores on the combined data (base case) in this study. There is a two-factor solution. The first component explains 39.26% of the variance in the data and is labelled "resource advantage". The three functions which are closely related to "resource advantage" are after-sales service, purchasing and operations. The KMO measure of sampling adequacy is .644 and thus indicates that factor analysis is appropriate. Cronbach's alpha is .6572, indicating a reasonable level of scale reliability. These functions are

TABLE 6.3 Factor analysis of "functional effectiveness" variables for base case

Component matrix[a]

| | Component 1 |
|---|---|
| Effectiveness of after-sales service | .782 |
| Effectiveness of purchasing | .682 |
| Effectiveness of operations | .674 |
| Effectiveness of distribution | .622 |
| Effectiveness of marketing | .513 |
| Effectiveness of R&D | .419 |

Extraction method: Principal Component Analysis.
[a] One component extracted.

Total variance explained

| Component | Initial eigenvalues | | | Extraction sums of squared loadings | | |
|---|---|---|---|---|---|---|
| | Total | % of variance | Cumulative % | Total | % of variance | Cumulative % |
| 1 | 2.355 | 39.257 | 39.257 | 2.355 | 39.257 | 39.257 |
| 2 | 1.158 | 19.292 | 58.549 | | | |
| 3 | .927 | 15.446 | 73.995 | | | |
| 4 | .725 | 12.077 | 86.071 | | | |
| 5 | .446 | 7.427 | 93.498 | | | |
| 6 | .390 | 6.502 | 100.000 | | | |

Extraction method: Principal Component Analysis.

further analysed on an industry basis where a comparison with these combined data shows how the relationship of functions with "resource advantage" is improved and changed at industry level.

## The Composition of the Unobserved Exogenous "Market Advantage" Variable

The ability of a firm to outperform its rivals with superior products and services gives it the ability to charge higher prices and/or increase market share (Porter, 1985) and thereby display a competitive advantage, reflected in above-industry-average business performance. The theoretical model of this study has called these "output values". Performance on these output values, it is theorised, is not heterogeneous. In other words, certain output values play a bigger role in determining business performance. The study so far has largely confirmed this situation.

A two-factor solution emerged. The first factor is labelled "market advantage", and TABLE 6.4 shows the results of a factor analysis of these

TABLE 6.4 Factor analysis of "market advantage" variables using combined data for the base case

Component matrix[a]

| | Component 1 |
|---|---|
| Customer responsiveness index | .767 |
| Quality index | .740 |
| Innovation index | .601 |
| Prices charged for goods and services | .330 |

Extraction method: Principal Component Analysis.
[a] One component extracted.

Total variance explained

| Component | Initial eigenvalues | | | Extraction sums of squared loadings | | |
|---|---|---|---|---|---|---|
| | Total | % of variance | Cumulative % | Total | % of variance | Cumulative % |
| 1 | 1.605 | 40.137 | 40.137 | 1.605 | 40.137 | 40.137 |
| 2 | 1.077 | 26.933 | 67.070 | | | |
| 3 | .801 | 20.030 | 87.100 | | | |
| 4 | .516 | 12.900 | 100.000 | | | |

Extraction method: Principal Component Analysis.

variables. Using the combined data, customer responsiveness, innovation, quality and price combine to explain 40.1% of the variability of the data. The KMO test of sampling adequacy is. 510 and Cronbach's alpha is .4506 (Cronbach's alpha improves to .5164 with price removed). The number of residuals greater than .1 is five.

## The Composition of the Unobserved Exogenous "Cost Advantage" Variable

Profitability of a firm is determined not only by its ability to generate revenues but also by its cost structure, as discussed previously. Resource advantage should theoretically relate not only to market-related advantages but also to cost-related advantages. A firm's functional mix of tangible and intangible resources and its ability to effectively use them should be related to its "cost advantage". Table 6.5 shows the results of a factor analysis of "cost advantage" variables.

A single-factor solution emerged. The above analysis shows that efficiency variables load well onto the "cost advantage" factor. The KMO

Table 6.5 Factor analysis of "cost advantage" variables using combined data for the base case

Component matrix[a]

| | Component 1 |
|---|---|
| Capital efficiency | .771 |
| Output costs | .759 |
| Labour efficiency | .749 |
| Capacity utilisation | .724 |

Extraction method: Principal Component Analysis.
[a] One component extracted.

Total variance explained

| Component | Initial eigenvalues | | | Extraction sums of squared loadings | | |
|---|---|---|---|---|---|---|
| | Total | % of variance | Cumulative % | Total | % of variance | Cumulative % |
| 1 | 2.255 | 56.381 | 56.381 | 2.255 | 56.381 | 56.381 |
| 2 | .627 | 15.683 | 72.064 | | | |
| 3 | .584 | 14.590 | 86.654 | | | |
| 4 | .534 | 13.346 | 100.000 | | | |

Extraction method: Principal Component Analysis.

test of sample adequacy is .768 and Cronbach's alpha is .741. The number of residuals above .1 is six, indicating a weak model fit.

## The Composition of the Unobserved Exogenous "Competitive Advantage" Variable

Competitive advantage has been defined as the ability of a firm to generate returns above the average rate for the industry. This structural equation model is suggesting that a firm's overall competitive advantage is related to underlying cost and market-related advantages, which in turn are related to resource advantages.

The factor analysis of "competitive advantage" is shown in TABLE 6.6. A single-factor solution emerged. The variables load well onto the "competitive advantage" factor and explain 61.4% of the variability of the data. The KMO measure of sampling adequacy is .561 and Cronbach's alpha is .680.

The combined structural equation model, which is inclusive of all the industries studied (i.e. the base case), is shown in FIGURE 6.3.

TABLE 6.6 Factor analysis of "competitive advantage" variables using combined data for the base case

Component matrix[a]

| | Component 1 |
|---|---|
| Return on sales against industry average | .889 |
| Return on investment against industry average | .856 |
| Market share performance compared to industry average | .564 |

Extraction method: Principal Component Analysis.
[a] One component extracted.

Total variance explained

| Component | Initial eigenvalues | | | Extraction sums of squared loadings | | |
|---|---|---|---|---|---|---|
| | Total | % of variance | Cumulative % | Total | % of variance | Cumulative % |
| 1 | 1.841 | 61.355 | 61.355 | 1.841 | 61.355 | 61.355 |
| 2 | .831 | 27.713 | 89.068 | | | |
| 3 | .328 | 10.932 | 100.000 | | | |

Extraction method: Principal Component Analysis.

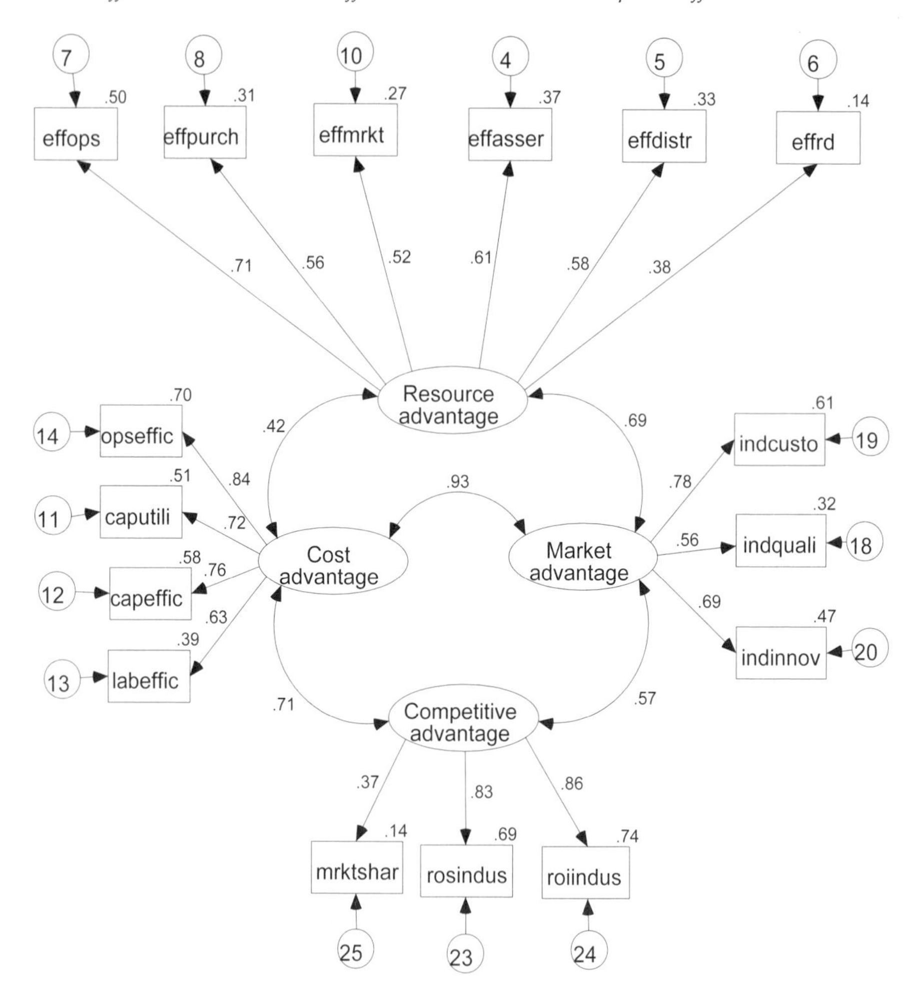


FIGURE 6.3 Combined structural equation model (base case)

The structural equation model generated a convergent and proper solution. Convergent validity of the model was examined by comparing each observed endogenous variable's pattern coefficient with its standard error (Anderson & Gerbing, 1988). All observed endogenous variables' coefficients were greater than twice their standard errors, providing evidence of convergent validity.

To further test the underlying theory of this study that the relationships between the unobserved exogenous variables "resource advantage", "cost advantage", "market advantage" and "competitive advantage" are indeed heterogeneous, a comparison was made between a minimum constrained and a maximum constrained version of the identified confirmatory model. In other words, with the identified model the variances and covariances were allowed to vary between the unobserved exogenous variables, and this was compared to the same model where these relationships were hypothesised not to vary. A comparison of the resultant function of log-likelihood, number of parameters and chi-square of the difference between these two models is given in TABLE 6.7.

The difference between these two models is significant at $p = .05$ and consequently the null hypothesis that the relationships between the unobserved exogenous variables do not vary is rejected, as predicted by this study's theory.

The model explains 74% of the variability of return on investment and 69% of the return on sales. The model explains only 14% of the variability of market share, which is probably a result of the definitional problems of what is the "market" as revealed in the triangulation of the market share responses. Cost advantage had a stronger relationship to competitive advantage with a covariance of .71 than did market advantage with a covariance of .57. Seventy percent of the variability of operational efficiency was explained by cost advantage and 61% of the variability in customer responsiveness was explained by market advantage. The resource advantage co-varied most with market advantage (.69), and resource advantage explained 50% of the effectiveness of the operations function. There was a strong co-variance between cost and market advantage.

These are the highlights of the combined structural equation model. The next step was the development of structural equation models for each of the industries for which sufficient data were available. The industry models were then compared with the combined model to test the hypothesis that the model fits the data better at industry level. The path diagrams of these models are shown in FIGURES 6.4–6.6.

TABLE 6.7 The difference between the maximum constrained and minimum unconstrained base case structural equation models

| | Minimum unconstrained model | Maximum constrained model | Difference |
|---|---|---|---|
| Log-likelihood | 1399.737 | 1444.319 | 44.582 (chi—obtained) |
| Parameters | 52 | 46 | 8 |
| Chi-square ($p = .05$) | | | 15.507 (chi—critical) |

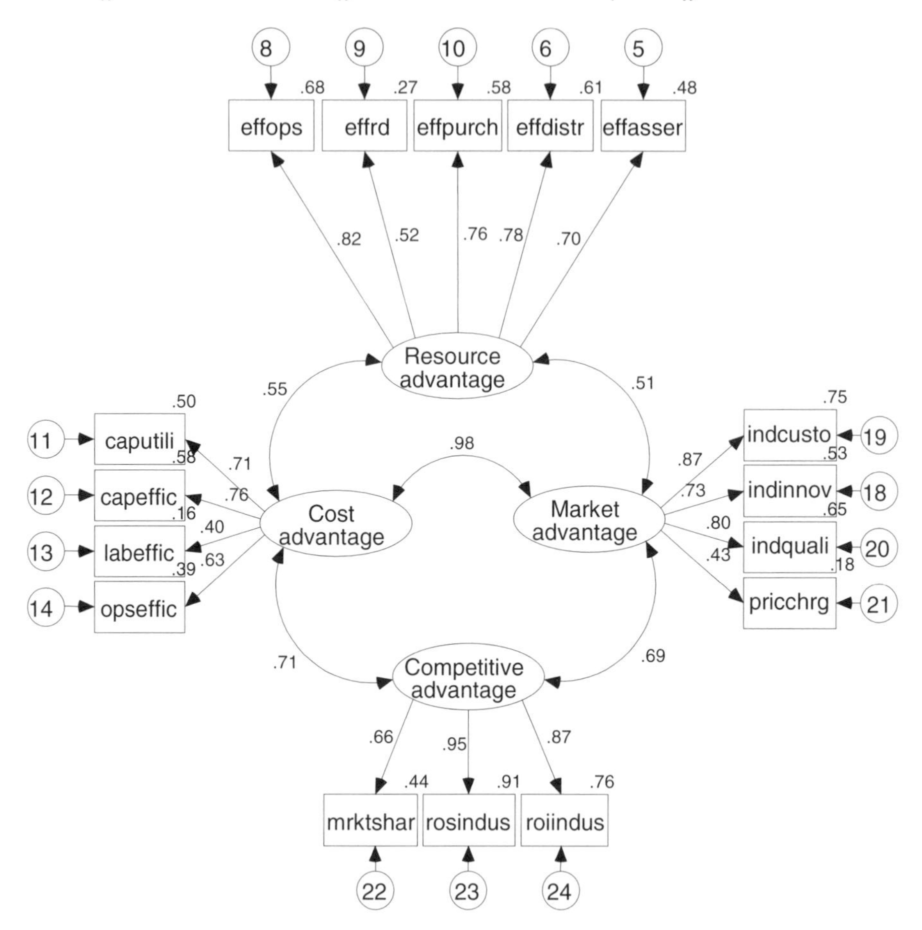


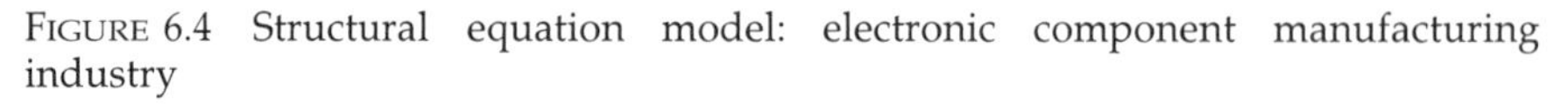
FIGURE 6.4 Structural equation model: electronic component manufacturing industry

## Testing the Controlling Proposition

> Competitive advantage is the product of a heterogeneous set of market, cost and resource advantage variables and such a model has better fit properties at industry level.

To test whether the structural equation models also confirm the "fit" between the concepts of resource, cost, market and competitive advantage concepts, each industry model was compared with the combined model to see whether models developed at industry level had a better fit with the

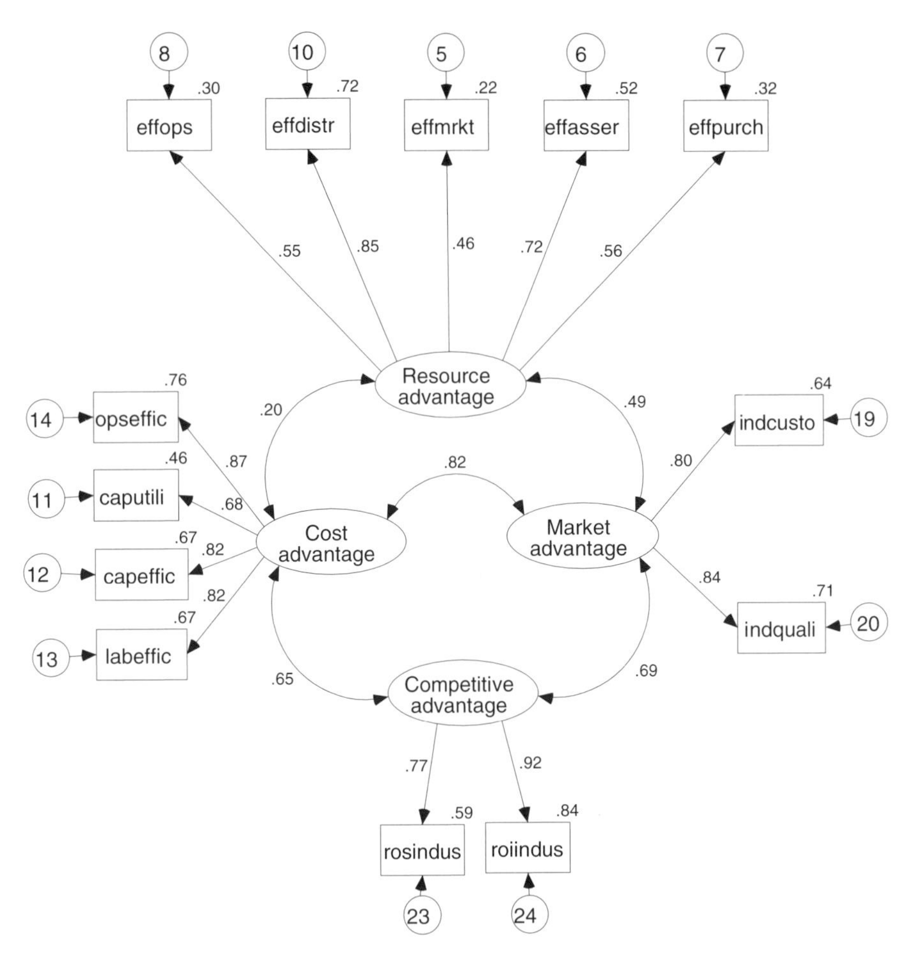


FIGURE 6.5 Structural equation model: automotive component manufacturing industry

data. This was carried out by calculating the significance of the difference in chi-squared between each industry model and the combined model.

> Ha: There is a significant difference between the fit of the model at a combined or industry level.

If the null hypothesis is rejected and the alternative accepted, this would mean that the specified model fits the data more appropriately at an industry level rather than across industries. This outcome would give additional support to the validity of the output-based view of the firm

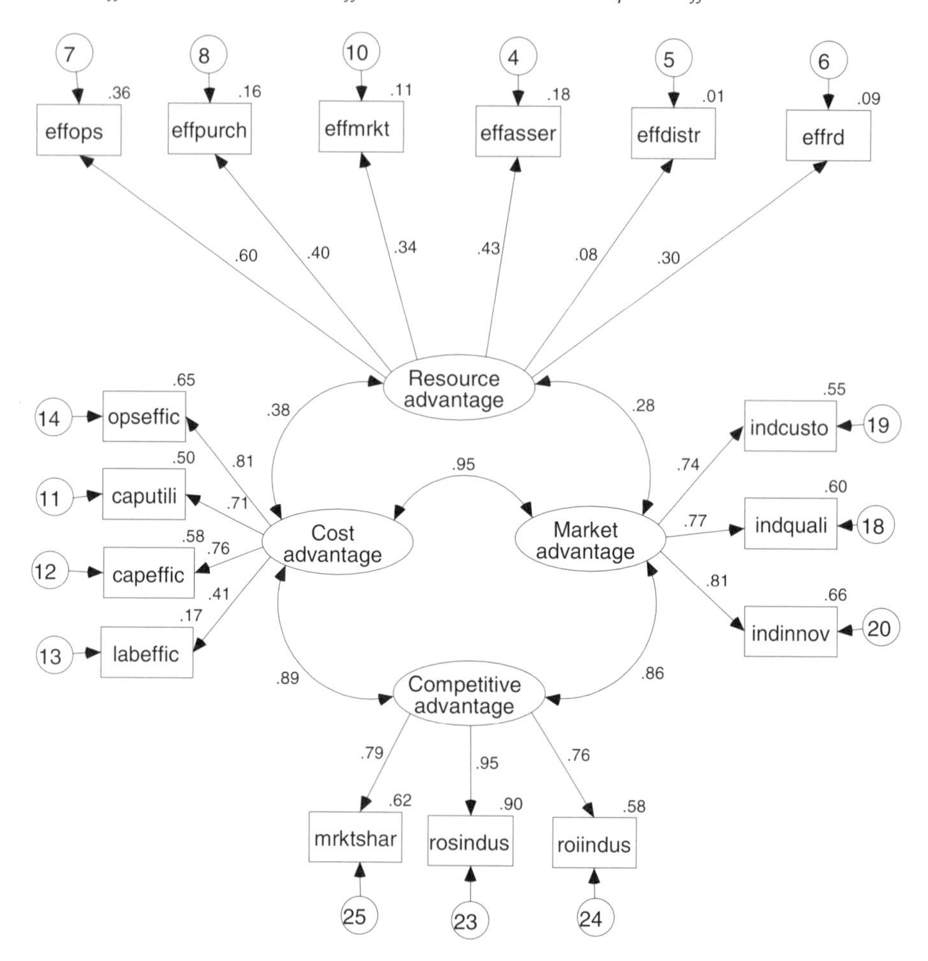


FIGURE 6.6 Structural equation model: logistics services industry

as defined in this study, as a way of explaining differences in firm performance. It would support the previous hypotheses of this study. Additionally it would give support to the notion that the priorities given to output values—efficiency, price and resources—differ between industries. Consequently the model should fit the data better when applied to industry-level data.

In interpreting the chi-square results in TABLE 6.8, consideration needs to be given to the criticisms that have been made of the chi-squared test in determining the likelihood of fit of the model to the data. The argument centres on the issue of sample size, where a large sample size will more

TABLE 6.8 Testing the difference between the fit of the base case and the UK electronic components, automotive parts manufacturing and logistics services industries using minimum unconstrained models

| | Log-likelihood | Parameters | Difference in $\chi^2$ |
|---|---|---|---|
| Combined data model (base case) | 1399.373 | 52 | |
| Electronic industry data model | 472.994 | 47 | 926.379 (chi—obtained)<br>11.071 (chi—critical) |
| Automotive industry data model | 281.318 | 39 | 1118.055 (chi—obtained)<br>22.362 (chi—critical) |
| Logistics services industry data model | 305.125 | 36 | 1094.248 (chi—obtained)<br>22.362 (chi—critical) |

readily result in a failure to reject the null hypothesis, and small sample sizes will more readily result in rejection of the null hypothesis (Bentler & Bonnett, 1980).

This weakness may be ameliorated by the fact that chi-squared is being calculated on the basis of differences in the log-likelihood ratio *between* two models, rather than *within* a single model. Nevertheless, the differences in sample size between the combined data and each industry separately are of necessity proportionately large, which may give rise to a concern that the null hypothesis is too readily rejected and thereby to a Type I error. As a result, additional emphasis should be given to the extent to which the log-likelihoods differ. The bigger the difference in the log-likelihood ratio, the smaller the probability that a Type I error has occurred.

The difference between the cross-industry (combined) model and the individual industry is significant at $p = .05$ in all cases and consequently the null hypothesis is rejected. The model fits the data significantly better when applied at the industry level. The difference in log-likelihood ratios is also well beyond the $p = .05$ level and consequently the difficulty with sample size is less likely to have caused a Type I error.

In conclusion, the structural equation models have shown that the relationships between the underlying variables vary significantly and that the models' fit with the data improves with lower levels of aggregation of data across industries. These findings support the theoretical model of this study, which suggested that not only would the relationships between resources, output values and efficiency vary with business performance, but that these relationships would vary by industry, thereby giving rise to a better fit of the model at industry level.

## Findings in Relation to the Literature

Given the underlying goal of this study to increase the explanatory power of why firms in the same industry have different business performances, the following is a comparison of two (from among many) prior studies with this study, in terms of that goal. These prior studies, are an examination of a relatively small element of the ground covered by this study. Consequently the appropriate parts from this study are extracted for comparative purposes.

### Innovation

In a study of the effect of important incremental innovations on market share, Banbury and Mitchell (1995) showed that the rate of significant and early innovation in the American implantable cardiac pacemaker industry explained a high level of market share ($R^2 = .74$). Clearly for this industry innovation is an important output value. For the electronic component manufacturing industry this study showed a significant correlation between market share and the success rates of new products (.517, $p < .01$). When all the innovation factors are regressed with market share in the electronic component manufacturing industry, the success rate of new products explains 26.7% of market share variability ($R^2 = 26.7$). When innovation is nested in the unobserved exogenous variable "market advantage" in the confirmatory structural equation model, $R^2 = .52$. Market share has $R^2 = .43$ when nested with "competitive advantage" in the same model.

The model developed in this study offers a richer explanation of market share, as it includes other output values beyond innovation and a wider range of measure of business performance. For example, variations in return on sales and return on investment are more strongly related to "competitive advantage" than market share. These findings would confirm and extend the results of the Banbury and Mitchell (1995) study that innovation is an important output value in explaining differences in business performances. However, it is also noteworthy that the degree to which this variable explains differences in firm performance varies by industry, an important element of this study's theoretical model. Innovation did not feature as a significant factor in market share performance in any of the other industries examined in this study, confirming the heterogeneous nature of the relationship of factors with business performance.

Nevertheless, innovation was an important factor in other measures of business performance. For example, in the financial services sector the innovation factor "success rate of new products" was significantly related to return on sales (.654, $p < .05$). In summary, this study confirms the

Banbury and Mitchell (1995) study but also extends it across industries and for more measures of business performance.

### Quality and Customer Responsiveness

Anderson and Zeithaml (1984) developed a series of regressions, one each for the growth, mature and decline stages of the product life cycle. Of their 25 variables, nine were common with this study. Their purpose was to see whether changes in business performance as measured by market share and return on investment were influenced by a significantly different set of betas on these variables. The values of $R^2$ for each stage of the product life cycle for each business performance measure are tabulated in TABLE 6.9 with the $R^2$ of this study.

Whilst Anderson and Zeithaml (1984) controlled for product life cycle, the products used were of necessity from different industries. This means that they assumed that each of the underlying variables that they used has a homogeneous relationship with business performance across industries. In other words the relationship of customer service, for example, with market share and return on investment is structurally the same between industries.

This study would suggest that this is not the case. On the other hand, this study has not allowed for differences between industries on the basis of product life cycle. Nevertheless, assessing each industry on its own merits controls for product life cycle influences. Of course, this raises the whole question of how product life cycles are defined—i.e. at what level (the individual item, the product group, the product category or the industry) (Dhalla & Yuspeh, 1976)—and how they are to be controlled for. It is possible that Anderson and Zeithaml (1984) were in fact identifying more in the way of differences in underlying relationships with business performance between industries.

TABLE 6.9 A comparison of the Anderson and Zeithaml (1984) regressions with this study

| Model type | Market share ($R^2$) | Return on investment ($R^2$) |
|---|---|---|
| Growth | .283 | .489 |
| Maturity | .278 | .456 |
| Decline | .432 | .497 |
| Electronic | .531 | .221 |
| Automotive | .277 | .600 |
| Finance | None | .407 |
| Logistics | .197 | .570 |

## In Relation to Contingency Theory

One definition of the contingency theory suggested that it was the "it depends" theory (Hambrick & Lei, 1985). This study suggests that there are some "rules" which appear to be uniform across industries in explaining differences in firm performance. In this regard the study shows some limited support for the extreme universal view. The rule, which appears to be generalisable and only at a high level of abstraction, is the heterogeneous nature of the relationship between output values, efficiency, price and business performance as well as the heterogeneous nature of the relationships between firm resources and performance on the output value, efficiency and price variables.

Heterogeneity appears to be a consistent theme irrespective of industry setting. With respect to the other end of the contingency spectrum, which claims that performance is entirely dependent on the unique contingencies facing the firm, this study would suggest that certain "patterns" of relationships are discernible within industry settings. Consequently this study would not go as far as the extreme situation-specific perspective. It would argue instead that there is validity in attempting to understand differences in firm performance through understanding patterns of competitive behaviour within industry settings. This study has suggested that these patterns may be usefully constructed from the priorities of relationships between output values, efficiency, price, and resources and business performance.

With respect to the congruency subset of contingency theory, this study has tentatively identified patterns of variables that need to be aligned in order to create superior performance (Venkatraman & Prescott, 1990). It confirms the study of Venkatraman and Prescott (1990), suggesting that the alignment of certain variables "has systematic implications for performance" (p. 18). The present study has, however, extended their investigation, which was primarily based on environmental and resource deployment variables, to include output value, efficiency and price variables. Firms which gave certain output values, efficiency and price priorities tended to perform better in a systematic fashion.

In relation to the competency approach, this study would give support to that of Hitt and Ireland (1986) that competencies arise within functions and that they arise on a differential basis. This study does not directly evaluate the sources of differential competencies, though it does provide a prioritisation mechanism for future study into the sources of heterogeneous distinctive functional competence.

## In Relation to the Resource-Based View of the Firm

This study provides evidence of the heterogeneous nature of resources in relation to business performance. It suggests that the resources that underpin functions have a differential impact on output value, efficiency and price outcomes. This is reflected in the heterogeneous nature of future investment plans of firms, the skill levels embedded in functions and the imitability of functions. It extends prior studies of the resource-based view by linking the value of the outputs of the firm to resources. It suggests that resources underpin the heterogeneous nature of functional effectiveness and impact, which in turn support cost and market competitiveness. This study highlights the importance of not treating resource types as homogeneous (Venkatraman & Prescott, 1990).

In conclusion this study is confirmatory of a number of studies which are typically narrower in scope than this one. It has highlighted the need for studies to identify relationships within industry contexts and to build more comprehensive models in the search for greater explanatory power of the differences in firm performance. In particular, it goes beyond most other studies by including simultaneously business performance, market and cost advantage, and finally resource advantage. It is very much like a large but still incomplete jigsaw puzzle, which confirms many prior pieces and relates them within a new and useful framework.

## Implications for Policy

This study has provided some evidence for the notion that the relationships of business performance to output values, efficiency and price are heterogeneous. Additionally the effectiveness of resources is also heterogeneously related to output values, efficiency and price. What causes superior functional performance is potentially related to the imitability of the underlying tangible and intangible resources connected to some common orchestrating theme. This is a key area for future research. As Miller (1996) observes, "The quality of configuration can have important normative implications. The heart of distinctive competence and competitive advantage may lie not in possession of specific organisational resources or skills; these can usually be imitated or purchased by others. Rather competitive advantage may reside in the orchestrating theme and integrative mechanisms that ensure complementarity among a firm's various aspects" (p. 509).

This study has provided some evidence that the outcome of any such orchestrating theme is heterogeneous. In other words, the orchestrating theme has "favourites" when it comes to output values, efficiency, price and functions. These favourites are also not consistent across industries, though the principle of heterogeneity apparently is. What then are the policy implications of these findings?

The first implication is that firms need to identify, from among a potentially large number of output values, which of those values are most closely associated to business performance. In particular, these output values directly influence marketplace performance, i.e. total revenues and price levels. Consequently, executives attempting to enhance the revenue-generating capabilities of the firm need to focus (e.g., in their marketing, R&D and operations policies) on the relatively few output values which will generate superior performance.

The second area for policy is the need to develop an understanding of those areas of efficiency that will lower the cost base of the firm relative to output, i.e. the sources of productivity. For example, labour efficiency was shown to be important to the automotive components and logistics industries and less so for the financial services industries.

In conclusion, understanding the nature of the relationships of output values, efficiency and price to business performance and then using these relationships as prioritisation mechanisms for underlying resources may be a useful logic behind policy formulation.

## A Summary of This Study's Contribution

This study has made a contribution in three main areas, namely to the development of theory, which is predominantly confirmatory (though it also contains theory development elements), to the application of theory through greater understanding of four UK industries, and in the area of methodology.

In the first area of theory, this study has built on a rich heritage of work which stems from two major lines of investigation. These are the contingency and resource-based theories. This study has attempted to combine these two approaches into a more comprehensive theoretical model which acknowledges the explanatory strengths of both prior types. It has uniquely argued that a comprehensive theoretical model of the differences in firm performance must simultaneously include an outward and inward perspective. In addition, it has suggested that the theory must allow for the heterogeneous nature of relationships between the outward-looking variables and the inward-looking variables.

It is the combination of the contingency and resource theories along the dimensions of market orientation and heterogeneity which is the unique theoretical contribution of this study. In the process the theoretical model developed in this study provided the basis for confirmation of the prior theoretical approaches and the injection of an element of theory development.

The four UK industries chosen for this study have not been examined in relation to output values, efficiency, price and resources in a simultaneous way before. The findings of this study indicate that the nature of the relationships varies significantly between these industries and between the manufacturing and service sectors. This study has given rise to additional insights into the nature of these relationships in these UK industries. For example the role of innovation was highlighted for the financial services industry and the predominant nature of operations in the electronic components industry to customer responsiveness and efficiency.

In the area of methodology this study has made a contribution by using a range of triangulation methods in an attempt to ascertain the degree of reliability and validity of the measures used. This study has been largely confirmatory of the findings of prior studies with regard to the use of subjective measures (Dess & Robinson, 1984). While financial performance gave the best triangulation results when measured as ratios, absolute measures such as market share were the least reliable.

## Future Research

This research could be expanded in a number of ways. In the first instance the source of resource advantage could be sought. This study has suggested a priority list of output values, efficiency outcomes and underlying functions and resources, which could be the starting point. The research question could be "why are certain functions more effective in generating the required output value and efficiency performances?". What combinations of tangible and intangible resources facilitate this performance? In addition, what configuration and coordination mechanisms are used to facilitate high performance across functional boundaries?

Future research could look at confirming this study's findings by expanding the number of industries investigated in the UK and internationally. For example, do the same industries in the USA give the same priorities on output values and functions as in the UK? How important is the national environment as an intervening variable?

Additionally, the level of operationalisation of variables that make up the output values and efficiency could be extended. In this way a more sensitive picture of these industries could be constructed.

In conclusion, this study has provided a tested theoretical framework within which further advances in knowledge can be made by deepening the search for sources of superior competitive ability, and expanding this framework across industries and national boundaries.

## Acknowledgements

The author would like to thank the co-editors of this chapter, namely Patricia Gorman Clifford and Robert Nixon, for their invaluable comments.

Special thanks go to Surrey European Management School for supporting this research.

## References

Anderson, J. & Gerbing, D. (1988). Structural equation modeling in practice: A review and recommended two-step approach. *Psychological Bulletin*, **103**(3), 411–423.

Anderson, C. & Zeithaml, C. (1984). Stage of the product life cycle, business strategy, and business performance. *Academy of Management Journal*, **27**(1), 5–24.

Ansoff, I. (1987). The emerging paradigm of strategic behaviour. *Strategic Management Journal*, **8**, 501–515.

Bain, J.S. (1959). *Industrial Organisation*. New York: Wiley.

Banbury, C. & Mitchell, W. (1995). The effect of introducing important incremental innovations on market share and business survival. *Strategic Management Journal*, **16**, 161–182.

Barney, J. (1986). Strategic factor markets: Expectations, luck, and business strategy. *Management Science*, 1231–1241.

Barney, J. (1991). Firm resources and sustained competitive advantage. *Journal of Management*, **17**(1), 99–120.

Bart, V. & Habib, M. (1991). Strategy, structure, and performance of U.S. manufacturing and service MNCs: A comparative analysis. *Strategic Management Journal*, **12**, 589–606.

Bentler, P. & Bonnett, D. (1980). Significance tests and goodness of fit in the analysis of covariance structures. *Psychological Bulletin*, **88**, 588–606.

Berry, W., Hill, T. & Klompmaker, J. (1993). Customer-driven manufacturing. *International Journal of Operations and Production Management*, **15**, 4–16.

Bourgeois, L. (1985). Strategic goals, perceived uncertainty, and economic performance in volatile environments. *Academy of Management Journal*, **28**(3), 548–573.

Chandler, A.D. (1962). *Strategy and Structure: Chapters in the History of the American Industrial Enterprise*. Cambridge, MA: MIT Press.

Corsten, H. & Will, T. (1993). Reflections on competitive strategy and its impact on modern production concepts. *Management International Review*, **33**(4), 315–334.

Dean, J. & Snell, S. (1996). The strategic use of integrated manufacturing: An empirical examination. *Strategic Management Journal*, **17**, 459–480.

Dess, G., Ireland, R. & Hitt, M. (1970). Industry effects and strategic management research. *Journal of Management*, **16**(1), 7–27.

Dess, G. & Robinson, R. (1984). Measuring organisational performance in the absence of objective measures: The case of the privately held firm and conglomerate business unit. *Strategic Management Journal*, **5**, 265–273.

Dhalla, N. & Yuspeh, S. (1976). Forget the Product Life Cycle concept! *Harvard Business Review*, 102–112.

Donaldson, L. (1987). Strategy and structural adjustment to regain fit and performance: In defense of contingency theory. *Journal of Management Studies*, **24**(1), 1–24.

Fiegenbaum, A., Hart, S. & Schendel, D. (1996). Strategic reference point theory. *Strategic Management Journal*, **17**, 219–235.

Ghemawat, P. (1991). *Commitment: The Dynamic of Strategy*. New York: Free Press.

Grinyer, P., McKiernan, P. & Yasai-Ardekani, M. (1988). Market, managerial and organisational correlates of economic performance in the U.K. electrical engineering industry. *Strategic Management Journal*, **9**(4), 297–318.
Hambrick, D. (1983). Some tests of the effectiveness and functional attributes of the Miles and Snow's Strategic Types. *Academy of Management Journal*, **26**(1), 5–26.
Hambrick, D. & Lei, D. (1985). Toward an empirical prioritisation of contingency variables for business strategy. *Academy of Management Journal*. **28**(4), 763–788.
Hill, T. (1993) *Manufacturing Strategy*. Basingstoke: Macmillan.
Hitt, M. & Ireland, R. (1985). Corporate distinctive competence, strategy, industry and performance. *Strategic Management Journal*, **6**, 273–293.
Hitt, M. & Ireland, R. (1986). Relationships among corporate level distinctive competencies, diversification strategy, corporate structure and performance. *Journal of Management Studies*, **23**(4), 401–416.
Hitt, M., Ireland, R. & Stadter, G. (1982). Functional importance and company performance: moderating effects of grand strategy type. *Strategic Management Journal*, **3**, 315–330.
Hofer, C.W. (1975). Towards a contingency theory of business strategy. *Academy of Management Journal*, **18**, 784–810.
Kim, J. & Arnold, P. (1992). Manufacturing competence and business performance: A framework and empirical analysis. *International Journal of Operations and Production Management*, **13**(10), 4–25.
Kim, Y. & Campbell, N. (1995). Strategic control in Korean MNCs. *Management International Review*, **35**(1), 95–108.
Kotha, S. & Nair, A. (1995). Strategy and environment as determinants of performance: Evidence from the Japanese machine tool industry. *Strategic Management Journal*, **16**, 497–518.
Lawrence, P. & Lorsch, J. (1967). *Organization and Environment*. Boston, MA: Harvard University Press.
Lenz, R. (1980). Environment, strategy, organisation structure and performance: Patterns in one industry. *Strategic Management Journal*, **1**, 209–226.
Levitt, T. (1960). Marketing myopia. *Harvard Business Review*, 45–56.
Mason, E. (1939). Price and production policies of large-scale enterprise. *American Economic Review*, 61–74.
Mathur, S. (1988). How firms compete: A new classification of generic strategies. *Journal of General Management*, **14**(1), 30–57.
Mazen, A., Hemmasi, M. & Lewis, M. (1987). Assessment of statistical power in contemporary strategy research. *Strategic Management Journal*, **8**, 403–410.
McGrath, R., MacMillan, I. & Venkatraman, S. (1995). Defining and developing competence: A strategic process paradigm. *Strategic Management Journal*. **16**, 251–275.
Mehra, A. (1996). Resource and market based determinants of performance in the U.S. banking industry. *Strategic Management Journal*, **17**, 307–322.
Miller, D. (1986). Configuration of strategy and structure: Towards a synthesis. *Strategic Management Journal*. **7**, 233–249.
Miller, D. (1987a). Strategy making and structure: Analysis and implications for performance. *Academy of Management Journal*. **30**(1), 7–32.
Miller, D. (1987b). The structural and environmental correlates of business strategy. *Strategic Management Journal*, **8**, 55–76.
Miller, D. (1990). *The Icarus Paradox*. New York: Harper Business.
Miller, D. (1996). Configurations revisited. *Strategic Management Journal*, **17**, 505–512.
Miller, D. & Friesen, P. (1982). Structural change and performance: Quantum versus

piecemeal–incremental approaches. *Academy of Management Journal*, **25**(4), 867–892.

Miller, D. & Friesen, P. (1983). Strategy making and the environment: The third link. *Strategic Management Journal*, **4**, 221–235.

Mintzberg, H., Ahlstrand, B. & Lampel, J. (1998). *Strategy Safari*. Hemel Hempstead: Prentice Hall Europe.

Olshavsky, R., Aylesworth, A. & Kempf, D. (1995). The price–choice relationship: A contingent processing approach. *Journal of Business Research*, **33**, 207–218.

Peteraf, M. (1993). The cornerstones of competitive advantage: A resource based view. *Strategic Management Journal*, **14**, 179–191.

Porter, M. (1980). *Competitive Strategy*. New York: Free Press.

Porter, M. (1985). *Competitive Advantage*. New York: Free Press.

Porter, M. (1996). What is strategy? *Harvard Business Review*, 61–78.

Ramaswami, S., Flynn, E. & Nilakanta, S. (1993). Performance implications of congruence between product-market strategy and market structure: An exploratory investigation. *Journal of Strategic Marketing*, **1**, 71–92.

Rumelt, R. (1991). How much does industry matter?'' *Strategic Management Journal*, **12**, 167–185.

Scherer, F. (1970). *Industrial Market Structure and Economic Performance*, Chicago, IL: Rand McNally.

Selznick, P. (1952). *The Organisational Weapon*. New York: McGraw Hill.

Skinner, W. (1974). The focussed factory. *Harvard Business Review*, 113–121.

Snow, C. & Hrebiniak, L. (1980). Strategy, distinctive competence and organizational performance. *Administrative Science Quarterly*, **25**, 317–336.

Van de Ven, A. & Ferry, D. (1997). *Measuring and Assessing Organisations*, New York: Wiley.

Venkatraman, N. (1990). Performance implications of strategic coalignment: A methodological perspective. *Journal of Management Studies*, **27**(1), 20–41.

Venkatraman, N. & Prescott, J. (1990). Environment–strategy coalignment: An empirical test of its performance implications. *Strategic Management Journal*, **11**, 1–23.

Venkatraman, N., Henderson, J. & Oldach, S. (1993). Continuous strategic alignment: Exploiting information technology capabilities for competitive success. *European Management Journal*, **11**(2), 139–149.

Wernerfelt, B. (1984). A resource-based view of the firm. *Strategic Management Journal*. **5**, 171–180.

Wheelwright, S. (1984). Manufacturing strategy: Defining the missing link. *Strategic Management Journal*. **5**, 77–91.

# 7

# Does Sticking to the Knitting Unravel Your Corporate Reputation?

SUZANNE M. CARTER, WM. GERARD SANDERS

## INTRODUCTION

Organizational members often make key strategic decisions on behalf of the firm. These actions are scrutinized by a variety of corporate constituents including shareholders, competitors, consumers, and government agencies among others. Constituents evaluate and judge both these managerial actions as well as other firm attributes deemed relevant (for example, level of social responsibility, commitment to the environment, innovativeness) and in turn form their perceptions of the corporate reputation of the firm (Bromley, 1993). Corporate reputation has been argued to be an important intangible asset (Hall, 1993) with the capability of providing a sustainable competitive advantage (Barney, 1991).

We argue that key strategic actions affecting and relating to the firm's core competencies serve to signal constituents about key managerial decisions and thus have an influence on how constituents perceive the firm's reputation. Furthermore, we maintain that when management follows prescriptions and norms that are deemed appropriate in the business and academic press, constituents are more likely to perceive these actions positively and thus rate the organization's reputation favorably. We examine two corporate strategic actions, specifically acquisitions and divestitures, during a period when

*Dynamic Strategic Resources: Development, Diffusion and Integration.*
Edited by Michael A. Hitt, Patricia Gorman Clifford, Robert D. Nixon and Kevin P. Coyne.

academicians (Rumelt, 1974; Prahalad & Hamel, 1990) and the business press (e.g., *Fortune, Forbes, Business Week,* etc.) strongly emphasized the importance of maintaining a set of core competencies.

Both acquisitive and divestiture activities provide a substantial amount of information to constituents regarding the scope of the firm (e.g., the breadth of its product market activities) and overall corporate strategy. Acquisitions allow firms to move into additional markets or functions, often increasing the scope of the firm. In contrast, divestitures allow firms to decrease the number of markets or functions served, often reducing the scope of the firm. Because the business press typically provides significant information on these strategic actions, corporate constituents are able to monitor these decisions and judge management's ability to enhance the value of the firm through effective handling of its scope of activities. For example, constituents should be in a position to form an opinion about whether these strategic activities enhance or detract from the firm's core competencies and therefore the organization's current and potential value. To the extent that these actions alter perceptions of the firm, they should also be important to the overall reputation of the company. Thus, our study examines how acquisitions and divestitures affect a firm's reputation and whether any such consequences are moderated by contextual factors, such as the firm's diversification level and its recent performance level.

Understanding how strategic actions affect corporate reputation is important to both scholars and practitioners alike. Although most research concerning strategic actions such as acquisitions and divestitures examines how these actions influence firm profitability (Chang, 1996), outcome measures other than financial performance are relevant and have long-term consequences as well (Barney, 1991; Fombrun, 1996). Indeed, recent research has found that corporate reputation is considered by CEOs to be the most important intangible asset available to the firm (Hall, 1993), and one that must be protected in order to sustain its advantages. It thus becomes essential to be able to anticipate constituent reaction to such well-publicized strategic actions. Regardless of the intentions of management, when critical constituents judge the firm's strategic actions, these judgments may result in decisions by constituents that influence the company's stock price (Higgins & Bannister, 1992), product sales (Herbig & Milewicz, 1995), and other key outcomes of the firm (Higgins & Diffenbach, 1989). Because of the costly nature of acquisitions and divestitures, recognizing how key constituents judge the organization's reputation in response to these activities should be critical to making such strategic decisions. Thus, determining the relationship of acquisitions and divestments to other types of performance measures, such as reputation, should help us to further our understanding of the benefits and detriments of changing the scope of the firm.

We begin with a brief theoretical overview of past research examining reputation assessments, acquisitions and divestitures. We then turn to a theoretical development of our arguments and an empirical test of the hypothesized relationships. Discussion of results and implications for future research are then set forth.

## THEORETICAL BACKGROUND

Constituents are provided with a variety of cues to assess corporate reputation. This assessment includes interpreting signals received from market and accounting data, institutional arrangements and strategic actions (Fombrun & Shanley, 1990). Market and accounting data that can be interpreted include market performance, market risk, dividend policy, accounting profitability, and accounting risk. Institutional signals include social responsibility, press coverage, and institutional ownership. Finally, strategic actions that may be interpreted as signals include such moves as product differentiation, market entry and changes in diversification level. Corporate constituents are able to use these signals to monitor preoccupations of management and thus make judgments regarding the firm's future prospects (Fombrun & Shanley, 1990). We focus on how strategic actions (i.e. those involving significant resource commitments), specifically acquisitions and divestitures, may be viewed and interpreted as signals by corporate constituents. Our interest in studying strategic rather than tactical actions is that strategic actions represent significant commitments of resources and are difficult to both implement and reverse, whereas tactical actions involve fewer resources and are relatively easier to implement and reverse (Hitt, Ireland & Hoskisson, 1999). Thus, strategic actions are more likely to be judged carefully by constituents and thus be reflected in the organization's reputation. Past research has provided evidence that diversification decisions do influence financial performance. We extend that work and study whether, after controlling for the effects of firm financial performance, there is a strong residual effect on the reputation of the firm.

The strategic management literature describes the firm as possessing resources and capabilities that should be configured to endow the firm with distinctive competencies (Andrews, 1987; Barney, 1991; Wernerfelt, 1984). Moreover, this perspective assumes that firms can use diversification as a vehicle to leverage their resources and capabilities to achieve competitive advantage and improve long-term performance (Andrews, 1987; Donaldson & Lorsch, 1983; Hamel & Prahalad, 1994; Haspeslagh & Jemison, 1991; Porter, 1987). Acquisitions are one mechanism that can be used by firms to transfer resources and capabilities from one firm to another, thereby creating value through spreading valuable resources to multiple businesses. Although firms can diversify through internal development of new lines of businesses, acquisitions have become a popular means of diversifying (Haspeslagh & Jemison, 1991).

Excessive diversification, however, can dissipate value. Such excessive diversification became common during the 1960s and early 1970s. This increase was precipitated by at least two key forces. Antitrust laws were established to reduce the ability of organizations to gain power within one industry. Tough antitrust enforcement likely resulted in firms investing available resources in the acquisition of unrelated businesses (Ravenscraft & Scherer, 1987) that would not lead to antitrust agency conflicts. Additionally, the Capital Asset Pricing Model (CAPM) was a popular financial tool during this time that was perhaps inappropriately applied to managing a portfolio of businesses to reduce risk (Naylor & Tapon, 1982).

While highly diversified firms (i.e., conglomerates) were the craze of the 1960s and early 1970s, research from the mid-1970s to the 1990s suggested that returns from such diversification had real limits. Indeed, a growing number of studies found that too much diversification was suboptimal (Jensen, 1986; Montgomery, 1985; Palepu, 1985). In addition, Rumelt's (1974, 1982) seminal work suggested that firms that diversify around a related set of businesses were more likely to achieve high levels of performance than were those that diversified into unrelated businesses. Other studies found that high levels of diversification result in increased bureaucratic costs (Jones & Hill, 1988), the necessity for multiple competitive logics that often exceed executive comprehension (Prahalad & Bettis, 1986), and eventually the need to restructure the firm (Hoskisson & Johnson, 1992; Hoskisson & Turk, 1990; Johnson, 1996). Moreover, scholars began to criticize extensive acquisition activity as being routinely value destroying (Porter, 1987; Shleifer & Vishny, 1991) and as attempts to unwisely engage in too much diversification (Jensen, 1986; Ravenscraft & Scherer, 1987).

While evidence of the detriments of excessive diversification had been mounting for several years, Prahalad and Hamel (1990) brought many of these academic concerns to the attention of the popular press through their publication in the *Harvard Business Review* of "The core competence of the corporation". They argued that organizations would be well advised to avoid the risks associated with managing a set of unrelated businesses, and instead "stick to the knitting" by relying on a set of core competencies (Prahalad & Hamel, 1990). Publications such as *Forbes* and *Business Week*, among others, also discussed the disadvantages of acquisitions and the benefits of focusing on core businesses (*Corporate Board*, 1991; Loderer & Martin, 1990; Oneal & Bremmer, 1990; Phalon, 1990; Prokesch & Powell, 1985; Zweig, 1995), further disseminating many scholars' research evidence. Consequently, it is no surprise that diversification generally, and acquisitions specifically, came to be disfavored in the business press (Fombrun & Shanley, 1990). Concurrent with this disfavor of diversification, divestitures became a popular way for firms to increase the focus on their core businesses by shedding businesses that were peripheral (Hoskisson & Turk, 1990; Koretz, 1989; Markides, 1995).

## Development of Hypotheses

Acquisitions and divestitures are interesting strategic initiatives with which to study the effects of corporate strategy on firm reputation. These corporate actions are very common among large US firms. For instance, in the US alone there were approximately 8000 acquisitions and divestitures in 1997 (*Mergers & Acquisitions*, January 1998). Moreover, by their very nature, these transactions are risky (Haspeslagh & Jemison, 1991; Pablo, Sitkin & Jemison, 1996) and research indicates that acquisition performance varies significantly (Jensen & Ruback, 1983; Mueller, 1987; Ravenscraft & Scherer, 1987). Indeed, there are numerous inherent difficulties associated with completing acquisitions and divestitures. For example, the acquiring company must often deal with culture clashes, top management turnover, unrealistic expectations for success, and other potentially value-destroying issues (Haspeslagh & Jemison, 1991). Perhaps because they often fail, acquisitions tend to result in subsequent divestitures (Porter, 1987; Ravenscraft & Scherer, 1987). Divestitures, on the other hand, are generally associated with increases in shareholder wealth (Dial & Murphy, 1995; John & Ofek, 1995; Markides, 1995).

While it appears clear that since the mid 1970s both academicians and the business press have been espousing the benefits of sticking with a core set of competencies and not diversifying beyond that set, the question remains as to how acquisitions and divestitures have been assessed by corporate constituents. We believe that when firms make changes that are seen as following the appropriate recommendations that are ascribed to at that time, constituents may view these moves as strategically appropriate, and as a result, increase their judgments of the firm's overall reputation. Accordingly, when firms make highly publicized moves, such as acquisitions and divestitures, then the degree to which these organizations are seen as "making the right moves" should affect the corporation's reputation. Constituents monitor these decisions and base their perceptions of the appropriateness of actions on their knowledge of the advantages and disadvantages of each of these decisions. The business press may influence constituents' judgments through its coverage of these strategic moves. The volume of media attention devoted to the activities, the degree to which these moves are discussed as appropriate, and the

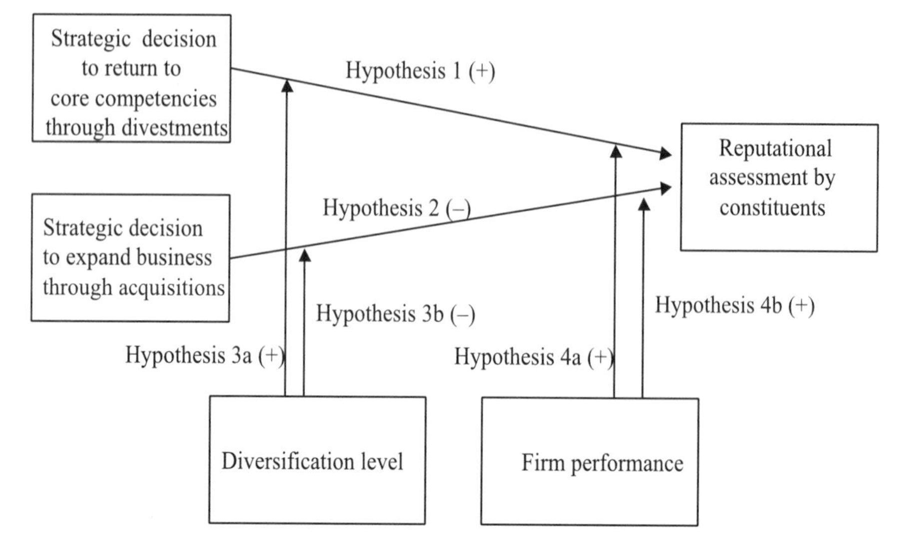


Fig 7.1 Hypothesized relationship between strategic actions and corporate reputation

tone and favorability of these moves as presented by the media may each influence constituents' views of these issues. Thus, the business press should significantly influence the constituents' views of whether the organization is making the appropriate decisions regarding the scope of the firm. FIGURE 7.1 illustrates our theoretical arguments that will be explored in detail below.

## DIVESTITURE ACTIVITY

Recent research has speculated that diversified firms generally improve performance when they divest of unrelated business units. John and Ofek (1995) studied large divestitures ($100 million plus) between 1986 and 1988 and found that performance increased more when divestitures were unrelated (different four-digit primary SIC code than the parent) than when related (*cf.* Comment & Jarrell, 1995). Additionally, Markides (1995) found that firms that were excessively diversified achieved higher levels of *ex-post* performance if they engaged in divestiture activities, suggesting that divestitures indeed add value to diversified firms by moving the firm closer to an optimum level of diversification. Dial and Murphy (1995) reported that even firms in declining industries have substantial opportunity for value creation through divestitures.

The business press has similarly added their support for "sticking to the knitting". Citing evidence from a survey conducted by economists at the University of Rochester, *Business Week* (Koretz, 1989) reported that firms whose restructuring involved focusing on core businesses were most likely to be successful. The article quoted Professor Gregg Jarrell as saying "The market's clear message is that it pays to concentrate on the few things you do best" (Koretz, 1989: 22). In a panel discussion of investment bankers, one representative was quoted as saying:

> There is basically a psychological component in merger and acquisition activity that is critically important. There has been a real question put on diversifying acquisitions. Compared with the average public company, conglomerates trade at a large discount. There is a real question mark as to the ability of managements to manage far-flung operations, and I think the companies that are focusing their activities and paring their activities are generally rewarded in terms of stock market valuation. (Quote from Lane as reported in *Mergers & Acquisitions*, 1993)

In sum, both the academic and business press have provided evidence that divestitures may be beneficial to the firm and are associated with increased firm performance. Because this argument has been espoused for over a decade, and evidence appears to have been disseminated widely, constituents are likely to be influenced by these findings and prescriptions, which in turn will affect their judgments of these strategic moves. We thus expect to see a positive relationship between divestitures and subsequent corporate reputation due to the widespread perception and empirical evidence that divestitures help the firm to focus on a core set of businesses. We hypothesize the following:

> Hypothesis 1: Firms that divest businesses will be perceived by constituents as attempting to focus on core activities, and thus, these actions will be associated with higher levels of subsequent corporate reputation.

## Acquisitions

Studies of the performance impact of acquisitions have generally found no gains, on average, to the acquiring firm, whether gains are assessed using market measures or accounting measures of performance. For example, in a synthesis of many studies of the effects of acquisitions on firm share price, Jensen and Ruback (1983) concluded that on average there is no positive association. In addition, studies by Ravenscraft and Scherer (1987) and Porter (1987) concluded that the effect of acquisitions on firm accounting profits is negative. Moreover, both of these studies found that acquisitions in one period lead to divestitures in later periods as firms attempt to correct ill-fated acquisitions (Porter, 1987; Ravenscraft & Scherer, 1987).

This research by scholars in the strategic management arena has been picked up by the business press and discussed in well-known media outlets, providing further evidence to practitioners and other business constituents that acquisitions are likely to be ineffective. For example, *Business Week* reported in 1985 that somewhere between a half and two-thirds of mergers do not work (Prokesch & Powell, 1985). Additionally, *Forbes* reported that diversifying into areas outside your experience might be dangerous (Phalon, 1990). *Business Week* also reported that "[The] historic surge of consolidations and combinations is occurring in the face of strong evidence that mergers and acquisitions, at least over the past 35 years or so, have hurt more than helped companies and shareholders .... The conglomerate deals of the 1960s and 1970s ... have since been thoroughly discredited, and most of these behemoths have been broken up" (Zweig, 1995: 122). Thus, given the findings of academic research demonstrating that acquisitions are generally value destroying (Jensen & Murphy, 1990) and widespread skepticism of such activity among the business press, we expect acquisitions to have a negative influence on subsequent reputation.[1]

> Hypothesis 2: Firms that acquire additional businesses will be perceived by constituents as reducing their emphasis on the core activities of the firm, and thus, these actions will be associated with lower levels of subsequent corporate reputation.

## Moderating Factors

We expect these relationships to be moderated by the firm's diversification level and recent performance. We will discuss each of these respectively.

### Diversification Level

A firm's prior level of diversification likely affects how constituents perceive divestitures and acquisitions. We argue that it is highly diversified firms that have the most to gain from divestitures (Markides, 1995). That is, highly diversified firms are more likely to have strayed from their core competencies than are more focused and integrated firms. Fombrun and Shanley (1990) found a negative relationship between unrelated diversification and subsequent corporate reputation, suggesting that constituents may not value organizations that have diversified beyond a set of core capabilities. Therefore, it is these firms that are most likely to receive reputational benefits from divestitures because these divestitures will likely reduce their excessive diversification level. Consequently, we expect that constituents will more highly value strategic decisions to divest among highly diversified firms than among those that are already rather focused in their diversification strategy. This would in turn result in greater reputational assessments for the highly diversified firms.

However, with respect to acquisitions, we would expect just the opposite. Because diversification is not highly valued by shareholders and financial analysts (Hoskisson & Turk, 1990), acquisitions should be more acceptable among focused firms than among diversified firms. Among focused firms, acquisitions may be rationalized as necessary expansion of market presence or attempts to secure important technology. However, among diversified firms acquisitions are likely to be characterized as further evidence of unnecessary diversification (*cf.* Fombrun & Shanley, 1990). That is, the greater the diversification level of the organization, the more negative we expect the relationship between acquisitions and corporate reputation to be.

In sum, a firm's diversification level may serve as a signal to corporate constituents, and may help constituents to assess the benefits of divestitures and acquisitions on the organization's reputation. In general, a firm that has a greater degree of diversification may be seen as in need of restructuring in order to return to its core competencies. Therefore, divestitures may be perceived as value-enhancing strategic decisions. Alternatively, acquisitions by a diversified firm may be signals that the firm is continuing to stray from its core competencies. Thus, it appears that diversification level may be a strong moderator of the relationships hypothesized above.

> Hypothesis 3a: The more extensive the level of diversification, the greater will be the positive relationship between divestitures and subsequent corporate reputation.
>
> Hypothesis 3b: The more extensive the level of diversification, the greater will be the negative relationship between acquisitions and subsequent corporate reputation.

### Recent Firm Performance

As implied in Figure 7.1, recent firm performance is also likely to serve a moderating role in the relationship between strategic actions and corporate reputation. While information and advice given by the academic and business press may play a significant role in helping constituents judge strategic actions, these constituents may view these actions differently depending on prior circumstances, such as previous financial performance. For example, past research has shown that when performance is particularly high or low, shareholders and other stakeholders routinely attribute that performance to the organization's top executives (Meindl, Ehrlich & Dukerich, 1985). That is, positive performance is often attributed to actions taken by the top management team rather than external circumstances beyond the control of management. Executives themselves tend to make similar attributions (Staw, McKechnie & Puffer, 1983; Salancik & Meindl, 1984). Similarly, poor performance is likely to increase shareholder scrutiny of the firm and the executive's role in such negative outcomes. We argue that when attributions regarding poor firm performance and the role executives played in such performance are strong, corporate strategic initiatives will be identified as further evidence of such a (perceived) causal link. Thus, when recent firm performance is poor, strategic actions such as divestitures and acquisitions are likely to be interpreted as signals of poor management. Alternatively, when performance is particularly good, executives benefit from the same tendency of stakeholders to attribute firm performance to managerial capabilities (Meindl, Ehrlich & Dukerich, 1985). Consequently, good recent performance is likely to result in stakeholders interpreting corporate strategic initiatives (e.g., divestitures and acquisitions) as signals that reinforce that attribution.

The implication of this attributional tendency is that constituents' assessments of the appropriateness of strategic actions are likely to be influenced not only by media coverage of these activities but also by the previous financial performance of the firm. The business press evidence that is provided to constituents regarding the appropriateness of acquisitions and divestitures may continue to affect constituents' views of the adequacy of these strategic decisions. However, we argue that with respect to both divestitures and acquisitions, it is likely that when recent performance is particularly good, attributional tendencies will encourage constituents to interpret these strategic decisions in a positive light. This is likely to result in an overall assessment of the strategic decision that is higher than it otherwise would be, due to the impact of the recent favorable performance of the firm. Alternatively, when recent performance is particularly poor, just the opposite attributions are likely. Again, constituents may be more likely to judge acquisition and divestiture activities undertaken by management more critically if the firm has had unfavorable firm performance recently, than had its performance been more favorable. Thus, while it is not clear whether these performance levels will completely counteract the evidence provided by academics and the media that "sticking to the knitting" is appropriate, it is still likely that performance will have at least a partially moderating influence on the organization's reputation. Thus:

> Hypothesis 4a: The higher the level of recent firm performance the greater will be the positive relationship between divestitures and subsequent corporate reputation.

> Hypothesis 4b: The higher the level of recent firm performance the more positive will be the relationship between acquisitions and subsequent corporate reputation.

## METHODOLOGY

### SAMPLE AND DATA

We drew our sample from the 1993 listing of *Fortune 500* firms. Information on corporate reputation was obtained from *Fortune*'s Most Admired survey. *Fortune* has surveyed experts regarding firm reputations of the *Fortune 500* firms in up to 32 industries from 1982 to the present. The *Fortune* survey, which has historically surveyed approximately 8000 executives, outside directors, and financial analysts, has been used in several cross-sectional academic studies to explore the determinants of corporate reputation (Fombrun & Shanley, 1990; McGuire, Sundgren & Schneeweis, 1988; Sobol & Farrelly, 1988). Data regarding acquisition and divestiture activity were collected from *Mergers & Acquisitions* (hereafter referred to as "the M&A database"). The M&A database contains information on all acquisitions and divestitures valued in excess of $5 000 000 made during this period, and was used to code acquisition and divestiture activity. This database also has the benefit of being the source for data in numerous previously published researches on acquisitions (Haunschild, 1993; Davis, Diekmann & Tinsely, 1994; Markides, 1995), which aids subsequent cross-study tests and comparisons. Executive ownership and board structure data were collected from firm proxy statements. Firm financial data were collected from Compustat. Combining these data gave us a sample size of 365 firms.

We lagged all independent and control variable data by one year. One year was chosen because it introduces causality into the model, but also limits the likelihood that exogenous factors affecting the process would go undetected. This one-year lag appears to be long enough for key corporate constituents to observe announcements of acquisitions and divestitures, analyze their appropriateness, and assess the consequences of these decisions on the firm's reputation. Similar lags were used by Fombrun and Shanley (1990) and Carter and Dukerich (1998).

## Measures

### Dependent Variable

Regarding *corporate reputation*, respondents of *Fortune*'s Most Admired survey are asked to rate only those firms in their own industry or economic sector (usually the ten largest companies in terms of sales for 32 industries). Eight attributes of reputation are used, and respondents rate the firms relative to their principal competitors on a scale of 0 to 10. These attributes include: (1) quality of management, (2) financial soundness, (3) quality of products or services, (4) ability to attract, develop, and keep talented people, (5) wise use of corporate assets, (6) value as long-term investment, (7) innovativeness, and (8) community and environmental responsibility. The scores of these eight attributes are then averaged to obtain an overall reputation score.

Brown and Perry (1994) argue that financial performance serves as a "halo" that surrounds the assessors of these reputations in the Most Admired survey. They conclude that removing this halo will provide clearer measures of the non-financial aspects of reputation. We employed the methodology used by Brown and Perry (1994), and removed the financial performance halo surrounding the reputation data. The halo-removed variable is a predicted measure of corporate reputation based on the residual determined after regressing the corporate reputation measure on a series of financial performance measures. The halo index was created using five financial and operating variables, computed as follows:

> Average return on assets (ROA, after tax) = $(\text{ROA}_{it} + \text{ROA}_{it-1} + \text{ROA}_{it-2})/3$; relative market to book value = market value/book value (firm) over market value/book value (industry); sales = natural logarithm of $\text{sales}_{it}$; growth = (percent change in $\text{sales}_t + \cdots +$ percent change in $\text{sales}_{t-2})/3$; and risk = long-term $\text{debt}_{it}/\text{equity}_{it}$. (Brown & Perry, 1994: 1350)

These financial performance measures were employed as independent variables in regression analyses on the *Fortune* attribute ratings. Coefficients generated in those regressions were used to calculate firm-specific residuals. These residuals, which represent the portion of the *Fortune* ratings not explained by prior financial performance, are the halo-removed ratings for the average rating, and are appropriate for use in research in which financial performance is also a variable of interest (Brown & Perry, 1994). The result is that the reputation data with the financial halo removed reported here should reflect factors other than financial performance. Additionally, utilizing this halo-removed measure reduces concerns for multicollinearity when entering the financial measure interactions into the equation. Finally, because respondents only reported reputation scores within their industry of expertise, these reputation measures were adjusted by industry as reported in *Fortune*, in order to adjust for the fact that some industries may be assessed higher than others. Sensitivity analysis found that similar industry adjustments for independent and control variables were unnecessary.

### Independent Variables

*Acquisition activity* was measured as the number of acquisitions completed during the previous three years. The number of acquisitions was determined by examining the M&A database for the number of transactions in which a firm acquired a controlling interest in another firm. *Divestiture activity* was measured as the number of divestitures during the previous three years. Divestitures were identified in the same manner as acquisitions. Both of these measures have been used previously by other researchers (Haunschild, 1993; Davis, Diekmann & Tinsley, 1994; Hitt *et al.*, 1996).

### Moderator Variables

*Diversification level* was measured using the entropy measure for total diversification (Palepu, 1985) such that $\text{diversification}_a = \Sigma\, P_{ia} \ln(1/P_{ia})$, where $P_{ia}$ is the proportion of a firm a's sales in business segment i. *Recent firm performance* was measured as total shareholder returns, defined as the sum of stock price gains plus dividends distributed during the prior year divided by the beginning stock price. Thus the measure captures the total gains to shareholder wealth during the period.

### Control Variables

*Firm size*, measured as the logarithm of firm sales, was included because it likely affects acquisition (Amburgey & Miner, 1992) and divestiture (John & Ofek, 1995) activity, as well as firm reputation (Fombrun & Shanley, 1990). A firm's financial condition may also affect how constituents perceive the reputation of the firm (Jensen, 1986; Hoskisson & Hitt, 1990; Fombrun & Shanley, 1990). To control for the capital structure of a firm, the *debt to equity ratio* was also included as a control (Jensen, 1986; Chatterjee & Wernerfelt, 1991). We included a second measure of firm performance (ROA) as a control in all models. ROA is a common measure of past performance in acquisition studies (Rumelt, 1974; Haunschild, 1993). Moreover, it was not highly correlated with *total return*, thus it does not pose problems of multicollinearity. Because vigilant board governance is assumed to enhance corporate performance (Jensen & Meckling, 1976), it may also improve

TABLE 7.1 Descriptive statistics[a]

| Variable | Mean | s.d. | 1 | 2 | 3 | 4 | 5 | 6 | 7 | 8 | 9 | 10 |
|---|---|---|---|---|---|---|---|---|---|---|---|---|
| Corporate reputation | 0.16 | 0.89 | | | | | | | | | | |
| Acquisition activity | 2.68 | 4.04 | .13 | | | | | | | | | |
| Divestiture activity | 0.55 | 0.92 | −.14 | −.08 | | | | | | | | |
| Diversification level | 0.71 | 0.52 | .08 | .32 | .11 | | | | | | | |
| Recent firm performance (%) | 19.20 | 20.60 | −.02 | −.04 | −.05 | .13 | | | | | | |
| Firm size (log) | 8.89 | 1.05 | .16 | .49 | .01 | .24 | .17 | | | | | |
| Debt-to-equity | 1.24 | 1.58 | −.21 | .42 | .12 | .19 | −.03 | .28 | | | | |
| ROA (%) | 5.45 | 6.69 | −.03 | −.16 | −.03 | −.23 | .21 | −.16 | −.36 | | | |
| Board outsiders | 0.78 | 0.10 | −.07 | −.03 | −.10 | .06 | .21 | .00 | .15 | −.06 | | |
| R&D intensity | 0.02 | 0.03 | .09 | .01 | .05 | .05 | .28 | .07 | −.20 | .47 | .02 | |
| CEO stock ownership (000) | 4006.00 | 16 024.00 | .06 | −.02 | −.12 | −.08 | .18 | .02 | −.07 | .17 | .05 | −.13 |

[a] Correlations greater than .13 and .10 are significant at $p < .01$ and $p < .05$, respectively.

the perceptions of corporate constituents. Therefore, we also included a measure of the proportion of board members who are outsiders (*board outsiders*), an indicator of how vigilant the board can be (Hoskisson & Turk, 1990).

*Research and development (R&D) intensity* has been shown to affect diversification activity (Chatterjee & Wernerfelt, 1991; Montgomery & Hariharan, 1991), and it may also affect the reputation of firms as perceived by key corporate constituents. Therefore, R&D intensity, measured as R&D spending divided by sales, was included as a control variable. Finally, the existence of appropriate financial incentives for the top executive can affect how constituents value the firm (Westphal & Zajac, 1998). Therefore, we included a control for *CEO stock ownership*, measured as the value of common shares owned by the CEO.

As previously mentioned, all independent and control variables were measured in the year prior to the measure of firm reputation. Because our measure of firm reputation is continuous, we used OLS regression to analyze the relationships hypothesized. TABLE 7.1 includes descriptive statistics of the variables.

## RESULTS

TABLE 7.2 summarizes our results. Control variables were entered in model 1, and the two main effects (acquisition and divestiture activity) were entered in model 2. Our findings suggest that there is indeed a strong relationship between corporate strategy and firm reputation and the addition of these variables was a significant improvement over the control model (change in $R^2 = .03$; $p < .01$). However, as reported in model 2, the results were contrary to hypotheses 1 and 2. Specifically, even after controlling for other factors including financial performance, divestitures were negatively associated with subsequent corporate reputation ($p < .05$), whereas acquisitions were positively associated with subsequent corporate reputation ($p < .01$).

As indicated in models 3 and 4, the relationships between corporate strategy (e.g., divestitures and acquisitions) and reputation were moderated by firm diversification level and recent firm performance (change in $R^2 = .04$, $p < .01$; change in $R^2 = .12$, $p < .001$ respectively). As reported in model 3, diversification level positively moderated the effects of both divestitures ($p < .05$) and acquisitions ($p < .05$) on firm reputation, giving support to H3a but contradicting H3b. As predicted in H4a and H4b, model 4 reports that recent firm performance had the expected positive moderating effect on the relationship between both divestitures ($p < .10$) and acquisitions ($p < .001$) on corporate reputation.

TABLE 7.2 Effects of corporate strategy on subsequent firm reputation[a]

| Independent variables | Model 1 | Model 2 | Model 3 | Model 4 |
|---|---|---|---|---|
| Divestiture activity | | −.10* (.05) | −.10* (.05) | −.11* (.05) |
| × diversification level | | | .15* (.09) | |
| × recent firm performance | | | | .002† (.001) |
| Acquisition activity | | .03** (.01) | .01 (.01) | .05*** (.01) |
| × diversification level | | | .03* (.01) | |
| × recent firm performance | | | | .004*** (.001) |
| Diversification level | .14 (.09) | .09 (.09) | .06 (.09) | .01 (.09) |
| Recent firm performance | −.002 (.002) | −.003 (.002) | −.003 (.002) | −.001 (.002) |
| Firm size (log) | .19*** (.05) | .13*** (.05) | .14*** (.05) | .16*** (.05) |
| Debt-to-equity | −1.80*** (.31) | −1.92*** (.33) | −1.77*** (.35) | −2.09*** (.33) |
| ROA (%) | −.01 (.01) | −.02* (.01) | −.02* (.01) | −.03** (.01) |
| Board outsiders | −.24 (.46) | −.31 (.46) | −.38 (.46) | −.31 (.44) |
| R&D intensity | 3.36* (1.82) | 3.47* (1.81) | 3.31* (1.81) | 5.55** (1.75) |
| CEO stock ownership (000) | .04 (.03) | .05 (.03) | .04 (.03) | .05* (.02) |
| Intercept | −1.15* (.55) | −.55 (.56) | −.52 (.57) | −.86 (.55) |
| Adjusted R-square | .10 | .13** | .14** | .22*** |
| Change in adjusted R-square | | .03 | .04 | .12 |

[a] Unstandardized regression coefficients; standard errors shown in parentheses. Significance levels:
† $p < .10$
* $p < .05$
** $p < .01$
*** $p < .001$.

## Post Hoc Analysis

One issue that we wanted to explore in greater depth was the possibility that the degree of relatedness of the acquisition or divestiture had a significant impact on constituents' judgments as to the appropriateness of the strategic action. In order to test for this possibility empirically, we checked to see what proportion of the acquisitions and divestitures in our sample were "related". We found that 76% of acquisitions were so classified while 77% of divestitures were "unrelated". In a sensitivity analysis, our results indicated that when we control for the type of acquisition or divestiture in our models, the results are materially the same as those reported above. Thus, it appears that relatedness of the acquisition or divestiture did not significantly influence our results. We now turn to a discussion of the complex pattern of results in the context of theory. Implications of our study on future research are also set forth.

## Discussion

It was argued here that management teams that adhere to prescriptions espoused by academicians and the business press should have higher levels of corporate reputation than those that deviate from such prescriptions. Surprisingly, our results found that when organizations followed the prescribed advice of the 1980s and 1990s to divest of businesses and limit acquisitions in order to maintain a set of core competencies as suggested by both academics and the business press, constituents rated these firms' reputations lower rather than higher. Specifically, we found evidence of a negative relationship between divestitures and subsequent reputation, and a positive relationship between acquisitions and subsequent reputation—even after controlling for previous levels of performance. We did find, however, that both level of diversification and recent financial performance influenced these relationships and, with only one exception, these results were in the predicted direction. Even so, there was considerable evidence that constituents judge firms' acquisitive and divestiture behavior differently than might be expected based on prior evidence as to the effectiveness of these diversification moves.

Our unexpected results suggest either that some important external constituents have not yet been convinced of the arguments by academics and business press regarding the effects of divestitures and acquisitions or that they have a somewhat different interpretation of these constructs and their effects than what is generally believed. This decoupling of theoretical and anecdotal prescriptions from constituent reaction has some precedent. Indeed, recent studies have noted that during the 1960s the stock market reacted positively to diversifying acquisitions, which further encouraged firms to diversify beyond their core competencies (Morck, Shleifer & Vishny, 1990). However, just the fact that the market's initial reaction encouraged further conglomerate activity did not mean that this activity was appropriate. As Shleifer and Vishny (1991: 58) suggested, "the mistaken market enthusiasm about particular events such as conglomerate mergers is a commonplace equilibrium occurrence in financial markets. The fact that the market thought that conglomerates were a good idea does not mean that they were". Although the market overall now seems to discount the price of firms that engage in acquisitions while rewarding those that engage in divestitures, corporate reputations do not seem to follow this pattern. Rather, our results indicate that firms engaging in acquisitions have higher subsequent reputations, while those engaging in divestitures have lower subsequent reputations. While it may appear that constituents are not convinced of the advice given by the business and scholarly press, it is likely that these constituents are taking other issues into consideration as well. Further evidence uncovered in our study may provide possible explanations for these conflicting results. We discuss these findings and their possible implications below.

Why should we have found such contradictory results? It could be that as far as individuals' perceptions (which is what constitutes corporate reputation) are concerned, acquisitions are seen as more proactive and positive while divestitures are viewed as admissions of prior failures regardless of the firm's change in scope. The strategic initiative of acquisitions may therefore be rewarded with higher levels of reputation while divestitures are penalized with lower levels of reputation. In addition, research suggests that the types of acquisitions taking place today are categorically different than in decades past. Specifically, acquisitions tend to be more related to the core business than they were in earlier decades (Davis, Diekmann & Tinsley, 1994). Thus acquisitions may be viewed as proactive expansion within an area of expertise.

Moreover, it certainly appears that it is important to look to contextual factors such as diversification level and recent performance when examining the influence of corporate strategy decisions on corporate reputation. Indeed, the results for our moderator variables support these conjectures. First, for both acquisitions and divestitures, diversification level positively moderated the relationship with reputation. That is, the greater the level of diversification the firm possesses, the higher constituents rated reputation in relation to acquisition and divestiture activities. It is possible that diversified firms may be viewed as possessing critical skills that enable them to create long-term value through both acquisitions and divestitures. As such, constituents may perceive these firms as portfolios of businesses that can be managed much like portfolios of individual investments. Thus, for diversified firms, acquisitions and divestitures may be viewed as natural and even necessary in the normal course of business. Recent research by Singh and Zollo (1997) supports the idea that some firms have particular skill at carrying out acquisitions. On the other hand, firms that are less diversified may be viewed as lacking the skills necessary to make such portfolio changes. Thus when determining corporate reputations, constituents may be more inclined to perceive that managers of highly diversified firms can better manage the difficulties associated with acquisitions and divestitures than can managers of less diversified enterprises.

The effects for recent firm performance likewise suggest that the perceived appropriateness of acquisition and divestiture activity is subject to firm context. Specifically, as past research has suggested, constituents often attribute recent positive performance to managerial talent. As a result, these constituents appear to be more likely to positively view acquisition and divestiture moves made by highly performing firms. Similar (but negative) attributions may be made for poorly performing firms. We believe that these attributional tendencies are not limited to the outcome variable (e.g., performance), but also to visible strategic initiatives sponsored by top executives. And indeed, our results provide evidence of this. Consequently, among poorly performing firms, strategic initiatives such as divestitures and acquisitions appear to be perceived negatively. These actions may be interpreted as further evidence of poor management. Furthermore, constituents may interpret decisions by these poorly performing firms as signals by management of the need to break with past strategies. That is, it may appear that management is admitting to failure regarding its past corporate strategy. However, among firms with good recent performance, just the opposite occurs. Strategic initiatives seem to be interpreted as confirmatory signals of quality management. Our results show that favorable performance seems to encourage constituents to view both acquisition and divestiture activity in a more positive light than might otherwise occur.

An important issue that this research partially addresses is the link between acquisitions and CEO status. Mueller (1987) argued that since there is little correlation between growth by acquisition and firm performance, but there is a significant association between firm size and executives' personal benefits, managers probably cause their firms to expand via acquisitions in order to achieve the personal benefits of increased *status* and pay. Our results actually provide a partial test of this speculation by examining how acquisition activity actually affects the corporate reputation of the firm. Previous research has noted that the reputation of the firm and the reputation of the managers of that firm are inextricably linked (Carter & Dukerich, 1998; Dutton, Dukerich & Harquail, 1994). Thus, improving the organization's reputation is bound to have a positive effect on the manager's individual status—and one way management can do this appears to be through acquisitive activity.

It is important to note that our research examined the judgments and perceptions of only one set of constituents relevant to the organization. The data on corporate reputation were collected from industry experts and financial analysts within the industry. While it is very likely that the respondents that typically complete the *Fortune* survey are deemed critical constituents by the organization, there is a possibility that the actions taken by the organization may not actually be aimed towards enhancing the reputation in the eyes of these particular constituents. However, it is likely that management does, at the very least, partially signal its intentions to these particular constituents. Moreover, many other constituents look to these experts to help them to assess an organization's success. Finally, it is important to note that this study only examined the largest firms in the *Fortune 500*. It is possible that the effects of divestitures and acquisitions on reputation may be different for smaller organizations not studied here. Smaller firms are not followed as diligently and broadly by financial analysts or the media and therefore may not receive the same scrutiny regarding specific strategic actions.

## IMPLICATIONS

There are several implications for scholars and practicing managers based on our study. First, the main effect for divestiture activity has important implications for organizations. Although scholars have previously espoused the benefits of divestitures on financial performance, they have often failed to consider how these moves may ultimately influence other measures of firm performance—such as corporate reputation. We now have evidence that constituents are not likely to view these moves in a positive light, unless there are contextual factors that encourage the constituents to attribute these strategic actions to superior managerial decision making or capabilities inherent within the ongoing diversification level of the organization. In as much as divestitures have been and appear to continue to be very popular strategic actions, firms must find ways to communicate the positive results of divestitures if they are going to attempt to restructure and simultaneously maintain their previous reputation levels. As organizational members attempt to be proactive as well as responsive to their environment, it is critical that they communicate their reasoning behind their divestiture activities.

Practicing managers and scholars alike should be careful to recognize that the firm's previous diversification level and financial performance will likely affect how constituents view acquisitions and divestitures. In other words, not all acquisitions and divestitures are alike. While some conglomerates may be able to retain their reputational status through many acquisition and divestiture actions, other more focused firms may have a more difficult time convincing constituents that they have the capabilities to manage changes in the scope of the firm. Furthermore, a highly performing firm may be no more likely to benefit financially from a single strategic initiative than a poorly performing firm, but our results suggest that constituents are likely to perceive that they are. Therefore, prescriptive advice regarding corporate strategic decisions without considering the characteristics of the organization is likely to be detrimental to the firm's reputation.

This study also has implications for research on acquisitions and divestitures. While there have been a great number of empirical studies examining the impact of diversification decisions on financial performance, it is important to begin to examine the influence of these decisions on firm outcomes other than financial performance. We found evidence that the influence of these decisions on corporate reputation differs from that on financial performance. As managers attempt to meet performance goals on a number of different dimensions, it is critical to be able to anticipate how certain strategic actions may influence these measures. Scholars can contribute to practicing managers' understanding of these issues by including other key performance dimensions, such as corporate reputation, in their studies.

This research also suggests that scholars and practitioners rethink how the idea of core competency is applied to acquisitions and divestitures. Prahalad and Hamel (1990) are quite specific in their view that scholars and practitioners often mistake core products for core competencies. Using archival measures of diversification and relatedness makes the misclassification of acquisitions and divestitures easy to do (*cf.* Robins & Wiersema, 1995). For example, researchers can easily classify a divested division as unrelated when in fact it possessed skills that were critical to the core competence of the firm. Moreover, business reporters and shareholders might also make similar misclassifications. Relying exclusively on current market and accounting returns, which are often positive, as evidence that divestitures are beneficial may be shortsighted in the same way that the markets' positive evaluations of conglomerate mergers during the 1960s was (Shleifer & Vishny, 1991). Prahalad and Hamel observe that some divestitures effectively cut off competencies (even core competencies) of firms that could lead to future positions of competitive advantage. Thus, another interpretation of our results could be that corporate constituents downgrade firms for divestitures because engaging in such activity can at times purge the firm of valuable resources and competencies.

## Conclusion

The surprising results reported here suggest that constituents may view proactive acquisitive behavior as value enhancing and, as a result, reward the organization with a higher level of reputation for this strategic activity. Additionally, these same constituents may view divestiture activity in a negative light and thus assess subsequent corporate reputation negatively. Both diversification level and firm performance have strong moderating relationships to these assessments, suggesting that constituents do not view all firms as equally likely to be able to manage the inherent difficulties associated with making changes to the diversification level of the organization. Unraveling the complexities of how diversification moves influence alternative performance measures such as reputation is an important step in our understanding of the influence of strategic actions on firm performance.

## Note

1. As noted by one of the editors, the processes described in the first two hypotheses could depend on the type of acquisition (i.e., relatedness). We explore this issue in a sensitivity analysis that is reported in the Results section.

## References

Amburgey, T.L. & Miner, A.S. (1992). Strategic momentum: The effects of repetitive momentum on merger activity. *Strategic Management Journal*, **13**, 335–348.

Andrews, K.R. (1987). *The Concept of Corporate Strategy*. Homewood, IL: Irwin.

Barney, J. (1991). Firm resources and sustained competitive advantage. *Journal of Management*, **17**(1), 99–120.

Bromley, D.B. (1993). *Reputation, Image, and Impression Management*. Chichester: Wiley.

Brown, B. & Perry, S. (1994). Removing the financial performance halo from Fortune's "Most Admired" companies. *Academy of Management Journal*, **37**(5), 1347–1359.

Carter, S. & Dukerich, J. (1998). Corporate responses to changes in reputation. *Corporate Reputation Review*, **1**(3), 250–270.

Chang, S. (1996). An evolutionary perspective on diversification and corporate restructuring: Entry, exit, and economic performance during 1981–89. *Strategic Management Journal*, **17**, 587–611.

Chatterjee, S. & Wernerfelt, B. (1991). The link between resources and type of diversification: Theory and evidence. *Strategic Management Journal*, **12**, 33–48.

Comment, R. & Jarrell, G.A. (1995). Corporate focus and stock returns. *Journal of Financial Economics*, **37**, 67–87.

*Corporate Board* (1991). Quantity and value of mergers and acquisitions activity goes down. *Corporate Board*, March/April, **12**(67), 28, 2p.

Davis, G.F., Diekmann, K.A. & Tinsley, C.H. (1994). The decline of the conglomerate firm in the 1980s: The deinstitutionalization of an organizational form. *American Sociological Review*, **59**, 547–570.
Dial, J. & Murphy, K.J. (1995). Incentives, downsizing, and value creation at General Dynamics. *Journal of Financial Economics*, **37**, 261–314.
Donaldson, G. & Lorsch, J.W. (1983). *Decision Making at the Top*. New York: Basic Books.
Dutton, J., Dukerich, J. & Harquail, C. (1994). Organizational images and member identification. *Administrative Science Quarterly*, **39**, 239–263.
Fombrun, C. (1996). *Reputation: Realizing Value from the Corporate Image*. Boston, MA: Harvard Business School Press.
Fombrun, C. & Shanley, M. (1990). What's in a name? Reputation building and corporate strategy. *Academy of Management Journal*, **33**(2), 233–258.
*Fortune* (1989–1992). Most admired corporations.
Hall, R. (1993). A framework linking intangible resources and capabilities to sustainable competitive advantage. *Strategic Management Journal*, **14**, 607–618.
Hamel, G. & Prahalad, C.K. (1994). Competing for the future. *Harvard Business Review*, July–August, 122–128.
Haspeslagh, P. & Jemison, D.B. (1991). *Managing Acquisitions: Creating Value through Corporate Renewal*. New York: Free Press.
Haunschild, P.R. (1993). Interorganizational imitation: The impact of interlock on corporate acquisition activity. *Administrative Science Quarterly*, **38**, 564–592.
Herbig, P. & Milewicz, J. (1995). The relationship of reputation and credibility to brand success. *Journal of Consumer Marketing*, **12**(4), 5–10.
Higgins, R. & Bannister, B. (1992). How corporate communication of strategy affects share price. *Long Range Planning*, **25**, 27–35.
Higgins, R. & Diffenbach, J. (1989). Communicating corporate strategy—the payoffs and the risks. *Long Range Planning*, **22**, 133–139.
Hitt, M., Ireland, R. & Hoskisson, R. (1999). *Strategic Management: Competitiveness and Globalization*. Cincinnati, OH: Southwestern.
Hitt, M., Hoskisson, R., Johnson, R. & Moesel, D. (1996). The market for corporate control and firm innovation. *Academy of Management Journal*, 1084–1119.
Hoskisson, R. & Johnson, R. (1992). Corporate restructuring and strategic change: The effect on diversification strategy and R&D intensity. *Strategic Management Journal*, **13**, 625–634.
Hoskisson, R. & Turk, T. (1990). Corporate restructuring: Governance and control limits of the internal capital market. *Academy of Management Review*, **15**, 459–477.
Jensen, M.C. (1986). Agency costs of free cash flow, corporate finance and takeovers. *American Economic Review*, **76**, 323–329.
Jensen, M.C. & Meckling, W.H. (1976). Theory of the firm: Managerial behavior, agency costs and ownership structure. *Journal of Financial Economics*, **3**, 305–360.
Jensen, M.C. & Murphy, K.J. (1990). CEO incentives: It's not how much you pay, but how. *Harvard Business Review*, May–June, 138–153.
Jensen, M.C. & Ruback, R.S. (1983). The market for corporate control: The scientific evidence. *Journal of Financial Economics*, **11**, 5–50.
John, K. & Ofek, E. (1995). Asset sales and increase in focus. *Journal of Financial Economics*, **37**, 105–126.
Johnson, R. (1996). Antecedents and outcomes of corporate refocusing. *Journal of Management*, **22**, 439–483.
Jones, G. & Hill, C. (1988). Transaction cost analysis of strategy–structure choice. *Strategic Management Journal*, **9**, 159–172.

Koretz, G. (1989). Going back to basics seems to be a smart move. *Business Week*, 20 November, 22.
Loderer, C. & Martin, K. (1990). Corporate acquisitions by listed firms: The experience of a comprehensive sample. *Financial Management*, Winter, **19**(4). 17 p.
Markides, C. (1995). Diversification, restructuring and economic performance. *Strategic Management Journal*, **16**, 101–118.
McGuire, J., Sundgren, A. & Schneeweis, T. (1988). Corporate social responsibility and firm financial performance. *Academy of Management Journal*, **31**(4), 854–872.
Meindl, J., Ehrlich, S. & Dukerich, J. (1985). The romance of leadership. *Administrative Science Quarterly*, **30**, 78–102.
*Mergers & Acquisitions* (1993). Will perkier economy stimulate more dealmaking in 1993? *Mergers & Acquisitions*, Jan–Feb., **27**(4), 14 (9).
Montgomery, C. (1985). Product-market diversification and market power. *Academy of Management Journal*, **9**, 789–798.
Montgomery, C.A. & Hariharan, S. (1991). Diversified expansion in large established firms. *Journal of Economic Behavior and Organization*, **15**, 71–89.
Morck, R., Shleifer, A. & Vishny, R. (1990). Do managerial objectives drive bad acquisitions? *Journal of Finance*, **45**, 31–47.
Mueller, D.C. (1987). *The Corporation: Growth, Diversification and Mergers*. New York: Harwood Academic Publishers.
Naylor, T. & Tapon, F. (1982). The capital asset pricing model: An evaluation of its potential as a strategic planning tool. *Management Science*, **10**, 1166–1173.
Oneal, M. & Bremner, B. (1990). The best and worst deals of the '80s. *Business Week*, 15 January, Issue 3141, 52, 5p.
Pablo, A.L., Sitkin, S.B. & Jemison, D.B. (1996). Acquisition decision-making processes: The central role of risk. *Journal of Management*, **22**, 723–740.
Palepu, K. (1985). Diversification strategy, profit performance, and the entropy measure. *Strategic Management Journal*, **6**, 239–255.
Phalon, R. (1990). The dangers of diversifying. *Forbes*, **146**(2), 60, 2p.
Porter, M. (1987). From competitive advantage to corporate strategy. *Harvard Business Review*, May/June, 43–60.
Prahalad, C.K. & Bettis, R. (1986). The Dominant logic. *Strategic Management Journal*, **7**, 485–501.
Prahalad, C.K. & Hamel, G. (1990). The core competence of the corporation. *Harvard Business Review*, **68**, 79–91.
Prokesch, S. & Powell, W. (1985). Do mergers really work? *Business Week*, 3 June, 88.
Ravenscraft, D. & Scherer, F.M. (1987). *Mergers, Sell-offs, and Economic Efficiency*. Washington, DC: Brookings Institution.
Robins, J. & Wiersema, M.F. (1995). A resource-based approach to the multibusiness firm: Empirical analysis of portfolio interrelationships and corporate financial performance. *Strategic Management Journal*, **16**, 277–300.
Rumelt, R.P. (1974). *Strategy, Structure, and Economic Performance*. Boston, MA: Division of Research, Graduate School of Business Administration, Harvard University.
Rumelt, R. (1982). Diversification, strategy and profitability. *Strategic Management Journal*, **3**, 359–369.
Salancik, G. & Meindl, J. (1984). Corporate attributions as strategic illusions of management control. *Administrative Science Quarterly*, **29**, 238–254.
Shleifer, A. & Vishny, R. (1991). Takeovers in the '60's and the '80's: Evidence and implications. *Strategic Management Journal*, Winter Special Issue, **12**, 51–59.
Singh, H. & Zollo, M. (1997). *Learning to acquire: Knowledge accumulation mechanisms*

*and the evolution of post-acquisition integration strategies.* Working paper, The Wharton School, University of Pennsylvania, Philadelphia, PA.

Sobol, M. & Farrelly, G. (1988). Corporate reputation: A function of relative size or financial performance? *Review of Business and Economic Research*, **24**(1), 45–59.

Staw, B., McKechnie, P. & Puffer, S. (1983). The justification of organizational performance. *Administrative Science Quarterly*, **28**, 582–600.

Wernerfelt, B. (1984). A resource based view of the firm. *Strategic Management Journal*, **5**, 171–180.

Westphal, J.D. & Zajac, E.J. (1998). The symbolic management of stockholders: Corporate governance reforms and shareholder reactions. *Administrative Science Quarterly*, **43**, 127–153.

Zweig, P. (1995). The case against mergers: Even in the '90s, most still fail to deliver. *Business Week*, 30 October, 122–130.

# 8

# Getting There by Lurches: The Rugged Road to Globalization

Paola Dubini, Ian C. MacMillan

## Introduction

Several elements indicate that the competitive landscapes on which companies compete increasingly show common characteristics. Political and institutional boundaries among countries are harmonizing, creating regions with high levels of interregional trade (United Nations, 1991); societies and lifestyles evolve toward similar patterns, leading to global homogenization of market structures (Vicari, 1989); industry structure increasingly allows companies to exploit economies of scale at the international level (Kobrin, 1991). The development and diffusion of communication networks facilitate the homogenization of market behavior, while reducing costs for companies associated with the growth of their international scope (Di Bernardo, Rullani & Vaccà, 1986). Globalization is thus seen as an inevitable result of international market development (Hawrylyshin, 1981), affecting industry dynamics as well as company behavior.

Similarly, discourse on the dynamics of global strategy for individual firms implies a progression toward full internationalization. Vernon (1966) ties the way a firm becomes global to the milestones in product life cycle (new, maturing, standardized). Johanson and Vahlne (1977, 1990) suggest a

*Dynamic Strategic Resources: Development, Diffusion and Integration.*
Edited by Michael A. Hitt, Patricia Gorman Clifford, Robert D. Nixon and Kevin P. Coyne.

progressive process in which firms accumulate experience in various countries and thereby are encouraged to further invest in those countries. This perspective holds that because the environment tends to a global state and because firms attempt to develop fit between their strategy and the environment (Andrews, 1971), companies will progressively have to adopt a global strategy, and to develop appropriate mechanisms to coordinate highly dispersed activities (Bartlett & Ghoshal, 1991). So companies operating in a global industry must eventually choose between seeking to become one of the dominant global players—secure in their dominance from any smaller player unless a technological discontinuity occurs—or being local and specialized. Companies stuck in the middle (Porter, 1980) will be either too small to exploit economies of scale or too big to be flexible enough or fast enough to tackle new opportunities in niche markets and will ultimately die. The rush of SGS-Thomson to become a "solid member of the top ten group" in the semiconductor industry is based on its perception that the industry is moving rapidly to a global consolidation phase in which survival requires reaching a significant critical mass.

The implication of extant theories on companies' global strategies is consistent with a view of globalization as a linear and irreversible path. In multidomestic industries, i.e. in industries in which competition in any local portion of the competitive landscape is independent from the competitive dynamics occurring in other portions of the competitive landscape, companies should manage their international activities as a portfolio (Porter, 1986). In these types of industries, the decision to increase its international scope is one of the options open to the company and not a necessity, as in the case of global industries. In global industries, the company's competitive results in a local portion of the competitive landscape are affected by the company's position in other local landscapes. As local portions of the competitive landscape tend to homogenize and the competitive environment in which the companies operate experiences a progressive increase in geographic scope (Rispoli, 1994), companies are irreversibly forced to adopt a global strategy, that is to say, to become ever more involved in economic activity in a growing number of countries (Welch & Loustarinen, 1988; Morrison, 1990) and to gradually increase the percentage of their activities within their value chains in those countries (Porter, 1985, 1986). In this view, a hybrid industry (that is, an industry in which, according to Porter's definition, both barriers and pressures to globalization are high) is just a transitory phase toward a global state.

However, if we look at the process from the point of view of individual companies struggling to pursue a global strategy (Baden-Fuller & Stopford, 1991), we see indications that contradict the assumption of progressive and irreversible movement, due to the role of the ruggedness of local competitive landscapes in affecting the process. Local ruggedness derives from the diversity of national markets, leading to a high variety of demand characteristics and competitive structures (Abrahamson & Fombrun, 1994; Miller & Chen, 1994, 1996), from specific distribution channels and from institutional as well as political barriers to the successful implementation of global strategies (Porter, 1986). More important, what movement does take place has highly idiosyncratic implications for the strategists of the firms involved, making the assessment of the possible alternative directions a crucial element in the development of global strategy (Manaresi, 1997). In this chapter, we use an extension of Baden-Fuller and Stopford's (1991) study of the major appliance industry to argue that the globalization process is far from orderly. From the point of view of the individual firm—as it copes with its path dependencies and attends to the dual-level problem of achieving fit in each local landscape while building fit globally—the process is highly idiosyncratic and depends deeply on specific facets of ruggedness in the local market landscapes that it serves. The problem for strategists is therefore to identify what features and characteristics of rugged local landscapes influence the ability of the firm to advance both local and global fit in the face of ever-evolving landscapes and the moves of competitors therein. In the following sections, we examine the issue of ruggedness of local competitive landscapes, the need for the companies to develop idiosyncratic competencies to maximise fit at the local level, and the difficulties associated with transfer of competencies across landscapes that in turn are experiencing structural changes.

## Global Strategy as a Problem of Dual Levels of Strategic Fit

In this chapter we look at globalization as a process of episodic adaptations to a series of evolving rugged landscapes (Levinthal, 1997). We suggest that global strategy for a specific firm is an evolutionary process of orchestrating fit at dual levels, simultaneous development of local fit within the local landscapes in which it competes, and global fit across the local landscapes. At any given time, every local landscape is characterized by a specific configuration of industry chains (Porter, 1985). Individual companies identify the specific activities they want to directly control as a way to maximize their share of contribution to the end-user value. In their choice of activity configuration, companies determine the variety of value-creating systems in which they can participate (Parolini, 1996). As the control of specific activities implies the creation of appropriate competencies to outperform competitors within the land-scape, this sets in place over time path-dependent competencies, a specific knowledge base (Cohen & Levinthal, 1990), idiosyncratic paradigms and trajectories (Nelson & Winter, 1982) and organizational routines (Barkema *et al.*, 1997) that can lever or inhibit the evolving global strategic fit. Thus the firm has a need to continuously be alert to the facets of specific rugged landscapes that could inhibit the development of global fit, as well as understand whether moves in local landscapes that it is contemplating will simultaneously advance strategic fit at global level. While this chapter focuses on the impact of local ruggedness on the deployment of idiosyncratic competencies across several competitive landscapes, it is worth mentioning that companies pursuing a global strategy do indeed develop global competencies that are successfully leveraged across several competitive landscapes, as in the case of Honda's ability to manufacture high-quality motors or Electrolux's speed in evaluating potential acquisitions. For the perspective taken in this chapter, it can be argued that the variety of competitive landscapes—in terms of ruggedness—offers the potential for learning and capability building (Barkema & Vermeulen, 1998) that can be leveraged across multiple landscapes as the company develops strategic finesse[1] (Ellis, 1994). Global competencies therefore derive from the successful management of specific activities along value chains in different local landscapes.

Because resources and competencies both limit and drive a company's growth (Penrose, 1959), patterns of globalization are influenced by the company's specific path-dependent competence base and by the nature of competitive ruggedness in different local markets (Levinthal, 1997). Achieving fit at the local level requires developing idiosyncratic core competencies for that level (Prahalad & Hamel, 1990). The development of competencies enabling fit maximization at the global level derives from the ability to manage better than competitors specific activities in the various value-creating systems in which the company participates in different landscapes. Achieving fit at both local and global levels is therefore constrained by the degree to which competencies developed to fit at the local level can be leveraged or transferred to other local landscapes and to the global landscape.

In each market in which they compete, companies are not only trying to increase the fit between their local strategy and the local market landscapes, but also trying to set a strategy for global fit at the macro level. If the global players have first developed in different countries, as is often the case, they are likely to seek idiosyncratic ways to design and implement their global strategy within a given industry. The extent to which global strategies are successful, therefore, depends on the dynamics associated with the individual landscapes as a result of discontinuities occurring in the environment (Bettis & Hitt, 1995; Hitt, Keats & DeMarie, 1998), on the idiosyncratic set of competencies available to the different actors as a consequence of their positioning in the different landscapes, and on their decisions concerning which activities to control in the different value-creating systems to which they belong. The identification of specific activities that can be successfully controlled across multiple landscapes is therefore a driver for fit maximization at global level.

As firms adapt idiosyncratically to their landscapes, selection occurs in parallel at both the local levels and the global level. The result at the industry level is an episodic streamlining of organizational forms, concentration of the industry, and the emergence of global players. The selection process is influenced by the starting position of the different actors within their specific rugged landscapes, and by gradual or sudden changes in the configuration of the landscape itself.

While firms need to be aware of the challenges of local adaptation and selection, they constantly run the danger of being selected out at the global level if they remain too focused on local competition. When firms in a specific country get locked into localized learning patterns that lead to country-specific development paths, this can significantly shape how competitive they are internationally. The differences in configuration of the value-creating systems and in the organizing principles in various countries lead to different organizational and learning capabilities at company levels in that country. Furthermore, national organizing principles (Kogut, 1991) may idiosyncratically influence how firms in that national context internationalize.

The firm competing in a global context therefore faces a dilemma. It must attempt to achieve fit in the many local landscapes in which it competes, yet at the same time continue to pursue global fit, so as to avoid being selected out at the global level. Levinthal's landscape theory suggests that the capacity of the firm to successfully adapt to global fit challenges is deeply influenced by the ruggedness of the local landscapes in which it has elected to compete, and the path-dependent effects this competition has had on its capability to achieve global fit. This means that we need to begin to understand the key dimensions that shape ruggedness.

## Dimensions Shaping the Ruggedness of Local Market Landscapes

To capture the dimensions that shape ruggedness we now draw on Parolini's (1996, 1999) extension of Porter's (1985) work on industry chains. The way a company competes in its local market landscapes depends on two elements (Parolini, 1996, 1999): the existing links in the industry chain in which it elects to compete, and the company's choices about which activities to control, that constitute its value-creating system.

## Configuration of Industry Chain

In any given local landscape, several value-creating systems may be simultaneously competing to woo end-users. In the United States, the sale of cars on the Internet is making inroads into the traditional car dealerships and is rapidly expanding, benefiting several actors involved in the industry chain, as used car inventory turnover increases and non-value-creating activities (such as transportation of used cars from regional warehouses to local dealers) can be eliminated.

Within a given competitive landscape, different value-creating systems may not be in competition; different distribution channels for the same product often attract different market segments, thus actually increasing the overall potential market for the product. In other cases, though, new value-creating systems provide value maximization for one or more actors involved, thus becoming over time the winning value configuration. Sony Playstation's success over Nintendo can be interpreted as superior industry-chain architecture benefiting all actors involved (Dubini & Rana, 1999). Although Nintendo had almost 90% of world market share in the console segment, Sony managed to become world leader in three years by using a technology upgrade to create a novel value-creating system that addressed new market segments through new distribution channels.

## Company's Choices of Which Activities to Control

The choice of which activities a firm wants directly or indirectly to control in order to generate competitive advantage affects the way it competes at the local level. In the refrigerator and washing appliance business in Italy, Electrolux controls all key activities from copper wire production to delivery to retailers, whereas in other countries it has decided on a more limited scope. Merloni's strategy of maintaining a tight relationship with equipment manufacturers has been helpful in its entry strategy in Russia and China.

Although the activities that need to be performed to satisfy a specific end-user need may be the same across different countries (reinforcing a decision to pursue a global strategy), the company's choices of configuration in specific countries may be different. Moreover, as Prahalad and Hamel (1994) suggest, competitive advantage may derive from controlling key activities that are not directly measured by market share at the end-user level. This means that choices that different actors along the industry chain make on which activities to control—and the relative significance of a specific activity in the value-creating system—may differ markedly from country to country. McDonald's had to develop a strategy of full integration when it entered Russia, because Russia had no logistical systems to deliver the appropriate raw materials with timing that met McDonald's requirements.

The two issues highlighted above obviously do not represent the only sources of ruggedness at the local level. For the purposes of our paper, though, the identification of activity configuration within the industry chain in a given portion of the competitive landscape and the choice of activity configuration by the company provide a parsimonious way to analyze the concurrent dynamics of competitive landscapes and global strategy development. The choice to take activities as opposed to actors as the unit of analysis—as Parolini's methodology suggests—is necessary to understand fit maximization at local and global level. The focus on the industry chain as opposed to a specific industry is necessary to understand the dynamics of relative importance of specific activities within value-creating systems, as ruggedness in different portions of the competitive landscape changes.

## The Global Evolution of the Major Appliance Industry[2]

To explore the theoretical arguments above, we revisit the case history of the global major appliance industry, an extension of the pan-European study conducted by Baden-Fuller and Stopford (1991; see also a more recent report by Feder, 1997).

For our purposes, the industry is a good representation of a rugged landscape as visualized by Levinthal. It is possible to identify very different initial positions by key players, a careful and fine-grained adaptation process at the local level, and an overall selection process at the global level of analysis, together with the existence of very different value-creating systems (due to product characteristics, manufacturing strategies, and distribution structures, not to mention regulations on environmental friendliness of products and cost of energy) in different parts of the world. According to traditional theory, the industry was a good candidate for globalization due to its maturity, the role of economies of scale (particularly in the manufacturing of key components) and scope related to brand and breadth of product range, the technological stability of the products and processes, and the relatively common basic need of end-users in different geographic markets (Grant, 1995). We believe that the analysis of local ruggedness in the different portions of the competitive landscape helps to explain why the globalization process was not as smooth as expected.

### Historical Review of the Major Appliance Industry

The industry at first developed autonomously in different periods and in different world regions. In North America, the industry started about 1910; in Europe and Japan, after World War II, using American technology; in

China, in the last decade. It is therefore possible to compare geographic markets at very different points in the life-cycle curve.

Technological innovation is gradual and incremental, rather than radical. With the exception of microwave ovens (that were designed to be a global standardized product and subsequently had to be modified to accommodate local cooking needs), no radically new product has been introduced in the global or regional markets in the past 30 years. Traditionally, local markets have been served with specific products developed with *ad hoc* technologies, refined through a series of architectural innovations (Henderson & Clark, 1990) based on a few original patents. With the exception of washing machines (in which the horizontal axis washing and spinning systems are significantly better in terms of cost-performance ratio than the vertical axis technology), no technological solution is significantly superior to the others. History and consumer habits have led to a dominant design in each major market (Anderson & Tushman, 1990). It is important to note that while modifications have been marginal and incremental, the products available in different parts of the world are very different in configuration, aesthetics and performance.

Serious intercontinental consolidation began in the mid-1980s, resulting from Whirlpool's acquisition of Philips in the Netherlands, Electrolux's acquisitions of Zanussi in Italy and White Consolidated in the United States, and Maytag's acquisition of Hoover in the United Kingdom. Japanese and Korean producers of microwave ovens began aggressive international marketing at the same time. As companies tried to pursue scale and scope economies and as the consumer markets favored full-range manufacturers, concentration occurred in North America, Europe and Japan/Korea. During the 1970s, Western Europe, North America, and Japan/Korea hosted approximately 400 manufacturers; they gradually converged around 15 groups in the last 20 years.

The emergence of new markets in Central and Eastern Europe, Latin America, and Asia—plus a flat demand and excess capacity in consolidated markets—precipitated intense competition among big international players during the early 1990s, seeking preemptive moves to gain resource position advantages in the emerging markets (Wernerfelt, 1984).

On the basis of their geographic scope of activities and their stated degree of willingness to pursue an international strategy, it is possible to cluster major appliance manufacturers into the following four categories.

- Three global players (Electrolux, Whirlpool, and Samsung) have reached a worldwide presence and are claiming to be pursuing a global strategy. From 1992 to 1995, the corporate slogan in the Electrolux annual report was first "at home everywhere" and then "the global appliance company". In its 1988 annual report, Whirlpool for the first time explicitly mentioned a determination to implement a global strategy, based on the assumption of linear and irreversible globalization (Whitwam, 1994):

> The heart of the strategy remains our studied belief that the process and product technologies of the major appliance industry are the same the world over. Of course, as we encourage and exploit those similarities, we will continue to respect the differences between national and regional markets in terms of consumer preferences for styling, features and other characteristics. (Whirlpool annual report, 1993)

- Six continental players (General Electric, Matsushita, Sanyo, Merloni, Bosch-Siemens, and Daewoo) are significant players on one continent—by virtue of a strong presence in most major markets within the continent—and are selectively present in major markets outside their domestic continent.
- Several multidomestic players (such as Maytag, Candy, El.Fi, Arcelik, and Toshiba) are significant players in a few key markets within a region and may have occasional presence outside their main continent.
- Several local players and niche players have been extremely selective in the definition of their scope and are either very strong internationally in a specific market segment (like Miele in dishwashers) or operate in local markets only.

## Globalization Stalled?

One would expect globalization in this industry to be proceeding apace, but it appears that the process may actually be reversing, if only temporarily.

Global players consistently underperform continentals: the globalization benefits that Baden-Fuller and Stopford found lacking in 1991 are still not accruing seven years later, and none of the global players are enjoying the potential benefits of their scale and scope. GE claims to be the industry leader in return on net assets and is selectively expanding in China and Brazil. Merloni has managed to achieve significant economic results from its Russian operations. Bosch-Siemens is heavily investing in South America now that it is no longer burdened by the onerous German exchange rates of the early 1990s.

Global players are experiencing significant implementation difficulties. Global strategies are increasingly affected by the variation occurring in different parts of the world. Both Whirlpool and Electrolux are addressing each region separately, both in strategic as well as in organizational terms. Whirlpool's 1996 annual report states:

> No single adjective accurately describes Whirlpool Corporation's 1996 performance, for at least two reasons. First, the operating conditions and

> our results varied widely around the world. Second, our commitment to create value, and against which we assess our accomplishments, resides on both short- and long-term horizons. (Whirlpool annual report, 1996)

Local players dominate emerging markets. Contrary to expectations, the biggest emerging markets such as China are witnessing the development of a local industry, while global players find it hard to sustain the huge costs associated with developing Chinese operations. In China's refrigerator industry, Chinese producers have built up market share faster than their Western counterparts and currently dominate.

## Sources of Local Ruggedness in the Globalization of the Major Appliance Industry

We contend that the main source of the apparent slow progress in the globalization process of the home appliance industry stems from specific facets of local ruggedness, in turn deriving from differences firms face in industry chains and in value-creating systems configurations in their specific regional landscapes. For the purposes of our analysis, we identify different levels (corresponding to links within the industry chain) representing separate industries in the traditional Porterian definition of competitive systems. Their different configuration in the various countries contributes to ruggedness in different local landscapes; as Porter (1986) suggests, downstream activities, i.e. activities related to wholesale and retail distribution and marketing to end-users, are more likely to affect company global strategies, although the example highlights how they affect product configuration and therefore backstream activities as well.

### At the Component Manufacturing Level

The main players in the major appliance industry—Whirlpool, Electrolux, and Matsushita—are backward-integrated in the production of key components, such as compressors[3] for refrigerators and motors for clothes washers and dishwashers. Embraco (a division of Whirlpool) and Electrolux Components are the suppliers to their parents but both also supply the international market.

### At the Appliance Manufacturing and Assembly Level

Four aspects of manufacturing and assembly are especially important. First, the differences in distribution channels and end-users' purchasing habits affect the competencies that manufacturers need in order to sustain competitiveness. Competition among local players in Europe, for example, has resulted in the emergence of two types of players. By operating several small and flexible plants, Italian manufacturers traditionally compete on flexibility and product range at low price, and have often grown by subcontracting for competitors on some product ranges. German manufacturers compete on quality and innovation and tend to exploit economies of scale by operating a few very big plants. Second, branding strategies, particularly for European manufacturers, are critical because of the variety of distribution channels and market segments. Third, the nature, bargaining power, and localization of distribution channels mean logistics play a key role in coordinating and integrating service in different parts of the world. Finally, major appliances are bulky and transportation costs account for nearly 4% of manufacturing costs, making it more likely for manufacturers to produce regionally.

### At the Distribution Level

Distribution channels aim at different market segments, and each segment calls for a specific array of service attributes to satisfy both channels and their customers (MacMillan & McGrath, 1996). Serving each channel and its associated end-user segments requires the development of specific know-how and idiosyncratic management skills on the part of the appliance producer, as some activities play a different role in various value-creating systems. For instance, advertising is crucial for sustaining competitive advantage in the free-standing segment, whereas it has only indirect impact on built-in sales. More important, logistics-related activities are heavily influenced by the nature of the channel they are aimed at. Hypermarkets have a higher bargaining power than small independent stores and enjoy specific services from producers' warehouses.

In the United States, real estate developers represent the main customers for major appliance manufacturers (almost 60% of the total market). Of the remaining sales (to end-users) about 30% to 40% of sales is done through major chains, such as Sears. Kitchen furniture stores and discount stores cover another 20% of sales to end-users. TABLE 8.1 shows the wide variety of relevance of different channels in Europe.

### At the End-User Level

Climatic conditions—and hence eating and dressing habits—vary in different parts of the world, leading to different requirements for basic functionalities. For instance, refrigerators in tropical countries need to be no-frost; dryers are necessary in cold and wet countries. The way people eat, cook, and dress imposes specific requirements on appliances. Washing

TABLE 8.1 Methods of distribution of major appliances in major European economies (largest percentages within country in bold)

| | Average Europe | Germany | France | UK | Italy | Spain |
|---|---|---|---|---|---|---|
| Mail order | 7% | **18%** | 4% | 5% | 0% | 0% |
| Wholesale | 6% | 5% | 5% | 7% | 9% | 3% |
| Hypermarkets | 8% | 4% | **20%** | 2% | 4% | **15%** |
| Department stores | 4% | 7% | 3% | 5% | 0% | 5% |
| Furniture stores/ products built into cabinets | 13% | 12% | 8% | 5% | **33%** | 8% |
| Specialty chains | **24%** | 8% | **36%** | **51%** | 10% | 13% |
| Independent stores | **28%** | **34%** | 16% | 11% | **35%** | **50%** |
| Others | 10% | 12% | 8% | **14%** | 9% | 6% |
| Total | 100% | 100% | 100% | 100% | 100% | 100% |
| Volume (1000 units) | 43 112 | 12 750 | 7925 | 6825 | 5971 | 4851 |

a pan in which an egg has been fried or a piece of meat has been roasted requires more energy than wiping soy sauce from a wok or rinsing a pan that has steamed some vegetables. Getting a red wine stain off a tablecloth is a real challenge, whereas a beer stain is not so much of a problem.

The average size and layout of households also influence the requirements for appliances. In the United States, bedrooms are one or even two floors up from where appliances are physically located, so it is not essential that an appliance be particularly silent. In Europe, most people live in apartments, and noise is an issue. In China and Japan, silence is essential. Companies also must consider household size and layout when planning service support. So far, servicing is performed on the end-user's premises because appliances are bulky and not easy to uninstall and transport.

### At the National Level

*Infrastructure* at the national level is critical: the speed of growth in the Chinese market depends on the speed of the electrification process of the rural areas. In much of Africa, infrastructure concerns dictate that refrigerators and freezers be equipped with a backup system that turns on if energy is cut off.

*Governments*, too, have a significant influence in many arenas (Doz, Bartlett & Prahalad, 1981). In the United States, a government decision against isobutane-based compressors made it impossible for German competitors to introduce them in American households. For the refrigerator industry, a major factor will be the upcoming decision of the Chinese government about which refrigerants will be permitted in Chinese compressors.

Thus we see that there are many places where local ruggedness of the landscape manifests itself in the globalization of major appliances. Our thoughts then turned to how these manifestations of ruggedness might have influenced the progress of globalization, causing us to seek underlying patterns that explain how local ruggedness influences the pace of globalization, as well as the unfolding of global strategies. As the following sections indicate, we claim that the challenges posed by specific local landscapes, and the tenaciousness of national boundaries, are major resilience elements in industry chain globalization; moreover, idiosyncratically rugged local landscapes are affected in different ways by discontinuities occurring in the environment. This, together with different configurations of industry chains in various countries, explains the lurching nature of the globalization process, affected by the sudden alignment of activities across several local landscapes. Two major consequences derive for companies striving to reach a dual fit at local and global level: the need to identify the activities across multiple value-creating systems that offer alignment potential and that enable the development of competencies to be leveraged on a global basis, and the spatial and temporal contingency of strategic opportunity in specific landscapes related to alignment potential.

## Irrefutable Challenges Posed by Specific Local Landscapes

Individual local landscapes cannot be ignored in the development of a global strategy. Any company's core competencies—which by definition are the result of the collective learning of the company (Prahalad & Hamel, 1990)—have been developed originally with respect to a specific business and then become part of the whole company's patrimony. Often, the superiority of a company *vis-à-vis* its competitors derives from competencies developed within a particularly demanding competitive environment (Porter, 1990) that have then been successfully leveraged across multiple competitive landscapes; we refer to these as global competencies. Companies pursuing a global strategy seek to exploit their competitive advantage on a global base; in doing so, however, they are continually distracted because at the local landscape level, they must attend to very specific and irrefutable adaptation processes. Paying attention to irrefutable challenges of local fit is not trivial, not just for competence-building purposes. It is from local landscapes that come the cash flows essential to support the firm's current and long-term investment activities (Kogut, 1989).

Our investigation of the major appliance industry suggests that the specific nature of the competitive landscapes at the local level is key to whether, how, and how fast globalization can occur. There are four reasons why that is so: dissimilarities of value-creating systems; imprinting that occurs because each company evolves by first dominating a specific domestic market; moves that are needed locally to cope with intense local competition but that often hinder globalization strategy; and resource competition that stems from the firm's other landscapes.

### Dissimilarities of Value-Creating Systems

The configuration of a specific value-creating system in one landscape can act as a serious barrier to globalization for a company and even for an industry chain as a whole. For instance, entering China requires that refrigerators be no-frost (like Japanese products), silent (like European products), small and cheap. A strong national industry has now emerged in China because European and US producers—lacking concomitantly low-cost, silent, small cheap refrigerators—found fit maximization in the China landscape inconsistent with fit maximization at the global level.

### Imprinting that Occurs from Dominating a Domestic Market

Our case analysis of the industry suggests that in general a globalizing firm grows by first dominating a domestic market that becomes bigger in scope, and acts as the arena for shaping and testing the company's value-creating system. Both Electrolux and Whirlpool use the fact that they have a solid competitive position in each key market in Europe and North America respectively as an argument for being true global players.

The nature of competitive ruggedness at the local level is key in imprinting the development of company assets and resources (Barney, 1991; Amit & Shoemaker, 1993) that eventually can be exploited more broadly. Global positioning may require early entry into emerging markets, but at the same time, competing in consolidated markets may demand a survival strategy of focusing resources. Moreover, Prahalad and Lieberthal (1998) argue that emerging and consolidated markets should not be managed in the same way.[4] Thus the path-dependent capabilities developed by a firm in its trajectory of success in its original domestic markets can lead to the development of core incompetencies or rigidities (Leonard-Barton, 1992) that render it unable to deliver critical product functionalities in other local—or emerging global—markets. To return to our example of Chinese refrigerators, consider the difficulties US firms are encountering in manufacturing appliances that are quiet enough for Asian markets. To achieve silent operation, it is not enough simply to put a quieter compressor in the refrigerator or a silent motor in the dishwasher. A whole new architecture of components needs to be developed, and doing so renders obsolete the existing refrigerator architecture, with all its attendant benefits of experience, scale, and scope that delivered success in the first market.

Past path dependencies developed while competing in local markets can therefore lead to dysfunctional capabilities that could become what we might call genetic flaws, making the current architecture of the product vulnerable to selection processes in other landscapes. That is what happened to Blockbuster Video in Germany. The company's ideology of avoiding all X-rated videos was successful in the United States but boomeranged in Germany, leading to unsatisfactory economic performance. German customers' resistance to being "protected" from video sex and violence was a major driver of the unsuccessful fit of the Blockbuster formula, as it affected the composition and spending patterns of the targeted market. This in turn had negative repercussions on the whole value-creating system. In our approach, fit maximization derives from superior configuration of value-creating systems; the case of Blockbuster indicates that a discrepancy of the industry chain configuration in the German market determines a non-optimal fit of the Blockbuster value-creating system in that country and therefore unsatisfactory performance. Blockbuster therefore faces the dilemma of fit maximization in Germany or search of local landscapes whose ruggedness fits with its global value-creating system configuration.

The design and implementation of country-specific value-creating systems for each local landscape requires idiosyncratic skills for managing specific activities. Working with independent stores scattered all over the country (Spain, Italy, Japan) versus working with powerful, highly efficient specialty chains (USA, UK, France) calls for different logistics structures and support activities. If a firm has developed highly successful management routines and processes (Nelson & Winter, 1982) in the base domestic business, abandoning or changing this "comfortable" competence to compete in other landscapes may be deeply resisted.

### Intense Pressure from Local Landscapes that Inhibit Attempts at Globalization

Actions necessary to defend local positions can force a player to costly competitive moves that hurt its global strategy. In 1994, when investments in emerging markets were booming, Electrolux (already the market leader in Europe) elected at significant cost to acquire AEG for two non-trivial reasons: first to preempt other global competitors from doing so (which would have given the competitors access to the limited-growth European regional market); and second, to allow Electrolux to strengthen its position *vis-à-vis* Bosch-Siemens (the third biggest competitor in Europe and first in Germany, where 40% of the European production of major appliances takes place). This strategic move therefore allowed the company to increase the fit within a growing domestic landscape, but at the same time diverted resources from the Chinese market, which at that time represented a key strategic window for the exploitation of the company's advantage on a global basis.

### Resource Pressures from the Firm's Other Landscapes that Inhibit Attempts at Globalization

In several cases, the kinds of resources needed to pursue a full-fledged global thrust were simply not available to the division that needed them. The prime examples were GE Appliance's and Samsung Appliance's difficulties in aggressively participating in China. Both divisions had conglomerate parents, and therefore faced fierce internal competition for resources from both related products and much more profitable unrelated products.

## Tenaciousness of National Boundaries

Part of the ruggedness of local landscapes may be determined by the persistence of barriers in specific countries. In fact four major elements appear to be critical in hindering globalization at individual country levels: country specificity of industry chains; immobility of brands and high cost of brand positioning; local imbeddedness; and problems stemming from inadequate infrastructure.

### Country-Specific Industry Chain Effects

In many industries—and definitely in the major appliance industry—the structure of the industry chain (Prahalad & Lieberthal, 1998), particularly distribution, is very country specific. Even though in most countries consolidation processes are occurring and the most aggressive players are developing internationalization strategies, distribution specificity plays a key role. There are two main reasons:

1. The activities performed at the retail distribution level (creation of an assortment, support to the end-user in the selection process, marketing, transportation, and installation) contribute to the end-user's perception of value.

2. Furthermore in each country, different distribution channels lead to value-creating systems that differ significantly in their cost structure. The factory cost for a dishwasher might be 100 units of currency for a freestanding model and 91 for the corresponding built-in model offering the same performance.[5] In Italy, the end-user is willing to pay a price ranging from 170 to 200 for the same built-in product. While one may argue that the 200 that end-users are willing to pay for a built-in model is the same as they would pay for a freestanding model once they had added on transportation and installation costs, there are still considerable differences in final prices and the structure of payoffs in the two value-creating systems.

## Immobility of Brands and High Cost of Building Brand Image Across Borders

As firms attempt to build global or regional brand image, they may be forced into costly alignment investments, as brands may not be positioned and perceived in the same way across different countries, due to the company's history of brand positioning. Although Zanussi, owned by Electrolux, is the overall market leader in major appliance *sales* in Italy, the Rex brand, which is also owned by Electrolux, is the leading *brand* in Italy. Rex was a brand originally owned by Zanussi, but since Electrolux is trying to create Zanussi as a pan-European brand, they have the dilemma of downplaying their leading brand in Italy to favor the pan-European brand they are trying to promote.

## Local Imbeddedness

In our case analysis we found instances when the firm was up against players that had a "home team advantage" in that particular country. This can manifest itself in many ways. *Government regulation* in the USA banned hydrocarbon refrigerants, thereby locking out German compressor manufacturers. Favored nation agreements put certain foreign competitors at an advantage. *Industry chain arrangements* proved an obstacle—for instance it is virtually impossible for European and North American producers to break into the Japanese distribution systems. *Public sentiment* worked against firms trying to build position. Italian appliances are perceived as low quality in the German market; all competitors have therefore introduced a specific brand for the German market. Whatever the reason, there were times when the effort and energy expended on overcoming local imbeddedness drained away significant resources that could be used in other landscapes.

### Problems of Infrastructure

In the case of developing economies, the sheer lack of infrastructure posed enormous problems in two ways. First, the rate of growth slowed abruptly once the markets in the electrified major cities of China, Latin America and Eastern Europe saturated. Second, there are no major transportation systems to serve the rural markets in industries where the product is heavy, bulky and difficult to transport. Further growth now depends on the rate of electrification and development of transportation systems.

## THE LURCHING NATURE OF GLOBALIZATION

In the previous sections, we have claimed that ruggedness in local landscapes is responsible for the development of idiosyncratic and path-dependent competencies, as companies pursue maximization of local fit through appropriate configuration of value-creating systems. Here we focus on the external variables enabling companies to leverage competencies—deriving from the superior management of specific activities within value-creating systems—across multiple landscapes.

"Firms with strong core competencies, often developed in their home country operations, can apply such competencies in international markets (Bartlett & Ghoshal, 1989). The competitive advantages that produce greater profitability in domestic markets provide motivation to apply the same competencies in international markets to further enhance the firm's profitability (Porter, 1990). The resource sharing among firms' multiple international operations in turn facilitates exploitation of common sets of core competencies to produce synergy (Grant, Jammine & Thomas, 1988)" (from Hitt, Hoskisson & Kim, 1997: 771). Each portion of the landscape is characterized by its own ruggedness. Because of this, external discontinuities (Bettis & Hitt, 1995; Hitt, Keats & DeMarie, 1998) on competitive dynamics may indeed have an impact on the global landscape, but affect each local landscape in a different way; idiosyncratic landscape dynamism also poses challenges for concurrent fit maximization at local as well as global level. For instance, the Montreal protocol on the environment has forced all component and refrigerator manufacturers to seek alternative refrigerants to the standard R12, but has resulted in a variety of alternative solutions becoming the standard in various parts of the world. While the industry experienced a change in the competitive structure on a global level—as low end players have been swept away from the industry—the effect of this environmental discontinuity has been an increase and not a reduction in competitive variance across landscapes.

Over time, as each locally rugged landscape changes and as companies extend their scope, portions of value-creating systems in different landscapes may suddenly align, allowing the companies who control the aligned activities to exploit their competencies across multiple landscapes. As firm-specific opportunities to enhance global position are highly contingent on idiosyncrasies in local landscapes that change constantly over time, the resulting process of globalization proceeds in "lurches' rather than moving forward incrementally.

## Idiosyncratic Time- and Space-Contingent Windows of Opportunity

As local landscapes change in a non-linear way, a constant stream of idiosyncratic opportunities arise for specific firms, and not others, to capture advantage in one or more landscapes, as alignment occurs between activities across multiple value-creating systems. Like the rare occasions during eclipses when all the planets are in alignment, there can be times when several local landscape conditions coming into alignment will allow a firm to undertake what Levinthal calls a long jump, and the resulting lurch may reconfigure the entire global landscape and put one company at an advantage over its competitors. Samsung became a global player through the manufacturing and sale of microwaves by taking advantage of emerging international alignment in consumer cooking behavior (the need to cook quickly and direct from the freezer for singles and working mothers). Samsung's new product fitted nicely with the distribution structures and purchasing processes it already had for its major appliances in various local landscapes. Why did the other global players allow this to happen? They were all deeply engaged in expensive and energy-sapping consolidation mergers taking place at the same time—which once again demonstrates the idiosyncratic spatial and temporal nature of many globalization opportunities.

Due to the lurching nature of the globalization process, opportunities for alignment in companies' global strategies are temporary, and alignment occurs for portions of the global landscape at a time. In the home appliance industry, a huge market window opened in the early 1990s, as a portion of the Chinese market reached the sufficient income level to afford a refrigerator or a washing machine. In two years, market penetration of appliances in urban China shifted from 4% to 89%; for products with an average lifecycle of 10 years, the attractiveness of the Chinese market changed dramatically after the opportunity window closed.

Local or global, idiosyncratic opportunities arise when, as a result of landscape dynamics, the firm can forge alignment between its competences and two types of shift in the landscape: shifts in industry chain activity configuration and shifts in value-creating systems.

### Industry Chain

When a shift in the industry chain occurs, this may allow a firm to align its competences to the reconfigured landscape. As electronic commerce expands beyond the United States, those key players in Europe that have made major investments in logistics and warehousing are exploring the sale of appliances through the Internet, in the hope that they can leverage their logistical capabilities and assets through electronic selling.

### Value-Creating Systems

Alternatively, a shift in value-creating systems may give rise to opportunity for alignment by the transfer of competences from one landscape to another, which is happening in Europe as consumers become increasingly attracted to built-in appliances. This has put Italian manufacturers at an advantage over competitors, given that already one-third of the sales in Italy are built-in appliances purchased through furniture stores.

The opportunity to create advantage out of alignment between firm competence and a shift in landscape need not be reactive, the firm may seize the opportunity to create alignment between a competence that it has and a target landscape. Since Whirlpool enjoyed a strong relationship with Sears in the United States, it was not surprising that the company was able to go out and create a similar competitive situation in Canada, once Canadian retail structures reflected those in the United States.

## Major Ways in which Firms Align Competences with Opportunities

Companies in our industry study employed four major ways to try to align competences with opportunities in their target landscapes:

1. *Transfer*. First was to transfer competences from one landscape to another, as described above (Italian built-in cabinet competences into the rest of Europe; Whirlpool into Canada following retail structure development).
2. *Build*. An alternative was to deliberately build competences in a targeted landscape, as did Merloni in developing suppliers in Russia. This can also take place at the global level, as the earlier description of Samsung's global microwave build-up illustrates.

3. *Buy*. Another alternative was to purchase the necessary competences in a target landscape, as illustrated by Electrolux's acquisitions of Zanussi, White and AEG.
4. *Take out options*. The final alternative we observed was to make real options investments (Bowman & Hurry, 1993; Dixit & Pindyk, 1994; McGrath, 1997) in arrangements like the joint ventures with the Chinese, or licensing agreements that reduce the huge investments required to transfer, build or buy, yet secure an opportunity to do so once uncertainty is reduced.

The taking out of real options is a critical alignment alternative. As Kogut (1989) writes, "A multinational corporation can be seen as consisting of proprietary assets from which it derives current cash flows, as well as of a set of options inherent in operating in multiple environments."

Companies cannot fully predict when alignment will take place and thus may need to treat entry into specific markets as option investments only to be fully exploited when alignment occurs. Options-like investments in new markets, new product architectures, and new technologies generate know-how and competencies that can be developed and transferred whenever specific activities along the industry chains in which the company competes align with the investment. Alignment cannot be fully predicted or controlled; it takes place episodically. Companies have to be prepared to make controlled options investments with no return in the short run in order to have the chance to commit heavily when alignment occurs. For instance, Maytag acquired Hoover in 1986 to get a foothold in Europe, then divested 10 years later to invest in a venture in China.

For all their benefits to competing in local landscapes, the above moves (transfer, build, buy, or take out options) in or across local landscapes do not necessarily advance global fit. Basic advances in global fit take place when the firm is able to expand its competitive strength in one or several landscapes in such a way that global fit is increased.

When certain competencies related to managing specific activities or operating at specific links of the industry chain become critical, companies that have mastered those competencies have an advantage over competitors who were not required to master them because the competitive dynamics and configuration of the industry activity chains at their local level were different. For example, in the mono-application smartcards value-creating systems, the activities related to the development of software applications necessary to personalize cards are currently high value-generating ones. Semiconductor manufacturers derive their margins from their ability to efficiently manufacture high volumes of memory cards at the lowest possible cost. As the industry develops and it is possible to offer multiple applications on the same card, a security standard is emerging, making personalization activities less critical than co-developing with potential customers the specifications for smarter cards. As a result, only one or a very few companies will have control over the security-related activities and will be able to leverage those competences across multiple value-creating systems and at the global level. For all the other competitors, any investments made to control personalization activities will no longer generate return.

## Fit Maximization at Local and Global Levels

In the previous sections, we have described strategy as the idiosyncratic, path-dependent process of designing value-creating systems within locally rugged competitive landscapes. In the process of fit maximization in each landscape, companies develop competencies necessary to master crucial activities along the industry chain. The development of a global strategy has been viewed as a way to increase and exploit the company's competence base across dynamic multiple landscapes. The possibility of exploiting competencies on a global level has been explained by the alignment of specific activities within value-creating systems in different landscapes (as a consequence of changes in ruggedness in some landscapes deriving from external variables or of company behavior) and by the ability of the firm to recognize alignment potential and therefore carefully select which activities to control in different value creating systems.

In some cases, fit maximization at specific local levels also increases fit at global level. This means that not only does the firm improve its position in a specific landscape, but it also enhances its global fit via one or more global levers (Yip, 1989) at the same time: extension of participation in major markets; increase in product standardization, increased ability to concentrate activities; enhancement of capacity to undertake uniform marketing across landscapes; and increased ability to integrate competitive moves across landscapes. Below we document some of the strategies that illustrate how moves at local levels were also able to enhance global fit in the home appliance industry.

### Extension of Market Participation

Any moves in local landscapes that extend the firm's presence in the major global markets will simultaneously advance global fit. We found moves in local landscapes that simultaneously enhanced participation in major global markets, and we also found that there was a range over which this enhancement of global participation occurred. At one end of the range was what we consider to be major extensions of presence, like Electrolux's almost simultaneous acquisition of Zanussi in Europe and White

Consolidated in the USA, both of which moves covered multiple products and markets. At the other end of the range were moves that we call "sphere of influence" extensions. Here the firm enters the market with an option-like move, whose purpose is for mutual forbearance[6] purposes or for foothold purposes.

In the major appliance industry, it is currently almost impossible to gain a significant market position in the United States or in Europe without exorbitant investments. Similarly, the Chinese market is no longer easy to enter, having temporarily matured. China will present a major growth opportunity for new players again only after electrification outside the major cities and improvements in transportation. In the meantime, incumbents may entrench their position with reconfigurations of the supply, distribution, and servicing structures. Unless current non-players in the Chinese market pursue "sphere of influence" type investments to keep the door open for later entry, they may remain locked out.

### Advancement of Product Standardization

We found that firms followed one of two possible strategies in attempting to advance the degree of product standardization across landscapes. The more obvious strategy was to seek the largest pool of customers in the combined landscapes and develop standard products to serve those segments common to every landscape with that homogeneous product—this was the strategy pursued so successfully by Samsung in microwaves. The alternative was to seek to standardize by producing a product for a large segment of one landscape and then creatively tailoring the marketing pitch of this standardized product to the appropriate segment (Baalbaki & Malhotra, 1993) in other landscapes. This is the current approach of GE appliances in Europe and Brazil. Because its big two-door refrigerators with ice dispensers, a standard in the USA, do not fit with European kitchen requirements for size, consumption levels, or noise, the company is a niche player in Europe, targeting high-end customers looking for the big, oversized status-symbol American refrigerators. This allows GE to enjoy a significant premium price,[7] a strategy comparable to that of Miele in the dishwasher segment.

### Enhanced Ability to Concentrate Activity

The global compressor manufacturers have found ways of concentrating manufacturing activities. For the completed and assembled product, firms like Merloni recognized that ruggedness of the local competitive landscape calls for tailored products, for logistics adapted to local distribution and infrastructure, or for control of country-specific distribution channels, so that cost advantages, benefits of economies of scale and scope, from the concentration of primary activities—typically manufacturing and assembly—had less impact on the final price than support costs such as promotion, transportation, service, and technical assistance. They have therefore focused on concentration of those support activities (defined by Parolini as activities that do not need to be replicated for every unit of product manufactured and sold) that can be planned and managed on a global scale and can be relocated, centralized, or outsourced with limited impact on the end-user's perceived value, but with significant cost advantages. So, for instance, Merloni has outsourced the production and inventorying of all instruction manuals for all appliances manufactured in its European plants.

### Enhanced Potential for Uniform Marketing Across Landscapes

When Whirlpool acquired Philips, it took it only four years to completely replace the post-acquisition "Philips–Whirlpool" brand into the "Whirlpool" brand in Europe. This was obtained through a massive advertising effort in Europe that set the stage for a global branding push. On the other hand, as we mentioned earlier, Electrolux is experiencing difficulty in building a pan-European, let alone a global, brand image.

### Enhancement of Potential to Make Integrated Competitive Moves Across Landscapes

As with enhancement of market position, the moves in this category fell into a range from moves that built potential to make concerted effort on several fronts to moves that built potential to reshape spheres of influence. A fascinating example that covers both ends of the range is the purchase of AEG by Electrolux. At the pan-European level it dramatically broadened Electrolux's ability to make concerted moves in Europe, particularly against Bosch-Siemens. At the global level the purchase in effect pre-empted any opportunity for North American or Asian players from establishing an enhanced sphere of influence in Europe.

In other cases, ruggedness of landscapes and the need for the company to maximize fit in each of them may result in the development of core rigidities (Leonard-Barton, 1992) hindering the firm's ability to maximize fit at the global level (Ruef, 1997); the ability to recognize alignment potential of activities across value-creating systems in different landscapes and the subsequent possibility of successfully transferring competencies and maximizing learning potential may be hindered by the magnitude of the options open as the company increases the scope of its activities (Hitt,

Hoskinsson & Kim, 1997). Most recent rumors about both Whirlpool and Electrolux refer to the possibility that the two companies reduce their scope by divesting from the components business.

Pursuit of a global strategy in a rugged landscape will occasionally lead to missteps or slowdowns, because alignment of a cluster of activities does not occur in every market. Lurches may reverse direction, as the firm discovers that its assumptions about the future directions of the global landscape are not met: "The global nature of selection pressures drives the companies in the industry over time toward the existence of an unique form. However, adaptation guides and limits the selection process by determining the set of organizational forms over which selection occurs. The speed at which selection drives the population to an unique form is slowed by the fact that organizations have moved toward the various local peaks associated with their particular starting point and therefore reduced the variation in organizational fitness level in the population" (Levinthal, 1997).

For instance, Whirlpool set up global R&D units in the United States, Italy, and Singapore but had to relocate the Singapore unit three years after the start-up. Electrolux has been aiming at becoming "the global appliance company" for the past three years, but the switch from European product lines to global product lines is slow and painful. The intensity of GE's efforts to gain a stable market position in Brazil has varied significantly over the years.

## Conclusions

In this paper, we show how local ruggedness constrains globalization, how its evolution creates opportunities for local fit between competences and evolving landscapes, and where such local adaptation also advances global fit.

The preceding discussion yielded several themes that we contend are worth consideration by those studying global strategy in any industry. First, globalization is a "personal" process. Because of path dependencies, each firm has a unique set of limitations and opportunities that emerge as the environment unfolds. We therefore suggest the revision of literature on the management of global companies (Prahalad & Doz, 1987; Bartlett & Ghoshal, 1991) and on the learning perspective applied to the internationalization process (Barkema & Vermeulen, 1998) in the light of the challenges posed by ever-changing local ruggedness, to further consider the limitations posed to the successful implementation of global strategies by the extreme variety of options available. Although it may be true that over time the industry globalizes in a converging way, the pace at which that happens and each firm's ability to cope are a function of the moves that the firm and its competitors can make, which in turn are paced by local ruggedness. Local ruggedness is determined by how the firm and its competitors are electing to compete within industry chains in different landscapes by defining their value-creating systems.

Second, the development of a global strategy is an evolutionary process, charted not so much by the firm's unilateral decisions as by the orchestration of the firm's attempts to fit both local and global landscapes in the face of competing countermoves and environment dynamics, so that globalization at firm and global levels is likely to proceed in lurches. Attending to ruggedness at the various local levels in which the firm participates is vital, because the specific structure of ruggedness sets up idiosyncratic constraints and opportunities that the firm must navigate as it strives for global fit. This suggests the revision of literature on the institutional and organizational solutions to manage international activities (Perlmutter, 1969; Hedlund, 1981, 1986; Bartlett & Ghoshal, 1989; Brandt & Hulbert, 1977; Picard, 1980; Negandhi & Baliga, 1981; Jarillo & Martinez, 1990; Nobel & Birkinshaw, 1998), in order to identify organizational solutions enabling the companies to assess alignment potential.

We contend that the specificity of the competitive landscapes at the local level is key to whether, how, and how fast globalization can occur. The industry on which we base our reasoning is mature, with established players and a stable technological environment; still we found that local rugged landscapes and their evolution present challenges to the players that decided to pursue a global strategy. Although we believe that the concluding remarks highlighted above are generally applicable to several industries, it can be argued that more dynamic landscapes or industries in the development phase will pose different challenges with regard to variety of activity alignment possibilities, obsolescence of global competencies, and ability of the players involved in predicting trajectories of globalization. Therefore, it becomes relevant to assess what are the activities within value-creating systems that have the best chances of aligning globally and favoring fit maximization at local as well as global level. Since fit maximization at both local and global levels is constrained by the degree to which competencies developed to fit at the local level can be leveraged or transferred to other local landscapes and to the global landscape, it is suggested that one should analyse difficulties in competence transfer (Dierickx & Cool, 1989; Szulanski, 1995) from the point of view of missed alignment of activities in different landscapes.

## Notes

1. "Strategic finesse is a long run step improvement in strength and position relative to competitors attained after persistent attention to individually small gains in performance or position". (Ellis, 1994: 50)

2. The focus of our analysis is the major appliance, or white goods, industry: companies that design, manufacture, distribute, and sell ranges, refrigerators, freezers, dishwashers, clothes washers, and dryers to individuals and families worldwide. The industry is only minimally related to the professional appliances industry, which is much more fragmented and characterized by distinct competitive arenas.
3. The compressor is the main component of a refrigerator and accounts for about 30% of direct material costs.
4. Again in this chapter, we are interested in exploring the nature of competitive ruggedness in different parts of the competitive arena and not so much in the structures that should be designed to compete in different parts of the competitive environment.
5. The difference in cost between freestanding and built-in products derives from the fact that built-in products do not have a complete front door. The kitchen cabinet manufacturer will normally insert built-in appliances and build the external door with the same material as the cabinet doors.
6. The mutual forbearance hypothesis argues that when competitors meet in multiple markets they will tend to reduce their aggressiveness in each market for fear of retaliation in the other market. By strategically investing in a market that has little short-run or long-run promise for direct returns, the firm can nonetheless build a position from which it can control competitors' behavior in other landscapes via punitive actions in the invested landscape. Such investments serve the purpose of increasing the investing firm's sphere of influence in both landscapes (McGrath, Chen & MacMillan, forthcoming).
7. GE refrigerators are a status symbol in many European countries and currently cost four to six times the average products.

## Acknowledgements

The authors wish to acknowledge the help of Antonello Garzoni, and Davide Ravasi who provided key insights in discussions about this paper.

## References

Abrahamson, E. & Fombrun, C.J. (1994). Macrocultures: Determinants and consequences. *Academy of Management Review*, **19**, 728–755.

Amit, R. & Shoemaker, P.J. (1993). Strategic assets and organizational rent. *Strategic Management Journal*, **14**, 33–46.

Anderson, P. & Tushman, M.L. (1990). Technological discontinuities and dominant designs: A cyclical model of technological change. *Administrative Science Quarterly* **35**, 604–633.

Andrews, K.R. (1971). *The Concept of Corporate Strategy*. Homewood, IL: Irwin.

Baalbaki, I.B. & Malhotra, N.K. (1993). Marketing management bases for international market segmentation: An alternate look at the standardization/customization debate. *International Marketing Review* **10**(1).

Baden-Fuller, C. & Stopford, J.M. (1991). Globalization frustrated: The case of white goods. *Strategic Management Journal*, **12**(7), 493–507.

Barkema, H.G. & Vermeulen, F. (1998). International expansion through start-up or acquisition: A learning perspective. *Academy of Management Journal*, **41**(1), 7–26.

Barkema, H.G., Shenkar, O., Vermeulen, F. & Bell, J.H.J. (1997). Working abroad, working with others: How firms learn to operate international joint ventures. *Academy of Management Journal*, **40**, 426–442.

Barney, J. (1991). Firm resources and sustained competitive advantage. *Journal of Management*, **17**(1), 99–120.

Bartlett, C.A. & Ghoshal, S. (1989). *Managing Across Borders: The Transnational Solution*. Cambridge, MA: Harvard Business School Press.

Bartlett, C.A. & Ghoshal, S. (1991). Global strategic management: Impact on the new frontiers of research. *Strategic Management Journal*, **12** (Special Issue), 5–16.

Bettis, R.A. & Hitt, M.A. (1995). The new competitive landscape. *Strategic Management Journal*, **16**, 7–19.

Bowman, E. & Hurry, D. (1993). Strategy through the option lens: An integrated view of resource investments and the incremental choice process. *Academy of Management Review*, **18**(4), 760–782.

Brandt, W.K. & Hulbert, J.M. (1977). Headquarter guidance in marketing strategy in the multinational subsidiary. *Columbia Journal of World Business*, **12**, 7–14.

Cohen, W.M. & Levinthal, D.A. (1990). Absorptive capacity: A new perspective on learning and innovation. *Administrative Science Quarterly*, **35**, 128–152.

Di Bernardo, B., Rullani, E. & Vaccà, S. (1986). Cambiamento tecnologico ed economia di impresa. *Economia e Politica Industriale*, **50**, 25–41.

Dierickx, I. & Cool, K. (1989). Asset stock accumulation and sustainability of competitive advantage *Management Science*, **35**(12), 1504–1513.

Dixit, A. & Pindyck, R. (1994). *Investment Under Uncertainty*. Princeton, NJ: Princeton University Press.

Doz, Y.L., Bartlett, C.A., Prahalad, C.K. (1981). Global competitive pressures and host country demands: Managing tensions in MNCs. *California Management Review*, **12**(3), 63–74.

Dubini, P. & Rana, M. (1999). Costruzione e difesa del vantaggio competitivo nel settore dei videogiochi. *Economia & Management*, (forthcoming).

Ellis, R.J. (1994). Strategic finesse: Incrementally decisive global strategies. *International Review of Strategic Management*, **5**, 49–69.

Feder, B.J. (1997). For white goods, a world beckons. *The New York Times*, 25 November (sec. 1B: 4).

Grant, R.M. (1995). *Contemporary Strategy Analysis: Concepts, Techniques, Applications*. Oxford: Blackwell.

Grant, R.M., Jammine, A.P. & Thomas, H. (1988). Diversity, diversification and profitability among British manufacturing companies 1972–1984. *Academy of Management Journal*, **31**, 771–801.

Hawrylyshin, B. (1981). Managerial realities of global interdependence. In *Management and the World of Tomorrow*, Proceedings of the 18th CIOS World Management Congress. London: Gower Press.

Hedlund, G. (1986). The hypermodern MNC: a heterarchy? *Human Resource Management*, **25**, 9–36.

Henderson, R.M. & Clark, K.B. (1990). Architectural innovation: The reconfiguration of existing product technologies and the failure of established firms. *Administrative Science Quarterly*, **35**, 9–30.

Hitt, M.A., Hoskisson, R.E. & Kim, H. (1997). International diversification: Effects on innovation and firm performance in product diversified firms. *Academy of Management Journal*, **40**(4), 767–798.

Hitt, M.A., Keats, B.W. & DeMarie, S.M. (1998). Navigating in the new competitive landscape: Building strategic feasibility and competitive advantage in the 21st century. *Academy of Management Executive*, **12**(4), 22–42.

Jarillo, J.C. & Martinez, I. (1990). Different roles for subsidiaries: The case of multinational corporations in Spain. *Strategic Management Journal*, **11**(7), 506–512.

Johanson, J. & Vahlne, J.E. (1977). The internationalization process of the firm: A model of knowledge development and increasing foreign market commitments. *Journal of International Business Studies*, **8**(1), 23–32.

Johanson, J. & Vahlne, J.E. (1990). The mechanism of internationalization. *International Marketing Review*, **7**(4), 11–24.

Kobrin, X. (1991). An empirical analysis of the determinants of global integration. *Strategic Management Journal*, **12** (Summer Special Issue), 17–31.

Kogut, B. (1989). Research notes and communications: A note on global strategies. *Strategic Management Journal*, **10**, 383–389.

Kogut, B. (1991). Country capabilities and the permeability of borders. *Strategic Management Journal*, **12**, 33–47.

Leonard-Barton, D. (1992). Core capabilities and core rigidities: A paradox in managing new product development. *Strategic Management Journal*, **13**, 111–125.

Levinthal, D. (1997). Adaptation on rugged landscapes. *Management Science*, **43**(7), 934–950.

MacMillan, I.C. & McGrath, R.G. (1996). Discover your products' hidden potential. *Harvard Business Review*, **74**(3), 58–73.

Manaresi, A. (1997). Forme organizzative e processi di internazionalizzazione. In G. Lorenzoni (ed.), *Architetture Reticolari e Processi di Internazionalizzazione*. Bologna: il Mulino, 12–35.

McGrath, R.G. (1997). A real option logic for initiating technology positioning investments. *Academy of Management Review*, **22**, 974–996.

McGrath, R.G., Chen, M.-J. & MacMillan, I.C. (1999). Multimarket maneuvering in uncertain spheres of influence: Resource diversion strategies. *Academy of Management Review* (forthcoming).

Miller, D. & Chen, M.J. (1994). Sources and consequences of competitive inertia: A study of the US airline industry. *Administrative Science Quarterly*, **39**, 1–23.

Miller, D. & Chen, M.J. (1996). The simplicity of competitive repertoires: An empirical analysis. *Strategic Management Journal*, **17**, 419–439.

Morrison, A.J. (1990). *Strategies in Global Industries: How US Businesses Compete*. Westport, CT: Quorum Books.

Negandhi, A.R. & Baliga, B.R. (1981). Internal functioning of American, German and Japanese multinational corporations. In L. Otterbeck (ed.), *The Management of Headquarters–Subsidiary Relations in Multinational Corporations*, Aldershot: Gower, 106–120.

Nelson, R.R. & Winter, S.J. (1982). *An Evolutionary Theory of Economic Change*. Cambridge, MA: Belknap Press.

Nobel, R. & Birkinshaw, J. (1998). Innovation in multinational corporations: Control and communication patterns in international R&D operations. *Strategic Management Journal*, **19**, 479–496.

Parolini, C. (1996). *Rete del Valore e Scelte Aziendali*. Milan: EGEA.

Parolini, C. (1999). *The Value Net*. New York: Wiley (forthcoming).

Penrose, E.T. (1959). *The Theory of the Growth of the Firm*. Oxford: Basil Blackwell.

Perlmutter, H.V. (1969). The tortuous evolution of the multinational corporation. *Columbia Journal of World Business*, January–February, 9–18.
Picard, J. (1980). Organizational structures and integrative devices in European multinational corporations. *Columbia Journal of World Business*, **15**, 30–35.
Porter, M.E. (1980). *Competitive Strategy: Techniques for Analyzing Industries and Competitors*. New York: Free Press.
Porter, M.E. (1985). *Competitive Advantage: Creating and Sustaining Superior Performance*. New York: Free Press.
Porter, M.E. (1986). *Competition in Global Industries*. Cambridge, MA: Harvard Business School Press.
Porter, M.E. (1990). *The Competitive Advantage of Nations*. New York: Free Press.
Prahalad, C.K. & Doz, Y. (1987). *The Multinational Mission: Balancing Local Demands and Global Vision*. New York: Free Press.
Prahalad, C.K. & Hamel, G. (1990). The core competence of the corporation. *Harvard Business Review*, **68**, 79–91.
Prahalad, C.K. & Hamel, G. (1994). *Competing for the Future*. Cambridge, MA: Harvard Business School Press.
Prahalad C.K. & Lieberthal, K. (1998). The end of corporate imperialism. *Harvard Business Review*, July–August, 69–79.
Rispoli, M. (1994). *Le Forme di Internazionalizzazione delle Imprese*. Venice: Il Cardo.
Ruef, M. (1997). Assessing organizational fitness on a dynamic landscape: An empirical test of the relative inertia thesis. *Strategic Management Journal*, **18**, 837–853.
Szulanski, G. (1995). *An empirical investigation of the barriers to transfer of best practice inside the firm*. Unpublished doctoral dissertation, INSEAD, France.
United Nations (1991). *World Investment Report. The Triad in Foreign Direct Investment*. New York: United Nations.
Vernon, R. (1966). International investment and international trade in the product cycle. *Quarterly Journal of Economics*, **80**, 190–207.
Vicari, S. (1989). *Nuove Dimensioni della Concorrenza: Strategie nei Mercati Senza Confini*. Milan: EGEA.
Welch, L.S. & Loustarinen, R. (1988). Internationalization: Evolution of a concept. *Journal of General Management*, **14**(2), 34–55.
Wernerfelt, B. (1984). A resource-based view of the firm. *Strategic Management Journal*, **5**, 171–180.
Whitwam, D. (1994). Right way to go global: An interview with Whirlpool CEO David Whitwam. *Harvard Business Review*, **72**(1), 45–56.
Yip, G.S. (1989). Global strategy in a world of nations? *Sloan Management Review*, **31**(1), 29–41.

# Organizational Resources: Development, Commitment and Governance

# 9

# Transition Processes Towards the N-Form Corporation: Strategic Implications for Knowledge Flows[1]

FRANS A.J. VAN DEN BOSCH, RAYMOND A. VAN WIJK

## INTRODUCTION

Firms are increasingly confronted with the strategic challenge of reconciling the exploitation/exploration dilemma regarding knowledge. On the one hand, firms have to exploit their existing knowledge base. On the other hand, without exploring new knowledge areas by knowledge sharing and knowledge creation, firms cannot maintain a competitive advantage. This paper contends that in dealing with this dilemma, organizational form, and in particular the N-form, matters. One way firms have tried to resolve the dilemma is by entering into strategic alliances and other partnerships to gain access to new knowledge and other resources (Day & Wendler, 1998; Ring, 1996; Ring & van de Ven, 1994; Sivula, van den Bosch & Elfring, 1997). However, when firms enter into these external networks, the organizational forms they traditionally have employed, such as the multidivisional M-form, are likely to remain unchanged. It

*Dynamic Strategic Resources: Development, Diffusion and Integration.*
Edited by Michael A. Hitt, Patricia Gorman Clifford, Robert D. Nixon and Kevin P. Coyne.

appears that these traditional organizational forms are less suitable for knowledge sharing and creation.

As a result, firms such as General Electric, Skandia, 3M, Asea Brown Boveri, Hewlett-Packard, Microsoft and Intel have spearheaded the adoption of new organizational forms, that is internal network forms of organizing, as an alternative to the rigid hierarchies of the functional U-form and the multidivisional M-form organizations. The pioneering efforts of protagonist CEOs of these firms, such as Jack Welch (General Electric), Andy Grove (Intel) and Percy Barnevik (ABB), have led to an increasing appreciation in practice and recognition among scholars of the importance of internal networks to increase levels of exploration and experimentation (March, 1991). In scholarly contributions it is claimed that internal network organizations—alternatively labeled as integrated network organizations, N-form corporations, or just N-forms—facilitate knowledge creation, organizational learning and knowledge sharing (e.g. Ghoshal & Bartlett, 1997; Hedlund, 1994). The internal or integrated network form of organizing can be described as "an organization model that allows companies to develop distributed capabilities and expertise, link those capabilities through rich horizontal flows of information, knowledge, and other resources, and develop the trust that is required as a glue to hold together their distributed, integrated organizations" (Ghoshal & Bartlett, 1997: 100). To facilitate these knowledge sharing and creation processes, N-forms are distinct in comparison to traditional organizational forms in light of *three mutually related perspectives*. These perspectives, treated here as conceptual lenses through which we will analyze N-forms, are organizational structure, management, and knowledge flows.

One of the most important characteristics of N-forms is that knowledge flows are primarily horizontal between interdependent organizational units rather than vertical, as they are in more traditional organizational forms (Ghoshal & Bartlett, 1997; Hedlund, 1994). This characteristic enables high levels of coordination and integration of knowledge (*cf.* Grant, 1996), which may lead to higher levels of exploration in firms with internal networks. While the M-form has been considered the most significant organizational innovation of the 20th century, based on the expected increasing importance of knowledge creation and sharing, the N-form might possibly be a candidate for such a position for the coming decades.

Although internal networks have penetrated a wide variety of industries and their scholarly recognition has increased, theories on how N-forms function have only recently begun to appear in the literature (e.g., Ghoshal & Bartlett, 1997; Hedlund, 1994; Miles & Snow, 1994; Nohria, 1996). In addition, except for Ferlie and Pettigrew's (1996) UK-based study of the National Health Service, empirical work regarding *transition processes* towards N-forms is largely lacking. Reflected in the fact that dynamic theories of strategy are still in their infancy (van den Bosch, 1997), few strategic insights are available regarding the transition processes towards N-forms, and the managerial capabilities required for this endeavor (Pettigrew, Conyon & Whittington, 1995).

As we contend that internal networks are important for the management of one of the most strategic resources, knowledge, the transition process towards N-forms deserves attention. That is why we address the *research question* of how transition processes towards internal networks or N-forms take place, and in particular how organizational structure, managerial and knowledge processes change during a firm's transition process towards the N-form corporation.

To answer this question, we will give a brief review of the theoretical contributions regarding N-forms, using three conceptual lenses. Next, we will present a longitudinal case study conducted within a large European multinational financial services firm. The case study highlights the transition process in terms of organizational structure, management processes and knowledge flows during the 1992 to mid-1998 period of a special business unit within the financial services firm. The selected business unit was founded with the purpose of knowledge creation and sharing within the firm. During the transition process the business unit evolved into an expanding internal network.

The paper is structured as follows. In the next section, the N-form will be analyzed from three perspectives. In the third section, a new knowledge flow metric to assess transition processes towards N-forms is proposed. In the fourth section, the results of the case study will be presented. The final section concludes with a discussion highlighting future research avenues and the managerial implications of our findings.

## THE N-FORM CORPORATION FROM THREE PERSPECTIVES

As a way to capture organizational form, Bartlett and Ghoshal (1989) and Nohria and Ghoshal (1997) have proposed a biological analogy to describe the organizational characteristics involved. Organizational form pertains not only to a basic anatomy (i.e. formal structure), but also to a physiology (i.e. interpersonal relationships and processes) and psychology (i.e. shared values and beliefs). In our analysis of internal networks, we will focus primarily on anatomy and physiology. The anatomy of internal networks or N-forms is captured by the first perspective to be discussed: organizational structure. The physiology will be analyzed from both the management and knowledge process perspectives. The psychology of internal networks will be addressed by discussing, among other things, how management processes can contribute to a trust-based organizational culture.

## Organizational Stucture of the N-Form

One of the underlying factors that accounts for the emergence of internal network forms is the dynamizing and globalizing landscape which requires firms to be flexible (Volberda, 1998), and which necessitates being locally responsive while maintaining a global profile (Bartlett & Ghoshal, 1989, 1993). According to Hitt, Keats and DeMarie (1998), in this new competitive landscape strategic flexibility, that is the capability of firms to proact or respond quickly to changing competitive conditions, is most important. In achieving strategic flexibility five major actions are required. One of these is developing new organizational structures. In this connection, Hitt, Keats and DeMarie (1998: 35) suggest the development of horizontal structures that are able "to integrate the different knowledge and expertise of team members from across the organization".

These horizontal structures have much in common with the organizational structure of N-forms. In theoretical contributions to N-forms, however, deliberately creating interdependencies across the organization is emphasized more than horizontal structures. The structure of internal networks is constituted by a decentralized, dense set of dispersed, differentiated, but interdependent organizational units (Hedlund, 1994). Because "knowledge is a resource that is difficult to accumulate at the corporate level and ... that those with the specialized knowledge and expertise most vital to the companies' competitiveness are usually located far away from corporate headquarters" (Bartlett & Ghoshal, 1993: 32), each unit has a certain stock of knowledge localized to, for example, a certain geographical area, a particular market, a certain technology, or even a particular problem. Besides having operational responsibility, each of these largely autonomous organizational units has a large amount of strategic responsibility as well. As each unit more or less performs different activities derived from different asset stocks, organizational units are decentralized specialists (Nohria, 1996) adhering to "economies of depth" rather than to economies of scale or scope (Hedlund, 1994). Since each unit is consequently more or less different concerning its specialism, the N-form corporation is internally disaggregated (Day & Wendler, 1998), enabling a multitude of search processes to build different capabilities and competences capable of being applied to alternative uses. These capabilities and competences enable N-forms to respond effectively to a range of future changes.

In addition to the differentiation of actors, activities, resources and knowledge, each unit is also dependent on the performance of other units and are required to collaborate. These interdependencies across the units enable the *leveraging* of competence (Sanchez, Heene & Thomas, 1996). The ability to leverage competence across its dispersed units is built on the presence of a high degree of trust, reciprocity, and a distributed power structure, as alternatives to the authority and price mechanisms of hierarchies and markets respectively (Handy, 1992; Nohria & Ghoshal, 1997). One way interdependencies are created and maintained within the N-form is by creating "people interdependence" (Hedlund, 1994). Temporary projects are important in such a context. These projects may be multifunctional, and may contain people from different organizational units. Hedlund (1994) pointed out that the recombination of the knowledge of people requires permanence in the personnel pool. A changing pool of people restricts knowledge sharing. Knowledge sharing requires know-who: "To draw on tacit reservoirs of expertise, a certain permanence of employment and relations is desirable" (Hedlund, 1994: 84). By deliberately creating interdependencies, the N-form is also able to realize "coordination flexibility". In line with Hedlund's (1994: 83) observation that in N-forms integrating mechanisms become more important than differentiating mechanisms, the interdependencies across people and across organizational units suggest that firms with different levels of interdependencies may also differ in their transition processes towards N-forms. In the discussion of the case study findings we will come back to this observation.

## Management Processes Within the N-Form

With regard to the various managerial levels within the network organization, Bartlett and Ghoshal (1993) and Ghoshal and Bartlett (1997) indicate that the managerial roles and processes at these levels differ substantially from those in firms with more traditional organizational forms, such as U- and M-forms. Rather than being the composers of the grand strategies, top management's role in the N-form corporation is setting out a vision (Bartlett & Ghoshal, 1993). In so doing, they provide the proper context, based on the creation of trust, shared by other management levels for the creation and sharing of knowledge (Hedlund, 1994), and for the building and leveraging of competences which are built on this knowledge.

Since strategic responsibility is decentralized to lower levels of management, it can be argued that the most appropriate level at which strategies are formed is shifted to middle management. Like other contributors (Floyd & Wooldridge, 1996; Nonaka & Takeuchi, 1995), Bartlett and Ghoshal (1993) stress the importance of *middle management* within the N-form corporation. The major function of middle management is to share resources, skills, and knowledge laterally among organizational units. Middle management in the N-form takes over the role of top management in traditional organizational forms in coordinating the knowledge stocks and flows within the firm. By means of these *lateral managerial mechanisms and relations*, the often long vertical path to and from headquarters in traditional organizational forms such as the M-form is circumvented. In turn, this results in a greater responsiveness to the compelling environmental demands. In that spirit, rather than being the recipients of knowledge and the implementors of resource *allocation* decisions made at the top, middle management in network organizations is responsible for the *leverage* of resources, competences and knowledge. Clearly, firms that have eliminated middle management to a large extent will be confronted with this lack of knowledge integration and leverage capacity in their transition process towards internal networks.

Through the pursuit of new opportunities present in the environment, front-line management's function in N-forms is to create these resources, skills and knowledge to the appropriateness of the deep environmental knowledge present at the localities of organizational units (e.g., market knowledge, technological knowledge), or the requirements elsewhere in the firm. In that vein, front-line management fosters the creation of knowledge, and the enhancement of the knowledge stocks present at the organizational unit.

## KNOWLEDGE FLOWS WITHIN THE N-FORM

Knowledge is essentially related to human action, and therefore context-specific and relational in that it depends on situational circumstances. Knowledge is created dynamically both by individuals and in social interaction among agents (Nonaka & Takeuchi, 1995). As Boisot (1998: 12) points out: "knowledge is a property of agents predisposing them to act in particular circumstances". As organizational form may enable or restrict knowledge creation, we will focus here on how N-forms create a context for actors to create knowledge.

Knowledge processes in N-form corporations involve knowledge creation and sharing by network actors resulting in increases of knowledge stocks (*cf.* Nonaka & Takeuchi, 1995) or knowledge assets (Boisot, 1998), and knowledge flows (Hedlund, 1994). Based on this premise, the key advantage of the N-form has been ascribed to "its ability to create value through the accumulation, transfer, and integration of different kinds of knowledge, resources, and capabilities across its dispersed organizational units" (Nohria & Ghoshal, 1997: 208). As the knowledge flows involved clearly differentiate the various organizational forms (Van Wijk & Van den Bosch, 1998), we will focus on knowledge sharing. This knowledge-sharing capability allows for the *integration* of knowledge which is *differentiated* across formal boundaries (Baker, 1992), and therefore provides the basis to both building and leveraging competence.

Since the constraints springing from bounded rationality prevent knowledge from being accumulated entirely at the corporate level, it is usually located in the localities of the network actors, such as international subsidiaries of multinational corporations (Nohria & Ghoshal, 1997). The widespread use of teams and projects, in which both organizational members and people outside the corporation are represented as human assets, enables the sharing and integration of knowledge and competence. These structural instruments enable horizontal knowledge flows. In more traditional organizational forms, such as the functional U-form and multidivisional M-form, knowledge flows are primarily vertical and unidirectional from headquarters to divisions, business units, and operating units. In N-forms, however, it has been argued that knowledge flows are to a large extent horizontal or lateral, and above all bi- or multidirectional (Hedlund, 1994; Quinn, Anderson, & Finkelstein, 1996). Therefore, to gain insight into the progress regarding sharing of knowledge in the transition process towards N-forms, monitoring the changing configuration of both horizontal and vertical knowledge flows is of strategic importance.

## A New Knowledge Flow Metric to Assess Transition Processes

Besides the organizational knowledge processes and managerial skills involved in developing the N-form corporation, there is also need for a new metric through which the transition process towards the N-form corporation can be described and analyzed. Traditional metrics, such as the degrees of formalization, centralization, specialization and standardization, are important to discriminate traditional organizational forms from new organizational forms, such as the N-form corporation. With the increasing importance of knowledge, and the advent of new knowledge processes in the N-form corporation, however, a new metric by which both practitioners and scholars are able to assess the dynamics of the knowledge flow configuration in use by firms may be useful.

Below, the H/V ratio is proposed as an example of such a new metric. The H/V ratio provides a measure to analyze the extent to which an organization operates under the strategic logic of an N-form corporation (Van Wijk & Van den Bosch, 1998). By relating the incidence of horizontal knowledge flows to the incidence of vertical knowledge flows, an assessment of the phase of the transition process towards internal network forms of organizing is possible. The knowledge flows include both explicit and tacit knowledge. The H/V ratio is formulated as

$$\text{H/V ratio} = \frac{\text{horizontal knowledge flows}}{\text{vertical knowledge flows}}$$

As suggested by the above-mentioned theoretical contributions to the N-form literature, firms with internal network forms or N-form corporations are likely to have an H/V ratio larger than 1, in which case horizontal knowledge flows have a higher perceived incidence than vertical ones. In contrast, it is expected that the H/V ratio of more traditional organizational forms, such as multidivisional forms, is likely to be lower than 1. An H/V ratio lower than 1 indicates that vertical knowledge flows have a higher perceived incidence compared to horizontal ones. This also suggests that when firms transform themselves and start adopting the logic of the N-form corporation to the demise of traditional organizational forms, the H/V ratio is likely to increase over time.

The transition process of multidivisional firms or M-form corporations towards firms operating internal network forms of organization or N-form corporations is likely to be complex and takes up a large amount of time. During this process organizational structure, management processes, and knowledge flows have to change in the direction of the N-form logic. To monitor and analyze this process, the H/V ratio might be helpful. The transition processes take place, however, at various levels of analysis within the firm, with different speeds. This means that different units of analysis, such as a business unit within a tightly integrated division or one in a loosely integrated division, portray different H/V ratios. Besides the H/V ratio at the firm level, an H/V ratio can be estimated for various other units of analysis within a firm. For example, the H/V ratio of a division in which the business units are highly interdependent regarding knowledge creation is likely to be higher in comparison to a division having rather independent business units.

FIGURE 9.1 provides a "snapshot" of the incidence of horizontal and vertical knowledge flows in a stylized multidivisional firm, having a strong corporate center and a central staff organization (e.g., performing R&D activities, legal department, etc.). For one division, division 3, the structure is further elaborated. This division consists of two business units. The solid lines depict examples of vertical knowledge flows. These solid lines represent hierarchical relations associated with unidirectional knowledge flows. The dotted lines depict examples of horizontal knowledge flows. These flows can be operationalized by multidirectional knowledge flows due to knowledge sharing. If all the knowledge required to perform, improve, and rejuvenate the activities of the two business units in the third division comes from outside these units, the H/V ratio of this division is low. If between these units a process of knowledge sharing and creation takes place, over time this development will be reflected in an increase of the division's H/V ratio. Similarly, if the same process takes place within the units themselves—that is, the units within the business unit start knowledge sharing—the H/V ratio of the business unit increases as well.

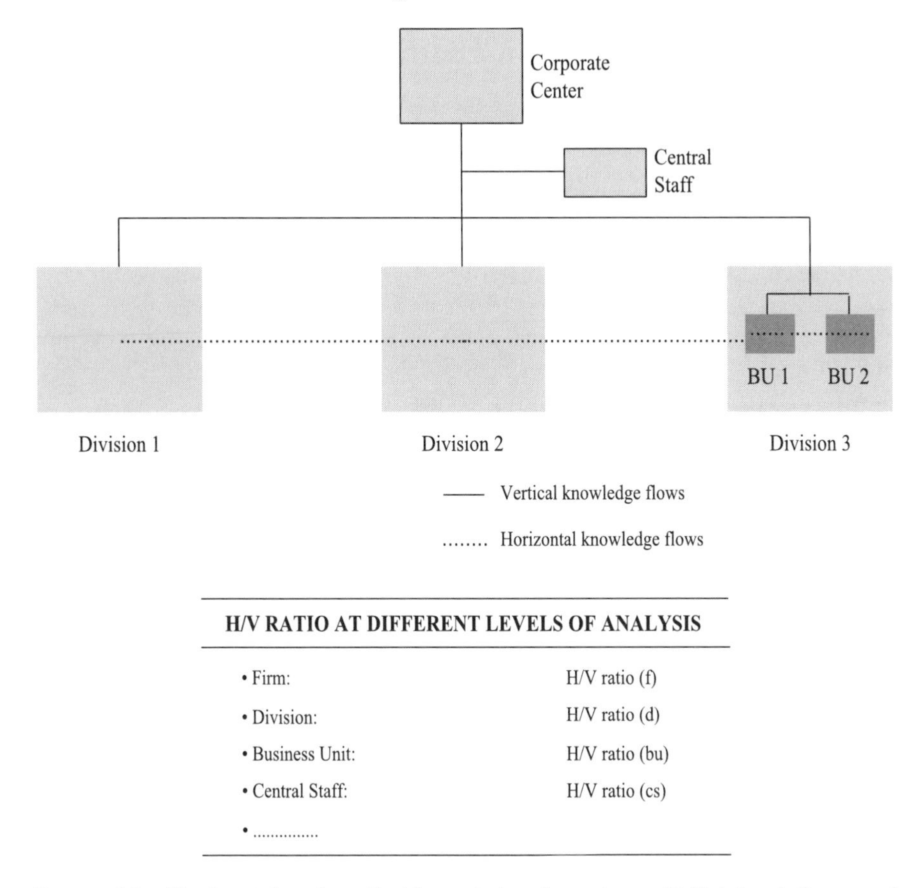


FIGURE 9.1 Horizontal and vertical knowledge flows in multidivisional firms, and H/V ratios at different units of analysis

The H/V ratio at the firm level can be considered, at least in principle, as an indicator of the average of the H/V ratios of all the organizational parts within the firm. Therefore, the H/V ratio at the firm level might be considered an indicator of the overall transition process of existing firms towards N-forms. Obviously, empirical research regarding this ratio is far more complicated than will be illustrated here in assessing the H/V ratio at the business unit level. For the purposes of acquiring insight into transition processes, however, a longitudinal analysis of the transition process including the H/V ratio of a business unit chosen for that purpose, as will be described in the next section, might be useful.

## Case Study of a Transition Process

A case study was conducted at Banco to gain insight into the transition processes of firms moving from a traditional organizational form to an N-form.[2] Banco is a large European multinational financial services firm, employing more than 10 000 people, whose aim is to provide financial services in a competitive national and international market. In 1997, it had a total income of more than 5 billion US dollars (interest, commission, and other income) in its consolidated Profit and Loss Account. Due to blurring industry boundaries, the financial services industry is increasingly becoming integrated, enabling Banco to benefit from synergistic effects. Therefore, Banco is structured accordingly, consisting of a central organization operating in the banking industry, some affiliated subsidiaries competing in related industries, such as insurance, and a substantial number of locally embedded units through which the clients are mainly served.

The longitudinal case study was conducted at Banco's facilitatory business unit, named Profac. The reason for this choice was that Profac was especially created by top management with the deliberate aim of increasing the creation of knowledge to be at the service of the rest of Banco. The founding of Profac illustrates that the role of top management is clearly of great importance in the creation of N-forms (Bartlett & Ghoshal, 1997). The analysis of the transition process of this business unit may provide new insights into the structural, managerial and knowledge flow issues involved during transition processes.

## Methodology

As did Ghoshal and Bartlett (1997) and Nohria and Ghoshal (1997) in their studies on internal networks, in the case study we made use of interviews and archival data. The data reported here stem from research conducted in late 1997 and early 1998. A total of 15 interviews were held with founding "fathers", present and previous management team members, and other coordinating employees to get acquainted with the transition process of the business unit into a growing and developing internal network. The semi-structured interviews focused on the transition processes in Profac, in particular the changing configuration of knowledge flows between the constituent subunits of the business unit, the management processes and skills involved, and factors that affected the transition process. The facilitatory Profac business unit was founded in 1992 with the explicit goal of "creating knowledge". The clients of Profac consisted of other organizational units within Banco, in particular the network of local units and the central organization, and a small number of external clients. Similar to the theoretical exposition of this paper, the transition process of Profac will be described from the above-mentioned perspectives, that is in terms of structural, managerial and knowledge-flow transition.

## STRUCTURAL TRANSITION

Profac has been transforming ever since its foundation in 1992. The structure of Profac has undergone substantial changes in its short history, which are illustrated in FIGURE 9.2. The major transition occurred in 1994/1995 when the old way of organizing was completely recast.

At its foundation in 1992, Profac employed 30 people and was organized along two exploratory Product Units (PUs) that stood in close relation to each other. Knowledge creation and sharing were considered to be the most important. Shortly after its foundation, Profac increased in size as a result of the incorpation of a number of groups from other parts of Banco. These groups gave rise to the creation of three new PUs within the existing organizational structure. With the inclusion of these three PUs, the number of employees rose from 30 to 60. Triggered by a process of compartmentalization of the PUs, this increase in organizational size had a negative impact on the creation and sharing of knowledge across Profac. The interviews revealed that this compartmentalization process led to a differentiation of norms and values.

As these developments inhibited the creation and sharing of knowledge horizontally across PUs, in 1994/1995 the structure of Profac was completely conceived anew by Profac's management team and in particular its CEO, as chairman of the management team. The purpose of this major organization was to regain the internal network form of organization and the exploratory focus of the year immediately following foundation. The five PUs were abolished, and instead three "Areas of Attention" ("Advice", "Development" and "Exploitation") were created to recast the organization and to change the rhetoric used in Profac. Partly because the number of employees increased to approximately 100, each area of attention had a number of interdependent "clusters" to retain, as the Chief Executive of Profac referred to it, "the subtlety of small groups". The number of clusters in an area of attention was deliberately variable in order to tailor Profac to changing client demands and technological advancements. That is, in one period of time there could be five clusters, whereas in a subsequent period there could be three or eight clusters, possibly regarding entirely different subjects and with a different composition of knowledge workers.

By the end of 1996, the number of employees had increased to 220. As in the previous period, the number of formal management layers, however, remained unchanged. With the establishment of projects cutting across

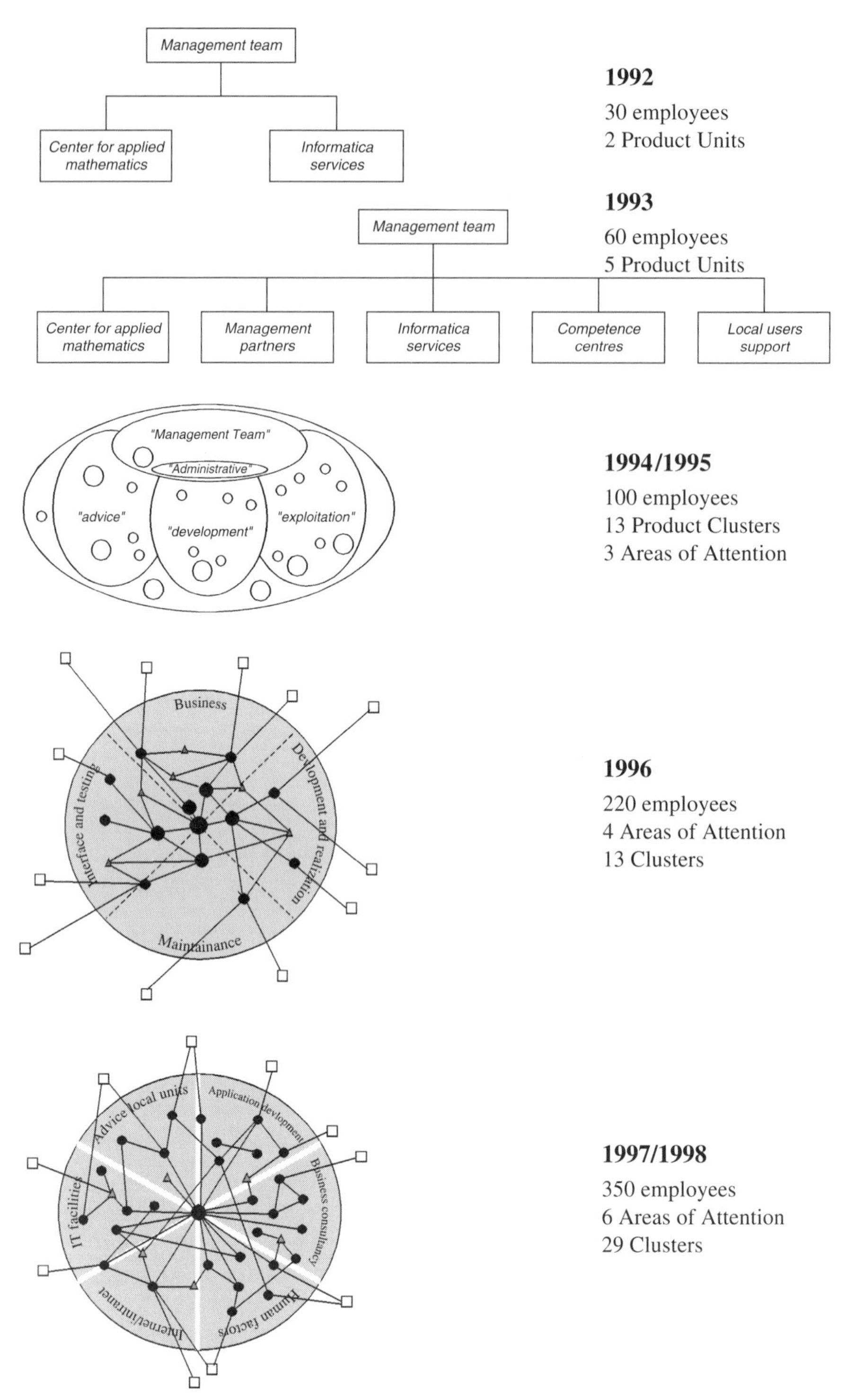


FIGURE 9.2 The transition process of the Profac Business Unit of Banco

clusters and areas of attention to ease collaboration, however, the number of organizational layers has increased by one. Although the increase in the number of employees led to an additional area of attention, the organizational setup remained intact. However, as the number of employees had increased to approximately 350 by the end of 1997, partly because of the inflow of people from another business unit of Banco, the number of areas of attention has been increased to six. The number of clusters within Profac has increased as well: from 13 in 1996 to 29 at the beginning of 1998.

## Transition of Management Processes

The structural transition process of the Profac business unit also had implications for the management processes in the business unit. In particular, the increase in employees had a substantial impact on the managerial function in that the span of control of managers increased rapidly over time.

During the main transition period in 1994/1995, an additional layer of coordinating personnel in the form of cluster coordinators was therefore added to free up some of the time of the management team, in that the manager of an area of attention was no longer able to oversee the activities of all employees. These cluster coordinators were not appointed formal management positions with formal management tasks (e.g., execution of performance appraisals, authority to sign for contracts of more than 5 000 US dollars). The Chief Executive of Profac described the cluster coordinators rather as the "functional feeders" of Profac. Their task is limited to overseeing and leading the activities in their cluster in order that the goals of Profac were adhered to. In addition, cluster coordinators also have an important role in establishing linkages across clusters and areas of attention. Thus, although there were three *organizational layers* (management team, cluster coordinators, employees), there was still only one formal *management layer* in the period 1994–1995.

In 1996, the number of organizational layers was increased by one with the establishment of project managers heading the projects of persons from different clusters and areas of attention. These project managers originated from one of the clusters participating in the project, and if the project was an encompassing one, one of the members of the Management Team functioned as project leader. As the number of employees increased from approximately 220 to 350 over the period 1996–1998, managers were confronted with serious time constraints. As a Management Team member observed, "If I do all my performance appraisal talks with the employees, I will be busy for one to two months." This development has currently led to extensive discussions to delegate formal management functions to the cluster coordinators. This discussion has focused, on the one hand, on the issue that the Management Team of Profac wanted to maintain only one formal layer of management to preserve Profac's flat structure and flexibility, and on the other hand, on the awareness that the increasing size of Profac requires additional management resources.

Currently, the Management Team of Profac appears to favor the latter point of the discussion. As the Chief Executive of Profac recognized, "The *way* of organizing matters, no matter what kind of structure you have. The processes are important." This way of organizing, emphasizing collaboration, communication, informality, and fluidity, has always been an integral part of the vision of Profac, as set out by the Chief Executive. All the changes in Profac have also occurred under this vision of the Chief Executive, who has been with Profac since its foundation.

## Knowledge Flows During the Transition Process

Over its six-year existence, the business unit has witnessed different developments regarding horizontal and vertical knowledge flows. These developments have been both the result and the cause of the managerial and structural changes that have taken place to reconceptualize the business unit. This reconceptualization process stems from continuous threats to its internal network form, which Profac confronted during the transition process. As a result, the H/V ratio, the relation between horizontal and vertical knowledge flows, changed over time as well.

Based on internal documents and interpreting the comments made in interviews, Figure 9.3 depicts a tentative representation of the development of the H/V ratio during the transition process. Shortly after Profac's foundation, the two PUs stood in close relation to each other and were able to share both explicit and tacit knowledge directly on a horizontal basis, either by face-to-face contacts or via Information Technology systems, across the boundaries of the respective PUs. With the incorporation of another three PUs in 1993, the increasing compartmentalization led quickly to progressive differences among the PUs, inhibiting the process of horizontal knowledge sharing across PU boundaries. Consequently, the H/V ratio decreased. As a Management Team member observed, "People in one Product Unit wear T-shirts, whereas people in another wear suits. This illustrates the difference in culture between the Product Units, and the resulting lack of communication and knowledge sharing between them."

The main transition period of 1994/1995 was instigated to reconceptualize the configuration of knowledge flows, and to increase the incidence of horizontal knowledge flows. The creation of areas of attention and clusters

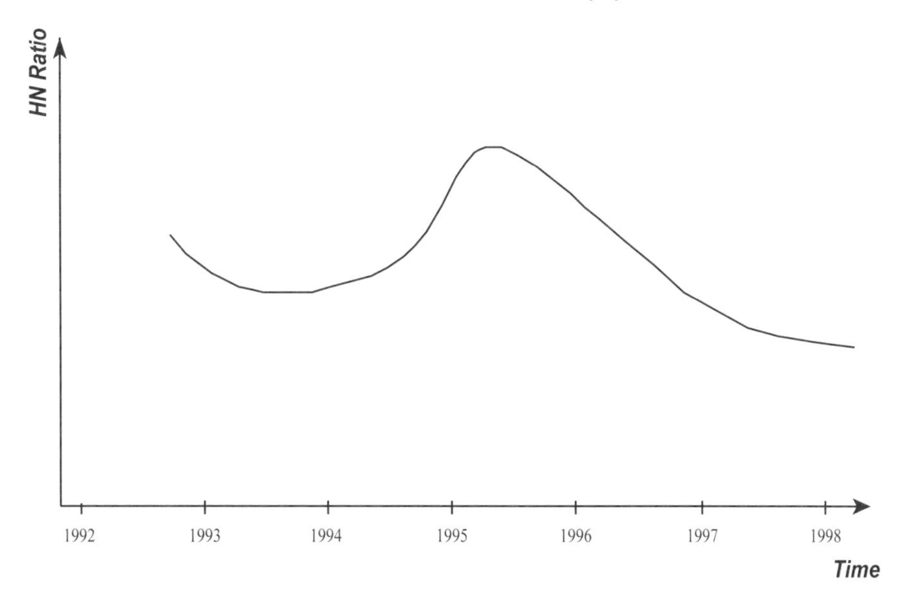


FIGURE 9.3 A tentative representation of the H/V ratio of Profac in transition. (Source: Based on longitudinal case study of Profac, 1992–1998)

aimed to resuscitate the idea of smallness within Profac, broke down artificial barriers. As a result, the sharing of knowledge across boundaries increased. Clusters remained small in order to ensure that the employees working for the clusters needed to consult each other to solve their problems. Knowledge sharing took place by means of formal routes as well as informal ones, such as, as the Chief Executive called it, "unintended meetings at the central coffee machine". Consequently, the H/V ratio increased during this period.

As the number of employees increased constantly, however, the areas of attention became also "islands" within Profac in terms of knowledge sharing. The creation of projects as a structural mechanism took place in 1996 to improve the transfer of knowledge across clusters and areas of attention. However, as more employees started working for Profac, projects were increasingly established within the confines of the areas of attention. This development led to a decrease in the incidence of horizontal knowledge flows, and therefore to a downward trend of the H/V ratio.

Based on the idea that employees carry with them tacit knowledge, we initiated an investigation of the transfer of people over the clusters and projects at the end of 1997. Our purpose was to establish the *transfer of tacit knowledge* across clusters and areas of attention. TABLE 9.1 contains the results. In analyzing the composition of all Profac's projects at a certain

TABLE 9.1 Snapshot of the composition of all Profac's projects (end of 1997)

| Composition of project | Employees | Cluster coordinators |
|---|---|---|
| What percentage of the projects have people from the same cluster? | 85% | 67% |
| What percentage of the projects have people from different clusters but within the same area of attention? | 3% | 6% |
| What percentage of the projects have people from different clusters and different areas of attention? | 12% | 27% |

Source: Survey of project administration initiated by authors.

point in time (end of 1997), three categories of projects were distinguished. The first category contains projects involving only people from the same cluster. The second category contains projects involving people from different clusters but belonging to the same area of attention. The last category contains projects involving people from across the different areas of attention. We expected that employees were less likely to work across areas of attention than were cluster coordinators. As the findings in TABLE 9.1 show, this was indeed the case. About 12% of employees work in projects containing people from more than one area of attention. In the case of cluster coordinators, this percentage rises to 27%. Furthermore, contrary to what we expected, the degree of cross-fertilization within projects, that is projects in which people from different clusters and areas of attention are present, was only 15% for the employees. For the cluster coordinators it amounted to 33%, clearly indicating their key role in knowledge sharing.

These preliminary findings suggest that most knowledge was transferred within these areas. Knowledge flows, in particular tacit knowledge flows between areas of attention, were less frequent. Only the large-scale projects, for example the project to prepare the Information Technology structure of Banco for the year 2000, used employees from various areas of attention. As a result, in 1997 the H/V ratio of horizontal knowledge flows to vertical ones decreased. The relative increase of vertical knowledge flows as opposed to horizontal ones was also strengthened by the incorporation of a substantial number of employees from another business unit of Banco. This other business unit had a hierarchical tradition, which was clearly reflected in the behavior of its employees. As a result, in joining Profac these hierarchically oriented employees witnessed substantial difficulty in working in an internal network.

## Discussion and Conclusion

Internal networks may be considered a new strategic variable in the management of firm resources to create a competitive advantage. However, empirical studies examining the transition processes of a firm's existing organizational form towards the N-form are lacking. This paper examined a longitudinal case study of such a transition process in a large multidivisional firm. The investigation took place from three complementary perspectives: organizational structure, management processes and knowledge processes. In particular, we addressed the strategic implications for the configuration of knowledge flows, using the H/V ratio as a new knowledge flow metric. In discussing the results of our analysis and case study, we focus on three topics: first, the usefulness of simultaneously looking at the transition process via three perspectives or conceptual lenses; second, the nature of the transition process; and third, issues highlighted in the transition process deserving managerial attention. These issues are the importance of knowledge flows for strategic change; organizational size as a potential inhibiting factor in the creation of internal networks; the measurement of knowledge flows; and finally, the impact of initial conditions on, for instance, the speed of the transition process.

Looking from *three perspectives* (organizational, managerial and knowledge) to the transition process towards the N-form corporation appeared fruitful. As the description and analysis of the transition process of Profac shows, for a proper understanding of N-forms these three perspectives must be considered mutually related. For example, it appeared that after getting the organizational form right, the subtlety of small groups with substantial horizontal knowledge flows was restored again. Subsequently, the next problem arose: the management processes required adjustments. In response to these problems, a new coordination layer was created by establishing cluster coordinators. This new coordination layer, however, appeared to be insufficient to counterbalance the decreasing horizontal knowledge flows across the boundaries between individual projects, clusters, and areas of attention. As Figure 9.3 depicts, this resulted in a downward trend of the H/V ratio. Clearly, an important lesson for creating knowledge-based strategies was learned in that organizational structure, management processes and knowledge flows are mutually related to each other. The *interconnectedness* of these three perspectives brings us to a discussion of the nature of the transition process.

As stated in the introduction, empirical work is scarce regarding the *nature of the transition process* towards N-forms. Having no empirical evidence at hand, a plausible assumption could be that these transition processes are of a more or less linear and incremental nature. As is revealed in the case study, the opposite may be more true. The message of

FIGURES 9.2 and 9.3 is that the nature of the transition process can be described as showing the alternation between two different types of transition phases: a progression phase and a regression phase. The first type, characterized by a *progression* towards the N-form, is a phase in the transition process in which the firm's organizational structure, as well as its management and knowledge processes, simultaneously develop towards N-form characteristics. The second type can be characterized by a *regression* from the N-form, with the reversed effect. TABLE 9.2 summarizes some key attributes of both transition phases as seen through the three conceptual lenses or perspectives.

Although a number of issues highlighted in the case study deserve more research attention, we will give an indication of the relevance for management practice of these issues. The first issue deserving attention is the possible influence of knowledge flows on *strategic change*. In this regard, Hærem, von Krogh and Roos (1996: 132) argue that "... it is the knowledge transfer processes which determine the change direction of a company." This suggests that the managerial ability to deliberately influence knowledge processes and flows will determine the success of the implementation of the intended strategy. Our research findings on the Profac case study support this relationship. They show how the managerial ability to change the intensity and directionality of knowledge flows indeed determines whether the deliberate strategy of creating and maintaining an internal network structure was successful. In the 1993–1994 period, Profac drifted away from an internal network strategy, as is reflected in the downward trend of the H/V ratio in FIGURE 9.3. This triggered Profac's CEO to take initiatives aimed at increasing horizontal knowledge flows. Thereby Profac's organizational structure was redirected towards an internal network in the 1994–1995 period. However, shortly after this major effort,

TABLE 9.2 Two phases in the transition process towards the N-form and some key attributes

| | Three perspectives to examine the transition process towards N-forms | | |
|---|---|---|---|
| | Organizational structure | Management processes | Knowledge flows |
| *Progression phase* towards N-form | Organizational structure is no bottleneck | Linking people | H/V ratio increases |
| *Regression phase* from N-form | Compartmentalization | Struggle with size | H/V ratio decreases |

Source: Based on a longitudinal case study of Profac, 1992–1998.

horizontal knowledge flows again became less prevalent (see FIGURE 9.3). Clearly, implementing an internal network as a knowledge-based strategy seems to be a major managerial challenge. As FIGURE 9.2 suggested, one of the most serious problems during the transition process of Profac was the growth of the number of employees: from 30 in 1992 to about 12 times that number in 1998. This fast growth process and, in particular, dealing with organizational size is the second issue deserving attention.

Although the relevance of *organizational size* to the creation of internal networks or N-forms did not belong among our research questions, in the description and analysis of the transition process of Profac it was found to have exerted a major impact on this process. That is why we would like to raise the question whether there is a kind of "natural" limit to functioning as an internal network. This idea of a "natural" limit is triggered by statements of companies. Due to the need for knowledge creation and sharing, in particular regarding tacit knowledge, a number of well-known international business services firms state that their offices should not have more than about 50 or 100 people. What evidence can be inferred from our research regarding this question? The transition process of Profac indeed suggests that size matters. Similarly, it appeared that deliberately changing organizational structure and management processes matters, in the sense that adopting organizational structure and management processes may partly and temporarily undo the effect of organizational size on the creation of the N-form. The Profac case provides interesting examples, such as the creation of areas of attention, clusters, additional coordinative organizational layers (cluster coordinators) and the addition of projects to the formal structure of Profac. These managerial efforts to cope with the increasing size of Profac have pushed Profac, albeit for a limited period of time, from the regression phase towards the progression phase (see TABLE 9.2). Needless to say, the issue of size deserves further research attention to create more understanding of how managerial efforts and organizational change can cope with growth in the creation of N-forms.

A third issue deserving attention is the measurement of *knowledge flows*. We focused mainly on managerial perceptions of intra-organizational knowledge flows. Although these perceptions undoubtedly reflect managerial cognition, attention should be paid to the incidence of actual knowledge flows as well. The H/V ratio can be used for this purpose. As tacit knowledge is strategically most important, a focus on tacit knowledge flows seems to be of particular interest. To get a quantitative indication of the incidence of tacit knowledge flows, the transfer of "knowledge workers" across the different parts of internal networks, such as clusters, areas of attention, etc., can be measured over time. As we showed in the Profac case (see TABLE 9.1), such an indication offers additional insights into knowledge flows in internal networks. From a more general perspective, the increasing necessity of creating knowledge-based strategies will definitely trigger the need for managerial metrics to measure and monitor knowledge flows. The suggested H/V ratio could be of help for that purpose.

A fourth and final issue deserving attention is the impact that *initial conditions*, or imprinting at founding (Stinchcombe, 1965) of distinct systems of control, might have on the transition process. As we suggested in the theoretical analysis of organizational structure of N-forms, firms with different levels of interdependencies may differ in their transition process, for instance, regarding speed. For example, a multidivisional firm with divisions characterized by substantial interdependencies between business units, and having higher divisional H/V ratios than is usual in its industry, possesses a positive initial condition. Such an initial condition is likely to favor such firms in their transition process towards internal networks. Organizational units having already a favorable "starting position" may function as the seeds and catalysts of the transition process at the firm level. The Profac case study illustrated this conjecture at the business level. As is described in the case study, the initial conditions were rather favorable. Fast growth, in the Profac case by a sudden inflow of employees not accustomed to working in an internal network environment, however, can reduce the impact of initial conditions. This impact of initial conditions on the transition process of firms makes these transition processes path dependent: a "one best way" of transition processes is likely not to be found.

In a Special Issue of the *Strategic Management Journal* on "Knowledge and the Firm" it is stated that: "... the process by which knowledge is created and utilized in organizations may be the key inimitable resource managers need to appreciate, if not understand ..." (Schendel, 1996: 3). We submit that internal networks or N-forms play a key role in this process. Our paper has contributed to the understanding of the process by which knowledge is created and utilized in firms in several ways. First, it presents an empirical investigation of knowledge flows in internal networks, including the development and application of a new managerial metric to measure and monitor knowledge flows. Second, it describes and analyzes how a concrete transition process of a business unit towards the N-form takes place within a large multidivisional firm. The analysis reveals an alternation between two transition phases: a progression towards and a regression from the N-form. Third, the analysis of the transition process also shows how and why managerial insights and efforts are needed to create, and in particular to maintain, N-forms as a competitive advantage in knowledge-intensive environments.

In conclusion, understanding and managing transition processes towards new organizational forms, in particular those suitable for knowledge creation and sharing such as N-forms, presents a challenge for both strategy scholars and managers, the former in their search for inimitable firm-specific resources, and the latter to acquire the appropriate managerial capabilities to create and maintain N-forms as a competitive advantage.

## Notes

1. This paper was one of the finalists for the 1998 McKinsey/SMS Best Conference Paper Prize. The authors participate in an international research project on New Forms of Organizing coordinated by Professor Andrew Pettigrew of Warwick University, UK. We gratefully appreciate the comments of the participants of this research project on earlier versions of this paper. We are also indebted to the managers of Banco's central organization, and the managers of the business unit Profac for their valuable support in preparing the case study. Furthermore, we acknowledge the valuable comments and suggestions of the participants of the 1998 SMS Conference who have shared their ideas with us. In particular, we would like to thank Trish Clifford, Kevin Coyne, Michael Hitt and Robert Nixon for their comments on our paper. Of course, the usual disclaimer applies.
2. For reasons of confidentiality, the subject of the case study is labeled "Banco". In order to preserve anonymity, references to citations made by organizational members in either interviews or magazines are omitted.

## References


Baker, W.E. (1992). The network organization in theory and practice. In N. Nohria & R.G. Eccles (eds), *Networks and Organizations: Structure, Form and Action*, Boston, MA: Harvard Business School Press, 397–429.

Bartlett, C.A. & Ghoshal, S. (1989). *Managing Across Borders: The Transnational Solution*. Boston, MA: Harvard Business School Press.

Bartlett, C.A. & Ghoshal, S. (1993). Beyond the M-form: Toward a managerial theory of the firm. *Strategic Management Journal*, **14** (Winter Special Issue), 23–46.

Bartlett, C.A. & Ghoshal, S. (1997). The myth of the generic manager: New personal competencies for new management roles. *California Management Review*, **40**(1), 92–116.

Boisot, M. (1998). *Knowledge Assets*. Oxford: Oxford University Press.

Day, J.D. & Wendler, J.C. (1998). The new economics of organization. *McKinsey Quarterly*, **X**(1), 4–18.

Ferlie, E. & Pettigrew, A.M. (1996). Managing through networks: Some issues and implications for the NHS. *British Journal of Management*, **7** (Special Issue), S81-S99.

Floyd, S.W. & Wooldridge, B. (1996). *The Strategic Middle Manager: How to Create and Sustain Competitive Advantage*. San Francisco, CA: Jossey Bass.

Ghoshal, S. & Bartlett, C.A. (1997). *The Individualized Corporation: A Fundamentally New Management Model*. San Francisco, CA: Harper.

Grant, R.M. (1996). Prospering in dynamically-competitive environments: Organizational capability as knowledge integration. *Organization Science*, **7**(4), 375–387.

Hærem, T., von Krogh, G. & Roos, J. (1996). Knowledge-based strategic change. In G. von Krogh & J. Roos (eds), *Managing Knowledge: Perspectives on Cooperation and Competition*, London: Sage 116–136.

Handy, C. (1992). Balancing corporate power: A new federalist paper. *Harvard Business Review*, **70**(6), 59–72.
Hedlund, G. (1994). A model of knowledge management and the N-form corporation. *Strategic Management Journal*, **15** (Summer Special Issue), 73–90.
Hitt, M.A., Keats, B.W. & DeMarie, S.M. (1998). Navigating in the new competitive landscape: Building strategic flexibility and competitive advantage in the 21st century. *Academy of Management Executive*, **12**(4), 22–42.
March, J.G. (1991). Exploration and exploitation in organizational learning. *Organization Science*, **2**(1), 71–87.
Miles, R.E. & Snow, C.C. (1994). *Fit, Failure and the Hall of Fame*. New York: Free Press.
Nohria, N. (1996). *From the M-form to the N-form: Taking stock of changes in the large industrial corporation*. Working paper 96-054, Division of Research, Harvard Business School, Boston, MA.
Nohria, N. & Ghoshal, S. (1997). *The Differentiated Network: Organizing Multinational Corporations for Value Creation*. San Francisco, CA: Jossey-Bass.
Nonaka, I. & Takeuchi, H. (1995). *The Knowledge-Creating Company*. Oxford: Oxford University Press.
Quinn, J.B., Anderson, P. & Finkelstein, S. (1996). New forms of organizing. In H. Mintzberg & J.B. Quinn (eds), *The Strategy Process*, New York: Prentice-Hall, 350–362.
Pettigrew, A.M., Conyon, M. & Whittington, R. (1995). *The New Internal Network Organisation: Process and Performance*. Successful proposal to the ESRC, UK.
Ring, P.S. (1996). Networked organization: A resource based perspective. *Acta Universitatis Upsaliensis, Studia Oeconomiae Negotiorum*, 39.
Ring, P.S. & van de Ven, A. (1994). Developmental processes of cooperative interorganizational relationships. *Academy of Management Review*, **19**(1), 90–118.
Sanchez, R., Heene, A. & Thomas, H. (1996). Towards the theory and practice of competence-based competition. In R. Sanchez, A. Heene & H. Thomas (eds), *Dynamics of Competence-based Competition: Theory and Practice in the New Strategic Management*, Oxford: Pergamon, 1–35.
Schendel, D.E. (1996). Editor's introduction to the 1996 Winter Special Issue: Knowledge and the firm. *Strategic Management Journal*, **17** (Winter Special Issue), 1–4.
Sivula, R.P., van den Bosch, F.A.J. & Elfring, T. (1997). Competence building by incorporating clients into the development of a business service firm's knowledge base. In R. Sanchez & A. Heene (eds), *Strategic Learning and Knowledge Management*. Chichester: Wiley, 121–137.
Stinchecombe, A. (1965). Social structure and organizations. In J.G. March (ed.), *Handbook of Organizations*, Chicago, IL: Rand McNally, 142–193.
Van den Bosch, F.A.J. (1997). Porter's contribution to more general and dynamic strategy frameworks. In F.A.J. van den Bosch & A.-P. de Man (eds), *Perspectives on Strategy: Contributions of Michael E. Porter*, Boston, MA: Kluwer Academic, 91–100.
Van Wijk, R.A. & van den Bosch, F.A.J. (1998). Knowledge characteristics of internal network-based forms of organizing. In S. Havlovic (ed.), *Academy of Management Best Paper Proceedings*, BPS: B1–B7.
Volberda, H.W. (1998). *Building the Flexible Firm: How to Remain Competitive*. Oxford: Oxford University Press.

# 10

# "Creative Destruction" or "Creative Cooperation"? A Tale of Two Industries

FRANK T. ROTHAERMEL

## INTRODUCTION

A generation ago, companies such as Compaq or Amgen did not exist. Amazon.com is less than five years old. Technological revolutions such as the microprocessor, biotechnology or the Internet, for example, have reshaped existing industries in dramatic ways or created entirely new industries. These technological discontinuities have had a tremendous impact on competition and company performance in the computer and pharmaceutical industries, as well as on book publishing and retailing, among many other industries.

In this paper, I advance and test two different models with respect to the nature of competition following a technological discontinuity. On the one hand, Schumpeter (1942: 83) considers capitalism as an economic system in which competition is driven by the perennial gale of "creative destruction". Underlying capitalism is an evolutionary process that follows a characteristic pattern. In periods of market equilibria, established firms earn economic profits based on innovative products or processes. These equilibria are transient since they are punctuated by discontinuities in which prevailing competences are made obsolete and new competences will command economic rents for innovating firms. The innovating firms will

*Dynamic Strategic Resources: Development, Diffusion and Integration.*
Edited by Michael A. Hitt, Patricia Gorman Clifford, Robert D. Nixon and Kevin P. Coyne.

eventually rise to become the new dominant firms in the period following the discontinuity. The innovators will dominate the market until a new discontinuity will make their competitive advantage obsolete, which hails a new round of creative destruction. Schumpeter observes that markets are not static but dynamic in nature and that any equilibrium must be transient since competition is a process driven by creative destruction:

> Capitalism ... is by nature a form or method of economic change and not only never is but never can be stationary. ... The fundamental impulse that sets and keeps the capitalist engine in motion comes from the new consumers' goods, the new methods of production or transportation, the new markets, the new forms of industrial organization. ... [This] industrial mutation ... revolutionizes the economic structure from within, incessantly destroying the old one, incessantly creating a new one. The process of Creative Destruction is the essential fact about capitalism ... it is not [price] competition which counts but the competition from ... *the new technology* ... competition which strikes not at the margins of the profits ... of existing firms but at their foundations and their very lives. (1942: 82–84; emphasis added)

Schumpeter views the perennial gale of creative destruction as the driving force behind the market system. On the other hand, not every innovation must necessarily lead to a Schumpeterian process of creative destruction. For example, in the biopharmaceutical industry we observe a process of "creative cooperation" between existing, traditional pharmaceutical companies and new biotechnology firms (NBFs), which have entered the market for drug discovery and manufacturing since the mid-1970s. In this paper, the Schumpeterian model of creative destruction is complemented by the notion of creative cooperation, which describes the phenomenon of extensive cooperation between incumbents and new entrants initiated ("created") by a technological discontinuity that leads to a search for mutually complementary assets. Complementary assets such as marketing, manufacturing, and after-sales service are often needed to ensure the successful commercialization of an innovation (Teece, 1986). Therefore, a technological discontinuity that leads to the process of creative cooperation destroys the existing industry structure but instead of destroying the incumbent firms with it—as in the extreme case of the Schumpeterian model —it creates an industry structure of extensive cooperation between incumbents and new entrants that allows for symbiotic coexistence in a newly defined industry. To discriminate between the two competitive models of creative destruction and creative cooperation, the notion of competence-enhancing versus competence-destroying technological discontinuity is helpful (Tushman & Anderson, 1986). However, the concept of competence-enhancing versus competence-destroying technological discontinuity is dichotomous as it relates to the technological competence of the firm. In order to fully understand the impact of a technological discontinuity on a firm and the resulting nature of competition in an industry, the discontinuity's total effect on a firm's technological and non-technological competences should be taken into account (Tripsas, 1997).

The two competitive models of creative destruction and creative cooperation discussed in this paper will allow us to better understand the nature of competition and its impact on firm performance following a technological discontinuity. The industry sample includes the mainframe computer and pharmaceutical industries. For each industry, one technological discontinuity is identified and its impact on the nature of competition and firm performance is empirically tested. More specifically, the identified technological discontinuity for the mainframe computer industry is the arrival of the PC in 1981, and for the pharmaceutical industry it is the emergence of the new biotechnology since the mid-1970s. The proposed model of the nature of competition following a technological discontinuity is operationalized through a recently developed test for structural change in univariate time series in each industry (Vogelsang, 1997).

## Technological Discontinuities

The term innovation is used very broadly in the literature (see, for example, Abernathy & Clark, 1985; Henderson & Clark, 1990; Nelson & Winter, 1977; Sahal, 1981; Schumpeter, 1942; Scherer & Ross, 1990). However, this paper deals with the question of what kind of competitive nature to expect following a discontinuity. To address this question, I will therefore narrow the scope from innovation in general to the more focused concept of technological discontinuities. Tushman and Anderson (1986) in their seminal article have laid important groundwork with regard to this concept. They define technological discontinuities as offering "sharp price-performance improvements over existing technologies. Major technological innovations represent technical advance so significant that no increase in scale, efficiency, or design can make older technologies competitive with the new technology" (1986: 441).

Technologies made obsolete by a technological discontinuity cannot compete on the basis of price and/or performance with the new products or processes. However, a technological breakthrough will often lead to an efficiency focus by firms locked into the old technology. With the appearance of the new technology, competition will cause the old technology to be utilized more efficiently and cost-effectively than ever before. Firms locked into the old technological paradigm will push the productivity frontier in their attempt to ward off new entrants based on the new technology. However, this efficiency focus within the old technological framework is often a sign of impending decline. For example, natural ice harvesting reached its peak in terms of productivity and efficient logistics only after the emergence of artificial refrigeration. The new technology caused the incumbents to respond with increased efficiency within the natural ice harvesting paradigm in their futile attempt to compete with producers of artificial refrigerated ice (Utterback, 1994). Therefore, a characteristic of a technological discontinuity is that the new technology will eventually prevail, since no price/performance improvement under the old technological paradigm will be able to make the older technology competitive with the new one.

Tushman and Anderson (1986) further categorize technological discontinuities as competence-destroying or competence-enhancing since they either destroy or enhance the technological competence of existing firms in an industry. Competence-destroying discontinuities "... require new skills, abilities, and knowledge in both the development and production of the product. The hallmark of competence-destroying discontinuities is that mastery of the new technology fundamentally alters the set of relevant competences within a product class ..." (1986: 442). On the other hand, competence-enhancing discontinuities "are order-of-magnitude improvements in price/performance that build on existing know-how within a product class. Such innovations substitute for older technologies, yet do not render obsolete the skills required to master the old technologies" (1986: 442). Almost every industry will experience some kind of discontinuity over time and the rate of occurrence of technological discontinuities is increasing (Bettis & Hitt, 1995). FIGURE 10.1 depicts schematically a technological discontinuity as two overlapping S-curves representing trajectories of two distinct

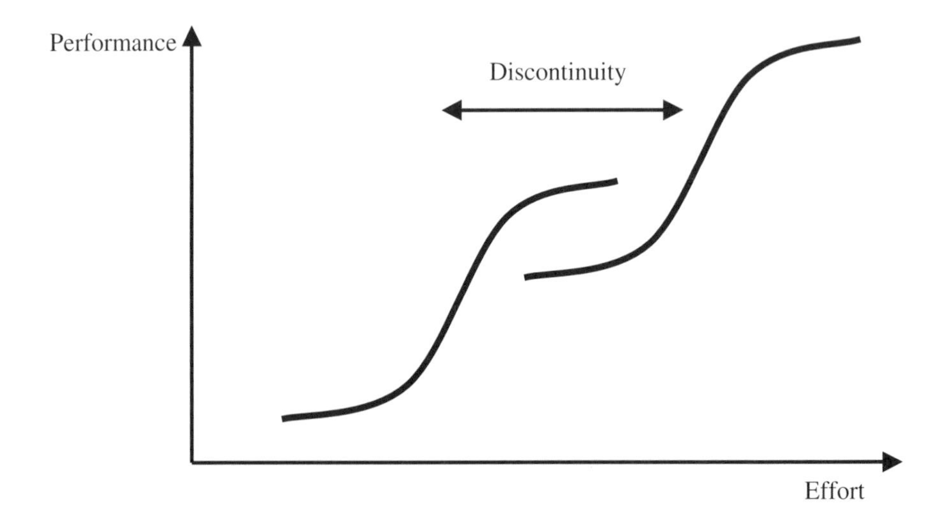


FIGURE 10.1 Schematic depiction of a discontinuity. Source: Foster (1986: 102)

technologies (Foster, 1986). Each technology takes off very slowly, then improves rapidly before it experiences diminishing marginal returns to R&D effort when approaching its physical limit. A discontinuity is not just a single point in time but is more accurately described as a time period, in which the old and new technologies coexist. At the beginning of a discontinuity, it is usually the case that the new technology does not perform as well as the old technology. However, over time the new technology will prevail.

A technological discontinuity is an event which redefines the competitive rules in an industry. Dramatic changes in the nature of competition and firm performance are initiated by a technological discontinuity (Hitt, Keats & DeMarie, 1998). Focusing on a technological discontinuity in two different industry settings allows us to test hypotheses with respect to the nature of competition and firm performance in the post-discontinuity period. The nature of competition prior to a technological discontinuity in time $T_0$ can be seen as some kind of steady-state competition, most likely based on either price or non-price competition; however, the prevailing competition in $T_0$ is not based on innovation or adaptation to a technological discontinuity during this period. This equilibrium is punctuated during the time period $T_1$ by a technological discontinuity. The technological discontinuity in $T_1$ will have a moderating effect on the steady-state competition prevalent in $T_0$. The way existing firms are impacted by a technological discontinuity determines, in the aggregate, the nature of competition in the industry in the post-discontinuous time period $T_2$. This relationship is depicted in FIGURE 10.2.

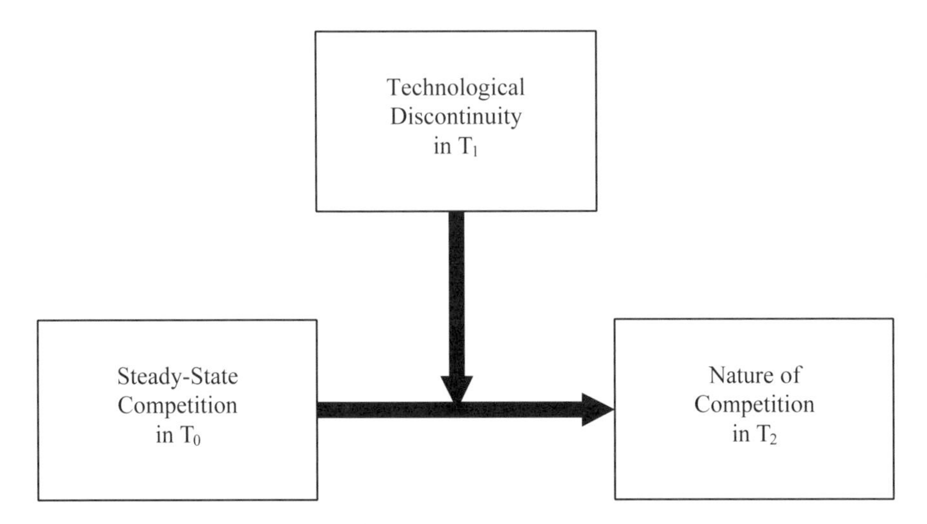


FIGURE 10.2 Technological discontinuity as mediator of nature of competition. Source: Rothaermel, (1999)

The effect of radical technological change on incumbents has been discussed extensively in the literature. For example, Abernathy and Clark (1985) develop a very useful framework for analyzing the competitive implications of an innovation. A firm's competitive advantage is built on tangible and intangible resources. Therefore, the significance of an innovation for the nature of competition depends on its "transilience", which is "its capacity to influence the firm's existing resources, skills and knowledge" (Abernathy & Clark, 1985: 5). The authors emphasize that innovation is not a simple phenomenon, rather it can be destructive, disruptive, and make obsolete on the one hand, but also it can be refining and improving on the other. This notion is reinforced by Tushman and Anderson's (1986) study of competence-destroying and competence-enhancing discontinuities. An important point with regard to the models of the nature of competition following a technological discontinuity advanced in this paper is that Tushman and Anderson find support for a dichotomy between competence-enhancing and competence-destroying discontinuities. This dichotomy relates to a firm's technological competence. Therefore, the Tushman–Anderson perspective does not account for the impact of a technological discontinuity on a firm's multiple competences.

However, in order to study the nature of competition following a technological discontinuity, it is important to distinguish between a firm's technological and non-technological competences (Pavitt, 1998). According to the value chain perspective, a firm consists of a chain of activities for transforming inputs into outputs (Porter, 1985). Each activity adds certain value to the product or service. The competitive advantage of a firm can only be understood by horizontally disintegrating the discrete activities a firm performs in transforming inputs into outputs. For example, a technological discontinuity can either destroy or enhance the R&D capability of incumbent firms (Tushman & Anderson, 1986). However, it is important to expand this analysis to include the effect of a technological discontinuity on non-technological competences such as marketing and distribution in order to understand its effect on incumbent firms and the nature of competition following a technological discontinuity (Mitchell, 1992; Pavitt, 1998; Tripsas, 1997). The combined effect of a technological discontinuity on an incumbent firm's technological and non-technological competences will influence firm behavior and on the aggregate determine the nature of competition prevailing in the post-discontinuity time period.

Neither industries nor companies are defined accurately by focusing only on a single core competence. Companies are a composition of asset bundles, some assets being more critical to survival and firm performance than others (Barney, 1991). Products are only the artifacts or outward manifestation of what a firm develops and produces. A firm's products are based on a unique blend of firm-specific technological knowledge and organizational forms that the firm utilizes to transform inputs into outputs. In particular, the innovating firm needs to assemble technological and non-technological assets to successfully commercialize on a technological breakthrough. Therefore, firms that possess dynamic core competences will experience a competitive advantage in a discontinuous environment. Dynamic core competences enable firms to adapt quickly to changes in their environment, since those firms hone their competences through meta-learning and continuous improvement over time (Lei, Hitt & Bettis, 1996). In addition, firms, in particular large ones, fail in adapting to technological discontinuities not because of a lack of technological knowledge or its understanding but because of a mismatch between a firm's system of coordination and control respectively to its available technological opportunities (Pavitt, 1998). The empirical finding of McKelvey (1996a) supports the view that neither firms nor industries are accurately defined by one core competence. She finds in her historical, in-depth case study of the parallel development of human growth hormone by the US biotechnology firm Genentech and the Swedish pharmaceutical company Kabi that a technological discontinuity can be simultaneously competence-enhancing as well as competence-destroying for firms in the same industry.

It is important to note that when considering the total impact of a technological discontinuity on a firm's value chain, a discontinuity can be competence-destroying for the firm's technological competences while at the same time competence-enhancing for the firm's non-technological competences (McKelvey, 1996b). For example, the emergence of biotechnology can be equated with a competence-destroying discontinuity in the way pharmaceuticals are discovered, developed, and manufactured according to the Tushman–Anderson framework. In particular, drug discovery and development is based on recombinant DNA in the biotechnology framework but on chemical screening in the traditional framework. The skills accrued under the chemical screening framework are obsolete within the genetic engineering framework. Since drug discovery is based on a completely different method within the biotechnology framework compared to the traditional chemical-based framework, one can identify the emergence of biotechnology as a competence-destroying technological discontinuity for existing pharmaceutical firms (Powell, Koput & Smith-Doerr, 1996). Therefore, according to the perennial gale of creative destruction, one would predict that the innovating biotechnology firms would rise to be the dominant players in the pharmaceutical industry. Yet, after about 25 years of commercialized biotechnology, Amgen as the most successful new entrant is only number 32 worldwide in terms of sales (Scrip's, 1998). It is crucial to note that the emergence of biotechnology did not destroy other competences of the traditional pharmaceutical companies such as FDA regulatory management, marketing, and sales and distribution, for example; in fact some of these capabilities actually became more valuable. These non-technological assets are enhanced since they are specialized with respect to commercializing biotechnology (Teece, 1986). In addition, the new entrants not only needed to gain access to downstream value chain activities in order to commercialize on biotechnology, but also stood in need for finance in order to conduct the capital-intensive biotechnology R&D (Pisano, 1991). In this situation, new entrants providing the new technology and incumbents providing the necessary market-related competences to commercialize on the new technology and capital to finance R&D will search out their mutually complementary assets through interfirm cooperation (Hitt *et al.*, 1998). Therefore, the emergence of biotechnology can be seen as both competence-destroying and competence-enhancing for existing pharmaceutical companies when considering its impact on the entire value chain of an incumbent pharmaceutical firm.

## "Creative Destruction" or "Creative Cooperation"?

In the following, I propose a framework which will help to explain the effects of a technological discontinuity on the nature of competition and firm performance. A firm exposed to a technological discontinuity must assemble technological and non-technological assets to successfully commercialize on a technological breakthrough (Pavitt, 1998). If a technological discontinuity destroys incumbent firms' technological competences without enhancing other non-technological competences, then we expect a Schumpeterian process of creative destruction to take place in this specific industry (Schumpeter, 1942). Exclusively competence-destroying technological discontinuities break the existing market structure. Subsequently, barriers to entry will be lowered and new firms will enter the industry by exploiting the competence-destroying technology. Therefore, exclusively competence-destroying discontinuities favor new entrants over incumbents. New entrants based on new competences commercialize on the innovative technology and thereby gain market share at the expense of incumbents. The incumbents are often unable to take advantage of the technological breakthrough since they are locked into the old technology in terms of skills, abilities, and expertise (Tushman & Anderson, 1986). Not only are the incumbents locked into the old technological framework, they might also find themselves locked out from the new technological paradigm (Schilling, 1998). Subsequently, the performance of incumbent firms declines and eventually they will exit the industry while new entrants enter the industry and eventually rise to dominance following a technological discontinuity (Schumpeter, 1942). For example, the emergence of the PC destroyed alternative word-processing methods such as mechanical or electronic typewriters (Utterback, 1994). Therefore, if a technological discontinuity is exclusively competence-destroying for incumbent firms then we will observe the Schumpeterian process of creative destruction. The above discussion is summarized in Hypothesis 1:

H1: The process of creative destruction will lead to a break in incumbent industry performance, which will decline following the break date.

The theoretically more interesting case with respect to the nature of competition is encountered when the technological discontinuity is competence-destroying with respect to the technological competence of incumbent firms but simultaneously competence-enhancing with respect to the non-technological competences of incumbent firms. In this constellation, incumbents are able to adapt to radical technological change through extensive cooperation with organizations embedded in the new technological paradigm. The technological discontinuity initiates a process of creative cooperation, which allows incumbents and new entrants to access their mutually complementary assets. The non-technological assets of incumbent firms are enhanced when they are specialized with respect to commercializing on the technological breakthrough. If this is the case, then the incumbents will benefit more from the technological breakthrough than the innovators (Teece, 1986). In this situation, new entrants also have a need to cooperate with incumbent firms in order to commercialize on the new technology. Therefore, extensive cooperation between incumbent and new entrant firms will follow a technological discontinuity that destroys the technological competence of incumbent firms while simultaneously enhancing their non-technological competences. Subsequently, incumbent firms are able to thrive in a competence-destroying discontinuous environment through strategically structuring their cooperation with new entrants. In particular, incumbents will thrive in a technologically discontinuous environment if they virtually rebuild their destroyed technological competences through cooperation with new entrants. On the other hand, new entrants virtually extend their downstream value chain through accessing the market-related competences of incumbent firms. In this situation, incumbent and new entrant firms are able to coexist in a symbiotic manner (Pisano, 1991). The process of creative cooperation presents an alternative view of the competitive process driven by innovation compared to the Schumpeterian model of creative destruction. On the aggregate, the extensive cooperation between incumbents and new entrants should lead to improved incumbent industry performance since their market-related technological competences are specialized with respect to the commercialization of the innovation (Mitchell, 1992; Teece, 1986). Hypothesis 2 captures the discussion above:

> H2: The process of creative cooperation will lead to a break in incumbent industry performance, which will improve following the break date.

Considering the total effect of a technological discontinuity on a firm's value chain, a discontinuity can be simultaneously competence-destroying for a firm's technological competences as well as competence-enhancing for a firm's non-technological competences. In this situation, I am able to derive a hypothesized framework describing the nature of competition and its outcome following a technological discontinuity. The processes of creative destruction and creative cooperation, including industry examples with a respective technological discontinuity in parentheses, are depicted in Figure 10.3.

## Research Sample

The research sample for this study comprises the mainframe computer and pharmaceutical industries. For each industry, one technological discontinuity is identified: the emergence of the PC in 1981 for the mainframe computer industry and the emergence of biotechnology since the 1970s for the pharmaceutical industry. The emergence of the PC based on the invention of the microprocessor transformed the computer industry. All dominant players in the pre-PC computer industry such as IBM, DEC, and others were all fully vertically integrated companies. This represented the

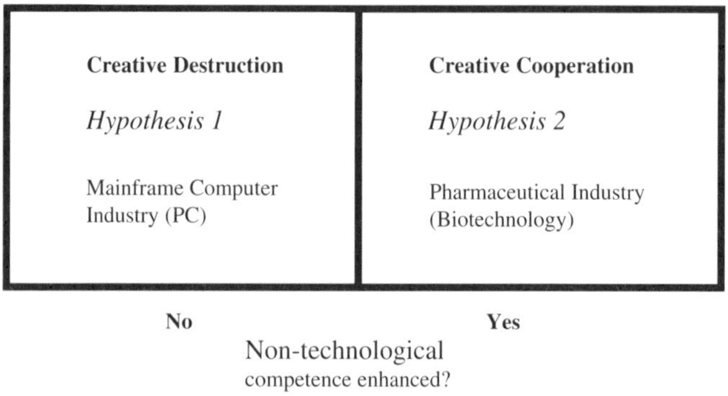

| **Creative Destruction**<br>*Hypothesis 1*<br>Mainframe Computer Industry (PC) | **Creative Cooperation**<br>*Hypothesis 2*<br>Pharmaceutical Industry (Biotechnology) |
|---|---|
| **No** | **Yes** |

Non-technological competence enhanced?

Figure 10.3 Proposed nature of competition following a competence-destroying technological discontinuity

so-called proprietary system approach. Each firm had its proprietary semiconductor chip implementation around which its computers were built. The company would then also design its proprietary operating system as well as application software for its computers. The entire package consisting of proprietary chip, computer hardware, operating system, and application software was then sold and serviced through the company's own sales, distribution, and service force. Therefore, a firm's value chain in the mainframe computer industry before the arrival of the PC encompassed all activities needed to transform inputs into outputs: chips, computers, operating systems, application software, and finally sales and distribution. All companies were vertically aligned and competed in this industry "as one proprietary block against all other companies' vertical proprietary blocks" (Grove, 1996: 41).

In 1981, the first PC built on microprocessor technology was introduced. In subsequent years, economies of scale in combination with incremental innovation lowered the price for computing power exponentially. Not only was the cost of computing lowered exponentially; the performance of PC-based computing increased also exponentially. Users shifted away from mainframe or minicomputers to PCs, in particular once the possibility of networking the PC emerged. Therefore, the PC can be identified as a competence-destroying discontinuity, since it brought a drastic price/performance decrease with it, based on an entire new product class. These two criteria were also used by Tushman and Anderson (1986) to identify competence-destroying technological discontinuities. The dramatic decrease in the price/performance ratio of the PC is depicted in FIGURE 10.4.

This technological discontinuity initiated by microprocessor technology changed the entire structure of the computer industry. The fully vertically

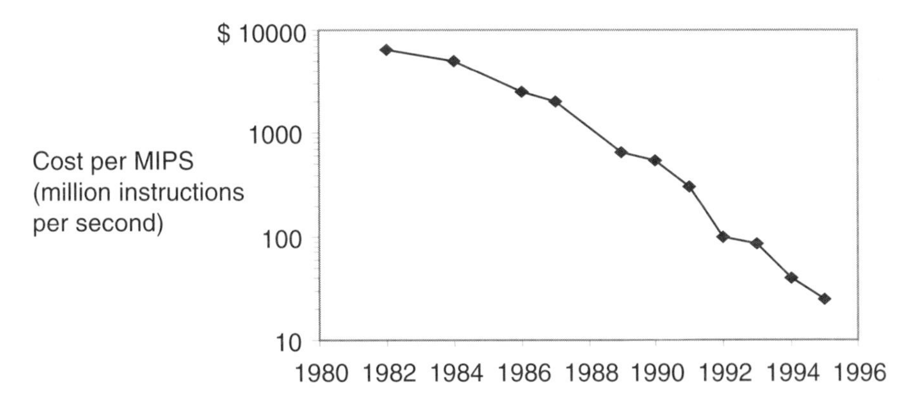


FIGURE 10.4 Decrease in cost per MIPS in the computer industry, 1980–95. Source: Grove (1996: 63).

integrated firms were now confronted with firms that would concentrate only on one or two activities of the value chain. For example, in the pre-PC era, the firm boundaries of a mainframe computer firm would include chip manufacturing, computer hardware, operating systems, application software, and sales and distribution. After the emergence of the PC, the computer industry was transformed from an industry where fully vertically integrated proprietary blocks competed with one another to an industry in which firms would compete within horizontal blocks. Each segment of the value chain was now represented by firms who focused on only one or two activities of the value chain. None of the emerging competitors had all value-chain activities in house. Therefore, competition was based on concentration on one or two core competences. For example, in microprocessor development and manufacturing Intel would compete with Motorola and other firms. In computer hardware a great number of firms—including Compaq, Dell, Hewlett-Packard and many other "clone" manufacturers—would compete based on the IBM PC standard. In operating systems, Microsoft would compete with IBM, Apple, and UNIX. In application software, Microsoft would compete with Borland, WordPerfect, Lotus, etc. Even in sales and distribution many more outlets emerged such as retail stores, superstores, dealers, and mail order, for example. In general, the emergence of the PC transformed the computer industry from a vertically aligned industry into a horizontally aligned industry (Grove, 1996). Therefore, it destroyed the technological competence of mainframe computer manufacturers since the new entrants would now compete on a new technology, the microprocessor. In addition, it also negatively affected the downstream activities of the mainframe computer firms since they now had to face competitors that competed on only one or two activities of the value chain. Therefore, the emergence of the PC is identified as an exclusively competence-destroying technological discontinuity for the existing mainframe computer companies. We expect the process of creative destruction to take place in the computer mainframe industry (Hypothesis 1).

The identified technological discontinuity in the pharmaceutical industry is the emergence of biotechnology in 1970s. For example, Genentech, founded in 1976, was the first company to commercialize on biotechnology. The emergence of biotechnology represents a technological discontinuity for traditional pharmaceutical firms in certain activities of their value chain. More specifically, firm competences for traditional pharmaceutical companies in research and drug discovery as well as drug development are destroyed. However, firm competences in other activities of the value chain, such as FDA regulatory management, as well as marketing and sales, are still valuable. The challenge for traditional pharmaceutical firms is to fit these new technologies based on recombinant DNA with their existing competences into their value chain in order to adapt to the new technological framework.

At the time of the emergence of the first biotechnology firms in the 1970s, the new entrants basically focused entirely on the research and drug discovery part of the value chain (Teitelman, 1989). Some companies developed diagnostic kits and brought them to the market; however, with regard to drug discovery and development, the focus of NBFs could be found in the first two activities of their value chain. Eventually the NBFs intended to integrate forward through the value chain. However, it took Amgen over 10 years to become a fully integrated pharmaceutical company. The nature of the biotechnology innovation initiated a process of creative cooperation. Through this process, the new entrants were able to gain access to the missing downstream activities of their value chain as well as capital. On the other hand, the traditional pharmaceutical companies made the new building block of genetic engineering fit their value chain, mainly through cooperative arrangements with new entrants but also through internal R&D (Zucker & Darby, 1997). The traditional pharmaceutical firms not only needed to understand the new technology but also needed innovative products, which NBFs potentially provided.

At the time of the entrance of the NBFs, none of the new firms had the necessary downstream activities either to manage their products through the FDA successfully or to market it to the physicians, hospitals, and HMOs. However, the downstream activities of the existing pharmaceutical companies were still intact. This made it possible that traditional pharmaceutical firms could benefit early on from the technological discontinuity "biotechnology". Even though their competence in research and drug discovery was destroyed, their competence in clinical trial development, FDA management, and marketing and sales was still valuable and even enhanced, since these skills could be used to commercialize on the new technology. This competence-enhancing effect can be explained by understanding the importance of the downstream activities in the pharmaceutical industry. At the time of the emergence of the NBFs, the existing pharmaceutical companies were the only firms capable of bringing these innovative drugs based on genetic engineering to the market. These downstream activities are specialized to the commercialization of biotechnology (Teece, 1986). Therefore, the downstream activities of the existing pharmaceutical companies were enhanced by the emergence of biotechnology. In this case, the emergence of biotechnology was competence-destroying for the technological competence of existing pharmaceutical companies while at the same time competence-enhancing for their non-technological competences when considering the total impact of a discontinuity on a firm's competences. This constellation leads to a process of creative cooperation (Hypothesis 2).

Partnership agreements are a critical vehicle for biotechnology innovation. External partnering is primarily used in the biopharmaceutical industry to move a discovery along the value chain through development, manufacturing, and eventually marketing and sales. Prior to 1970, only three biotechnology cooperative agreements were formed, and during the 10 years between 1970 and 1979 about 120 agreements were created. However, during the early 1980s the average number of agreements was 66 per year and this number rose to 132 per year for the period 1985 to 1988. Since 1989, the number remained at about 100 annually (Greis, Dibner & Bean, 1995). In 1995 and 1996 alone, 287 strategic alliances were formed (Lee & Burrill, 1996). The dramatic increase in the use of strategic alliances to commercialize on biotechnology is depicted in FIGURE 10.5.

Almost 70% of CEOs of all publicly traded NBFs and 50% of privately held NBFs anticipated to have at least one strategic alliance completed by the end of 1997 (Lee & Burrill, 1996). In addition, strategic partnering also has a strong international component: almost one-third of all strategic alliances of US firms are with foreign companies (Greis, Dibner & Bean, 1995). According to venture financing trends in early 1996, investors preferred NBFs that would focus on multiple novel products in their product pipeline rather than on companies focusing on becoming a fully integrated drug development company and full-scale commercial

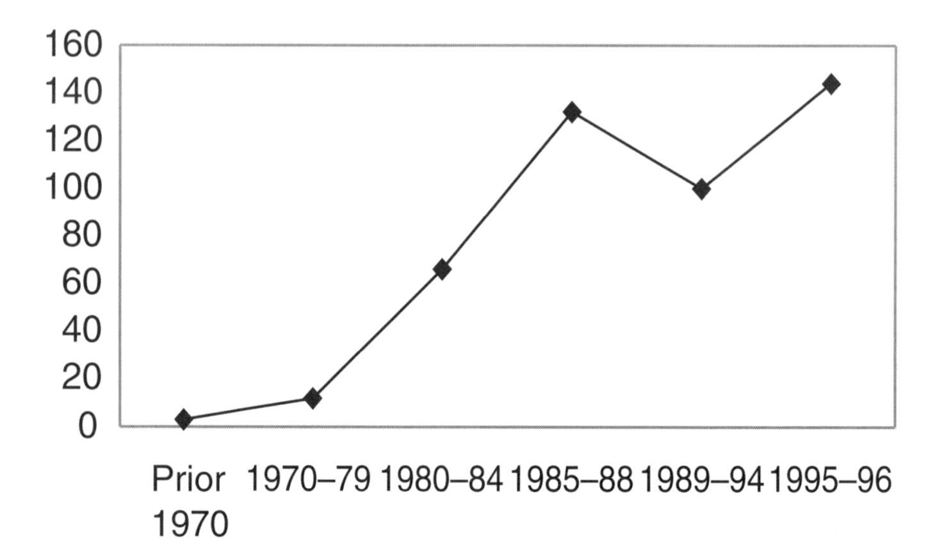


FIGURE 10.5 Average number of cooperative arrangements in the biopharmaceutical industry, 1970–96. Source: Rothaermel (1999).

manufacturer (Lee & Burrill, 1996). This in turn also drives the need for NBFs to partner with established pharmaceutical companies for production, marketing, and sales capability. Both new biotechnology entrants and incumbent pharmaceutical firms have an incentive to search out their mutually complementary assets.

Given Tushman and Anderson's (1986) dichotomous view of technological discontinuities, one would assume that the emergence of biotechnology was competence-destroying to existing pharmaceutical firms, and therefore we would expect the Schumpeterian process of creative destruction to take its course. However, after more than 20 years of commercialized biotechnology, we have not seen new biotechnology entrants replacing existing, traditional pharmaceutical firms. On the contrary, we have seen a process of creative cooperation between new biotechnology and existing pharmaceutical companies. This process of creative cooperation will lead to an improved industry performance for existing pharmaceutical firms (Hypothesis 2).

## Research Method and Data

The proposed model of the nature of competition following a technological discontinuity was tested in the computer mainframe and pharmaceutical industries, using a recently developed test for structural change in univariate time series (Vogelsang, 1997). To operationalize the proposed model, I examined a time series of quarterly net income of firms participating in the mainframe and pharmaceutical industries from 1965 to 1997. The time of emergence of the PC and biotechnology technological discontinuities lies about in the medium range of the respective time spans. I identified all the participating firms in the market for mainframe computers and pharmaceuticals through analyzing Standard & Poor's industry reports from 1965 through 1997. Several companies exited the market, while others merged and formed new companies. In the final sample, I ended up with seven from initially nine companies in the mainframe computer industry. However, the remaining seven companies represent close to 100% market share in the mainframe computer industry during 1965–97. In the pharmaceutical industry, I initially identified 19 companies; however, due to mergers, my final sample includes 14 companies representing close to 100% market share of the US pharmaceutical industry (Table 10.1 depicts the research sample).

To test the advanced hypotheses, I investigated a time series of the industry performance variable quarterly net income. According to Hypothesis 1, a process of creative destruction leads to a decline in industry performance. This implies that the time series should exhibit a

TABLE 10.1 Industry sample, 1965–97

| Mainframe computer industry | Pharmaceutical industry |
|---|---|
| Control Data | Abbott Laboratories |
| Digital Equipment | Eli Lilly |
| Honeywell | Merck |
| IBM | Miles Laboratories |
| NCR | Pfizer |
| Sperry | Robines (A.H.) |
| Unisys | Schering-Plough |
| | Searle (G.D.) |
| | Smithkline Beecham |
| | Squibb |
| | Sterling Drug |
| | Syntex |
| | Warner-Lambert |

statistically significant structural break some time after the emergence of the technological discontinuity. Since an overall decline in industry performance is predicted, the coefficient of the indicator variable for the break date is expected to be negative. On the other hand, Hypothesis 2 predicts that a process of creative cooperation will lead to an improvement in industry performance. This implies that the time series should also exhibit a statistically significant break date some time after the emergence of the technological discontinuity. Since an overall improvement in industry performance is predicted, however, the coefficient of the indicator variable for the break date variable is expected to be positive.

Since I chose quarterly net income as industry performance variable, I was able to utilize 130 and 131 observations, comprising a time series from 1965 through 1997. I obtained a time series of quarterly net income for each firm of the two industries from Standard & Poor's 1998 Compustat database, which contains financial information about publicly traded companies based on annual reports and SEC 10K filings. The integrity and utility of the data series contained in the Compustat database has been validated (Davis & Duhaime, 1992). The time series for quarterly net income for the industry sample was arrived at by aggregating the results for each firm. I then estimated the following regression model to test for a structural break in the time trend assuming a deterministic trending process:

$$y_t = \alpha + \beta t + \delta DT_t + \mu_t \qquad (10.1)$$

where $y_t$ represents quarterly industry net income, t is the time trend, and $DT_t$ is an indicator variable depending on the date of the structural break ($T_B$), where $DT_t = t - T_B$ if $t > T_B$, 0 otherwise. The null hypothesis states that

$\delta = 0$, meaning $y_t$ is determined by a deterministically trending process without an exogenous shock leading to a structural shift in the deterministic time trend. The research hypothesis states that $\delta \neq 0$, meaning that $y_t$ is trend stationary with a one-time break in the deterministic trend function, which occurs at an unknown date. I identified the year of a structural break by applying a maximum Chow test on the indicator variable "year" (Quandt, 1960). Once I had identified the break date, I additionally applied a Wald-type test for detecting shifts in the trend function (i.e. quarterly net income) based on recent advancements in econometric theory in order to avoid biases caused by estimating the break date (Vogelsang, 1997). Since the break date $T_B$ is unknown, however, I had to adjust the critical values using Vogelsang's (1997) method of Wald-type tests for detecting breaks in the trend function of dynamic time series. This Wald-type test has been employed to detect structural breaks in the growth rate of real GDP for a number of countries (Ben-David & Papell, 1995). I propose that either the process of creative destruction or that of creative cooperation is in force if the null hypothesis ($\delta = 0$) is rejected. The sign of the coefficient of the indicator variable will discriminate between the process of creative destruction and the process of creative cooperation. If the sign is negative, the process of creative destruction is taking place. On the other hand, if the sign is positive, the process of creative cooperation is in full force.

## Creative Destruction in the Mainframe Computer Industry

The break date of the quarterly net income time series in the mainframe computer industry is selected by choosing the value of $T_B$ for which the squared t-statistic for the coefficient of the indicator variable "year" is maximized (Quandt, 1960). The year identified for a structural break in the time series of quarterly net income in the mainframe computer industry is 1985. This holds true, regardless whether the full sample or a truncated sample ending 1990: 4 excluding negative values for quarterly net income is applied. The regression results are reported in Table 10.2.

Even after adjusting the critical value using the Wald-type tests proposed by Vogelsang (1997), the indicator variable "year" representing the break date is still very highly significant at $p < 0.001$. In addition, the sign is negative, as expected. The mainframe computer industry experienced a structural break in industry performance in 1985. As predicted, the process of creative destruction has led to a structural break in industry performance, which declined following the break date. In addition, the process of creative destruction has been rather intense, given that the break date is only four years after the emergence of the PC in 1981. Therefore, this evidence

TABLE 10.2 Results for regression model

Results of the regression model $y_t = \alpha + \beta t + \delta DT_t + \mu_t$, where $y_t$ represents quarterly net income, t is the time trend, and $DT_t$ is an indicator variable depending on the date of the structural break ($T_B$), where $DT_t = t - T_B$ if $t > T_B$, 0 otherwise. The t-statistics are reported in parentheses.

| Industry sample | Break date | Intercept | Time trend, t | $DT_t$ | $R^2$ |
|---|---|---|---|---|---|
| Computer mainframe industry | 1985 | −68.03<br>(−0.26) | 19.96***<br>(4.01) | −236.28***<br>(−4.61) | 0.14 |
| Pharmaceutical industry | 1987 | −40.55<br>(−0.78) | 12.52***<br>(13.66) | 174.17***<br>(14.27) | 0.93 |

*** Significant at $p < 0.001$.

strongly supports Hypothesis 1. If a technological discontinuity is exclusively competence-destroying for incumbent firms, we observe the Schumpeterian process of creative destruction, which will lead to the dominance of new entrants and the decline in performance of incumbent firms. The scenario has indeed been played out in the mainframe computer industry.

## Creative Cooperation in the Pharmaceutical Industry

The date for a structural break in quarterly net income for the pharmaceutical industry is also identified through applying a maximum Chow test (Quandt, 1960). The break date for the pharmaceutical industry is 1987. In addition, the sign of the coefficient of the indicator variable year is positive, as expected. Even after applying the Wald-type tests for detecting structural breaks in univariate time series to avoid biases caused by estimating the break date (Vogelsang, 1997), the indicator variable "year" representing the break date is still very highly significant at $p < 0.001$. The process of creative cooperation has led to a break in industry performance, which improved significantly following the break date. The statistical evidence strongly supports Hypothesis 2.

Since the emergence of biotechnology was simultaneously competence-destroying as well as competence-enhancing based on the proposed value chain perspective, the pharmaceutical industry experienced a structural break in quarterly net income in 1987. In addition, the process of creative cooperation has been rather intense, given that the positive impact of biotechnology is already recognizable only seven years after the first IPO of a biotechnology firm (Genentech in 1980). The traditional pharmaceutical companies responded not only quickly but also very successfully to the new technology. The response mainly took the form of co-opting new biotechnology firms through cooperative arrangements. If a technological discontinuity is simultaneously competence-destroying and competence-enhancing for incumbent firms, we observe a process of creative cooperation that leads to improved industry performance of incumbent firms. This process of creative cooperation has taken place in the pharmaceutical industry.

## Discussion and Conclusion

The notion of creative cooperation provides a different view of the competitive process driven by innovation. In particular, it presents an alternative perspective to the Schumpeterian model of competition driven by innovation initiating a process of creative destruction. The process of creative cooperation helps us to explain what we observe in high-technology industries like the biopharmaceutical industry. In addition, the process of creative cooperation might foreshadow what to expect in high-technology industries experiencing a technological discontinuity that simultaneously destroys and enhances incumbent firms' competences. The process of creative cooperation might be a piece of the puzzle to reconcile simultaneous competition and cooperation, i.e. "co-opetition" (Brandenburger & Nalebuff, 1996).

The findings in this paper also support Abernathy and Clark's (1985) concept of "low transilience" innovation, which allows incumbent firms to benefit from innovation. An example of a "low transilience" innovation is a process innovation that requires discontinuous change in the product design technology while existing market linkages remain unchanged. Abernathy and Clark (1985) find that in this situation, incumbents will not only survive but also experience significant advantages relative to new entrants. This study also finds support for Tripsas's (1997) notion of incumbent survival through complementary assets, and Mitchell's (1992) differentiation of the importance of technical versus market-related capabilities when adapting to a new technology. In addition, this paper reinforces the importance of analyzing the impact of an innovation on incumbents in its total impact, including all linkages between different firm competences (Henderson & Clark, 1990; Tripsas, 1997).

Yet, this paper carries the analysis a step further since it includes the element of firm cooperation as a way for incumbents to adapt to radical technological change. For example, incumbents may focus on adapting to "disruptive technologies" (Christensen, 1997) through cooperation with new entrants. A technological discontinuity that simultaneously destroys and enhances the competences of incumbent firms will lead to a symbiotic relationship between incumbents and new entrants. It is important to note that in this situation, incumbents will—on the average—be able to profit more from the discontinuity than new entrants providing the technology. This result presents empirical support for Teece's (1986) hypothesis with respect to the importance of complementary assets in commercializing an innovation. Future research should attempt to apply the notion of creative cooperation to other industry settings in order to enhance its external validity.

This notion of creative cooperation as an alternative perspective to the Schumpeterian model of creative destruction also has important implications for strategic management. In particular, the two models of the nature of competition presented in this paper help the manager to understand what kind of competitive climate to expect following a technological discontinuity. More importantly, it will allow the manager to make future-oriented decisions as soon as a discontinuity is perceived. For example, managers of incumbent firms in industries experiencing a technological discontinuity that simultaneously enhances and destroys the firm's competences, should gain a competitive advantage by searching out those strategic alliance partners that leverage the incumbent's enhanced downstream, market-related competences. This strategy should also enable incumbent firms to "buy time" in order to build the upstream, technical-related competences. In addition, new entrants may choose a cooperative strategy as the only possible way to enter an otherwise non-contestable industry. One limitation of this study is, however, that it is unable to say anything with respect to interfirm performance differentials. To study interfirm performance differentials in industries experiencing a discontinuous technological change in their environment is a much-needed expansion of this stream of research. In conclusion, given that the future will hold many more technological discontinuities—occurring in ever-shorter time intervals—the perspective presented here can indeed help us to understand the nature of competition in the post-discontinuity time period. This is a first step in allowing strategic managers to build and sustain a competitive advantage in the context of a highly dynamic environment.

## References

Abernathy, W.J. & Clark, K.B. (1985). Innovation: Mapping the winds of creative destruction. *Research Policy*, **14**, 3–22.

Barney, J. (1991). Firm resources and sustained competitive advantage. *Journal of Management*, **17**, 99–120.

Ben-David, D. & Papell, D.H. (1995). The great wars, the great crash, and steady state growth: Some new evidence about an old stylized fact. *Journal of Monetary Economics*, **36**, 453–475.

Bettis, R.A. & Hitt, M.A. (1995). The new competitive landscape. *Strategic Management Journal*, **16**, 7–19.

Brandenburger, A. & Nalebuff, B. (1996). *Co-opetition*. New York: Doubleday.

Christensen, C.M. (1997). *The Innovator's Dilemma: When New Technologies Cause Great Firms to Fail*. Boston, MA: Harvard Business School Press.

Davis, R. & Duhaime, I.M. (1992). Diversification, vertical integration, and industry analysis: New perspectives and measurement. *Strategic Management Journal*, **15**, 511–524.

Foster, R. (1986). *Innovation: The Attacker's Advantage*. New York: Summit Books.

Greis, N.P., Dibner, M.D. & Bean, A.S. (1995). External partnering as a response to innovation barriers and global competition in biotechnology. *Research Policy*, **24**, 609–630.

Grove, A.S. (1996). *Only the Paranoid Survive*. New York: Doubleday.

Henderson, R.M. & Clark, K.B. (1990). Architectural innovation: The reconfiguration of existing product technologies and the failure of established firms. *Administrative Science Quarterly*, **35**, 9–30.

Hitt, M.A., Dacin, M.T., Levitas, E., Arregle, J.-L. & Borza, A. (1998). *Partner selection in emerging and developed market contexts: Resource-based and organizational learning perspectives*. Working paper, Texas A&M University, Lowry Mays College and Graduate School of Business, College Station, TX.

Hitt, M.A., Keats, B.W. & DeMarie, S. (1998). Navigating the new competitive landscape: Building strategy flexibility and competitive advantage in the 21st century. *Academy of Management Executive*, **12**(4), 22–42.

Lee, K.B. Jr. & Burrill, G.S. (1996). *Biotech 97: Alignment*. Palo Alto, CA: Ernst & Young, LLP.

Lei, D., Hitt. M.A. & Bettis, R. (1996). Dynamic core competences through meta-learning and strategic context. *Journal of Management*, **22**, 549–569.

McKelvey, M.D. (1996a). *Evolutionary Innovations: The Business of Biotechnology*. Oxford: Oxford University Press.

McKelvey, M.D. (1996b). Discontinuities in genetic engineering for pharmaceuticals? Firm jumps and lock-in systems of innovation. *Technology Analysis and Strategic Management*, **8**, 107–116.

Mitchell, W. (1992). Are more good things better, or will technical and market capabilities conflict when a firm expands? *Industrial and Corporate Change*, **1**, 327–346.

Nelson, R.R. & Winter, S. (1977). In search of useful theory of innovation. *Research Policy*, **6**, 36–76.

Pavitt, K. (1998). Technologies, products, and organization in the innovating firm: What Adam Smith tells us and Joseph Schumpeter doesn't. *Industrial and Corporate Change*, **7**, 433–452.

Pisano, G.P. (1991). The governance of innovation: Vertical integration and collaborative arrangements in the biotechnology industry. *Research Policy*, **20**, 237–249.

Porter, M.E. (1985). *Competitive Advantage: Creating and Sustaining Superior Performance*. New York: Free Press.

Powell, W.W., Koput, K.W. & Smith-Doerr, L. (1996). Interorganizational collaboration and the locus of innovation: Networks of learning in biotechnology. *Administrative Science Quarterly*, **41**, 116–145.

Quandt, R.E. (1960). Tests of hypothesis that a linear regression system obeys two separate regimes. *Journal of the American Statistical Association*, **55**, 324–330.

Rothaermel, F.T. (1999). *"Creative Destruction" or "Creative Cooperation"? An Empirical Investigation of Technological Discontinuities and Their Effect on the Nature of Competition and Firm Performance*. Unpublished doctoral dissertation: University of Washington.

Sahal, D. (1981). *Patterns of Technological Innovation*. London: Addison-Wesley.

Scherer, F.M. & Ross, D. (1990). *Industrial Market Structure and Economic Performance*. Boston: Houghton Mifflin.

Schilling, M. (1998). Technological lockout: An integrative model of the economic and strategic factors driving technology success and failure. *Academy of Management Review*, **23**, 267–284.

Schumpeter, J.A. (1942). *Capitalism, Socialism and Democracy*. New York: Harper & Row.

*Scrip's 1998 Yearbook, Volume 1: Industry and Companies*. PJB Publications.

Standard & Poor's (1965–1997). *Industry Reports*. New York: Standard & Poor's.

Standard & Poor's (1998). *Compustat*. Englewood Cliffs, NJ: McGraw-Hill.

Teece, D.J. (1986). Profiting from technological innovation: Implications for integration, collaboration, licensing and public policy. *Research Policy*, **15**, 285–305.

Teitelman, R. (1989). *Gene Dreams: Wall Street, Academia, and the Rise of Biotechnology*. New York: Basic Books.

Tripsas, M. (1997). Unraveling the process of creative destruction: Complementary assets and incumbent survival in the typesetter industry. *Strategic Management Journal*, **18**, 119–142.

Tushman, M.L. & Anderson, P. (1986). Technological discontinuities and organizational environments. *Administrative Science Quarterly*, **31**, 439–465.

Utterback, J.M. (1994). *Mastering the Dynamics of Innovation*. Boston, MA: Harvard Business School Press.

Vogelsang, T.J. (1997). Wald-type tests for detecting breaks in the trend function of a dynamic time series. *Econometric Theory*, **13**, 818–849.

Zucker, L.G. & Darby, M.R. (1997). Present at the biotechnological revolution: Transformation of technological identity for a large pharmaceutical firm. *Research Policy*, **26**, 429–446.

# 11

# Design as a Strategic Alliance: Expanding the Creative Capability of the Firm

BIRGIT H. JEVNAKER, MARGARET BRUCE

## INTRODUCTION

In this article we offer a view that the capacity to collaborate with creative design experts has become more central to competitive success. In order to create desirable extended products that can compete in internationalized markets, firms need to exploit a wider range of skills beyond their traditional core competencies. For example, collaboration with communication experts, product designers, and art directors can provide a leading edge, such as happened with the Absolut Vodka now famous for its pure content, its bottle, its arts campaigns and its creative advertising. Like Swatch (Swiss plastic watches), Absolut illuminates how a business can be entirely *reconceived* through creative imagination and design.[1] Concurrently a plethora of new and imaginative strategic alliances is transforming industries from transportation to communication, information technology, health and life sciences, media and entertainment, aerospace and beyond (Doz & Hamel, 1998). In this new world of diverse expertise, networks, coalitions, and alliances, a special case of strategic interest is partner interactions with design experts. Design challenges are more pertinent for

*Dynamic Strategic Resources: Development, Diffusion and Integration.*
Edited by Michael A. Hitt, Patricia Gorman Clifford, Robert D. Nixon and Kevin P. Coyne.

business than ever before in the well-equipped part of the world. Firms need to make their core businesses visible and meaningful to many stakeholders even when competing on intangible competencies and values (Itami, 1987). Consumers are more demanding and more design aware. Rapid changes in technology provide new products and changes in existing ones, and the pressure to speed up the market introduction of new products also affects business (Bowen *et al.*, 1994). Some firms compete on their abilities to generate a new platform of innovative products that are so sophisticated in their hardware, their software/service and also their people content as to capture the new opportunities that make customers leverage their own value creation (Wallin, 1997). Talented designers can foresee this and design the users' experience.

Designing intelligently extended products or services which are attractive and easy to use is difficult. Even more challenging is reconceiving the core concepts and philosophy of a business, and even reshaping its industry (Hamel & Prahalad, 1994). By using design experts, companies can differentiate and reinvent or improve their product and service offerings, since designers seek to integrate tangible and intangible assets. They can excite and entice consumers and they can provide a strong message to the market place. Imaginative designers can also identify and create a distinct identity, a meta product, or even brand the whole firm and its core products to sustain an innovative profile. Thus advanced design has potential strategic interest; it can make business values and strategy visible to the firm's stakeholders (Olins, 1989). Design is complex (Lawson, 1990) and refers to the activity of designing, that is, the creation of something that is novel, making it visible through various representations (Walsh *et al.*, 1992). In addition, design refers to the artifact and can qualify this as "good design". Designers' expertise is used in product design, engineering, graphic design, fashion design, communication, advertising and events, retail design, etc. Therefore, different design disciplines exist and are utilized by companies.

Up to now, few managers have been accustomed to working with designers, and few possess a qualified design expertise in-house (Walsh *et al.*, 1992). Not surprisingly, relatively few firms excel in product design (Lorenz, 1986, 1990). In order to mobilize and tailor corporate design, this paper focuses on the industrial design alliance as an intermediate and somewhat overlooked collaborative approach that may be beneficial for both companies and their design associates if its potential is realized. Forming strategic design alliances so as to produce a steady flow of innovative products is one approach to leverage design expertise. Advanced industrial design can create new values through an interdisciplinary creative and synthesizing approach that connects and transforms the hard technology with soft values and makes these visible in material or other form. This chapter examines firms' collaboration with industrial product designers in creating innovative new product lines. From a strategic viewpoint, it is essential that industrial design may foster a new and unique combination of the firms' strategic assets, since this expertise relates to the global scene (Hayes, 1990) and also regional industrial cultures (Sparke, 1986a) as well as to the future (Blaich, 1993). However, new product designs may also be misaligned to the firm's strategy, competencies and established market outlets, and managing design strategically is therefore critical (Dumas, 1993).

Yet industrial designers have been portrayed as unfamiliar experts who are hard to integrate in design and commercializion of product innovations (Lorenz, 1990; Dumas, 1993; Blaich, 1993). Based on Barney (1997) and Hitt, Hoskisson and Nixon (1993), we want to shed light on *how* the value-creating but rarely integrated design resources are, in fact, advantageous and of strategic interest. The purpose of this paper is to generate new insight by examining industrial design alliances as a strategic way of organizing a sustainable creative design capability. Since products and communications may be imitated, the dynamic capability to *repeatedly* create and sustain attractive product innovations through complex design partnerships is seen as more valuable. Despite potential advantages, it is uncertain what is actually gained in practice and especially whether firms do build up a sustainable design capability through alliances (see Bruce & Jevnaker, 1998). A recent survey of UK firms indicates that investment in external design expertise reaps commercial advantages (Roy & Potter, 1993), but other research shows that design expertise is not well integrated with business process (Walsh *et al.*, 1992; Dumas, 1993; Svengren, 1995). Furthermore, design expertise is sourced in an *ad hoc* manner or based on cost, rather than based on a longer-term or strategic perspective (Olins, 1987; Bruce & Morris, 1995) and viewed as a source of investment.

In contrast, the central theme of this paper is to argue that industrial design in relation to business firms is a challenging task. It may be conceived as a strategic relational activity and fragile corporate asset that has to be nourished and protected in order to attain a sustainable design capability. Over time, this may eventually lead to a competitive advantage, but the change processes and relationships seem to be somewhat intricate. Clear patterns have not yet been identified as to how design development is organized in design-intensive firms (Dumas, 1993; Svengren, 1995). Rather, a *diverse* design practice is suggested in innovative firms (Thackara, 1997). Interestingly, the organizing of industrial design as a value-creating but often mobile competence *beyond company borders* may challenge the core competence view of the firm which tends to regard the internal growth resources as most valuable for competitive strengths (*cf.* Prahalad & Hamel, 1990). By contrast, an alternative view would be that critical competencies may reside in outside expertise and networks (Jevnaker, 1996; Dyer & Singh, 1998). A mobile strategic competence for the focal firm is not unthinkable in industrial design, it has been observed in different industrial settings (Bruce & Jevnaker, 1998). However, the ability to manage and to extract value from the partnership is uncertain. Research suggests that strategic alliances and networks are no quick fix, since industrial coordination is not achieved by mergers and acquisitions but has to be created by working closely in a strategic network (Jarillo, 1993) and through long-term investments (Kanter, 1989).

Based on company cases, the aim of this paper is to start the identification of possible patterns in companies' cooperation with industrial designers. More cumulative insights into this phenomenon may be enabled by comparing more than one company's alliance with external design expertise over time, looking for contrasts as well as similarities. The first part of the paper relates design to strategy in order to uncover the most significant gap in our current knowledge on design/business interfaces (Dumas, 1993; Svengren, 1997). More specifically, a model for strategic sourcing of design is delineated and recent trends regarding the use of design expertise in business are also introduced. The next section provides a preliminary conceptual framework for thinking about the benefits and costs of alliances with outside design experts. This relates to previous research on design management (see Jevnaker, 1994; Bruce & Jevnaker, 1998) and on sources of innovation (Leonard-Barton, 1995), as well as being influenced by the capability-based strategy perspective of the firm (Teece, Pisano & Shuen, 1990; Barney, 1997). Three companies (Ingersoll-Rand, HÅG and Ericsson) operating in the different European countries of Britain, Norway and Sweden are then compared in terms of how they have developed and used design alliances. Ingersoll-Rand produces highly engineered tools for construction and other industries, HÅG manufactures steel office furniture systems, and Ericsson is a telecommunications company. Engineering and industrial design are used by all three companies. In each case, industrial design expertise is outsourced to create new products that have a range of "added values" (i.e. easy to use, aesthetically pleasing and performing well functionally) and these have led to competitive advantages as well as renewal challenges for each firm. However, the relationship with the external design firms is managed quite differently. The differences among the companies illuminate the backstage design alliancing as a *cumulative* versus a *disruptive* process in terms of whether the industrial design developments accumulate and converge into distinctive and coherent product innovations. This also suggests that a relational advantage is captured to a different degree. Finally, the paper discusses how and why future capabilities were being developed and extended by the firms.

## Strategic Sourcing of Design

Our present understanding of use of design expertise is messy and needs to be further explored. In the following, various forms of design sourcing are discussed in relation to the firm's creative and coordinative capability in design. A capability may be understood as the way resources, talents and processes are combined and used (*cf.* Teece, Pisano & Shuen, 1990), that is the aptitude to foster design as value-creating activities. For example, how even design-intensive giants such as IBM, Sony or Philips have been able to tap and take advantage of their industrial product designers varies over time and place (Heskett, 1980; Lorenz, 1990; Sakakibara, 1998).

Design expertise may be located as an in-house resource, outsourced, or organized through various combinations of internal and external expertise (*cf.* Williamson, 1985). Though less surveyed, the location of design resources seems to differ according to design traditions, supply and demand factors, corporate and interfunctional policies (Hitt, Hoskisson & Nixon, 1993), and cultural differences in interfirm endeavors. In Japan and Germany, for example, in-house design is often found in exemplary design-conscious firms, such as Sony and Braun and other high-tech firms (Masuda, 1996; Kretschmann, 1996). In the UK, outsourcing of design expertise is on a more arm's-length basis (Bruce & Morris, 1995); whereas close and long-term client-design relationships may be found in northern Italy and Scandinavia (Kicherer, 1990; Jevnaker, 1993; Bruce & Morris, 1995). In this chapter, the focus is on companies' cooperative alliances with external design experts over time. A *"design alliance"* is a cooperative business relationship between a company and its key source of design expertise (or one of its key sources).

Trends indicate that design expertise is increasingly outsourced by companies (Bruce & Morris, 1995), and new forms of collaboration with external designers that combine in-house and outside expertise have emerged (Aldersey-Williams, 1996). This is evident in business settings that traditionally have relied on internal resources, such as Japan and Germany (*Design Management Journal*, 1996). Although not much studied, the purpose of outsourcing and alliances may be manifold, such as access to creative capacity, speed to market, and complementary knowledge, as well as perhaps learning and assistance in finding future opportunities.

The issue of design alliances is interesting because this may contribute to business and design development, as well as to theory-building on design. Often competitive advantages simultaneously demand levels of novelty, perceived quality, recognized offerings, low cost, and fast response times that traditionally organized companies cannot deliver, according to networks researcher Jarillo (1993). We suggest that firms may expand and extend their creative capabilities through alliances with knowledgeable and dedicated individuals or groups that can relate, improvise and act skillfully and quickly to this new landscape. Exemplary businesses seem to derive their strengths from distinctive relations with customers, employees and suppliers (Kay, 1993). This is more easily said than done. The customer signals (market-pull) as well as the firm's technological driving forces (technology-push) need to be attended to, interpreted and transformed in a beneficial manner. This double linking is critical for successful innovation (Burgelman & Sayles, 1986), but the difficulty is what to keep and what new to introduce. The dilemmas of change and stability, or balancing exploration and exploitation (March, 1991), are well-known in management literature (Baden-Fuller & Volberda, 1997), but how to judge and handle them is less explored.

It is precisely here that creative and somewhat detached design agents are critical, since they may overcome the stickiness or inertia of past action. Henderson and Clark (1991) found that development groups of established firms had serious problems in changing the components within a principal product model (architectural innovation). Designers are typically trained in creative *reconfigurations* through continuous experimentation and critical reviews of past, present and future opportunities and requirements. Designers bring these accumulated types into the unique business situation tailoring, or misaligning, the new designs (often more than one alternative) to the specific requirements of the particular problem setting (see, e.g., Schön, 1988). Furthermore, design experts and creative management or teams may, at best, stretch to create something *more*, both in the overall configuration *and* in the often overlooked details (since "the devil is in the details"):

> Design creates corporate distinctiveness in an otherwise product and image surfeited marketplace. It can create a personality ... so it stands out ... It communicates value to the customer, makes selection easier, informs and entertains (Kotler & Rath, 1984).

Thus, design may be of strategic importance, bringing in new competence-based action perspectives and also hitherto irrelevant knowledge (Kreiner, 1999), making these overlooked aspects relevant for the focal firm. Indeed, creating something that has not been seen before, at least not exactly in the same manner (Walsh *et al.*, 1992), often involves not only diversity, but serendipity (Burgelman & Sayles, 1986) and playful experimentation or foolish technology (March, 1976). In line with Kreiner (1999), we suggest that this knowledgeable action cannot be "managed in" merely by instructions or control mechanisms; it needs to be cultivated and stimulated by more than a good brief. The strategic management literature does not specify how advantages of talented design may be fostered and disadvantages reduced, although design commits future resources and a steady stream of such decisions may emerge in a distributed manner in organizations (Olins, 1989).

Previous research indicates that very few firms have built up a conscious management capacity and coordinating structure to sustain and leverage design as a creative capability. Rather, design decisions and design actions are fragmented, even in design-committed firms; see, for example, accounts from Sony and Philips (Lorenz, 1990; Blaich, 1993) and a British research study on 16 manufacturing and service firms (Dumas & Whitfield, 1989). Against this background, we suggest that when the firm lacks the relevant design expertise or needs a fresh injection of complementary design thinking to its accumulated design and business competence, then design alliances may be especially valuable. When new design ideas are of high strategic importance, we suggest that the strategic sourcing of best available external (or internal, if better) design expertise is especially critical; in fact, a combination may be of special interest due to its creative dynamics (see TABLE 11.1).

Hence design expertise is perhaps an extreme case of external sourcing and boundary spanning (Ashkenas *et al.*, 1995). Key characteristics of collaboration and strategic alliances, in general, are mutual interdependence and the need for complementary inputs and flexible interaction (Kanter, 1989; Barney, 1997). However, little is known about the nature and

TABLE 11.1 Need for strategic sourcing of design expertise

| | | Corporate design capability—creative and coordinative deployment | |
|---|---|---|---|
| | | *Low* | *High* |
| Strategic importance of new design concepts | *Low* | Little investment (risk of ignorance) | Candidates for outsourcing (risk of *ad hoc* approach) |
| | *High* | Design and learning alliance (risk of underinvestment) | Internal R&D, and/or dynamic combination of design and business expertise including design alliances, and fresh talents? (risk of cacophony) |

Source: Adapted from Jevnaker (1999) and inspired by Leonard-Barton (1995: 144) and Durand (1997); the need for design alliances and the risks of ignorance, underinvestment, etc., are added owing to the suggested difficulties of organizing, managing and fostering innovative designs.

organization of design alliances. As is typical for today's fluid and uncertain alliances (Doz & Hamel, 1998), the benefits and strategic foundations of design alliances are unclear. In line with Edith Penrose (1959), we need to explore what services designers offer to business. No precise theory specifies how and why one company organizes design as compared to another company. The organizational economics literature even treats creativity as a constancy and so this is not explored in relation to business transactions (Jevnaker, 1995b; Williamson, 1985: 244). Critical factors for the success of managing design relations such as personal chemistry between designer and client to facilitate creativity (Bruce & Docherty, 1993) are, surprisingly often, neglected in the current perspectives on corporate and marketing strategy (Walsh *et al.*, 1992; Dumas, 1993; Svengren, 1997). Design as a creative source might be seen as an opportunity for product or image differentiation and innovation, but past research gives limited insight into the working relationships between business firms and designers.

Moreover, it is not clear how design alliances provide a unique strategic advantage to the firm (Barney, 1997) and how benefits gained relate to the organization of design capability. In other words, how is design integrated into core business processes, so as to establish a design capability to create value not just once, but continually, in today's innovation marathon (Jelinek & Schoonhoven, 1990)? One focus of this paper is to discuss how an innovative design development may actually be facilitated (or not) through an alliance with outside design expertise.

## Design Expertise in Business: Some Problems

The present gap in corporate design competence relates to creative, cognitive and coordinative deployment abilities. One recurrent problem is the term "design". This causes ambiguities because it has more than one common meaning (see, e.g., Walker, 1989; Hollins & Hollins, 1991; Sparke, 1986a). Moreover, definitions are often tied to the design professions themselves (Gorb, 1990). Borja de Mozota (1992) refers to the different cognitive structures of designers and managers, which are so deeply rooted that this inhibits the integration of design with business processes. Interface problems between designers and managers have been articulated elsewhere (e.g., Souder, 1988). Often, management is unfamiliar with the broad range and content of specialized design disciplines (Jevnaker, 1996). This is echoed in Prone's (1995) comment that:

> Presidents and CEOs tend to direct their attention to the larger numbers within creative services on any pro-forma—advertising, merchandising, promotion—and hence, they rarely analyze the real return on investment of

> upgraded design. They tend to see effective design as a random application of aesthetics: sometimes the target gets hit, other times not. (Michael Prone, principal at the Design Firm of Collona, Farrell; Prone, 1995)

Another common shortcoming is to focus on the object as the visible artifact in design rather than on the intangible expertise and creative processes that brought about the new "designs". Design management is seldom described as a corporate process that poses strategic problems and challenges to managers as well as to designers; how this is done in theory and practice is far from well known (Dumas, 1993; Svengren, 1995).

It has more or less bypassed the strategic management field, the corporate communication literature and the product development literature (reviewed by Dumas, 1993; Svengren, 1995, 1997; Hart, 1995) that some companies apparently compete precisely on their ability to create and market designed products which serve the users well, not just once but repeatedly, and integration of design expertise seems to be a crucial factor in their success (Svengren, 1995). Gorb and Dumas (1987) suggest that "design aware firms" have a clear sense of how their design competence affects their business, so that design becomes infused into the norms and practices of the company. For the majority of businesses, however, they suggest that design is utilized in an unplanned and *ad hoc* manner. "Silent design", they suggest, is the more common practice, whereby decisions are made without realizing the impact these have on design, for example marketing may allocate a design budget without identifying the full costs of the project. Often the visual elements of a company's corporate image—exhibitions, logo, merchandise, signage, web sites, etc.—are not coordinated to maximize their impact.

According to Dumas (1993), the design model seems to advocate an exclusivity of the process of design where the designer wants to expand his or her role "by the human tendency to grab more as less becomes available ... making integration less and less likely". For example, if the firm does not intend to change more than the product's shape, designers may introduce new materials, colors and configurations of components, to give a product identity that may not fit with the firm's overall product strategy and thus lead to misalignments. To outsource design may thus be risky if design commits major product configuration decisions with investment consequences. Using design partners can also be risky if the focal firm leaves its future navigation unconsciously to the partner or uses an *ad hoc* sourcing approach (see Table 11.1). By contrast, the team-based model of modern product development may overlook the influence of talented individuals and particular creative interplays among a few core persons, such as the relationship between the design consultancy and its business clients.

How do the agents actually deal with these potential problems that may emerge between designers and their clients? As in other difficult fields of social action, one possibility is to develop an interactive and reciprocal relationship, and this is elaborated in the rest of the paper.

## A Conceptual Framework for Design Alliances

### What is a Design Alliance?

A design alliance, in the context of this paper, is thus a collaborative and interactive business relationship between a company and its design resource. In line with Barney's work on strategic alliances (1997), the design alliance is a cooperative strategy between originally independent partners, that is a voluntary relationship. The parties to the alliance are mutually dependent in terms of inputs, co-production and rewards, but remain independent in terms of ownership and equity. In general, knowledge-based alliances are typically seen as means to gain an improved and flexible resource position (in inputs, process or outputs) more rapidly than would be feasible through internal competencies and resource accumulation. Alliances are vehicles to faster or otherwise improved value creation through access to and synergy of resources (Barney, 1997). A design alliance can be of potential strategic importance by providing skills, knowledge and expertise that is recognized as a corporate asset. The various design talents are considered in relation to the firm's particular business need.

Design alliances are not new, indeed the design pioneer Henry Dreyfuss formed long-term relationships with clients from the late 1920s onwards (Lorenz, 1986; Freeze, 1998), but they have recently attracted interest for their role in global competition. The "new hybrids" describe external collaborations between internal and external design-related competencies across organizational borders (Aldersey-Williams, 1996). International examples are Korean Samsung's close partnership with the British–American industrial design consultancy, IDEO, or IBM's long-term relationship with the Milan-based industrial designer Richard Sapper, which involved a collaboration across three continents between the US, Japan and Italy (Sakakibara, 1998). In the IT business, in companies such as Apple and IBM, internal design resources collaborate with external expertise (Parsey, 1995; Sakakibara, 1998).

One of the main motives for design alliances is that of cooperating with outside expertise to take advantage of the best available design knowledge of product use (Ainamo, 1996), since this may create a favorable edge in products, brands and communications. Yet finding and recruiting the best available and flexible design ally seems to be a strategy that only some international firms have exploited (Walsh *et al.*, 1992; Aldersey-Williams, 1996).

With the downsizing of companies, the trend to outsourcing design expertise has already occurred, certainly in the US and UK (Bruce & Morris, 1995). Decisions have to be made as to the nature of the relationship with the design supplier. The main issues are whether this is to be built up on a cooperative as well as a shorter- or longer-term basis. For the external designer, it may be a major challenge to grasp problems and discover opportunities that may be unknown, even by the client company.

## What May Design Alliances Bring to the Firm?

Benefits of design alliances can be identified and these are discussed below.

*Closer access to design expertise.* Unique or improved products that differentiate the firm can be generated from design alliances, as well as access to ideas, know-how and new technologies that may also reduce the time to market. Since design knowledge resides in human experts—it is not fully codified nor easily transferable—firms need to nurture this competence over time. Only a few firms have access to design expertise in-house, and tailor-made design skills are not easily bought, nor quickly developed. One way to building a sustainable design competence is to develop an alliance with design experts.

*Managing uncertainty in design development.* In general, alliances or other collaborative relationships are seen as beneficial from an economic viewpoint when neither "buy" (classical contracts) nor "make" (through internal resources) is considered to be feasible and efficient. This applies especially to situations in which it is difficult to specify *a priori* the problem, the procedures and tools needed, and the kind of solutions sought. Through collaboration in the design process, the parties may learn to cope with this uncertainty and ambiguity in ways that are fruitful for both, e.g. through an evolving brief.

*Ongoing design and business interactions.* Design is a key asset in the era of new knowledge-based competition, that is where the critical resources are no longer money, buildings or raw materials. In this context, the particular bundle of intangible design- and business-related resources, as embodied in products (product idea/concept, "meta-product") and in people (managers, experts, users, dealers, etc.), are seen as core sources of competitive advantage. These assets need to be mobilized into some form of unified or distinctive combinations, which may require ongoing interactions between design and the firm's core competencies. Over time and with more than one project, the firm and its management may be better able to create a productive climate for both parties.

*Visualization and product decisions.* Often industrial design implies critical trade-offs, in terms of design focus. Interestingly, design expertise is an invisible as well as a visible resource and is a specialized development activity. In addition to creating the meaningful "X-factor" (the character or personality of products) and the suitable interface with the user, design also can coordinate visually other resources (technical features, materials, components, marketing attributes, packaging, etc.). This linking of core aspects of design and its management makes design a powerful competence to possess.

*Design—"First mover" advantage.* A distinctive design approach in a business setting is a fairly new concern (on the business agenda in the late 1980s and early 1990s). However, in the current competitive environment of product affluence, globalization, customer sophistication and new technology opportunities, design is becoming essential in some industries. A design partner may be a possible route to attaining "first mover" advantage.

*Flexible tailoring.* If firms use professional design infrequently, or do not need design experts in-house, an alliance with a design consultant may be especially beneficial. A variety of collaborative approaches are feasible and depend on the firm's need for design solutions that are tailor-made or the ease of access to an external design supplier. Long-term relationships with design partners have some advantages, such as familiarity with client's needs, possession of appropriate skills, accumulating company-relevant knowledge, etc.

*Strengthen name, image and reputation.* By investing in design, the firm may strengthen its market position through, for example, brand building and projecting a quality image. This can be a highly valuable asset when recognized and preferred by the customer, dealer, etc. Moreover, benefits may accrue from using a highly reputable design company. Design can also be coordinated to encompass products, communications and the overall corporate environment. Managing design to create a coherent corporate identity can differentiate the firm.

*Other benefits.* Design alliances can also help a firm manage the risks and share the costs (Barney, 1997) associated with more radically innovative design work or new business developments. Sometimes the investment required to exploit a design opportunity can be large or the payback may not be delivered for some time. In this situation, sharing the costs and commitments within an alliance may spread the risks and increase the potential benefits. Royalty agreement is a contractual arrangement that is often practiced in such situations.

The above discussion suggests that using design alliances strategically can bring commercial benefits and serve to differentiate the company. Building a cooperative relationship with the design company may be appropriate where a tailor-made solution and flexibility are required. Where new ideas are sought, more classical market mechanisms may be used, such as outsourcing, buying models from fairs or arranging design competitions. However, when technical coordination is needed, the arm's length/market approach cannot deal with this (Williamson, 1985). Barney (1997) pinpoints that firms have an incentive to cooperate in strategic alliances when the value of their resources and assets combined is greater than the value of their resources and assets separately. This notion of resource complementarity may benefit both parties (not just the client).

Over time, as a design–client relationship evolves a set of advantages may accrue for the firm and also the designer, e.g. through repeat business, royalties and reputation, but so far, no full understanding or theory of this type of alliance development exists that specifies conditions and crucial relations. Disadvantages of design alliances are also possible. If either party does not contribute according to expectations, then diminishing returns may result over time. The parties may also misuse the trust-based relationship (Williamson, 1985). Another possibility is that complacency may reduce the creative flows between the parties and so lead to disbenefits.

Company cases can help to understand how design relationships enfold and create value over time, so as to form a strategic design alliance. The next part of the paper considers three cases.

## Data and Methodology

### Cases

A set of relevant cases have been documented in a new case anthology (Bruce & Jevnaker, 1998) and this was used as a basis for suitable cases. First, we wanted to compare business cases where industrial design was emerging, or was perceived as a new expertise of potential strategic and economic value for the firm. By examining two engineering-driven firms, the challenge of configuring and integrating outside design expertise into the engineering ranks and core competencies of the technology firms are explored. By contrast, a third case study, from a manufacturer of metal office furniture, helps to identify the driving forces of a dynamic and long-term design partnership that has become a strategic source of corporate innovation. This design collaboration is driven by independent design professionals and a product development team (including engineering), which allows input from expertise outside the domain of furniture manufacturing.

The purpose of the three cases selected was to compare the design relationships as these developed over time in three product companies:

Ingersoll-Rand (UK), Ericsson (Sweden) and HÅG (Norway). In each company, senior managers, product development managers and other key personnel involved with making design decisions were interviewed, using a semi-structured questionnaire. The questionnaire covered such issues as company strategy, attitudes to design, project development and management of design resource, e.g. sourcing, liaison with design firm, evaluation, etc. The designers involved in the projects were also interviewed to ascertain their views and attitudes as to the management of the project, their understanding of the company strategy and their project management competencies. Different researchers collected the material from the companies.

A within-case description is often considered preferable before comparing multiple cases so as to enable the reader to grasp each story within one particular context, including its connections between agents and events. Thus a compact version of design alliances relating to the three independent companies (Ingersoll-Rand, Ericsson and HÅG) is presented before the cross-comparisons. In the company cases, the various approaches companies have adopted to utilize design skills are described. The challenge of resourcing and utilizing design competence is dealt with in different ways. TABLE 11.2 summarizes the three cases and provides an overview of each.

TABLE 11.2 Key aspects of three product companies' design alliances

| Key aspects | Product Design Alliance as to Ingersoll-Rand | LM Ericsson | HÅG |
|---|---|---|---|
| Time period | Industrial design from Dec. 1991 to 1993. Medium-term ally | Industrial design from 1984. Several stop-go processes. Short-term allies. | Industrial and furniture design from 1974 onwards, long-term and future |
| Target market for new product designs | Construction industry, professional users | Personal end-users in global markets of mobile cellular phones | Contract market and end-users for office chairs. |
| Comments | Strategic investment linked to new product safety regulations | Engineering-led product development | Entrepreneur-led integrated design investments in the short and long term. |

Source: The Ericsson case is based on Svengren (1995, 1997) and additional own observation of LM Ericsson management's presentations. The Ingersoll-Rand and HAG cases are based on the Bruce and Morris and the Jevnaker chapters in Bruce and Jevnaker (1998).

## CASE 1: TOOLMAKER INGERSOLL-RAND'S NEW INDUSTRIAL DESIGN PARTNERSHIP

Changes in European health and safety legislation presented opportunities for the development of new products for the construction industry. A product development team was set up with the mission of producing a product that was "best in class" for power, vibration and ergonomics. The Project Engineer had been working on a new vibration-reducing device, Vibra-Smooth, and he wanted a product that would utilize this technology. This meant taking a risk because this was a radical departure from existing products. Industrial design was required to ensure that the new product would meet ergonomic and market needs. External industrial designers would have to be relied upon because the company did not have its own in-house industrial designers and this would add to the project's risk.

In addition to this aspect of the perceived risk was that of the short product development time. To be "first in the market" with a new product and to beat potential competition, the product had to be ready for market launch within a year. A team approach was adopted to help achieve this target; the team consisted of the European Marketing Manager, the Product Engineering Manager and the Production Manager. This core team was given the authority to make crucial decisions and had to report to a steering committee of directors to keep them informed of major developments. This authority meant that the members of the team were highly committed to the project. Each member of the team contributed on an equal footing and the project leader's duties were rotated. All of this helped instill a feeling of trust and openness to foster cross-fertilization of ideas.

Sourcing appropriate design skills was a major issue as the company did not have the appropriate industrial design skills to achieve the objectives of the project. They faced a dilemma: whether or not to develop the Vibra-Smooth technology, which would delay the market launch, or to introduce a product without this technology but which would meet the deadline. The team decided to look for a design supplier that would be able to advise them about the complexities of expanding Vibra-Smooth into a new product design. Not only were the design skills critical in sourcing the new design supplier, but their commitment to the project was also critical. As the European Marketing Manager expressed it:

> We wanted someone to come to the party that had to take some of the responsibility and put his stake in as well. We wanted someone who was part of the team.

By chance, a local design company that had a good reputation and had strong engineering know-how approached the company at this time. Their approach was to have an open rapport with the client and to work closely with the client to facilitate an open and creative working relationship.

However, the product did reach the market in 18 months from conception to launch and it was highly successful, becoming market leader and winning a number of prestigious design awards. The approach to design and product development was just as important an outcome as the product itself. A multi-disciplinary team with effective interaction with the customer base and the autonomy to make decisions quickly was critical to the success of the project. As the European Marketing Manager commented:

> During the project, many things were learnt, which will apply to the next project—continuous improvement is the name of the game! This product is the start of the "right" product image for the company—the image of the future will be one of modern styling coupled with super efficiency.

## Case 2: LM Ericsson's Mobile Phones—Challenge of Design Integration

Ericsson was one of the first companies to venture into mobile phones in the early 1980s and was proactive in developing the market for these products. The design of mobile phones has evolved and changed over time, essentially to reduce the weight and size of the product, whilst improving its performance. As well as changes to the product design, competition has become more intense, which makes the design of the product distinctive and critical for sales. Within the company, substantial organizational changes occurred throughout the history of its involvement with mobile phones (Svengren, 1995).

The culture of the mobile phone division was regarded as less engineering dominated than other groups within Ericsson. Marketing and sales, R&D, finance and general management were all located in one place. It was distinctive in other ways, namely in responding to rapid product development and market cycles, in high-volume production and in being end-user oriented. A switch of design company was also made to try to foster a close collaboration between the R&D operations and a local industrial design firm.

It was decided by the product development team that the next "breakthrough" product should focus on ergonomic design, that is the keypad, display, size, form and colors. At the same time, the product should be able to work globally and be heavily branded, that is have a distinctive identity that could differ from other Ericsson products. The mission was to develop "high product quality following four design characteristics: compactness, elegance, balance and credibility".

In 1992 the marketing and product managers in the division gained the authority to oversee the product design and marketing for subsequent products. They began by sourcing an industrial design firm that could exploit the technological advances of Ericsson and that had an international outlook, as well as project management skills and a knowledge of mass production techniques. Such a company was found and collaboration began.

However, the new R&D Manager in the division was skeptical about the role of the industrial design firm in development and so their task was limited to work on the surface elements of the phone, rather than to control the whole of the design.

One of the major competitors launched a distinctive design on the market. This created "shock waves" and the reaction was to set up an industrial design manager to integrate industrial design at a strategic level in product development. The Managing Director stated that:

> We can no longer have a situation where the technicians come to marketing with a ready product. ... We have to see the whole product and the development process where industrial design is an important issue. As such, industrial design should be equal to other activities of product development (Svengren, 1998: 175–176).

In summary, this case highlights the complexity that a global company within a fast-moving market has to face. Quick decisions and fast moves are needed. However, the product development was engineering led and did not exploit industrial design expertise in an optimum way. As the market demand for mobile phones was so high and everything that could be produced was sold, there was little incentive to change. But once the market had become more competitive and growth rates had leveled out, design became critical as a major source of differentiation.

## Case 3: HÅG's Office Chairs Fit for Humans Through Long-Term Ergonomic Design Alliance

HÅG maintains that people are not made for sitting still. The challenge is to reduce the risk of musculo-skeletal disorders. Thus, making chairs for sitting is a kind of paradox for this furniture-maker, established in 1943. Since the end of the 1970s, this paradox has been acknowledged by HÅG and even exploited as a challenging international business opportunity. The solution is to make chairs more movable and fit for humans. Moreover, the firm communicates a consistent message to its selected markets emphasizing that the world needs to be refurnished. Given this background, dynamic design thinking would seem natural and critical. However, historically, ergonomic chair design has been more or less neglected by the furniture-making industry (Sparke, 1986b). At HÅG, this type of design thinking did emerge during the mid-1970s, partly by serendipity and partly by conscious search for new ideas. Most critical were particular driving forces and creative relationships putting the new ideas on the corporate agenda and making them strategic.

To understand the driving forces, we need to look back to 1974. A new marketing manager was recruited through a consultant relationship, and he started to revitalize the company that at that time had serious financial problems. One of the first things he did was to search for the best chair designer through his networks at the Norwegian design center, where he had worked previously. Interestingly, he dared to take in a young furniture/industrial designer, Peter Opsvik, who was said to be the best, though less established than other designers considered. This piece of advice was not a common perception at the time; it came through one special relationship contact at the national design center. The designer agreed to come to help HÅG, and once he had contributed to a redesign of one of HÅG's office chairs, the former top manager and owner had intended to terminate his contract. However, this particular job was merely a beginning, according to the new marketing manager. The relationship with this young designer was not discontinued; rather, it was strengthened into a range of projects and frequent communication.

Peter Opsvik is today well known as highly innovative in the furniture design environment and his product designs are exhibited in several countries. At the time when HÅG's marketing manager called on him, he had already designed the first ergonomically planned children's chair in the world (the Tripp Trapp) and he was generally inspired by ergonomic thinking as a fundamental point of departure in chair making. Opsvik had met ergonomic experts in Essen and had also worked at Tandberg's Radio factory; he had ideas beyond the conventional furniture design domain. At HÅG, he met a Danish surgeon who had written a pamphlet on "Seated Man" with examples from seating challenges related to children.

HÅG has absorbed this way of thinking which today is fused into its organizational culture. A range of initiatives has stimulated this progress, such as continued investments in competence on ergonomics and design, and repeated communication and promotion to both internal and external audiences, including the refinement of a visual and verbal rhetoric around the company's ethos (Jevnaker, 1993). Interestingly, all staff as well as strategic partners participate repeatedly in HÅG's own Academy which makes it a truly learning organization. A proactive entrepreneurial top manager (the former marketing manager) has been the design champion and is a wellspring of communicative ideas. More subtle is perhaps his ability to recruit new expertise as well as keeping up the social glue of the whole firm (he knows everyone by first name and often even their families). In the firm, this top driving force has been complemented with a team of excellent and committed managers such as the head of product development and head of marketing. To sum up, there are several factors that are important for HÅG's continued renewal, but most critical seem to be the constant stream of innovative product designs combined with a courageous, attractive and consistent market communication in international markets. These core assets are supplemented with just-in-time distribution systems and other efforts to improve its services. From close to bankruptcy in the early 1970s, HÅG has achieved considerable growth and is currently the leading producer of office and visitors' chairs in Scandinavia. More than 75% of sales are to markets outside Norway. Although a small corporation in international terms, HÅG has managed to be highly competitive in its markets.

## RESULTS

In general, design-based benefits are attributed to the abilities (or disabilities) of design experts to improve the quality, usability, aesthetic expression and communicative identity. An alternative view is to stress the business and managerial side (Gorb, 1990; Dumas, 1993). Surprisingly often, the creative relationships among clients and designers are not considered. In the following, the potential benefits of the client–design relationship are examined with reference to the three alliance cases (see TABLE 11.3).

*Closer access to design expertise.* Whether design resources are located inside or outside the firm, one particular challenge identified in past literature is to connect design and business expertise in ways that may yield a long-term synergy and competence, and make strategic use of design resources in value-creating corporate processes (e.g. Blaich, 1993; Jevnaker, 1994; Svengren, 1997; Kristensen, 1998). Mutual benefits accrue to both design firms and their clients from design alliances. Both Ingersoll-Rand and HÅG did benefit from a *close access* to outside design expertise, whilst Ericsson had problems with managing the project due to management moves, staff turnover and other reasons.

Ingersoll-Rand gained its close access to expertise *during* the project work, while HÅG has benefited from a continuously close access to its key design alliance *beyond* project work. This nuance may be of importance for the firm's continued design capability. At HÅG, a range of knowledge-based events, informal phone calls and visits indicate that there is a rich contact between the designer and the firm over time. This is not obvious. The former top manager wanted to disconnect the partnership when finished

Table 11.3 Company comparisons of design alliances

| Benefits | Design Alliance as to Ingersoll-Rand | Ericsson* | HÅG |
|---|---|---|---|
| Closer access to design expertise | High degree during project work | Low degree due to stop–go processes | High degree beyond project work |
| Managing ambiguity | Did learn to cope with equivocal and complex trade-offs | Problems with linking marketing and design to engineering | Managed ambiguous areas, creative climate harnessed |
| Ongoing design/business interactions | Intensive and project-based | Disrupted efforts in repeated projects | Intensive and partly detached beyond projects |
| Visualization and product decisions | Rapid visual tools explored, intense interaction | Visual tools and design features explored, interrupted contacts | Visual tools, intense interactions and verbal rhetoric explored |
| Designed innovation—"first mover advantage" | Became market leader and won design awards | Smaller personal cellular phones, not sustainable | Pioneered ergonomic chair design; market leader in Scandinavia; product and design awards |
| Flexible tailoring | Flexible, highly committed and increasingly more familiar expertise | Both familiar and not familiar; explored new sources | Creative, flexible, and highly familiar, outside design expert as insider but also intellectually autonomous |
| Strengthening product name and reputation | To a high degree | To a medium degree, yet high market share | To a high degree, design excellence |
| Achieving a comprehensive visual image | Not analyzed | Well-known concern, but design not comprehensive | To a high degree, well-known and distinct corporate profile |
| Learning and overspill of knowledge | New design centre, increased design awareness among managers | Design management seminars, top management signals increased commitment to integrate design | Creative studio, corporate academy, 12 design partners, multiple contact debriefings, design as corporate value |

* Source: Our interpretation based on Svengren (1995, 1997).

with the first project: "now you can send the designer home"! The integrated and longer-term concerns were also visible at Ingersoll-Rand, according to the project leader:

> We had the objective of starting a product design facility in Europe that went beyond this initial project. We wanted someone who was part of the team (Bruce & Morris, 1998: 78).

*Managing ambiguity*. All three companies used the design alliance as a way of *reducing ambiguity* (more than uncertainty) in the design development, since all firms did not know in advance what the problem was and how to specify it in relation to design, the methods and approaches needed, and the solutions that might be best for the customers, as well as the product firm and other stakeholders such as safety regulatory bodies. This is as expected in alliances (Barney, 1997), and accords with the reciprocal contract problems of design partners (see Jevnaker, 1996, 1999). What is more interesting is that the parties handled these uncertainties and ambiguities in different ways as part of the ongoing interaction, suggesting that this next point is highly critical.

*Ongoing design/business interaction*. In order to explore the new design opportunities and direct further search, repeated contacts/meetings were held and several decision points were established in all cases, although the details on the relational level are more richly described in the Ingersoll-Rand and the HÅG cases. In fact, incidents of non-disclosure emerged at Ericsson. For a long time the design collaboration was rather chaotic because the industrial designers did not receive any information nor any clear goals for their work; according to Svengren (1998), the designers were not allowed access to future plans, nor were they invited to discuss the concept of the product and its marketing. In the other cases, the *intense ongoing and interactive problem-solving efforts* were crucial for progress in design development. For example, industrial design consultant Bob Buxton working for Ingersoll-Rand describes the process in this way:

> You have to tell the client everything, otherwise at the end of the project, the product is not acceptable. This takes a lot of time, and typically we have put more time in than we wanted to. (Bruce & Morris, 1998: 79)

This responsible self-representation nurturing the client orientation was found also in other interviews with experienced industrial design consultants (see Jevnaker, 1996) and relates to the significant gap of design knowledge in business (Blaich, 1993).

*Visualization and product decisions*. Product concepts were transformed into material reality by testable models in these cases. The visualization (sketches, drawings, prototypes) provided a shared creative space.

However, the pace of development may compress the important 3-D modeling stage and, despite warning from the designer, this happened in the Ingersoll-Rand project, resulting in a small ridge or aesthetic flaw, but the client did not regard this as likely to affect customer sales.

*Designed innovation—first-mover advantage.* At Ingersoll-Rand and HÅG, the designers and product leaders strove for the best available product design solutions. Both companies also gained a leading edge through their innovative product designs. Ericsson was already very successful and was, for some time, not dedicated to involving its design alliances fully into product strategies and innovation. This hindered design improvements and interfunctional coordination.

*Flexible tailoring.* Innovative designs sometimes do not fit with the firm's established structures for procurement, manufacturing, distribution, etc. (Dumas, 1993). In the cases studied, the industrial designers took great effort in adapting the design solutions to get them right for the end-user as well as the manufacturing company. However, tailoring is hindered when designers are not included in strategy plans and discussions.

*Strengthen name, reputation and image.* By investing in industrial design, Ingersoll-Rand and HÅG created new values that were appreciated through prizes and media attention, gaining a reputation for leading-edge user-friendly products. HÅG also achieved a comprehensive visual corporate profile and creative marketing by extending their innovative design thinking to graphics, interiors, exhibitions, etc. By contrast, the Hotline concept of Ericsson's mobile phones created ambiguities in marketing and communication not playing up to the engineering strengths of Ericsson.

*Learning and overspill of knowledge.* In all three cases, learning and an overspill of knowledge were indicated but to a different degree. Design awareness emerged among managers and this was fostered or further explored: at Ericsson in design management seminars, at Ingersoll-Rand in their planned European Design Centre. At HÅG a range of design learning activities were cultivated, e.g. through the product development's debriefing process, in international marketing training, and generally through the company's learning academy.

## DISCUSSION

The novel focus in these cases was especially linked to improving the *end-user* situation. The companies and the designers worked cooperatively to interpret and improve the usability of the companies' products. Not surprisingly, a knowledge-based alliance is naturally dependent on each party's expertise, but these cases also bring forward the individual creative energy as well as the relational knowledge flow and creativity.

The strategy- and entrepreneur-led design investments paid off while the engineering-led development did not allow designers fully to the table. In the former cases, an integrated product design approach has emerged as the design strategy was not seen in isolation from other perspectives. Both the company and the design experts cooperated closely to meet ergonomic *and* market needs, as well as making the product design technically feasible. In this kind of design development, visualization and model-testing play a particular role, as also found by Leonard-Barton (1991).

The designers' and co-developers' absorption in the creative design process seems crucial and has a personal as well as a relational dimension. Although the technology bases, resources and time pressures were different, each party's continued commitment and interaction brought fresh ideas to the alliance. The utter absorption in their projects is found in creativity research on individuals (Csikszentmihalyi, 1996), but incidents of interactive absorption of creative partnerships are less well documented.

Although intense collaboration and interaction are significant in these cases, individual talents were also visible. In fact, the cases do not underline any big contradiction between creative individuals and innovative groups. HÅG's development was triggered by its entrepreneurial manager and his search for the best furniture designer as well as his insistence on sustaining the working relationship with Norwegian designer Peter Opsvik. This designer had no problem in dealing with HÅG's product development teams and also visited suppliers to better understand their capacities. Interestingly, Opsvik had been exposed to ergonomics during a study visit to Germany. Hence, this case illuminates the role of working within a wider network, which includes a deliberate search for knowledge and more random factors. This accords with new literature on strategic networks (Jarillo, 1993) and highlights the ability to take advantage of serendipity in innovation. The catalytic effect of unanticipated phenomena is important in the creation of wholly new products (Burgelman & Sayles, 1986).

What is also essential in these cases is the determination to search for something new and better, an intrinsic motivation that is found in creativity research (Csikszentmihalyi, 1996). The designers and others in the product development team had the vision to develop a radical product. This takes *courage* at an early stage in the product's development. The extrinsic rewards came later: Ingersoll-Rand became market leader and HÅG has pioneered ergonomic chair design and is a market leader in its field in Scandinavia. These first mover advantages of Ingersoll-Rand and HÅG were not luck, but the results of hard and intensive creative work and close cooperation.

What is refreshing is the recognition of design and the learning between the design and client companies that can occur when new and successful designs emerge. As may be observed within the design alliances of

Ingersoll-Rand as well as HÅG, the knowledgeable parties expand their knowledge (*cf.* Nonaka & Takeuchi, 1995) and probe-and-learn within an ongoing interactive process *framed by the relationship*, so that both may perform better together than each may do alone (Jevnaker, 1996). Interestingly, this type of intensive workshop of value creation among a smaller core group (or, we may add, a dyad) has recently been called the value shop (Stabell & Fjeldstad, 1998) to distinguish it from the more linear value chains.

Hitherto we do not know what makes some design alliances more innovative or "hot" than others. To achieve synergy in a somewhat compressed timespace through dialogue and creative interaction among people with diverse expertise is one possible speculation. New design approaches are more empathic to end-users, e.g. exploring the future in the present through contextual research learning how consumers are doing things (Ireland & Johnson, 1995). Intensive ongoing interaction on usability issues was found and this accords with Thompson's conception of an intensive technology (Thompson, 1967; Jevnaker, 1993) or a passing-ball-game (Jevnaker, 1996; Barney, 1997) or "shuttling" (Thölke & Lowe, 1996), which seems to be a common ingredient of effective design alliances.

Based on insights into the three companies' design alliances, it is worth noting that both the complementary (diverse) expertise and the partly overlapping business/technology expertise seemed to be critical inputs within these creative dynamics. More importantly, the parties tended to see the world differently, and this may evoke tensions. At HÅG, these tensions are no surprise; they are expected and exploited. These are similar to what Nissan's design director has called creative abrasion (Hirschberg, 1998, also cited in Leonard-Barton, 1995: 63) and these creative dialectics were also found in four other Norwegian design alliance cases (Jevnaker, 1995a,b). Perhaps recognized talented experts may be more tolerated when they voice disagreement? HÅG's management has apparently learned to foster and deal with a diverse group of design personalities and the associated creative abrasion, that is when "different ideas rub against each other" (Leonard-Barton, 1995: 63). By contrast, in the Ericsson case, the above types of tensions and uncertainties did not seem to be dealt with effectively, and interactions with outside designers were disrupted from time to time.

The cases indicate the benefits that close cooperation can bring for both parties of the design alliance when it is fostered and harnessed. For the client, the design firm can provide fresh insights and bring new knowledge and skills, which in these settings typically have to be combined with the company's own skills and processes. Even in the more autonomous furniture design projects, it was beneficial to combine competencies in order to gain more effective use of materials, improve the aesthetics and ensure efficient production. For the design firm, there are novel problems to work on, which may involve the design firm acquiring and developing new know-how. So, both the designer and the client may undergo a learning process to achieve the final result.

If the alliance is successful, there may be an overspill of design know-how into other projects, both for the design firm to use for other clients and for the company to discover new applications. A successful design outcome can strengthen a design alliance. In some cases, clients are moving into the designer's company, or co-locating to be closer to their external design resource, for example Korean Samsung with the British–American design consultancy IDEO (Jevnaker, 1996). Cost savings may be made, particularly by the client, where information and development costs can be shared by parties of the alliance, rather than being borne totally by the client. However, some companies are reluctant to foster such close ties with their design suppliers and prefer a more "arm's length" relationship; cultural differences may account, to some extent, for differences in approaches to the management of design alliances. Nonetheless the design alliance could be the company's major source of creativity and push the firm ahead of its competition. Such personalized sources of creative know-how are difficult to imitate, and special relationships and personalities are visible in design alliances.

## Implications

As stressed by Robert Blaich (Philips and Herbert Miller's former head of design), managing design to make the crucial connections between business functions and between design and corporate is complex (Blaich, 1995). It is still not known whether locating design outside the firm may enhance rather than reduce these functional barriers. Leonard-Barton (1995) notes that firms, in general, are better trained in competitive behavior than in cooperation. However, the external designers may receive some hostility from internal staff and have problems in becoming acknowledged as the idea source or co-creator for the product. Grounded on the presented results, the following three implications can be put forward.

### Strategy and Design

Industrial design experts were found to be concerned with creating and signaling new qualities for the client's customers and this empathy with the users gave managers entirely new perspectives on their core business. Since design as a creative and differentiating competence has been neglected in both business practice (Lorenz, 1986, 1990) and management theory (Kotler

& Rath, 1984), design needs to be thought about strategically. The cases reinforce the view that designers seldom are directly involved in the formulation of their clients' strategic plans for design. Even though, their designs may influence the company's strategic direction. As illuminated at Ingersoll-Rand and HÅG, designers and co-developers can reconceive and make new sense of the business that can provide a leading edge. Indeed, the product and its meaning can become the most powerful symbol for the company. Design acts upon intangible values making a good connection between the symbolic and the tangibles, whether it is care for the user or other concerns. Through its philosophy of ergonomic and environmental designs, the chair-maker, HÅG, attempted to "refurnish the world". This company demonstrates that design can build a distinctive and attractive profile by innovating and continually improving product lines.

Based on the three cases, it may be argued that it is possible to obtain an advanced industrial design competence only after considerable collaborative practice or exposure, due to the highly tacit design skills and many interdisciplinary tradeoffs involved in designing within complex and non-routine industrial development settings (Heskett, 1980; Schön, 1988; Blaich, 1993). This has important strategic implications, since this learning barrier also protects others from gaining rapid access to advanced and design-tailored advantages. Less sophisticated surface design features are more easy to imitate.

## Location of Design Expertise

In the late industrial and digital society with uncertain but fairly *constant changes*, it may be more valuable (more benefits than costs) to cooperate with outside expertise, rather than to be self-reliant, in order to take advantage of the best available design knowledge. This may help to build a favorable edge in products, brands and communications relative to the uncertain creation of wealth in business settings. However, the location issue is secondary to other concerns. It seems favorable to take advantage of the best available design expertise—wherever that is located—and also leverage the design competencies in firms (Walsh *et al.*, 1992; Svengren, 1995). The case material gives evidence that seeds for innovative growth may emerge from multiple sources, but design alliances seem to play a crucial role: designers may have developed abilities to *discover* or create the new ideas, but also to *transform* these into meaningful concepts that may benefit their business clients. Hence, this flow of expertise and relationally based design process can be a crucial source of innovation. Leonard-Barton (1995) prefers to use another metaphor, "wellsprings", which may flow from outside as well as from inside the firm.

## Investment in Design Relationships

The initial contact between the designers and companies appears as more or less random, though some evidence for active search for excellent design input was found. Sourcing of appropriate design expertise is complex. Managers do not realize the potential of the expertise they are sourcing (if sufficient absorptive competence is not present: *cf.* Cohen & Levinthal, 1980). Thus initiatives from designers are valuable, such as happened in the Ingersoll-Rand case. Long-term or intensive relationships between a client and a design partner can help. The industrial design collaboration in all three cases illuminates what it takes to expand the firm's product design capability. What is important, in addition to access to talented designers, are the continued efforts and sustained investments made to nurture the design competence. The cases highlight the effort needed to develop a *momentum* (Itami, 1987) and capitalize on design relationships over time. The ambitions and needs of the firms vary, but a long-term investment appears necessary if design is to take on a strategic role. For instance, Richard Sapper was given the title of industrial design consultant for IBM in 1980, but the development of distinctive computer notebooks only "took off" in the 1990s (Sakakibara, 1998). Peter Opsvik's relationships with HÅG and Stokke (another client) started in 1974 and 1967, respectively, but the strategic significance of the innovative product lines did not occur before the mid-1980s.

Moreover, the capability-based perspective of the firm suggests that sources of competitive advantage are the capabilities and resources that are difficult to imitate, such as talents, skills and knowledge (Barney, 1997), and what economists call "time-compressed diseconomies" may be crucial for competitive advantage (Dierickx & Cool, 1989). As indicated in Table 11.2, the future design capabilities of the companies are highly influenced by their current investments in building up and sustaining design alliances.

## Conclusion: Fundamentals of Design Relationships

Thus far, we know very little about creative coordination. Design may trigger further inquiry in this direction: how do companies foster creative design work and desirable solutions by taking advantage of heterogeneous contributors? What are the ingredients of a successful design alliance? How can creativity and novelty, originality, taste or uniqueness be managed successfully? These three cases support earlier findings in the design and innovation literature that top and middle management commitment is required if design is to be taken seriously as a strategic resource. Also, these top managers recognized that the designers could communicate with other managers, marketers, dealers, etc., to convey effectively the values of the product. One of the main problems that affects design investment is its acknowledgement as a distinctive competence.

Recipes for success do not exist because they relate to the individuals concerned and the context in which they operate. Design–client relationships are, in essence, tailor-made. The design alliances may even be expanded in such a manner that they blur with the company's creative strategic core, though this may not be tolerated. Moreover, the actions and processes within these working relationships are quite hidden, emerging within the secrecy of the product development processes. The personalized and tacitly evolving design alliances are difficult for outsiders to explore, which may make them competitively interesting (*cf.* Barney, 1997) but also intricate to grasp for research. Nonetheless, some fundamental rules for effective partnering of client and design companies can be stated. Perhaps the most important is that of courage to allow for openness and the frank exchange of ideas. Acknowledgment of design as a valuable, or equal, partner in the development of projects is a fundamental aspect of creative relationships. Learning from experience is another significant feature. Companies may utilize design in an *ad hoc* manner and repeat the same mistakes and encounter the same types of problems, rather than continually improving and learning from these.

The company cases indicate that establishing long-term relationships between client and design experts can foster trust, acknowledgment and learning. This may allow contradictions to be disclosed and synthetically resolved. Creative dialectics were important in all three cases, but design-related tensions also emerged and improvements in design were disrupted. Some of the industrial design relationships portrayed in the cases show how design can produce substantive competitive advantages. These findings may be valid for other companies, since they accord with the creative dynamics described by Nissan International Design's President Jerry Hirschberg (1998; see also Leonard-Barton, 1995).

Unless these fundamentals of design relationships are heeded, then design will continue to have an uneasy relationship with business. We have argued that creative knowledge is located in the design alliance formed between the client and the design firm and that this can become a strategic competence which impacts on the company's innovative ability and potential business performance. From HÅG, Ericsson and Ingersoll-Rand, we learn that design alliances may constitute creative capabilities that are fragile and intangible. Developing capabilities in design is a continuous process, but can reap rewards when harnessed over time. Once destroyed, they may perhaps never be rekindled and the company will have recognized, but too late, that it has lost its creative and competitive edge.

## Note

1. The story of Absolut has been told in a comprehensive Swedish TV programme. Moreover, one of the consultants involved who was responsible for the art campaign gave additional insights in speeches to various audiences in Oslo during 1998.

## Acknowledgement

Research support from the Research Council of Norway is gratefully acknowledged (FAKTA program for design/business issues; VARP-P2005 program for integrated product development research).

## References

Ainamo, A. (1996). *Industrial design and business performance. A case study of design management in a Finnish fashion firm.* Doctoral thesis, Helsinki School of Economics and Business Administration. (Ainamo also has an article on this subject in Bruce & Jevnaker (1998.)

Aldersey-Williams, H. (1996). Design at a distance: The new hybrids. *Design Management Journal*, **7**(2), 43–49.

Ashkenas, R., Ulrich, D., Jick, T. & Kerr, S. (1995). *The Boundaryless Organization: Breaking the Chains of Organizational Structure*. San Francisco, CA: Jossey-Bass.

Baden-Fuller, C. & Volberda, H. (1997). Strategic renewal in large complex organizations: A competence-based view. In A. Heene & R. Sanchez (eds), *Competence-based Strategic Management*, Chichester: Wiley.

Barney, J.B. (1997). *Gaining and Sustaining Competitive Advantage*. Reading, MA: Addison-Wesley.

Blaich, R. with Blaich, J. (1993). *Product Design and Corporate Strategy: Managing the Connection for Competitive Advantage*. New York: McGraw-Hill.

Blaich, R. (1995). Design management: Unfinished business for this millennium. Speech and Abstract presented under *The Challenge of Complexity*, 3rd International Conference on Design Management, 21–22 August, Helsinki: University of Art and Design Helsinki (UIAH).

Borja de Mozota, B. (1992). Design education and research: A theoretical model for the future. *Design Management Journal*. **3**(4), 19–25.

Bowen, H.K., Clark, K.B., Holloway, C.A. & Wheelright, S.T. (eds) (1994). *The Perpetual Enterprise Machine: Seven Keys to Corporate Renewal Through Successful Product and Process Development*. New York: Oxford University Press.

Bruce, M. & Docherty, C. (1993). It's all in a relationship: a comparative study of client–design consultant relationships. *Design Studies*. **14**(4), 402–422.

Bruce, M. & Jevnaker, B.H. (eds) (1998). *Management of Design Alliances: Sustaining Competitive Advantage*. Chichester: Wiley.

Bruce, M. & Morris, B., with Svengren, L. & Kristensen, T. (1995). *Strategic Management of Design Consultancy: Comparisons from Sweden, Denmark and Britain*. Manchester: School of Management, UMIST.

Bruce, M. & Morris, B. (1998). A comparative study of design professionals. In M. Bruce & B.H. Jevnaker (eds), *Management of Design Alliances: Sustaining Competitive Advantage*, Chichester: Wiley.

Burgelman, R. & Sayles, L.R. (1986). *Inside Corporate Innovation*. New York and London: Free Press.

Cohen, W.M. & Levinthal, D.A. (1980). Absorptive capacity: A new perspective on learning and innovation. *Administrative Science Quarterly*, **35**, 128–152.

Csikszentmihalyi, M. (1996). *Creativity: Flow and the Psychology of Discovery and Invention*. New York: Harper Collins.

*Design Management Journal* (1996). Design management and consulting. *Design Management Journal*, **7**(2).

Dierickx, I. & Cool, C. (1989). Asset stock accumulation and sustainability of competitive advantage. *Management Science*, **35**(12), 1504–1513.

Doz, Y.L. & Hamel, G. (1998). *The Alliance Advantage. The Art of Creating Value Through Partnering*. Boston, MA: Harvard Business School Press.

Dumas, A. (1993). *The effect of management structure and organisational process on decisions in industrial design*. Doctoral dissertation, London Business School.

Dumas, A. & Whitfield, A. (1989). Why design is difficult to manage: A survey of attitudes and practices in British Industry. *European Management Journal*, **7**(1), 50–56.

Durand, T. (1997). Strategizing for innovation: Competence analysis in assessing strategic change. In A. Heene & R. Sanchez (eds) *Competence-based strategic management*. Chichester: Wiley, 127–150.

Dyer, J.H. & Singh, H. (1998). The relational view: Cooperative strategy and sources of interorganizational competitive advantage. *Academy of Management Review*, **23**(4), 660–679.

Freeze, L. with Powell, E. (1998). Design management lessons from the past: Henry Dreyfuss and American business. In M. Bruce & B.H. Jevnaker, (eds), *Management of Design Alliances: Sustaining Competitive Advantage*. Chichester: Wiley.

Gorb, P. (ed.) (1990). *Design Management*. Papers from the London Business School. LBS Design Management Unit, London: Architecture Design and Technology Press.

Gorb, P. & Dumas, A. (1987). Silent design. *Design Studies*, **8**(3).

Hamel, G. & Prahalad, C.K. (1994). *Competing for the Future*. Boston, MA: Harvard Business School Press.

Hart, S. (1995). Where we've been and where we're going in new product development research. In M. Bruce & W.G. Biemans, (eds), *Product Development:. Meeting the Challenge of the Design–Marketing Interface*, Chichester: Wiley, 15–42.

Hayes, R. (1990). Design: Putting class into "World Class". *Design Management Journal*, **1**(2), 8–14.

Henderson, R.M. & Clark, K.B. (1991). Architectural innovation: The reconfiguration of existing product technologies and the failure of established firms. *Administrative Science Quarterly*, **35**(1), 9–30.

Heskett, J. (1980). *Industrial Design*. London: Thames and Hudson.

Hirschberg, J. (1998). *The Creative Priority*. New York: Harper Collins.

Hitt, M.A., Hoskisson, R.E. & Nixon, R.D. (1993). A mid-range theory of interfunctional integration, its antecedents and outcomes. *Journal of Engineering and Technology Management*, **10**, 161–185.

Hollins, G. & Hollins, B. (1991). *Total Design: Managing the Design Process in the Service Sector*. London: Pitman.

Ireland, C. & Johnson, B. (1995). Exploring the future in the present. *Design Management Journal*, **6**(2), 57–64.

Itami, H. with Roehl, T. (1987). *Mobilizing Invisible Assets*. Cambridge, MA: Harvard University Press.

Jarillo, J.K. (1993). *Strategic Networks: Creating the Borderless Organization*. Oxford: Butterworth-Heinemann.

Jelinek, M. & Schoonhoven, C.B. (1990). *The Innovation Marathon: Lessons from High Technology Firms*. Oxford: Blackwell (1993 paperback edition, Jossey-Bass, San Francisco, CA).

Jevnaker, B.H. (1993). Inaugurative learning: Adapting a new design approach. *Design Studies*, **14**(4), 379–401.

Jevnaker, B.H. (1994). *Building organizational capabilities in design. Lessons from the '94 Olympic Games*. Working paper 124/1994, Bergen: Foundation for Research in Economics and Business Administration (SNF).

Jevnaker, B.H. (1995a). *Den skjulte formuen. Industridesign som kreativ konkurransefaktor (The Hidden Treasure)*. SNF-report 36/95, Bergen: Foundation for Research in Economics and Business Administration (SNF) (in Norwegian).

Jevnaker, B.H. (1995b). *The Hidden Treasure—Competitive advantage through design alliances*. Working paper 58/1995, Bergen: Foundation for Research in Economics and Business Administration (SNF).

Jevnaker, B.H. (1996). *Industridesign som kreativ konkurransefaktor: En forstudie*. SNF-Report 54/96, Bergen: Foundation for Research in Economics and Business Administration (SNF) (in Norwegian).

Jevnaker, B.H. (1999). Integrating product innovations: Dilemmas of design expertise and its management. *Proceedings*, Conference on *Design Cultures*, European Academy of Design Sheffield Hallam University, 2, 1–46.

Kanter, R.M. (1989). *When Giants Learn to Dance: Mastering the Challenges of Strategy Management and Careers in the 90's*. London: Unwin.

Kay, J. (1993). *Foundations of Corporate Success: How Business Strategies Add Value*. Oxford: Oxford University Press.

Kicherer, S. (1990). *Olivetti: A Study of the Corporate Management of Design*. London: Trefoil Publishers.

Kotler, P. & Rath, G.A. (1984). Design: a powerful but neglected strategic tool. *Journal of Business Strategy*. **5**(2), 16–21.

Kreiner, K. (1999). Knowledge and mind: The management of intellectual resources. *Advances in Management Cognition and Organizational Information Processing*, **6**, 1–29.

Kretschmann, D. (1996). Consulting in Germany: Where we stand. *Design Management Journal*, **7**(2), 43–49.

Kristensen, T. (1998). The contribution of design to business: A competence-based perspective. In M. Bruce & B.H. Jevnaker, (eds), *Management of Design Alliances: Sustaining Competitive Advantage*, Chichester: Wiley, 217–241.

Lawson, B. (1990). *How Designers Think*. London: Butterworth Architecture.

Leonard-Barton, D. (1991). Inanimate integrators: A block of wood speaks. *Design Management Journal*, **2**(3), 61–67.

Leonard-Barton, D. (1995). *Wellsprings of Knowledge*. Boston, MA: Harvard Business School Press.

Lorenz, C. (1986). *The Design Dimension*. Oxford: Basil Blackwell.

Lorenz, C. (1990). *The Design Dimension*, new revised edition. Oxford: Basil Blackwell.

March, J.G. (1976). The technology of foolishness. In J.G. March & J.P. Olsen, (eds), *Ambiguity and Choice in Organizations*. (2nd edn, 1979), Bergen: Universitetsforlaget, 69–81.

March, J.G. (1991). Exploration and exploitation in organizational learning. *Organization Science*, **2**(1), 71–87.

Masuda, F. (1996). Trends in design consulting in Japan. *Design Management Journal*, **7**(2), 43–49.

Nonaka, I. & Takeuchi, H. (1995). *The Knowledge-Creating Company*. New York and Oxford: Oxford University Press.
Olins, W. (1987). Mysteries of design management revealed. In J. Bernsen, (ed.), *Design Management in Practice*. European/EEC Design Editions, Copenhagen/Barcelona: Danish Design Council & Foundation BCD.
Olins, W. (1989). *Corporate Identity: Making Business Strategy Visible Through Design*. London: Thames and Hudson.
Parsey, T. (1995). Design as strategy. Speech and Abstract from *The Challenge of Complexity*. 3rd International Conference on Design Management, Helsinki: UIAH.
Penrose, E. (1959). *The Theory of the Growth of the Firm*. London: Basil Blackwell.
Prahalad, C.K. & Hamel, G. (1990). The core competences of the corporation. *Harvard Business Review*, May–June, 79–91.
Prone, M. (1995). The design proposal in a changing world ... Ensuring its success and value. *Design Management Journal*, **6**(3), 69–73.
Roy, R. & S. Potter. (1993). The commercial impact of investment in design. *Design Studies*, **14**(2), 171–193.
Sakakibara, K. (1998). Global new product development: The case of IBM notebook computers. In M. Bruce & B.H. Jevnaker, (eds), *Management of Design Alliances: Sustaining Competitive Advantage*. Chichester: Wiley.
Schön, D.A. (1988). Designing: Rules, types and worlds. *Design Studies*, **9**(3), 181–190.
Souder, W.E. (1988). Managing relations between R&D and marketing in new product development projects. *Journal of Product Innovation Management*, **5**, 6–19.
Sparke, P. (1986a). *An Introduction to Design and Culture in the Twentieth Century*. London: Routledge.
Sparke, P. (1986b). *Furniture, 20th Century Design*. London: Bell & Hyman.
Stabell, C. & Fjeldstad, O. (1998). Configuring value for competitive advantage: On chains, shops and networks. *Strategic Management Journal*, **19**(5), 413–437.
Svengren, L. (1995). *Industriell design som strategisk ressurs* (in Swedish). Doctoral dissertation, Lund University Press, Lund, Sweden.
Svengren, L. (1997). Industrial design as a strategic resource: A study of industrial design methods and approaches for companies' strategic development. *The Design Journal*, **0**(1), 3–11.
Svengren, L. (1998). Integrating design as a strategic resource: The case of Ericsson Mobile Communications. In M. Bruce & B.H. Jevnaker (eds), *Management of Design Alliances*, Chichester: Wiley, 159–178.
Teece, D., Pisano, G. & Shuen, A. (1990). *Firm capabilities, resources, and the concept of strategy*. Economic Analysis and Policy Working Paper, EAP-38. Berkeley: University of California.
Thackara, J. (1997). *Winners! How Today's Companies Innovate by Design*. Amsterdam: BIS.
Thölke, J. & Lowe, A. (1996). *The social psychological processes of "shuttling", "legitimising" and "surveillancing"; the hidden processes of successful product renewal. A grounded theory approach. Hidden vs. Open Rules in Product Development*. NPD workshop report from TU Delft.
Thompson, J.D. (1967). *Organizations in Action*. New York: McGraw-Hill.
Walker, J.A. (1989). *Design History and the History of Design*. London: Pluto Press.
Wallin, J. (1997). Customers as the originators of change in competence building: A case study. In A. Heene, & R. Sanchez, (eds), *Competence-based Strategic Management*. Chichester: Wiley, 111–126.
Walsh, V., Roy, R., Bruce, M. & Potter, S. (1992). *Winning by Design: Technology, Product Design and International Competitiveness*. Oxford: Blackwell Business.
Williamson, O.E. (1985). *The Economic Institutions of Capitalism*. New York: Free Press.

# 12

# The Timing of Strategic Alliances

PAUL E. BIERLY III, ERIC H. KESSLER

## INTRODUCTION

The competitive landscape of many industries has changed dramatically in the last two decades (Bettis & Hitt, 1995). New technologies are transferred across national and organizational boundaries at a faster rate with the help of more advanced information and communication systems (Hamel & Prahalad, 1994; D'Aveni, 1994). Additionally, many industry boundaries are being broken down as diverse knowledge bases from traditionally separate industries are being integrated, such as the merging of the computer and telecommunications industries. This condition, referred to as industry fusion, puts firms in the position of facing new and powerful competitors with different industry recipes for success and a rapidly changing industry structure (Bierly & Chakrabarti, 1999; Spender, 1989). In these more dynamic competitive landscapes it is often very difficult to maintain a competitive position in each of the different technological areas that are integrated to make more sophisticated products.

Partnerships and a network type of structure can help a firm maintain a superior competitive position in this type of dynamic environment (Ohmae, 1989; Chesbrough & Teece, 1996; Hamel, Doz & Prahalad, 1989). Firms can focus on the areas they do well (i.e., core competencies) and rely on partners in other areas. Partners can be valuable in helping to understand the changing rules of the game. They also improve a firm's strategic flexibility since the firm has committed fewer resources to each of the different

*Dynamic Strategic Resources: Development, Diffusion and Integration.*
Edited by Michael A. Hitt, Patricia Gorman Clifford, Robert D. Nixon and Kevin P. Coyne.

technologies. Moreover, strategic alliances provide many firms with new sources of competitive advantage, such as access to complementary technologies, access to new markets, and reduction of risk (Hagedoorn, 1993). In this chapter, we use a broad definition of strategic alliances to include all "partnerships between firms whereby their resources, capabilities, and core competencies are combined to pursue mutual interests in developing, manufacturing, or distributing goods or services" (Hitt, Ireland & Hoskisson, 1999; 314). This broad definition includes joint ventures, where a new separate entity is created. Koza and Lewin (1998) describe alliances as having either exploitation or exploration objectives. Alliances formed to reduce information asymmetries have exploration objectives, which involve the motive of exploring new opportunities. They are pursued to provide a framework for learning, engage in innovation and basic research, and build new capabilities. Alliances formed to establish a market position have exploitation objectives, which involve the motive to exploit an existing capability. They are pursued to increase the productivity of capital and assets, engage in cost reduction, and refine existing capabilities and technologies.

In this chapter we tackle one specific issue concerning strategic alliances: the *timing* of the initiation of the alliance in the product development process. More specifically, our research question is: what factors lead a firm to form alliances earlier in the development process and what factors lead a firm to form alliances later in the development process? In general, the importance of timing to competitive advantage is well documented in the strategy literature (Lieberman & Montgomery, 1988; Stalk & Hout, 1990). For example, many have explored issues related to early-mover versus late-mover advantages when developing new technologies and entering new markets (Golder & Tellis, 1993; Kerin, Varadarajan & Peterson, 1993). However, there is little in the literature addressing timing issues specific to the formation of technology-based strategic alliances. These issues are important for several reasons. During earlier stages of development, the technology associated with the product is usually based more on basic than on applied science, the knowledge is usually more abstract and less detailed, and there is more uncertainty associated with development. Clearly alliances formed in the earlier development stages involve higher risk.

The new product development process can be viewed as a continuous learning experience (Leonard-Barton, 1995). However, if a partner does not participate in the development process until the later stages, it will be difficult, if not impossible, to learn the tacit knowledge associated with the process, which usually requires "learning-by-doing" (Wheelwright & Clark, 1992). A firm involved in the development of new technologies from the beginning will have a better understanding of the technology in the long run, and will be better able to integrate the new knowledge with its existing knowledge base. Forming alliances in the earlier development stages shows commitment to the development of certain capabilities and such strategic actions may have importance by either blocking direct competitors or countering their previous moves.

We test the above research question by examining a large number of alliances in the pharmaceutical industry, where partnerships have become increasingly important in the successful integration of knowledge and the development of new products (Henderson & Cockburn, 1994; Powell, 1998; Barley, Freeman & Hybels, 1992). All of the alliances in this study involve a large pharmaceutical firm, which we designate the focal firms of the study. The partners of the focal firms range dramatically in size from being very small biotechnology firms to other large pharmaceutical or chemical firms. Narrowly focusing on alliances with large pharmaceutical firms as the focal firms ensures that we are studying firms in similar situations. Factors that are hypothesized to influence the timing of the strategic technology partnerships are: (a) alliance-based factors, (b) firm-based factors, and (c) partner-based factors.

## Hypotheses

### Alliance-Based Factors

The type and purpose of the alliance will influence the timing of when the partners form the alliance. By timing we refer to the new product development stage of the most important drug involved in the alliance. The primary purpose of the alliance may be to share technologies, co-market products, help each other with manufacturing, assist in entering new markets, etc. (Hagedoorn, 1993). Firms typically form strategic alliances when the purpose of the alliance addresses the current stage of development of the drug. For example, a marketing alliance may be formed during the early stages of drug development when the primary focus is on the design of the drug, but such an alliance would involve high uncertainty and would be difficult to control with a formal contract. Thus, marketing alliances are more likely to be formed later in the development process, after the characteristics of the drug are better known.

We specifically propose that alliances that are formed for the purpose of promoting and integrating research will be formed earlier in the product development process than alliances formed to support other portions of the value chain, such as manufacturing and marketing. Clearly, more research and development occurs earlier in the new product development process than later. Even with a fully integrated new product development team, more research and development is conducted earlier in the overall process and other activities usually associated with "downstream" areas are conducted later in the process (Wheelwright & Clark, 1992). R&D alliances formed early in the new product development process will be more influential in the initial design of the drug and the direction of subsequent research and development.

> H1: R&D-oriented strategic alliances will be initiated earlier in the product development and approval process than non-R&D alliances.

However, among R&D alliances, some alliances that focus on certain types of knowledge bases will be formed earlier in the product development process than others. Specifically, alliances that are associated with a more abstract, turbulent and newer knowledge base will often be formed earlier in the development process than alliances associated with a more mature, stable and explicit knowledge base. Alliances associated with newer technologies represent greater departures from the existing practices of companies (Damanpour, 1991; Henderson & Clark, 1990; Meyers & Marquis, 1969), are more uncertain, and require partnership throughout the entire process so that different knowledge areas can be best understood and integrated.

The field of biotechnology is an example of a more abstract, newer knowledge base, when compared to the field of organic chemistry associated with traditional pharmaceutical firms. Biotechnology can be characterized as a competence-destroying innovation, from the perspective of the established pharmaceutical companies (Powell, Koput & Smith-Doerr, 1996; Zucker & Darby, 1997). The knowledge base associated with biotechnology is markedly different than the knowledge base of most traditional pharmaceutical companies. Success in the field of biotechnology requires expertise in the area of molecular biology and other very specific areas. Established pharmaceutical companies generally have a strong knowledge base in the areas of organic chemistry and pharmacology. Additionally, most research in biotechnology is at the basic science level and involves more tacit knowledge, whereas most research of pharmaceutical companies is at the applied science and development level and involves more explicit knowledge. Thus, when a pharmaceutical firm enters into a partnership that focuses on biotechnology, the most critical challenge for them is the difficult task of integrating the different knowledge bases (Powell, 1998; Pisano, 1991). Entering an alliance earlier in the new product development process will allow the pharmaceutical firm the opportunity to learn, transfer, and integrate the more abstract and tacit knowledge from the biotechnology company. If the pharmaceutical firm waits too long in the process to form the alliance, it will not be able to understand and integrate the different knowledge bases effectively.

The above argument is based on the assumption that learning is a very important objective of a strategic alliance, consistent with arguments by Hamel (1991) and Hamel, Doz and Prahalad (1989). This assumption is particularly relevant in the situation of an alliance between a pharmaceutical company and a biotechnology company because it would be very difficult to acquire the abstract and tacit knowledge associated with biotechnology and apply it without understanding it (Powell, 1998; Zucker & Darby, 1997). However, another reason why alliances that focus on a newer technological base are initiated earlier in the development process has to do with the smaller target partner. A small firm developing a radical new technology is likely to need financial assistance from a larger partner early in the development process.

> H2: Alliances that focus on a newer technological base (e.g., biotechnology) will be commenced earlier in the development and approval process than those that focus on older, established technological bases (e.g., non-biotechnology).

We propose that certain types of governance modes will be used more frequently during different stages of the development and approval process. There are three general types of governance modes for strategic alliances: nonequity (contractual) alliances, equity alliances, and joint ventures (Barney, 1997). *Nonequity alliances* are contractual alliances that do not include an equity position, such as R&D agreements, marketing agreements, technology swaps, and manufacturing arrangements. Nonequity alliances provide more flexibility for the partners (less commitment), are usually less sophisticated, and are usually shorter-term (Hagedoorn, 1993; Hagedoorn & Narula, 1996). This type of governance mode is very efficient for explicit, simple arrangements. However, for complex alliances involving uncertainty associated with the transfer and integration of intangible and tacit knowledge, nonequity alliances are usually inadequate because contracts can not be written that provide adequate control of the partnership (Kogut, 1988; Hennart, 1988). Also, nonequity alliances may provide little disincentive for partners to cheat since there is less commitment to the other partner (Williamson, 1975).

*Joint ventures* are partnerships where a new, independent company is created by the combination of the resources of the two parent firms. Joint ventures are an effective mode of governance for transferring and integrating tacit knowledge and developing a long-term relationship (Kogut, 1988; Hennart, 1988). They are also effective in aligning the strategic goals of partners to minimize cheating. However, they usually involve a high degree of commitment and limit firms' strategic flexibility (Hagedoorn, 1993). A potential problem with joint ventures is that the partners will have different learning rates, causing one firm's competitive advantage to erode as critical tacit knowledge is leaked (Hamel, 1991; Beamish & Banks, 1987; Kogut, 1988). Additionally, many of these arrangements are not successful because of conflicting cultures, control systems, and human resource practices (Ohmae, 1989).

*Equity alliances* are partnerships where a contractual agreement is supplemented with one of the partners purchasing a portion of its partner's equity capital. Occasionally, both partners have an equity position in each other and the equity position may also include a position on the board of directors. These arrangements are effective at increasing the commitment among the partners, since they are not relying solely on a contract. Compared to nonequity alliances, the firm taking the equity position has better access to information, can better monitor performance and has more control (Pisano, 1989). Compared to joint ventures, there is less commitment and more flexibility, since they are not as permanent (Hagedoorn, 1993; Hagedoorn & Narula, 1996). However, it is more difficult to transfer and integrate knowledge than using a joint venture where employees are working together and interacting continuously. Concerning flexibility and ease of knowledge transfer, equity alliances can be viewed as mid-range alliances between nonequity alliances and joint ventures.

In the early stages of development, where creativity and idea generation are critically important, a looser, more flexible, and more "organic" management structure is usually preferred over a tighter, more bureaucratic form. Organic structures are lower in vertical differentiation, formalization, and centralization. As a result, organic structures create a more conducive context for the flexibility, adaptation and cross-fertilization needed to foster creativity and inventive activities (Kanter, 1988; Damanpour, 1991; Spender & Kessler, 1995). On the other hand, a tighter, more controlling, and more formal management structure is usually better during the later stages of development, where implementation and idea exploitation are most important, to ensure speed and focus (Kanter, 1988). Consistently, we propose that alliances involving products in an earlier stage of development and approval are more likely to be equity arrangements than alliances involving products in later stages. During these earlier stages of development, the technology associated with the product is usually based more on basic than on applied science, the knowledge is usually more abstract, and there is more uncertainty. Under these conditions, negotiating a contract is difficult and an equity or joint venture arrangement may ease the flow of knowledge across firm boundaries and increase control. However, in the early stages of development it may be very difficult to get different companies with different areas of expertise to work closely together. A joint venture during these early stages where ideas may still be vague may create a large amount of conflict. The benefits are uncertain and often less than the high costs of commitment, governance and reduced flexibility.

H3: A larger proportion of strategic alliances in the earlier stages of the development and approval process will be equity alliances, compared to alliances in the later stages of development and approval.

## Firm-Based Factors

As discussed above, the earlier stages of development are associated with more basic science and abstract knowledge. For a firm to form a partnership under such conditions of uncertainty, it would need to have a high level of "absorptive capacity" to be able to understand, interpret and integrate a partner's knowledge (Cohen & Levinthal, 1990). Absorptive capacity is particularly important in evaluating and assimilating tacit knowledge, which by definition is especially difficult to transfer across organizational boundaries. Absorptive capacity can be increased by internal R&D in the specific area, production experience, and advanced technical training (Cohen & Levinthal, 1990). The growth of absorptive capacity is path dependent in the sense that it builds on prior commitment and knowledge development. Additionally, a high level of absorptive capacity is needed to evaluate a partner's knowledge assets to ensure it is worthwhile to enter the partnership. Evaluating a partner is particularly problematic in the early stages of development when the knowledge is more tacit and abstract, because these intangible assets may not be appreciated. Higher levels of absorptive capacity are needed more during this period than later in the development process when the knowledge is more explicit and easier to measure.

H4: Firms with greater absorptive capacity will enter alliances earlier in the development and approval process than firms with less absorptive capacity.

We propose that the profitability of the large pharmaceutical firms involved in alliances and the timing of the alliance will be negatively correlated. Nohria and Gulati (1996) illustrated that organizational slack is an important catalyst for organizational innovation because it (a) allows the relaxation of controls, (b) represents funds that can be approved even during uncertain times, and (c) allows experimentation. (They also point out that excessive slack may lead to diminished discipline and control, which may result in decreased innovation.) A large pharmaceutical firm that is more profitable typically has more resources available for a long-term investment and is less concerned with an immediate pay-off. On the other hand, a large pharmaceutical firm that is less profitable is under more pressure to invest in a project that will have a quick pay-off and may not have the luxury to invest in a project that will take several years, even if it may be profitable. Also, a larger amount of financial resources may be demanded of the firm that invests earlier, because the development costs in the earlier stages tend to be very high.

> H5: Firms that are more profitable will be more likely to enter alliances earlier in the development and approval process than firms that are less profitable.

Additionally, we propose that the size of a firm will influence the timing of an alliance. Larger firms, especially if they are broadly diversified, are better positioned to invest in a specific risky long-term venture because they can spread the risk across more projects. Larger firms usually have more resources available for long-term projects. Smaller firms may not have enough income from existing products to fund long-term investments.

> H6: Larger pharmaceutical firms will enter alliances earlier in the development and approval process than smaller pharmaceutical firms.

Forming partnerships early in the development phase typically involves high uncertainty and frequent change, as plans are continuously modified based on new knowledge and a changing environment. In such dynamic and uncertain environments, firms must maintain strategic flexibility (Harrigan, 1985; Kogut, 1985; Bierly & Chakrabarti, 1996b). Strategic flexibility can be defined as "the capability of the firm to proact or respond quickly to changing competitive conditions and thereby develop and/or maintain competitive advantage" (Hitt, Keats & DeMarie, 1998). Strategic flexibility is especially important given the new competitive landscape firms face (e.g., rapidly evolving information and communication technologies, increasing globalization), because these changes mandate that strategists balance the stable and fluid states of their organizations. However, there are many different types of mobility barriers that may limit flexibility (see Aaker & Mascarenhas, 1984, for a detailed list). Financial flexibility is limited with a lack of liquidity and high long-term debt because these conditions restrict the availability of funds for initiating the partnerships and limit the firm's ability to redirect funds as needed to respond to environmental changes (Aaker & Mascarenhas, 1984). Manufacturing flexibility is limited if the firm has already engaged large capital expenditures on the commitment to a given process or technology (Ghemawat, 1991). High capital intensity particularly limits flexibility if the plant and equipment are product-specific and difficult to resell.

H7: Firms with a higher degree of strategic flexibility will enter alliances earlier in the development and approval process than firms with lower strategic flexibility.

## Partner-Based Factors

Size differences between the two partners have implications concerning control of the partnership. Greater differences in size will usually result in one company being a more dominant leader. Alliances with two equally sized partners may lack a leader and may endure more conflict because they have less-defined roles and there is "equal right to fight". Alliances with a dominant partner tend to be more stable and successful (Killing, 1982). From the perspective of the large pharmaceutical company, they would prefer to have more control in the more uncertain situation of forming a partnership early in the development process. From the perspective of smaller partners, they might need resources immediately and thus enter into alliances at an earlier time than if they were larger and more financially independent.

H8: Firms will enter alliances earlier in the development and approval process when the partners are of less equal size than when the partners are of more equal size.

Alliances initiated earlier in the development process are more likely to be a higher proportion of domestic alliances than alliances initiated later in the development process for two reasons. First, when the partners are geographically (and politically) close, the large pharmaceutical firm will be better able to monitor the alliance and thus be better positioned to maintain control throughout the long and uncertain development process. Second, similarities of firms in a partnership are important for maintaining a long-term relationship. Similar cultures, control systems, communication patterns and pay systems will enable the two partners to work in harmony over a long period. Maintaining this harmony will be more critical for those alliances initiated early in the development process because of the uncertainty and longevity of those alliances.

H9: Firms will be more likely to enter alliances earlier in the development and approval process when the partners are located in the same country than when the partners are foreign.

A pharmaceutical firm will be more comfortable forming a partnership with a partner if the partner is more stable and reliable. Firms that are more profitable are less likely to radically change their strategy, have lower turnover of key personnel, and tend to exhibit more consistent behavior (Leonard-Barton, 1995; Miles *et al.*, 1978; Snow & Hrebiniak, 1980). A partnership with a more profitable firm diminishes the risk exposure of the partnering firm. This is much more important earlier in the product development process than later, since the partnership must last for a longer time.

> H10: Firms will be more likely to enter alliances earlier in the development and approval process when the partners are more profitable than when the partners are less profitable.

Pharmaceutical companies that form partnerships in the early stages of development want partners that are committed to the new technology and have a strong knowledge base in the area. R&D expenditures of the partner are indicators of their commitment and knowledge level. High R&D expenditures also indicate a more financially stable company that will be able to thrive throughout the lifetime of the partnership.

> H11: Firms will be more likely to enter alliances earlier in the development and approval process when the partners invest more in R&D than when the partners invest less in R&D.

Above we argued for the need for the pharmaceutical firms to have strategic flexibility when entering partnerships in the early stage of development. The same arguments also hold for the partner firms. If they are to survive in a partnership throughout the long development process, they must have the flexibility to adapt to a changing environment. Financial flexibility and manufacturing flexibility are just as important for the partner as for the large pharmaceutical companies.

> H12: Firms will be more likely to enter alliances earlier in the development and approval process when the partners have high levels of strategic flexibility than when the partners have low levels of strategic flexibility.

## METHODS

This study analyzes the differences of 652 strategic alliances in the pharmaceutical industry from 1988 to 1995. (The sample size decreases for certain regression models because some data, especially financial data, were not obtainable for some of the firms.) Our specific focus is from the perspective of large pharmaceutical companies; thus, we included most of the largest pharmaceutical firms from the US, Japan, and Europe. To ensure we were studying similar firms, we did not include conglomerates that had high revenue from non-pharmaceutical areas. The sample includes alliances with a wide variety of partners including other pharmaceutical companies of various size and location, biotechnology companies, and companies from related industries. The Windhover Information Inc. Pharmaceutical Strategic Alliances database is the data source concerning specific information about the alliances and COMPUSTAT is used for financial data. The Windhover database is internationally recognized as one of the most complete and reliable databases of its kind.

Bivariate correlations and regression analysis were used to analyze the data. Bivariate correlations were employed to examine the strength and direction of dyadic relationships between variables. Regression analyses were then employed to test the hypotheses in a more reliable manner because they account for the interdependencies among the variable and control for their effects. Four regression models are used to test the hypotheses. The first model tests the effects of alliance-based factors on the stage of research and development when the alliance is initiated. The second model tests the effects of firm-based factors of the large pharmaceutical firms on the stage of development. The third model tests the effects of partner-based factors on the stage of development. The fourth model includes all of the variables used in this study. The first three models allow us to compare alliance-based, firm-based and partner-based factors. The fourth model is best for testing the hypotheses, since it is the most general and comprehensive model; unfortunately, it is less powerful since there are some lost data points.

## Variables

The following variables are used in this study:

**STAGE**: This is an ordinal variable that ranges from 1 to 10, and is used to differentiate alliances depending on the new product development stage of the most important drug involved in the alliance, as determined by Windhover's industry experts. The 10 stages are: (1) R&D, (2) Preclinical trials, (3) IND files, (4) Clinical trials, (5) Phase I, where drug safety is analyzed in human volunteers, (6) Phase II, where drug efficacy is analyzed in a sample of patients, (7) Phase III, which includes advanced trials to accumulate drug efficacy data, (8) NDA filed, (9) Registered, (10) Marketed. In most cases, there is more uncertainty during the earlier R&D stages and less uncertainty in the final stages of approval.

**RDALL**: This dichotomous variable separates alliances with the primary purpose of conducting R&D from all other types of deals, such as those that focus primarily on marketing, manufacturing, licensing, and product swaps. R&D-based alliances are given a value of 1 and all others are given a value of 0.

**BIOTECH**: This dichotomous variable separates alliances involving the development, manufacturing or distribution of a biotechnology product (value of 1) from those that do not (value 0). Biotechnology can be defined as "a body of knowledge and a set of techniques for using live organisms such as bacteria, yeast, fungi, plant cells, and animal cells in production processes" (Pisano, 1996). We differentiate biotechnology from other drug categories because knowledge in the biotechnology area tends to be more related to basic science, more abstract and tacit than the knowledge base of the established pharmaceutical industry (Powell, Koput & Smith-Doerr, 1996; Barley, Freeman & Hybels, 1992). Powell, Koput and Smith-Doerr (1996) argue that the knowledge bases are so different that biotechnology represents a competence-destroying innovation to the pharmaceutical industry.

**EQUITY**: The dichotomous variable EQUITY differentiates alliances that involve some degree of equity sharing from all other alliances. Equity alliances are given a value of 1 and all others are given a value of 0. Equity alliances include alliances where either one or both companies have an equity stake in the other.

**JV**: This dichotomous variable, standing for joint venture, differentiates alliances that create a new independent entity from all other alliances. Joint venture alliances are given a value of 1 and all others are given a value of 0.

**RDS, PRDS**: The R&D intensity of the focal firm (RDS) and its partner (PRDS) is defined as the ratio of annual R&D dollars spent by a firm to the firm's total sales. R&D intensity is an excellent measure of how aggressive a firm is in its pursuit of developing new products and its attempt at internal learning (Bierly & Chakrabarti, 1996a). It is also a measure of "absorptive capacity", which is the degree to which firms can understand, interpret and apply external knowledge (Cohen & Levinthal, 1990).

**ROS, PROS**: The profitability of the focal firm (ROS) and the partner firm (PROS) is measured by the ratio of a firm's annual income to its total revenue.

**EMP, PEMP**: The size of the focal firm (EMP) and its partner (PEMP) is measured by the total number of employees at the end of the year that the alliance was initiated. This variable is preferable to using annual revenues as a measurement of size because it reduces multicollinearity; annual revenues are used as part of a ratio for several other variables. As expected, the variables measuring the number of employees of the focal and partner firms were highly correlated with their revenue (0.79 and 0.96, respectively).

**CR, PCR**: The current ratio of the focal firm (CR) and its partner (PCR) is defined as the ratio of current assets to current liabilities. The current ratio of a firm indicates its liquidity and strategic flexibility (Aaker & Mascarenhas, 1984; Bierly & Chakrabarti, 1996b). Financial flexibility in the form of liquid assets enables firms to rapidly redirect funds as needed to respond to environmental changes.

**CAPINT, PCAPINT**: The capital intensity of the focal firm (CAPINT) and its partner (PCAPINT) is measured by the ratio of a firm's net plant, property and equipment to total sales. Capital intensity is another measure of strategic flexibility because the intensity of a firm's capital assets can be a barrier to a firm's capability to change its strategy to respond to environmental change (Harrigan, 1985). The higher the level of capital intensity, the more difficult it will be for a firm to rapidly change its strategy in response to environmental conditions. Ghemawat (1991) refers to high levels of capital intensity as a firm's commitment to its present strategy, precisely because these predominantly sunk costs reduce the firm's flexibility.

**DTEQ, PDTEQ**: The overall debt position of the focal firm (DTEQ) and its partner (PDTEQ) is measured by the ratio of total debt to shareholder equity. This variable is also a measure of a firm's leverage and strategic flexibility, particularly its ability to invest in large, long-term research projects (Aaker & Mascarenhas, 1984).

**RSIZE**: This variable is used to determine the size of the larger organization in the alliance, relative to the partner. It is measured by the ratio of the revenues of the two firms.

**DOMESTIC**: This dichotomous variable identifies whether or not the company and partner are from the same country. Domestic alliances are given a value of 1 and international alliances are given a value of 0. The assumption is that two firms from the same country will be closer in both geographic distance and cultural similarity.

## Results

### Correlation Analysis

Table 12.1 displays the descriptive statistics and the correlation matrix. A negative correlation with STAGE, our dependent variable, indicates that a higher value of the specific independent variable is associated with alliances being initiated at an earlier stage of the product development and approval process. As expected, STAGE is highly negatively correlated with RDALL ($r = -0.54$, $p < 0.001$), indicating that alliances with a primary focus on R&D tend to be initiated earlier in the development process than other types of

TABLE 12.1 Descriptive statistics and correlation matrix[a]

| Variable | N | Mean | SD | 1 | 2 | 3 | 4 | 5 | 6 | 7 | 8 |
|---|---|---|---|---|---|---|---|---|---|---|---|
| 1 STAGE | 570 | 5.06 | 3.64 | 1.00 | | | | | | | |
| 2 RDALL | 650 | 0.52 | 0.50 | −.54*** | 1.00 | | | | | | |
| 3 BIOTECH | 648 | 0.31 | 0.46 | −.35*** | .34*** | 1.00 | | | | | |
| 4 EQUITY | 651 | 0.13 | 0.34 | −.24*** | .19*** | .28*** | 1.00 | | | | |
| 5 JV | 652 | 0.07 | 0.26 | −.03 | −.20*** | −.07† | −.07* | 1.00 | | | |
| 6 RDS | 406 | 0.11 | 0.08 | −.07 | .12* | .01 | .06 | .01 | 1.00 | | |
| 7 EMP | 406 | 38.0 | 15.7 | −.08 | .00 | .12* | .05 | −.03 | −.20*** | 1.00 | |
| 8 ROS | 406 | 0.15 | 0.08 | −.10* | .17*** | .11* | .00 | −.03 | .35*** | .16*** | 1.00 |
| 9 CR | 406 | 26.9 | 292 | −.03 | .03 | −.06 | −.04 | .10† | .89*** | −.09† | .22*** |
| 10 CAPINT | 406 | 0.38 | 0.15 | −.04 | .14** | .16** | .22*** | −.10† | .15** | −.34*** | .12* |
| 11 DTEQ | 406 | 43.0 | 45.0 | .06 | .02 | .00 | .02 | .03 | −.07 | .04 | −.38*** |
| 12 RSIZE | 373 | 5888 | 35655 | −.05 | .06 | .11* | .12* | −.04 | .03 | −.05 | .04 |
| 13 PEMP | 246 | 14.5 | 30.8 | .32*** | −.20*** | −.29*** | −.15* | .10 | .21** | −.01 | .17* |
| 14 DOMESTIC | 640 | 0.48 | 0.50 | −.07† | .07† | .10* | .13*** | −.10* | −.06 | .07 | .12* |
| 15 PROS | 256 | −22.7 | 289 | −.01 | −.07 | −.11† | −.17** | .02 | −.05 | .06 | −.06 |
| 16 PRDS | 247 | 0.11 | 1.06 | −.01 | .06 | .11† | .17** | −.02 | .05 | −.05 | .05 |
| 17 PCR | 264 | 6.41 | 8.50 | −.29*** | .16** | .21*** | .21*** | −.05 | −.02 | −.04 | .10 |
| 18 PCAPINT | 256 | 8.16 | 85.1 | −.03 | −.04 | −.01 | .04 | −.02 | −.02 | .07 | −.07 |
| 19 PDTEQ | 244 | 39.7 | 151 | .06 | −.09 | −.05 | .00 | .04 | .02 | .00 | .06 |

TABLE 12.1 (continued)

| Variable | 9 | 10 | 11 | 12 | 13 | 14 | 15 | 16 | 17 | 18 | 19 |
|---|---|---|---|---|---|---|---|---|---|---|---|
| 1 STAGE | | | | | | | | | | | |
| 2 RDALL | | | | | | | | | | | |
| 3 BIOTECH | | | | | | | | | | | |
| 4 EQUITY | | | | | | | | | | | |
| 5 JV | | | | | | | | | | | |
| 6 RDS | | | | | | | | | | | |
| 7 EMP | | | | | | | | | | | |
| 8 ROS | | | | | | | | | | | |
| 9 CR | 1.00 | | | | | | | | | | |
| 10 CAPINT | −.22*** | 1.00 | | | | | | | | | |
| 11 DTEQ | −.08 | .22*** | 1.00 | | | | | | | | |
| 12 RSIZE | −.01 | .14* | .02 | 1.00 | | | | | | | |
| 13 PEMP | .27*** | −.14† | −.15† | −.08 | 1.00 | | | | | | |
| 14 DOMESTIC | −.13** | .14** | .04 | .01 | −.06 | 1.00 | | | | | |
| 15 PROS | .01 | −.23** | −.07 | −.78*** | .04 | −.06 | 1.00 | | | | |
| 16 PRDS | −.01 | .22** | .06 | .77*** | −.05 | .06 | −.99*** | 1.00 | | | |
| 17 PCR | −.05 | .13† | −.04 | .02 | −.26*** | .08 | −.02 | .02 | 1.00 | | |
| 18 PCAPINT | −.01 | −.01 | −.04 | .26*** | −.03 | .07 | −.30*** | .44*** | −.03 | 1.00 | |
| 19 PDTEQ | .01 | .08 | −.02 | −.03 | .16* | −.08 | .02 | −.02 | −.04 | .00 | 1.00 |

[a] Significance levels:
† $p < .10$
* $p < .05$
** $p < .01$
*** $p < .001$.

alliances. BIOTECH is also highly negatively correlated with STAGE ($r = -0.35$, $p < 0.001$), indicating that biotechnology alliances, with their more abstract, newer knowledge base, tend to be initiated earlier in the development process than other types of alliances. EQUITY (but not JV) is significantly negatively correlated with STAGE ($= -0.24$, $p < 0.001$), indicating that alliances initiated earlier in the development process, where there is more uncertainty, are more likely to be equity alliances than those initiated later in the development process.

With only one exception, the firm-based factors were not significantly correlated with STAGE. Neither RDS (measuring absorptive capacity), EMP (measuring size), nor the three measures of strategic flexibility (CR, CAPINT, and DTEQ) were significantly correlated with STAGE. The only firm-based factor significantly correlated with STAGE was ROS ($r = -0.10$, $p < .05$), indicating that firms that are more profitable are more likely to enter alliances in the earlier stage of development.

Two of the partner-based factors were highly correlated with STAGE. The size of the partner firm (PEMP) was positively correlated with STAGE ($r = 0.32$, $p < 0.001$), indicating that the large pharmaceutical firms were more likely to enter alliances early in the development process with smaller firms. Two large firms are more likely to form an alliance later in the development process, and those alliances are probably more often focusing on marketing, not R&D. Interestingly, the relative size difference of the two partners (RSIZE) was not significantly correlated. Neither the national origin of the partner (DOMESTIC), profitability of partner (PROS), nor R&D intensity of partner (PRDS) were significantly correlated with STAGE. The other partner-based factor that was significantly correlated with STAGE was the current ratio of the partner, PCR ($r = -0.29$, $p < 0.001$). This finding indicates that the pharmaceutical firms are more likely to form an alliance early in the development process with a partner that is liquid and financially sound, and has strategic flexibility, as compared to other firms that are not. None of the other partner-based measures of strategic flexibility were significantly correlated with STAGE.

The correlation matrix reveals other interesting relationships among the different independent variables, even though these correlations of potential interest are not specifically related to the purpose of this chapter. For example, it is interesting to note that R&D alliances (RDALL) are positively associated with an equity mode of governance (EQUITY; $r = 0.19$, $p < 0.001$) and negatively associated with a joint venture mode of governance (JV; $r = -0.20$, $p < 0.001$). A similar trend is also found for biotechnology alliances. Thus, it appears that the strategic focus of the alliance as well as the technological base of the alliance influence its mode of governance. Another interesting observation is that the profitability of pharmaceutical firms (ROS) is associated with high spending on R&D (RDS;

r = 0.35, p < 0.001) and the size of the firm (EMP; r = 0.16, p < 0.001). Thus, it appears that in this industry a more aggressive technology strategy and the strategic advantages of size, such as economies of scale in research and marketing, are critical success factors.

## Regression Analysis

Table 12.2 displays the results from the four regression models with STAGE as the dependent variable. Model 1, which includes the four alliance-based independent variables, explains more variance ($R^2 = 0.343$, adjusted $R^2 = 0.338$, $p < 0.001$) than the models with firm-based and partner-based variables (Models 2 and 3). All four of the alliance-based factors used in

Table 12.2 Regression analysis with STAGE as the dependent variable (beta statistic shown)[a]

| | Model 1 | Model 2 | Model 3 | Model 4 |
|---|---|---|---|---|
| 1 RDALL | −.478*** | | | −.483*** |
| 2 BIOTECH | −.167*** | | | −.156† |
| 3 EQUITY | −.086* | | | .079 |
| 4 JV | −.103** | | | −.126† |
| 5 RDS | | −.273 | | .152 |
| 6 EMP | | −.136* | | −.120 |
| 7 ROS | | −.016 | | .030 |
| 8 CR | | .207 | | −.088 |
| 9 CAPINT | | −.019 | | −.085 |
| 10 DTEQ | | .072 | | .064 |
| 11 RSIZE | | | .175 | −2.08* |
| 12 PEMP | | | .206** | .011 |
| 13 DOMESTIC | | | −.006 | −.079 |
| 14 PROS | | | −5.93** | −4.17 |
| 15 PRDS | | | −6.44** | −2.15 |
| 16 PCR | | | −.312*** | −.275*** |
| 17 PCAPINT | | | .953** | .291 |
| 18 PDTEQ | | | −.014 | .002 |
| Model $R^2$ | .343 | .030 | .247 | .620 |
| Adjusted $R^2$ | .338 | .014 | .209 | .545 |
| F | 73.1*** | 1.82† | 6.55*** | 8.26*** |
| N | 566 | 355 | 169 | 110 |

[a] Significance levels:
† p < .10
* p < .05
** p < .01
*** p < .001.

Model 1 (RDALL, BIOTECH, EQUITY, and JV) are statistically significant variables, initially supporting Hypotheses 1, 2 and 3. R&D and biotechnology alliances tend to be formed earlier in the development process, relative to non-R&D and non-biotechnology alliances, and a higher proportion of these alliances are equity alliances than alliances formed later in the development process. However, they do not fully support Hypothesis 3 insofar as the joint venture variable is also significant. This reveals the unhypothesized finding that, similar to equity alliances, joint ventures are also formed earlier rather than later in the development process.

Model 2 is a regression model with firm-based variables as independent variables. What is most striking about this model is that these factors explain almost none of the variance of the dependent variable, STAGE ($R^2 = 0.030$, adjusted $R^2 = 0.014$)! Thus, the decision by the pharmaceutical company to enter alliances earlier or later in the development process does not appear to be influenced by specific characteristics of the firm. Hypotheses 4, 5, 6 and 7 are not supported by this model.

Model 3 is a regression model with partner-based variables as independent variables. These variables explain a significant amount of variance in the dependent variable, STAGE ($R^2 = 0.247$, adjusted $R^2 = 0.209$, $p < 0.001$). The size (PEMP), profitability (PROS), R&D intensity (PRDS), current ratio (PCR), and capital intensity (PCAPINT) of the partner are all significant variables in the model, and all in the proposed direction. Hypotheses 10 and 11 are initially supported and Hypothesis 12 is initially supported by two of the three measures of strategic flexibility (PCR and PCAPINT, but not PDTEQ). Since RSIZE is not a significant variable, Hypothesis 8 is not supported by this model. Thus, the size of the partner appears to be more important than the relative sizes of the two companies involved in the alliance, since partner size (PEMP) was significant and relative size (RSIZE) was not. Additionally, Hypothesis 9 was not supported by this model since the variable DOMESTIC was not significant.

Model 4 is a regression model with all of the variables in our study included. This model explains a large amount of variance in the dependent variable, STAGE ($R^2 = 0.620$, adjusted $R^2 = 0.545$, $p < 0.001$). Since the adjusted $R^2$ in Model 4 is significantly larger than in Model 1, this further supports the importance of the partner-based factors. Model 4 indicates that the type of alliance, the liquidity of the partner firm, and the relative size of the partner are the most powerful factors in determining at which stage of development that an alliance is initiated. R&D alliances (RDALL, statistically significant) and biotechnology alliances (BIOTECH, marginally significant) tend to be formed earlier in the development process, supporting Hypotheses 1 and 2, respectively. Alliances with partners of dissimilar size (high RSIZE) tend to be formed earlier in the development process and alliances with similar sized partners (low RSIZE) tend to be formed later in the development process, supporting Hypothesis 8. As noted above, partner size measured by the number of employees is statistically significant in Model 3, and relative size, measured as a ratio of revenues, is not significant; the reverse is true in Model 4. A partial explanation of this may be the multicollinearity of variables. For example, adding the biotechnology variable to Model 4 is partially accounting for size, since most biotechnology companies are relatively small (PEMP and BIOTECH, $r = -.29$, $p < .001$).

Alliances with a partner with high liquidity, measured by its current ratio (PCR), tend to be formed earlier in the development process, partially supporting Hypothesis 12. It is interesting to note that current ratio, which measures liquidity and is a short-term indicator, is a significant variable, but capital intensity and debt-to-equity ratio, the other measures of strategic flexibility that are long-term indicators, are not significant (except that capital intensity is significant in Model 3). This may indicate that the short-term financial position of a partner is critical, but long-term investments by partners (e.g., in new sophisticated equipment) may be valuable and a source of knowledge.

Some of the hypotheses that are not supported also provide interesting insights. All of the hypotheses associated with firm-based variables (Hypotheses 4–7) are not supported statistically by Model 4, indicating that the external context influences the timing of alliances more than internal conditions. Hypothesis 3, which predicted that a larger proportion of equity alliances (EQUITY) would occur earlier in the development process, was not supported (as it was in Model 1); instead Model 4 has the independent variable JV marginally significant, indicating that more joint ventures are used earlier in the development process. Thus, it appears that the benefit joint ventures offer in facilitating the transfer and integration of knowledge outweigh the high degree of commitment and reduced strategic flexibility associated with this method of governance.

## Conclusion

The strongest and most consistent findings of this study are that alliance-based factors, and to a lesser extent partner-based factors, are strong predictors of the timing of strategic technology partnering, whereas factors specific to the firm had little effect on timing decisions. There are several implications of these observations that are important for strategic concerns. First, alliances should be conceptualized as tools or means to an end rather than as ends in themselves. This is because alliances tend to be initiated at different times depending upon their (a) strategic purpose, (b) technological base, and (c) type of governance structure. We also know that the mode of governance for an alliance is itself determined by a complex set of factors, such as strategic focus, nationality, and technological base (Bierly & Kessler, 1998). The equation gets even more complex when the nature of the partner (e.g., flexibility and relative size) is considered. Thus the strategic value of an alliance varies as a function of its context. On the basis of these differences, we are tempted to propose a finer-grained terminology for describing partnering behavior and refer to alliances as early-stage alliances (or early-stage equity alliances, joint-ventures, etc.), later-stage alliances, or perhaps some shade of gray in between. Such terminology would better capture the strategic implications of partnering behavior by taking into account the characteristics of alliances (e.g., purpose, technological base, governance structure) that influence its functionality and dynamics. Although it would be premature to propose a formal typology based on one single-industry study, further research can build on these results to explore other dimensions and derive aggregate factors from which we can derive important strategic distinctions between types of technology partnerships.

Second, because firm-based factors were much poorer predictors of timing than factors relating to the nature of the alliance and the partners in the alliance, it may make more sense to speak of timing decisions as context-driven rather than firm-driven. That is to say, it seems to be more important *what* you are doing than *who* you are *per se* when considering partnerships in the technology field. This finding suggests an environmental contingency explanation for the timing of strategic technology partnerships. Environmental contingency theory argues that an organization should seek to achieve a fit between its strategy and its task and institutional environment (e.g., Miles *et al.*, 1978). Of course, due to the similarity of firms in the sample, this claim should be regarded as preliminary and needs to be further investigated. Nevertheless, there were important differences between firms in the sample and these differences had little impact on the dependent variable.

Third and most generally, the *timing* of partnerships is an important factor to consider from both a practical and an academic perspective. Similar to timing issues surrounding the development of a new product (Kessler & Chakrabarti, 1996) or the entry into a market (Kerin, Varadarajan & Peterson, 1993), there appears to be a complex set of factors underlying the timing of entry into alliances. As a result, timing should be considered whenever analyzing the functionality of strategic partnering. Moreover, correlation analysis presented in this study suggests that there may be a link between timing and firm profitability. Thus it may be appropriate for more research and more attention to be dedicated to this area.

Taken as a whole, we argue that these findings concerning the timing of technology partnering have important implications related to the theme of this book. This is because partners, partnerships, and technological learning gleaned from partnerships can all be viewed as resources of the firm. They all play a role in expanding the knowledge base of the firm and are strategically valuable since they are more intangible resources that are difficult to imitate. The text posits that firms must tailor their strategy to fit evolving environmental demands and constraints. In this chapter we argue that the context of technological partnerships in the product development process is the primary driver of timing decisions. Thus, firms can act on these findings by tailoring the timing of partnerships to their strategic purpose, technological base, and mode of governance. Furthermore, the effective use of strategic alliances, including the timing of alliances, can be a critical vehicle for increasing the firm's strategic flexibility, allowing the firm to evolve as the environment shifts.

## References


Aaker, D.A. & Mascarenhas, B. (1984). The need for strategic flexibility. *Journal of Business Strategy*, **5**(2), 74–82.

Barley, S.R., Freeman, J. & Hybels, R.C. (1992). Strategic alliances in commercial biotechnology. In N. Nohria & R.G. Eccles (eds), *Networks and Organizations*, Boston, MA: Harvard Business School Press, 311–347.

Barney, J.B. (1997). *Gaining and Sustaining Competitive Advantage*. Reading, MA: Addison-Wesley.

Beamish, P.W. & Banks, J.C. (1987). Equity joint ventures and the theory of the multinational enterprise. *Journal of International Business Studies*, **18**(2), 1–15.

Bettis, R.A. & Hitt, M.A. (1995). The new competitive landscape. *Strategic Management Journal*. **16** (Summer Special Issue), 7–19.

Bierly, P. & Chakrabarti, A. (1996a). Generic knowledge strategies in the US pharmaceutical industry. *Strategic Management Journal*, **17** (Winter Special Issue), 123–135.

Bierly, P. & Chakrabarti, A. (1996b). Technological learning, strategic flexibility, and new product development in the pharmaceutical industry. *IEEE Transactions on Engineering Management*, **43**(4), 368–380.

Bierly, P. & Chakrabarti, A. (1999). Dynamic knowledge strategies and industry fusion. *International Journal of Technology Management*, forthcoming.

Bierly, P.E. & Kessler, E.H. (1998). Governance of interorganizational partnerships: A comparison of US, European and Japanese alliances in the pharmaceutical industry. In M.A. Hitt, J.E. Ricart & R.D. Nixon (eds), *Managing Strategically in an Interconnected World*, Chichester: Wiley, 185–206.

Chesbrough, H.W. & Teece, D.J. (1996). When is virtual virtuous? Organizing for innovation. *Harvard Business Review*, January–February, 65–73.

Cohen, W.M. & Levinthal, D.A. (1990). Absorptive capacity: A new perspective on learning and innovation. *Administrative Science Quarterly*, **35**, 128–152.

Damanpour, F. (1991). Organizational innovation: A meta-analysis of effects of determinants and moderators. *Academy of Management Journal*, **34**, 555–590.

D'Aveni, R.A. (1994). *Hypercompetition*. New York: Free Press.

Ghemawat, P. (1991). *Commitment: The Dynamic of Strategy*. New York: Free Press.

Golder, P.N. & Tellis, G.J. (1993). Pioneering advantage: Marketing logic or marketing legend. *Journal of Marketing Research*, **30**, 158–170.

Hagedoorn, J. (1993). Understanding the rationale of strategic technology partnering: Interorganizational modes of cooperation and sectoral differences. *Strategic Management Journal*, **14**, 371–385.

Hagedoorn, J. & Narula, R. (1996). Choosing organizational modes of strategic technology partnering: International and sectoral differences. *Journal of International Business*, **27**(2), 265–284.

Hamel, G. (1991). Competition for competence and interpartner learning within international strategic alliances. *Strategic Management Journal*, **12**, 83–103.

Hamel, G. & Prahalad, C.K. (1994). *Competing for the Future*. Boston, MA: Harvard Business School Press.

Hamel, G., Doz, Y. & Prahalad, C.K. (1989). Collaborate with your competitors—and win. *Harvard Business Review*, **67**(1), 133–139.

Harrigan, K.R. (1985). *Strategic Flexibility*. Lexington, MA: Lexington Books.

Henderson, R.M. & Clark, K.B. (1990). Architectural innovation: The reconfiguration of existing product technologies and the failure of established firms. *Administrative Science Quarterly*, **35**, 9–30.

Henderson, R. & Cockburn, I. (1994). Measuring competence? Exploring firm effects in pharmaceutical research. *Strategic Management Journal*, **15** (Winter Special Issue), 63–84.

Hennart, J.F. (1988). A transaction costs theory of equity joint ventures, *Strategic Management Journal*, **9**, 361–374.

Hitt, M.A., Ireland, R.D. & Hoskisson, R.D. (1999). *Strategic Management: Competitiveness and Globalization*, 3rd edition. Cincinnati, OH: South-Western College Publishing.

Hitt, M.A., Keats, B.W. & DeMarie, S.M. (1998). Navigating in the new competitive landscape: Building strategic flexibility and competitive advantage in the 21st century. *Academy of Management Executive*, **12**(4), 22–42.

Kanter, R.M. (1988). When a thousand flowers bloom: Structural, collective, and social conditions for innovation in organizations. In B.M. Staw & L.L. Cummings (eds), *Research in Organizational Behavior*, Vol. 10, Greenwich, CT: JAI Press, 169–211.

Kerin, R.A., Varadarajan, P.R. & Peterson, R.A. (1993). First mover advantages: A synthesis, conceptual framework, and research propositions. *Journal of Marketing*, **56**, 33–52.

Kessler, E.H. & Chakrabarti, A.K. (1996). Innovation speed: A conceptual model of context, antecedents and outcomes. *Academy of Management Review*, **21**(4), 1143–1191.

Killing, J.P. (1982). How to make a global joint venture work. *Harvard Business Review*, May–June.

Kogut, B. (1985). Designing global strategies: Profiting from operational flexibility. *Sloan Management Review*, **26**(5), 27–38.

Kogut, B. (1988). Joint ventures: Theoretical and empirical perspectives. *Strategic Management Journal*, **9**, 319–332.

Koza, M.P. & Lewin, A.Y. (1998). The co-evolution of strategic alliances. *Organization Science*, **9**(3), 255–264.

Leonard-Barton, D. (1995). *Wellsprings of Knowledge: Building and Sustaining the Sources of Innovation*. Boston, MA: Harvard Business School Press.

Lieberman, M.B. & Montgomery, D.B. (1988). First mover advantages. *Strategic Management Journal*, **9**, 41–58.

Meyers, S. & Marquis, D.G. (1969). *Successful Industrial Innovations.* Washington, DC: National Science Foundation.

Miles, R.E., Snow, C.C., Meyer, A.D. & Coleman, H.J. (1978). Organizational strategy, structure, and process. *Academy of Management Review,* **3**, 546–562.

Nohria, N. & Gulati, R. (1996). Is slack good or bad for innovation? *Academy of Management Review,* **39**(5), 1245–1264.

Ohmae, K. (1989). The global logic of strategic alliances. *Harvard Business Review,* March–April, 143–154.

Pisano, G.P. (1989). Using equity participation to support exchange: Evidence from the biotechnology industry. *Journal of Law, Economics and Organization,* **5**(1), 109–125.

Pisano, G.P. (1991). The governance of innovation: Vertical integration and collaborative arrangements in the biotechnology industry. *Research Policy,* **20**, 237–249.

Pisano, G. (1996). Biotechnology: A technical note. In R.A Burgelman, M.A. Maidique & S.C. Wheelwright (eds), *Strategic Management of Technology and Innovation,* Chicago, IL: Irwin, 415–418.

Powell, W.W. (1998). Learning from collaboration: Knowledge and networks in the biotechnology and pharmaceutical industries. *California Management Review,* **40**(3), 228–240.

Powell, W.W., Koput, K.W. & Smith-Doerr, L. (1996). Interorganizational collaboration and the locus of innovation: Networks of learning in biotechnology. *Administrative Science Quarterly,* **41**, 116–145.

Snow, C.C. & Hrebiniak, L.G. (1980). Strategy, distinctive competence, and organizational performance. *Administrative Science Quarterly,* **25**, 317–336.

Spender, J.-C. (1989). *Industry Recipes: An Inquiry into the Nature and Sources of Managerial Judgement.* New York: Blackwell.

Spender, J.-C. & Kessler, E.H. (1995). Managing the uncertainty of innovation: Extending Thompson (1967). *Human Relations,* **48**, 35–56.

Stalk, G. & Hout, T.M. (1990). *Competing Against Time: How Time-based Competition is Reshaping Global Markets.* New York: Free Press.

Wheelwright, S.C. & Clark, K.B. (1992). *Revolutionizing Product Development.* New York: Free Press.

Williamson, O.E. (1975). *Markets and Hierarchies: Analysis and Antitrust Implications.* New York: Free Press.

Zucker, L.G. & Darby, M.R. (1997). Present at the biotechnology revolution: Transformation of technological identity for a large incumbent pharmaceutical firm. *Research Policy,* **26**, 429–446.

# 13

# Governance of R&D—Transaction Cost, Resources, Inertia and Social Capital

THOMAS KEIL

## INTRODUCTION

The competitive environment in an increased number of industries can be characterized as complex and dynamic. Rapid, often discontinuous, technological change, increased cost of innovation, and convergence of basic technologies pose challenges to a wide variety of firms. In such environments a large number of firms are reconsidering which activities to perform internally and which activities to outsource (Dillmann, 1996; Pisano, 1988; Schneider & Zieringer, 1991). Among the activities considered for outsourcing is research and development. While some authors herald advantages of external technology sources, such as improved time to market or decreased cost (Chatterji, 1996; Jonash, 1996), others warn of the risks such as technological dependence or loss of competitiveness inherent in such organizational arrangements (Ulset, 1996). A more balanced analysis of the advantages and disadvantages of internal and external possibilities to govern research and development would seem imperative.

*Dynamic Strategic Resources: Development, Diffusion and Integration.*
Edited by Michael A. Hitt, Patricia Gorman Clifford, Robert D. Nixon and Kevin P. Coyne.

For research and development, the analysis of governance modes has been dominated by transaction cost arguments (Pisano, 1990, 1991; Robertson & Gatignon, 1998; Tapon, 1989). This paper reviews the transaction cost frameworks for research and development governance. It points out that among other weaknesses, transaction cost analysis tends to be ahistorical and asocial. The paper develops complementary arguments derived from resource-based theory, social capital theory and evolutionary theories. It is proposed how the firm-specific history of governance modes and different levels of social capital are related to the choice of governance modes for research and development.

The paper starts with a brief conceptual analysis. A review and critique follows on how the transaction cost framework has been applied for the analysis of research and development governance. Next, the resource-based view of research and development governance is outlined. The paper then develops a dynamic social perspective of the process of research and development governance. The paper ends with conclusions.

## Governance of Research and Development

In the scholarly as well as in the practice-oriented literature, the question of research and development governance has been discussed under headings such as research and development outsourcing, technology development modes, or governance of innovation (Dillmann, 1996; Pisano, 1990, 1991; Robertson & Gatignon, 1998). Common to these studies is that they analyze when a firm should pursue research and development in-house and when it might be better to resort to external partners. The studies' main difference can be found in their conceptualization of what alternatives a firm might have.

For this paper, research and development governance is defined as the organizational form that is used for research and development activities. In principle, firms can choose from a number of alternatives that lie between two extreme cases. One extreme is that a firm pursues research and development activities completely internally,[1] that is, it does not work with any external partners. At the other extreme, the firm does not pursue any research and development activity internally but purchases research and development services in the market, that is from external providers. Between these two extremes, several *intermediate* or *hybrid* (Williamson, 1975, 1985) forms can be found. Characteristic of the intermediate arrangements is that research and development is carried out collaboratively with an external partner. This collaboration can be based, for instance, on contracts or can take place in a newly formed joint venture. In practice, governance arrangements are significantly more complicated, often involving the exchange of cross-licensing of existing knowledge on top of agreements about the development of new technology. The simplifications made are for analytical purposes.

## Transaction Cost View of R&D Governance Decisions

For analysis of research and development governance, the dominant framework has been transaction cost analysis. Building on the work of Coase (1937), transaction cost analysis has been developed in the seminal works of Williamson (1975, 1985). The transaction cost framework starts from the assumption that not only internal production is costly, but also market transactions come at a cost. Transaction costs include search costs, negotiation costs, control costs, and costs of adaptation. The decision to retain an activity within the boundaries of the firm, to use markets, or an intermediate arrangement,[2] should be based on a comparison of the transaction costs incurred in each.

Assuming the existence of bounded rationality and opportunism, transaction cost theory argues that three attributes of transactions need to be considered to determine the optimal governance mode (Williamson, 1985: 52–61). The most important characteristic of a transaction is the need for transaction specific investments (Picot, 1991). The more a transaction requires investments that cannot be redeployed to other uses, the lower are the incentives for an external party to make these investments. Thus, transaction specificity suggests an activity to be conducted within the boundaries of the firm.

In transaction cost analysis, uncertainty is the second important characteristic of transactions. Using an external party for research and development leaves the firm with two alternatives. The first is that it could draft a contract that covers all contingencies that might arise in the course of the project. If a transaction contains uncertainty, in reality this is virtually impossible. Alternatively, the firm can act in good faith and leave potential issues for negotiation between the two parties once they arise. However, this might create ample opportunity for opportunism. To avoid the negative effects of uncertainty, transaction cost analyses would suggest internalizing activities that are associated with high uncertainty.

The third characteristic is the frequency of the transaction. Specialized governance structures might often be needed to govern transactions that might need considerable transaction-specific investments (Williamson, 1985). However, specialized governance structures are costly to devise. Therefore, frequency is important to recover the cost of devising these governance structures. By the same token, frequency can make the use of hierarchies more efficient. If research and development activities occur frequently, the fixed cost of research and development can be spread over a larger number of projects. In conclusion, Schneider and Zieringer (1991) point out that frequency mainly amplifies the effects of asset specificity and uncertainty.

Transaction cost analysis has been applied and adapted in the context of research and development (e.g., Mang, 1998; Pisano, 1990, 1991; Schneider & Zieringer, 1991; Tapon, 1989). For research and development, the first and probably most important aspect is uncertainty. Uncertainty might take several forms (Tapon, 1989). The first form of uncertainty can be described as outcome uncertainty. Research and development activities might produce results that were not predicted. How these results get appropriated is difficult to negotiate *ex ante* (Pisano, 1988: 61–63). In cases of weak appropriability regimes (Teece, 1986), the partner providing the technology might easily utilize the technology elsewhere. Even if the expected results are produced, partners might reuse these results against the will of the other firm elsewhere in an unforeseen way. Even in cases of patent protection, the knowledge gained by developing the technology remains with the developing firm. This knowledge can be used then for further developments.

Considerable uncertainty exists also concerning the inputs into the research and development activities. For instance, personnel requirements are difficult to assess *ex ante*. Uncertainty might also exist regarding equipment that is needed for the research and development activities. In some cases, related technology development might be needed that was not foreseen.

Uncertainty makes it impossible to negotiate an all-encompassing contract. Renegotiations at various project stages are a normal procedure (Pisano, 1990). The risk of potential adaptations is another result from the uncertainty inherent in research and development activities. Due to the difficulty in predicting the outcome of a long-term development project, substantial adaptations of the output might be necessary to be able to use this output (Schneider & Zieringer, 1991). Uncertainty makes investment in assets that cannot be redeployed for other uses increasingly risky. If during a project problems between the partners arise, the research and development already incurred can easily lead to a lock-in into a suboptimal relationship (Ulset, 1996: 66).

In research and development projects, information asymmetry (Steensma, 1996a) poses an additional source of transaction cost. The partner carrying out the research and development work is almost always in a better position to judge the state of the project and the potential outcome. This holds especially true during the project. Potential for opportunistic behavior exists. Control and intervention mechanisms to deter opportunistic behavior are costly and often impractical, as selective control and intervention without creating disincentives for innovation are difficult if not impossible to construct (Ulset, 1996: 66).

In transaction cost analysis of research and development, frequency plays a role. Different predictions for the effects of frequency have been proposed. Schneider and Zieringer (1991: 81–89) suggest that search and negotiation costs can be reduced if activities are outsourced regularly. However, regular need for research and development activities carries also a potential for reduced internal cost, as fixed cost can be divided over a large number of projects. A regular use of one subcontractor might easily lead into a lock-in and dependence (Pisano, 1990).

For research and development, Pisano (1990) has pointed to the importance of small numbers bargaining. The negotiation position of the sponsor firm during a research and development project depends critically on the availability of alternative suppliers for the research and development activity. Already at the beginning, the potential number of sources is limited. In the course of the project, this problem receives further weight. In a research project, some of the generated knowledge is usually tacit. The codified descriptions and artifacts that are the normal output from research and development projects do not easily transfer this form of knowledge. Thus, switching to alternative suppliers is further impeded. The bargaining position of the supplier is improved if the generated knowledge is specialized to the supplier. Thus, even fewer other suppliers would have the necessary knowledge to continue the project. Particularly, if the knowledge is important for or specific to the buyer, this dependence is increased. As Pisano (1990) points out, this phenomenon might extend over generations of technology. The path-dependent nature of technology (Dosi, 1982) might make the switching to other sources difficult.

Arguments from transaction cost economics have been recently complemented with agency theory and incomplete contract arguments (Ulset, 1996). Some of the problems inherent in outsourcing knowledge-intensive activities might be offset by the right incentive structures. This argument is in line with the work of Brynjolfsson (1994) which draws on incomplete contract theory (Grossman & Hart, 1986; Hart, 1991, 1995). Brynjolfsson (1994) shows how ownership incentives improve the behavior of an agent in situations in which the agents holds inalienable assets. Agency theory suggests that hybrid arrangements that carry both elements of hierarchies and markets might be preferable for research and development activities as they balance the monitoring cost with risk (Hennart, 1993).

Transaction cost analysis and its extensions have been criticized from various perspectives. Granovetter (1985, 1992) argued that transaction cost analysis ignores an important aspect of economic behavior, namely its social embeddedness. While economic rationales play an important role for economic activities, this activity is taking place in a network of social relationships and might be at least partially motivated by non-economic goals such as approval, status or power. Recently, several empirical studies have shown how social ties affect inter-firm relationships (Gulati, 1995a, 1995b; Uzzi, 1996, 1997). For research and development in the pharmaceutical industry, Pisano and Mang (1993: 125) found that firms pursuing research and development outsourcing did not use detailed contracts, but relied on renegotiation in good faith. Thus, trust can act as a safeguard that decreases the "propensity towards opportunism" (Nooteboom, 1996; Nooteboom, Berger & Noorderhaven, 1997). As Granovetter (1985) argues, transaction cost arguments overestimate the power of "rational" control mechanisms over the power of social control mechanisms such as self-regulation, shared norms, moral obligation, trust, reputation and identity (Larson, 1992). Ghoshal and Moran (1996) extend this criticism. They argue that Williamson's treatment of opportunism leads to suboptimal decisions if applied to normative decisions. This line of criticism can be summarized that transaction cost economics arguments are based on too strict assumptions regarding human rationality, motivation, and behavior. Transaction cost arguments neglect the social character of economic transactions.

Further criticisms of transaction cost economics arguments have been brought forward. One criticism is that transaction costs are difficult if not impossible to determine reliably in real-world situations (Dillmann, 1996). In her dissertation, Nicholls-Nixon (1993: 23) points out that transaction cost arguments cannot explain subsequent performance differences within projects that employ the same governance mode. Especially, the *ex-post* behavior of the parties is neglected (Sobrero, 1996). Transaction cost analysis further neglects the history of transactions in which any transaction is embedded (Gulati, 1995a). Thus, transaction cost economics arguments remain largely static (Hennart, 1988).

Bühner and Tuschke (1996) have brought another criticism forward. They argue that within the original transaction cost analysis (Williamson, 1975), first a core activity area is determined. This core of the firm is not subject to transaction cost considerations, but has to be kept within the firm. Later frameworks[3] have ignored this distinction and applied the arguments on all activities the firm may potentially carry out. However, the strategic value of an activity cannot be determined based on transaction cost arguments alone. Other theories need to be used to determine this value before transaction cost arguments can be applied. Langlois and Robertson (1995) have made a similar argument. They argue that for some activities of the firm, the cost advantage to internal organization is effectively infinite. These activities are idiosyncratic and non-contestable.

## RESOURCE-BASED PERSPECTIVE

The transaction cost perspective has been complemented by arguments derived from the resource-based theory of strategic management (Eisenhardt & Schoonhoven, 1996; Madhok & Tallman, 1998; Mang, 1998). The resource-based literature builds on the seminal work of Edith Penrose (1959). Firms are viewed as bundles of resources. These resources differ in their potential to generate rents for the firm (Grant, 1991; Peteraf, 1993; Prahalad & Hamel, 1990; Wernerfelt, 1984). Those firms that possess resources with greater rent potential should achieve higher performance.

In the normative version of the resource-based theory of strategic management, the firm is viewed to focus on those technologies and competencies[4] that are rare, inimitable, difficult to substitute, and valuable (Barney, 1991). All other competencies can and should be considered for outsourcing (Quinn & Hilmer, 1994). As Bühner and Tuschke (1996) point out, the resource-based view could be used as a criterion to determine the core area of the firm for which transaction cost considerations should not be applied.

Early resource-based arguments have been criticized as rather static (Teece, Pisano & Shuen, 1997) and not taking issues of organizational inertia into consideration (Rumelt, 1995). More recent refinements develop a more dynamic theory (Lei, Hitt & Bettis, 1996; Teece, Pisano & Shuen, 1997). They argue that the firm's competencies have to evolve over time. In this view, it is critical that a firm develops the capability to change and adopt its core competencies. An additional refinement of the resource-based view is derived from looking at the firm as a dynamic competence system. In this view, the focus is no longer on single competencies, but on understanding the interdependencies between competencies (Heene & Sanchez, 1997; Sanchez & Heene, 1997; Sanchez, Heene & Thomas, 1996). Not only the change of the single competence is analyzed, but also the change of the relationship between competencies is introduced as an additional important parameter.

The resource-based view has normative implications for research and development governance. The basic logic for these implications is that a firm should internally develop those technologies or competencies that are providing it with competitive advantage. All other technologies can be accessed from external partners. Chiesa and Barbeschi (1994) have developed a more sophisticated scheme of resource-based implications for research and development governance. They argue that two characteristics of technology are important for choosing the research and development governance mode. First, it is important to consider if the firm's advantage is based on the application of a single technology or on the integration of multiple technologies. Second, the value of the new knowledge area is important. Chiesa and Barbeschi (1994) distinguish between core knowledge, competence refreshing knowledge and non-core knowledge.[5] The authors argue that non-core knowledge can be acquired directly from the market. For competence-refreshing knowledge, collaborative modes might be superior as the firm increases its ability to integrate the new knowledge with its existing knowledge. Complete internal development would seem imperative if a firm that is focusing on a single technology tries to create core knowledge.

Recent resource-based theory has stressed the importance of intermediate, that is collaborative, modes of research and development governance. Madhok and Tallman (1998) argue that firms do not necessarily enter into collaborative relationships to minimize the expected cost of development, as transaction cost theorists would argue. Rather, firms might enter relationships in the expectation of creating superior value through the combination of complementary resources and capabilities (Zajac & Olsen, 1993). Firms can create and appropriate value in inter-firm relationships by leveraging their internal resource pool with complementary resources (Stein, 1997) or through learning new competencies from the partner (Hamel, 1991; Hamel, Doz & Prahalad, 1989; Kogut, 1988). In some industries, the convergence of formerly separate technologies requires firms to draw upon technologies in which they have no or only very weak capabilities. In this context, cooperative research and development might be driven by the motive to access these capabilities from a partner (Doz & Hamel, 1997, 1998). In other cases, the absorption of knowledge and capabilities from a partner might be the driving force to enter a close relationship with an external partner rather than relying on internal development or using arm's-length licensing arrangements (Hagedoorn & Narula, 1996; Osborn & Baughn, 1990). Transferring tacit knowledge might be easier in organizational arrangements that foster intense interaction and collaboration (Kogut & Zander, 1992).

Recent empirical research supports the notion that the competence characteristics influence the governance choices in research and development projects (Irwin, Hoffman & Lamont, 1998; Steensma, 1996b) and the formation of technology development-oriented alliances (Eisenhardt & Schoonhoven, 1996; Sakakibara, 1997). However, several criticisms of the resource-based view have also been brought forward. It has been argued that resource-based theory largely ignores the firm environment (Verdin & Williamson, 1994). Porter argues that in the resource-based perspective, empirical papers sometimes suffer from being tautological (Porter, 1991).

Summarizing the discussion of the transaction cost and resource-based view, one can conclude that both theories, at least in their pure form, lack important elements. In both theories, problems of research and development governance are reduced more or less to questions of a suitable economic setup, that is finding partners with suitable resources and capabilities and designing the right governance modes to work with them. In the next section it is argued that this view is too narrow. Process matters in several respects. For instance, the choice of governance modes might be bound by the governance history of the firm (Pisano, 1988). To understand the research and development governance decisions, a longitudinal, evolutionary perspective would seem necessary. Further, economic action is embedded in social networks (Granovetter, 1985). Thus, economic and social goals often coexist and need to be included into the analysis.

## Towards a Dynamic, Social View of Research and Development Governance

This section outlines a dynamic, social perspective on governance of research and development. It analyzes the single transaction in the context of previous transactions the firm has been and is engaged in. In addition, it includes the evolution of the environment into the analysis. The underlying research question is how the development of the firm and its environment affect the governance of research and development. Four propositions are developed that are summarized in Figure 13.1. These four propositions concern two basic mechanisms that affect the firm's choice of research and development governance modes. The first mechanism is best described through the notion of inertia (defined as indisposition to motion, exertion or change). It is argued that firms exhibit inertia in research and development governance. Forces are discussed that might lead a firm to overcome this inertia. This mechanism is formalized in propositions 1 and 2 and is depicted in the upper half of Figure 13.1. The second mechanism describes how social capital introduces additional inertia into research and development governance. It is formalized in propositions 3 and 4. The lower half of Figure 13.1 depicts the underlying relationships.

Taking an evolutionary perspective sheds further light on the assumption of bounded rationality (Simon, 1947) in decision-making that is inherent in the transaction cost view. In some instances, decisions might not be the outcome of a rational evaluation process, but rather applications of an existing routine to a situation, whether appropriate or not. This proposition has been made by authors in evolutionary economics (Nelson & Winter, 1982) and organizational evolution (Stuart & Podolny, 1996) alike. Routines form through previous operating experience (Nelson & Winter, 1982). They might constrain actions by acting as perceptual filters. In the same vein, Powell (1998) argues that firms build up skills at forming external relationships. Knowledge how to cooperate implies that information is filtered by a specific context, by experience, and by interpretation. The

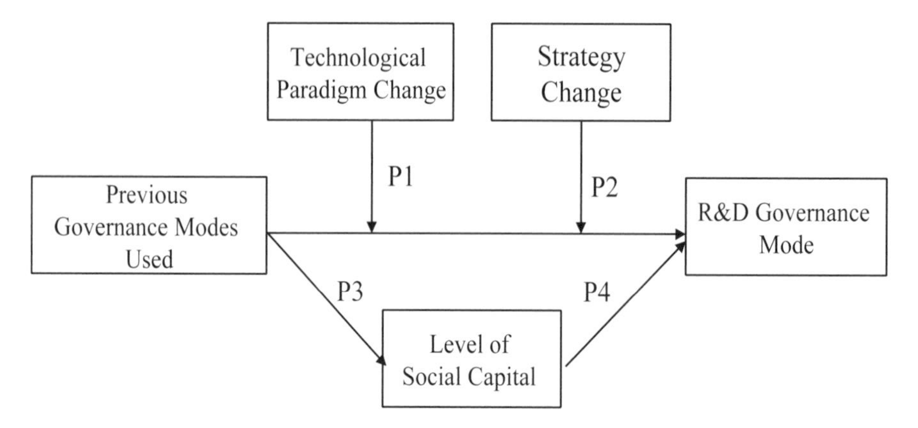


FIGURE 13.1 Governance history, social capital, and R&D governance modes; P1–P4 are Propositions 1–4 below

knowledge and skills built up influence the variety of design choices the firm has (Penning & Harianto, 1992).

Not only routines can limit the degrees of freedom for the firm. Research and development decisions are path dependent. Over time, the governance of transactions may become inseparably linked with the governance of other transactions in which the firm is already engaged (Argyres & Liebeskind, 1999). For instance, ongoing supplier relationships might exist and need to be taken into consideration. Existing relationships might suggest keeping an activity with an external supplier rather than internalizing it to avoid endangering sunk costs. The cost of actually resolving partnerships has been studied mainly from the transaction cost perspective. Sunk costs include, for instance, relationship-specific tangible resources, but also the time spent on learning to collaborate with the particular partner. Existing commitments to governance modes might also limit the degree of freedom with other parties. Existing alliances with one firm might, for instance, forestall the formation of a closer alliance with a third party. As previously argued, the cumulative nature of knowledge development might also lock firms into a relationship. Knowledge accumulates mostly in the firm that carries out the research and development activity. Part of this knowledge is tacit and can be transferred only with great difficulty across firm boundaries (Kogut & Zander, 1992, 1993). Tacit knowledge often requires intense collaboration (Steensma, 1996a) to be transferred and governance modes that allow for intense interaction. This argument suggests that within a knowledge trajectory, firms might only gradually be able to change from one governance mode to another.

Empirical evidence for the persistence in research and development governance is scarce and mixed. Nerkar (1997) shows that firms exhibit persistence in their research and development activity. However, his analysis is limited to the knowledge domain rather than the governance mode. Stuart and Podolny (1996) show that the evolution of technological capabilities is characterized by local search, that is, firms persist in collaboration or non-collaboration patterns.

Two authors have empirically analyzed persistence in the use of governance modes up to this point. The findings of these studies are contradictory. In a multi-industry study, Steensma (1997) finds support for the hypothesis that experience with particular governance modes is related to the continued use of this governance mode. In contrast, Pisano (1990) does not find a significant influence of the sourcing history of the firm. However, Pisano's results might be industry specific. Pisano (1988) analyzes pharmaceutical firms after the emergence of the biotechnology paradigm. He tested whether sourcing patterns in large pharmaceutical companies persist over paradigm changes. It is probable that the radical nature of the change might have caused the firms to break with their routines. This interpretation is supported by the study of Powell, Koput and Smith-Doerr (1996). In a study of new biotechnology firms[6] they found that firms persist in using collaborative agreements. They conclude that the firms develop considerable absorptive capacity and skills in managing collaborations, as well as increased awareness of new projects and a reputation as a reliable partner. These benefits make it more probable that firms persist in their behavior of entering into collaborative research and development. The interpretation that firms persist in their routines until a dramatic change forces them to reconsider these routines is also in line with punctuated equilibrium models of organizational change (Gersick, 1991; Haveman, 1992; Romanelli & Tushman, 1994). Thus, our first proposition is as follows:

> Proposition 1: The relationships between the propensity of a firm to use a particular research and development governance mode and the firm's sourcing history will be moderated by paradigm changes in the technological environment.

Dramatic change is not limited to technological change. It might also be caused by forces from within the firm or by forces in the environment other than technology. While relatively seldom, firms do change strategic direction over time. In many cases, this change might be due to changes within the environment that fundamentally alter the business logic (Hagedoorn & Schakenraad, 1990). In the environment, dramatic change might take, for instance, the form of deregulation. In the telecommunication sector, the recent deregulation has forced a number of firms to reconsider their research and development strategy to avoid losing ground against new competitors. The appointment of a new CEO or complete top management team often initiates dramatic internally caused changes in the strategy of a firm. Madhavan, Koka and Prescott (1998) show how dramatic change in the industry environment is related to structural change in inter-firm networks. They find that dramatic change is related to altered structures while less dramatic change is related to reinforcement of existing structures. Part of a strategic reorientation might be a reconsideration of research and development governance decisions. Similarly, Koza and Lewin (1998) point out that strategic alliances, which can be one form of research and development governance, should be viewed in the context of the evolution of firm strategy. As in the case of dramatic changes in the technological paradigm, dramatic strategic change might lead to a break with existing problem-solving routines. Thus, we present our second proposition:

> Proposition 2: Fundamental changes in the strategic orientation of the firm will moderate the relationship between the research and development governance history of a firm and the propensity to use a particular governance mode.

Additional forces might influence the choice of research and development governance mode. As firms cooperate in research and development projects, social capital (Bordieu, 1986; Coleman, 1988) is built between the partners. Social capital can be defined as "the sum of the actual and potential resources embedded within, available through, and derived from the network of relationships possessed by an individual or social unit" (Nahapiet & Ghoshal, 1998: 243). However, social capital is not only a resource, but it acts likewise as a constraint on the partners to perform according to each other's expectations (Walker, Kogut & Shan, 1997). Thus, social capital is an example of social control replacing contractual control mechanisms (Ghoshal & Moran, 1996). The function of social capital in posing expectations on a partner and limiting the partner's variety of acceptable actions is of special interest for this paper. A high level of uncertainty about appropriate means and outcomes characterizes many research and development activities (Tapon, 1989). Social control would seem important to counter the potential threat of opportunism. One might expect that social capital plays an important role for firms that engage in research and development-related cooperation. In line with this argument, several authors find that social capital plays an important role in the formation of inter-firm networks of biotechnology start-ups (Liebeskind *et al.*, 1996; Powell, Koput & Smith-Doerr, 1996; Walker, Kogut & Shan, 1997).

In this paper, the social capital argument is extended towards the question of governance. To do so, a closer look at the social capital construct is needed. Social capital is a multidimensional construct (Putnam, 1995). Nahapiet and Ghoshal (1998) distinguish between three main dimensions of social capital, which they term structural, relational, and cognitive. The structural dimension of social capital refers to the overall pattern of relationships between the actors in a social network (Burt, 1992; Koka & Prescott, 1998). For instance, a firm that has a large number of relationships with other firms would have a higher social capital than a firm with a low number of relationships. The relational dimension describes the nature of the single dyadic relationship (Granovetter, 1992; Koka & Prescott, 1998). Trust, shared norms and obligations characterize relationships with a high level of relational social capital. The cognitive dimension refers to shared representations, interpretations, and systems of meaning (Nahapiet & Ghoshal, 1998).

Different modes of governance can be expected to relate to different levels of social capital that a firm can accumulate by using them. For the structural dimension of social capital, this point is obvious. If a firm does not enter into a relationship with an external partner, that is, it completely internalizes research and development, it cannot build high levels of social capital through the relationship. Thus, the firm should exhibit a low level of social capital. In line with this argument, Walker, Kogut and Shan (1997) show that the change of social capital is related to the number of relationships a firm enters.

A more fine-grained view of the relationship between governance and social capital can be gained by taking the other two dimensions into account. The relational dimension of social capital comprises at least trust, norms and sanctions, obligations and expectations, and identity and identification (Nahapiet & Ghoshal, 1998). The formation of trust in inter-organizational relationships has been linked to interaction between the firms (Larson, 1992; McAllister, 1995; Ring & Van de Ven, 1994; Van de Ven & Walker, 1984). Also, joint norms and sanctions (Larson, 1992), obligations and expectations (Gulati, 1995a), and network identity develop largely through intense interaction between firms. Various governance modes provide different opportunities for interaction (Hagedoorn, 1990). Intermediate forms of governance provide for more interactions than do market-based governance forms. Equity-based forms of governance such as joint ventures might provide the best opportunities to interact (Osborn & Baughn, 1990).

Analyzing the cognitive dimension of social capital further strengthens the arguments made for the relational dimension of social capital. The formation of shared cognition in organizations takes place through challenges posed by a firm's environment, sociopolitical processes within the firm, and changes in key decision makers' values and assumptions (Lyles & Schwenk, 1992; Walsh, 1995). Often, these cognitive structures manifest themselves in organizational cultures (Sackmann, 1992) and organizational language (von Krogh & Roos, 1995). Shared cognition between organizations requires information and knowledge exchange to build shared interpretations and joint language. Thus, firms have to engage in an inter-organizational learning process (Sobrero & Schrader, 1998). Governance modes are expected to differ with respect to organizational learning (Steensma, 1996a). Authors agree that intermediate forms of governance provide better learning opportunities than purely market-based forms of governance (Osborn & Baughn, 1990; Osborn & Hagedoorn, 1997). However, a more fine-grained analysis between equity and non-equity arrangements is less clear-cut. Joint ventures might offer advantages due to the greater amount of interaction (Osborn & Baughn, 1990). On the other hand, non-equity arrangements might provide a more effective environment for discovery of new knowledge due to their greater flexibility (Osborn & Hagedoorn, 1997). For this reason, we will only distinguish between intermediate forms of governance and market-based, or hierarchical, forms of governance.

If governance modes provide different opportunities to accumulate social capital, a firm's history of research and development governance can be expected to be related to the level of social capital a firm possesses. For instance, a firm that has been conducting mainly in-house research and development should exhibit a much lower level of social capital than a firm that has been actively participating in collaborative development projects. Accordingly:

> Proposition 3: For research and development, the level of social capital a firm has accumulated will be related to the governance modes employed in previous research and development activities.

In proposition 3, it has been argued that the level of social capital is related to the governance modes used in previous research and development activities. Now, it will be argued that this level of social capital that has been accumulated affects the choice of governance for current activities. More specifically it is argued that firms with a high level of social capital can be expected to exhibit a higher propensity to use intermediate forms of governance. Again the different dimensions of social capital help to structure the reasoning for this expected relationship.

Being embedded in a larger number of relationships should provide the firm with superior access to information about new collaborative opportunities. Social networks provide the function of making potential partners aware of each other's needs, capabilities, and alliance requirements (Gulati, 1995b; Van de Ven, 1976). Through this informational function, social networks and social capital reduce uncertainty regarding the partner and the risk of intermediate forms of governance.

Aside from the structural element of access to relevant information about potential collaboration partners, the cognitive dimension of social capital also plays a role. Access to information is necessary for understanding a situation or opportunity, but not sufficient. The interpretation or sense making might be even more important (Weick, 1995). Interpretation of information is related to the existing knowledge. Thus, shared knowledge would increase the probability of a similar interpretation of information. High levels of cognitive social capital should enable the firm to better frame common problems and explore avenues of joint research and development. By having a common language and a common understanding of problems, firms are better able to develop cooperative research and development modes.

Trust is probably the most studied element of the relational dimension of social capital. Gulati (1995a) argues that through interaction firms develop knowledge-based trust as well as cognitive trust. Trust increases the predictability of the partner's behavior. Thus, the propensity to internalize the activity is reduced. In relationships that exhibit a high level of trust, less reliance on hierarchical contracts should be found. In a study of alliances in biopharmaceuticals, new materials manufacturers, and automotive businesses, Gulati (1995a) finds that firms with prior alliances with the same partner are more likely to choose non-equity-based alliances.

Based on the discussion up to this point, one might ask if a high level of social capital is likely to lead to market-based, rather than intermediate forms of governance. However, this would seem unlikely, as one core aspect of social capital is that it "requires the maintenance of and reinvestment in the structure of prevailing relationships" (Walker, Kogut & Shan, 1997: 109). Even if the relational dimension of social capital would suffice to use purely market-based arrangements, this would reduce the future level of social capital. Thus, in a dynamic view, the firm would in an iterative process gravitate towards intermediate forms of governance. Therefore:

> Proposition 4: A high level of social capital will be related to a higher propensity to use intermediate modes of governance for research and development.

## Conclusions

For research and development activities, this paper has built a complementary, evolutionary and social perspective of governance mode choice. It has been argued that research and development governance cannot be understood through static snapshot views of transaction cost or resource positions alone. Rather, the governance history and the social networks the firm is embedded in have to be taken into account.

The main contribution of this paper is to show how a longitudinal and social view of research and development governance can significantly increase our understanding of governance phenomena. The paper shows how firms can use different organizational arrangements to develop technology, a critical resource for many firms. The arguments in this paper suggest that a firm should not consider research and development activities as a cost factor that ought to be minimized, but rather as a strategic resource. Especially in rapidly changing environments, competitiveness might be critically dependent on managing research and development activities optimally. To gain advantage from research and development activities, a firm would need to analyze the strategic potential of knowledge areas before committing to governance modes that might be difficult to alter later. As part of this analysis, also social relations should also be considered. By making an aspect such as social capital explicit, a firm might be able to improve the quality of decisions.

It should be noted that the arguments made in this paper are not intended to replace transaction cost or resource-based analysis. While social goals as well as persistence play a role in firm behavior, they do not replace rational analysis in the firm. Rather, the two perspectives should be seen as complementary. Firms or better individuals in firms can be expected to attempt rational behavior. However, rationality is bounded (Simon, 1947) and might take a wider range of arguments into account than purely economic arguments (Granovetter, 1985).

The model that was proposed in this paper is on a different level of analysis than transaction cost or resource-based explanations of governance choice. One might think the single decision is embedded into a process of previous and future governance decisions. While for analytical modeling purposes compelling, it is incorrect to view governance mode choices independently from the processes they are embedded in.

It would seem important to point out at least one important limitation of the arguments made in this paper. For research and development, it has been argued that social capital plays the strongest role in environments that are characterized by uncertainty. Thus, one would expect the explanatory power of these arguments to be stronger in technology-intensive industries. In environments in which the research and development activities play only a minor role, the routine-based persistence might not take place. If, for instance, research and development projects are undertaken only on a sporadic basis, routines for governance decisions might never form. Also the formation and reliance on high levels of social capital would seem less probable in this context.

In future research, scholars might empirically examine the mechanisms introduced in this paper in greater detail. In particular, the concept of social capital would require intense empirical attention. Theoretical extensions of the above arguments might analyze how social capital is context dependent or how it might be transferred from one context to another.

In conclusion, this paper has been developing a dynamic perspective of how previous governance history and social capital affect governance choices for research and development. This view is useful in complementing the predominant transaction cost and resource-based arguments.

## Acknowledgements

This research was supported by grants from the Academy of Finland, IVO Foundation, NESTE Foundation, and Wihuri Foundation. The paper has been significantly improved by comments from Erkko Autio, Pia Hokkanen, Tomi Laamanen, Markus Nordberg, Annaleena Parhankangas, Paul Robertson, and the editors of this book. All remaining errors and shortcomings, however, remain the sole responsibility of the author.

## Notes

1. In transaction cost economics, this solution is referred to as hierarchical governance.
2. In its original form transaction cost analysis only considers markets or hierarchies as possible governance modes. Only later extensions have expanded this analysis to also include intermediate forms such as alliances (Hennart, 1993; Powell, 1990; Williamson, 1991).
3. For instance Picot (1991). The approach in his paper is interesting as he uses the strategic importance of an activity as a variable to determine the transaction cost. Thus, he tries to build strategic considerations into the transaction cost framework.
4. For simplicity, the term competencies is used in the following to encompass resources, capabilities and competencies. This follows the definition proposed by Henderson and Cockburn (1994).
5. Chiesa and Barbeschi (1994) define core knowledge as knowledge that "contributes to perceived customer value, to the build-up of competence and is highly appropriable in itself, or to the creation of a unique pattern of knowledge accumulation and co-ordination." Competence-refreshing knowledge lacks the appropriability but can contribute together with existing knowledge to innovations. Non-core knowledge refers to available basic knowledge.
6. New biotechnology firms are firms that have been founded for the purpose of researching and developing new products that exploit biotechnology (Liebeskind *et al.*, 1996). Powell and Brantley (1992) argue that these firms have emerged due to the fact that biotechnology was a competence-destroying innovation for established firms in client industries such as chemicals and pharmaceuticals.

Incumbent firms lacked an understanding of biotechnology and thus used the new biotechnology firms to get access to biotechnology.

## References

Argyres, N.S. & Liebeskind, J.P. (1999). Contractual commitments, bargaining power, and governance inseparability: Incorporating history into the transaction cost theory of the firm. *Academy of Management Review*, **24**(1), 49–63.

Barney, J. (1991). Firm resources and sustained competitive advantage. *Journal of Management*, **17**(1), 99–120.

Bordieu, P. (1986). The forms of capital. In J.G. Richardson (ed.), *Handbook of Theory and Research for the Sociology of Education*, New York: Greenwood.

Brynjolfsson, E. (1994). Information assets, technology, and organization. *Management Science*, **40**(12), 1645–1662.

Burt, R.S. (1992). The social structure of competition. In N. Nohria & R.G. Eccles (eds), *Networks and Organizations: Structure, Form, and Action*, Boston, MA: Harvard Business School Press, 57–91.

Bühner, R. & Tuschke, A. (1996). Outsourcing. *Die Betriebswirtschaft*, **57**(1), 20–30.

Chatterji, D. (1996). Accessing external sources of technology. *Research Technology Management*, **39**(2), 48–56.

Chiesa, V. & Barbeschi, M. (1994). Technology strategy in competence-based competition. In G. Hamel & A. Heene (eds), *Competence-based Competition*, Chichester: Wiley, 293–314.

Coase, R. (1937). The economic nature of the firm. *Economica*, **IV**, 386–405.

Coleman, J. (1988). Social capital in the creation of human capital. *American Journal of Sociology*, **94**, S95–S120.

Dillmann, L. (1996). *Outsourcing in der Produktentwicklung*. Frankfurt: Lang.

Dosi, G. (1982). Technological paradigms and technological trajectories. *Research Policy*, **11**, 147–162.

Doz, Y. & Hamel, G. (1997). The use of alliances in implementing technology strategies. In M.L. Tushman & P. Anderson (eds), *Managing Strategic Innovation and Change*, New York: Oxford University Press, 556–580.

Doz, Y.L. & Hamel, G. (1998). *Alliance Advantage: The Act of Creating Value Through Partnering*. Cambridge, MA: Harvard Business School Press.

Eisenhardt, K.M. & Schoonhoven, C.B. (1996). Resource-based view of strategic alliance formation: Strategic and social effects in entrepreneurial firms. *Organization Science*, **7**(2), 136–150.

Gersick, C.J.G. (1991). Revolutionary change theories: A multilevel exploration of the punctuated equilibrium paradigm. *Academy of Management Review*, **16**(1), 10–36.

Ghoshal, S. & Moran, P. (1996). Bad for practice: A critique of the transaction cost theory. *Academy of Management Review*, **21**(1), 13–47.

Granovetter, M. (1985). Economic action and social structure: The problem of embeddedness. *American Journal of Sociology*, **91**(3), 481–510.

Granovetter, M. (1992). Problems of explanation in economic sociology. In N. Nohria & R.G. Eccles (eds), *Networks and Organizations: Structure, Form, and Action*, Boston, MA: Harvard Business School Press, 25–56.

Grant, R.M. (1991). The resource-based theory of competitive advantage: Implications for strategy formulation. *California Management Review*, **33**(3), 114–135.

Grossman, S. & Hart, O. (1986). The costs and benefits of ownership: A theory of vertical and lateral integration. *Journal of Political Economy*, **94**, 691–719.

Gulati, R. (1995a). Does familiarity breed trust? The implications of repeated ties for contractual choice in alliances. *Academy of Management Journal*, **38**(1), 85–112.
Gulati, R. (1995b). Social structure and alliance formation patterns: A longitudinal analysis. *Administrative Science Quarterly*, **40**(4), 619–652.
Hagedoorn, J. (1990). Organizational modes of inter-firm co-operation and technology transfer. *Technovation*, **10**(1), 17–30.
Hagedoorn, J. & Narula, R. (1996). Choosing modes of governance for strategic technology partnering: International sectoral differences. *International Journal of Business Studies*, 265–284.
Hagedoorn, J. & Schakenraad, J. (1990). Inter-firm partnership and co-operative strategies in core technologies. In C. Freeman & L. Soete (eds), *New Explorations in the Economics of Technological Change*, London: Pinter, 3–37.
Hamel, G. (1991). Competition for competence and interpartner learning within international strategic alliances. *Strategic Management Journal*, **12**, 83–103.
Hamel, G., Doz, Y.L. & Prahalad, C.K. (1989). Collaborate with your competitors—and win. *Harvard Business Review*, **67**, 133–139.
Hart, O. (1991). Incomplete contracts and the theory of the firm. In O.E. Williamson & S.G. Winter (eds), *The Nature of the Firm—Origins, Evolution, and Development*, New York: Oxford University Press, 138–158.
Hart, O. (1995). *Firms, Contracts, and Financial Structure*. Oxford: Clarendon Press.
Haveman, H.A. (1992). Between a rock and a hard place: Organizational change and performance under conditions of fundamental environmental transformation. *Administrative Science Quarterly*, **37**(1), 48–75.
Heene, A. & Sanchez, R. (eds). (1997). *Competence-Based Strategic Management*. Chichester: Wiley.
Henderson, R. & Cockburn, I. (1994). Measuring competence? Exploring firm effects in pharmaceutical research. *Strategic Management Journal*, **15**, 62–84.
Hennart, J.-F. (1988). A transaction costs theory of equity joint ventures. *Strategic Management Journal*, **9**, 361–374.
Hennart, J.-F. (1993). Explaining the swollen middle: Why most transactions are a mix of "market" and "hierarchy". *Organization Science*, **4**(4), 529–547.
Irwin, J.G., Hoffman, J.J. & Lamont, B.T. (1998). The effect of the acquisition of technological innovations on organizational performance: A resource-based view. *Journal of Engineering and Technology Management*, **15**, 25–54.
Jonash, R.S. (1996). Strategic technology leveraging: Making outsourcing work for you. *Research Technology Management*, 19–25.
Kogut, B. (1988). Joint ventures: Theoretical and empirical perspectives. *Strategic Management Journal*, **9**(4), 319–332.
Kogut, B. & Zander, U. (1992). Knowledge of the firm, combinative capabilities, and the replication of technology. *Organization Science*, **3**(3), 383–397.
Kogut, B. & Zander, U. (1993). Knowledge of the firm and the evolutionary theory of the multinational corporation. *Journal of International Business Studies*, **24**, 625–645.
Koka, B.R. & Prescott, J.E. (1998). Strategic alliances as social capital: A theory of the nature of social capital and its effect on firm performance. Paper presented at the Academy of Management Conference, San Diego, CA.
Koza, M.P. & Lewin, A.Y. (1998). The co-evolution of strategic alliances. *Organization Science*, **9**(3), 255–264.
Langlois, R.N. & Robertson, P.L. (1995). *Firms, Markets and Economic Change—A Dynamic Theory of Business Institutions*. London: Routledge.
Larson, A. (1992). Network dyads in entrepreneurial settings: A study of the

governance of exchange relationships. *Administrative Science Quarterly*, **37**(1), 76–104.

Lei, D., Hitt, M.A. & Bettis, R. (1996). Dynamic core competences through meta-learning and strategic context. *Journal of Management*, 22, 549–569.

Liebeskind, J.P. Oliver, A.L. Zucker, L. & Brewer, M. (1996). Social networks, learning, and flexibility: Sourcing scientific knowledge in new biotechnology firms. *Organization Science*, **7**(4), 428–443.

Lyles, M.A. & Schwenk, C.R. (1992). Top management, strategy and organizational knowledge structures. *Journal of Management Studies*, **29**(3), 155–174.

Madhavan, R., Koka, B.R. & Prescott, J.E. (1998). Networks in transition: How industry events (re)shape interfirm relationships. *Strategic Management Journal*, **19**(5), 439–459.

Madhok, A. & Tallman, S.B. (1998). Resources, transactions and rents: Managing value through interfirm collaborative relationships. *Organization Science*, **9**(3), 326–339.

Mang, P.Y. (1998). Exploiting innovation options: an empirical analysis of R&D-intensive firms. *Journal of Economic Behavior & Organization*, **35**, 229–242.

McAllister, D.J. (1995). Affect- and cognition-based trust as foundations for interpersonal cooperation in organizations. *Academy of Management Journal*, **38**(1), 24–59.

Nahapiet, J. & Ghoshal, S. (1998). Social capital, intellectual capital, and the organizational advantage. *Academy of Management Review*, **23**(2), 242–266.

Nelson, R.R. & Winter, S.G. (1982). *An Evolutionary Theory of Economic Change*. Cambridge, MA: The Belknap Press.

Nerkar, A.A. (1997). *The development of technological competence within firms: An evolutionary perspective*. Unpublished Dissertation, University of Pennsylvania, Philadelphia, PA.

Nicholls-Nixon, C.L. (1993). *Absorptive capacity and technology sourcing: Implications for responsiveness of established firms*. Unpublished Dissertation, Purdue University, Lafayette, IN.

Nooteboom, B. (1996). Trust, opportunism and governance: A process and control perspective. *Organization Studies*, **17**(6), 985–1010.

Nooteboom, B., Berger, H. & Noorderhaven, N.G. (1997). Effects of trust and governance on relational risk. *Academy of Management Journal*, **40**(2), 308–338.

Osborn, R.N. & Baughn, C.C. (1990). Forms of interorganizational governance for multinational alliances. *Academy of Management Journal*, **33**(3), 503–519.

Osborn, R.N. & Hagedoorn, J. (1997). The institutionalization and evolutionary dynamics of interorganizational alliances and networks. *Academy of Management Journal*, **40**(2), 261–278.

Penning, J.M. & Harianto, F. (1992). Technological networking and innovation implementation. *Organization Science*, **3**(3), 356–382.

Penrose, E. (1959). *The Theory of the Growth of the Firm*. Oxford: Oxford University Press.

Peteraf, M.A. (1993). The cornerstones of competitive advantage: A resource-based view. *Strategic Management Journal*, **14**, 179–191.

Picot, A. (1991). Ein neuer Ansatz zur Gestaltung der Leistungstiefe. *Zeitschrift für betriebswirtschaftliche Forschung*, **41**(4), 336–357.

Pisano, G.P. (1988). *Innovation through markets, hierarchies, and joint ventures: Technology strategy and collaborative arrangements in the biotechnology industry*. Unpublished Dissertation, University of California, Berkeley, CA.

Pisano, G.P. (1990). The R&D boundaries of the firm: An empirical analysis. *Administrative Science Quarterly*, **35**, 153–176.

Pisano, G.P. (1991). The governance of innovation: Vertical integration and collaborative arrangements in the biotechnology industry. *Research Policy*, **20**, 237–249.

Pisano, G.P. & Mang, P.Y. (1993). Collaborative product development and the market for know-how: Strategies and structures in the biotechnology industry. In R.A. Burgelman & R.S. Rosenbloom (eds), *Research on Technological Innovation, Management and Policy*. Greenwich, CT: JAI Press, 109–136.

Porter, M.E. (1991). Towards a dynamic theory of strategy. *Strategic Management Journal*, **12** (Winter Special Issue), 95–117.

Powell, W.W. (1990). Neither market nor hierarchy: Network forms of organization. In B.M. Staw & L.L. Cummings (eds), *Research in Organization Behavior*, Volume 12, Greenwich, CT: JAI Press, 295–336.

Powell, W.W. (1998). Learning from collaboration: Knowledge and networks in the biotechnology and pharmaceutical industries. *California Management Review*, **40**(3), 228–240.

Powell, W.W. & Brantley, P. (1992). Competitive cooperation in biotechnology: Learning through networks? In N. Nohria & R. Eccles (eds), *Networks and Organizations: Structure, Form and Action*, Boston, MA: Harvard Business School Press, 365–394.

Powell, W.W., Koput, K.W. & Smith-Doerr, L. (1996). Interorganizational collaboration and the locus of innovation: Networks of learning in biotechnology. *Administrative Science Quarterly*, **41**(1), 116–145.

Prahalad, C.K. & Hamel, G. (1990). The core competence of the corporation. *Harvard Business Review*, **68**, 79–91.

Putnam, R.D. (1995). Bowling alone: America's declining social capital. *Journal of Democracy*, **6**, 65–78.

Quinn, J.B. & Hilmer, F.G. (1994). Strategic outsourcing. *Sloan Management Review*, **35**, 43–56.

Ring, P.S. & van de Ven, A.H. (1994). Developmental process of cooperative interorganizational relationships. *Academy of Management Review*, **19**(1), 90–118.

Robertson, T.S. & Gatignon, H. (1998). Technology development mode: A transaction cost conceptualization. *Strategic Management Journal*, **19**, 515–531.

Romanelli, E. & Tushman, M.L. (1994). Organizational transformation as punctuated equilibrium: An empirical test. *Academy of Management Journal*, **37**(5), 1141–1166.

Rumelt, R.P. (1995). Inertia and transformation. In C.A. Montgomery (ed.), *Resource-based and Evolutionary Theories of the Firm: Towards a Synthesis*, Boston: Kluwer, 101–132.

Sackmann, S.A. (1992). Culture and subcultures: An analysis of organizational knowledge. *Administrative Science Quarterly*, **37**(1), 140–161.

Sakakibara, M. (1997). Heterogeneity of firm capabilities and cooperative research and development: An empirical examination of motives. *Strategic Management Journal*, **18** (Summer Special Issue), 143–164.

Sanchez, R. & Heene, A. (eds) (1997). *Strategic Learning and Knowledge Management*. Chichester: Wiley.

Sanchez, R., Heene, A. & Thomas, H. (eds) (1996). *Dynamics of Competence-based Competition*. Oxford: Elsevier Science.

Schneider, D. & Zieringer, C. (1991). *Make-or-buy-Strategien für F&E: transaktionskostenorientierte Überlegungen*. Wiesbaden: Gabler.

Simon, H.A. (1947). *Administrative Behavior*. New York: Macmillan.

Sobrero, M. (1996). Strategic management of interorganizational relations in new product development. Paper presented at the 16th annual international SMS conference, Phoenix, AZ, 10–13 November.

Sobrero, M. & Schrader, S. (1998). Structuring inter-firm relationships: A meta-analytic approach. *Organization Studies*, **19**(4), 585–615.

Steensma, H.K. (1996a). Acquiring technological competencies through inter-organizational collaboration: An organizational learning perspective. *Journal of Engineering and Technology Management*, **12**, 267–286.

Steensma, H.K. (1996b). *Strategic options in technology procurement: A theoretical integration and empirical analysis.* Unpublished Dissertation, Indiana University, Bloomington, IN.

Steensma, H.K. (1997). *Internalizing external technology: A model of governance mode choice.* Working paper, Indiana University, Bloomington, IN.

Stein, J. (1997). On building and leveraging competences across organizational borders: A socio-cognitive framework. In A. Heene & R. Sanchez (eds), *Competence-based Strategic Management*, Chichester: Wiley, 267–284.

Stuart, T.E. & Podolny, J.M. (1996). Local search and the evolution of technological capabilities. *Strategic Management Journal*, **17**, 21–38.

Tapon, F. (1989). A transaction cost analysis of innovations in the organization of pharmaceutical R&D. *Journal of Economic Behavior and Organization*, **12**, 197–213.

Teece, D.J. (1986). Profiting from technological innovation: Implications for integration, collaboration, licensing and public policy. *Research Policy*, **15**, 285–305.

Teece, D.J., Pisano, G. & Shuen, A. (1997). Dynamic capabilities and strategic management. *Strategic Management Journal*, **28**(7), 509–533.

Ulset, S. (1996). R&D outsourcing and contractual governance: An empirical study of commercial R&D projects. *Journal of Economic Behavior and Organization*, **30**, 63–82.

Uzzi, B. (1996). The sources and consequences of embeddedness for the economic performance of organizations: The network effect. *American Sociological Review*, **61**, 674–698.

Uzzi, B. (1997). Social structure and competition in interfirm networks: The paradox of embeddedness. *Administrative Science Quarterly*, **42**(1), 35–67.

Van de Ven, A.H. (1976). On the nature, formation and maintenance of relations among organizations. *Academy of Management Review*, **1**(1), 24–36.

Van de Ven, A.H. & Walker, G. (1984). The dynamics of interorganizational coordination. *Administrative Science Quarterly*, **29**(4), 598–621.

Verdin, P.J. & Williamson, P. (1994). Core competences, competitive advantage and market analysis: Forging the links. In G. Hamel & A. Heene (eds), *Competence-based Competition*, Chichester: Wiley, 77–110.

Von Krogh, G. & Roos, J. (1995). *Organizational Epistemology.* New York: St. Martin's Press.

Walker, G., Kogut, B. & Shan, W. (1997). Social capital, structural holes and the formation of an industry network. *Organization Science*, **8**(2), 109–125.

Walsh, J.P. (1995). Managerial and organizational cognition: Notes from a trip down memory lane. *Organization Science*, **6**(3), 280–321.

Weick, K.E. (1995). *Sensemaking in Organizations.* London: Sage.

Wernerfelt, B. (1984). A resource-based view of the firm. *Strategic Management Journal*, **5**, 171–180.

Williamson, O.E. (1975). *Market and Hierarchies: Analysis and Antitrust Implications.* New York: Free Press.

Williamson, O.E. (1985). *The Economic Institutions of Capitalism.* New York: Free Press.

Williamson, O.E. (1991). Comparative economic organization: The analysis of discrete structural alternatives. *Administrative Science Quarterly*, **36**(2), 269–296.
Zajac, E.J. & Olsen, C.P. (1993). From transaction cost to transactional value analysis: Implications for the study of interorganizational strategies. *Journal of Management Studies*, **30**(1), 131–145.

# 14

# Salient Options: Strategic Resource Allocation Under Uncertainty

RITA GUNTHER MCGRATH, PAOLA DUBINI

## INTRODUCTION

Strategic renewal requires organizational commitment to new, often highly uncertain, strategic projects (Ghemawat, 1991; Guth & Ginsberg, 1990; Christensen & Bower, 1996). As is widely recognized, however, the actual process of strategic commitment is not very well understood, and departs in many critical respects from extant theoretical models (Brown & Eisenhardt, 1997).

In the boundedly rational economic perspective, managers are presumed to favor those projects that they believe have the highest probability of delivering economic performance (March & Simon, 1958; Allison, 1971). As is well understood, these beliefs are often derived through processes that are not objectively rational. Present value rules, for instance, are ritualistically referred to and ignored (Bettis & Hitt, 1995; Dixit & Pindyck, 1994). Risks are viewed in light of a "managerial", not statistical, logic (March & Shapira, 1987). Resource commitments are made from alternatives remaining after a path-dependent and cumulative process has truncated the range of potential choices (Nelson & Winter, 1982; Teece *et al.*, 1994; Christensen & Bower, 1996). And the recognition of the need to make

*Dynamic Strategic Resources: Development, Diffusion and Integration.*
Edited by Michael A. Hitt, Patricia Gorman Clifford, Robert D. Nixon and Kevin P. Coyne.

a choice at all is hindered by an assortment of cognitive and emotional biases (Kiesler & Sproull, 1982).

From a different point of view, the non-rational idiosyncrasy of the resource allocation process derives from the confrontation of interest groups to gain access and control resources (Crozier, 1964). In this view, decisions are made which best suit the preferences of those in power, namely those who have gained control over critical organizational contingencies (Thompson, 1967; Salancik & Pfeffer, 1974; MacMillan, 1978; MacMillan & Jones, 1986). Creating commitment, particularly to uncertain new undertakings, is viewed as a delicate process of negotiating with those in power at various levels in the organization, in order to gain their sympathy, interest and conviction (Bower, 1970; Burgelman, 1983). The political dynamic in these more intuitive than rational models is often held accountable for a systematic tendency to under-invest in exploration (March, 1991), or conversely to commit to projects which are economically undesirable as a function of selfishness or ego involvement (Levinthal & March, 1993; Hayward & Hambrick, 1997). A major motivator is the desire on the part of the dominant coalition to preserve the status quo.

Evidence from empirical studies is mixed. On the one hand, championing processes that lead decision makers in companies to make commitments to new projects are seen as crucial, lending support to the more intuitive, political view (Burgelman, 1983). On the other, recent studies of managerial decision making show that economic considerations do enter into the decisions in a major way (Dixit & Pindyck, 1994). The resulting situation is that the allocation process is recognized as one that is not premised on strictly rational decision processes, yet simultaneously that a purely political, intuitive perspective on the process is also not adequate.

In this paper, we explore whether real options reasoning might be a useful way to bring together these perspectives. Real options reasoning, as suggested by previous authors (Bowman & Hurry, 1993; Mitchell & Hamilton, 1988; McGrath, 1997), offers a logical basis for seemingly irrational choices on the part of managers (using conventional logic) and also suggests ways in which seemingly intuitive decisions can have a rational basis.

Four differentiating characteristics of a real options approach from more conventional approaches are (1) recognition that investments can provide a firm with access to future benefits that are not evident at the time of the investment (for instance, by creating the conditions in which an organization reduces uncertainty or creates knowledge); (2) containment of downside costs while preserving upside opportunity; (3) creating the conditions for proprietary action (typically through path-dependent resource accumulation or knowledge development); and (4) emphasis on the value of managerial flexibility (see, for example, Sanchez, 1993).

Our purpose is to add empirical evidence to a growing theoretical literature in strategy. We empirically demonstrate that real options reasoning suggests a way to integrate models of the resource allocation process. Real options reasoning can account for a variety of anomalies poorly explained by conventional approaches. It can explain, for instance, why strategists make intuitive choices that appear to be economically illogical, revealing these to be quite sensible. For instance, the common practice of imposing high corporate hurdle rates on proposed projects implicitly recognizes that irreversible commitments can have long-term consequences beyond those of the project under consideration, regardless of its net present value. This represents a way of compensating for the cost of lost flexibility (Dixit & Pindyck, 1994). Flexibility is particularly important under uncertain conditions, as initiatives seldom work out as planned, meaning that the ability to redirect enhances value.

We begin by considering a resource allocation process in which top management is driven by rational profit maximization; we then consider a resource allocation process in which either the project is promising high returns or needs top management commitment, in which case it has to demonstrate the capacity to create new opportunities. We then contrast these theoretical relations with a real options reasoning perspective. These contrasting theoretical models are tested by comparing a series of structural models on data from 239 uncertain strategic projects.

## Corporate Commitment: Alternative Perspectives

Given limited, and often scarce, resources, senior managers are constantly in the position of making tradeoffs among competing opportunities. In explaining why managers make the choices that they do, scholars tend to rely on one or the other of two dominant perspectives: the economically rational and the politically intuitive.

### Rational Decision Processes

Under what economists famously call norms of rationality, managers should allocate resources to those projects with the highest chances of delivering economic performance (March & Simon, 1958; Allison, 1971). This means projects that can contribute economic "rents" to the firm, where rents refer to sustainable supra-normal returns, in excess of industry norms (Alchian, 1991).

The capacity to generate rents is associated with the ability to deliver returns in excess of the firm's cost of capital, thus increasing the value of the firm overall (Stewart, 1991). This is presumed to be a core objective for managers, hence a key motivation for their behavior. Rents may derive from the creation of idiosyncratically productive combinations of resources (Penrose, 1959; Peteraf, 1993) that make the company unique in the eyes of its targeted market. Expectations for high rents are best justified when those in a firm perceive that it has created uniquely productive strategic assets (Peteraf, 1993; Amit & Schoemaker, 1993).

A key driver of "Ricardian" rents is represented by the firm's ability to operate with greater efficiency than its rivals. If the sources of this superior productivity are associated with path-dependent, difficult-to-imitate routines and resource combinations, the "Ricardian" rents that ensue are likely to be durable, and to provide one basis for a lasting competitive advantage (Dierickx & Cool, 1989; Barney, 1991; Nelson & Winter, 1982).

Another driver for the judgment that a project might have high rent potential stems from its option value. Real options reasoning speaks to classes of investments in real assets that have a similar structure and investment logic as do investments in financial options (Dixit & Pindyck, 1994). Initial investments create the right but not the obligation to participate in future opportunity, yet should events prove the opportunity not to be attractive, executives may elect not to make further investments. Among the most powerful ideas in real options reasoning is thus the notion that projects have option value, above and beyond the value that might be derived by explicit calculation up-front. The often substantial follow-on investments to capture the opportunity are usually referred to as investments in "exercising" the real option (see Trigeorgis, 1996).

As with a financial option, in which increases in volatility increase the value of the option, option value for an uncertain new project grows as the variance of potential returns becomes greater (McGrath, 1997). This is because the potential upside gain increases, while the downside loss (the price of the option) remains limited to the investment in creating the real option. Similar to a financial option is the idea that a real option may be held, traded or combined with other real options, which can generate returns for the firm even if exercise does not occur (Kogut, 1991). Thus, a technology may be licensed, a joint venture may be sold, a new business division may be spun off, or a complementary partner may be found, all ways in which a real option can generate future value, even if it is not exercised (Kogut & Kulatilaka, 1994).

The value of a real option is also associated with knowledge and resource creation effects. As idiosyncratic knowledge is a basic source of competitive advantage (Nonaka, 1991: 96; Conner & Prahalad, 1996), new projects should be evaluated and supported in terms not only of the short-term rent they can generate, but also on the basis of the amount of idiosyncratic knowledge they can mobilize and generate, thus contributing to organizational learning (March, 1991; Argyris & Schon, 1996). Investing in new projects can help a firm better understand and respond to new market needs, can yield superior insight into new technologies and can position a firm favorably with respect to industry standards and other contingencies. Moreover, knowledge capitalization and real options reasoning can overcome difficulties in assessing new project potential by adding a process dimension to it, as Block and MacMillan (1985) suggest.

A major difference between decisions using a real options logic and decisions relying on conventional decision rules (such as the present value rule) is that they are seen as sequential. Small investments in a project are made in order to create the right, but not the obligation, to participate in future opportunities. In case of success, the option is "exercised" (Trigeorgis, 1996) and the company commits itself to a full-scale new project. In the event of failure, losses are limited. Investing in real options can create a preemptive strategy to occupy a competitive space; from the point of view of the internal power coalition, it is a parsimonious way to explore new possibilities without challenging the dominant group.

This way of looking at the economic rationality model accommodates projects with a highly uncertain outcome by including the option value variable. As Bettis and Hitt (1995) observe, managers increasingly find themselves confronted with genuine uncertainty (as opposed to risk), where uncertainty is characterized as "unknowability, where the mean and distribution of outcomes cannot be reasonably assumed" (p. 12). New projects are notorious for their uncertainty. Success might depend, for example, on market evolution and attractiveness rather than anything the firm's managers do (Stuart & Abetti, 1987; Sandberg & Hofer, 1987). Such developments are hard to predict. As Eisenhardt and Zbaracki (1992) point out, short-term rent potential assessments are inadequate to the tasks of assigning a value to such projects (although tools such as net present value models are alive and well in business school textbooks (Brealey & Myers, 1981)).

What this suggests is that either short-term productivity or longer-term option value could drive senior management judgments with respect to the economic attractiveness of a project. It is therefore possible to make the following hypothesis:

> H1: Resource commitment to projects will be greater to the extent that they are perceived by top management as having the potential to generate rents, which in turn are seen to stem from either productivity or option value.

The first hypothesis suggests that, other things being equal, managers will find those projects that have rent potential to be most deserving of commitment. Economic potential on its own, however, is known to be insufficient to drive corporate resource allocation (Bower, 1970). McGrath (1995), for instance, found little relationship between the economic potential of projects and the level of corporate enthusiasm for them. In a four-year field study of the histories of 23 corporate ventures within a single financial services organization, she gathered data on rent potential, a construct she termed "market worth". She also gathered evidence on the level of political interest in the venture, measuring the salience of each venture to senior executives. She found that four of the projects had high rent potential, yet the firm never really made a commitment to them. Five other projects received considerable commitment, yet showed little market potential. All nine of the ventures in the sample which showed low company commitment were discontinued (some by being sold off), even though nearly half of them had high market impact scores. Thus, good-looking numbers don't seem to be enough to assure survival within the firm.

A further danger with purely economic models is that they are associated with better and enhanced exploitation of existing resources. It is likely that existing customers, technologies and market opportunities would be favored over constructs such as option value in the resource allocation process. Given the observed complex negotiation process leading to resource allocation, other elements seem to be important. In order to account for this element, scholars have suggested a process in which rational considerations are combined with what Frederickson (1985) termed an "intuitive" approach.

## The Intuitive Perspective

In an intuitive perspective, the economic potential of a project is only one driver of senior-level commitment, and often not the most important driver at that (Bower, 1970; Burgelman, 1983). In this view, although economic considerations do have a part to play, heuristics manifest in intuitive and experiential considerations are also extremely important. Moreover, such "non-rational" processes are thought to increase in both frequency and utility as the level of uncertainty increases and the time available for making choices shortens (Eisenhardt, 1989).

One implication of departing from the rational model of decision making is that the notion of firms as unitary decision makers must be left behind. Instead, the personal experience of individuals, their previous successes, cognitive biases, interpersonal affiliations, preferences and egos are seen to strongly influence the commitments they make. The reasons, in other words, for supporting a project are idiosyncratic, and may vary a good deal from firm to firm and from one decision maker to another. The result is that the process of generating firm-level commitment to a strategic project is fundamentally political (Pettigrew, 1973; Day, 1994; MacMillan, 1978).

In a political system, resource allocation flows follow the interests, desires and maneuverings of the most powerful people (Salancik & Pfeffer, 1974; Pfeffer, 1992). Projects that those in power in a firm believe to be important get more attention, have greater legitimacy, and are defended more vigorously and with a wider variety of tactics than projects considered unimportant (Eisenhardt & Bourgeois, 1988). Under economic rationality, economic criteria such as rent potential are seen to act as the key drivers for the attention and interest of senior managers. Intuitive reasoning, in contrast, suggests that managers may have many reasons other than economic potential to find a project interesting and worthy of support.

Stated in a different way, it can be argued that there are two paths leading to resource allocation. Either projects are extremely promising in terms of rent potential, or it is necessary that they are heavily championed by top management, who might use experience to assess the long-term potential of the new project, and power to see that it receives resources. While rent potential associated with a new project can be assessed in a relatively objective way within the company (and therefore can be defended by the project team members), top management attention and support is necessary for projects whose outcome cannot be predicted and whose real potential will become apparent only in process. Therefore

> H2: Other things being equal, high rent potential projects are likely to receive resource commitment without the intervention of senior managers, but high option value projects are likely to depend upon senior level salience to receive support.

We have thus suggested that resource commitment decisions are multifaceted. On the one hand, expectations for market success should have a positive influence, as we suggested in the first hypothesis. On the other, senior-level salience should have a positive influence, as we suggest in the second hypothesis. This brings us to the point of considering whether real options reasoning might help us define the connection between judgments of economic rationality and judgments of interest to senior managers.

## Real Options Reasoning and Corporate Knowledge Mobilization

Over the years, adherents of different perspectives on strategic resource allocation have delighted in critiquing one another (see Eisenhardt &

Zbaracki, 1992). We thus have considerable empirical research that shows that economic models poorly describe reality, yet also considerable empirical research that suggests that a purely political process can be damaging, dysfunctional, and distasteful (Gandz & Murray, 1980; Eisenhardt & Bourgeois, 1988).

Recently, an alternative view of the strategy process has emerged that offers some promise of integrating economic and intuitive rationales for the support of projects. This is a view of the strategic commitment process as one of opening, exercising and exiting "real" options (Bowman & Hurry, 1993; Kogut, 1991; Mitchell & Hamilton, 1988; McGrath, 1997).

In this model, the economic and the intuitive perspectives on resource allocation no longer need be in conflict. Rather, they mutually reinforce organizational learning dynamics. Real options reasoning suggests that option value need not be only another factor in present value calculations, nor need it be so difficult to anticipate that it can only rely on political maneuverings to result in resource commitment. Projects that are not promising in terms of present value might have enough option value to excite a positive intuitive response. Indeed, Dixit and Pindyck (1994) and Trigeorgis (1996) show that incorporating an option value term explains actual managerial investment behavior better than straightforward calculation of NPV does.

The primary conclusion they draw from real options reasoning is that it may make sense for a project to be allocated resources when it is perceived to open new opportunity spaces, even without the immediate expectation of a payoff in terms of short-term rents. Further, this expected option premium is sensed intuitively by managers, who often characterize it in terms of an experience-based sense of attractiveness. In this respect, the resource allocation process is company specific and path dependent, as each company has its own knowledge base and learning mechanisms and as the resource allocation process of top management is influenced by individual experience and group political dynamics. Moreover, this idiosyncrasy is manifest in the different things that are of interest to senior management—judgments of rent potential and option value, for example, are likely to vary by manager, resulting in differential levels of excitement and enthusiasm, or salience.

Differences in perceived option value underpin much of the theory of entrepreneurial insight (Knight, 1921) in which differential willingness to take risk under uncertainty yields returns to the entrepreneur who is willing to take risks that others are not. Several factors contribute to these differences in perception. First, under uncertainty, different decision makers are likely to utilize different indicators of future value, rendering judgments of this value heterogeneous. For instance, as prospect theory (Kahneman & Tversky, 1979) holds, whether an envisaged future is perceived as a gain or a loss to the perceiver is likely to influence judgments about its worth. Further, assumptions about likely future trajectories are apt to differ depending upon the organizational location and background of the person making the judgments, and are apt to be heavily influenced by such variables as organizational level, functional experience, age and position in the social network within the company. In other words, since the assessment of option value is largely a matter of deriving assumptions from the data, different individuals are likely to make different value judgments.

We therefore propose a third influence on resource allocation to new projects, consistent with the following hypotheses:

> H3: Salience to top managers will increase as a function of either increases in rent potential or increases in option value for an uncertain project.

In the empirical discussion that follows, we develop and test the proposed relations in the three hypotheses with three different structural models, each of which adds or removes a possible path to resource commitment on the part of managers in the firm. We present all three models in an attempt to tease out the subtleties in the relations among the constructs.

## Methods

### Sample

We measure the effects of strategic resource allocation decisions at project level with survey instruments collected for a sample of 239 uncertain new projects. For the most part, the relationship between company and project in our dataset is 1 : 1. About 20 companies contributed data for more than one project, but no company contributed data for more than three projects. The multiple-project companies all gave us projects in different, unrelated lines of business. This limits the risk of a single-company bias. All respondents were fluent in English and completed surveys in English. Prior to completing the surveys, respondents were instructed on the firm-specific interpretation to be used of potentially confusing terms (such as "the offering" or "customers and clients").

Each project had a team working on it and a senior executive as project leader; all projects were identified by senior executives (not necessarily the project leader) as strategically important. Projects were solicited from a variety of sources, including executives personally known to members of the research team and their colleagues, and executives associated with programs operating at our research institutions. To be included in the sample, a project had to meet the following criteria: (1) it must be considered by at least one senior executive in the firm to represent a significant strategic initiative; (2) it must have at least three full-time employees working on it (the average being four to five people per team); (3) it must be uncertain, in that one or more of the markets, processes, technologies or products to be developed must be new for the parent firm; (4) all group members with significant project responsibilities must commit to providing survey data; and (5) it must be currently underway, with outcomes as yet unknown. Although the reader should be aware that this is a convenience sample, these criteria were developed to avoid biases stemming from retrospective recall, unrepresentative sampling and *post-hoc* selective sampling that are characteristic of much research into new products and new projects (see March & Sutton, 1997; Brown & Eisenhardt, 1995).

## Survey Reliability and Validity

All employees with a significant responsibility for achieving project goals (whether or not they were dedicated full-time to the project)—i.e. all project team members—completed a survey questionnaire, which contained items measuring each of the theoretical constructs discussed above. The organizations providing data did so with the expectation that they would be able to use the results diagnostically (note that presentation of results occurred only after data collection); for this reason, some companies went through the data gathering process a few times during the development of the project. In these cases, only the results for the first round have been used. All managers involved contributed considerable time and several companies contributed funding. This clearly distinguishes the surveys used here from randomly mailed questionnaires. It further suggests a substantial level of interest in and commitment on the part of respondent firms to making sure that the data provided accurately reflect what was actually happening in a project. All responses were held in strict confidence.

Respondents scored each item on 1 to 5 Likert-type scales, where higher scores are always associated with higher levels of the construct. The respondent set's average response for each item was first calculated. Then these average scores for each item were totaled and averaged across items for each section of the questionnaire representing a construct, thus providing an overall grand average for each construct. This is similar to the approach employed by Gresov, Drazin and van de Ven (1989). They point out a major advantage: when scores are totaled across several items in a large sample, with group responses to large number of items, biases of individual responses are averaged out and the resulting interpretation of results is conservative (see also McGrath, MacMillan and Venkataraman, 1995, for a more recent application of this approach).

The Cronbach Alpha for each construct exceeded the recommended level of .7 (Nunnally, 1978) for all respondents. The recommended .7 level was also achieved for the five largest national sub-samples in the data (analyzing only responses from nationals of the United States, the United Kingdom, Italy, Finland, and Japan). This suggests that the reliability of the measures holds across different cultures.

Many other checks for validity and reliability were conducted. Harmon's single-factor test for common method bias (Podsakoff & Organ, 1986) was performed. Items from the different constructs separated cleanly, meaning that no item from one construct loaded greater than .5 on a factor associated with another construct. This reduces concerns regarding common method bias. Discriminant validity was also checked. In every case, the correlations within construct were greater than the correlations across constructs, reducing concerns regarding common response bias. In short, the results of a number of widely accepted tests reveal support the reliability and validity of the measures used here.

## CONSTRUCTS

Five constructs were analyzed for this study. **Resource commitment** represents the amount of budget, staff and other assets respondents perceive as dedicated to the project, in competition with other projects (Alchian & Demsetz, 1972: 790). This is the dependent variable in our study. **Salience** represents the amount of visible and public attention senior executives are perceived to be paying to the project (Guth & MacMillan, 1986; MacMillan & Jones, 1986). **Rent potential** is a probability estimate of the likelihood of generating rents at project maturity (Alchian, 1991; Barney, 1986; Amit & Schoemaker, 1993; Bowman, 1974). **Productivity** is a judgment of the extent to which the project will achieve unusual efficiency gains, relative to current firm performance and relative to competitors (Peteraf, 1993). Finally, **option value** is a measure of the extent to which the project is perceived to open new opportunities for the firm (Bowman & Hurry, 1993; Kogut, 1991) as well as offering knowledge exploration and exploitation potential (March, 1991). The items representing each construct, and associated Cronbach Alpha coefficients, are presented in the Appendix. A correlation matrix for each of the variables was calculated. This is presented in TABLE 14.1. The variables were not significantly skewed.

TABLE 14.1 Descriptive statistics and correlation matrix (N = 239)[a]

| | Mean | SD | Salience | Rent | Option value | Resource commitment |
|---|---|---|---|---|---|---|
| Productivity | 3.21 | 0.76 | .19** (.002) | .41*** (.0001) | −0.07 ns | .15* (0.02) |
| Salience | 3.99 | 0.70 | | .23*** (.0002) | .15* (.02) | .59*** (.0001) |
| Rent potential | 66.1 | 14.00 | | | −.11 (.08) | .21** (.0014) |
| Option value | 1.67 | 1.44 | | | | .13* (.05) |
| Resource commitment | 3.35 | 0.75 | | | | |

[a] Significance levels:
*p < .05
**p < .01
***p < .001
ns = not significant.

The variable representing the option value construct has a relatively low score and a high standard deviation. This suggests that for our sample there is considerable variety in the perceived option value for each project. It also suggests that respondents' estimation of option value is conservative, given the relatively low mean.

An important result in the correlation matrix is that option value is negatively correlated (though not significantly, even at the .10 level) with rent potential. This matters, because an argument is sometimes forwarded that option value is simply another term in a standard NPV calculation and can be treated as such. This result supports the idea that managers evaluate option value differently from rent potential and make a firm distinction between them. There is similarly no significant correlation between option value and productivity, suggesting that future opportunities and today's efficiency objectives do not stem from the same source.

Rent potential, as expected, is positively and significantly correlated with salience, productivity and resource commitment. There is also a positive and significant correlation between resource commitment and salience, consistent with the idea that those projects which have intuitive appeal, as evidenced in their ability to command the attention, support and backing of those in power, will tend also to obtain access to needed resources (Eisenhardt, 1989). In the analysis that follows, we develop and compare structural models for three alternative paths to resource commitment.

## Structural Analysis of Alternative Models

We used the LISREL procedure in SAS to develop three structural models that test alternative relationships between salience, rent potential and option value in the allocation of resources to uncertain new projects. A word on the occasionally confusing interpretation of "fit" in structural models may be in order at this point. With structural modeling, the equivalent of the null hypothesis is that the paths defined in the structural model do not adequately represent the relationships in the data. A high chi-square and a p-value, therefore, of less than .05 can therefore be taken as evidence of poor fit, while a p-value of greater than .05 is usually accepted as evidence of adequate fit (Bollen, 1989). Our approach to the empirical analysis was therefore to derive a set of relationships from extant theory, assess the results and reject those models with poor fit.

### Model 1: Economic Rational Reasoning

This model tests H1, the hypothesis that projects with the greatest economic potential will attract the most attention and consequently commitment from senior managers. Rent potential can be seen to be relatively shorter-term (deriving from productivity gains) or longer-term (deriving from option value). Option value, in other words, is characterized in this model as simply another term in an NPV-type benefit calculation. Table 14.2 presents the results of the analysis, with the resultant model graphically depicted in Figure 14.1.

Table 14.2 Results for Model 1: Economic rational reasoning

| | | |
|---|---|---|
| Rent potential = | 0.4083 *Productivity | – 0.0826* Option value + residual |
| Standard Error | 0.0589 BETA2 | – 0.0589 BETA1 |
| T value | 6.9310 | – 1.4020 |
| Salience = | 0.2355 *Rent potential | + residual |
| Standard Error | 0.0630 GAM2 | |
| T value | 3.7384 | |
| Resource commitment = | 0.5867 *Salience | + residual |
| Standard Error | 0.0525 GAM1 | |
| T value | 11.1777 | |
| Fit criterion | 0.0587 | |
| Goodness of fit index | 0.9778 | |
| Chi square | 13.9656 | |
| Prob > chi**2 | 0.0158 | |
| Bollen (1989) Non-normed Index Delta2 = 0.9475 | | |

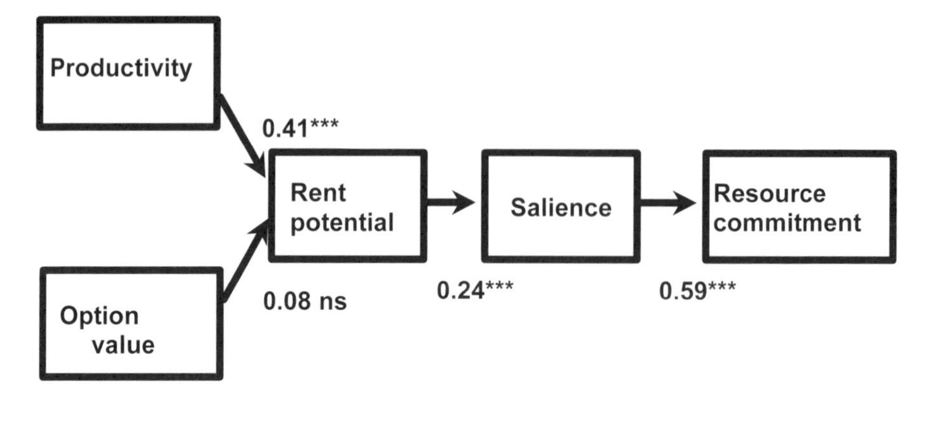


**Chi-square = 13.97 (p = .016)**
**Significance levels are explained in Table 14.1**

FIGURE 14.1 Economic rational reasoning

Since the p-value for this model is only .016, it does not exhibit good fit to the data, although some of the paths in this model (notably between productivity and rent potential, rent potential and salience, and salience and resource commitment) are significant.

## Model 2: Separate Routes to Resource Commitment

In Model 2, we test the argument that economic rationality and intuition of option value, that becomes manifest in salience, comprise two separate paths to the attainment of resource commitment. Results are presented in TABLE 14.3 and graphically depicted in FIGURE 14.2. This model addresses H2, namely that high rent potential projects can find support independent of senior level salience (since they make economic good sense), while projects with option value need salience to receive support. This addresses the issue of whether both the economic rationality school and the intuitive school are correct and in parallel. In other words, the two approaches may represent separate paths to the attainment of resource commitment.

Unfortunately, the chi-square for Model 2 is 22.3 with $p = .0005$, meaning that the parallel path model doesn't fit the data well. The paths between productivity and rent potential and between option potential and salience are significant, but the model overall does not explain resource commitment well enough.

TABLE 14.3 Results for Model 2: Separate routes to resource commitment

| | | | |
|---|---|---|---|
| Rent potential = | 0.4140 *Productivity | + residual | |
| Standard Error | 0.0590 BETA1 | | |
| T value | 7.0171 | | |
| Salience = | 0.1503 *Option value | + residual | |
| Standard Error | 0.0641 BETA2 | | |
| T value | 2.3455 | | |
| Resource commitment = | 0.5700 *Salience | + 0.0711 *Rent potential | + residual |
| Standard Error | 0.0523 GAM1 | + 0.0523 GAM2 | |
| T value | 10.8991 | + 1.3591 | |
| Fit criterion | 0.0938 | | |
| Goodness of fit index | 0.9654 | | |
| Chi square | 22.3171 | | |
| Prob > chi * *2 | 0.0005 | | |
| Bollen (1989) Non-normed Index Delta2 = 0.8986 | | | |

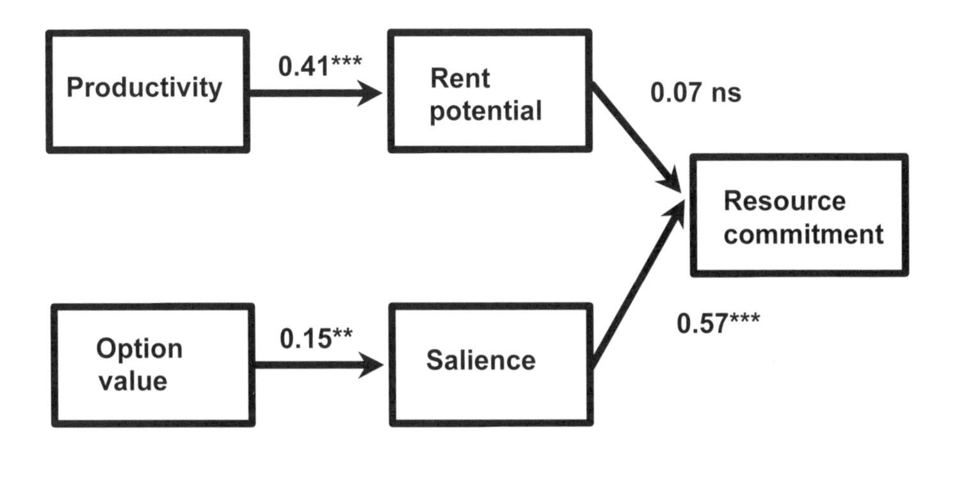


FIGURE 14.2 Separate routes to resource commitment

We have thus tested two hypotheses with respect to resource allocation, and found that neither appears to explain resource commitment well. This suggests that our third hypothesis may have more promise, which we test using a third model.

## The Proposed Model

In the third model, we test how the intuitive model mingles with the rational model to take into account company specificity—in terms of resources—and path dependence in the resource allocation process. Results are presented in TABLE 14.4, and graphically depicted in FIGURE 14.3.

TABLE 14.4 Results for Model 3: The salient options model

| | | | |
|---|---|---|---|
| Rent potential = | 0.4140 *Productivity | + residual | |
| Standard Error | 0.0590 BETA1 | | |
| T value | 7.0171 | | |
| Salience = | 0.2554 *Rent potential | + 0.1788 *Option value | + residual |
| Standard Error | 0.0620 GAM2 | + 0.0620 BETA1 | |
| T value | 4.1216 | + 2.8858 | |
| Resource commitment = | 0.5867 *Salience | + residual | |
| Standard Error | 0.0523 GAM1 | | |
| T value | 11.2203 | | |
| Fit criterion | 0.0330 | | |
| Goodness of fit index | 0.9874 | | |
| Chi square | 7.8424 | | |
| Prob > chi**2 | 0.1651 | | |
| Bollen (1989) Non-normed Index Delta2 = 0.9834 | | | |

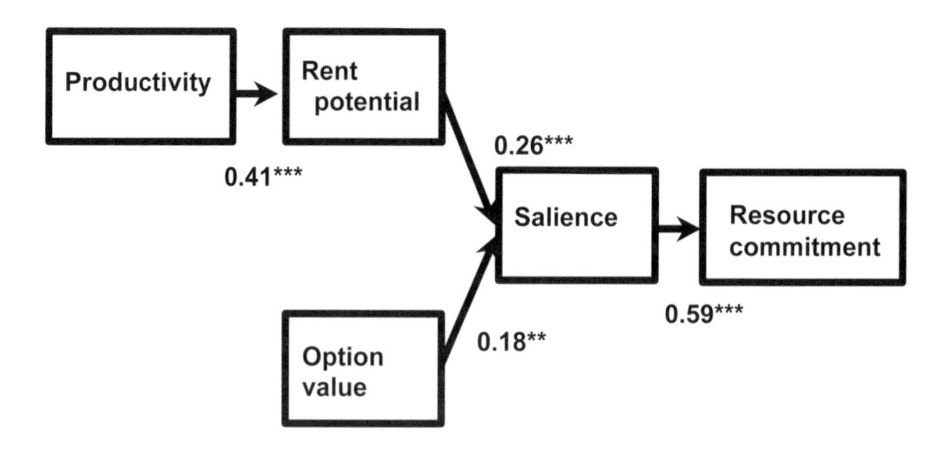


FIGURE 14.3 The proposed salient options model

In Model 3, salience is a positive and significant driver of resource commitment. Salience, however, can be generated either by near-term rent potential (as the positive and significant path suggests) or by longer-term option value (again, a positive and significant path). This suggests that, as advocates of an intuitive view have long argued, salience is essential in securing initial resource commitment to uncertain new projects. Projects with significant option value need time, that salience grants, to engage in exploration of the idea until rent potential can be more objectively assessed.

Salience can be created from either of two possible paths. A project with attractive rent potential is likely to receive more attention, and subsequently more resource commitment, than a project with a less attractive profile. Alternatively, however, projects with high option value can also generate salience, and subsequent resource commitment, even in the absence of near-term rent potential. The latter projects we term "salient options". This model, with a chi-square of 7.84 ($p = .165$), fits the data well.

Having tested three alternative theoretical models before offering the model presented in FIGURE 14.3 as the proposed model, we next tested other alternatives. The procedure we followed was to systematically remove one path at a time, then add one path at a time to the proposed model (Model 3) to see if fit improves by dropping a path or adding a path. None of the alternative models we tested fits the data better than the proposed model.

## DISCUSSION

Model 3 allows us to articulate a more refined set of relations than those proposed in the initial discussion and the first two hypotheses. It essentially suggests that without salience, there will be no resource commitment to an uncertain project, and without either rent potential or option value, there will be little salience. In this study, we integrate constructs that are central to three core streams in the strategic resource allocation literature and show not only that they matter, but how and with what effects.

From the rational economic point of view, one would expect idiosyncratic economic potential to be an important driver of commitment. Our results suggest that this is so, but that pure economic potential may not be enough. Economic potential, represented here by rent potential, is indeed important. Economic potential on its own, however, is not enough to drive corporate resource allocation. Unless the economic potential of a project is sufficiently compelling to senior executives that they find it salient, resource commitment will not necessarily follow. This point regarding salience reinforces the arguments made by Christensen (1997) and others, that innovative projects need to be able to create salience to receive commitment, and that this is often difficult in the confines of a business preoccupied with established opportunities rather than new ones.

Our results strongly support the arguments long offered by scholars suggesting a more intuitive view of the strategic commitment process than that of the economic rationality school. Salience, the extent to which a project generates enthusiasm and attention on the part of senior executives, is indeed a powerful predictor of resource commitment. Our results further shed some light on the likely drivers of salience.

Our data suggest that salience is significantly affected by the perceived economic benefit to the firm of engaging in a project, rather than the pure self-interest of senior decision makers. Thus, high rent potential projects are likely to be seen as interesting and relevant. Interestingly, so too are projects with high option value, even if their shorter-term prospects will not substantially enhance the bottom line.

This suggests that real options reasoning offers a useful complement to more conventional views of resource allocation. Executives in our study are supportive not only of those projects with clear and immediate economic potential, but also of those projects that can create option value. The construct in itself is particularly useful in the case of new projects, as it allows the development of evaluation criteria to assess the economic potential in light of potential opportunities, rather than shorter-term considerations.

## IMPLICATIONS

The results of our study offer several implications for future theoretical and normative directions in strategic resource allocation.

They first support those who argue that there is a need to modify some of the assumptions implicit in a strictly rational economic rationality perspective. Those who question the assumption of an efficient internal market for limited corporate resources are supported by our results (see Eisenhardt & Zbaracki, 1992). Salience, a judgmental construct, is seen to powerfully influence resource allocations.

Instead of a process in which the most economically attractive projects are funded to the extent that the corporate coffers allow, the salience effect introduces an idiosyncratic and path-dependent element in allocation decisions, since it takes into consideration the specificity of the company resource base, organizational dynamics and management composition. This offers empirical support for Van de Ven's (1986) observation that new initiatives represent ideas that must be "managed into good currency" whether they are economically attractive or not. It also serves as a reminder that economic potential alone does not necessarily generate resource commitment. Rather, salience must be generated as well.

As some new-project champions are apt to forget, the struggle to capture the hearts and minds of senior managers is as relevant to the long-term outcome of the strategic resource allocation process as the struggle to capture market share or make a technological breakthrough (see Block & MacMillan, 1993). In addition to minding the economic store, then, venture champions need to take into account competition for scarce space on the managerial agenda.

This suggests that future theories of corporate-level resource allocation should characterize managerial salience as a scarce resource in short supply, every bit as much as they might so characterize such resources as highly skilled people or physical assets. This suggests a form of internal market for salience. Projects intended to provide a source of corporate renewal compete in this market not only with other projects, but also with all other calls on the attention and interest of senior executives. Indeed, as Hitt *et al.*, (1996) find, the greater the number of other activities distracting managers from new initiatives and innovative projects, the less innovation a firm is likely to pursue.

Much activity relevant to the market for corporate control (such as mergers, acquisitions, takeovers and various forms of alliance) can potentially have a serious distractive effect. This suggests significant limitations to the ability of managers to continue new business development in the face of other events that are highly salient to them.

An encouraging result of our study is that at least in our sample, executives appear to be willing to invest in uncertain projects with long-run option potential. This offers hope of firms being able to avoid the dangers of excessive short-term focus and "simplification" in the corporate repertoire (Miller, 1993). Were executives not to be prepared to take option potential into account, the negative present values likely to accompany the typical high option value project could easily doom exploratory projects with the potential to build the future of the firm. The salience of options, however, suggests that firms do attend to uncertain projects that create the opportunities of the future.

Our results also have implications for those attempting to mobilize senior-level resource commitment for a new project (Day, 1994). They suggest that a different case for salience needs to be made depending on whether a project has the potential to deliver near-term rents, or whether it is instead an option on the possibility of creating rents at some as yet undetermined time in the future. The options case, because it is so often characterized as intuitive or visceral, may require far more careful elaboration than a case promising to deliver proximate and certain results. After all, in allocating resources to an option, senior managers must divert resources that could have been devoted elsewhere, such as in the existing business. The option case, therefore, needs to be made with precision. The items used to tap the option value construct in our survey might offer a practical point of departure for creating such an argument.

More important from the perspective of the future development of strategic resource allocation theory is to distinguish between option value for a proposed project, and net present value for the same project. As scholars working in this area have demonstrated (see, for example, Trigeorgis, 1996; Kogut, 1991) the two are not always related in an obvious way. Option value, for instance, can be greater for a high-variance project than for a more certain one, even if its mean expected value of future cash flows is lower.

The effects of variance on option value suggest ways in which senior managers might use real options reasoning to make their intuitions more consciously strategic. There is substantial utility for most firms operating in uncertain environments to make variance-increasing, as well as mean-increasing, investments. This is consistent with the view forwarded by March (1991) and Levinthal and March (1993) who argue that to remain viable over the long run, firms need to engage in both variance-reducing, exploitative behavior, and variance-increasing, exploratory behavior (see also Tushman & O'Reilly, 1997).

This brings us to the question of actually managing projects with high option potential. Recall that the value of an option is driven by variance, specifically the ability to gain access to a large potential upside while constraining potential downside loss (McGrath, 1997). In evaluating proposed projects, our results suggest that managers find the high upside potential of option value salient. As the project is actually executed, however, the ability to contain losses in the event that optimistic expectations prove unfounded is equally important.

The distinction between projects with high option value and projects with high rent potential is an important one, because the imperative with an option is to control downside potential variance as far as possible, while increasing potential upside variance as far as possible. In practice, this means that many low-cost options may be funded, provided that they are funded with parsimony (Hambrick & MacMillan, 1984). Even if such initiatives fail, they can still contribute to the economic wellbeing of the firm through residual learning, technological spillovers or skill-building effects (McGrath, 1995; Maidique & Zirger, 1985). Block and SubbaNarasimha offer empirical evidence with respect to corporate ventures. They note that "overall firm performance in venturing is most likely determined by the size of the losses in the losers, rather than percentage of ventures that are profitable" (working paper, cited in Block & MacMillan, 1993: 334). Understanding that managing options requires different processes than managing immediate rent potential projects is therefore important.

## Conclusion

We began this inquiry with the hope of exploring how real options reasoning might be operationalized empirically, and examined with respect to the corporate resource allocation process. We found considerable empirical support for a role for rent potential (an economic driver) and option value (an intuitive driver) in capturing senior management salience. Salience, in turn, is seen to have a powerful effect on which projects within a firm are likely to secure commitment. At the level of the firm, allocating the limited space on the agenda, or scarce salience, to projects is likely to involve at least some degree of politics and negotiation.

Real options reasoning suggests why organizations might engage in some degree of ''foolish'' experimentation (March, 1991) without the assumption of immediate payback, but with the goal of building routines aimed at knowledge maximization and progressive uncertainty reduction. It also suggests the mechanism through which intuition is converted to action. Making commitments to real options, under the right circumstances, leads to the reduction of uncertainty through experiential learning. This uncertainty reduction can yield sufficient information that it becomes clear to decision makers that the option is ''in the money'', meaning that it is a high rent potential project. Rapid investments to exercise (capitalize on the opportunity) may then be made, investments that might appear to an outsider to be abrupt (see Eisenhardt & Zbaracki, 1992: 33).

Finally, this study adds additional empirical evidence to the growing stream of research suggesting that real options reasoning shows how strategic practices that might seem to be illogical can make eminent sense. For instance, projects with very long time horizons and highly uncertain payoffs may be supported for their inherent option value, provided they are consistent with the company's learning mechanisms. So, too, option value, or the lack thereof, can explain withdrawal and exit behavior that make no sense in a net present value perspective. For instance, as Gimeno *et al.*, (1997) found, the decision to exit a business may have less to do with whether it is delivering adequate returns to the capital it uses than with other alternatives available to the decision maker (in their study, an individual entrepreneur). Similarly, as McGrath (1995) found in her study of corporate ventures, projects which are unable to capture managerial salience may well find themselves spun off or sold off, whether or not they appear to be attractive investments from an economic point of view.

In short, this study adds to a stream that suggests that real options reasoning itself offers a high-potential option for gaining greater insight into actual strategic decision-making and other kinds of strategic resource allocations.

## Acknowledgements

The authors gratefully acknowledge the financial support of the Chazen Institute of Columbia Business School, the Accelerating Competitive Effectiveness (ACE®) Program of the Wharton School's Snider Entrepreneurial Center, and a grant from the Ewing Marion Kauffman Foundation. Ian C. MacMillan provided guidance and useful comments.

## References

Alchian, A.A. (1991). Rent. In J. Eatwell, M. Milgate & P. Newman, (eds), *The World of Economics*. New York: W.W. Norton, 591–597.

Alchian, A.A. & Demsetz, H. (1972). Production, information costs and economic organization. *American Economic Review*, **62**, 777–794.

Allison, G.T. (1971). *Essence of Decision: Explaining the Cuban Missile Crisis*. Boston, MA: Little, Brown.

Amit, R. & Schoemaker, P. (1993). Strategic assets and organizational rent. *Strategic Management Journal*, **14**, 33–46.

Argyris C. & Schon D.A. (1996). *Organizational Learning II. Theory, Method and Practice.* Reading, MA: Addison-Wesley.

Barney, J.B. (1986). Strategic factor markets: Expectations, luck, and business strategy. *Management Science*, **32**, 1231–1241.

Barney, J.B. (1991). Firm resources and sustained competitive advantage. *Journal of Management*, **17**, 99–120.

Bettis, R.A. & Hitt, M.A. (1995). The new competitive landscape. *Strategic Management Journal*, **16** (Special Issue), 7–19.

Block, Z. & MacMillan, I.C. (1985). Milestones in successful business planning. *Harvard Business Review*, September–October.

Block, Z. & MacMillan, I.C. (1993). *Corporate Venturing: Creating New Businesses Within the Firm*. Cambridge, MA: Harvard Business School Press.

Bollen, K.A. (1989). *Structural Equations with Latent Variables*. New York: Wiley.

Bower, J.L. (1970). *Managing the Resource Allocation Process*. Boston, MA: Harvard Business School Press.

Bowman, E.H. (1974). Epistemology, corporate strategy and academe. *Sloan Management Review*, **15**.

Bowman, E.H. & Hurry, D. (1993). Strategy through the option lens: An integrated view of resource investments and the incremental-choice process. *Academy of Management Review*, **18**, 760–782.

Brealey, R. & Myers, S. (1981). *Principles of Corporate Finance*. New York: McGraw-Hill.

Brown, S. & Eisenhardt, K.M. (1995). Product development: Past research, present findings and future directions. *Academy of Management Journal*, **20**, 343–378.

Brown, S.L. & Eisenhardt, K.M. (1997). The art of continuous change: Linking complexity theory and time-paced evolution in relentlessly shifting organizations. *Administrative Science Quarterly*, **42**, 1–34.

Burgelman, R.A. (1983). A process model of internal corporate venturing in the diversified major firm. *Administrative Science Quarterly*, **18**, 223–244.

Christensen, C. (1997). *The Innovator's Dilemma*. Cambridge, MA: Harvard Business School Press.

Christensen, C. & Bower, J. (1996). Customer power, strategic investment, and the failure of leading firms. *Strategic Management Journal*, **17**, 197–219.

Conner, K. & Prahalad, C.K. (1996). A resource-based theory of the firm: Knowledge vs. opportunism. *Organization Science*, **7**(5), 477–501.

Crozier, M. (1964). *The Bureaucratic Phenomenon*, Chicago, IL: University of Chicago Press.

Day, D.L. (1994). Raising radicals: Different processes for championing innovative corporate ventures. *Organization Science*, **5**, 148–172.

Dierickx, I. & Cool, K. (1989). Asset stock accumulation and sustainability of competitive advantage. *Management Science*, **35**, 1504–1513.

Dixit, A. & Pindyck, R. (1994). *Investment Under Uncertainty*. Princeton, NJ: Princeton University Press.

Eisenhardt, K.M. (1989). Making fast strategic decisions in high-velocity environments. *Academy of Management Journal*, **32**, 543–576.

Eisenhardt, K.M. & Bourgeois, L.J. II (1988). Politics of strategic decision making in high velocity environments: Toward a midrange theory. *Academy of Management Journal*, **31**, 737–770.

Eisenhardt, K. & Zbaracki, M.J. (1992). Strategic decision making. *Strategic Management Journal*, **13**, 17–37.

Frederickson, J.W. (1985). Effects of decision motive and organizational performance level on strategic decision processes. *Academy of Management Journal*, **28**, 821–843.

Gandz, J. & Murray, V.V. (1980). The experience of workplace politics. *Academy of Management Journal*, **23**, 237–251.

Ghemawat, P. (1991). *Commitment: The Dynamic of Strategy*. New York: Free Press.

Gimeno, J., Folta, T.B., Cooper, A.C. & Woo, C.Y. (1997). Survival of the fittest? Entrepreneurial human capital and the persistence of underperforming firms. *Administrative Science Quarterly*, **42**, 750–783.

Gresov, C., Drazin, R. & van de Ven, A. (1989). Work-Unit Task uncertainty, design and morale. *Organization Studies*, **10**, 45–62.

Guth, W.D. & Ginsberg, A. (1990). Guest editors' introduction: Corporate entrepreneurship. *Strategic Management Journal*, **11**, 5–15.

Guth, W.D. & MacMillan, I.C. (1986). Strategy implementation versus middle management self-interest. *Strategic Management Journal*, **7**, 313–327.

Hambrick, D. & MacMillan, I.C. (1984). Asset parsimony—Managing assets to manage profits. *Sloan Management Review*, Winter, 67–74.

Hayward, M.L.A. & Hambrick, D.C. (1997). Explaining the premiums paid for large acquisitions: Evidence of CEO hubris. *Administrative Science Quarterly*, **42**, 103–127.

Hitt, M.A., Hoskisson, R.E., Johnson, R.A. & Moesel, D.D. (1996). The market for corporate control and firm innovation. *Academy of Management Journal*, **39**, 1084–1119.

Kahneman, D. & Tversky, S. (1979). Prospect theory: An analysis of decision under risk. *Econometrica*, **47**(2), 263–292.

Kiesler, S. & Sproull, L. (1982). Managerial responses to changing environments: Perspectives on problem sensing from social cognition. *Administrative Science Quarterly*, **27**, 548–570.

Knight, F. (1921). *Risk, Uncertainty and Profit*. 1971 Midway reprint, Chicago, IL: University of Chicago Press.

Kogut, B. (1991). Joint ventures and the option to expand and acquire. *Management Science*, **37**, 19–33.

Kogut, B. & Kulatilaka, N. (1994). Operating flexibility, global manufacturing, and the option value of a multinational network. *Management Science*, **40**, 123–139.

Levinthal, D. & March, J.G. (1993). The myopia of learning. *Strategic Management Journal*, **14**, 95–112.

MacMillan, I.C. (1978). *Strategy Formulation: Political Concepts*. St Paul, MN: West Publishing.

MacMillan, I.C. & Jones, P. (1986). *Strategy Formulation: Power and Politics*. St Paul, MN: West Publishing.

Maidique, M.A. & Zirger, B.J. (1985). The new product learning cycle. *Research Policy*, **14**, 299–313.

March, J.G. (1991). Exploration and exploitation in organizational learning. *Organization Science*, **2**, 71–87.

March, J.G. & Shapira, Z. (1987). Managerial perspectives on risk and risk taking. *Management Science*, **33**, 1404–1418.

March, J.G. & Simon, H.A. (1958). *Organizations*. New York: Wiley.

March, J. & Sutton, R. (1997). Organizational performance as a dependent variable. *Organization Science*, **8**, 698–706.

McGrath, R.G. (1995). Advantage from adversity: Learning from disappointment in internal corporate ventures. *Journal of Business Venturing*, **10**, 121–142.

McGrath, R.G. (1997). A real options logic for initiating technology positioning investments. *Academy of Management Review*, **22**, 974–996.

McGrath, R.G., MacMillan, I.C. and Venkataraman, S. (1995). Defining and developing competence: A strategic process paradigm. *Strategic Management Journal*, **16**, 251–275.

Miller, D. (1993). The architecture of simplicity. *Academy of Management Review*, **18**, 116–138.

Mitchell, G.R. & Hamilton, W.F. (1988). Managing R&D as a strategic option. *Research-Technology Management*, **27**, 15–22.

Nelson, R.R. & Winter, S.J. (1982). *An Evolutionary Theory of Economic Change*. Cambridge, MA: Belknap Press.

Nonaka, I. (1991). The knowledge creating company. *Harvard Business Review*, November–December, 96–104.

Nunnally, J. (1978). *Psychometric Theory*, 2nd edition. New York: McGraw-Hill.

Penrose, E. (1959). *The Theory of the Growth of the Firm*. New York: Wiley.

Peteraf, M.A. (1993). The cornerstones of competitive advantage: A resource-based view. *Strategic Management Journal*, **14**, 179–192.

Pettigrew, A. (1973). *The Politics of Organizational Decision Making*. London: Tavistock.

Pfeffer, J. (1992). *Managing with Power*. Boston, MA: Harvard Business School Press.

Pfeffer, J. & Salancik, G.R. (1974). Organizational decision making as a political process: The case of the university budget. *Administrative Science Quarterly*, **19**, 135–151.

Podsakoff, P.M. & Organ, D. (1986). Self-reports in organizational research: Problems and Prospects. *Journal of Management*, **12**, 531–544.

Salancik, G.R. & Pfeffer, J. (1974). The bases and use of power in organizational decision making: The case of a university budget. *Administrative Science Quarterly*, **19**, 453–473.

Sanchez, R. (1993). Strategic flexibility, firm organization and managerial work in dynamic markets: A strategic options perspective. In P. Shrivastava, A. Huff, & J. Dutton, (eds), *Advances in Strategic Management*, Volume 9. Greenwich, CT: JAI Press, 251–291.

Sandberg, W.R. & Hofer, C.W. (1987). Improving new venture performance: The role of strategy, industry structure, and the entrepreneur. *Journal of Business Venturing*, 2(1), 5–29.

Stewart, G.B. (1991). *The Quest for Value*. New York: Harper Collins.
Stuart, R. & Abetti, P.A. (1987). Start up ventures: Towards the prediction of initial success. *Journal of Business Venturing*, 2(3), 215–231.
Teece, D., Rumelt, R., Dosi, G. & Winter, S. (1994). Understanding corporate coherence: Theory and evidence. *Journal of Economic Behavior and Organization*, **23**, 1–30.
Thompson, J. (1967). *Organizations in Action: Social Science Bases of Administrative Theory*. New York: McGraw-Hill.
Trigeorgis, L. (1996). *Real Options: Managerial Flexibility and Strategy in Resource Allocation*. Boston, MA: MIT Press.
Tushman, M.L. & O'Reilly, C.A. III (1997). *Winning Through Innovation*. Boston, MA: Harvard Business School Press.
Van de Ven, A.H. (1986). Central problems in the management of innovation. *Management Science*, **32**, 590–607.

## APPENDIX: CONSTRUCT OPERATIONALIZATION

| Construct | Items |
|---|---|
| Resource commitment | Agreement (1 = to no extent, 5 = to a great extent) with the following statements:<br>• The project has no difficulty in the internal competition for funds<br>• The project has no difficulty in the internal competition for staff<br>• The project has no difficulty in having its budget approved<br>Cronbach Alpha: .89 |
| Rent potential | Probability (scale of 0–100) of achieving:<br>• Success for the project<br>• Higher profits than competitors<br>• Better margins than competitors<br>• Higher revenues than competitors<br>• Significant savings for customers<br>• Unusually high profits<br>• Margin improvement<br>• Increased revenues<br>• Significant savings for the firm<br>Cronbach Alpha: .84 |
| Productivity | Agreement (1 = strongly disagree, 5 = strongly agree) with the following statements:<br>• This project will allow us to do more work without increasing headcount<br>• This project will allow us to gain economies of scale<br>• This project reduces the number of steps required to complete a transaction<br>• This project will reduce our turnaround time<br>• This project will allow us to make better use of assets we already own<br>• This project reduces the amount or cost of input resources<br>• This project will allow us to achieve a lower cost per unit of output<br>• This project eliminates or reduces post-sales service requirements |

(*continued*)

| Construct | Items |
|---|---|
| | • This project will lower our fixed costs<br>• This project will reduce our costs of distribution<br>• This project will reduce our costs for storage or inventory<br>• This project will reduce our costs of operations<br>Cronbach Alpha: .93 |
| Salience | Agreement (1 = to no extent, 5 = to a great extent) with the following statements:<br>• The project has strong support at the Board level<br>• The project is being aggressively championed by senior managers of the corporation<br>• The project has strong support from top management<br>• The project has support from other divisions or businesses in the corporation<br>Cronbach Alpha: .83 |
| Option value | Agreement (1 = to no extent, 5 = to a great extent) with the following statements:<br>Undertaking this project will accomplish the following:<br>• Help us learn new manufacturing, production or operations skills<br>• Help us learn about new market segments<br>• Help us learn about international market opportunities<br>• Help us learn what product features and attributes our customers really care about<br>• Help leverage our existing distribution capacity<br>• Help utilize excess operations capacity<br>• Leverage our skills in design and customization<br>• Leverage our skills in operations<br>• Leverage our skills in service and distribution<br>• Leverage our skills in sourcing<br>• Extend the reach of our products and services<br>• Extend brand awareness of our offering<br>• Provide a new source of differentiation for our company<br>• Capitalize on brand loyalty<br>• Leverage our advertising<br>• Build our reputation in a new business area<br>• Put us in a favorable position with respect to future industry standards<br>• Allow us to gather better information on customers and competitiveness<br>• Develop new sources of supply<br>• Enhance our image<br>• Provide ideas for new products or services<br>• Give us advantage in sourcing from suppliers<br>• Give us an advantage in accessing distributors<br>Cronbach Alpha: .89 |

# 15

# The Influence of Leveraging Tacit Overseas Knowledge for Global New Product Development Capability: An Empirical Examination[1]

MOHAN SUBRAMANIAM, N. VENKATRAMAN

## INTRODUCTION

In recent years, the nature of competition by organizations has intensified. Competition has become more knowledge-based with the sources of competitive advantage unmistakably shifting from physical assets to intellectual resources (Prahalad & Hamel, 1990; Quinn, 1992). While this emergent knowledge-based competition has affected a wide spectrum of organizations, it has raised some especially significant challenges for firms competing internationally. This is because the home-based sources of knowledge or "ownership advantages" that had long

*Dynamic Strategic Resources: Development, Diffusion and Integration.*
Edited by Michael A. Hitt, Patricia Gorman Clifford, Robert D. Nixon and Kevin P. Coyne.

provided organizations their predominant impetus to compete in international markets (Dunning, 1980) are no longer adequate today. Global rivals now wrest competitive initiative through leveraging knowledge from multiple country sources for new product ideas, manufacturing know-how and technologies. Indeed with increasing globalization of our economy, the ability to transfer and deploy knowledge across borders has become one of the central competitive concerns for many organizations.

However, our understanding of how organizations effectively transfer and deploy knowledge across borders remains limited in many ways. Prior studies have viewed knowledge flows between headquarters and subsidiaries of multinational companies (MNCs) largely as control or administrative mechanisms (e.g. Egelhoff, 1988; Gupta & Govindrajan, 1993; Nobel & Birkinshaw, 1998). Consequently, not much is understood about how organizations leverage knowledge across borders to create competitive advantage. Also lacking is an understanding of how organizations transfer and deploy knowledge across borders for specific business process capabilities (such as new product development, global manufacturing, customer service, and so on) with the focus of prior research being on general aspects of knowledge transfer.

On the other hand, the competitive implications of knowledge to organizations have recently attracted a lot of attention in the strategic management literature (e.g., Cohen & Levinthal, 1990; Grant, 1996; Spender, 1996; Zander & Kogut, 1995). The significance of *tacit* knowledge to a firm's competitiveness has been of particular interest (Nonaka, 1994). Tacit knowledge largely "indwells" in the minds of people as perspectives or images of reality (Polyani, 1966). The inherent difficulties in its codification and transfer pose significant barriers for rival organizations to replicate this kind of knowledge, making tacit knowledge an important strategic resource (Conner & Prahalad, 1996). However, the competitive implications of tacit knowledge have not yet been adequately tested in the global setting. Some studies have recognized that tacit knowledge is especially difficult to transfer and deploy across borders (Kogut & Zander, 1993; Teece, 1977, 1983) because of its "sticky" properties (von Hippel, 1994), but not much is understood about how firms overcome this difficulty and leverage tacit knowledge from geographically dispersed sources. Also lacking are empirical studies validating the widely conjectured influence of leveraging tacit knowledge on firm capabilities.

Considering these gaps in our understanding, this study investigates the influence of transferring and deploying tacit knowledge across country borders on a firm's capabilities in developing new *global* products—or products for multiple country markets.

## Background and Motivation for the Study

Two reasons drive the choice of global new product development as the setting to examine how the transfer and deployment of knowledge across borders influences firm capabilities. The first reason is that identifying and evaluating market requirements of multiple countries and then transferring and deploying that knowledge across borders is at the kernel of the global new product development process (Takeuchi & Porter, 1986). As global products cater to multiple countries, their success in global markets requires both adaptation to unique country requirements and standardization across them (Bartlett & Ghoshal, 1989; Prahalad and Doz, 1987). Adaptation is important to penetrate different country markets while standardization is important to achieve operational efficiency. Knowledge of unique country conditions that allow MNCs to address these conflicting requirements typically lies dispersed in their overseas subsidiaries (Ohmae, 1990). Hence the ability to develop new global products fundamentally depends on how proficiently MNCs transfer and deploy knowledge from multiple country sources.

A second reason is that global product development is of growing significance to several organizations today because of the advantages it provides over competitors who manage new product development either as purely a domestic process, or as a portfolio of independent activities in different countries (Ghoshal, 1987; Porter, 1986; Yip, 1995). For example, products catering to multiple markets as opposed to merely one domestic market exploit greater economies of scale to gain cost advantages (Buzzell, 1968; Levitt, 1983; Porter, 1980). Moreover, integrating new product development activities across countries offers several other strategic benefits: it eliminates duplication of efforts and saves costs, making products more competitive (Porter, 1986); it enables firms to launch new products simultaneously in multiple country markets, thereby reducing the risks of preemptive entry by multinational rivals in those markets (Chen & Stucker, 1997; Hamel & Prahalad, 1985); and it also allows firms to leverage ideas generated in one geographic market into other geographic markets (Bartlett & Ghoshal, 1989). Such compelling advantages have in fact made global new product development a central aspect of a firm's global strategy (Yip, 1995).

Despite its significance, however, global new product development has not been sufficiently examined empirically by prior research. Research on *global products* has focused mostly on the feasibility of standardization across markets rather than on how global products could be effectively developed (e.g., Boddewyn, Soehl & Picard, 1986; Cavusgil, Zou & Naidu, 1993; Samiee & Roth, 1992). Studies of *global R&D* have centered on location, coordination, or evolution of R&D activities worldwide (see Cheng & Bolon,

1993 for a review) rather than on global new product development. Research on the *diffusion of knowledge within MNCs* (e.g., Bartlett & Ghoshal, 1989; Gupta & Govindrajan, 1993) has also not highlighted how various approaches MNCs adopt to transfer and deploy knowledge across borders specifically influence their global new product development capabilities. Hence we believe that global new product development is a useful context in which to investigate the influence on firm capabilities of knowledge transfer and deployment across borders.

## Conceptual Framework

We frame our inquiry using the resource-based view of the firm and consider knowledge as a critical resource within firms (Barney, 1991; Peteraf, 1993). Accordingly, we see a firm's capability being derived from its routines, or the regular activities through which the firm uniquely leverages its knowledge resource (Amit & Schoemaker, 1993; Nelson & Winter, 1982). We further contend that firms leverage unique and difficult-to-imitate overseas knowledge for greater global new product development capabilities through employing routines that leverage tacit overseas knowledge.

### Definitions

We define tacit overseas knowledge as *"the knowledge of the differences among overseas markets that is difficult to codify and transfer in a systematic way"*. We focus on knowledge concerning *the differences among overseas markets* because addressing unique requirements of multiple countries is a fundamental issue facing firms developing global products (Cavusgil, Zou & Naidu, 1993; Jain, 1989). Furthermore, the notion of *the difficulty in codification and transfer* is a central attribute of tacit knowledge (Grant, 1996; Nonaka, 1994; von Hippel, 1994; Zander & Kogut, 1995).

We define global new product development capability as *"the ability to consistently and successfully introduce new products simultaneously in multiple country markets"*. We focus on *consistency* of new product introductions, as random or sporadic new product successes are not adequate for firms to create or maintain market dominance (Leonard-Barton, 1992; Nobeoka & Cusumano, 1997). We also incorporate the notion of *successful introduction,* as market success is a fundamental aspect of any business process capability (Amit & Schoemaker, 1993; Barney, 1991). Finally, we also recognize *simultaneous* introduction in multiple markets, as integrating product development activities across countries and developing products that concurrently meet the requirements of several countries is quintessential to the global new product development process (Porter, 1986; Yip, 1995).

## Leveraging Tacit Overseas Knowledge for Global New Product Development Capability

In concurrently meeting the requirements of multiple country markets, addressing the differences between countries becomes a central issue for the process of global new product development (Jain, 1989). Knowledge concerning the differences between countries could be *tacit* or *explicit* (Subramaniam, Rosenthal & Hatten, 1998). Many national requirements and their differences entail explicit knowledge, as they are based on universally accepted and objective criteria. For instance, transmission systems for televisions differ between countries based on universally accepted engineering specifications such as PAL, SECAM, or NTSC. Similarly, cordless telephones need to respond to regulatory laws for distinct frequency ranges in different countries. These differences are not subject to individual interpretations or perspectives, and can be easily codified.

On the other hand, many differences between national and regional markets involve tacit knowledge, such as differences in cultures, tastes, habits and customs (Jain, 1989; Subramaniam Rosenthal & Hatten, 1998). Takeuchi and Porter (1986) describe how cultural differences made Campbell soup unpopular in Brazil. Housewives apparently felt they did not fulfill their "proper" role if they served soup they could not call their own, and hence preferred using dehydrated soup starters (of competitors) to which they could add their own ingredients. The understanding of such differences among country requirements is tacit, as it is based upon personal perspectives and interpretations of individuals.

As tacit knowledge lacks objective criteria for consistent description, it could have several alternative interpretations, each with different implications for the design tradeoffs of the new global product being developed. For instance, preferences in shapes of television cabinets vary with cultures. Some country markets prefer sleek designs, while others prefer more bulky designs (Subramaniam, Rosenthal & Hatten, 1998). Moreover, the specifics of what is perceived as "sleek" could involve several possible interpretations, making comprehensive codification of the knowledge base driving them very difficult (von Hippel, 1994). Unlike explicit differences such as PAL/SECAM/NTSC, insights to arrive at these interpretations evolve with experience and largely reside in the minds of subsidiary managers located in those countries.

Tacit aspects of overseas market knowledge and plants are hence more difficult to interpret and transfer from overseas subsidiaries to design headquarters, or where global new product development projects are conducted (Kogut & Zander, 1993; Nonaka, 1994). Consequently, such knowledge is less likely to be equally possessed by all competitors. As product innovations primarily occur by exploiting consumer preferences or needs in ways not perceived by or known to others, the opportunities for such differential interpretation are greater when exploiting tacit aspects of overseas knowledge. On the other hand, explicit aspects of overseas knowledge, such as knowledge about switching frequency range regulations of cordless telephones, are more likely to be equally possessed by all competitors because of the relative ease in transferring such knowledge across borders. Hence, although explicit aspects of overseas knowledge are undoubtedly very important and necessary to acquire when designing global products, they are not sufficient to create superior capabilities as they provide lesser opportunities for differential interpretation, and thus less likelihood for innovation.

Furthermore, for ongoing innovation, the ability to continually spot new opportunities from a tacit knowledge base of overseas markets[2] is less likely to be imitated as tacit knowledge is not easily diffused (Zander & Kogut, 1995). Such knowledge is also cumulative, building upon prior knowledge and becoming more in-depth over time (Cohen & Levinthal, 1990; Nonaka, 1994), making it difficult to replicate unless comparable time and experience is devoted (Dierickx & Cool, 1989). Addressing more tacit, as compared to explicit, overseas knowledge for designing a global product is hence more likely not only to provide a lead in continually generating product innovations, but also to deter others from quick imitation, and thus increase the probabilities of market success (Banbury & Mitchell, 1995). *Hence, we assert that leveraging greater tacit overseas knowledge enhances a firm's global new product development capability.*

## Operational Framework and Hypotheses

We operationalize the degree of tacit overseas knowledge leveraged by organizations in terms of the routines employed for developing global products. We contend that successful patterns among these routines will reflect an *interaction* among two critical activities in the global new product development process. These activities are: (a) addressing more tacit as compared to explicit differences among countries, and (b) employing rich information processing mechanisms. We focus on *interactions* among these activities as we argue that both these activities are necessary, and neither on its own is sufficient to leverage tacit overseas knowledge (see Figure 15.1).

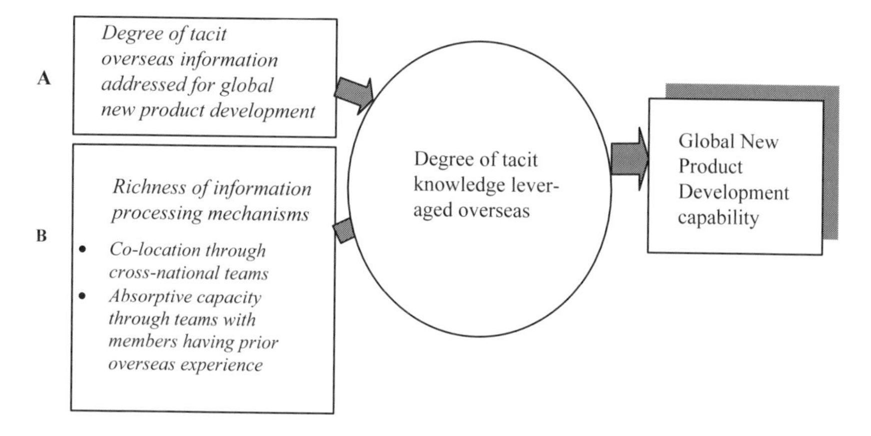


**Key:**

☐ Observed and measured constructs

◯ Interactions representing the routines leveraging tacit overseas knowledge — unmeasured but estimated in the analysis

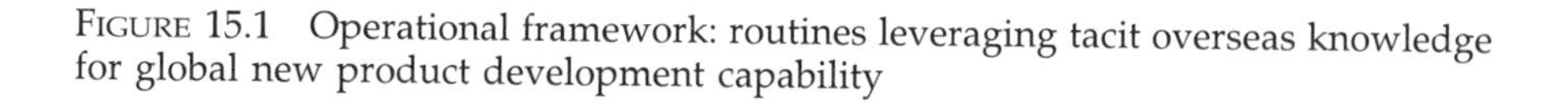

FIGURE 15.1 Operational framework: routines leveraging tacit overseas knowledge for global new product development capability

## ADDRESSING TACIT DIFFERENCES AMONG COUNTRIES

In managing the global new product development process, organizations have a choice in terms of addressing tacit or explicit differences among countries for their global product design. At a conceptual level, this choice reflects Galbraith's (1977) notion of work units opting to confront greater uncertainty in their tasks[3] by choosing to focus on more ambiguous or complex information that is difficult to acquire when conducting their tasks (van de Ven & Delbecq, 1974). At a more operational level, Subramaniam, Rosenthal & Hatten (1998) provide evidence for MNCs routinely exercising such a choice. Through various case studies they document how global new product development processes vary in terms of tacit and explicit differences among countries addressed for the global product designs. In fact, they noticed these variations occurring across different global new product development processes and product categories even within MNCs.

Given that MNCs have such a choice, addressing more tacit as compared to explicit differences among countries becomes a necessary condition to leverage tacit overseas knowledge in the global new product development process. However, to effectively acquire and deploy tacit overseas information the global new product development process also requires rich information processing mechanisms, because of the difficulty in acquiring and deploying tacit information from overseas locations (Kogut & Zander, 1993).

## Information Processing Mechanisms

We adopt two complementary theoretical perspectives of information processing, based on the concepts of co-location (Nonaka, 1994) and absorptive capacity (Cohen & Levinthal, 1990). Co-location and the resultant face-to-face contact among individuals enhance the media richness of information transfer (Daft & Lengel, 1986). It is one of the primary ways of sharing tacit information to create new knowledge (Nonaka, 1994; Nonaka & Takeuchi, 1995) and represents a critical aspect of information processing capacity. Absorptive capacity, or the ability to absorb new information and create new knowledge based on prior related knowledge, is another important aspect of information processing capacity (Cohen & Levinthal, 1990; Garud & Nayyar, 1994). We capture the concept of co-location through the existence of cross-national teams, and the concept of absorptive capacity through the existence of teams with members having prior overseas experience.

## Routines for Tacit Knowledge Leverage as Interactions

We motivate our argument for routines as interactions—or the necessity to *both* address tacit overseas information *and* employ rich information processing mechanisms to leverage tacit overseas knowledge—through an example. Consider Sanyo (a Japanese manufacturer) which reportedly positions its cordless telephone based on "soft appearance". Knowledge about what constitutes "soft appearance" in multiple countries is tacit, as this knowledge is difficult to codify and transfer from overseas locations. This is because there are numerous possible interpretations of what "soft appearance" means in different country contexts. A comprehensive understanding of all the possible nuances of "soft appearance" resides only in the minds of the overseas managers concerned and is based upon their own personal experiences and beliefs.

A global new product development team at Sanyo's headquarters is unlikely to acquire all the nuances of what its overseas managers know about "soft appearance" in different countries if the team chooses to employ lean[4] information processing mechanisms, such as written memos or reports to acquire that information. The depth and breadth of what the overseas managers understand about "soft appearance" is very difficult to comprehensively document in memos and reports. However, such a tacit knowledge base is more likely to be effectively leveraged by the global new product development team if it employs richer mechanisms, such as face-to-face contact with overseas managers (Daft & Lengel, 1986; Nonaka, 1994). With these richer media of information exchange, various possible design alternatives could be reviewed in considerably more detail, and the depth and breadth of what the overseas managers understand about "soft appearance" could be effectively utilized in the global product design process. However, a rich medium of exchange by itself is also insufficient to leverage tacit overseas knowledge, unless the design teams choose to address tacit aspects of country requirements in their global design process. Hence, we contend that leveraging tacit overseas knowledge is a function of an interaction between addressing tacit differences among countries and the global new product development process employing rich information processing mechanisms.

## Hypothesis 1: Leveraging Tacit Overseas Information Through Co-location

We argue that addressing more tacit as compared to explicit differences among countries through co-locating domestic and overseas managers will result in greater tacit knowledge being leveraged by the global new product development process. Co-location can be achieved in the global new product development process by way of employing cross-national teams. Through co-location and the resulting face-to-face contact among domestic and overseas team members, various nuances about the tacit differences among countries can be effectively shared and deployed for the new product design. The example of Sanyo capturing knowledge about differences in the perceptions of "soft appearance" among countries through face-to-face contact of team members reinforces our argument. As co-location also increases the socialization and interpersonal contact among the project team members, cross-national teams become effective means for processing tacit information (Nonaka, 1994). Consequently, addressing more tacit as compared to explicit differences among countries through cross-national teams will result in higher global new product development capabilities. Hence:

> H1: The interaction between (a) the degree of tacit overseas information addressed by the project team, and (b) co-locating domestic and overseas managers, will positively influence global new product development capability.

## Hypothesis 2: Leveraging Tacit Overseas Information Through Absorptive Capacity

Another choice for the global new product development process is to influence its absorptive capacity through strengthening the prior knowledge about overseas market conditions in project teams (Cohen & Levinthal, 1990). This can be achieved by composing project teams that include domestic members with prior experience in overseas markets. Nonaka and Takeuchi (1995) provide some examples of how Nissan, while designing their global car, employed teams with engineers who were earlier posted in European markets and had acquired tacit knowledge about the driving conditions in those markets. This prior experience and the consequent prior tacit knowledge about the overseas markets concerned enhanced the team's ability to absorb new related knowledge about those markets. Addressing more tacit differences among countries through teams with domestic members having prior experience in overseas markets should thus lead to greater global new product development capabilities. Hence:

> H2: The interaction between (a) the degree of tacit overseas information addressed by the project team, and (b) absorptive capacity, will positively influence global new product development capability.

## Methodology

Our research design consisted of a cross-sectional survey using key informants. The survey was administered to key members of global new product development teams, namely members who had an important role to play in the global new product development process. A single informant acting on behalf of the team provided information about each global new product development process. The survey was administered across multiple industries in the consumer packaged goods, consumer durables and industrial product sectors. Its scope was restricted to *manufactured* products. The new products selected for this survey were those which were introduced in the market in the last five years and had existed in the market for at least one year.

### Sampling

Sampling of companies and their global new product development processes presented some unique problems. Not all MNCs develop global products and all product development projects among MNCs also do not develop global products. Hence we concluded that sending questionnaires randomly to a set of MNCs was not likely to result in adequate meaningful responses. We first created a target sample base of companies that were likely developers of global products. Then we identified managers who were involved with global new product development projects and could serve as key informants for this study.

We created a target sample base of 152 companies through multiple approaches. First, we solicited the help of ACNielsen, a major market research company in the US for identifying 90 of their client companies involved in global new product development. Based on discussions with their representatives, we selected a list of marketing and R&D managers of these companies who were likely to be involved in global new product development. Second, we identified 22 more MNCs that were corporate sponsors of six research centers of the university where this research was conducted. From these corporate sponsors we obtained a list of their managers who were likely to be involved in global new product development. Third, we added 40 more MNCs that were known to be developing global products from prior academic and business articles. For these companies we created a mailing list of informants from the *Directory of Corporate Affiliations.*

We then invited these 152 MNCs to participate in our study. Fifty-seven of them participated, giving us a response rate of 37.5%. An independent t-test comparing mean revenues (obtained from secondary sources) of the responding and non-responding companies revealed no significant differences (at $p < .05$), ruling out any significant response bias. As many of these MNCs were involved in developing several distinct categories of global products, we encouraged them to give us multiple responses. We received a total of 102 responses from different divisions and product categories from these 57 MNCs. We discarded 12 of these responses: three pertained to non-manufactured products (software and franchise expansion), five responses were about new products not yet launched, and four more were incomplete. This left a total of 90 usable responses from 45 multinational companies. Of these 90 responses, 43 were from the consumer packaged goods sector, 23 from the consumer durables sector, and 24 from the industrial products sector (see Appendix 1 for details of the companies and product categories).

The sampling process was by design non-random since global new product development is not widely practiced and is a strategic choice adopted by different MNCs. However, our sample represented a broad cross-section of product categories and firms. Several of the firms represented are leading multinational companies who account for a significant portion of the global economy. Twenty-two of these companies were ranked in the 1997 *Fortune 1000* list in terms of revenue. Of these

22 companies, eight were ranked in the top 100 list, of which four were in the top 50 list. Many of these companies have been cited in prior studies as exemplary global competitors (for example, see Yip, 1995). A majority of the companies in the sample were US-based. Three companies in the sample were based in Europe, one in Japan and one in South Korea.

## Key Informants

We used key informants to provide data on global new product development processes. Selecting appropriate informants is critical, as the reliability of information about activities related to a group or an organization depends on whether the selected persons have the requisite knowledge, or are from a vantage point to do so. All managers who responded to our survey were members of global new product development teams and were also in the upper middle management level of their companies. A majority of the informants (62%) were senior managers having titles of Directors, Vice Presidents and Presidents. This is indicative of the vantage point they had in providing information on the complex and multi-level activities concerning global new product development. Also, 92% of the informants represented the functions of R&D/Engineering, Marketing and General Management. These are critical functions for new product development.

## Survey Instrumentation

We developed the survey instrument in several phases. The first phase consisted of several hours of interviews with managers involved in the practice of global new product development. These interviews gave us a first-hand appreciation of how the practice of global new product development was actually conducted in multinational companies. With this understanding serving as a background, we then systematically searched the literature on new product development, international business, strategic management and organization theory for relevant scales. This search resulted in only a few scales that were applicable to the conceptual framework and hypotheses of this study. For a majority of the constructs, however, we developed new scales.

## Measures

The measure for the dependent variable—global new product development capability—was developed based on integrating key indicators from prior related studies. These indicators include (a) *frequency of new product introductions* (Nobeoka & Cusumano, 1997), (b) *order of market entry* (Banbury & Mitchell, 1995), (c) *simultaneous entry in multiple markets* (Porter, 1986), (d) *the ability to be responsive to market requirements*, (e) *the ability to be competitive in terms of price* (Bartlett & Ghoshal, 1989), and (f) *the ability to penetrate new overseas markets* (Yip, 1995) (see Appendix 2, Construct 1).

The measure for the degree of tacitness was adapted from Zander and Kogut (1995). Three dimensions from their study relevant to this context were *complexity*, *codifiability* and *observability* of the information on the differences among countries. That is, when the information on the differences among countries considered for developing the global product was more complex, less codifiable and more difficult to observe, that information was considered more tacit relative to explicit. Based on these concepts, we developed some fine-grained measures to capture the construct (see Appendix 2, Construct 2).

We measured co-location as the existence of cross-national teams through a dummy variable denoting the presence/absence of overseas managers in the project teams (see Appendix 2, Construct 3). Similarly, we measured absorptive capacity as the existence of domestic team members having prior overseas experience through a dummy variable denoting the presence/absence of domestic managers with prior overseas experience in the project team (see Appendix 2, Construct 4).

## Pilot Testing

We pilot-tested the face validity of these scales with 16 managers involved with global new product development. We spent a minimum of two hours with each of these managers, discussing every question and indicator with them so as to ascertain that their interpretation of the question was consistent with the meaning of the construct. Based on their feedback, we reworded some of the questions for better clarity and ease of understanding.

## Measurement Properties

All the constructs using multiple indicators were tested for their reliability. Cronbach alphas for all the constructs were well above the recommended value of 0.7 (see Appendix 2). Furthermore, the constructs were tested for their convergent and discriminant validity. Each construct was paired with another construct, and all the pair combinations were factor-analyzed using varimax rotation. The indicators of each construct loaded only on its own construct for all the pairs of constructs. Hence, convergent and discriminant validity requirements were satisfied for these constructs (detailed results available on request). We further developed a measure for business performance as a means to test the predictive validity of our dependent variable. Following Venkatraman and Ramanujam (1987), this measure captured multiple dimensions of business performance—namely, how satisfied managers were with respect to competition about their division's growth in sales, growth in market share, return on investment and return on sales. A significant zero-order correlation of 0.49 ($p < .01$) between global new product development capability and business performance confirmed the predictive validity of the dependent variable.

## Control Factors

We used seven variables to control for factors other than the tacit overseas knowledge leveraged by the project team that may have an influence on global new product development capability. The first two variables—*brand image in overseas markets*, and *overseas market share*—were chosen as they co-vary with global new product development capability. They co-vary because several "other" factors that influence a firm's overseas brand image and overseas market share also influence its global new product development capability. Hence using these control variables enables controlling for several of these "other" factors that are not possible to comprehensively enumerate and incorporate in the framework. We controlled for *industry represented* through two dummy variables demarcating whether the product was a consumer packaged good, a consumer durable, or an industrial product. The remaining control variables were chosen because their influence on global new product development capability can be inferred from prior studies. The higher a firm's *global marketing infrastructure* the better the firm is structured to compete globally (Porter, 1986), and hence is more likely to have greater global new product development capabilities. Similarly, the greater *the number of countries targeted* for global new product development, the greater the firm's chances for simultaneous introductions in multiple markets—and hence the greater its likelihood for higher global new product development capability. Next, the higher the *market concentration*, the lower the likely market rivalry, and hence the higher the odds of the new global product being successful in the market place (Porter, 1980). Finally, we used *permeability of managers across borders* to represent an organizational level contextual factor believed to enhance the flow of knowledge across borders for greater chances of innovation. Based on Bartlett and Ghoshal (1989), this construct represents how frequently managers from headquarters and overseas subsidiaries of the focal organization visit one another and interact informally with one another (see Appendix 2, Constructs 5–10).

## Results

Table 15.1 summarizes the means, standard deviations and the zero-order correlations among the constructs used for testing the hypotheses.

Correlations among the degree of tacitness and each of the information-processing mechanisms—co-location through cross-national teams, and absorptive capacity through teams with members (managers) having prior overseas experience—are below 0.1, ruling out any possible multi-collinearity effects. We used multiple regression analysis to test our hypotheses.[5] Table 15.2 presents the results of the regression analysis.

Model 1 is the test for the control variables. Together the control variables contribute to an adjusted $R^2$ of 0.564 and the F-statistic is highly significant ($p < .001$). This confirms our *a priori* expectations of the influence of the selected control variables on global new product development capability. Model 2 is the test of the main effects of the degree of tacitness in overseas information and cross-national teams. The results reveal that the main effects are *not* significant, and taken individually neither the degree of tacitness in overseas information nor cross-national teams is significant. Model 3, which is a test of Hypothesis 1, confirms that the interaction between the degree of tacitness in overseas information and cross-national teams is significant at $p < .001$. The F-statistic for the increase in $R^2$ over Model 1 is also highly significant (at $p < .001$). These results strongly support Hypothesis 1.

Model 4 tests the influence of the main effects of the degree of tacitness in overseas information and teams with members having prior overseas experience. The results reveal that the main effects are not significant. Model 5, which tests Hypothesis 2, confirms that the interaction between the degree of tacitness and teams with domestic members having prior overseas experience is significant at $p < .05$. The increase in $R^2$ of Model 5 over Model 1 is also significant at $p < .01$. These results support Hypothesis 2. Overall, both our hypotheses are supported.

## *Ex-post* Analysis: Sensitivity to the Organizational Context

In our analysis so far we explained the variance in the global new product development capabilities among firms for specific *product categories* based upon how their *project teams* leveraged tacit overseas knowledge—through either co-location or absorptive capacity. We focused our attention at the *level of the project teams* because it is at this level that knowledge actually gets deployed into the development of new global products, reflecting the firm's capabilities in this process. However, knowledge deployed by the project

TABLE 15.1 Means, standard deviations and zero-order correlations[a]

| | 1 | 2 | 3 | 4 | 5 | 6 | 7 | 8 | 9 | 10 | 11 | 12 |
|---|---|---|---|---|---|---|---|---|---|---|---|---|
| Mean | 5.15 | 0.7 | 0.81 | 0.47 | 0.29 | 4.9 | 4.53 | 4.07 | 6.89 | 3.64 | 4.71 | 5.89 |
| Standard deviation | 1.49 | 0.46 | 0.40 | 0.5 | 0.46 | 1.61 | 1.52 | .96 | 5.03 | 1.85 | 1.53 | 1.38 |
| 1. Degree of tacitness | 1.00 | | | | | | | | | | | |
| 2. Co-location (cross-national teams) | –.019 | 1.00 | | | | | | | | | | |
| 3. Absorptive capacity (team members with prior overseas experience) | .066 | .097 | 1.00 | | | | | | | | | |
| 4. Industry represented (A) | –.115 | .104 | –.027 | 1.00 | | | | | | | | |
| 5. Industry represented (B) | .091 | .068 | .084 | –.60** | 1.00 | | | | | | | |
| 6. Brand image | –.048 | .167 | –.038 | .279** | .035 | 1.00 | | | | | | |
| 7. Overseas market share | 0.04 | .012 | –.067 | .060 | .035 | .662** | 1.00 | | | | | |
| 8. Global marketing infrastructure | –.016 | .147 | .344** | .050 | .046 | .212* | .135 | 1.00 | | | | |
| 9. Number of countries targeted | –.092 | –.073 | .070 | .099 | –.001 | –.070 | –.047 | –.133 | 1.00 | | | |
| 10. Market concentration | .167 | .244* | .057 | .005 | .081 | .083 | .118 | .015 | –.066 | 1.00 | | |
| 11. Permeability of managers across borders | .035 | .243* | .312** | .067 | –.080 | .099 | .169 | .015 | –.068 | –.005 | 1.00 | |
| 12. Global new product development capability | .039 | .253* | .151 | .092 | .078 | .656** | .616** | .206* | .038 | .244* | .333** | 1.00 |

[a] Significance levels:
* $p < .05$
** $p < .01$.

TABLE 15.2 Regression results (N = 90)[a]

| | Model 1 | Model 2 | Model 3 | Model 4 | Model 5 | Model 6 | Model 7 |
|---|---|---|---|---|---|---|---|
| *Unstandardized Beta coefficients* | | | | | | | |
| Control variables: | | | | | | | |
| Geographic scope | .039* | .042* | .047* | .020† | .038* | .043† | .028 |
| Industry represented (A) | −.199 | −.247 | −.231 | −.106 | −.142 | −.258 | −.137 |
| Industry represented (B) | −.045 | −.019 | −.022 | −.122 | −.052 | .058 | .058 |
| Global infrastructure | .129 | .106 | .09 | .065 | .129 | .002 | .002 |
| Market concentration | .127* | .09† | .05 | .122* | .122* | .116* | .116* |
| Overseas market share | .226** | .249** | .299*** | .237** | .223** | .286*** | .286*** |
| Brand image | .410*** | .383*** | .341*** | .426*** | .41*** | .431*** | .431*** |
| Permeability of managers across borders | .235*** | .207** | .232*** | .233*** | .285*** | (dropped) | (dropped) |
| Independent variables: | | | | | | | |
| (A) Degree of tacitness | | .024 | .034 | .03 | .026 | .005 | .025 |
| (B) Cross-national teams | | .389 | .475† | | | .675* | |
| (C) Teams with members having prior overseas experience | | | | .214 | .185 | | .579* |
| Interaction between A and B | | | **.587*****[b] | | | | |
| Interaction between A and C | | | | | **.379***[b] | | |
| | | | | | | **.529*****[b] | |
| | | | | | | | .116 |
| *Model statistics* | | | | | | | |
| $R^2$ | .604 | .619 | .685 | .625 | .644 | .626 | .57 |
| Adjusted $R^2$ | .654 | .570 | .639 | .575 | .592 | .577 | .514 |
| F | 15.09*** | 12.51*** | 15.03*** | 12.64*** | 12.34*** | 12.87*** | 10.09*** |
| Change in $R^2$ (from model 1) | | | .081 | | .044 | | |
| F for change in $R^2$ | | | **6.68*****[b] | | **3.25****[b] | | |

[a] Significance levels:
† $p < .1$
* $p < .05$
** $p < .01$.
*** $p < .001$
[b] These results are commented upon in the text.

team is also influenced by its organizational context, as knowledge transfer occurs at multiple levels in an organization (Nonaka, 1994; Hedlund, 1994). We were thus interested in testing the sensitivity of our results on project-level activities to their organizational contexts.

We tested our results by removing the contextual variable *permeability of managers across borders* from our models. This contextual variable captures how frequently headquarters and overseas subsidiary managers visit and informally interact with one another. Models 6 and 7 in Table 15.2 test the interactions between the degree of tacitness in overseas information—and co-location and absorptive capacity respectively—after dropping this contextual variable. The results for Model 6 show that our findings remain unchanged with respect to Hypothesis 1. That is, the interaction between the degree of tacitness and cross-national teams remains significant even after removing permeability of managers across borders from the model. However, Model 7 in Table 15.2 reveals that the interaction between the degree of tacitness and absorptive capacity loses its significance *when permeability of managers across borders* is dropped from the model. Our interpretation of this result is that the approach of leveraging tacit overseas knowledge through absorptive capacity appears to be effective only in an organizational context wherein there is a high permeability of managers across borders.[6]

## Discussion

Global new product development capability is a key driver of a successful global strategy. Prior research, while clearly emphasizing the significance of the global new product development process in effectively competing in today's global environment (e.g., Bartlett & Ghoshal, 1989; Takeuchi & Porter, 1986; Yip, 1995), has not focused on how this capability could be effectively developed. Adopting a resource-based approach, our study highlights how organizations can create this critical capability by leveraging overseas knowledge. Our findings provide compelling evidence that leveraging tacit overseas knowledge significantly influences a firm's global new product development capability. This specific effect of tacit knowledge leverage is observed beyond the effects of several other factors related to organization structure, global positioning and market structure, that have been conventionally understood to influence organizational performance. We find organizations leverage tacit overseas knowledge by addressing more tacit as opposed to explicit differences among countries through rich information-processing mechanisms.

Differences among countries have long been understood to make the process of developing global products difficult (e.g., Boddewyn, Soehl &

Picard, 1986; Buzzell, 1968). Moreover, cultural differences among countries have also been singled out for creating this difficulty (Jain, 1989). However, the competitive implications of the choices firms make in terms of the nature of differences among countries they choose to address have been neither examined nor noticed by prior studies. Our results confirm that those firms that effectively leverage knowledge regarding tacit differences among countries—or knowledge that is difficult for others to acquire and leverage—are more likely to possess greater global new product development capabilities. On the other hand, those firms who choose to leverage only knowledge regarding explicit differences—or knowledge that is easy for most competitors to acquire and leverage—are less likely to have greater global new product development capabilities. Hence, while knowledge about explicit differences among countries may be necessary, it is not sufficient to create differential capabilities. These results support some of the core tenets of the resource-based view of the firm—that is, firm capabilities are a function of resources that are unique and difficult to replicate. Tacit overseas knowledge clearly appears to be one such resource for global new product development capability. By leveraging tacit overseas knowledge, organizations can use the global new product development process to build rare and difficult-to-imitate resources that produce competitive advantage.

## Integrating the Content and Process Aspects of Knowledge

Our results also confirm that the *interactions* between the content of knowledge and the process by which it is acquired influence global new product development capabilities. The content of knowledge refers to the nature of overseas information addressed for the global product design—tacit or explicit. The process of knowledge acquisition refers to the information-processing mechanisms employed to transfer and deploy overseas information into the global product design. In the absence of main effects and the significance only of interaction effects, we find support for a widely held but untested assertion that *both* the content and process aspects of knowledge are equally important in creating an inimitable resource (Garud & Nayyar, 1994; Grant, 1996; Nonaka, 1994). Dierickx and Cool (1989) epitomize this view by arguing that both the "stocks" and "flows" make the knowledge asset unique and inimitable, with the "flows" clearly influencing the "stocks".

Put differently, our results reveal that merely addressing tacit differences among countries is not sufficient to generate high global new product development capabilities. Global new product development projects also need rich information-processing mechanisms—considering the difficulty in acquiring information on tacit differences among countries. Similarly, the results also reveal that rich information-processing mechanisms by themselves are not necessarily associated with high global new product development capabilities. This is possibly because these mechanisms—namely cross-national teams and teams with members having prior overseas experience, only provide a platform for firms to transfer and deploy tacit knowledge. The platform in itself does not appear to be effective unless utilized to leverage tacit knowledge. It is also likely that MNCs may have attained parity in instituting these information-processing mechanisms. Consequently, these mechanisms by themselves have limited value in the current competitive context of these organizations unless employed to leverage information and knowledge that is unique and difficult for their rivals to acquire.

## The Influence of the Organizational Context

The results also suggest that the approach employed by global new product development teams to leverage tacit overseas knowledge is sensitive to the context of the organization. Employing teams with members having prior overseas experience appears to be effective only in those organizations that have a high permeability of managers across borders, with headquarters and subsidiary managers frequently visiting and informally interacting with one another. This result is yet tentative, as it is not supported in our study by a significant three-way interaction between the degree of tacitness, teams with members having prior overseas experience, and permeability of managers across borders. However, this observation warrants more subsequent examination as it implies that a group's absorptive capacity is dependent not merely on the prior experience of its members but on how closely related the group is to its sources of new knowledge. Lane and Lubatkin (1998) describe this phenomenon as *relative absorptive capacity*—after finding in a sample of pharmaceutical and biotechnological alliances that a student firm's ability to absorb new knowledge from a teacher firm is influenced by how closely the teacher and student firms are related. Hence, it is likely that the headquarters and overseas subsidiaries of firms may require a tight linkage for their teams composed with members having prior overseas experience to be effective at absorbing tacit overseas knowledge.

## Contributions and Conclusions

This study makes several important contributions to theory, methodology and business practice. From a theoretical standpoint, it contributes to the global strategy literature by providing new insights on a critical aspect of competing globally that has not been addressed by prior studies. By considering knowledge as a key resource within organizations, this study also integrates the resource-based view of the firm with the emerging knowledge-based view of the firm. The knowledge-based view of the firm believes that the competitive advantage of a firm lies in its ability to create, store and apply knowledge (Spender, 1996; Zander & Kogut, 1995). Of particular interest to this research stream has been the significance of tacit knowledge within organizations. Tacit knowledge is now widely believed to be an important and untapped source of competitive advantage. This study is one of the first to provide empirical evidence on the critical role of tacit knowledge in influencing firm capabilities. From a methodological perspective, this study develops new measures for key constructs such as tacit knowledge and firm capabilities. From a managerial perspective, this study provides guidelines to managers in making some critical choices in the process of global new product development.

Two limitations of this study may be apparent to a reader. One is our use of a single informant. However, as we focused on very specific project team-level activities (unlike broader issues like organizational culture where there could be considerable heterogeneity among different sub-units), and collected information from a knowledgeable project team member, we mitigate the general weakness associated with a single informant (Venkatraman & Grant, 1986). Another related problem could be a common method bias. However, considering that all the hypotheses were based upon interaction effects rather than main effects, it is unlikely that the common method bias would have influenced our results. In other words, it is unlikely that managers would have an "interaction-based theory" in their minds that could be systematically biasing their responses and these results.

To conclude, our study sheds light on some important but unaddressed aspects of innovation processes of firms competing in the global market. We examined the patterns of routines by which firms successfully leverage overseas knowledge for global new product development. Our evidence confirms that leveraging tacit overseas knowledge is associated with greater global new product development capabilities. Our results also reveal that effectively leveraging tacit overseas knowledge entails global new product development teams addressing tacit differences among countries and employing rich information-processing mechanisms to transfer and deploy this tacit information. Rich information-processing mechanisms include co-locating domestic and overseas managers through cross-national teams and building absorptive capacity in the global new product development process through teams with domestic members having prior overseas experience. Our findings also suggest that leveraging tacit overseas knowledge using teams with members having prior overseas experience may be effective only in those organizations where headquarters and subsidiary managers frequently visit and informally interact with one another. At a more fundamental level this study confirms a core tenet of the resource-based view of the firm—that firm capabilities are a function of unique and difficult-to-imitate resources.

## Notes

1. This study has been supported by the Carnegie Bosch Institute through a grant on the topic "Knowledge in International Corporations". This material is also based on the work supported by the National Science Foundation under grant number SBR-9422284 to the second author. Any opinions, findings, conclusions or recommendations expressed in this material are those of the authors and do not necessarily reflect the views of the National Science Foundation. We wish to thank Michael Lubatkin, Steve Floyd, William Schulze, Mark Youndt, and Luis Martins for their comments on earlier drafts of this paper.
2. As tacit understanding is largely derived by personal experiences its creation is idiosyncratic and often leads to detection of opportunities not spotted by other competitors. For example, Sanyo spotted a new opportunity for developing cordless telephones with an electromagnetic battery recharging feature (as opposed to the conventional means of physical contact terminals) by interpreting a reason based on tacit differences among country markets. Facing frequent complaints about cordless telephone batteries failing to recharge in the US market, they discovered the problem to be associated with a cultural trait peculiar to the US market—of consumers "snacking" while using the telephone and hence soiling the physical contacts for battery recharging. This consumer trait was apparently not observed in Japan, their home market.
3. In Galbraith's (1977) notion of a "fit" in information processing, organizations can choose to encounter either high or low levels of uncertainty in their tasks as long as they possess appropriate information processing capacities.
4. Based on Daft and Lengel (1986), we view richness of information processing mechanisms as a continuum, with *lean* mechanisms connoting the low end of that continuum. Hence, while face-to-face contact is an example of a rich medium of information of exchange, written memos are an example of a lean medium of information exchange.
5. Factor analysis with varimax rotation confirmed that all multiple indicator variables loaded on a single factor. Considering the factor scores as weights, the respective weighted averages of the indicators were used to compute the value of each multiple indicator variable. Furthermore, as suggested by Venkatraman (1989), interactions were computed by multiplying respective independent variables after transforming them by centering them around their mean to avoid multicollinearity problems.
6. The significance of the interaction terms does not change when other control variables are dropped from the model. We also tested for a three-way interaction between the degree of tacitness addressed, teams with members having prior overseas experience and the permeability of managers across borders, and did not find it to be significant. It is also important to note that permeability of managers across borders and project teams with domestic members having prior overseas

experience are distinct constructs. Permeability of managers across borders represents the degree to which middle managers of the organization regularly visit overseas locations and informally interact with managers at those locations, whereas project teams with members with prior overseas experience represent teams composed with domestic managers who were posted in an overseas office for *at least one year*. While it is likely that organizations with high permeability of managers across borders may have many managers who were posted overseas, those organizations may still choose not to involve these managers in project teams. As such, permeability of managers across borders is an organizational-level variable, and team composition with domestic members having prior overseas experience is a project-level variable.

## References


Amit, R. & Schoemaker, P. (1993). Strategic assets and organizational rents. *Strategic Management Journal*, **14**, 33–46.

Banbury, C.M. & Mitchell, W. (1995). The effect of introducing important incremental innovations on market share and business survival. *Strategic Management Journal*, **16**, 161–182.

Barney, J.B. (1991). Firm resources and sustained competitive advantage. *Journal of Management*, **17**(1), 99–120.

Bartlett, C.A. & Ghoshal, S. (1989). *Managing Across Borders*, Boston, MA: Harvard Business School Press.

Boddewyn, J.J., Soehl, R. & Picard, J. (1986). Standardization in international marketing: Is Ted Levitt in fact right? *Business Horizons*, **29**(6), 69–75.

Buzzell, R. (1968). Can you standardize multinational marketing? *Harvard Business Review*, **46**, 102–113.

Cavusgil, S.T., Zou, S. & Naidu, G.M. (1993). Product and promotion adaptation in export ventures: An empirical investigation. *Journal of International Business Studies*, 479–506.

Chen M. J. & Stucker, K. (1997). Multinational management and multimarket rivalry: Toward a theoretical development of global competition. *Academy of Management Proceedings, Boston*, 2–6.

Cheng, J.L.C. & Bolon, D.S. (1993). The management of multinational R&D: A neglected topic in international business research. *Journal of International Business Studies*, 1–18.

Cohen, W.M. & Levinthal, D.A (1990). Absorptive capacity: A new perspective on learning and innovation. *Administrative Science Quarterly*, **35**, 128–152.

Conner, K.R. & Prahalad, C.K. (1996). A resource-based theory of the firm: Knowledge versus opportunism. *Organization Science*, **7**(5), 477–501.

Daft, R.L. & Lengel, R.H. (1986). Organizational information requirements, media richness and structural design. *Management Science*, **32**, 554–571.

Dierickx I. & Cool, K. (1989). Asset stock accumulation and sustainability of competitive advantage. *Management Science*, **35**, 1504–1511.

Dunning, J.H. (1980). Toward an eclectic theory of international production. *Journal of International Business Studies*, Spring–Summer, 9–31.

Egelhoff, W. (1988). *Organizing the Multinational Enterprise: An Information Processing Perspective*, Cambridge, MA: Ballinger.

Galbraith, J.R. (1977). *Organization Design*, Reading, MA: Addison-Wesley.

Garud, R. & Nayyar, P.R. (1994). Transformative capacity: Continual restructuring by intertemporal technology transfer. *Strategic Management Journal*, **15**, 365–385.
Ghoshal, S. (1987). Global strategy: An organizing framework. *Strategic Management Journal*, **8**(5), 424–440.
Grant, R.M. (1996). Prospering in dynamically-competitive environments: Organizational capability as knowledge integration. *Organization Science*, **7**(4), 375–387.
Gupta, A.K. & Govindrajan, V. (1993). Coalignment between knowledge flow patterns and the strategic systems and processes within MNCs. In P. Lorange, B. Chakravarthy, J. Roos & A. van de Ven (eds), *Implementing Strategic Processes: Change, Learning and Cooperation*, London: Basil Blackwell.
Hamel, G. & Prahalad, C.K. (1985). Do you really have a global strategy? *Harvard Business Review*, July–August, 139–148.
Hedlund, G. (1994). A model of knowledge management and the N-form corporation. *Strategic Management Journal*, **15**, 73–90.
Jain, S. (1989). Standardization of international marketing strategy. *Journal of Marketing*, **53**(1), 70–79.
Kogut, B. & Zander, U. (1993). Knowledge of the firm and the evolutionary theory of the MNC. *Journal of International Business Studies*, **24**(4), 625–645.
Lane, P.J. & Lubatkin, M. (1998). Relative absorptive capacity and inter-organizational learning. *Strategic Management Journal*, **19**(5), 461–478.
Leonard-Barton, D. (1992). Core capabilities and core rigidities: A paradox in managing new product development. *Strategic Management Journal*, **13**, 111–126.
Levitt, T. (1983). The globalization of markets. *Harvard Business Review*, **61**, 92–102.
Nelson, R. & Winter, S. (1982). *An Evolutionary Theory of Economic Change*. Cambridge, MA: Belknap Press.
Nobel, R. & Birkinshaw, J. (1998). Innovation in multinational corporations: Control and communication patterns in international R&D operations. *Strategic Management Journal*, **19**(5), 479–496.
Nobeoka, K. & Cusumano, M.A. (1997). Multi-project strategy and sales growth: The benefits of rapid design transfer in new product development. *Strategic Management Journal*, **18**(3), 169–186.
Nonaka, I. (1994). A dynamic theory of organizational knowledge creation. *Organization Science*, **5**(1), 14–37.
Nonaka, I. & Takeuchi, H. (1995). *The Knowledge Creating Company*. New York: Oxford University Press.
Ohmae, K. (1990). *The Borderless World: Power and Strategy in the Interlinked Economy*. New York: Harper Perennial.
Peteraf, M.A. (1993). The cornerstone of competitive advantage: A resource-based view. *Strategic Management Journal*, **14**(3), 179–192.
Polyani, M. (1966). *The Tacit Dimension*. London: Routledge & Kegan Paul.
Porter, M.E. (1980). *Competitive Strategy: Techniques for Analyzing Industries and Competitors*. New York: Free Press.
Porter, M.E. (1986). Competition in global industries: A conceptual framework. In M.E. Porter (ed), *Competition in Global Industries*, Boston, MA: Harvard Business School Press, 16–60.
Prahalad, C.K. & Doz, Y. (1987). *The Multinational Mission: Balancing Local Demands and Global Vision*. New York: Free Press.
Prahalad, C.K. & Hamel, G. (1990). The core competence of the corporation. *Harvard Business Review*, **68**(3), 79–91.
Quinn, J. B. (1992). *Intelligent Enterprise: A Knowledge and Service Based Paradigm for Industry*. New York: Free Press.

Samiee, S. & Roth, K. (1992). The influence of global marketing standardization on performance. *Journal of Marketing*, **56**(2), 1–17.
Spender, J.C. (1996). Making knowledge the basis of a dynamic theory of the firm. *Strategic Management Journal*, **17**, 45–62.
Subramaniam, M., Rosenthal, S.R. & Hatten, K.J. (1998). Global new product development: Preliminary findings and research propositions. *Journal of Management Studies*, **35**(6), 773–796.
Takeuchi, H., & Porter, M.E. (1986). The roles of marketing in global strategy. In M.E. Porter (ed.), *Competition in Global Industries*, Boston, MA: Harvard Business School Press.
Teece, D.J. (1977). Technology transfer by multinational firms: The resource cost of transferring technological know-how. *Economic Journal*, June, 242–261.
Teece, D.J. (1983). Technological and organization factors in the theory of the MNE. In M. Casson (ed.), *The Growth of International Business*, London: George Allen & Unwin.
Van de Ven, A.H. & Delbecq, A.L. (1974). A task contingent model of work-unit structure. *Administrative Science Quarterly*, **19**(2), 183–197.
Venkatraman, N. (1989). The concept of fit in strategy research: Toward verbal and statistical correspondence. *Academy of Management Review*, **14**(3), 423–444.
Venkatraman, N. & Grant, J.H. (1986). Construct measurement in organizational strategy research: A critique and proposal. *Academy of Management Review*, **11**(1), 71–87.
Venkatraman, N. & Ramanujam, V. (1987). Measurement of business economic performance: An examination of method convergence. *Journal of Management*, **13**(1), 109–122.
Von Hippel, E. (1994). Sticky information and the locus of problem solving. *Management Science*, **40**(4): 429–439.
Yip, G.S. (1995). *Total Global Strategy*. Englewood Cliffs, NJ: Prentice-Hall.
Zander, U. & Kogut, B. (1995). Knowledge and the speed of transfer and imitation of organizational abilities: An empirical test. *Organization Science*, **6**(1), 76–92.

## APPENDIX 1 COMPANIES AND PRODUCT CATEGORIES REPRESENTED IN THE SAMPLE

See table on page 398.

| Sr. no., company | Product category |
|---|---|
| 1. 3M | Sponges, Cosmetics |
| 2. Abbot Laboratories | Baby food |
| 3. Alberto Culver | Shampoo |
| 4. Bausch & Lomb | Contact lenses |
| 5. Becton Dickinson | Digital thermometers, insulin injectors |
| 6. Black & Decker | Cordless drills |
| 7. British-American Tobacco | Cigarettes |
| 8. Brown Group | Children's footwear |
| 9. Caterpillar Company | Hydraulic excavators |
| 10. Cummins | Diesel engines |
| 11. Daewoo | Dishwashers, hydraulic excavators, forklift trucks, machine tools |
| 12. Duracell | Batteries |
| 13. Eastman Kodak | Films, digital cameras |
| 14. Fuji Xerox | Copiers |
| 15. GE Appliances | Refrigerators |
| 16. Gillette | Writing instruments, razors |
| 17. Hallmark Cards | Greeting cards |
| 18. Hélène Curtis | Cosmetics |
| 19. Hershey Foods | Chocolate confectioneries |
| 20. Hewlett-Packard | Medical imaging devices, printers, digital cameras |
| 21. Honeywell | Temperature control systems |
| 22. Jafra Cosmetics | Cosmetics |
| 23. Johnson & Johnson | Toothbrushes |
| 24. Liptons | Food products |
| 25. L'Oréal | Cosmetics |
| 26. Lucent Technologies | PBX systems |
| 27. Maytag | Dishwashers, refrigerators |
| 28. Mead Johnson | Baby foods |
| 29. Motorola | Cellular telephones |
| 30. Nortel | PBX systems |
| 31. Ocean Spray Cranberries | Food products |
| 32. Oral-B | Toothbrushes |
| 33. Osram Sylvania | Fluorescent lamps |
| 34. Parker Pen Company | Writing instruments |
| 35. Philips | Digital cameras |
| 36. Polaroid | Digital cameras, films |
| 37. Reckitt & Colman | Air fresheners |
| 38. Reebok | Athletic shoes |
| 39. Siemens | Induction motors, generators |
| 40. SmithKline Beecham | Toothpaste |
| 41. Tambrands | Tampons |
| 42. Tennant | Machine tools |
| 43. Trane Company | Room air-conditioners |
| 44. Whirlpool | Refrigerators, washing machines |
| 45. Wyeth-Ayerst International | Baby food |

# Appendix 2 Constructs and their Measures

1. Global new product development capability (Cronbach alpha: .84)

With respect to your key competitors, please rate how your *product category currently fares*, on the following dimensions:

- Frequency of new global product introductions
- Being first in the market with new product introductions
- Ability to introduce new versions simultaneously in several markets
- Ability to respond to unique requirements of different countries
- Ability to price competitively
- Ability to penetrate new overseas markets

Measured on a 1–7 scale: Much worse than the competition—About the same—Much better than the competition

2. Degree of tacitness in overseas information (Cronbach alpha: .81)

Please indicate the characteristics of the information acquired *from overseas locations* (about differences among overseas markets, manufacturability in overseas plants, etc.) The information *your project acquired:*

| | |
|---|---|
| Was simple | Was complex |
| Was easy to comprehensively document in manuals or reports | Was difficult to comprehensively document in manuals or reports |
| Was easy to comprehensively understand from written documents | Was difficult to comprehensively understand from written documents |
| Was easy to precisely communicate through written documents | Was difficult to precisely communicate through written documents |
| Was obvious to all competitors | Had subtle nuances known only to a few competitors |
| Was easy to identify without personal experience in the overseas locations | Was difficult to identify without personal experience in the overseas locations |

←——————————→

Measured on a 1–7 scale

Note: This question was preceded by two other questions that provided the survey respondents the background for this construct. These questions were:

1. How significant for your project was the following information to develop the new global product? (on a 1–7 scale: Was of no significance—Was of great significance)
2. How new or novel was the following information used by your project for developing the new global product? (on a 1–7 scale: Not at all new—Substantially new)

For each of these questions, the indicators were:

- Information on overseas market preferences
- Information on the feasibility of manufacturing various design alternatives in overseas plants
- Information on differences among overseas markets

| 3. Co-location—represented as teams being either domestic or cross-national |
| --- |
| Dummy variable—measured as 1 if there were overseas members in the team, 0 otherwise |

| 4. Absorptive capacity—represented as teams having domestic members with prior overseas experience, or not having domestic members with prior overseas experience |
| --- |
| Dummy variable—measured as 1 if the team had domestic members who were posted in overseas offices for at least a year, 0 otherwise |

5 and 6. Brand image in overseas markets, and overseas market share (control variables)

With respect to your key competitors, please rate how your *product category currently fares*, on the following dimensions:

- Brand image in key overseas markets
- Market share in key overseas markets

Measured on a 1–7 scale: Much worse than the competition—About the same—Much better than the competition

| 7. Global marketing infrastructure (control variable) |
|---|
| Marketing/sales offices that supported your product category<br>Measured with respect to "presence in important country markets" of this indicator, on a 1–5 scale: In none (0%)—In very few (<10%)—In some (10–50%)—In most (50–90%)—In almost all (90–100%) |

| 8. Market concentration (control variable) |
|---|
| The market served by the global product:<br>Had many competitors ⟷ Had few competitors<br>Measured on a 1–7 scale |

| 9. Number of countries targeted (control variable) |
|---|
| Requirements of how many countries were important considerations for the new global product's design? |

| 10. Permeability of managers across borders (control variable) (Cronbach alpha: .88) |
|---|
| How prevalent were the following practices in your Division (at the time of the project)?<br>• Regular visits to HQ by overseas managers (middle management)<br>• Regular visits to overseas subsidiaries by HQ managers (middle management)<br>• Informal interactions between HQ and overseas subsidiary middle managers<br>Measured on a 1–7 scale: Very rare—Moderately prevalent—Extremely prevalent |

# 16

# What is the Role of Performance Goals in Product Development? A Study of Japanese Camera Manufacturers

Kentaro Koga, Antonio Davila

## Introduction

The present paper empirically explores the role of performance goals in product development. The study investigates the target costing practices of camera manufacturers in Japan. Target costing is an innovative control system that seeks to minimize those manufacturing costs which are determined in product development (Cooper, 1995; Society of Management Accountants of Canada, 1994).

Setting performance goals as well as managing the organizational process to achieve those goals is an essential aspect of today's business management. This is even true in product development where high uncertainty regarding the performance may diminish the meaningfulness of the goals. White and Locke (1981) document that R&D professionals and managers perceive performance goals as an important cause of successful R&D. Nonetheless, academic researchers, and often managers, do not explicitly

*Dynamic Strategic Resources: Development, Diffusion and Integration.*
Edited by Michael A. Hitt, Patricia Gorman Clifford, Robert D. Nixon and Kevin P. Coyne.

understand why performance goals are set, and what role the goals play in product development.

Achieving good performance in product development is a key pillar for strategy implementation. The impact of product development on business performance has been magnified by shortened product lifecycle (Patterson, 1993). Additional pressure on product development comes from time-based competition where companies try to gain first-mover advantage. Today, firms have to launch the right product at low cost since they have substantially less time to correct mistakes after the development process. Performance goals can facilitate appropriate implementation of the business strategy in product development.

There are three possible roles of performance goals. First, the performance goal can be a benchmark that sets rewards for product designers to mitigate the agency problem (Demski & Feltham, 1978). Second, the performance goal can signal the prediction for the actual performance and facilitate the planning and coordination among the business functions involved in product development (Anthony, 1988). Third, the performance goal can be a catalyst for organizational learning among the workers, such as product designers and process engineers, who try to achieve the goal (Imai, Nonaka & Takeuchi, 1985).

The present paper empirically explores whether performance goals in product development play these roles. Specifically, the study investigates the target costing practices of 35 compact camera development projects of seven Japanese manufacturers between 1991 and 1996.

Statistical analyses examine the consistency between each role and empirical evidence individually because the roles may not be mutually exclusive. The results indicate that performance goals are catalysts for organizational learning among the workers who try to achieve them (the third role). The challenging (i.e., lower) cost targets are associated with successful cost reduction accomplishment. Challenging targets initiate intensive interactions between product designers and process engineers. Moreover, the challenging targets trigger frequent monitoring of the gap between the target and cost estimate. Intensive interactions and frequent monitoring, in turn, lead to low-cost product and process designs.

This paper contributes to the literature by investigating performance goals, an important aspect of product development that has been overlooked. In addition, in contrast with other studies, the paper incorporates different perspectives on organization (i.e., agency, coordination and organizational perspectives) and compares them in terms of the consistency with empirical evidence. The paper is also relevant to practitioners because the findings are contrary to the conventional wisdom which maintains that performance goals must be achieved (Tanaka, 1993); challenging goals lead to good actual performance even though the goals may not be met.

The remainder of the present paper is organized as follows. The next section reviews the literature. Section three outlines the research method. Section four reports the statistical results. The final section concludes the paper with a discussion on the implication of the findings to practitioners and possible extensions to the study.

## LITERATURE REVIEW

### DESCRIPTION OF TARGET COSTING AND PRODUCT DEVELOPMENT PROCESS

#### Target Costing

The present paper empirically explores the role of performance goals in product development. Specifically, the study investigates the practice of target costing, an innovative control system that seeks to minimize those manufacturing costs which are determined in product development. Target costing is an ideal application of goal setting to explore in this study because, in target costing, the cost target is the central force from which the development activities emanate.

Academic researchers (e.g., Cooper, 1995; Cooper & Slagmulder, 1997; Kato, 1993) and writers in the business press (e.g., *Economist*, 1996; Worthy, 1991) argue that the use of target costing reduces product manufacturing costs. Cooper (1994a) claims that target costing is more effective in managing manufacturing costs during product development than other approaches. Hiromoto (1988) identifies target costing as ''[a]nother hidden edge'' which sustained the competitiveness of Japanese corporations in the global market during the 1980s.

Target costing's principle can be expressed by a simple equation:

$$\text{Product costs} = \text{Selling price} - \text{Profit margin} \qquad (16.1)$$

Target costing takes the selling price and profit margin as given, and derives the target of product costs satisfying the equation. Selling price is set by extensive market research on customers and competitors (Cooper, 1994b). Profit margin is determined by long-term business strategy so that the product fulfills the required return on assets (Sakurai, 1990). The resulting target of product costs is fixed at the beginning of the product development process to drive the development activities.

Alternatively, a firm may take what Cooper (1994a) calls the ''conventional approach'', in which product designers develop the product first, and then estimate the costs. The profit margin results from the estimated product costs and selling price as in Eqn (16.2):

$$\text{Profit margin} = \text{Selling price} - \text{Product costs} \tag{16.2}$$

Another approach, the cost-plus principle, simply adds up the estimated product costs and desired profit margin to determine the selling price as in Eqn (16.3):

$$\text{Selling price} = \text{Product costs} + \text{Profit margin} \tag{16.3}$$

Target costing's characteristics are not limited to the practice of setting the cost target. After setting the target, product designers frequently estimate the product costs and compare the estimate with the target to measure the performance of cost reduction (Cooper, 1994b; Fisher, 1995). Regularly, the cost estimate exceeds the target. Tanaka (1993) maintains that the estimate must come closer to the target through cost reduction activities during product development. When the gap between the target and estimate does not narrow, however, the target is revised to an attainable level.

### Product Development Process

FIGURE 16.1 presents the average product development process of the sample of 35 compact camera development projects. The entire development process, which lasts an average of 18.9 months, comprises seven stages.

In the *advanced engineering* and *concept study* stages, product designers and marketing personnel examine the technical and commercial feasibility of the prospective camera, respectively. During the *product planning* stage, the product designers plan the major features of product design such as component layout and specifications of important parts. Performance goals including the cost target are set as well. In *product design*, the product designers work on the engineering drawings of each part. The *process engineering* stage includes design of manufacturing tools, part dies and assembly lines. The two *pilot runs* are the final development stages before mass production. During each run, product and process designs are checked to see whether they can withstand the demands of mass production.

## TECHNOLOGY MANAGEMENT LITERATURE

The technology management literature identifies several factors that characterize product development performance. Overall, the studies are

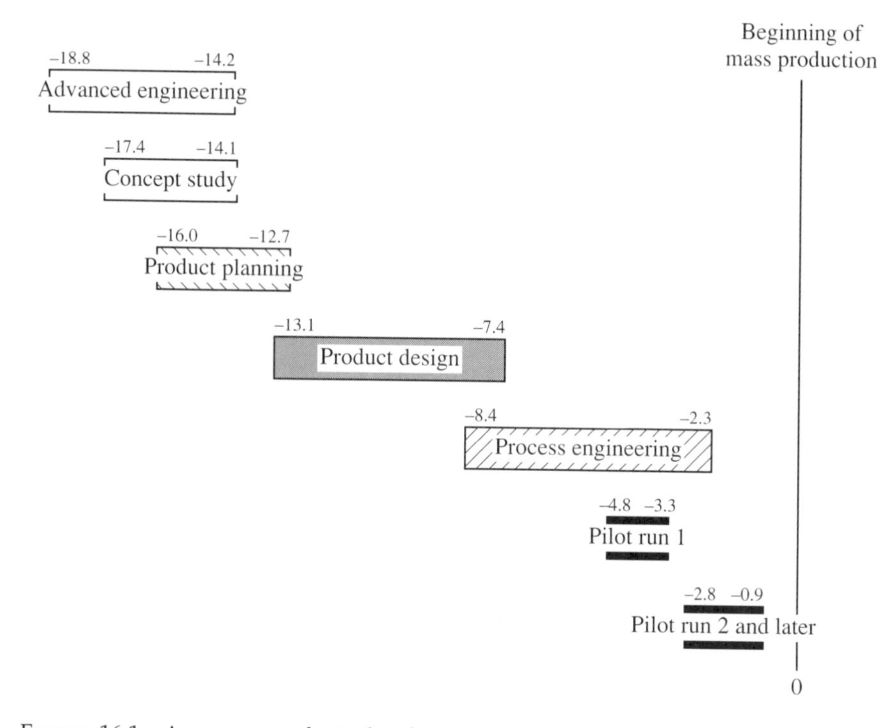


FIGURE 16.1 Average product development process of sample (months before beginning of mass production)

based on the coordination and organizational learning perspectives. No study empirically explores the role of performance goals.

In their study of the automotive industry, Clark and Fujimoto (1991) examine product development lead time, development productivity and product quality. For product quality they construct a measure called total product quality (TPQ), which is a weighted average index made from customer satisfaction rankings, defect ratio, expert evaluation on design quality, and market share. Clark and Fujimoto find that the three performance measures are positively correlated with one another. They also identify factors associated with good performance: integrated problem-solving, "heavyweight" project management and manufacturing capability. These factors contribute to better coordination among business functions, especially between product design and process engineering, which, in turn, leads to the internal integrity of the product.

Hitt, Hoskisson and Nixon (1993) develop a theoretical model describing organizational factors that affect product development performance, defined as the ability for a firm to appropriate value from innovation.

They identify interfunctional integration as a key driver in facilitating communication to improve time-to-market and to cope with design and demand uncertainty. Firms may use loose coupling, integrators, cross-functional appointments and training, multifunctional teams and cultural indoctrination to promote interfunctional integration.

Iansiti (1995a, 1995b) studies the product development projects of mainframe computer manufacturers. He focuses on product development lead time and development productivity as performance measures of the development projects. Iansiti finds that development lead time is shorter and development productivity is higher in projects with "system-focused" technology integration. System-focused technology integration takes "an early focus on systemic interactions between knowledge bases and a tendency to explore how the system as a whole will behave before making commitments to individual fundamental choices" (Iansiti, 1997: 95). In other words, a system focus first puts together the entire system of a product's technologies, and then works on individual components. Iansiti underscores the importance of product planning that coordinates development activities.

Concentrating on product development lead time, Eisenhardt and Tabrizi (1995) show that in the computer industry fast development is associated with the "experimental approach" incorporating frequent iterations, more testing, frequent milestones and powerful leadership. These authors conclude that experimental product design is relevant to less predictable products in uncertain settings such as personal computers, because the experiments generate new ideas and initiate organizational learning. Eisenhardt and Tabrizi also examine the effect of rewards on development lead time. Contrary to their research hypothesis, the projects with rewards took longer than the projects without rewards. (This result is significant for development projects of less predictable products at the 0.1 level; it is not significant for projects of stable products at a conventional level.)

In summary, the technology management literature suggests that shorter product development lead time and higher development productivity are associated with better interface between product designers and process engineers (Clark & Fujimoto, 1991; Hitt, Hoskisson & Nixon, 1993), more elaborate product planning (Iansiti, 1995a, 1995b), more frequent iterations, testing and milestones (Eisenhardt & Tabrizi, 1995), and more powerful leadership of the project manager (Clark & Fujimoto, 1991; Eisenhardt & Tabrizi, 1995). These factors lead to better coordination across business functions (Hitt, Hoskisson & Nixon, 1993), and enhance organizational learning. The impacts of the factors differ, however, depending on the uncertainty of product technology.

No study empirically explores the role of performance goals *in the context of product development* in spite of the fact that goal setting is a prevalent practice in today's product development. Also, each of the past studies is founded on one perspective on organization without attention to the others. This paper contributes to the literature by investigating performance goals, an important aspect of product development that has been overlooked. In addition, this paper incorporates three major perspectives on organization (i.e., agency, coordination and organizational learning perspectives) and compares them in terms of the consistency with empirical evidence.

## Three Perspectives on the Role of Performance Goals

### Agency Perspective

The performance goal in product development can be a benchmark that sets rewards for product designers. Often, the compensation is determined by whether the actual performance meets a certain threshold. This role is based on the perspective of agency theory (Jensen & Meckling, 1976).

The agency literature assumes that there is a conflict of interests between the principal and agent. Also, it is assumed that the agent knows more about his or her effort and ability than the principal. Upon this framework, analytical research from the agency perspective designs incentive schemes to maximize the total value created through the relationship between principal and agent (Baiman, 1982).

Demski and Feltham (1978) show that under moral hazard or adverse selection, the compensation contract based on a performance goal is Pareto superior to the contract linearly tying rewards to actual performance if the investigation cost is sufficiently small. Codero (1991) and Gupta and Wilemon (1990) suggest that rewards motivate product designers to accelerate the product development process. Similarly, Davila (1998) documents that, in product development of the medical devices industry, project managers receiving variable compensation linked to their actual performance perceive their performance to be higher than that of their peers on a straight salary.

From the agency perspective, the principal needs to compensate the risk-averse agent for the risk of variable rewards by a fixed portion of compensation; without such a fixed portion, the agent will not work for the principal (Kreps, 1990). An incentive scheme that imposes substantial risk on the agent is costly because the fixed portion becomes large. Accounting and management textbooks based on agency perspective recommend performance goals that are "tight, but attainable", suggesting that the optimal goal is the one that is reached about 50% of the time (Atkinson *et al.*, 1997; Emmanuel, Otley & Merchant, 1990; Greenberg & Baron, 1997), though, taking the agency perspective, Daily (1998) claims that the performance goal should be achieved much less than 50% of the time if the gap between the performance goal and actual performance is tied to an implicit reward. Accordingly, whether the performance goal plays the benchmark role for rewards can be examined by the frequency of the actual performance attaining the goal. Specifically, the agency perspective predicts the following proposition:

P1: The performance goal is achieved 50% of the time.

### Coordination Perspective

The performance goal in product development can signal the prediction for the actual performance and facilitate the planning and coordination among the business functions involved in product development. For instance, by referring to the cost target, procurement officers can infer what kind of material is necessary, and begin searching potential suppliers early. Likewise, when the cost target is changed during product development, the revised target can help the marketing personnel predict the actual performance of product manufacturing costs. Marketing can decide the selling price, and prepare the sales promotion policy accordingly. In these cases, the cost target *by itself* signals the prediction for the actual performance, and thereby facilitates planning and coordination; the procurement officers and marketing personnel coordinate their activities using the target. (Alternatively, the coordination can be attained by the interactions among the workers who try to achieve the performance goal. This paper classifies the interactive process as organizational learning role. By contrast, coordination role refers to the case in which the business functions use *only* the information of cost target to coordinate their activities.)

Anthony (1988: 92) claims that a budget with an explicit goal "serves as a device for coordinating the activities" among managers. Using an analytical model, Kanodia (1993) shows that the performance goal can be used to coordinate operations when managers have private information about their operating environments. Gersick (1988) empirically finds that clear goals synchronize the energies and attention of a team.

In order to fulfill the coordination role, the performance goal should be a good predictor for the actual performance. Hence, the predicting power of the goal for the actual performance is an indicator of how well the goal serves the role of coordination. A positive relationship between the goal and actual performance is a necessary condition for the predicting power. Hence, the coordination perspective leads to the following proposition:

P2: The performance goal is positively associated with the actual performance.

## Organizational Learning Perspective

The third possible role is a catalyst for organizational learning among the workers who try to achieve the performance goal. The explanation behind the organizational learning perspective is that challenging goals trigger interactions among the workers, such as product designers and process engineers, thereby enhancing the capability of knowledge creation (Nonaka & Takeuchi, 1995). For instance, product designers frequently ask questions of, seek advice from, and jointly solve problems with process engineers so that the product designers can take manufacturability into account in product design (Ulrich & Eppinger, 1995).

Documenting the process of emergent strategies in Johnson & Johnson, Simons (1987) finds that recurring comparisons between the budget (i.e., performance goal) and the actual performance are associated with the interactions among the managers in the process. Interaction involves intensive reviews, dialogs and debates that lead to creative searching, testing and sharing of new ideas (Simons, 1995). Allen (1977) shows that high-performing product development projects rely on frequent interactions within the organization. Studying five product development projects of Japanese manufacturers, Imai, Nonaka and Takeuchi (1985) conclude that a challenging goal is essential for successful development.

In line with the organizational learning perspective, the social psychology literature documents a positive linear relationship between the level of goal difficulty and actual performance (e.g., Locke, 1968; Locke *et al.*, 1989; Tubbs, 1986). In a study of miners, Buller and Bell (1986) find that performance goals stimulate the search and development of task strategies. Using a management game, Earley, Wojnaroski and Prest (1987) show that extensive search of task strategies leads to better actual performance. Consequently, the organizational learning role of performance goals can be examined by the relationship between the level of goal difficulty and the actual performance. The organizational learning perspective predicts:

> P3: The level of goal difficulty is positively associated with the actual performance.

The three perspectives on the role of performance goals are not mutually exclusive. It is possible that the performance goal plays multiple roles. Accordingly, it is necessary to examine the consistency between each perspective and empirical evidence individually. It is difficult to test the three propositions jointly because they refer to different aspects of the product development process.

## Research Method

### Unit of Analysis

The unit of analysis of the present research is a product development project. The study examines cost targets, cost estimates and actual costs for the projects.

### Sample Selection

This paper investigates projects of 35 mm compact cameras developed in Japan between 1991 and 1996. Competition in the compact camera business provides an ideal environment for the study of target costing.

Effective cost management is the key success factor in the compact camera business. The technology of compact cameras is quite mature, leaving little room for innovative features. Therefore, manufacturers offer essentially identical product functionality. Since the price points of compacts are well defined in each global region (e.g., in Japan, the price points of compacts are 19 800, 29 800, 39 800, 49 800 and 59 800 yen), firms compete over the amount of discount they offer to camera wholesalers and retailers, and eventually to consumers. As a consequence, the compact camera market is intensively price competitive, and effective cost management is imperative for survival.

There are several other advantages from studying compact cameras. First, compact cameras are complex enough to require elaborate cost management practices, yet not so complex that the practices cannot be documented.

Second, cameras have been manufactured by stable and similar manufacturing technologies in the industry for the past 10 years. Thus, the performance variation stems from how well the cost management practices are employed, and not from innovative manufacturing technologies.

The period between 1991 and 1996 also suits the purpose of this research because the recession of the Japanese economy triggered a domestic price-cutting race, which spread to the rest of the world. Between 1991 and 1996, due to the market condition, cost management was an even more critical strategic concern for Japanese camera manufacturers than in other periods.

Seven Japanese camera manufacturers (names disguised to protect confidentiality) provided data on 49 product development projects. According to the market research by Yano Keizai Kenkyuzyo (1995), the combined Japanese market share of the seven firms was 84.8% in 1994. The target sample included all the projects of the participating firms except for those in which product development was outsourced to a non-subsidiary firm (i.e., non-*keiretsu* firm). The target sample also does not include camera development projects that were abandoned in the process of product development. The number of such abandoned projects was very small because the camera manufacturers maintain a full-line business strategy, positioning one product in each price point. In order to maintain the homogeneity within the sample, this paper's sample includes only 35 platform development projects (Clark & Wheelwright, 1993) that contain at least 50% of new parts, calculated on the basis of product manufacturing costs.

TABLE 16.1 summarizes the profile of the cameras in the sample. Panel A reports the composition of the sample by firms. Firms B and F developed only a few cameras by themselves. The development of the rest of their product lines was outsourced to non-subsidiary firms. Outsourced products are excluded from the sample. Panel B presents the composition by market launch years. There are few observations before 1993 because several development projects of earlier years were excluded from the sample due to missing archival records. Within the sample, only one camera was launched in 1996 since in that year the camera manufacturers devoted most of their product development resources to the new photography standard, Advanced Photo System (APS). APS cameras are not included in the study because of their technological novelty. According to Panel C, the mean and median list prices are 47 474 and 46 000 yen, respectively. There is a large standard deviation in the projected sales volume due to observations with extremely high volume. The mean and median maximum zoom lengths are 87 and 80 mm, respectively.

## DATA COLLECTION

This study collected data of three research variables: cost target, cost estimate and actual performance of product manufacturing costs (actual costs, hereafter). Data were collected from two sources. The firms' archival records provided information on actual costs. A survey of the managers of camera development projects provided information on cost targets and cost estimates; one questionnaire was completed for each development project in the sample. The product development function of each participating firm keeps records on the cost targets and cost estimates. The project managers were encouraged to refer to these records. The survey instrument also sought information of the attributes of each camera such as product functionality.

## MEASUREMENT OF RESEARCH VARIABLES

### Cost Target and Cost Estimate

All the camera manufacturers in this research include only manufacturing costs in the cost target and cost estimate; development, marketing and

TABLE 16.1 Profile of cameras in the sample ($n = 35$)

Panel A: Composition by firms

| Firm | Frequency (Number of observations in sample) | Number of responses to survey |
|---|---|---|
| A | 5 | 8 |
| B | 3 | 3 |
| C | 5 | 8 |
| D | 7 | 7 |
| E | 5 | 8 |
| F | 3 | 7 |
| G | 7 | 8 |
| Total | 35 | 49 |

Panel B: Composition by market launch years

| Year | Frequency |
|---|---|
| 1991 | 3 |
| 1992 | 4 |
| 1993 | 9 |
| 1994 | 9 |
| 1995 | 9 |
| 1996 | 1 |
| Total | 35 |

Panel C: Summary statistics of major product attributes

| | Mean | Standard deviation | Minimum | Median | Maximum |
|---|---|---|---|---|---|
| List price (Yen) | 47 474 | 10 898 | 24 800 | 46 000 | 66 000 |
| Projected sales volume (1000 units) | 690 | 490 | 200 | 480 | 2400 |
| Maximum zoom length (mm) | 87 | 27 | 32 | 80 | 140 |

distribution costs are excluded. Direct manufacturing costs comprise direct labor, and direct material and part costs. Indirect manufacturing costs are mainly tool and die costs, and costs associated with manufacturing support functions (e.g., quality assurance). Tool and die costs are generally allocated to products by the projected unit sales volume. Other indirect costs are pooled together in each manufacturing site and allocated using a volume-based measure such as total direct costs; no firm employs activity-based costing (Kaplan & Cooper, 1998).

Although the camera firms acknowledge that the actual costs change during mass production, all firms set the cost target as the *average* cost over the projected sales volume. The cost estimate is projected upon the same basis.

The product manufacturing costs are estimated through aggregation of expected component and assembly costs. Regularly, the aggregated cost estimate exceeds the target.

Each product designer redesigns the component he or she is responsible for, and the process engineers reconsider the manufacturing process to reduce the manufacturing costs. The redesigning and revising process is called Value Engineering (VE). After VE, the manufacturing costs are estimated again to be compared with the target. When there is still a gap, VE activities repeat. The process goes through several iterative steps of VE, re-estimation of the manufacturing costs, and comparison with the target (see FIGURE 16.2). Accordingly, data of the cost target and cost estimate were collected for four different stages of product development: product planning, product design, process engineering and pilot runs.

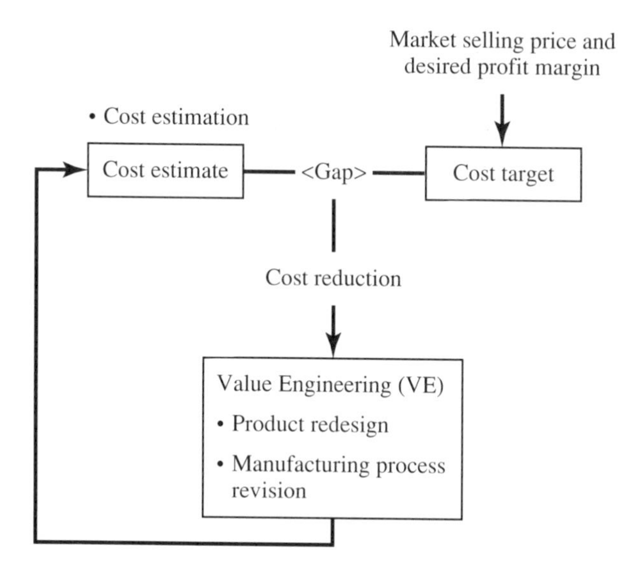


FIGURE 16.2 Procedure of target costing

### Actual Performance of Product Manufacturing Costs

The actual costs decline during mass production along the experience curve. Thus, this study gathered data of the actual costs at three points in time: 3rd, 6th and 12th months of mass production.

Since data of cost targets, cost estimates and actual costs are highly confidential, this paper uses percentile indices that disguise the monetary amount. The indices are set relative to the beginning cost target of each camera development project (i.e., cost target in the product planning stage).

## Statistical Results

Since the three perspectives on the role of performance goals are not mutually exclusive, the statistical analyses examine the consistency between each perspective and empirical evidence individually.

### Examination of Agency Perspective

The performance goal from the agency perspective is used as a benchmark that sets rewards for product designers. Accounting and management textbooks based on the agency perspective suggest that the optimal goal is the one that is reached about 50% of the time. Accordingly, the agency perspective predicts that the performance goal is achieved 50% of the time (P1).

Table 16.2 reports the summary statistics of cost targets, cost estimates, their changes and actual costs. In Panel A, the mean cost target stays stable around 100 throughout the product development process. The median is constant at 100. By contrast, the mean cost estimate starts at 106 and moves substantially up to 111 (see Panel B). The mean cost estimate immediately before mass production (i.e., pilot runs) overruns the target by 10. The Wilcoxon signed-ranks test shows that the gap between the target and estimate in pilot runs is statistically significant (Wilcoxon statistic 162.5, two-tailed p value 0.00). The empirical evidence does not coincide with Tanaka's (1993) claim that the gap must narrow in the process of target costing.

Moreover, the actual costs during mass production are even higher; the mean levels of the 3rd, 6th and 12th months of mass production are 129, 119 and 113, respectively (see Panel D). Figure 16.3 presents how the mean cost target, cost estimate and actual costs move throughout product development and mass production.

TABLE 16.2 Summary statistics of cost target, cost estimate and actual costs[a]

| | Mean | Standard deviation | Minimum | Median | Maximum |
|---|---|---|---|---|---|
| Panel A: Cost target during product development | | | | | |
| Product planning | 100 | — | 100 | 100 | 100 |
| Product design | 101 | 2 | 100 | 100 | 109 |
| Process engineering | 101 | 2 | 100 | 100 | 109 |
| Pilot runs | 101 | 3 | 100 | 100 | 109 |
| Panel B: Cost estimate during product development | | | | | |
| Product planning | 106 | 8 | 100 | 103 | 126 |
| Product design | 109 | 12 | 93 | 104 | 145 |
| Process engineering | 110 | 14 | 93 | 106 | 154 |
| Pilot runs | 111 | 15 | 95 | 106 | 154 |
| Panel C: Change between product planning and pilot runs | | | | | |
| Cost target | 1 | 3 | 0 | 0 | 9 |
| Cost estimate | 5 | 12 | −13 | 0 | 35 |
| Panel D: Actual costs during mass production | | | | | |
| 3rd month | 129 | 24 | 95 | 127 | 174 |
| 6th month | 119 | 20 | 92 | 116 | 173 |
| 12th month | 113 | 19 | 88 | 111 | 165 |

[a] Cost target, cost estimate and actual cost are indexed against the cost target in product planning using percentile scale. Cost target and cost estimate are the figures at the end of each product development stage.

TABLE 16.3 reports that 14, 17 and 31% of the sample achieved the cost target by the 3rd, 6th and 12th months of mass production, respectively. The camera manufacturers consider that the actual costs in the 6th month roughly represent the *average cost over the entire sales volume*. This approximation is relevant for three reasons. First, the product lifecycle of a compact camera is between 18 and 24 months. Second, the manufacturers produce large numbers of cameras in the first six months of mass production to meet high demand immediately after the market launch. Third, the experience curve flattens later in the product lifecycle. In the 6th month, the number of development projects that achieved the target is only 17% of the sample (see TABLE 16.3).

In summary, the number of camera development projects that achieved the cost target is much smaller than 50% of the sample. These results contradict the conventional wisdom which maintains that performance goals must be achieved (Tanaka, 1993). The findings are surprising, given that effective cost management is the key success factor in the compact camera business due to the severe price competition.

Indeed, the seven project managers who were interviewed prior to data collection alluded that targets are not set at realistic levels; they are set

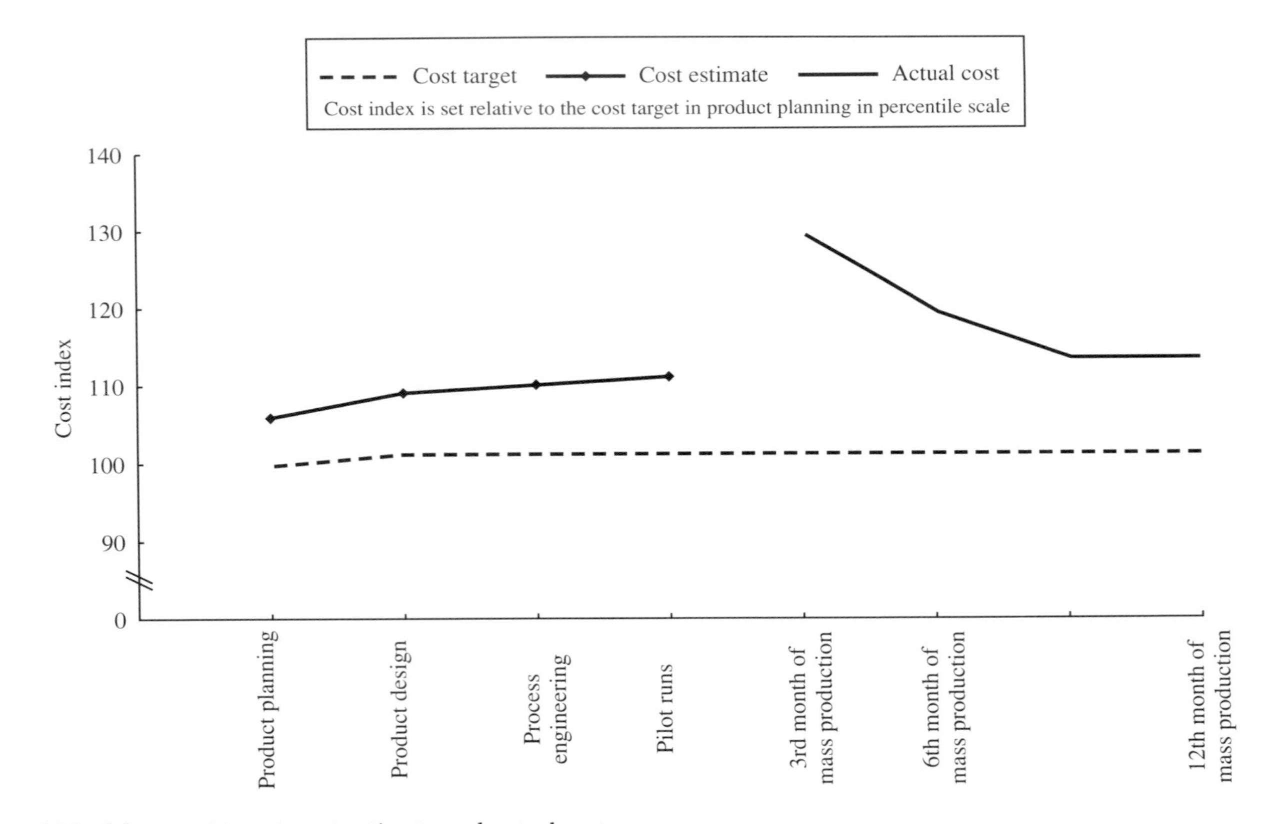


FIGURE 16.3 Mean cost target, cost estimate and actual costs

TABLE 16.3 Sample composition as to cost target achievement[a]

| Timing | Target achieved | Target not achieved |
|---|---|---|
| Pilot runs | 13[b] (37%) | 22 (63%) |
| 3rd month of mass production | 5 (14%) | 30 (86%) |
| 6th month of mass production | 6 (17%) | 29 (83%) |
| 12th month of mass production | 11 (31%) | 24 (69%) |

[a] Frequency for each response in upper rows; percentage within sample in lower rows in parentheses.
[b] Target achievement in pilot runs based on cost estimate, not actual costs.

ambitiously. For example,

> It is desirable to meet the cost target, but we understand that this is very difficult. I recognize the target as a [stretched] goal that makes everybody happy: consumers, retailers, our marketing, manufacturing and product design teams. However, we cannot make everybody happy every time.

Evidence shows that the product designers as well as the project manager were not punished when the actual costs fell short of the cost targets. First, the camera manufacturers do not have explicit incentive schemes that tie objective performance of actual costs to the product designers' and the project manager's rewards. Second, it is unlikely that the head of the product development function of each firm used information on actual costs when evaluating the designers subjectively, because firms do not deliver actual cost data to this function. The lack of linkage between the compensation of the product designers and the project manager, and the actual costs, does not support the agency perspective that asserts the relationship between the rewards and actual performance (e.g., Jensen & Meckling, 1976; Demski & Feltham, 1978).

The finding that only 17% of the camera development projects in the sample achieved the cost target by the 6th month of mass production is not consistent with P1 which predicts that the performance goal is met 50% of the time. The cost targets in the sample are not suitable for a benchmark for setting rewards. (Examination of the agency perspective is built on accounting and management textbooks' inference that performance goals should be reached about 50% of the time. This paper's finding against the agency perspective may be a consequence of the false claim about the 50% achievement, instead of the agency perspective itself.)

## Examination of Coordination Perspective

The performance goal can signal the prediction for the actual performance and facilitate planning and coordination among the business functions involved in product development. In order to fulfill the coordination role, the performance goal should be a good predictor for the actual performance. The predicting power requires a positive relationship between the goal and the actual performance (P2).

In target costing, ideally, the actual costs attain the cost target so that the target predicts the actual costs perfectly. In this paper's sample, however, a surprisingly small number of camera development projects achieved the target (see TABLE 16.3). It may be the case that the target is set at the level with a "discount" from the prediction of actual costs. If the "discount" level is shared by the business functions involved in product development, the target can signal the predicted costs. Also, the cost estimate instead of the cost target may take the role of signaling the prediction. Accordingly, the predicting power of the cost target, as well as the cost estimate, for the actual costs is examined by regression analyses.

In each regression, the dependent variable is the actual costs in the 3rd, 6th or 12th month of mass production. The independent variable which predicts the actual costs is either the cost target in pilot runs, the cost estimate in product planning, or the cost estimate in pilot runs. (For the purpose of presentation, this paper reports results for one cost target and two cost estimates. These are chosen because product planning and pilot runs are the beginning and final stages of product development, respectively. Results for the intermediate stages lie between those of product planning and pilot runs.) The regression includes firm indicator variables to incorporate the possibility that the "discount" levels differ by firms. (In the regressions, the indicator variable of Firm D is dropped. Firm D has the lowest means of actual costs in the 3rd, 6th and 12th months of mass production.) The t-statistic of the coefficient estimate for the cost target (or cost estimate) indicates whether the target (or estimate) is positively associated with the actual costs. In addition, the $R^2$ measures the extent of the predicting power.

TABLE 16.4 reports the results of ordinary least squares (OLS) regressions. In Panel A, the independent variable is the cost target in pilot runs. Its coefficient estimate is not significant at a conventional level in the regression with the actual costs in the 6th month of mass production, the proxy for the average cost over the entire sales volume. The target is

TABLE 16.4 Regression of actual costs on cost target and cost estimate[a,b]

Panel A: Cost target in pilot runs as independent variable

| Variable | Actual costs in 3rd month of mass production[c] | Actual costs in 6th month of mass production[c] | Actual costs in 12th month of mass production[c] |
|---|---|---|---|
| Cost target in pilot runs | 0.56<br>(0.35) | 1.82<br>(1.22) | 3.25<br>(2.33)** |
| F statistic | 2.53** | 1.25 | 1.76 |
| $R^2$ | 0.40 | 0.24 | 0.31 |
| Adjusted $R^2$ | 0.24 | 0.05 | 0.14 |

Panel B: Cost estimate in product planning as independent variable

| Variable | Actual costs in 3rd month of mass production[c] | Actual costs in 6th month of mass production[c] | Actual costs in 12th month of mass production[c] |
|---|---|---|---|
| Cost estimate in product planning | 1.05<br>(1.65) | 0.94<br>(1.53) | 1.02<br>(1.67) |
| F statistic | 3.14*** | 1.40 | 1.30 |
| $R^2$ | 0.45 | 0.27 | 0.25 |
| Adjusted $R^2$ | 0.31 | 0.08 | 0.06 |

Panel C: Cost estimate in pilot runs as independent variable

| Variable | Actual costs in 3rd month of mass production[c] | Actual costs in 6th month of mass production[c] | Actual costs in 12th month of mass production[c] |
|---|---|---|---|
| Cost estimate in pilot runs | 0.77<br>(2.54)** | 0.82<br>(2.91)*** | 0.79<br>(2.77)*** |
| F statistic | 4.02*** | 2.49** | 2.15* |
| $R^2$ | 0.51 | 0.39 | 0.36 |
| Adjusted $R^2$ | 0.38 | 0.23 | 0.19 |

[a] Each regression includes six firm indicator variables. Coefficient estimate in upper row; t-statistic in lower row in parentheses.
[b] Significance level is two-tailed for coefficient estimate, one-tailed otherwise:
*$p < 0.1$.
**$p < 0.05$.
***$p < 0.01$.
[c] Dependent variable.

significantly associated with the actual costs only in the 12th month at the 0.05 level (t-statistic 2.33).

In the regression with the actual costs in the 12th month of mass production, $R^2$ is 0.31. The contribution of the cost target in pilot runs to $R^2$ is even smaller because the regression includes firm indicator variables. The $R^2$ of the regression with only firm indicator variables is 0.18, suggesting that the incremental contribution of the target to the $R^2$ is 0.13. Accordingly, the predicting power of the cost target is not sufficient for the business functions involved in product development to coordinate their activities using the target by itself.

In Panel B, the independent variable is the cost estimate in product planning. The coefficient estimates are not significant in any regressions at a conventional level. By contrast, in Panel C, the cost estimate in pilot runs is significant for all three regressions at the 0.05 level (t-values 2.54, 2.91 and 2.77 for the 3rd, 6th and 12th months of mass production, respectively). Even in these regressions, however, the values of $R^2$ do not exceed 0.51, which do not suggest a strong predicting power ($R^2 = 0.51$, 0.39 and 0.36 for the 3rd, 6th and 12th months of mass production, respectively).

Overall, the predicting power of the cost target or cost estimate for the actual costs is limited. The findings do not provide sufficient evidence for P2 claiming that the performance goal is positively associated with the actual performance.

The present paper conducts an additional test of coordination perspective by examining the relationship between the changes in cost target and selling price. In target costing, the cost target is set by Eqn (16.1) that represents the principle of target costing. Through the equation, target costing links the product manufacturing costs with the selling price, and facilitates the coordination between the product design function, which is responsible for reducing manufacturing costs, and marketing, which is responsible for setting the price. Hence, the equation is in accord with the coordination role of the performance goal.

Coordination between the product design and marketing functions would become easier if the relationship in Eqn (16.1) holds throughout the product development process. Thus, unless the profit margin changes, the coordination perspective predicts that the change in cost target is positively associated with the change in selling price. (When the desired profit margin per product changes substantially, the cost target and price could move opposite to each other. The positive association between the cost target and price, however, should take place more often than the inverse association.)

In order to examine this proposition, this paper employs a one-way analysis of variance (ANOVA) in which the change in cost target is the dependent variable, and the change in selling price is the independent variable. The change in price is coded as either upward change, no change or downward change. The survey instrument did not seek quantitative data on the change in selling price.

TABLE 16.5 reports that the change in cost target is significantly related to the change in selling price at the 0.05 level (F statistic 4.41, p value 0.02). A Duncan multiple-range test (p value 0.1) shows that when the price moves upward, the target increases significantly more than in the case of no price change; yet, contrary to the prediction based on coordination perspective, when the price is changed downward, the cost target moves upward, though the change is not significantly different from the no-change case. Indeed, no camera development project in the sample lowered the target. (One camera development project, which was excluded from the research sample, reduced the cost target by less than 1%. This camera, however, was a derivative product, not a new platform.) The result that downward change in price is associated with upward change in cost target casts doubt on the perspective that the cost target facilitates coordination between the product design and marketing functions.

The findings from the regressions and ANOVA are not consistent with the coordination perspective of performance goals. The regression results show that the cost target is only marginally associated with the actual costs, not supporting P2. The ANOVA result indicates that the cost target and selling price are not linked in a way that facilitates coordination between the product design and marketing functions.

## EXAMINATION OF ORGANIZATIONAL LEARNING PERSPECTIVE

The performance goal in product development can be a catalyst for organizational learning by triggering interactions among the workers who try to achieve that goal. Organizational learning perspective predicts that challenging goals lead to better actual performance. This proposition is in

TABLE 16.5 Analysis of variance of cost target change by selling price change

| Selling price change | Frequency | Mean of cost target change | | |
|---|---|---|---|---|
| | | | F statistic | 4.41 |
| | | | p value | 0.02 |
| Up | 11 | 2[a] | | |
| No change | 20 | 0 | | |
| Down | 4 | 2 | | |

[a] Significantly different from no change case at 0.1, one-tailed.

line with the social psychology literature which documents that challenging goals improve the quality of task strategies. The organizational learning perspective predicts that the level of goal difficulty is positively associated with the actual performance (P3).

This paper measures the performance of actual costs as the ratio of actual costs to cost target. When the actual costs are lower than the target (i.e., good performance), the ratio is smaller than 1; when the actual costs are higher than the target (i.e., bad performance), the ratio is greater than 1. The cost target is used as the benchmark of actual costs because the latter are affected by factors besides cost reduction activities, such as product functionality (e.g., whether the camera was equipped with panoramic picture feature) and projected sales volume, a camera with larger projected sales volume incurring lower indirect manufacturing costs. The cost target incorporates these factors. Thus, the ratio of actual costs to cost target is a reasonable measure of the actual performance.

Raw data of cost targets, however, are not ideal as a benchmark of actual performance because the difficulty of achieving the targets may differ from one project to another. Accordingly, this paper adjusts the cost targets so that they represent the "average" level of difficulty in the sample. The adjusted target with "average" difficulty is estimated using an OLS regression analogous to hedonic price analysis.

Specifically, the adjusted cost target is the predicted value from the regression in which the raw data of cost targets are regressed on factors affecting product manufacturing costs. The factors included in the regression are product functionality, projected sales volume, new product development and manufacturing technologies, and geographical locations of assembly and part procurement. Features of major product functionality that are likely to influence manufacturing costs as well as the location of assembly site (i.e., Japan versus Southeast Asia) are operationalized using indicator variables. The product features considered are remote control and exterior styling in three-dimensional shape (i.e., curved shape); the indicator variable for exterior styling in three-dimensional shape is coded 0 for no adoption, 1 for partial adoption and 2 for full adoption. The relevant features were identified through interview of a project manager of each camera manufacturer prior to the questionnaire survey. Maximum zoom length and projected sales volume are transformed logarithmically to be included in the adjustment. New development and manufacturing technologies are proxied by the camera's market launch date (measured as the number of months from the beginning of 1990); recent camera development projects should benefit from new technologies. The proportion of parts procured outside Japan is measured by the percentage of non-Japanese parts on the basis of product manufacturing costs.

TABLE 16.6 Regression of final adjustment of cost target[a,b]

| Variable | Log of cost target[c] |
|---|---|
| Constant | 2.42<br>(5.17)*** |
| Product functionality: | |
| Log of maximum zoom length | 0.64<br>(6.13)*** |
| Remote control | 0.18<br>(2.69)*** |
| Three-dimensional exterior styling | 0.20<br>(4.01)*** |
| Log of projected sales volume | −0.17<br>(−4.50)*** |
| Market launch date | −0.01<br>(−5.41)*** |
| Southeast Asia assembly site | −0.14<br>(−1.81)* |
| Percentage of non-Japanese parts (× 0.001) | 0.50<br>(0.27) |
| F statistic | 29.33*** |
| $R^2$ | 0.88 |
| Adjusted $R^2$ | 0.85 |

[a] Coefficient estimate in upper row, t-statistic in lower row in parentheses.
[b] Significance level is two-tailed for coefficient estimate, one-tailed otherwise:
*$p < 0.1$
**$p < 0.05$
***$p < 0.01$.
[c] Dependent variable.

TABLE 16.6 presents the results of adjustment. The predicted value from the regression is the adjusted cost target. The adjusted target represents "average" difficulty in the sample, and is the benchmark for the performance of actual costs. Specifically, the performance of actual costs is measured as the ratio of actual costs to adjusted target. Also, the residual from the regression is used as the variable for target difficulty; a negative residual indicates that the target is more difficult (i.e., lower) than "average".

TABLE 16.7 reports the results of the regressions in which the ratio of actual costs to adjusted target is regressed on the target difficulty. The regressions also include firm indicator variables to control for the firm effects. In all the regressions, the coefficient estimates of target difficulty are positive and significant at the 0.05 level (t-values 2.04, 2.56 and 2.51 for the

TABLE 16.7 Regression of cost to adjusted target ratio on target difficulty[a,b]

| Variable | Cost to adjusted target ratio in 3rd month of mass production[c] | Cost to adjusted target ratio in 6th month of mass production[c] | Cost to adjusted target ratio in 12th month of mass production[c] |
|---|---|---|---|
| Intercept | 1.08<br>(16.68)*** | 1.04<br>(16.48)*** | 1.01<br>(15.16)*** |
| Target difficulty | 0.48<br>(2.04)** | 0.59<br>(2.56)*** | 0.61<br>(2.51)** |
| Number of firm variables included | 6 | 6 | 6 |
| Firm of significant indicator variable at 0.1, and sign | A, +<br>E, +; G, + | A, +<br>E, +; F, + | E, + |
| F statistic | 3.60*** | 2.43*** | 2.29** |
| $R^2$ | 0.48 | 0.39 | 0.37 |
| Adjusted $R^2$ | 0.35 | 0.23 | 0.21 |

[a] Coefficient estimate in upper row; t-statistic in lower row in parentheses.
[b] Significance level is two-tailed for coefficient estimate, one-tailed otherwise:
** $p<0.05$
*** $p<0.01$.
[c] Dependent variable.

3rd, 6th and 12th months of mass production, respectively). The more difficult (i.e., the lower) the cost target is, the lower the actual costs relative to the adjusted target. Consequently, more challenging targets are associated with better performance of actual costs. The findings support P3 predicting that the level of goal difficulty is positively associated with the actual performance. Empirical evidence is consistent with the organizational learning role of performance goals.

Interviews with project managers also endorse the organizational learning perspective. Several project managers said that they intensify target-costing activities, such as intensive interactions with process engineers and frequent cost estimations, when the managers foresee difficulty in reducing costs. For instance,

> When I am not confident to meet the cost target, I check and double-check the cost estimate. I also invite process engineers to the estimation process. Extensive checks not only enhance credibility of the cost estimate number, but generate good cost reduction ideas that lie in the "white space" between the process engineers and [product designers].

> I start getting feedback from process engineers and procurement officers earlier if the [cost target] is set tight. Talking with the process engineers is not pleasant, because they [process engineers] and we [product designers] think differently. However, I know that early interactions end up with satisfying results.

Koga (1998) documents that frequent cost revisions and intensive interactions between product designers and process engineers are associated with lower actual costs. Cost revisions are an informal form of cost estimations. In cost estimations, the costs of each product component and assembly process are estimated from scratch; in contrast, in cost revisions, the project manager partially revises the cost estimate figure through daily interactions with product designers, process engineers and procurement officers. Intensive interactions take the forms of frequent questions, reports and approvals of design decisions, as well as advice and joint problem-solving between product designers and process engineers. Together, Koga's findings and this paper's results indicate that challenging cost targets lead to lower actual costs through intensive interactions among the workers involved, and frequent monitoring of the gap between the cost target and cost estimate. The effectiveness of target costing should stem from the interactive process of reviews, dialogs and debates about the gap between the goal and actual performance.

## CONCLUSION

The present paper empirically explores the role of performance goals in product development. The study analyzes data of target costing practices collected from Japanese camera manufacturers' archival records and a questionnaire survey.

The paper investigates the cost targets of camera development projects from three perspectives: agency, coordination and organizational learning. Specifically, the study examines whether the empirical evidence is consistent with each perspective.

The statistical results do not support the agency perspective. A surprisingly small number of camera development projects achieved the cost target. The project manager and the product designers, however, were not penalized over time. The findings are also not consistent with the coordination perspective. The predicting power of the cost target by itself as well as the cost estimate for the actual costs is marginal.

This paper does, however, find evidence consistent with the organizational learning perspective. The more challenging (i.e., lower) the cost target is, the better the performance in terms of actual costs. Interviews with project managers reveal that difficult targets initiate intensive interactions between product designers and process engineers. Moreover, challenging targets trigger frequent monitoring of the gap between the target and cost estimates. Intensive interactions and frequent monitoring, in turn, should lead to low-cost product and process designs.

This paper is relevant to practitioners because the findings are contrary to the conventional wisdom which maintains that performance goals must be achieved; challenging goals lead to good actual performance even though the goals may not be met. At the same time, however, the evidence indicates that performance goals alone cannot generate good actual performance. In the camera development projects, challenging goals are accompanied by interactive control (Simons, 1995) in which the workers involved interact with one another through reviews, dialogs and debates about the gap between the cost target and cost estimate. In interactive control, performance goals are vehicles of creative searching, testing and sharing of new ideas. The effectiveness of target costing should stem from this interactive process in product development.

This study identifies opportunities for future research. First, it finds that the level of target difficulty is positively associated with the performance of actual costs; the more difficult the cost target is, the better the performance in terms of actual costs. The study, however, does not investigate whether there is an optimal level of goal difficulty. When the goal is too challenging, the workers may not acknowledge credibility in the goal (Simons, 1995). If this is the case, there is a tradeoff between the interactions among the workers, which are triggered by the difficult goal, and the goal's credibility. Future research can explore this tradeoff regarding the goal difficulty.

Second, this research can be replicated in other industries. Compact cameras are products with moderate complexity. Performance goals may play a significant coordination role for more complex products, such as automobiles, in which a greater number of workers are involved in product development. Studies of other industries will gauge the external validity of this paper's findings.

## ACKNOWLEDGMENTS

We are grateful to the camera manufacturers which participated in the research. We also appreciate Walter Kuemmerle's encouragement to pursue the research question of this paper. The present paper benefited from helpful comments to the earlier draft from Jay Barney, Shin'ichi Hirota, Marco Iansiti, Bob Kaplan, Bob Simons, workshop participants at Waseda University, and especially Patricia Clifford and Robert Nixon (co-editors) and Sid Balachandran. The research was generously funded by Harvard

Business School's Division of Research and Arthur Andersen LLP Foundation.

## References

Allen, T.J. (1977). *Managing the Flow of Technology*. Cambridge, MA: MIT Press.

Anthony, R.N. (1988). *The Management Control Function*, revised edn. Boston, MA: Harvard Business School Press.

Atkinson, A., Banker, R.D., Kaplan, R.S. & Young, S.M. (1997). *Management Accounting*, 2nd edn. Upper Saddle River, NJ: Prentice-Hall.

Baiman, S. (1982). Agency research in managerial accounting: A survey. *Journal of Accounting Literature* **1**, 154–213.

Buller, P.F. & Bell, C.H. Jr. (1986). Effects of team building and goal setting on productivity: A field experiment. *Academy of Management Journal*, **29**, 305–328.

Clark, K.B. & Fujimoto, T. (1991). *Product Development Performance: Strategy, Organization, and Management in the World Auto Industry*. Boston, MA: Harvard Business School Press.

Clark, K.B. & Wheelwright, S.C. (1993). *Managing New Product Development and Process Development*. New York: Free Press.

Codero, R. (1991). Managing for speed to avoid product obsolescence: A survey of techniques. *Journal of Product Innovation Management*, **8**, 283–294.

Cooper, R. (1994a). *How Japanese manufacturing firms implement target costing systems: A field-based research study*. Working paper, Claremont Graduate School, Claremont, CA.

Cooper, R. (1994b). *Nissan Motor Company Ltd: Target costing system*. Case study 9–194–040. Boston, MA: Harvard Business School.

Cooper, R. (1995). *When Lean Enterprises Collide: Competing Through Confrontation*. Boston, MA: Harvard Business School Press.

Cooper, R. & Slagmulder, R. (1997). *Target Costing and Value Engineering*. Portland, OR: Productivity Press.

Daily, D.J. (1998). *The impact of targets on performance: Archival evidence from a multi-unit firm*. Working paper, Boston College, Chestnut Hill, MA.

Davila, A. (1998). *The information and control functions of management control systems in product development: Empirical and analytical perspectives*. Doctoral dissertation, Harvard Business School, Boston, MA.

Demski, J.S. & Feltham, G.A. (1978). Economic incentives in budgetary control systems. *Accounting Review*, **53**(2), 336–359.

Earley, P.C., Wojnaroski, P. & Prest, W. (1987). Task planning and energy expended: Exploration of how goals influence performance. *Journal of Applied Psychology*, **72**, 107–114.

*Economist* (1996). In faint praise of the blue suit. *Economist*, 13 January, 59–60.

Eisenhardt, K.M. & Tabrizi, B.N. (1995). Accelerating adaptive processes: Product innovation in the global computer industry. *Administrative Science Quarterly*, **40**(1), 84–110.

Emmanuel, C., Otley, D. & Merchant, K. (1990). *Accounting for Management Control*, 2nd edn. London: Chapman & Hall.

Fisher, J. (1995). Implementing target costing. *Journal of Cost Management*, **9**(2), 50–59.

Gersick, C.J.G. (1988). Marking time: Predictable transitions in group tasks. *Academy of Management Journal*, **31**, 9–41.

Greenberg, J. & Baron, R.A. (1997). *Behavior in Organizations*, 6th edn. Upper Saddle River, NJ: Prentice-Hall.

Gupta, A.K. & Wilemon, D.L. (1990). Accelerating the development of technology-based new products. *California Management Review*, **32**(2), 24–44.

Hiromoto, T. (1988). Another hidden edge: Japanese management accounting. *Harvard Business Review*, **64**(4), 22–26.

Hitt, M.A., Hoskisson, R.E. & Nixon, R.D. (1993). A mid-range theory of interfunctional integration, its antecedents and outcomes. *Journal of Engineering and Technology Management*, **10**, 161–185.

Iansiti, M. (1995a). Science-based product development: An empirical study of the mainframe computer industry. *Production and Operations Management*, **4**(4), 335–359.

Iansiti, M. (1995b). Technology integration: Managing technological evolution in a complex environment. *Research Policy*, **24**, 521–542.

Iansiti, M. (1997). *Technology Integration: Making Critical Choices in a Dynamic World*. Boston, MA: Harvard Business School Press.

Imai, K., Nonaka, I. & Takeuchi, H. (1985). Managing the new product development process: How Japanese companies learn and unlearn. In K.B. Clark, R.H. Hayes, & C. Lorenz (eds), *The Uneasy Alliance: Managing the Productivity–Technology Dilemma*, Boston, MA: Harvard Business School Press.

Jensen, M.C. & Meckling, W.H. (1976). Theory of the firm: Managerial behavior, agency costs, and ownership structure. *Journal of Financial Economics*, **3**(4), 305–360.

Kanodia, C. (1993). Participative budgets as coordination and motivational devices. *Journal of Accounting Research*, **31**(2), 172–189.

Kaplan, R.S. & Cooper, R. (1998). *Cost and Effect: Using Integrated Cost Systems to Drive Profitability and Performance*. Boston, MA: Harvard Business School Press.

Kato, Y. (1993). *Genka-kikaku: Senryakuteki Kosuto Manejimento (Target Costing: Strategic Cost Management)*. In Japanese. Tokyo: Nihon Keizai Shinbun.

Koga, K. (1998). *Determinants of effective product cost management during product development: Opening the black box of target costing*. Working paper, Harvard Business School, Boston, MA.

Kreps, D.M. (1990). *A Course in Microeconomic Theory*. Princeton, NJ: Princeton University Press.

Locke, E.A. (1968). Toward a theory of task motivation and incentives. *Organizational Behavior and Human Performance*, **3**, 157–189.

Locke, E.A., Chah, D.O., Harrison, S. & Lustgarten, N. (1989). Separating the effects of goal specificity from goal level. *Organizational Behavior and Human Decision Processes*, **43**, 270–287.

Nonaka, I. & Takeuchi, H. (1995). *The Knowledge-Creating Company: How Japanese Companies Create the Dynamics of Innovation*. Oxford: Oxford University Press.

Patterson, M.L. (1993). *Accelerating Innovation: Improving the Process of Product Development*. New York: Van Nostrand Reinhold.

Sakurai, M. (1990). The influence of factory automation on management accounting practices: A study of Japanese companies. In R.S. Kaplan (ed.), *Measures for Manufacturing Excellence*, Boston, MA: Harvard Business School Press.

Simons, R. (1987). Planning, control, and uncertainty: A process view. In W.J. Bruns, Jr. & R.S. Kaplan (eds), *Accounting and Management: Field Study Perspectives*, Boston, MA: Harvard Business School Press.

Simons, R. (1995). *Levers of Control: How Managers Use Innovative Control Systems to Drive Strategic Renewal*. Boston, MA: Harvard Business School Press.

Society of Management Accountants of Canada (1994). *Implementing Target Costing*. Hamilton, Ontario.

Tanaka, T. (1993). Genka-kikaku (Target costing). In Japanese. In T. Tanaka & Y. Kobayashi (eds) *Kanri-Kaikeiron: Gaidansu (A Guide to Management Accounting Theories)*, Tokyo: Chuo Keizaisha.

Tubbs, M.E. (1986). Goal setting: A meta-analytic examination of the empirical evidence. *Journal of Applied Psychology*, **71**, 474–483.

Ulrich, K.T. & Eppinger, S.D. (1995). *Product Design and Development*. New York: McGraw-Hill.

White, F.M. & Locke, E.A. (1981). Perceived determinants of high and low productivity in three occupational groups: A critical incident study (1). *Journal of Management Studies*, **18**(4), 375–387.

Worthy, F.S. (1991). Japan's smart secret weapon. *Fortune*, 12, August, 72–75.

Yano Keizai Kenkyuzyo (1995). *Nihon Maketto Shea Jiten (Japanese Market Share Directory)*. In Japanese. Tokyo: Yano Keizai Kenkyuzyo.

# 17

# Unnatural Acts: Building the Mature Firm's Capability for Breakthrough Innovation

RICHARD LEIFER, MARK RICE

## INTRODUCTION

The contemporary competitive environment has been and continues to be driven by technological revolution, globalization, hypercompetition, extreme emphasis on price, quality and customer satisfaction with a resultant increasing focus on innovation (Hitt, Keats & De Marie, 1998). These factors cause increased competitive complexity and dynamism requiring an increasing emphasis on innovation as a strategic competence.

The competitive landscape began to change drastically during the 1980s when technology-rich US firms experienced increasing difficulty competing in various industries such as semiconductor memory chips, office and factory automation, and consumer electronics (Morone, 1993). Some have attributed these failures to an inferior capacity, relative to competitors, for achieving continuous and incremental improvements in products and processes targeted at increased quality and decreased costs. In response, in the past decade US firms have focused on incremental innovation in existing products or processes, with an emphasis on cost competitiveness and quality improvements (Betz, 1993; Hamel & Prahalad, 1991; Morone,

*Dynamic Strategic Resources: Development, Diffusion and Integration.*
Edited by Michael A. Hitt, Patricia Gorman Clifford, Robert D. Nixon and Kevin P. Coyne.

1993). There are indications, however, that a focus on incremental innovation is an incomplete approach. Firms that hold the largest market share in one product generation often fail to maintain leadership when technologies shift (Bower & Christensen, 1995). Long-term competitive advantage comes from conflicting, yet ultimately complementary, activities: (1) maintaining a steady stream of incremental and continuous improvements in established business lines, and (2) setting aside existing successful products for new innovations (Hitt, Keats & DeMarie, 1998). Thus, developing new businesses and products based on breakthrough (also termed discontinuous, radical, game-changer) innovations becomes critical to long-term, competitive advantage.

The distinction between incremental and breakthrough innovation probably stems from the definition of innovation proposed by Schumpeter (1934) who suggested that an innovation idea is the catalyst for a departure from existing practice supplanting standard operating procedures. March (1991), drawing on Schumpeterian themes, makes a distinction between exploration and exploitation. Exploitation has to do with refining or expanding existing products or processes while exploration has to do with something fundamentally new, including new products, processes, or combinations of the two. Hence, breakthrough innovations are those that depart from the past and result in new products or services. Incremental innovations usually emphasize cost or feature improvements in existing products or services (Betz, 1993; Hamel & Prahalad, 1991; Morone, 1993). In contrast, breakthrough innovation concerns the development of new businesses or product lines based on new ideas or technologies (Morone, 1993) or substantial cost reductions that transform the economics of a business.

Although there may be significant risk and uncertainty associated with incremental innovation, it is more identifiable and manageable compared with the uncertainty associated with breakthrough innovation. Hence, management practices utilized in the development of incremental innovations can be clearly defined and systematized. With respect to project planning, for example, a number of researchers have identified various stage-gate processes for incremental innovation development, which are widely understood and utilized in our sample companies (Cooper, 1990; Marquis, 1969). Since uncertainty is relatively proscribed, managers can define a continuum of project activities punctuated by a series of decision-making gates, where go/no-go decisions can be made.

By comparison, the uncertainty associated with breakthrough innovation is much greater. There is uncertainty about whether the technology will work, what the markets are and what the applications might be. This uncertainty is difficult to manage in a systematic manner. Although the concept of breakthrough innovation frequently appears in the literature

(Wheelwright & Clark, 1992) in terms of its importance or definition, there are relatively few ideas of how to manage it.

Block and MacMillan (1993) and McGrath and MacMillan (1995) point to differences between managing incremental and breakthrough innovation. It has been noted that breakthrough and incremental innovation processes require different organizational capabilities (Henderson & Clark, 1990). Approaches to market learning are fundamentally different as well (O'Connor & Veryzer, 1998). Hence, we contend that the processes and practices appropriate for managing incremental innovation may be inadequate, and, in some cases, dysfunctional for the development and commercialization of breakthrough innovation where uncertainty, risks and potential rewards are much higher.

Attempting to migrate the disciplined processes developed for incremental innovation into the breakthrough innovation domain may be inappropriate due to differences of the phenomena being managed. Managers of the companies in our study reported difficulty in trying to do this. The lack of clear managerial prescriptions in the literature and the confusion of the managers in our sample companies of how to manage breakthrough innovation provide the motivation for this study. In this paper we describe and categorize a variety of practices in use and in so doing uncover critical issues facing managers with indications of approaches to solving them. Our goal is to provide managers with a starting point for experimentation with new practices and tactics for improving breakthrough innovation effectiveness and to provide researchers with fruitful directions for further study.

In this study, we define a breakthrough innovation project as a formally established project, with an explicit budget and organizational identity, viewed as offering the potential for a factor of 5–10 times (or more) improvement in product performance, an entirely new set of product performance features or a significant (>30%) reduction in cost. This definition was derived from three sources: (1) review of the various definitions of breakthrough innovation in the literature (e.g. Leifer, 1997), (2) discussions among the research team members based on the various perspectives of their disciplines, and (3) intense discussion with industry representatives on the Discontinuous Innovation Subcommittee of the Research-on-Research Committee of the Industrial Research Institute.

## Research Methods

The project was a multiple case, four-year longitudinal study of 12 on-going breakthrough innovation projects (1995–1998) in 10 large, mature firms: Air Products, Analog Devices, DuPont, GE, GM, IBM, Nortel, Otis Elevator,

Polaroid, and Texas Instruments. The study was underwritten by the Sloan Foundation and sponsored by the Industrial Research Institute (IRI), a professional association of *Fortune 500* research and development managers. The multiple case study design allowed us to explore the similarities and differences of management practices across industries, companies and projects.

The study team included six faculty and several doctoral students from various disciplines. The study was deliberately designed as an exploratory, theory-building study rather than a conventional, theory-testing study. A panel of informants from each company met with the study team for in-depth interviews. The informants typically comprised the technical inventor or discoverer, project manager, project champion, and a senior manager. Each interview was taped and transcribed, resulting in many thousands of pages of transcripts. In addition, the research team had access to project documentation, reports and business cases.

## Multiple Comparison Case Study Methodology

This research project employs a multiple case study methodology. Case study research involves the examination of phenomena in natural settings. The case study method is especially appropriate for research in new topic areas, with a focus on "how" or "why" questions concerning a contemporary set of events (Eisenhardt, 1989). Case study research that employs multiple cases should follow a replication logic (Yin, 1994). The complexity of case study research and the high level of interpretation that is necessary create an advantage for the use of research teams. Multiple investigators can bring a variety of experience and complementary insights to the research. A mix of different perspectives can increase the likelihood of discovering novel insights. Convergence of opinions from various researchers can enhance confidence in the findings, and conflicting views can keep the research from premature closure (Eisenhardt, 1989).

## Field Study Sample Selection

Each participating firm nominated one or more projects for research consideration. To be included, a project was viewed by the R&D and project managers of the firm as a "game-changer", i.e. that it meets the characteristics of breakthrough innovation defined above. The project had to be formally established, with a project team and a budget. The participating companies in conjunction with the research team selected one or two projects for inclusion in the study. Although we gathered contextual information at the firm level, the project was the unit of analysis. At the point we began gathering data the projects were in various phases of development, although none were close to commercialization. As will become clear below, it is difficult to characterize the stage of development of the projects because breakthrough projects do not seem to follow clear stages of development. Over the four-year study, the following projects were commercialized or are now in the public domain: BIOMAX™ (a DuPont degradable material); the TI digital mirror device; Analog Devices' air bag actuator; the IBM SiGe chip; and the Otis Elevator bi-directional elevator. For the remainder, the identities of the breakthrough innovations are cloaked to protect the competitive position of the companies.

## Findings and their Relationship to the Literature

We begin with an opening discussion of the nature of the breakthrough innovation life cycle to provide a context for our findings.

### The Nature of the Breakthrough Innovation Life Cycle

Our team developed timelines for each project. The timeline for Project 7, presented in Figure 17.1, provides a typical picture of the general findings related to the breakthrough innovation life cycle derived from all 12 field projects.

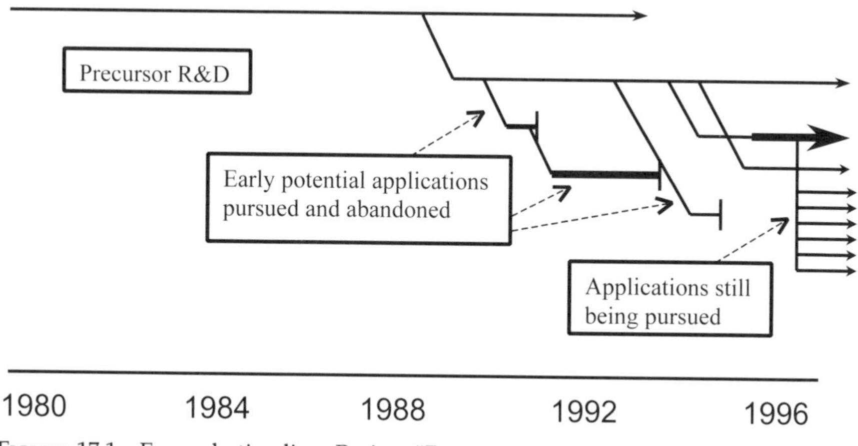


Figure 17.1 Example timeline: Project #7

In this case, the stream of technology research and development activities that preceded the formation of the commercialization project team began in 1980. The lines represent the applications pursued, and the thickness of the lines represents changes in the level of commitment of human and financial resources. The life cycle diagram indicates that Project 7 waxed and waned throughout its history. In the late 1980s and early 1990s several streams of development activity reached dead ends and were abandoned, requiring the team to generate ideas for new high-potential avenues to explore. The development effort often took off in directions unanticipated at the project outset, particularly in response to discontinuous events related to changes in personnel, the formation of internal and external alliances, and key funding milestones. In late 1996, the technology was successfully transferred from the R&D business development organization to a business unit for manufacturing. Uncertainty about target markets and requirements for adoption by lead users remains high; hence, a variety of market applications continue to be pursued. Although initial target applications were not judged to be adequate for achieving an acceptable threshold of revenues, initial market response was sufficient to warrant moving forward. In fact, one of our follow-up interviews revealed that visibility in the marketplace derived from initial product launches stimulated the identification of new and more promising application domains suggested by potential customers.

This project is typical of all the projects studied. The life cycle of breakthrough projects is profoundly different from that of continuous improvement projects. They are long term (typically 10 years or longer) and sporadic, with many stops and starts, deaths and revivals. Projects are non-linear. These projects were fraught with uncertainty about the technology, potential market applications, customers, and organizational/management issues. Finally, all the projects were context dependent. The development process was significantly influenced by personalities, personal preferences, organizational culture and informal networks.

On the basis of this discussion, we conclude that management processes for breakthrough innovation are substantially different from those for incremental innovation. For example we found that there is a desire to apply the stage gate system for managing product development developed by Cooper (1990). Cooper indicates that his system can be applied for the development of new products, not just extensions or incremental improvements. However, in practice, the stage gate system engenders a sense of linearity with clearly specified stages and gates, whereas breakthrough innovation is characterized by non-linearity and uncertainty. The breakthrough implementation tactics we observed and which we describe below were designed to address the uncertainty and non-linearity problems of breakthrough innovations.

## TACTICS FOR FOSTERING BREAKTHROUGH INNOVATION

Our aim in this section is to examine our findings in the context of the strategy literature. We are focused on tactics that can be implemented in the organizations of today for increasing breakthrough innovation effectiveness. These five implementation tactics were based on an analysis of the empirical data. The first three tactics refer to necessary activities in the process of launching a radical innovation project, and the fourth tactic protects innovation projects from organizational pressure and resistance. The fifth tactic reflects our observations that, in current practice, breakthrough innovation relies on individual initiative rather than a systematic organizational process. The five tactics discussed are:

1. Stimulating attractive ideas
2. Promoting opportunity recognition
3. Evaluating and screening breakthrough innovations
4. Creating incubating organizational structures
5. Catalyzing individual initiative

### 1. Stimulating Attractive Ideas

Burgelman (1983) identified two kinds of strategic activities: (1) those induced by the firm's current concept of corporate strategy, and (2) autonomous strategic activities that fall outside the scope of the current strategy. It is useful to examine idea stimulation in our data set in the context of Burgelman's two kinds of strategic activities. The 10 firms employed a variety of mechanisms to stimulate breakthrough innovation ideas that led, eventually, to the 12 projects. Among these were: (1) Articulating holy grails, (2) Articulating strategic intent, (3) Issuing a request for proposals, (4) Promoting connections to external sources of technical information, (5) Conducting technology forecasting exercises, (6) Convening think tanks, (7) Creating an idea generation "sand box", and (8) Rotating talent.

The first three mechanisms were used by management to communicate to the entire organization the importance of idea generation. This first kind of strategic activity targeted at stimulating breakthrough innovation ideas can be thought of as a "strategic push". Six projects emerged, partially due to strong articulation by senior management of the need for new ideas. The responses to these three mechanisms relate to Burgelman's (1983) first kind of strategic activity, i.e. activity induced by the firm's current concept of corporate strategy.

The remaining five mechanisms were used to enhance the idea-generating productivity of specific individuals or groups within the organization. They provide a context that supports (1) an organizational response to "strategic push", as well as (2) the second kind of strategic activities identified by Burgelman (1983), i.e. autonomous strategic activities that fall outside the scope of the current strategy. The specific ideas that are generated may fall within or outside of current corporate strategy, but the strategic choice by senior management to create a facilitative, supportive context for stimulating idea generation brings the activity itself into the strategic framework of the firm. We discuss below how several of these mechanisms were utilized.

*Articulating holy grails.* In seven of the 12 field study projects, there was a shared awareness among researchers and research managers of a technical "holy grail" within their industries. A "holy grail" is a potential technical breakthrough that is generally recognized as a catalyst for transforming an industry, if it can be achieved. For example, in the auto industry a dramatic improvement in fuel efficiency to 80 miles per gallon would provide substantial competitive advantage to the firm that achieved the technical breakthroughs required for achieving this holy grail. In the people mover industry, current elevator technology limits the height of buildings. If that technical limitation could be overcome, it would be possible to erect buildings substantially higher than possible today, such as the proverbial "mile high building". In the information storage industry, creating the capacity to have gigabytes of memory on a floppy disk was seen as a holy grail.

*Articulating strategic intent.* In four cases articulation of strategic intent created a heightened awareness of the need for idea generation and alertness to new ideas. Although articulating strategic intent can take the form of articulating the importance of pursuing a holy grail as a strategic goal, it can alternatively be expressed in less specific terms—a more general call to arms. For example, in one case, the CEO pushed for new businesses in the white spaces between existing business units. In another, the CEO challenged the company to identify new applications of the firm's breakthrough technology for a market in which the company was not currently active.

*Issuing a request for proposals.* In five companies, competitive pressures threatening the core businesses of the firm, or the perceived need for new strategic opportunities, caused senior management to issue a request for proposals, either to the company or to a business unit, to pursue breakthrough innovations. In two cases, hundreds of proposals were submitted for evaluation and screening.

*Promoting connections to external sources of technical information.* The innovation literature argues consistently that external information gathering (Utterback & Brown, 1972; Tushman & Nadler, 1986; Gluck, 1988; Betz, 1993; Martin, 1984) creates a foundation for idea generation. In five of the 12 field study cases, proactively connecting to external sources of information had a significant impact on the generation of the initial idea. External sources included a scientific paper read by a senior research scientist; ideas submitted by external sources; a scientific paper on a secondary area of interest for a scientist; a "brown-bag" lunch with a university researcher; and awareness of an innovation in an adjacent market.

*General observations about the practice of idea generation.* With one exception, idea-generating mechanisms were applied sporadically and in an *ad hoc* fashion, rather than systematically, continuously and strategically. When the idea generation activity was generally undertaken through individual initiative, and not incorporated into institutional processes, that idea generation mechanism ceased with the retirement or departure of the individuals. Results indicate an opportunity for senior managers to create a facilitating context and strategic push, as effective stimuli for the generation of breakthrough ideas.

## 2. Promoting Opportunity Recognition

We found opportunity recognition was typically an event that followed idea generation and triggered the ensuing process of evaluation and screening. The critical role of opportunity recognition in the process of developing and commercializing a breakthrough innovation emerges from a number of sources. To take advantage of shifts in technology, market, and competition, the opportunity first needs to be recognized and interpreted within the context of the firm's environment (Myers & Rosenbloom, 1993). Since companies sensitive to environmental shifts are best positioned for discontinuous change (Utterback, 1994), success comes from an ability to imagine markets that do not presently exist, and then to invest in their development ahead of the competition (Hamel & Prahalad, 1991). To accomplish this, companies need to develop the ability to sense, communicate, and appreciate the early signs of change (Gluck, 1988).

It is interesting that all the researchers cited above refer to the capacity of the company, or of management in general, for opportunity recognition. In contrast, we found opportunity recognition was based on individual initiative rather than a capacity or practice of the firm (Rice and Kelley, 1997). Kirzner (1973) defines the pure entrepreneur as a "decision-maker whose entire role arises out of his alertness to hitherto unnoticed [profit] opportunities", or in the words of Rumelt (1984), "sources of potential rents". In our research, opportunity recognition related to breakthrough innovation was highly dependent on individual initiative and capacity, rather than routine practices and procedures of the firm. It was not a random act, but was generally reactive in nature and unusual, rather than proactive and routine.

In nine of the 12 projects, a low- to mid-level research manager performed the initial act of opportunity recognition. In two of the 12 projects, senior scientists, who had control over discretionary resources to support initial feasibility testing of real or potential innovations, recognized the opportunity. In essence, these two individuals played dual roles, as researcher and research manager, rather than as a researcher only. In only one of 12 cases was a senior technical manager responsible for the initial opportunity recognition, and in no cases did a senior corporate manager fulfill this function. The initiative of individuals set in motion activities that resulted in the establishment of a project to commercialize the breakthrough innovation.

In the majority of cases, the scientists who envisioned, worked toward and/or accomplished the breakthrough innovations had some idea (typically general and somewhat vague) of the application domain(s) for their innovations, but limited understanding of the market (Rice & Kelley, 1997). In eight of the 12 cases, the idea generator was not the opportunity recognizer. The scientists' research managers, who recognized the opportunities associated with their breakthrough innovations, had sufficient understanding of the potential market or application, which, when combined with their technical expertise, allowed them to recognize the business opportunities. The frequent interaction between the first-line research managers and the scientists who were the idea generators made it likely that they would be in the best position to learn of the breakthrough ideas and make the connections to potential business opportunities. Unless someone close to the idea understands its implications, there is little chance it will reach the "radar screen" of higher-level managers.

The leap in thinking required of these research managers to recognize an opportunity is reflected in the comments of one research manager:

> We didn't know much about market size at the time. The market is big. It's enormous. It would be a killer technology in [this application domain] based upon my physical understanding of what would be required in that industry.

Breakthrough innovation opportunity recognition appears not to occur in a formal way, but rather is part of the organization's informal network and organizational culture. The report of an initial opportunity recognition that led to the establishment of one project is illustrative. Two research managers for two scientists involved in the initial research independently contacted two individuals within the business development group about an upcoming technical review of the research. They suggested that the business development people come to hear about an interesting idea. One of the two was too busy too attend. The other stated: "I get a notice every day for all the technical reviews going on here. I've got so many other things to do that I do not go unless somebody tells me to go. I was invited in [by the scientist's research manager] who said that this [technology] has the potential for making [product X]. I would not have normally gone to that review." It is likely that the initiation of this project would have been delayed, or missed altogether, without the occurrence of the opportunity recognition event.

In all cases, the desire to pursue an identified opportunity caused the research manager to reach out to other parts of the organization for support or resources. Given the high degree of technical and/or market uncertainty, the research manager sought confirmation of his perception of the opportunity. In addition, successful pursuit of the opportunity would over time require a significant commitment of the company's resources, which in turn would require decision makers with authority to commit resources to develop the innovation. The research manager became the catalyst for leading others in the organization to recognize the opportunity.

### 3. Evaluating and Screening Breakthrough Innovations

There was evidence in our study of competing for the attention and financial support of senior management via corporate requests for proposals, and proposals to venture boards, but this competition was not driving the evaluation and screening process. In fact, the concern of managers involved in our study was focused on how to evaluate and screen innovations much earlier in the process, before making proposals to venture boards typically becomes an issue.

A critical facet of managing the breakthrough innovation process is knowing that the pursuit is worth the risk. R&D managers recognize that the evaluation process for fundamental new lines of business differs significantly from that of extension projects. Yet our field studies offered limited evidence that there is a deliberate process or strategy for evaluating these projects differently. Screening was either undertaken as part of the normal project evaluation process, or treated in an *ad hoc* fashion. We note that in some cases, traditional evaluation criteria and methods were used, but were generally not perceived by the technologists and managers at the project level to be relevant to them.

The primary purpose of screening and evaluation activities was to support decision making related to resource (financial and human) allocation and, as necessary, acquisition. In all 12 cases, a positive outcome of the initial screening and evaluation process caused a commitment of internal human and financial resources from the discretionary funds of a research manager to continue exploratory work. At this point, uncertainty on one or more dimensions (technical, market, organizational, financial) was so high that the initial commitment simply reflected a conviction on the part of the research manager that the magnitude of the potential opportunity was large enough to warrant additional technical development.

In all cases, evaluation and screening at the project level was ongoing, initially centering on achievement of technical milestones, failure to achieve those milestones, or discovery of unanticipated technical hurdles (O'Connor & Veryzer, 1998). It also occurred with respect to market learning that came through interactions with early adopters and through the experience of "lead users" with prototypes. By comparison, evaluation and screening by senior management occurred in the context of periodic budgetary reviews and was conducted by an individual senior manager, a project "board of directors", and/or a venture review board, but still based on primarily technical considerations rather than on formal "business cases".

For breakthrough innovations initial assumptions could be made about market and economics related issues, but generally there were one or more critical issues related to technical uncertainty that took precedence. These needed to be resolved in order to be able to embody the technology into some sort of prototype that could be used for market learning. Hence, the focus of screening and evaluation activities in early project stages was predominantly technical. The primary evaluative questions driving the radical innovation projects in this study included the following:

- "What is the magnitude of the impact this technology can have on the market?"
- "What will this technology enable?"
- "Can this technology deliver the magnitude of benefit that is needed?"
- "What are the technical hurdles we must overcome to get this thing (or process) to work?"
- "What are the projected performance characteristics?"
- "What yield from the manufacturing process must be achieved to make the economics of the business attractive?"

The focus of this set of questions was on the return of new value, in a variety of ways, to the market (O'Connor & Veryzer, 1998). The long-run profit potential was assumed to be significant even though not currently quantifiable. In comparison, typical screening criteria for an incremental improvement investment relate to how much promise the project offered to the firm, characterized as, "What is the profit impact?" or "How fast will it grow?" or "How much market share can we expect to grab?". The focus of each of these questions is on a return to the firm over a given, usually specified, and relatively short timeframe.

For breakthrough innovations we found an emphasis on a more experimental, hands-on approach and a reliance on past experience to assess the value of the technology to the market (Rice, O'Connor, Peters &

Morone, 1998). Potential customers, or lead users, were not the only vehicle for this as perspectives of many constituents were sought, including leading members of the technical community, senior management at both the corporate and business unit levels, and line managers connected to the current customer base. There was a heavy reliance on "probes" to potential early adopters and others who were relatively sophisticated in relevant technical arenas, including: (1) professional conferences and meetings, where data are presented for the technology community's reaction and to gain potential customer interest; (2) the demonstration of the product via early prototypes for reaction within the firm; and (3) evaluations by potential customers of early working versions over extended trial periods.

These probes were more experimental in nature than analytical, and were designed for technical and market learning more than market evaluation (O'Connor & Veryzer, 1998). The purpose was not to assess the impact on sales, but rather to assess the degree to which potential users will experience value-in-use. Typically several potential applications were pursued, usually serially, to test technical and market assumptions. Positive results of these activities were critically important for gaining support internally, both to sustain financial support of senior management and to increase the receptiveness of business unit managers, who would eventually manage the product emerging from the project.

## 4. Creating Incubating Organizational Structures

Galbraith (1982) and Quinn (1985) state that organizations pursuing innovation require a specially designed structure that enables them to develop significant innovations not consistent with the existing organization concept. The appropriate structure is likely to be different in various situations and at different times. A structural design may need to be changed as conditions change (Twiss, 1986). A number of authors recommend that separate structures should be maintained: an operating structure for routine lines and an innovating structure for new innovative products (Galbraith, 1982; Burgelman & Sayles, 1986; Kanter, 1989). They argue that the mainstream mode of operation is too slow and conservative to allow for development of projects characterized by high uncertainty, high intensity and high autonomy. Innovative new projects are not likely to benefit from the existing organization's experience base (Kanter, 1989).

Breakthrough innovation seems to work best, especially in the front end of the process, when separated from ongoing business activities. For most operating businesses, breakthrough innovation is an unnatural act, because the uncertainty is too high, the time horizon too long, and the investment too large given the inherent risks. Breakthrough innovation projects are badly aligned with the reward structure of operating businesses. The costs occur in the present, but the benefits will not arrive for, perhaps, 10 years or more. Thus, regardless of potential long-term benefit for the firm, within the short time horizons of operating units the impact of breakthrough innovation is negative, i.e. depressing short-term profitability. For all these reasons mechanisms for protecting projects—incubating arrangements—functioned to allow projects to develop outside organizational pressures and to find resources not normally associated with project development.

We found that successful breakthrough innovations developed in a variety of incubating arrangements. These incubating "homes" allowed innovations to develop enough maturity to be attractive to the operating units while being protected from short-term organizational performance metric requirements. The relative effectiveness of the various options varied with context. In early development the home of the incubating organization is typically Corporate Research and Development (CRD), or a new business development group operating within CRD or a business unit, or a new ventures group operating at the corporate level.

Incubating arrangements frequently operated across internal and external organizational boundaries to bring needed resources into the project. Partnering was used for risk reduction throughout the breakthrough innovation development process. Participation of internal and external partnering organizations varied but had a significant impact. A wide variety of partners were observed, including government. In eight out of 12 cases, government agencies were a major source of funds after the project was formalized. Government funds were used to extend, expand and accelerate projects, but in only one case was government funding a trigger or motivation for the project. There was widespread use of alliances for a variety of purposes, including manufacturing, application development, market probing, and joint development of technology (Rice, O'Connor, Peters & Morone, 1998). A broad spectrum of partners were involved, including other large firms, universities, government laboratories and small high-tech firms. Strategic alliances served to contribute knowledge about markets and technology as well as help managers gain visibility and legitimacy for their projects. They aided in monitoring the environment, and provided access to related cutting-edge technologies that could provide entrance into new markets.

All of this points to the importance of a resource view of the breakthrough innovation process. Since these innovations typically require expertise, funding, and the use of organizational resources (such as time in a fabrication facility, or on a manufacturing line) outside normal resource allocation processes, the success of breakthrough innovations depends on the ability of project managers, champions and sponsors to find and acquire those resources.

## 5. Catalyzing Individual Initiative

In contrast to the literature that describes institutionalization of the incremental innovation process, we found that successful breakthrough innovation depended on the actions of individuals. Rather than relying on organizational systems to manage the process (as might be expected with incremental innovation), individuals were the prime movers and sustainers. We identified several types of key actors: creative scientists, opportunity recognizers, multiple champions and supporters, and project team leaders and members. All of these individuals demonstrate a common characteristic—a passion for and belief in the innovation. This passion overcomes and protects the innovation from organizational forces that naturally resist new ideas.

*Creative scientists or engineers.* Competitive advantage through technical leadership requires recruiting and development a cadre of talented scientists and engineers, who have both technical skills and creative, out-of-the-box, idea-generating capabilities (Morone, 1993). In nine of the 12 projects, a single hero scientist or creative engineer had the initial technical insight that set off the chain reaction of events leading to the breakthrough innovation. Often, it was a creative, cognitive act that linked disparate bits of information together.

In organizations that had positions of research fellows, hero scientists (technical champions) emerged from the ranks of senior research fellows or technical people with high prestige. The support and championing of the breakthrough innovation arena was tolerated and protected by their status. Nevertheless, there was still immense difficulty and the majority of these hero scientists simply stuck out their necks when advocating their breakthrough innovations. This of course comes at a risk, but the champions we observed were so passionate about their projects that they paid scant attention to the potential downside to their careers.

*Opportunity recognizers.* Taking the technical idea and recognizing the potential application or market opportunity was a critical event within the breakthrough innovation process. As indicated earlier in this paper, in eight of our 12 cases, first-line technical managers (themselves experienced engineers or scientists), not senior managers, were the individuals who first recognized the opportunity, even though they were not the ones who came up with the idea. These innovation recognizers were convinced of the significant potential impact of the innovation and had the confidence to champion it in the larger organization.

We also found that first-line managers were not always heard and sometimes gave up, i.e. the opportunity recognizers were not necessarily the champions. They may make the links and communicate the nature of the opportunity to someone else, but then choose not to fight the battles that so often arise with unfamiliar, uncomfortable or alien topics. Thus, although a creative capacity was necessary, it was not sufficient to achieve progress. A determination to get the attention of the larger organization and to fight for the resources to pursue the opportunity was also important.

*Multiple champions and supporters.* We observed the importance of multiple champions, playing multiple roles. As Day (1994) and Venkataraman, MacMillan and McGrath (1992) found, champions play multiple roles or there are multiple champions playing different roles. As the literature suggests and our data confirm, champions played a key role in driving these projects forward, especially in the face of obstructionism from other parts of the organization or when intensity and perseverance were required to overcome hurdles.

We identified several types of champions: technical champions, project champions, senior management champions, and business unit champions. Multiple champions are necessary to support and protect breakthrough innovations because organizational resistance comes from all sides and the projects by and large do not have organizational legitimacy (Dougherty & Heller, 1994). Although it might seem a reasonable strategy to somehow coordinate the activities of these multiple champions, we found little of this happening. Champions seemed to act individually, though simultaneously, in support of the innovations. While occasionally a single person assumed multiple championing roles, more often than not different people played each championing role. Finding champions was critical to breakthrough innovation success.

Informal networks emerged as critical in all 12 innovations for gaining resources. These networks occurred both vertically and horizontally within the organization, including within R&D, between R&D and the business units, and between the company and customers, suppliers and government. Informal networking played a prominent role in idea generation, idea evaluation, generating political/financial support, gaining access to scarce resources, e.g. manufacturing capacity, connecting with friendly customers for alpha testing, and attracting government funding. Due to the innovation's need for legitimacy, protection and access to resources as discussed above, champions tied into organizational networks were critical to overcoming these barriers. One project champion captured the importance of informal networks:

> It's important to know who the right people are in the company to get assistance and support; there's a secret way the company operates. Because of the way in which managers have grown up around here, you have these internal networks and you work them and that's what makes the place work.

## Conclusions

Based on a four-year study of 12 breakthrough innovation projects in 10 large mature firms, we concluded that there were significant differences in characteristics and management practices between breakthrough and incremental innovation projects. Best-practice management of incremental projects suggests a well-defined, linear path with clear go/no-go decision points, e.g. the stage gate model (Cooper, 1990). In contrast, breakthrough projects are highly uncertain and unpredictable, non-linear (with many detours, starts and stops), stochastic, and managed more through individual initiative rather than through formal, established organizational processes. Due to these dynamics, championing/sponsorship of senior management and reduced reliance on financial and market numbers as criteria for project continuation, at least early on, seem critical for long-term project success. The front ends of these projects seem to be extended compared to incremental projects, with extensive exploring and experimenting, probing and learning, rather than targeting and developing. Our data further indicate that when projects reach a dead end in one line of exploration, they frequently cycle back to the front end again, exploring another idea or market opportunity.

We identified a set of implementation tactics for coping with these phenomena, as summarized in Table 17.1. These implementation tactics were not applied in an isolated or sequential manner, but in a highly interactive manner. For example, both incubating organizational structures and senior manager championing reinforce each other, serving to protect radical innovation projects from the pressures and practices of the ongoing business. Idea generation is often the trigger for subsequent opportunity recognition, either by the idea generator or by a second individual in close proximity, and opportunity recognition in turn stimulates a set of initial evaluations. Due to overall uncertainty in the early years of these projects, idea generation is an ongoing and interactive part of early opportunity recognition and evaluation/screening and development activities. Hence, these tactics are used to promote and protect the discovery process that in the short term increases uncertainty but that for successful projects will, in the long term, reduce uncertainty sufficiently so that the project can be transferred into an operating unit that utilizes traditional management practices.

Conventional management techniques are unsuitable until uncertainty is sufficiently reduced. It appears that the primary imperative driving these projects was to reduce uncertainty to the point where conventional management practices could be applied or where it became apparent that the project should be abandoned. From our observations of the projects included in this study, it appeared that much of the breakthrough

TABLE 17.1 Summary of implementation tactics and their effects

| Implementation tactic | Implementation tactic effect |
|---|---|
| 1. Stimulating attractive ideas | Ensures a stream of high-quality ideas for triggering breakthrough innovations; creates a strategic context for push, develops goals as pull |
| 2. Promoting opportunity recognition | Sensing, recognizing, and supporting potential opportunities; low to mid-level research managers most likely to play this role as they are closest to on-going research |
| 3. Evaluating and screening breakthrough innovations | Criteria for continuing and supporting project; early development evaluated on technical considerations rather than on traditional business cases |
| 4. Creating incubating organizational structures | Protects the innovation from organizational resistance until it is strong enough to compete for resources and support on its own merits |
| 5. Catalyzing individual initiative | Technically creative individuals, champions and supporters necessary for ideas, recognition, securing resources, and organizational support and protection. Getting innovation on the "radar screen" of organizational decision-makers critical to continued project existence |

innovation process was not deliberately managed. While it may be true that conventional management techniques are inappropriate, we believe a more systematic approach can and will be developed. This more systematic approach, which can be derived from an understanding of the dynamics and characteristics of the breakthrough innovation project life cycle, can incorporate the five implementation tactics identified in this study:

1. Senior management can develop and articulate the need for breakthrough ideas, delineate "white-space" opportunities, and set "holy grail" challenges.
2. Senior management can support opportunity recognition of breakthrough ideas with the recruitment, development and placement of technically prestigious individuals, well networked in the company, to act as sentries and scouts, identifying and ferreting out new ideas.
3. Senior management can evaluate and screen breakthrough projects with different metrics compared with those used for incremental projects. Evaluation based on technical feasibility, at least early on, will keep a project alive against ongoing financial pressures. Further, senior

management can support alternative methods for accessing information used in the evaluation and screening process, e.g. experimentation and probes with potential customers for early market data.

4. Senior management can support and protect breakthrough projects by developing incubating organizational structures in which projects can mature sufficiently to be able to withstand the scrutiny of more traditional project evaluation reviews. These incubating arrangements may be implemented within R&D centers, business development groups, or separately run departments or divisions. Finding partners and creating alliances with complementary technologies or capabilities supports resource acquisition and helps spread the risk inherent in breakthrough projects.
5. Individuals play a critical role in developing and sustaining breakthrough innovations. Even in companies with effective incubating arrangements, senior management needs to support and protect breakthrough innovation projects visibly and vocally. Senior management can cultivate a set of individuals who operate within the organizational system and culture but at the same time challenge the organization by questioning current products and processes, thereby providing a catalyst for the initiation of breakthrough innovations and a medium for their development. Senior management can assist the process by making sure these unconventional, sometimes difficult individuals are identified, supported and rewarded. However, unless senior management plays the roles defined above, these out-of-the-box thinkers and actors may not emerge to play their roles.

Breakthrough innovation activity by its very nature is largely incompatible with mainstream business activity. Without stimulation and sponsorship by senior management, the flow of breakthrough innovation activity will be severely restricted by the culture and the drivers that serve to optimize mainstream business activity. Without the protection of senior management via championing and the creation of incubating structures and mechanisms, breakthrough innovation will fail to reach maturity.

Problems of organizational legitimacy result in difficulties in obtaining necessary resources, funding, personnel, time, support, access to organizational support services, etc. In a sense, the success of breakthrough innovations depends on obtaining a minimum support level of these resources. Most of the mechanisms for supporting the project—multiple champions, informal networks, hero scientists, top management support, discretionary resources, and external alliances, as well as government funding—are designed to obtain needed project resources. Many project members agreed that without government resources, for example, the project would have died due to malnutrition.

There are researchers who are skeptical about the capability of large established firms to pursue breakthrough innovation. Our findings suggest that senior management has the opportunity to exercise strategic decision making that can result in fostering, tolerating or squelching the development and commercialization of breakthrough innovations. The five implementation tactics identified in this study can be used to proactively manage the balance of core, mainstream business activity as against the breakthrough innovation activity that can provide the seeds for future business development.

Our study extends the existing literature by providing a foundation for developing appropriate management practices, rather than simply highlighting their existence and importance. We hope that this research effort will stimulate the development of additional managerial techniques and a systematic approach for implementing them that will allow firms to maximize the yield from their breakthrough innovation initiatives.

## Acknowledgements

The authors recognize the contributions of their colleagues who have been part of the Rensselaer Radical Innovation Research Project Team: Ronald Gutmann, Christopher McDermott, Joseph Morone, Gina O'Connor, Lois Peters, and Robert Veryzer, and our industry partners, particularly Miles Drake and Al Schmidt, who have co-chaired the subcommittee of the Research-on-Research Committee of the Industrial Research Institute, which engaged in an ongoing collaboration with the research team. In addition we recognize the Sloan Foundation for its substantial financial support for the project.

## References

Betz, F. (1993). *Strategic Technology Management*. New York: McGraw-Hill.

Block, Z. & MacMillan I.C. (1993). *Corporate Venturing*. Boston, MA: Harvard Business School Press.

Bower, J.L. and Christensen, C.M. (1995). Disruptive technologies: Catching the wave. *Harvard Business Review*, January–February, 43–53.

Burgelman, R.A. (1983). A process model of internal corporate venturing in the diversified major firm. *Administrative Science Quarterly*, **28**(2), 223–244.

Burgelman, R.A. & Sayles, L.R. (1986). *Inside Corporate Innovation*. New York: Free Press.

Cooper, R. (1990). The new product process: A decision guide for management. *IEEE Engineering Management Review*, June, 19–33.

Day, D.L. (1994). Raising breakthroughs. *Organization Science*, **5**(2), 148–168.

Dougherty, D. and Heller, T. (1994). The illegitimacy of successful product innovations in established firms. *Organizational Science*, **5**(2), 200–218.

Eisenhardt, K.M. (1989). Building theories from case study research. *Academy of Management Review*, **14**(4), 532–550.

Galbraith, J.R. (1982). Designing the innovating organization. *Organizational Dynamics*, **10**(3), 4–25.

Gluck, F.W. (1988). Breakthrough innovation through creative leadership. In R.L. Kuhn (ed.), *Handbook for Creative and Innovative Managers*, New York: McGraw-Hill.

Hamel, G. & Prahalad, C.K. (1991). Corporate imagination and expeditionary marketing. *Harvard Business Review*, **69**(4), 81–92.

Henderson, R.M. and Clark, K.B. (1990). Architectural innovation: The reconfiguration of existing product technologies and the failure of established firms. *Administrative Science Quarterly*, **35**, 9–30.

Hitt, M., Keats, B.W. & DeMarie, S.M. (1998). Navigating in the new competitive landscape: building strategic flexibility and competitive advantage in the 21st century. *Academy of Management Executive*, **12**(4), 22–42.

Kanter, R.M. (1989). Swimming in newstreams: mastering innovation dilemmas. *California Management Review*, **31**(4), 45–69.

Kirzner, I.M. (1973). *Competition and Entrepreneurship*. Chicago and London: University of Chicago Press.

Leifer, R. (1997). Organizational and managerial correlates of radical technological innovation. In D. Kocaoglu and T. Anderson (eds), *Innovation in Technology Management*, Portland International Conference on Management of Engineering and Technology, 134–137.

March, J. (1991). Exploration and exploitation in organizational learning. *Organizational Science*, **2**(1), 71–87.

Marquis, D.G. (1969) The anatomy of successful innovations, *Innovation*, November.

Martin, M.J.C. (1984). *Managing Technological Innovation and Entrepreneurship*, Reston, VA: Reston Publishing Company.

McGrath, R.G. & MacMillan, I.C. (1995). Discovery driven planning. *Harvard Business Review*, July–August, 44–54.

Morone, J.G. (1993). *Winning in High Tech Markets*, Boston, MA: Harvard Business School Press.

Myers, M.B. & Rosenbloom, R.S. (1993). Research management and corporate renewal. *Conference on the Future of Industrial Research*, February 1993, Harvard Business School, Boston, MA.

O'Connor, G.C. & Veryzer, R.W. (1998). Linking advanced technologies to market opportunities: The nature and process of market visioning. *Product Development Management Association 1998 Conference Proceedings*, 67–78.

Quinn, J.B. (1985). Managing innovation: controlled chaos. *Harvard Business Review*, **63**(3), 73–84.

Rice, M.P. & Kelley, D.J. (1997). Opportunity recognition in the domain of discontinuous innovation: An exploratory study, presented at the 1997 Babson College—Kauffman Foundation Entrepreneurship Research Conference.

Rice, M.P., O'Connor, G.C., Peters, L.J. & Morone, J.G. (1998). Managing discontinuous innovation. *Research Technology Management*, May–June, 52–58.

Rumelt, R.P. (1984). Toward a strategic theory of the firm. In X. Lamb (ed.), *Competitive Strategic Management*, Englewood Cliffs, NJ: Prentice-Hall, 556–570.

Schumpeter, J.A. (1934). *The Theory of Economic Development*. Cambridge, MA: Harvard University Press.

Tushman, M.L. & Nadler, D. (1986). Organizing for innovation. *California Management Review*, **28**(3), 74–92.

Twiss, B.C. (1986). *Managing Technological Innovation*. London: Pitman.

Utterback, J.M. (1994). Breakthrough innovation and corporate regeneration. *Research Technology Management*, **37**(4), 10.

Utterback, J.M. & Brown, J.W. (1972). Monitoring for technological opportunities. *Business Horizons*, **15**(5), 5–15.

Venkataraman, S., MacMillan, I.C. & McGrath, R.G. (1992). Progress in research on corporate venturing. In D.L. Sexton & J.D. Kasarda (eds), *State of the Art of Entrepreneurship*, Boston, MA: PWS-Kent Publishing, 487–519.

Wheelwright, S.C. & Clark, K.B. (1992). Creating project plans to focus product development. *Harvard Business Review*, March–April, 70–82.

Yin, R.K. (1994). *Case Study Research*. Thousand Oaks, CA: Sage.

# Index